FROM OLD ENGLISH
TO STANDARD ENGLISH

Studies in English Language series

A Course Book in English Grammar, 2nd Edition – Dennis Freeborn

From Old English to Standard English, 3rd Edition – Dennis Freeborn

Style: Text Analysis and Linguistic Criticism – Dennis Freeborn

Varieties of English, 2nd edition – Dennis Freeborn with Peter French and
    David Langford

Analysing Talk – David Langford

English Language Project Work – Christine McDonald

FROM OLD ENGLISH TO STANDARD ENGLISH

A Course Book in Language Variation across Time

Third edition

Dennis Freeborn

palgrave
macmillan

First edition published 1992
Second edition published 1998
Third edition published 2006 by
PALGRAVE MACMILLAN
Houndmills, Basingstoke, Hampshire RG21 6XS and
175 Fifth Avenue, New York, N.Y. 10010
Companies and representatives throughout the world

PALGRAVE MACMILLAN is the global academic imprint of the Palgrave
Macmillan division of St. Martin's Press, LLC and of Palgrave Macmillan Ltd.
Macmillan® is a registered trademark in the United States, United Kingdom
and other countries. Palgrave is a registered trademark in the European
Union and other countries.

ISBN-13: 978–1–4039–9880–4
ISBN-10: 1–4039–9880–9

This book is printed on paper suitable for recycling and made from
fully managed and sustained forest sources. Logging, pulping and
manufacturing processes are expected to conform to the environ-
mental regulations of the country of origin.

A catalogue record for this book is available from the British Library.

Library of Congress Cataloging-in-Publication Data
Freeborn, Dennis.
   From Old English to standard English : a coursebook in language variation across
time / Dennis Freeborn. — 3rd ed.
      p. cm. — (Studies in English language)
   Includes bibliographical references (p.) and index.
   ISBN 1–4039–9880–9 (pbk.)
     1. English language— History—Problems, exercises, etc. 2. English
language—Variation—Problems, exercises, etc. 3. English
language—Standardization—Problems, exercises, etc. I. Title. II. Series: Studies in
English language

PE1075.5.F74 2006
427.009—dc22   2006045218

10 9 8 7 6 5 4 3 2
15 14 13 12 11 10 09 08

Printed and bound in China

Contents

Preface to the third edition

The principal changes in the third edition of the book are:

- The use, in the transcriptions and quotations, of new fonts that more accurately reproduce the letter shapes of handwriting in Old English and Middle English manuscripts, and also an early printing font that is used for some 17th- and 18th-century texts. The transcription of the originals with their abbreviations (intended to be more or less exact) is followed by another transcription using the conventions of modern printed versions of Old and Middle English texts. However, please note that, while care has been taken to reproduce the handwriting as exactly as possible, the available fonts do not contain all the scribal variations in the shape of letters and abbreviations to be found in the manuscripts. Sometimes, therefore, there cannot be a completely exact match in some of the detail.
- The addition of an outline of the development of writing hands in six sections: Sections 3.2, 7.4, 12.2, 14.2, 15.1 and 17.3.
- A number of illustrative facsimiles have been added, and the whole text has once more been thoroughly checked and revised.
- Extensive supplementary materials are now provided on a new companion website.

Companion website

Lecturers, teachers and students have access to a companion website for the book at: www.palgrave.com/language/freeborn/.

Audio downloads

MP3 files are provided containing readings of extracts from a selection of the OE, ME and MnE texts. The text numbers spoken on the recording refer to the first edition, but they have been changed in the enlarged second and third editions. The new numberings in this book are shown in brackets in the following list of text recordings:

A broad phonetic transcription follows each recorded text in this book.
The readings are by Dr Alison Wray and Dennis Freeborn.

Text Commentary Book

This contains the worked examples and textual analyses of many Activities from the book. They are indicated after the relevant texts with the sign 📖. It also provides additional material on:

- Old English pronunciation
- Old English grammar
- Additional transcriptions and translations of selected facsimiles
- English spelling today (previously a postscript chapter in the second edition).
- The development of English spelling (previously a postscript chapter in the second edtion).

Word Book

This contains a complete word-list in alphabetical order for each Old and Middle English text, and for selected Early Modern English texts from the 15th to the 18th centuries. The lists for the Old English texts give the base form of inflected words and a translation, so that students can refer to an Old English dictionary or grammar more easily. Those for the Middle and Early Modern English texts include the derivation of each word. The *Word Book* also contains lists of loan-words from the early 13th to the 20th centuries. These are collated and reproduced again under each language of origin.

There is also a list of words in present-day English which are derived from Old English (reflexes).

Preface to the second edition

The text of the first edition has been completely revised and enlarged to include nearly two hundred historical texts, of which more than half are reproduced in facsimile. The facsimiles are primary sources of our knowledge of the language, illustrating the development of handwriting, printing, punctuation and spelling in a way which is not possible using modern printed versions of old texts.

The practice of modernising the spelling of modern printed texts of earlier English like, for example, the 15th-century *Paston Letters* and Shakespeare's late 16th- and early 17th-century plays has obscured important and interesting changes that have taken place. Literary texts are generally printed with modern spelling and punctuation, and though editions of Old and Middle English retain much of the original spelling, they usually add present-day punctuation.

The texts

The core of the book is the series of texts exemplifying the changes in the language from Old English to the establishment of Standard English. The texts have been selected for a number of reasons. The Old English texts are almost all from the *Anglo-Saxon Chronicle*, and so provide something of the historical context of the language a thousand years ago. Some texts have aspects of language itself as their subject. As we have no authentic records of the spoken language before the invention of sound recording, letters and diaries of the past are included, because they are likely to provide some evidence of informal uses of English. Some literary texts have been chosen, but the series does not constitute a history of English literature.

Readership

The first edition was intended for students of English Language at Advanced Level, but since publication in 1992 the book has been used in university departments of English, both in Britain and in over thirty overseas countries. As a result, the enlarged text aims to provide more material and commentary which is suitable for study in higher education. For example, chapter 6 demonstrates how a relatively short extract from an early Middle English text can be analysed to demonstrate the evidence for changes from Old English in spelling, pronunciation, vocabulary and grammar that had occurred. The Text Commentary Book contains a short chapter which takes the opening lines of Chaucer's *Prologue to the Canterbury Tales* as data for a practical exercise in using the evidence of rhyme to discover changes in pronunciation.

Activities

The Activities are designed to encourage students to find out for themselves – to answer the question 'how do you know?' and to consider possible reasons for what they observe. They are able to study data at first hand and to consider hypotheses, rather than to accept the answers to problems of interpretation that others have given. The process of analysing the texts in itself demonstrates how our knowledge of earlier English has been arrived at. The surviving corpus of Old and Middle English texts is all the evidence we have about the language as it was. There are no grammar books, descriptions of pronunciation, spelling books or dictionaries of English before the 16th century. The tasks in the Activities are no more than suggestions, and teachers will omit, modify and add to them as they think useful.

Many of the simpler, basic activities in the first edition have, however, been omitted, and teachers will readily devise them if they are needed.

Levels of study

It is helpful to consider three levels of study which may be followed according to students' needs, or to the amount of time available for study.

- At the first, observational level, features of the language can be simply noted and listed as interesting or different.
- At the second, descriptive level, such features are identified more specifically, using appropriate descriptive terms from a model of language.
- At the third, explanatory level, they are placed in their relation to general processes of language change, and in their social, political and historical context.

Language change

The English language, like all living languages, is in a continuous state of variation across time. The language of one generation of speakers will differ slightly from another, and at any one time there are 'advanced' and 'conservative' forms, whether they belong to regional, educational or class dialects. Change takes place at every level of language:

- Lexical level – new words are needed in the vocabulary to refer to new things or concepts, while other words are dropped when they no longer have any use in society.
- Semantic level – the meaning of words changes - *buxom* once meant *obedient*, *spill* meant *kill*, and *knight* meant *boy*.

- Syntactic level – a word-for-word translation of some Old English is unlikely to read like grammatical contemporary English, because word order and grammatical structure have changed as well as vocabulary.
- Phonological level – pronunciation in particular is always being modified and varies widely from one regional or social group to another.

The process of change has, however, considerably slowed since the 18th century, because the spelling system and grammatical structure have been standardised and are therefore highly resistant to further change.

Standard English

Standard English has a unique and special status. Its prestige is such that for many people it is synonymous with 'the English language'. This book sets out to show what the origins of present-day Standard English were in the past. It is concerned principally with the forms of the language itself, and makes reference to the historical, social and political background to the establishment of Standard English in outline only.

Commentaries

Analytic commentaries are provided for some of the texts in the book. Each commentary is a case-study based upon the text itself, which provides some of the evidence for change in the language. Other texts are provided without commentary.

Symbols

Languages

OE	Old English
Œ 1	Transcription using Old English letter shapes and abbreviations
Œ 2	Transcription using present-day printing conventions and filling out abbreviations
ME	Middle English
EMnE	Early Modern English
MnE	Modern English
Fr	French
OF	Old French
ONF	Old Northern French
AN	Anglo-Norman
ON	Old Norse
MS	manuscript
fr	from
WW	word-for-word translation

Grammar

m	masculine (gender)
f	feminine
n	neuter
nom	nominative (case)
acc	accusative
gen	genitive
dat	dative
sg	singular (number)
pl	plural
S	subject (in clause structure)
P	predicator
C	complement
O	object
Od	direct object
Oi	indirect object
A	adverbial
cj	conjunction
ccj	co-ordinating conjunction
scj	subordinating conjunction
Ø	stands for a deleted element in grammatical analysis
RP	Received Pronunciation

Writing and printing

Letters in caret brackets identify written letters of the alphabet, e.g. ⟨e⟩.

Letters in square brackets identify spoken sounds, using the symbols of the International Phonetic Alphabet (IPA), e.g. [ə], [ʃ], [iː].

An explanation and list of IPA symbols can be found in *Gimson's Pronunciation of English*, 5th edition revised by Alan Cruttenden, (London: Edward Arnold, 1994), p. 32, and in Dennis Freeborn with Peter French and David Langford, *Varieties of English: A n Introduction to the Study of Language* (Basingstoke: Palgrave Macmillan, 1993), Ch. 4, pp. 67–8.

Texts and facsimiles

Chapter 1

Chapter 2

Chapter 3

Chapter 4

Chapter 5

Chapter 6

Chapter 7

Chapter 8

Chapter 9

Chapter 10

Chapter 11

Chapter 15

Chapter 16

Chapter 17

Chapter 18

Chapter 19

Chapter 20

Chapter 21

1 Introduction

1.1 English today

Four hundred years ago, at the turn of the 16th and 17th centuries, English was spoken almost exclusively by the English in England, and by some speakers in Wales, Ireland and Scotland, and this had been so for hundreds of years since the language was first brought to Britain in the 5th century.

English today is a worldwide international language. It is spoken as a mother tongue by about 400 million people in the British Isles, Canada, the United States of America, Australia and New Zealand. It is a second language for many others in, for example, India and Pakistan and in some African states, where it is used as an official language in government and education.

New Englishes

Many different national and regional varieties of English have therefore developed, and will continue to do so. They have been called 'new Englishes', with their own characteristics of vocabulary, grammar and pronunciation, in the different states of Africa, India and Pakistan, Singapore and the Philippines for example.

Standard English

In Britain there are many regional and social dialects, but there is one variety which is not confined to any geographical region. It originally developed as a common system of writing, but it is also the dialect of what is called 'educated speech':

> Educated English naturally tends to be given the additional prestige of government agencies, the professions, the political parties, the press, the law court and the pulpit – any institution which must attempt to address itself to a public beyond the smallest dialectal community. It is codified in dictionaries, grammars, and guides to usage, and it is taught in the school system at all levels. It is almost exclusively the language of printed matter. Because educated English is thus accorded implicit social and political sanction, it comes to be referred to as STANDARD ENGLISH ... (Quirk et al., Longman 1985 *A Comprehensive Grammar of the English Language*, p 18)

The object of this book is to provide an outline of how the English language, and Standard English in particular, has developed into its present form. It says little about the changes since the late 18th century, because the standard language which had been established in written English by that time has not changed significantly,

1.4 How can we learn about Old English and later changes in the language?

The evidence for changes in the language lies in the surviving manuscripts of older English going back to the 8th century, and in printed books since the end of the 15th century. A lot of older English texts have been reprinted in modern editions, and so can be readily studied.

All our knowledge of pronunciation, however, has to be inferred from written evidence. So we can never reproduce for certain the actual pronunciation of English before the invention of sound recording in the late 19th century, but we try to make a reasonable guess by putting together different kinds of evidence.

1.5 Changes of meaning – the semantic level

Some people believe that words have 'real meanings', and object to evidence of change in current usage. Favourite words for teachers today are, for instance, *aggravate* and *disinterested*, which have taken on the meanings of *annoy* and *uninterested* in addition to those of *make worse* and *impartial*. It is argued that the new meanings are wrong, and an appeal is made to the **derivation** or **etymology** of a word – that is, what its original meaning was in the language it came from. Here is an example from the 'Letters to the Editor' columns of a newspaper. The first writer is arguing that Latin should be taught in schools; the second is one of the replies that were printed later:

Activity 1.2

Discuss the argument and the response. The dictionary definitions (from the OED) of the words mentioned in the letters are printed below.

1st letter

It is demonstrably more easy to explain the function of a word when you know what it means. The very word 'education' provides me with a wonderful example. In Latin e from ex meaning 'out' and ducare 'to lead' – literally, therefore to lead out (to lead out of ignorance into the light of knowledge).

(*The Independent*, 14 November 1987)

2nd letter

Knowing the derivation of the word education is of as much help to us in deciding how children should be educated as knowing the derivation of, say, 'hysteria' would be in choosing a treatment for that condition. May I suggest that your etymologically minded correspondents look up 'treacle' in a good dictionary? They will then know what to do if ever bitten by a snake.

(*The Independent*, 25 November 1987)

Dictionary definitions:

education

Latin *educare* (*to lead out*)

1 The process of nourishing or rearing a child or young person, an animal. (*obsolete*)
2 The process of bringing up (young persons); the manner in which a person has been brought up; with reference to social station, kind of manners and habits acquired, calling or employment prepared for, etc. (*obsolete*)
3 The systematic instruction, schooling or training given to the young in preparation for the work of life; by extension, similar instruction or training obtained in adult age. Also, the whole course of scholastic instruction which a person has received.
4 [*From sense 3, influenced by sense 2 and sometimes by the quasi-etymological notion 'drawing out'.*] Culture or development of powers, formation of character, as contrasted with the imparting of mere knowledge or skill.

hysteria

hysteria – modern (1801) medical Latin, formed as abstract noun to *hysteric* – a functional disturbance of the nervous system.

hysteric from Latin *hysteric-us*, from Greek ὑστερικ-ός *belonging to the womb, suffering in the womb, hysterical*, from ὑστέρα *womb*.

treacle

Middle English *triacle*, from Old French *triacle* (*antidote against a venomous bite*). The sense development in English has proceeded further than in other languages.

1. A medicinal compound, originally a kind of salve, composed of many ingredients (*obsolete*)
   I almoost haue caught a Cardynacle
   By corpus bones but I haue triacle . . .
   (Chaucer's *Pardoner's Prologue*, 1386)

2. The uncrystallized syrup produced in the process of refining sugar.

To understand that words change their meaning over time is to understand that words such as *aggravate* and *disinterested* can have two current meanings. Many words have changed so much that their original meaning seems quite remote, and it is interesting to use a dictionary to trace the sequence of meanings, and to see how one leads to another. For example, the earliest written record of the word *buxom* in the OED is dated 1175, and spelt *buhsum*:

Beo **buhsum** toward gode
Be obedient to God

It is recorded in a modern dictionary of Anglo-Saxon as *bocsum*, meaning *flexible, obedient*, and its first syllable *boc-/buh-* came from the OE word *bugan*, meaning *to bow down* or *bend* – that is, *bocsum/buhsum* means 'bow-some', 'pliable'. Its present-day meaning is defined in the *Concise Oxford Dictionary* as 'plump and comely'. How did *buxom* change its meaning from *obedient* to *plump and comely*, and what then is its 'true meaning'? Here is the sequence:

I   easily bowed or bent

1 Morally
  (a)   **obedient**
    *Be **obedient** to God*
    This meaning survives into the 19th century:
      To be **buxom** and obedient to the laws and customs of the republic
      (*George Borrow*, 1843)

  (b)   **submissive, humble, meek**
    þaꞇ lauedi til hir lauerd lute
    Wit **buxum** reuerence and dute   (c. 1300, *Cursor Mundi*)
    The lady bowed to her lord
    *With **humble** and fearful reverence*

  (c)   **gracious, indulgent, favourable; obliging, amiable, courteous, affable, kindly**
    Meek and **buxom** looke thou be
    And with her dwell
    (c. 1460, Mystery Play, *The Annunciation*, Angel to Joseph)

  (d)   **easily moved, prone, ready, willing**
    And many a beggere for benes **buxum** was to swynke   (Langland *Piers Plowman*, 1377)
    *And many a beggar was **willing** to toil for (a meal of) beans*

2 Physically
  flexible, pliant, unresisting
    Then gan he scourge the **buxome** aire so sore
    That to his force to yielden it was faine   (Spenser, *The Faerie Queene*, 1576)

II   blithe, jolly, well-favoured

3 **bright, lively, gay**
    A Souldier firme and sound of heart, and of **buxome** valour
    (Shakespeare, *Henry V*, 1599)

4 **Full of health, vigour and good temper; well-favoured, plump and comely, 'jolly', comfortable-looking (in person). (Chiefly of women).**
    She was a **buxom** dame about thirty   (*Scott Peveril of the Peak*, 1823)

These meanings overlapped for centuries in the course of the development of the present-day meaning of the word, which is confined to references to women as 'comfortable-looking in person'. It cannot be said that the 'real meaning' today is *obedient*, though it was for Samuel Johnson. He wrote in his *The Plan of a Dictionary* (1747),

> And *buxom*, which means only *obedient*, is now made, in familiar phrafes, to ftand for *wanton*, becaufe in an antient form of marriage, before the reformation, the

bride promifed complaifance and obedience in thefe terms, 'I will be bonair and *buxom* in bed and at board.'

(*bonair* derived from OF *bonnaire* – gentle, courteous, affable; shortened from *debonnaire*.)

The meaning *wanton* for *buxom* is mentioned in the *Oxford English Dictionary* as 'apparently only contextual' and is not recorded as one of the word's meanings.

When Johnson illustrated his proposal to quote 'obsolete meanings', he used lines from Milton's *Paradise Lost*, again using the word *buxom*:

– He with broad fails
Winnow'd the *buxom* air –

The entry for *buxom* in Johnson's *Dictionary* published in 1755 is as follows; you will see that the present meaning of the word (*plump and comely*) has not yet evolved:

BU'XOM. adj. [bucfum, Sax. from bugan, to bend. It originally fignified *obedient*, as *John de Trevifa*, a clergyman, tells his patron, that he is *obedient and* buxom *to all his commands*. In an old form of marriage ufed before the Reformation, the bride promifed to be *obedient and buxom in bed and at board*; from which expreffion, not well underftood, its prefent meaning feems to be derived.]

1. Obedient; obfequious.
   He did tread down, and difgrace all the Englifh, and fet up and countenance the Irifh; thinking thereby to make them more tractable and *buxom* to his government. *Spenfer's Ireland.*
   He, with broad fails,
   Winnow'd the *buxom* air.   *Milton*

2. Gay; lively; brifk.
          I'm born
   Again a frefh child of the *buxom* morn,
   Heir of the fun's firft beams.   *Crafhaw.*
       Zephyr, with Aurora playing,
   As he met her once a maying,
   Fill'd her with thee, a daughter fair,
   So *buxom*, blithe, and debonnair.   *Milton.*
          Sturdy fwains,
   In clean array, for ruftick dance prepare,
   Mixt with the *buxom* damfels, hand in hand,
   They frifk and bound.   *Philips.*

3. Wanton; jolly.
       Almighty Jove defcends, and pours
   Into his *buxom* bride his fruitful fhow'rs.   *Dryden's Virgil.*
       She feign'd the rites of Bacchus! cry'd aloud,
   And to the *buxom* god the virgin vow'd.   *Dryden's Æneid.*

Here are some more examples of words whose present-day meaning has evolved from a quite different original:

Word	Original meaning (now obsolete)
bachelor	A young knight, not old enough, or having too few vassals, to display his own banner, and who therefore followed the banner of another; a novice in arms
beam	A tree
career	The ground on which a race is run, a racecourse
cloud	A mass of rock; a hill
danger	Power of a lord or master, jurisdiction, dominion; power to dispose of, or to hurt or harm
dizzy	Foolish, stupid
eerie	Fearful, timid
fowl	Any feathered vertebrate animal; = bird
gentle	Well-born, belonging to a family of position; originally used synonymously with *noble*
girl	A child or young person of either sex, a youth or maiden
harlot	A vagabond, beggar, rogue, rascal, villain, low fellow, knave
horrid	Bristling, shaggy, rough
knave	A male child, a boy
knight	A boy, youth, lad. (only in OE)
lady	One who kneads bread
loft	Air, sky, upper region
meat	Food in general; anything used as nourishment for men or animals; usually, solid food, in contradistinction to *drink*
mess	Portion of food
naughty	Having or possessing naught; poor, needy
nice	Foolish, stupid, senseless
organ	A musical instrument
parliament	A speech; a talk, colloquy, conversation, conference, consultation
pen (writing)	A feather of a bird, a plume
quell	To kill, slay, put to death, destroy
read	To have an idea; to think or suppose *that*, etc.
rid	To clear (a way or space), esp. to clear (land) of trees, undergrowth, etc.
sad	Satisfied; sated, weary or tired (of something)
sell	To give, to hand over something
silly	Deserving of pity, compassion, or sympathy
spill	To put to death; to slay or kill
starve	To die; to die a lingering death, as from hunger, cold, grief, or slow disease
team	The bringing forth of children; childbearing
town	An enclosure; a field, garden, yard, court
want (vb)	To be lacking or missing; not to exist
worm	A serpent, snake, dragon

Activity 1.3

See if you can pair off the following words with their original meanings listed alphabetically below.
(*The correct pairings are printed at the end of the chapter.*)

Words	Meanings
coin	animal, beast
deer	cloud
dreary	cunning, crafty, wily, artful, astute
giddy	gory, bloody
honest	held in honour; respectable
nerve	mad, insane, foolish, stupid
pretty	reason as a faculty of the mind
sincere	sinew or tendon
skill	true, correct, exact
sky	wedge, corner, angle

Activity 1.4

(i) Choose some of the words in the preceding lists and trace their successive meanings in a dictionary.

(ii) The words in the following list have all changed their meaning in time. Choose some words from the list and use a dictionary to trace the successive changes of meaning.

can (*vb*)	flour	meal (*to eat*)	Pope	shut	toil
castle	harvest	medley	prestige	sleuth	toy
chore (*n*)	holiday	mole (*spot*)	pudding	slogan	try
control	kind (*n*)	mood	rather	smite	very
deal (*n*)	left(-*hand*)	moss	saucer	soft	walk
delicate	lewd	must (*vb*)	sergeant	solve	weird
faint	lord	pastor	shall	spoon	whine
false	lose	pester	share (*n*)	stomach	win
fear	may (*vb*)	pharmacy	shroud	stool	womb

The original meanings are listed in the Text Commentary Book

Answer to Activity 1.3: Correct pairing of words and meanings

Word	Original meaning	Source	Earliest recorded date
coin	wedge, corner, angle	F *coin* (*wedge, corner*)	1350
deer	animal, beast	OE deor	*c.*950
dreary	gory, bloody, cruel,	OE dreorig	8th C (*Beowulf*)
giddy	mad, insane, foolish, stupid	OE gidig	*c.*1000
honest	held in honour; respectable	OF honeste	1325
nerve	sinew or tendon	L nervus	1538
pretty	cunning, crafty, wily, artful, astute	OE prættig	*c.* 1000
sincere	true, correct, exact	L sincerus	1536
skill	reason as a faculty of the mind	ON skil	1200
sky	cloud	ON sky	1220

The date is that of the earliest occurrence of the word recorded in the *OED*.
OF = Old French; ON = Old Norse; F = French; L = Latin

2 The English language is brought to Britain

2.1 Roman Britain

In the middle of the 5th century Britain had been a province of the Roman Empire for over 400 years, and was governed from Rome. The official language of government was **Latin**. It would have been spoken not only by the Roman civil officials, military officers and settlers, but also by those Britons who served under the Romans, or who needed to deal with them. The term **Romano-British** is used to describe those 'Romanised' Britons and their way of life.

The native language was **British**, one of a family of **Celtic** languages. Its modern descendants are **Welsh** and **Breton** in Brittany (Britons migrated across the Channel in the 6th century to escape the Anglo-Saxon invasions). There were also speakers of **Cornish** up to the 18th century. Irish and Scots **Gaelic** today come from a closely related **Celtic** dialect. None of these languages resembles English, which comes from the family of **West Germanic** languages.

The Saxons had been raiding the east coast of Roman Britain for plunder since the early 3rd century, and a Roman military commander had been appointed to organise the defence of the coastline. He was called, in Latin, *Comes litoris Saxonici*, the 'Count of the Saxon Shore'. But Roman power and authority declined throughout the 4th century, and we know that a large-scale Saxon raid took place in AD 390.

2.2 *The Anglo-Saxon Chronicle*

Here are two short texts that were originally written down in the 9th century in what we now, from our point of view, call **Old English** (OE), but which was simply *Englisc* at the time. They are from *The Anglo-Saxon Chronicle*, which was first written down in the south-west of England, probably towards the end of the 9th century, copies then being sent to different regional centres. The text has survived, in whole or in part, in eight separate manuscript versions, each reflecting the concerns of the places and institutions in which they were kept and copied, and so the different versions of the *Chronicle* have interesting local variations. The annals range from references to incidents centuries before, obviously written down from oral tradition, some of which are reproduced in Chapters 2 and 3, to vigorous descriptions of contemporary affairs, for example Text 34 in Chapter 5. The early annals must not be read as accurate historical reporting.

Extracts and facsimiles from it in this book are taken from the versions known as *The Peterborough Chronicle* and *The Parker Chronicle*. The differences between them provide useful evidence for changes in the language that were taking place a thousand or more years ago.

The two texts following will give you a first impression of Old English. Text 4 is the beginning of the description of the island of Britain from the *Peterborough Chronicle*. Text 5 tells how the Britons had been conquered by the Romans in AD 47. The word-for-word translations (WW) are followed by paraphrases in Modern English (MnE).

Text 4: The opening of the **Peterborough Chronicle** *(facsimile)*

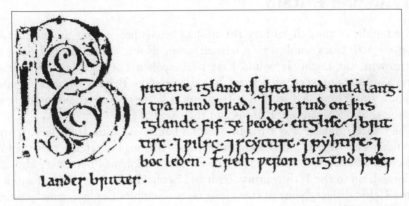

ŒE 1

Bꝛittene iȝland iſ ehta hunð mila lanȝ.
⁊ tꝑa hunð bꝛað. ⁊ heꝛ ꝛinð on þis
iȝlanðe fif ȝeþeoðe. enȝliſc. ⁊ bꝛit
tiſc. ⁊ ꝑilꝛc. ⁊ ſcyttiꝛc. ⁊ pyhtiꝛc. ⁊
boc leðen. Eꝛeſt peꝯon buȝenð þiſeꝯ
lanðeꝯ bꝛitteꝯ.

(See section 3.1.2.1 for a description of the letter shapes.)

ŒE 2

Brittene igland is ehta hund mila lang.
& twa hund brad. & her sind on þis
iglande fif geþeode. englisc. & brit
tisc. & wilsc. & scyttisc. & pyhtisc. &
boc leden. Erest weron bugend þises
landes brittes.

WW of-Britain island is eight hundred miles long.
& two hundred broad. & here are in this
island five languages. english. & british. & welsh. & scottish. & pictish. &
book latin. First were inhabitants of-this
land britons.

MnE The island of Britain is eight hundred miles long and two hundred broad. There are
five languages, English, Brito-Welsh, Scottish, Pictish and Latin. The first inhabitants
of this land were the Britons.

The scribe copied *fif geþeode* (*five languages*) and then divided the list into six. He
had mistaken what should have been one language (*Brito-Welsh*) for two. The Old
English words *brittisc* and *wilsc* referred to the same people.

📖 The vocabulary of Text 4 is listed in the Word Book.

Text 5a: Parker Chronicle *for AD 47 (facsimile)*

ŒI .xlvii. Ðer clauðiuſ oþeꞃ ꞃomana
cýninga bꞃetene lonð ge
ꞃohte ꞑ þone mæꞃtan ðel
þæſ ealonðeſ on hiſ gepalð on
feng ꞑ eac ſpelce oꞃcaðꞃ þa
ealonð ꞃomana cýneðome
unðeꞃ þeoððe

ŒII .xlvii.   Her Claudius oþer romana
cyninga bretene lond ge
sohte & þone mæstan del
þæs ealondes on his gewald on
feng & eac swelce orcadg þa
ealond romana cynedome
under þeodde

WW

47. Here Claudius second of-romans
kings of-britain land
attacked & the most part
of-the island into his power
seized & also orkney the
island to-romans empire
subjected

MnE

AD 47. In this year Claudius, the second Roman emperor, invaded Britain and conquered most of the land. He also subjected the Isle of Orkney to the rule of the Roman Empire.

The *Peterborough Chronicle* account differs in its detail:

Text 5b: Peterborough Chronicle *for* AD 47

Œ 2

·xlvii· Her Claudius romana cining gewat mid here on brytene·
& igland geeode· & ealle pyhtas· & walas underþeodde romana rice·

WW

47. Here Claudius romans' king went with army in britain.
& island over-ran. & all picts. & welsh made-subject-to romans' empire.

MnE

AD 47. In this year the Roman emperor Claudius invaded Britain with his army and overran the island. All the Picts and Welsh were also made subject to the Roman empire.

The vocabulary of Texts 5a and 5b is listed in the Word Book.

Texts 4 and 5b are recorded on the CD/cassette tape accompanying the book:

> briːtənə iːjlənd is ɛhta hʊnd miːla laŋ ənd twaː hʊnd
> braːd ənd heːr sɪnd ɔn θɪs iːjlənd viːf jəðeːədə ɛŋglɪʃ
> ənd brɪtɪʃ ənd wɪlʃ ənd ʃytːɪʃ ənd pʏçtɪʃ ənd boːk
> leːdən ɛːrəst weːrən buːɣənd θɪsəs lændəs briːtəs
>
> heːr klaʊdɪʊs roːmaːnə kɪnɪŋg jəwaːt mɪd hɛrə ɔn
> brɪtənə ənd iːjlənd jəeːədə ənd æːlːə pʏhtas ənd walas
> ʊndərθeːədːə roːmaːnə riːtʃə

2.3 How the English language came to Britain

By AD 443, the Roman legions had been withdrawn from Britain to defend Rome itself, so when the Romano-British leader Vortigern invited the Angles Hengest and Horsa to help defend the country, they found Britain undefended, and open not only for raiding and plunder but for invasion and settlement.

2.3.1 The coming of the Angles, Saxons and Jutes

This was not a peaceful process. Bede (673–735) describes what happened in his *Historia Ecclesiastica Gentis Anglorum* (*History of the English Church and People*), written in Latin and completed in 731.

> It was not long before such hordes of these alien peoples crowded into the island that the natives who had invited them began to live in terror. . . . They began by demanding a greater supply of provisions; then, seeking to provoke a quarrel, threatened that unless larger supplies were forthcoming, they would terminate the treaty and ravage the whole island. . . . These heathen conquerors devastated the surrounding cities and countryside, extended the conflagration from the eastern to the western shores without opposition, and established a stranglehold over nearly all the doomed island. A few wretched survivors captured in the hills were butchered wholesale, and others, desperate with hunger, came out and surrendered to the enemy for food, although they were doomed to lifelong slavery even if they escaped instant massacre. Some fled overseas in their misery; others, clinging to their homeland, eked out a wretched and fearful existence among the mountains, forests, and crags, ever on the alert for danger.
>
> (Translation from the Latin by Leo Sherley-Price, Penguin, 1955)

Bede, at the age of 7, had been given into the care of the Abbot of the monastery of Saints Peter and Paul at Wearmouth and Jarrow in Northumberland, where he spent the rest of his life as a priest. He became one of the most eminent scholars and teachers of his age, with an astonishing range of writings on theology, history, chronology, metrics and grammar. It is as a historian that he is remembered now. The *Historia Ecclesiastica Gentis Anglorum*, an account of the history of Christianity in England from the beginning up to his own day, is a primary source for understanding the origins of the English people.

Activity 2.1

In the following accounts of the coming of the Angles (Texts 6, 7 and 8), abbreviated words in the manuscript have been filled out in the transcriptions, but the punctuation is the original. Here are some suggestions for study:

(i)   Compare the word-for-word translations with the Old English facsimiles.

    (a)   List some OE words that are still used in MnE (some will be different in spelling); and

    (b)   list some OE words that have not survived into MnE;

    (c)   list those letters of the alphabet that are not used in MnE or that have changed a lot in shape;

    (d)   comment on the punctuation.

(ii)   Read the MnE version, and consider some of the reasons why the word-for-word translation does not read like present-day English.

Text 6a: Peterborough Chronicle *for* AD *443 (facsimile)*

Œ 1	Œ 2

ᚦep ren
ᴅon bpyτpalaρ oρepᴵᵃᵉτo
ρome· ⁊ heom ρulτumeρ
bæᴆon pıᴆ peohτaρ· ac hı
þæp neρᴆon nænne· ρoρþan
ᴆe hı ρeopᴆoᴆan pıᴆ ætlan
huna cınınᵹe· ⁊ þa renᴆon
hı τo anᵹlū· ⁊ anᵹel cẏn
neρ æᴆelınᵹaρ ᴆeρ ılcan
bæᴆon·

Her sen
don brytwalas ofer sæ to
rome. & heom fultumes
bædon wiþ peohtas. ac hi
þær nefdon nænne. forþan
þe hi feordodan wiþ ætlan
huna cininge. & þa sendon
hi to anglum. & angel cynnes
æðelingas þes ilcan
bædon.

WW Here sent britons over sea to rome. & them of-help asked against picts. but they there had-not none. because they fought against attila of-huns king. & then sent they to angles. & of-angle-kin peoples princes the same asked.

MnE 443. In this year the Britons sent overseas to Rome and asked the Romans for forces against the Picts, but they had none there because they were at war with Attila, king of the Huns. Then the Britons sent to the Angles and made the same request to the princes of the Angles.

Text 6b: Parker Chronicle *for* AD *443 (facsimile)*

Œ 1

hep renðon bpýtpalaᵹ to pome ꝺ heð fultomeᵹ bæðon pıþ pıhtaᵹ ac hı þaᵹ
næpðan nanne. ᵹoþþan ðe hı fýᵹbeðon pıþ ætla huna cýnınᵹæ. ꝺ þa renðon hı
to anᵹlū ꝺ anᵹel cýnneᵹ æðelınᵹaᵹ ðæᵹ ýlcan bæðan.

Œ 2

her sendon brytwalas to rome & heom fultomes bædon wiþ pihtas ac hi þar
næfdan nanne. forþan ðe hi fyrdedon wiþ ætla huna cyningæ. & þa sendon hi
to anglum & angel cynnes æðelingas ðæs ylcan bædan.

📖 The vocabulary of Texts 6a and 6b is listed in the Word Book.

Text 7: Peterborough Chronicle *for* AD *449 (facsimile)*

Œ 1

Œ 2

Œ 1

Þeɾ maɾtia_
nuſ ꝼ ualentin⁹ onꝼengon
ɾice ꝼ ɾixaðon.vii.. pint.
ꝼ on þeoɾa ðaᵹū ᵹelaðoðe
pyɾtᵹeoɾn anᵹel cin hiðeɾ.
ꝼ hi þa coman on þɾim ceo_
lum hiðeɾ to bɾytene. on
þam ſteðe heoppineˢ ꝼleot.
Se cyninᵹ pyɾtᵹeoɾn ᵹeꝼ
heom lanð on ſuðan eaſ_
tan ðiſſum lanðe. ꝼiððan
þe hi ſceolðon ꝼeohton ꝼið
pyhtaſ. Ðeo þa ꝼuhton
ꝼið pyhtaſ. ꝼ heoꝼðon ſi_
ᵹe ſpa hpeɾ ſpa heo co_
mon. Ðy ða ſenðon to
anᵹle heton ſenðon maɾa
ꝼultum. ꝼ heton heom ſec_
ᵹan bɾytpalana nahtſci_
pe. ꝼ þeſ lanðeſ cyɾta.
Ðy ða ſona ſenðon hiðeɾ
maɾe peoɾeð þam oðɾu
to ꝼultume. Ða comon
þa men oꝼ þɾim meᵹðū
ᵹeɾmanie. Oꝼ alð ſeaxū.
oꝼ anᵹlum. oꝼ iotum. Oꝼ
iotū comon cantpaɾa. ꝼ piht
paɾa. þ iſ ſeo meᵹð þe nu
eaɾðaþ on piht. ꝼ þ cyn on
peſt ſexum þe man nu ᵹit
hæt iutna cyn. Oꝼ ealð
ſeaxum coman eaſt ſeaxa.
ꝼ ſuð ſexa ꝼ peſt ſexa. Oꝼ
anᵹle comon ſe á ſyðð an
ſtoð peſtiᵹ betpix iutū
ꝼ ſeaxum. eaſt anᵹla. mið
ðel anᵹla. meaɾca. ꝼ ealla
noɾþhymbɾa. Ðeoɾa he.
ɾetoᵹan pæɾon tpeᵹen
ᵹebɾoðɾa. henᵹeſt. ꝼ
hoɾſa.

Œ 2

Her martia-
nus & ualentin onfengon
rice & rixaðon.vii. wintra.
& on þeora dagum gelaðode
wyrtgeorn angel cin hider.
& hi þa coman on þrim ceo-
lum hider to brytene. on
þam stede heopwines fleot.
Se cyning wyrtgeorn gef
heom land on suðan eas-
tan ðissum lande. wiððan
þe hi sceoldon feohton wið
pyhtas. Heo þa fuhton
wið pyhtas. & heofdon si-
ge swa hwer swa heo co-
mon. Hy ða sendon to
angle heton sendon mara
fultum. & heton heom sec-
gan brytwalana nahtsci-
pe. & þes landes cysta.
Hy ða sona sendon hider
mare weored þam oðrum
to fultume. Ða comon
þa men of þrim megðum
germanie. Of ald seaxum.
of anglum. of iotum. Of
iotum comon cantwara. & wiht-
wara. þæt is seo megð þe nu
eardaþ on wiht. & þæt cyn on
west sexum þe man nu git
hæt iutna cyn. Of eald
seaxum coman east seaxa.
& suð sexa & west sexa. Of
angle comon se a syððan
stod westig betwix iutum
& seaxum. east angla. middel angla. mearca. & ealla
norþhymbra. Heora he-
retogan wæron twegen
gebroðra. hengest. &
horsa.

WW 449.   Here martianus & valentinus took kingdom & reigned 7 winters. & in their
days invited vortigern angle people hither. & they then came in three ships hither to
britain. at the place heopwinesfleet. The king vortigern gave them land in south east
of-this land. provided that they should fight against picts. They then fought against
picts. & had victory wherever they came. They then sent to anglen ordered send
more help. & ordered them say britons' cowardice. & the land's goodness. They then
at-once sent hither greater force to others as help. Then came these men from three

nations germany. From old saxons. from angles. from jutes. From jutes came kent-people. & wight-people. that is the race which now dwells in wight. & the race among west saxons that one now still calls jutes' race. From old saxons came east saxons & south saxons & west saxons. From anglen came it ever since stood waste between jutes and saxons. east angles. middle angles. mercians & all northumbrians. Their leaders were two brothers. hengest. & horsa.

| MnE | 449. In this year Marcian (*Eastern Roman Emperor*) and Valentinian (*Western Roman Emperor*) came to power and reigned seven years. In their days Vortigern invited the Angles here and they then came hither to Britain in three ships, at a place called Ebbsfleet (*in Kent*). King Vortigern gave them land in the south-east of this country, on condition that they fought against the Picts. They fought the Picts and were victorious wherever they fought. Then they sent to Anglen, and ordered the Angles to send more help, and reported the cowardice of the Britons and the fertility of the land. So the Angles at once sent a larger force to help the others. These men came from three Germanic nations – the **Old Saxons**, the **Angles** and the **Jutes**. From the Jutes came the people of **Kent** and the **Isle of Wight** – that is, the people who now live in the Isle of Wight, and the race among the West Saxons who are still called Jutes. From the **Old Saxons** came the men of **Essex, Sussex** and **Wessex**. From **Anglen**, which has stood waste ever since, between the Jutes and Saxons, came the men of **East Anglia, Middle Anglia, Mercia** and the whole of **Northumbria**. Their leaders were two brothers, Hengest and Horsa.

The vocabulary of Text 7 is listed in the Word Book.

Text 8: **Peterborough Chronicle** *for AD 455 (facsimile)*

Œ 1

Þer hen
ᵹeſt ꝉ horſa ꝼuhton wið
þyrtᵹerne þā ciningе
on þære ſtope þe iſ cpe_
ðen æᵹeleſþrep. ꝉ hiſ bro_
ðoꞃ horſan man oꝼſloh.
ꝉ æꝼteꞃ þonn ꝼenᵹ to
ꞃice henᵹeſt. ꝉ æſc hiſ
ꞃunu.

Œ 2

Her hen
gest & horsa fuhton wiþ
wyrtgerne þam cininge
on þære stowe þe is cwe-
den ægelesþrep. & his broþor horsan man ofsloh.
& æfter þonn feng to
rice hengest. & æsc his
sunu.

WW 455. Here hengest & horsa fought with vortigern the king in the place that is called aylesford. & his brother horsa one slew. & after that came to kingdom hengest. & æsc his son

MnE 455. In this year Hengest and Horsa fought against king Vortigern at a place called Aylesford, and Hengest's brother Horsa was killed. Then Hengest became king and was succeeded by his son Æsc.

📖 The vocabulary of Text 8 is listed in the Word Book.

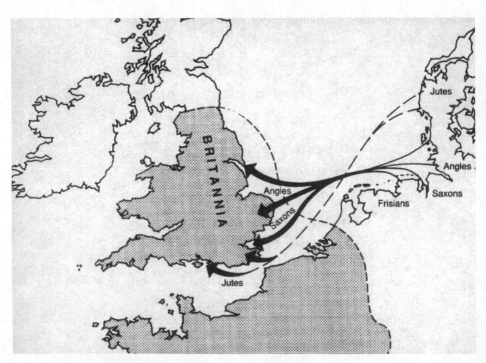

Map 1   The invasions of the Angles, Saxons and Jutes

2.3.2 'Englaland' established

The complete conquest of *Englaland* – 'the land of the Angles' – took another two centuries. There are tales of a Romano-British king called Arthur who led successful resistance in the 470s, winning battles that are recorded in Welsh heroic legends. He would have been a Romano-British noble, and was probably a commander of cavalry. Twelve victories against the Saxons are recorded, and much of the country remained under British rule for some time. But Arthur's name does not appear in the *Anglo-Saxon Chronicle*, and his historical existence is still disputed, though the chronicle does tell of other battles that took place. For example:

Text 9a: Peterborough Chronicle *for* AD *519 (facsimile)*

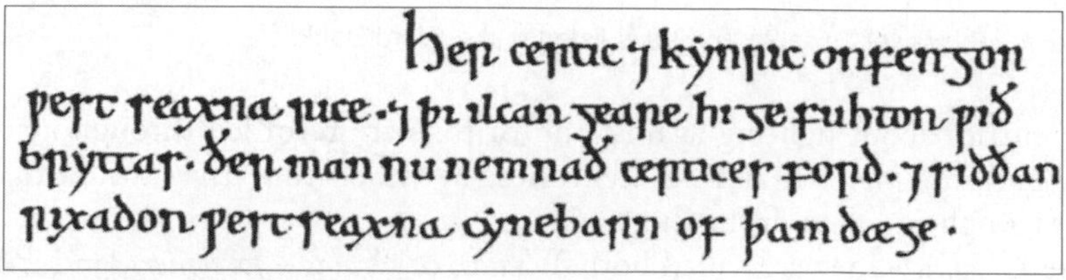

OE 1

Ꝺeꞃ ceꞃꞇıc ⁊ kẏnꞃıc onꝼenꝣon
ƿeꞅꞇ ꞅeaxna ꞃıce· ⁊ þı ılcan ꝣeaꞃe hı ꝣeꝼuhꞇon ƿıþ
bꞃẏꞇꞇaꞅ· ðeꞃ man nu nemnað ceꞃꞇıceꞅ ꝼoꞃð· ⁊ ꞅıððan
ꞃıxaðon ƿeꞅꞇ ꞅeaxna cẏnebaꞃn oꝼ þam ðæꝣe·

OE 2

**Her certic & kynric onfengon
west seaxna rice. & þi ilcan geare hi gefuhton wiþ
bryttas. ðer man nu nemnað certices ford. & siððan
rixadon west seaxna cynebarn of þam dæge.**

WW

519. Here certic & cynric took
west saxons' kingdom. & the same year they fought against
britons. where one now names certic's ford. & afterwards
ruled west saxons' princes from that day.

> **Activity 2.2**
>
> Compare the *Peterborough Chronicle* text above with the following version from the *Parker Chronicle*. What differences are there? Can you suggest any reason for these differences?

Text 9b: Parker Chronicle *for* AD *519 (facsimile)*

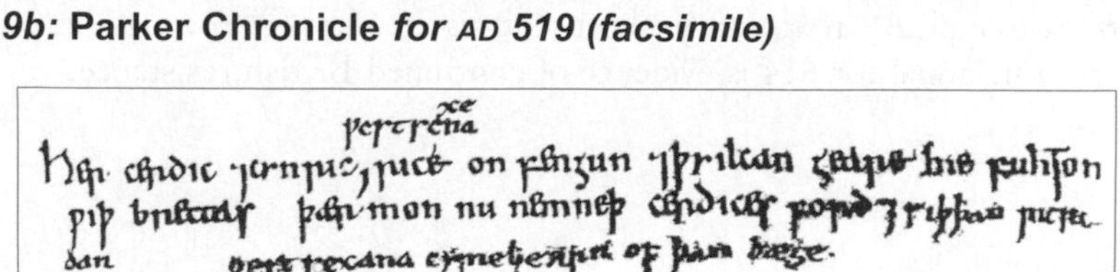

Œ 1

xe
peſt ſena
Ƿeր ceրdic 7 cẏnրic,րice onꝼengun· 7 þẏ ılcan ᵹeaրe hie ꝼuhton
pıþ bրettaſ· þæր mon nu nemneþ ceրdiceſ ꝼoրd· 7 ſıþþan pıcſa-
dan peſt ſexana cẏnebeaրn oꝼ þam dæᵹe·

ŒE 2

Her cerdic & cynric west sexena rice onfengun. & þy ilcan geare hie fuhton wiþ brettas. þær mon nu nemneþ cerdices ford. & siþþan ricsadan west sexana cynebearn of þam dæge.

WW

519. Here cerdic & cynric west saxons' kingdom seized. & the same year they fought against britons. where one now names cerdic's ford. 7 after ruled west saxons' princes from that day.

The vocabulary of Texts 9a and 9b is listed in the Word Book.

Similar entries about fighting against the Britons are recorded throughout the 6th century and into the 7th and 8th centuries, by which time they would have been driven as a fighting force from England.

In the *Chronicle* they are called both *Wealas*, or *Walas* – *foreigners*, and *Bretwalas*. *Walas* is the origin of the modern words *Wales*, *Welsh* and *Cornwall* (*Cornwalas*). The singular noun *wealh* was also used to mean *slave* or *serf*, which is an indication of the status of the Britons under Anglo-Saxon rule. For example, the entry for 755 in the *Parker Chronicle* tells of Cynewulf, King of Wessex:

ŒE 1

ꝺ ſe cẏnepulꝼ oꝼt mıclum ᵹeꝼeohtum ꝼeaht pıþ bրetpalum.

ŒE 2

7 se cynewulf oft miclum gefeohtum feaht wiþ bretwalum.

& that Cynewulf often great battles fought against brito-welsh.

and mentions in passing how a Welsh hostage became caught up in a local fight against Cyneheard, a prince of Wessex,

ŒE 2

hıe ſımle ꝼeohtende pæրan oþ hie alle læᵹon butan anum bրẏttıſcum ᵹıſle.
ꝺ he ſpıþe ᵹepundad pæſ.

ŒE 2

hie simle feohtende wæran oþ hie alle lægon butan anum bryttiscum gisle.
& he swiþe gewundad wæs.

they continuously fighting were until they all lay (dead) except one British hostage.
& he badly wounded was.

Here are two typical 7th-century short entries in the *Peterborough* and *Parker Chronicles*. The annal for 614 is evidence of continued British resistance.

Text 10a: Peterborough Chronicle *for* AD *611 (facsimile)*

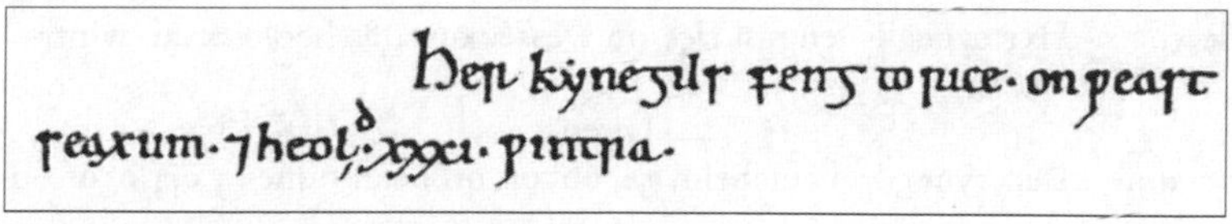

� kÿneʒilꞅ ꞅeꞇꞃꞅ ꞇo ꞃice. on ꝥeaꞃꞇ ꞃeaꞃum. ⁊heolꝺ. xxxi. ꝑintꞃia.

| ŒE 1 | Ꝺen kÿneʒilꞅ ꞅeng ꞇo ꞃice· on ꝥeaꞃꞇ ꞃeaxum· ⁊ heolꝺ ·xxxi· ꝑintꞃia· |

| ŒE 2 | Her kynegils feng to rice. on weast seaxum. & heold .xxxi. wintra. |

| WW | 611. Here cynegils took to kingdom. among west saxons. & held 31 winters. |

| MnE | 611. In this year Cynegils succeeded to the West Saxon kingdom and reigned for 31 years. |

Text 11a: Peterborough Chronicle *for* AD *614 (facsimile)*

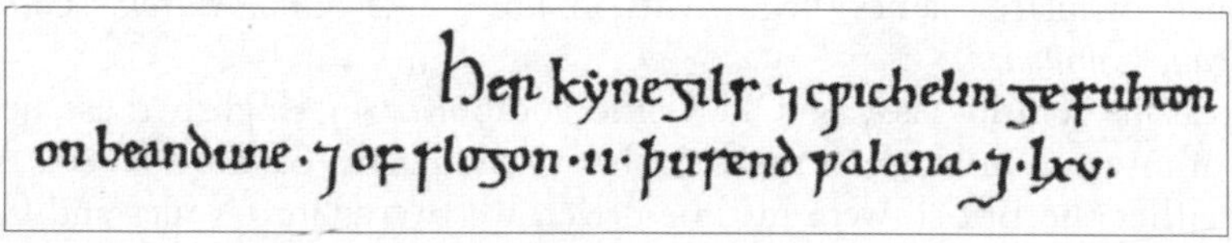

ᛒecp kÿneʒilꞅ ⁊cꝑichelm ʒe ꞅuhꞇon on beanꝺune. ⁊ oꞅ ꞅloʒon ·ii· þuꞃenꝺ ꝑalana ⁊·lxv·

| ŒE 1 | Ꝺen kÿneʒilꞅ ⁊ cꝑichelm ʒeꞅuhꞇon on beanꝺune· ⁊ oꞅꞅloʒon ·ii· þuꞃenꝺ ꝑalana· ⁊ ·lxv· |

| ŒE 2 | Her kynegils & cwichelm gefuhton on beandune. & ofslogon .ii. þusend walana. & lxv. |

| WW | 614. Here cynegils & cwichelm fought at beandune & slew 2 thousand welsh. & 65. |

| MnE | 614. In this year Cynegils and Cwichelm fought at Beandune and slew two thousand and sixty-five Welsh. |

Texts 10b and 11b: Parker Chronicle *for* AD *611 and 614 (facsimile)*

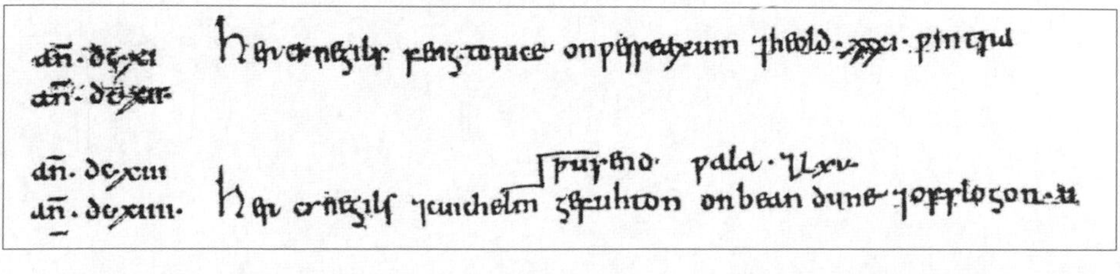

Œ 1	ðc.xi.	Þeп cýnegilſ ſeng тo pice on peſſeaxum. ⁊ heolð .xxxi. pïïⅼⅼ⋃ⱼⴰ.
Œ 2	dc.xi.	Her cynegils feng to rice on wesseaxum. & heold .xxxi. wintra.

Œ 1		⌐þuſenð pala· ⁊ lxv
	ðc·xⅲ·	Þeп cýnegilſ ⁊ cuichelm geſuhтon on bean ðune· ⁊ oſſloзon ·ⅱ·

| Œ 2 | dc.xiiii. | Her cynegils & cuichelm gefuhton on bean dune. & ofslogon .ii. þusend wala. & lxv |

📖 The vocabulary of Texts 10a and 10b, and of 11a and 11b, is listed in the Word Book.

2.3.3 Celtic words in English today

There is no surviving evidence of the British or Celtic language as it was used in the 5th century, and only a few Old Celtic words are to be found in MnE, such as *ass*, *bannock*, *brock* (i.e. badger), *crag*, *tor*. There is a larger number of Celtic place names of rivers and settlements; the best known include *Avon*, *Carlisle*, *Cornwall*, *Devon*, *Dover*, *Esk*, *Exe*, *London*, *Thames*, *Usk* and *Wye*.

OE *cumb*, like modern Welsh *cwm*, meaning *small valley*, *hollow*, is of Celtic origin. It occurs in many place names, like *Batcombe*, *Eastcomb*, *Salcombe* and *Winchcombe*. A number of place names begin with *Cum-*, like *Cumwhitton*, *Cumdivock*, *Cumlongan*, *Cumloden*.

The reasons for this lack of Old Celtic vocabulary in English must lie in the absence of integration between the British and the Anglo-Saxon invaders. As Bede records, either the British were in time driven westwards into Wales and Cornwall or they remained a subject people of serfs. The dominant language would therefore be English.

tor	Probably a Celtic name; cf. Gaelic torr – a rocky peak	847
brat	Irish *brat* – cloth, cloak	950
dun (a)	OE. *dun*, perhaps from Celtic: cf. Irish and Gaelic *donn* – brown	953
ass	There were two OE words for ass – *esol* and *assa*. OE *assa* was probably from the Celtic (cf. Old Northumbrian *asal*, *assal*, *assald*)	1000
bannock	Gaelic *bannach*	1000
brock	Gaelic *broc* – badger	1000

📖 Later Celtic loan-words from Scots Gaelic, Irish Gaelic and Welsh are listed in the Word Book.

3 Old English (I)

We call the language Old English (OE) during the Anglo-Saxon period and up to about 1100–1150, after the Norman Conquest. Our knowledge about it depends upon the survival of a number of manuscripts from which the grammar and vocabulary of the language have been reconstructed by scholars, working from the 16th century onwards (for a 16th-century example, see Section 3.1.6), but especially in the 19th and 20th centuries. They have provided us with the dictionaries and grammars of OE and the editions of OE texts to which we can refer.

3.1 Written Old English

3.1.1 Runes

The writing system for the earliest English was based on the use of signs called **runes**, which were devised for carving in wood or stone by the Germanic peoples of Northern Europe. The best surviving examples are to be seen in the Scandinavian countries – Sweden, Norway and Denmark – and in the islands of Shetland and Orkney. Few examples of rune-stones have survived in Britain, but the best known is a large 18-foot high cross now in the church at Ruthwell, Dumfriesshire in Scotland. On four sides of the Ruthwell Cross are some runic inscriptions in the Northumbrian dialect, which are part of an OE poem called *The Dream of the Rood* (*rood* comes from the OE word *rod* meaning *cross*), in which the Cross relates the events of the Crucifixion. The Ruthwell Cross probably dates from the 8th century.

3.1.1.1 Runes, writing and reading

One version of the runic alphabet is shown on p. 26.

One version of the runic alphabet is shown on p. 26.

Activity 3.1

Use the chart of the runic aphabet to transcribe the following words from the Ruthwell Cross fragment. They appear at the top of the south-west face of the Cross (see the drawing):

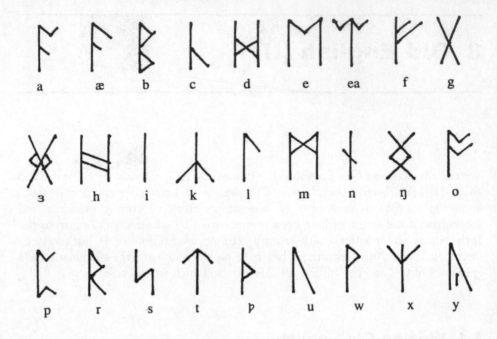

ᚪ ᚫ ᚠ ᛒ ᛣ ᚻ ᛗ ᛐ ᚠ ᚷ
a   æ   b   c   d   e   ea f   g

ᚸ ᚻ ᛁ ᛣ ᛚ ᛗ ᚾ ᛝ ᚩ
ᴣ   h   i   k   l   m   n   ŋ   o

ᛈ ᚱ ᛋ ᛏ ᚦ ᚢ ᚹ ᛉ ᚣ
p   r   s   t   þ   u   w   x   y

ᛏᚱᛁᛋᛏ   ᚠᚫᛋ   ᚠᚾ   ᚱᚩᛞᛁ   ᚻᚹᛖᚦᚱᚫ

ᚦᛖᚱ   ᚠᚢᛋᚫ   ᚠᛠᚱᚱᚪᚾ   ᛣᚹᚩᛗᚢ

ᚫᚦᚦᛁᛚᚫ   ᛏᛁᛚ   ᚪᚾᚢᛗ

Œ	KRIST ᚣÆS ON RODI ᚻᚣEÐRÆ ÐER FUSÆ FEARRAN KᚣOᴍU ÆÐÐILÆ TIL ANUᴍ
WW	CHRIST WAS ON CROSS WHETHER (= yet) THERE EAGER FROM-AFAR CAME NOBLE-(MEN) TO ONE-ALONE
MnE	Christ was on the cross yet eager noblemen came there from afar to him alone

The diagram shows the way in which part of the inscription is carved on the south-west side of the Ruthwell Cross.

This part of the inscription in the Northumbrian dialect of OE corresponds to the following lines from the poem *The Dream of the Rood* in the West Saxon dialect:

> crist wæs on rode
> hwæþere þær fuse feorran cwoman
> to þæm æþelinge

> Christ was on cross
> yet there eager-(men) from-afar came
> to the prince

In the Northumbrian version, the word *æþþilæ* is an adjective, nominative case, masculine plural, and so 'noble-men'. In the West Saxon poem, *æþelinge* is a noun, dative case, masculine singular following the preposition *to*.

The 'noble men' in the extract are Joseph and Nicodemus; cf the account in St John's Gospel, chapter 19: 38–9 – 'After that, Pilate was approached by Joseph of Arimathea, . . . who asked to be allowed to remove the body of Jesus. . . . He was joined by Nicodemus . . .'.

3.2 The development of writing hands (i)

Paleography
Handwriting is studied in **paleography**, which provides part of the evidence for the dating and placing of manuscripts in Old English through Middle English to Early Modern English. Descriptions of handwriting styles are made in later chapters (see sections 7.4, 12.2, 14.2, 15.1 and 17.3 and texts 34, 36, 38, 43, 52, 55, 86), but not using detailed paleographic terms. Scholars of paleography can identify the details between styles and the writing of individual scribes, but this is a specialised field of study (a number of relevant publications for reference are listed in the bibliography).

Letter shapes
In paleographic studies, the upper part of a letter which rises above the body of lower-case letters, e.g. in *b d f h k l*, is called an **ascender**, and the lower part of a letter which projects below the body of lower-case letters, e.g. in *g j p q*, us called a **descender**. There are several distinguishing features in the shape of letters which combine to differentiate one hand from another. You may find this list of features useful:

- **minim** letters are those which were made with a single downstroke of a pen – ⟨m n u ı⟩. Words with several adjacent minim letters could be difficult to read if written closely together, especially as letter ⟨ı⟩ was not dotted. For example:

   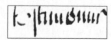

are not at first glance clearly *dominio, immunitate, divinum, testimonium,* nor is the following phrase easily read as **Numquid sicut dies hominis.**

This phrase is written in a formal early 14th-century Text hand (see section 7.4). Notice how in this particular English style of Text hand, the tops of the perpendicular strokes end in lozenge-shaped **serifs**, but the feet are squared level, without serifs. In most Text hand styles, the feet of letters have serifs also.

(This feature of letter shapes has survived into present-day printing fonts, with serifs – **hominis** – or without (called *sans serif*) – hominis)

- Ascenders and descenders may be embellished with **hooks** or **loops.**
- They may also be **upright** or **sloped.**
- The shape of the body of a letter may be either **round** or **angular.**
- Common letter combinations are often joined in **ligatures**, like the following examples:
  - (i) in an Old English hand – ſh ſl ſſ ſk ſi ſl
  - (ii) in a 16th-century Secretary hand (see section 15.1): ﬀ ſ ﬅ ſ ſ ﬀ ſ ﬀ ﬅ

Anglo-Saxon writing

During the Anglo-Saxon period before 1066, the scripts of manuscripts in Latin were written using styles of writing illustrated in the following facsimile from a Latin bible of about 850. The letter shapes for titles and headings are called **square** or **rustic capitals and uncials**, the text is in **Carolingian minuscules**. Capitals and uncials are categorised as **majuscules** – that is, there are very few parts of the letter above or below the line. A **minuscule** is a script of lower-case letters. **Uncials** are rounded capitalised letters derived from the shapes of Roman letters.

Carolingian minuscule, the hand commonly used in earlier Old English documents, was developed under Alcuin of York at the Abbey of Saint Martin at Tours in the late 8th century, during the reign of Charlemagne (hence the name *Carolingian* or *Caroline*). Lower-case letters used today are based on the script developed there. It was established in OE writing during the 10th century in a form known as **insular minuscule**.

text – Carolingian minuscules	
rustic capitals	
uncials	
text – Carolingian minuscules	

square capitals	# INCPEIVSDE SECDA
text – Carolingian minuscules	enior electae dominae etnaisciusquos ego diligo inueritate etnonego solus sedetcom

Insular minuscule

Writing in which each letter is formed separately and not joined to the others is called a **book hand** and can be seen in many of its varieties in the facsimiles. The style of book hand that developed in England is known as **insular**, because it was used by Anglo-Saxon scribes in the island of Britain, in contrast with Continental styles. It continued after the Norman Conquest of 1066 until about 1200. (For example, see the letter shapes ⟨ꝼ⟩, ⟨p⟩ and ⟨ᵹ⟩ in the *Ormulum* of *c*.1200 in Text 36, Chapter 5.)

Some of the letters of the alphabet in the facsimile texts in Chapter 2 are not at first easily recognisable. In Text 4, reproduced again here, for example, notice letters ⟨p⟩ (with a descender stroke) and ⟨ꞇ⟩ (with no ascender) in *Brittene*, ⟨ᵹ⟩ in *igland*, ⟨ɑ⟩ in *ehta*, ⟨ð⟩ in *hund* and ⟨ꝼ⟩ in *fif*.

There are three forms of ⟨s⟩, 'insular s' ⟨ꞅ⟩ in *sind*, 'long s' ⟨ſ⟩ in *is*, and the familiar 'round s' in *þis*.

The Roman alphabet used to write Old English

Written English as we know it had to wait for the establishment of the Church and the building of monasteries in the 7th century in which the monks wrote manuscripts in Latin, the language of the Church. Therefore the Roman alphabet was used to match letters to the nearest equivalent sound in English. But no Roman letter was available for some OE sounds, so other non-Roman letters were adopted. Three of them are always used in modern printed OE texts:

- ⟨æ⟩ – a vowel pronounced [æ] and called *ash* – derived from Latin. It is today popularly known as 'short a', as in MnE *cat*.
- ⟨þ⟩ – a consonant pronounced [θ] or [ð]; the letter is called *thorn* from its runic name (see section 3.1.1 on runes), now replaced by ⟨th⟩.
- ⟨ð⟩ – a consonant also pronounced [θ] or [ð]; the letter is called *eth* – derived from Irish writing and now replaced by ⟨th⟩.

  (Letters ⟨þ⟩ and ⟨ð⟩ tended to be interchangeable, and did not separately represent the voiced or voiceless ⟨th⟩ consonant.)

Some of the other non-Roman letters that you will see in the facsimiles are:

- ⟨ƿ⟩ – pronounced [w] and called *wynn* from its runic name. This letter is not usually used in printing OE today, and the familiar letter ⟨w⟩ is substituted. Letter <w> was not part of the OE alphabet. The consonant sound [w] was represented in the earliest OE writing by ⟨u⟩ or ⟨uu⟩ ('double-u'), and was then replaced by ⟨ƿ⟩, wynn. It is distinguished from thorn by having no ascender.
- ⟨ᵹ⟩ – the Roman letter ⟨g⟩ was written ⟨ᵹ⟩ (called *yogh*) and pronounced [ɡ], [j], [ɣ] or [x], depending on the sounds that preceded or followed it.
- ⟨⁊⟩ – this sign was used as shorthand for *and*, like the ampersand ⟨&⟩ today. It resembles a figure 7.

The OE alphabet therefore consisted of:

Vowel letters: a æ e ı o u ẏ
Consonant letters: b c ꝺ ꝼ ᵹ h l m n p ꞃ ꞅ/ſ/s ꞇ þ/ð ƿ x
k q z *were rarely used*
g, j *and* v *were not yet in use.*

Present-day printed OE texts almost always use ⟨g⟩ for ⟨ᵹ⟩, ⟨w⟩ for ⟨ƿ⟩ and only one form of ⟨s⟩.

Here is a brief summary of some of the developments, which can be checked against the facsimiles in Chapters 7 to 18, which discuss Middle and Early Modern English, including examples of early printing from the late 15th century onwards.

Later changes in letter shapes

- ⟨ƿ⟩ (wynn) was replaced by ⟨w⟩ or ⟨uu⟩ by *c.* 1300.
- ⟨ð⟩ (eth) had disappeared by about the same time.
- ⟨þ⟩ (thorn) survived much longer, into the 15th century, but often in modified forms, some without its ascender, looking like wynn ⟨ƿ⟩ (when wynn was no longer used), and others like ⟨y⟩. In that case, letter ⟨y⟩ was often dotted, ⟨ẏ⟩, for the vowel [i].
- ⟨g⟩ – the closed continental or 'carolingian' letter was introduced for the consonant [ɡ].
- ⟨ᵹ⟩ (yogh) came to be used for a number of different sounds, e.g. for [x], as in *riᵹt* [rɪxt] (*right*), for [j] as in *ᵹou* (*you*), or for [w] as in *laᵹe* (*law*). In form it was later written <ȝ>.
- ⟨r⟩ – the insular form ⟨ꞃ⟩ was replaced by two forms, one like figure 2 – ⟨ꝛ⟩ (e.g. Text 37, Laȝamon's *Brut*), and a 'continental' form like ⟨r⟩ (e.g. Text 38, *The Owl & the Nightingale*).
- ⟨s⟩ – the insular form ⟨ꞅ⟩ was dropped, but 'long s' ⟨ſ⟩ continued to be used into the 18th century in writing and printing, as well as the surviving 'round ⟨s⟩' (e.g. see the facsimiles in Chapters 17–19).
- ⟨ꞇ⟩ – the familiar present-day form ⟨t⟩ with a vertical stroke above the cross-bar, begins to appear in the 13th century.
- ⟨a⟩ – becomes closed to ⟨ɑ⟩ in the 13th century.

- ⟨ı⟩ was originally not dotted, ⟨i⟩. It could be easily confused next to 'minim letters' ⟨m⟩, ⟨n⟩ and ⟨u⟩, so there were two alternative changes. Either
  1 ⟨y⟩ was used for the vowel, or
  2 a slanting line like an accent was adopted as a diacritic mark, ⟨í⟩, which was taken over by early printers in the late 15th century and then reduced to the dot, ⟨i⟩ (see, for example, Caxton's printing in Texts 93 and 94, Chapter 14).
- ⟨æ⟩ had been replaced by ⟨a⟩ by the end of the 13th century.

Abbreviations

You will have noticed some abbreviations in the facsimiles in Chapter 2. They were continued from the writing of Latin manuscripts. The commonest are:

- A line, or "macron", over a letter shows the omission of ⟨m⟩ or ⟨n⟩, eg *oþrū* for *oþrum*.
- The omission of ⟨er⟩, ⟨re⟩ or ⟨ur⟩ is shown by different loops above the line – ⟨ʼ⟩, ⟨ꝛ⟩.
- þᵗ = *þat*; þʳto – *þerto*; þʳ – *þer*; ꝑ = *per*.

There are others which can be seen in the facsimiles in later chapters.

3.2.1 Long & short vowels & consonants in OE

3.2.1.1 *Vowels*

OE vowel letters represented both **long** and **short** OE vowels, that is, pairs of vowels with similar **quality** contrasted in **quantity**, or length (though linguists are not in fact agreed as to whether long and short vowels in OE differed only in quantity, and not in quality also).

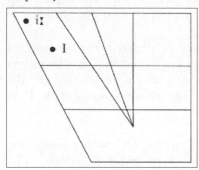

Vowel chart 1
MnE long [iː] and short [ɪ]

There are long and short vowels in present-day English pronunciation, but their length is determined by their 'phonetic environment' – the sounds that precede or follow. For example, the [ɑ] in *cart* is shorter than the [ɑː] in *card* because the voiceless [t] of *cart* causes the vowel to be cut off, whereas the voiced [d] of *card* does not. But there are no pairs of words in which only the length (quantity) of the vowel changes meaning. Even between vowels that are very similar, like the [i] of *peat* and the [ɪ] of *pit*, there is always a difference of quality, as this diagrammed vowel chart illustrates:

📖 The Text Commentary Book has a more detailed description.

There are two kinds of evidence that the length of the same vowel sounds in OE was **phonemic**, that is, that length of vowel alone in a word produced a difference of meaning:

- There are some **minimal pairs** of words, spelt identically, but with different meanings, for example:

long vowel		short vowel	
OE	*MnE*	*OE*	*MnE*
hām	home	ham	ham
īs	ice	is	is
rōd	rood	rod	rod

The possibility that they were in fact homonyms, spelt and pronounced identically, like MnE *bear* (*animal*) and *bear* (*carry*), is disproved by the second piece of evidence:

- The pronunciation of the vowels in MnE *home, ice* and *rood* has clearly changed considerably, from [ɑ:] [i:] and [o:] in OE, to [əʊ] [aɪ] and [u:] today, so there must have been significant differences in the pronunciation of the OE vowels for some to have changed and not others. (The changing or 'shifting' of long vowels took place gradually over the period from the 14th to the 17th centuries, and has been called the **Great Vowel Shift** by linguists. It is described in section 15.6.)

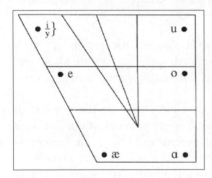

Vowel chart 2
OE single vowels

The number of OE pure or single vowels (as opposed to glides or diphthongs) was fourteen, twice the number of vowel-letters used in the OE alphabet, for each letter was used to represent both a long and a short vowel. Their position on a vowel chart will help you to remember their relationship.

The contrast between the systems of single vowels in OE and MnE can be seen in a vowel chart of the twelve MnE RP (Received Pronunciation, see section 17.1) vowels.

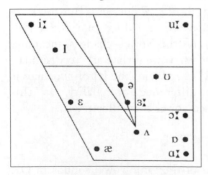

Vowel chart 3
MnE single vowels (RP)

Here are a few OE words containing examples of short and long vowels. The MnE **reflexes** (that is, words that have developed from an earlier stage of the language) have either different long vowels or diphthongs. (There are other changes you can see, but these are not a result of the long–short contrast; sound changes are rather more complex than this simplified account.)

OE		MnE		OE		MnE	
and	[a]	*and*	[a]	fīf	[iː]	*five*	[aɪ]
tā	[ɑː]	*toe*	[əʊ]	pytt	[y]	*pit*	[ɪ]
bæc	[æ]	*back*	[æ]	fȳr	[yː]	*fire*	[aɪə]
strǣt	[æː]	*street*	[iː]	oxa	[ɔ]	*ox*	[ɒ]
sunne	[ʊ]	*sun*	[ʊ] or RP [ʌ]	gōs	[oː]	*goose*	[uː]
cū	[uː]	*cow*	[au]	west	[ɛ]	*west*	[ɛ]
ribb	[i]	*rib*	[ɪ]	gēs	[eː]	*geese*	[iː]

In printing OE texts today, long vowels are conventionally marked with a macron, ā ǣ ē ī ō ū ȳ, but in this book long vowels are only marked when the information about length is relevant.

3.2.1.2 Consonants

OE had both short and long consonants. The pronunciation of **continuants** – that is, consonants that can be held on, like the fricatives [f], [h], [s] – can obviously be made longer or shorter. But **plosive** (**stop**) consonants, like [p] and [t], were also doubled in spelling to indicate a pronunciation similar to that of, for example, the MnE ⟨-pp-⟩ combination in a compound word like *hop-pole*, or ⟨-tt-⟩ in *part-time*, or the sequence -gg- in the phrase *big game*. There are only a few minimal pairs to prove the contrast, e.g.

hopian	[hopiən]	*to hope*
hoppian	[hop:iən]	*to hop*
cwelan	[kwɛlən]	*to die*
cwellan	[kwɛl:ən]	*to kill*

but the present and past tenses of certain verbs also formed minimal pairs with single and double consonants. They had the same long vowel in OE, but they have different vowels in their MnE reflexes, and are no longer minimal pairs. For example:

	present tense	*past tense*
OE	blēde	blēdde
MnE	bleed	bled
OE	fēde	fēdde
MnE	feed	fed
OE	mēte	mētte
MnE	meet	met

In all three OE verbs, the vowels of both present and past tenses are long [eː]. Both the vowels have since changed, but OE [eː] has shifted to [iː] in the present tense, and has shortened to [ɛ] in the past tense in MnE. The only difference between the two words in OE is in the length of the [d] or [t] consonant, therefore this must in some way have caused the later divergence of the vowels. It is further evidence that there were long and short consonants in OE.

3.2.1.3 OE letters and sounds

Here is a list of the letters of the OE alphabet, with a brief indication of their probable pronunciation. A few letters in OE, ⟨c⟩, ⟨ȝ⟩, ⟨f⟩, ⟨þ⟩, ⟨ð⟩, represented more than one sound, but pronunciation and spelling were much closer then than in MnE.

OE letter	OE word	OE sound (IPA)	Modern word with similar sound
vowels			
⟨i⟩	bringan (*bring*)	[ɪ]	*bring*
	rīdan (*ride*)	[iː]	*machine*
⟨y⟩	hyll (*hill*)	[ʏ]	German *schütten*
	hӯf (*hive*)	[y]	German *grün*
⟨e⟩	elm (*elm*)	[e]	*elm*
	fēdan (*feed*)	[eː]	German *gegen*
⟨æ⟩	æsc (*ash*)	[æ]	*ash*
	clǣne (*clean*)	[æː]	
⟨a⟩	sacc (*sack*)	[a]	American English *pot*
	ȝāt (*goat*)	[ɑː]	*cart*
⟨o⟩	fox (*fox*)	[ɔ]	*fox*
	ȝōs (*goose*)	[oː]	German *wohnen*
⟨u⟩	ful (*full*)	[ʊ]	*full*
	fūl (*foul*)	[uː]	*fool*
⟨ea⟩	earnian (*earn*)	[ɛə]	(no equivalent)
	ēast (*east*)	[ɛːə]	
⟨eo⟩	eorþ (*earth*)	[eə]	
	prēost (*priest*)	[eːə]	
consonants			
⟨p⟩	pullian (*pull*)	[p]	*pull*
⟨b⟩	brid (*bird*)	[b]	*bird*
⟨t⟩	tæȝl (*tail*)	[t]	*tail*
⟨d⟩	doȝȝa (*dog*)	[d]	*dog*
⟨c⟩	col (*coal*)	[k]	*coal, king*
or	cirice (*church*)	[tʃ]	*church*
⟨ȝ⟩**	ȝift (*gift*)	[g]	*gift*
or	ȝeonȝ (*young*)	[j]	*young*
or	boȝ (*bough*)	[ɣ]	–
⟨cȝ⟩	hecȝ (*hedge*)	[dʒ]	*hedge*

OE letter	OE word	OE sound (IPA)	Modern word with similar sound
⟨x⟩	æx (*axe*)	[ks]	*axe*
⟨f⟩	fot (*foot*)	[f]	*foot*
	lufu (*love*)	[v]	*love*
⟨þ⟩ ⟨ð⟩	þæc or ðæc (*thatch*)	[θ]	*thatch*
	feþer or feðer (*feather*)	[ð]	*feather*
⟨s⟩ ⟨ʃ⟩ and ⟨ſ⟩ ⟨ʃ⟩	sendan (*send*)	[s]	*send*
or	ceosan (*choose*)	[z]	*choose*
⟨sc⟩	sceap (*sheep*)	[ʃ]	*sheep*
⟨h⟩	sihþ (*sight*)	[ç]	German *nichts*
or	boht (*bought*)	[x]	German *nacht*
⟨l⟩	leþer (*leather*)	[l]	*leather*
⟨m⟩	mona (*moon*)	[m]	*moon*
⟨n⟩	niht (*night*)	[n]	*night*
⟨r⟩	rarian (*roar*)	[r]	*roar*
⟨p⟩**	pæter (*water*)	[w]	*water*

**Letters ⟨g⟩ and ⟨w⟩ are normally used for ⟨ȝ⟩ and ⟨p⟩ in modern printed editions of OE texts.

📖 There is a more detailed introduction to the pronunciation and spelling of OE in the Text Commentary Book.

3.2.2 The conversion to Christianity

In the 7th century much of the north of England was converted to Christianity by monks from Ireland, while Augustine had been sent by the Pope in 595 to preach Christianity to the English, and had begun in the south, in Kent. Here are the *Chronicle* annals that record the events:

Text 12a: Peterborough Chronicle *for AD 595 (facsimile)*

(The first sentence is in Latin.)

Hoc tempore monasteriū sci bene
dicti a longobardis destructū ē· Her gregorius pa_
pa sende to brytene augustinū mid wel manengum
munucum· þe godes word engla þeoda godspellodon·

Œ 2	Hoc tempore monasterium sancti benedicti a longobardis destructum est· Her gregorius papa sende to brytene augustinum mid wel manegum munucum· þe godes word engla þeoda godspellodon·

WW	595. At-this time monastery of-saint benedict by longobards destroyed was. Here gregory pope sent to britain augustine with very many monks. who god's word to-english nation preached.

MnE	595. At this time the monastery of St Benedict was destroyed by the Lombards. In this year Pope Gregory sent Augustine to Britain with very many monks, who preached God's word to the English nation.

Text 12b: Parker Chronicle *version (facsimile)*

Œ 1	Þer Ʒreʒoriuſ papa ſende to brytene Auʒuſtinū miđ pel maneʒŭ munecū þe ʒođer poþđ enʒla đeođa ʒođſpelleđon·

Œ 2	her Gregorius papa sende to brytene Augustinum mid wel manegum munecum þe godes word engla đeoda godspelledon·

📖 The vocabulary of Texts 12a and 12b is listed in the Word Book.

Text 13a: Peterborough Chronicle *for* AD **601** *(facsimile)*

Œ 1	her ſende ʒreʒoriuſ papa auʒu / ſtine apcebiſcope pallium on brytene· ꝥ pel maneʒa ʒođcunde laþepaſ him to fultume· ꝥ paulin⁹ biſcop ʒe hpirfeđe eađpine norþ hymbra cininʒ to fulluhte·

Œ 2	Her sende gregorius papa aug- ustine arcebiscope pallium on brytene· 7 wel manega godcunde larewas him to fultume· 7 paulinus biscop ge- hwirfede eadwine norðhymbra cining to fulluhte·

(The pallium was a vestment given by the Pope to mark the appointment of an archbishop.)

WW Here sent gregory pope augustine archbishop pallium in britain & very-many religious teachers him for help & paulinus bishop converted edwin northumbrians' king to baptism.

MnE 601. In this year Pope Gregory sent the pallium to Archbishop Augustine in Britain, and very many religious teachers to help him; and Bishop Paulinus converted Edwin King of Northumbria and baptised him.

Text 13b:* Parker Chronicle *version (facsimile)

Œ 1 Ðer rende gregoriur pap augurtino. ærce bircepe pallium in
bretene ꝓelmonige godcunde lareopar him to rultome.
ꝓpaulins birc ghperrde eðpine norþhymbra cyning to rulpihTe :·

Œ 2 Her sende gregorius papa augustino. ærce biscepe pallium in
bretene 7 welmonige godcunde lareowas him to fultome.
7 paulinus biscop gehwerfde edwine norþhymbra cyning to fulwihte.

📖 The vocabulary of Texts 13a and 13b is listed in the Word Book.

The monks had adapted the Roman alphabet from Latin to write English, which means that the spelling of OE gives us a good idea of its pronunciation. We know the probable sounds of Latin represented by the Roman alphabet, because there has been a continuous tradition of speaking Latin, to the present day. This also provides the evidence for the different OE dialects, because different spellings for the same words are likely to indicate differences of pronunciation or word-form.

3.2.3 Evidence of dialectal variation

Here are two versions of the earliest known poem in English. It is to be found in the OE version of Bede's *History of the English Church and People* (see section 2.3.1), which was translated from Latin into English in the late 9th century as part of a great revival of learning under King Ælfred (see section 3.4.2). The poem, a hymn to God the Creator, is all that survives of the work of the poet Cædmon, who lived in the 7th century. (For a discussion of OE verse, see Chapter 4.)

Text 14: Cædmon's hymn

West Saxon dialect

Nu we sculan herian heofonrices weard
Metodes mihte and his modgeðonc
weorc wuldorfæder; swa he wundra gehwæs
ece dryhten, ord onstealde.
He ærest gesceop eorðan bearnum
heofon to hrofe, halig scyppend;
ða middangeard, moncynnes weard,
ece dryhten, æfter teode
firum foldan, frea ælmihtig.

Northumbrian dialect

Nu scylun hergan hefænricæs uard
Metudæs mæcti end his modgidanc
uerc uuldurfadur, sue he uundra gihuæs
eci dryctin, or astelidæ.
He ærist scop ælda barnum
heben til hrofe, haleg scepen;
tha middungeard moncynnes uard,
eci dryctin, æfter tiadæ
firum foldu, frea allmectig.

WW

Now we must praise heaven-kingdom's Guardian
Creator's might and his mind-thought
work Glory-father's; as he of-wonders each
everlasting Lord, beginning established.
He first shaped of-earth for-children
heaven as roof, holy Creator;
then middle-earth, mankind's Guardian,
everlasting Lord, after determined
for-men earth, Ruler almighty.

West Saxon dialect

nu: we: ʃulən hɛrɪən heəvənriːʧəs weərd
metədəs mɪçt ənd hɪs moːdjəðɔŋk
weərk wuldərvædər
zwɑ: he: wundra jəhwæs
eːʧə dryçtən ɔrd ɔnstɛəldə
he: æːrəst jəʃɛoːp ɛərðən beərnum
heəvən toː hroːvə, hɑːlɪj ʃypːənd
ðɑ: mɪdːənjeərd, mɔnkynːəs weərd,
eːʧə dryçtən, æftər teːədə
viːrəm vɔldən, vreːə ælmɪçtɪj

Northumbrian dialect

nu: ʃylən hɛrgən hɛvænriːʧæs wɑrd
metudæs mæktɪ ɛnd hɪs moːdjɪdɑnk
wɛrk wuldurfadur,
swe: he: wundra jɪhwæs
eːʧɪ dryktɪn, ɔːr ɑːstɛlɪdæ
he: æːrɪst ʃoːp ælda barnum
hɛbən tɪl hroːvə, hɑːlɛj ʃepən
θɑ: mɪdːunjeərd mɔnkynːəs wɑrd,
eːʧɪ dryktɪn, æftər tiːadæ
fiːrum fɔldu, freːa ɑlːmeçtij

📖 The vocabulary of Text 14 is listed in the Word Book.

🎧 Text 14 is recorded on the CD/cassette tape accompanying the book.

3.2.4 *A Testimonie of Antiquitie*

A small book called *A Testimonie of Antiquitie* was printed in London in 1567. Its purpose was to provide evidence, in a contemporary religious controversy, about the Church sacraments. It reproduced, with a translation, a sermon 'in the Saxon tongue' by Ælfric (*c.* 955–*c.* 1010), Abbot of Eynsham near Oxford and a famous English preacher and grammarian.

The book is of interest to students of language, because the translation provides an example of 16th-century Early Modern English (EMnE) in both style, spelling and printing, while the Old English sermon is reproduced in a type face which copies

OE manuscript letter forms. Here is the beginning of Ælfric's sermon in *A Testimonie of Antiquitie*, with its 16th-century translation, and the list of 'The Saxon Caracters or letters, that be moste straunge' printed at the end of the book:

Text 15: *From* A Testimonie of Antiquitie *(1567) (facsimile)*

The epiſtle begin-
neth thus in the Saxon tonge.

Ælfric abb. gret Sigeferþ
freondlice; Me is gesæd þ
ðu rædest beo me þ ic oþen
tæhte on Englircen geppi-
ten . oþen eopen ancon æt
ham mið eop tæhþ. fonþan
ðe he rputelice rægþ þ hit
rie alefð. þ mærre pneortar
pel motan pifigen . anð min
geppiten piþcpeþeþ ðyren.

That is , Elfricke abbot doth
ſend frendlye ſalutation to Si-
geferth . It is tolde me that I
teach otherwyſe in my Engliſh
writynges, thē doth thy anker
teach, which is at home wyth
thee. For he ſayth playnly that
it is a lawfull thing for a prieſt
to marye , and my wrytynges
doth ſpeake agaynſt thys. &c-

¶ *The Saxon Caraĉters or letters,
that be moſte ſtraunge, be here
knowen by other common Caraĉters ſet ouer them.*

d. th. th. f. g. i. r. ſ. t. w.
¶ ð. ð. þ. f. g. ı. n. r. t. p.
y. z. and. that.
ẏ. Ʒ. ⁊. þ.

¶ Æ. Æ. Th. Th. E. H. M.
¶ Æ. Æ. Ð. þ. E. H. M.
S. W. And.
S. p. ⁊.

¶ *One pricke ſignifieth an vnperfect
point , this figure ; (which is lyke
the Greeke interrogatiue) a full
pointe, which in ſome other ölde
Saxon bookes, is expreſſed wyth
three prickes, ſet in triangle wyſe
thus* ∴

Transcription of the OE:

Œ 1
Ælfric abb. gret Sigeferþ
freondlice; Me is gesæd þ
ðu rædest beo me þ ic oþen
tæhte on Englircen geppi-
ten . oþen eopen ancon æt
ham mið eop tæhþ . fonþan
ðe he rputelice rægþ þ hit
rie alefð. þ mærre pneortar
pel motan pifigen . anð min
geppiten piþcpeþeþ ðyren.

Œ 2
Ælfric abbod gret Sigeferþ
freondlice; Me is gesæd þæt
ðu sædest beo me þæt ic oþer
tæhte on Engliscen gewri-
ten . oþer eower ancor æt
ham mid eow tæhþ . forþan
ðe he swutelice sægþ þæt hit
sie alefd. þæt mæsse preostas
wel motan wifigen . and min
gewriten wiþcweþeþ ðysen.

WW | Ælfric abbot greets Sigeferth
friendlily; to-me is said that
thou saidest about me that I other
taught in English wri-
tings than your anchorite at
home with you teaches. because
he clearly says that it
is permitted. that mass priests
well may wive. and my
writings against-speak this.

An *anchorite* is a religious hermit; see section 7.3.
Oþer . . . oþer = otherwise . . . than = differently from

3.3 Dialects and political boundaries

The English were not a politically unified nation until the 10th century, and as they originally came from different parts of western Europe (see Text 7, section 2.3.1 and Map 1), they spoke different dialects of West Germanic. They settled in different

Map 2   The Heptarchy

parts of Britain, but they were able to communicate with each other, since dialects are, generally, varieties of a language that differ in details of pronunciation, vocabulary or grammar, but usually not enough to prevent understanding.

However, what constitutes *a language* or *a dialect* in a particular society is likely to be determined by social or political rather than linguistic criteria. Some languages defined in this way may be mutually intelligible, while some dialects may not be. For example, is Scots a language, or a dialect of English? (See Text 179 in Chapter 20 for an example of literary Scots.)

The country during the 7th and 8th centuries is sometimes called the **Heptarchy** – that is, the country of seven kingdoms (Greek *hepta* = seven): Northumbria, Mercia, East Anglia, Essex, Kent, Sussex and Wessex. Wars were frequent, in which one or other of the kingdoms might dominate the others. For example, Wessex against Mercia in 628:

Text 16a: Peterborough Chronicle *for AD 628 (facsimile)*

Œ 1

hep kýneʒilſ ˥ cpichelm ʒe ꝼuhton
pið penðan æt cipnceaſtpe. ˥ ʒe þinʒoðon þa.

Œ 2

Ðep kýneʒilſ ˥ cpichelm ʒeꝼuhton
wið pendan æt cirnceastre. & geþingodon þa.

WW

628.   Here cynegils & cuichelm fought
with penda at cirencester & settled then.

MnE

628.   In this year Cynegils (King of Wessex) and Cwichelm fought
against Penda (King of Mercia) at Cirencester, and then they agreed terms.

Text 16b: Parker Chronicle *for AD 628 (facsimile)*

Œ 1

Ðep cýneʒilſ ˥cuichelm ʒeꝼuhtun piþ penðan æt cipenceaſtpe. ˥ʒe
þinʒoðan þa :

Œ 2

Her cynegils & cuichelm gefuhtun wiþ pendan æt cirenceastre. &
geþingodan þa.

📖 The vocabulary of Texts 16a and 16b is listed in the Word Book.

Map 3   Dialects of Old English

This does not mean, however, that there were seven different dialects. The evidence from OE manuscripts suggests that there were three or four: **Northumbrian** and **Mercian**, which together are called **Anglian**, from the West Germanic dialect of the Angles; **Kentish** and **West Saxon**, developing from the dialects of the Jutes and Saxons.

All living languages are in a continuous state of change and development, and OE was no exception between the 5th and 12th centuries. So any mention of the forms of OE words, or features of pronunciation, illustrates one dialect of the language at one stage of its development in a generalised way. It is usual to use the late West Saxon dialect of the 10th to 11th centuries to describe OE, because West Saxon was by then widely used as a standard form for the written language, and most surviving manuscripts are written in West Saxon.

3.4 Danish and Norwegian Vikings

3.4.1 Invasion, warfare and settlement

The *Peterborough Chronicle* records an event in AD 787 which proved to be an ominous portent of things to come:

Text 17a: **Peterborough Chronicle** *for AD 787 (facsimile)*

> Heɼ nam bɼeohtɼic cininʒ
> oꝼꝼan dohteɼ eadbuɼʒe· ꝥ on hiɼ daʒum comoᵹ
> æɼeɼt ·iii· ɼcipu noɼðmanna oꝼ heɼeða lande· ꝫ þa ɼeʒe
> ɼeꝼa þæɼ to ɼad· ꝫ he polde dɼiꝼan to ðeɼ cininʒeɼ tune
> þȳ he nȳɼte hpæt hi pæɼon· ꝫ hine man oꝼ ɼloh þa· Ðæt
> pæɼon þa eɼeɼtan ɼcipu denircɼa manna þe anʒel cȳn
> neɼ land ʒe ɼohton·

Œ 1

> Ðeɼ nam bɼeohtɼic cininʒ
> oꝼꝼan dohteɼ eadbuɼʒe·ꝫ on hiɼ daʒum comoN
> æɼeɼt ·iii· ɼcipu noɼðmanna oꝼ heɼeða lande· ꝫ þa ɼe ʒe
> ɼeꝼa þæɼ to ɼad· ꝫ he polde dɼiꝼan to ðeɼ cininʒeɼ tune
> þȳ he nȳɼte hpæt hi pæɼon· ꝫ hine man oꝼ ɼloh þa· Ðæt
> pæɼon þa eɼeɼtan ɼcipu denircɼa manna þe anʒel cȳn
> neɼ land ʒeɼohton·

Œ 2

> Her nam breohtric cining
> offan dohter eadburge· & on his dagum comon
> ærest ·iii· scipu norðmanna of hereðalande· & þa se ge
> refa þær to rad· 7 he wolde drifan to ðes ciniges tune
> þy he nyste hwæt hi wæron· & hine man ofsloh þa· Ðæt
> wæron þa erestan scipu deniscra manna þe angel cyn
> nes land gesohton·

WW

> 787. Here took breohtric king
> offa's daughter eadburh. & in his days came
> first 3 ships of-northmen from horthaland. & then the
> reeve there to rode. & he wished drive to the king's manor
> because he knew-not what they were. & him one slew there. That
> were the first ships danish men's that angle-people's
> land sought.

Text 17b: **Parker Chronicle** *for AD 787 (facsimile)*

> Hŕ nom —— beohtɼic cɼning oꝼꝼan dohtov eadbuɼʒe·
> ꝫ on hiɼdaʒum cuomon æheɼt ·iii· ɼcipu ꝫ þa ɼeʒeɼefa· þæɼto
> ɼad ꝫ hie polde dɼiꝼan to þæɼ cɼningf tine þɼhhuɼftæ hpæt
> hie pæɼon ꝫ hiɾe mon oꝼɼloʒ þæt pæɼon þa ðɼeɼtan ɼcipu
> deniɼcɼa monnd ꝫ eanʒel cɼnnf lond ʒɼohton ꞉~

Œ 1

·ꝺccclxxviii· heþ hine be ſtæl ſe heþe on
miðne pinteþ ofeþ tpelftan niht to cippanhame·
⁊ geþiꝺan peſt ſeaxna lanꝺ ⁊ geſetton· ⁊ mycel þæſ
folceſ ofeþ ſæ aꝺþæfꝺon· ⁊ þæſ oðeþ þone mæþtan
ꝺæl hi geþiꝺon butan þa cynge ælfþeꝺe litle peþeꝺe
un yðelice æfteþ puꝺū foþ· ⁊ on moþfeſtenum

⁊ þæſ oN
eaþtþon pþohte ælfþeꝺ cyninᵹ lytle peþeꝺe ᵹepeoþc
æt æðelinᵹa iᵹe· ⁊ of þam ᵹepeoþce þæſ pinnenꝺe þið
þone heþe· ⁊ þumeþ ſetena ſe ꝺel þe þæþ nehſt þæſ·
þa on ðeþe feoþeðan pucan ofeþ eaþtþon he ᵹeþaꝺ
to ecᵹbþihteþ ſtane be eaþton ſealpuꝺu· ⁊ him comon þæþ
onᵹean fumoþfæte ealle· ⁊ pillfæte· ⁊ hamtun fcyþ fe
ꝺæl þe hiþe beheonan fæ þæþ· ⁊ hif ᵹefæᵹene pæþon·
⁊ he foþ ymb ane niht of þam picum to æᵹlea· ⁊ þæþ
ymb ane niht to eðan ꝺune· ⁊ þæþ ᵹefeaht þið ealne he/
þe ⁊ hine ᵹeflymðe· ⁊ him æfteþ þaꝺ oð þet ᵹepeoþc· ⁊
þæþ fæt ·xiiii· niht· ⁊ þa fealꝺe fe heþe him ᵹiflaf· anꝺ
mycele aðaf· þet hi of hif þice polꝺon· ⁊ him eac ᵹehe/
ton þet heoþa cynᵹ fulpihte onfon polꝺe·

Œ 2

.dccclxxviii. Her hiene bestæl se here on
midne winter ofer twelftan niht to cippanhamme.
& geridan west seaxna land & gesetton. & mycel þæs
folces ofer sæ adræfdon. & þæs oðres þone mæstan
dæl hi geridon butan þam cynge ælfrede (& he) litle werede
unyðelice æfter wudum for. & on morfestenum

& þæs on
eastron wrohte ælfred cyning lytle werede geweorc
æt æþelinga ige. & of þam geweorce wæs winnende wið
þone here. & sumer setena se del þe þær nehst wæs.
þa on ðere seofeðan wucan ofer eastron he gerad
to ecgbrihtes stane be easton sealwudu. & him comon þær
ongean sumorsæte ealle. & willsæte. & hamtun scyr se
dæl þe hire beheonan sæ wæs. & his gefægene wæron.
& he for ymb ane niht of þam wicum to æglea. & þæs
ymb ane niht to eðan dune. & þær gefeaht wið ealne here & hiene geflymde. & him æfter rad oð þet geweorc. &
þær sæt .xiiii. niht. & þa sealde se here him gislas. and
mycele aðas. þet hi of his rice woldon. & him eac geheton þet heora cyng fulwihte onfon wolde.

WW

878. Here it(self) stole-away the host in
mid winter after twelfth night to chippenham.
& overran west saxons' land & occupied. & much of-the
folk over sea drove. & of-the other the most
part they subdued except the king Ælfred (& he) with-small band
with-difficulty through woods went & in moor-fastnesses.

& after at
easter built alfred king with-little company fortress
at Athelney & from that fortress was fighting against
the host. & of-somerset the part that there nearest was.
then in the seventh week after easter he rode
to egbertstone by east of-selwood & to-him came there
back of-somerset-men all. & wiltshire & hampshire
the part that of-it on-this-side-of sea was. & of-him glad they-were.
& he went after one night from those camps to iley. & later
after one night to edington. & there fought against all the
host & it put-to-flight. & it after rode up-to the fortress. &
there sat 14 nights. & then gave the host him hostages and
great oaths. that they from his kingdom wished. & him also
promised that their king baptism receive would.

(*the host* = the invading Danish army)

Text 19b: Parker Chronicle version

.dccclxxviii.   Her hiene bestæl se here on midne winter ofer
tuelftan niht to cippanhamme. ˀ geridon wesseaxna lond ˀ
gesæton. ˀ micel þæs folces ofer sæ adræfdon. ˀ þæs oþres
þone mæstan dæl hie geridon buton þam cyninge Ælfrede ˀ he
lytle werede unieþelice æfter wudum for. ˀ on morfæstenum.
ˀ þæs on eastron worhte Ælfred cyning lytle werede geweorc æt
eþelinga eigge. ˀ of þam geweorce was winnende wiþ þone here.
ˀ sumursætna se dæl se þær niehst wæs. þa on þære seofoðan
wiecan ofer eastron he gerad to ecgbryhtes stane be eastan
seal wyda. ˀ him to com þær ongen sumorsæte alle. ˀ wilsætan.
ˀ hamtun scir se dæl se hiere behinon sæ wæs. ˀ his gefægene
wærun. ˀ he for ymb ane niht of þam wicum to iglea. ˀ þæs ymb
ane to eþan dune. ˀ þær gefeaht wiþ alne þone here ˀ hiene
gefliemde. ˀ him æfter rad oþ þæt geweorc. ˀ þær sæt .xiiii.
niht. ˀ þa salde se here him fore gislas. ˀ micle aþas. þæt
hie of his rice uuoldon. ˀ him eac geheton þæt hiera kyning
fulwihte onfon wolde.

📖 The vocabulary of Texts 19a and 19b is listed in the Word Book.

Activity 3.2

Examine the differences between the pairs of words in the two *Chronicle* versions
listed on p. 48, and discuss the possible reasons for them.

(This topic is discussed in section 4.3.4.)

Peterborough	Parker	Peterborough	Parker
æglea	iglea	hire	hiere
Ælfred	Ælfrede	ige	eigge
æþclinga	eþelinga	land	lond
æþelinga ige	eþelinga eigge	litle, lytle	lytle
beheonan	behinon	mycel, mycele	micel, micle
butan	buton	morfestenum	morfæstenum
cippanhamme	cippanhamme	ongean	ongen
comon	com	scyr	scir
cyng, cynge, cyning	cyninge (*also* kyning)	sealde	salde
dæl, del	dæl	seofeðan	seofoðan
ealle, ealne	alle, alne	sumorsæte	sumursætna
easton	eastan	twelftan	tuelftan niht
ecgbrihtes stane	ecgbryhtes stane	ðere	þære
geflymde	gefliemde	þet	þæt
geridan, geridon	geridon	wæron	wærun
gesetton	gesæton	west seaxna	wesseaxna
geweorc	geweorce	willsæte	wilsætan
hamtun scyr	hamtun scir	wrohte	worhte
heora	hiera	unyðelice	unieþelice
hi	hie		

3.4.1.1 The Danelaw

After years of continuous war, Ælfred, King of Wessex, finally defeated the Danes and negotiated treaties with them. By the time of Ælfred's death in AD 899, at the end of the 9th century, only Wessex remained independent. The rest of England, north and east of the old Roman road called Watling Street (from London to Chester), was shared between the English and the Danes, and became known as the **Danelaw**.

The dots on Map 4 mark the sites of towns and villages with whole or part Norse names. The larger dots show names ending in the Norse *-by*, e.g. *Whitby*, *Grimsby*, and smaller dots show names with both OE and ON elements, e.g. *Grimston* (*Grim* is a Norse name, and *-tun* the OE for 'settlement'). The large number of ON place names is one of the clearest pieces of evidence for the settlement of Danish or Norwegian Vikings in the Danelaw. (There is a further reference to OE and ON place names in section 3.5.3.)

It was left to Ælfred's son Edward and his three grandsons who succeeded to the kingship of Wessex in turn, Æthelstan, Edmund and Eadred, to create through warfare a unified England under Wessex (see, for example, the accounts of Æthelstan's victory at the Battle of Brunanburh (937) in sections 3.5.4 and 4.1). But Scandinavian attacks continued throughout the first half of the 10th century, and were recorded in the *Chronicle*.

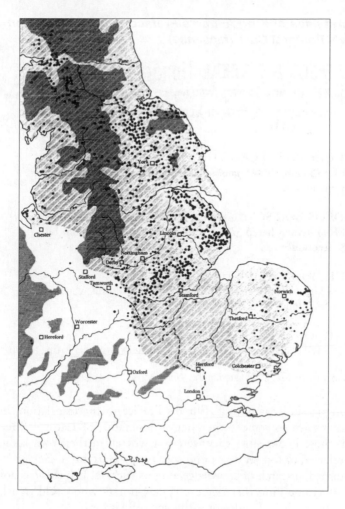

Map 4   The Danelaw

3.4.2 King Ælfred and the revival of learning

Ælfred the Great (848–99) was not only a great military leader, but also a scholar, anxious to restore the tradition of letters, which had decayed during the long years of warfare after the destruction of many monasteries. Among other translations, he wrote an English version of the Latin *Cura Pastoralis* of Pope Gregory (540–604) to provide spiritual education for the clergy. A copy was sent to every bishop. Here is the beginning of the copy sent to Bishop Wærferth at Worcester:

Text 20: First lines of King Ælfred's Preface to the West Saxon version of Gregory's Pastoral Care (facsimile)

Œ 1 ☩ ÐEOS BOC SEAL TO ꝡIOᵹORA LEASTRE
ÆLFRed̶ kýnin̊ᵹ hated̶ ᵹretan pæpfepð bircep hir pond̶um luf
lice ⁊ fpeond̶lice . . .

Œ 2 ☩ ÐEOS BOC SCEAL TO WIOGORA CEASTRE
ÆLFRed kyning hateð gretan wærferð biscep his wordum luf
lice & freondlice . . .

WW ☩ THIS BOOK SHALL TO WORCESTER
ALFred king calls (to) greet Wærferð bishop (with) his words lovingly & friendlily

MnE THIS BOOK IS TO GO TO WORCESTER
King Ælfred sends greetings to Bishop Wærferth with his loving and friendly words

📖 The vocabulary of Text 20 is listed in the Word Book.

The following facsimile is part of Ælfred's Preface to the translation, in which he describes his resolve to remedy the clergy's ignorance of Latin – 'they had little benefit from those books since they were not written in their own language'. King Ælfred has referred to former days of prosperity and learning in England, when men came from abroad in search of knowledge and instruction. But this has now changed, and when he became king there were very few priests who could translate a letter from Latin into English. He deplores this loss of wisdom.

Text 21: From King Ælfred's Preface to the West Saxon version of Gregory's Pastoral Care (facsimile)

OE 1 · ᵹeðenc hƿelcé ƿitu uſ ða be comon ꝼoꞃ ðíꞅꞅe poꝛulde . ðaða
ƿe hit nohꝼæðeꞃ ne ꞅelꝼe ne luꝼodon . ne eac oðꞃum monnū ne leꝼdon ;
ðone naman ænne ꝕe luꝼodon ðætte ƿe cꞃiꞅtne ꝕæꝛen : ⁊ ꞅꝛiðe ꝼeaꝛa
ða ðeaꝛaꝛ ; ða ic ða ðiꞅ eall ᵹemunde: ða ᵹemunde ic eac hú ic ᵹe ꞅeah
æꝛ ðæm ðe hit eall ꝼoꞃ heꞃᵹod ꝕæꝛe . ⁊ ꝼoꞃ bæꝛned . hu ða ciꞃicean ᵹiond
eall anᵹel cẏnn ꞅtodon maðma ⁊ boca ᵹeꝼẏlde . Onð eac micel meniᵹeo ᵹo
ðeꞅ ðioꝛa ⁊ ða ꞅꝛiðe lẏtle ꝼioꞃme ðaꝛa boca ꝛiꞅton . ꝼoꞃðæm ðe hie
⁊ ᵹ ꝕæꞅ
hioꝛa nanꝛuht ón-ᵹiotan ne meahton ./ ꝼoꞃðæm ðe hẏ næꝛon ón hio
ꝛa aᵹen ᵹeðiode apꝛitene . Sꝛelce hie cꝛæðen . uꝛe ẏldꝛan ða ðe ðaꞅ
ꞅtoꝛa æꝛ hioldon . hie luꝼodon ꝛiꞅdom ⁊ ðuꝛh ðone hie beᵹeaton ꝛelan
[⁊ úꞅ læꝼdon]

OE 2 and WW translation

Geðenc	hwelc	witu		us		ða	becomon	for	ðisse	worulde,	ða ða
Think	*what*	*punishments*		*upon us*		*then*	*came*		*in this*	*world,*	*when*

we	hit	nohwæðer	ne	selfe	ne lufodon	ne	eac	oðrum	monnum	ne lefdon;
we	*it*	*neither*		*ourselves*	*loved*	*nor*	*also*	*to other*	*men*	*allowed;*

ðone	naman	ænne	we	lufodon	ðæt	we	Cristne	wæren,	⁊	swiðe	feawa
the	*name*	*only*	*we*	*loved*	*that*	*we*	*Christian*	*were,*	*&*	*very*	*few*

ða	ðeawas.	Ða	ic	ða	ðis	eall	gemunde,	ða	gemunde	ic	eac
the	*virtues.*	*When*	*I*	*then*	*this*	*all*	*remembered*	*then*	*remembered*	*I*	*also*

hu ic geseah,
how I had seen,

ærðæmðe	hit	eall	forhergod	wære	⁊	forbærned,	hu	ða	ciricean	giond
before	*it*	*all*	*ravaged*	*was*	*&*	*burnt,*	*how*	*the*	*churches*	*throughout*

eall	Angelcynn	stodon	maðma	⁊	boca	gefylde.	Ond	eac	micel
all	*England*	*stood*	*with treasures*	*&*	*books*	*filled.*	*And*	*also*	*great*

menigeo Godes
multitude of God's

ðiowa	⁊	ða	swiðe	lytle	fiorme	ðara		boca	wiston,	forðæmðe	hie
servants	*&*	*these*	*very*	*little*	*benefit*	*from those*		*books*	*knew*	*because*	*they*

hiora	nanwuht	ongiotan	ne meahton,	⁊ þæt wæs	forðæmðe	hy	næron	on
of them	*nothing*	*understand*	*were able*	*& that was*	*since*	*they*	*were not*	*in*

hiora
their

agen	geðiode	awritene.	Swelce	hie	cwæden:	ure	yldran	ða ðe	ðas
own	*language*	*written.*	*Such*	*they*	*said*	*Our*	*forefathers*	*who*	*these*

stowa	ær	hioldon,	hie	lufodon	wisdom,	⁊	ðurh	ðone	hie
places	*formerly*	*held,*	*they*	*loved*	*knowledge,*	*&*	*through*	*it*	*they*

begeaton welan
acquired wealth

⁊	us	læfdon.
&	*to us*	*left (it)*

MnE Think what punishments then came upon us in this world when we neither loved it ourselves nor allowed it to other men – we loved only to be called Christians, and very few loved the virtues. When I remembered all this, then I also remembered how, before it was all ravaged and burnt, I had seen how the churches throughout all England stood filled with treasures and books, and there was also a great multitude of God's servants – they had very little benefit from those books, because they could not understand anything of them, and that was since they were not written in their own language. As if they had said, 'Our forefathers who formerly held these places loved knowledge, and through it they acquired wealth and left it to us.'

Ælfred's late 9th-century West Saxon shows some differences from the later 'classical' West Saxon of the 11th century, which became a common written standard. One example is the spelling of *giond, iowa, fiorme, hiora, ongiotan, geðiode, hioldon*, with the *-io-* diphthong. If you look up these words in a dictionary of OE, you will find them under *geond, eow, feorm, heora, ongietan, geðeode, heoldon*, which must mark a change in the pronunciation of the vowel.

📖 The vocabulary of Text 21 is listed in the Word Book.

3.5 Effects of Viking settlement on the English language

The settlement of the Norsemen and the occupation of the Danelaw had important effects on the English language.

3.5.1 Old Norse vocabulary

'Old Norse' is the name now given to the group of Scandinavian languages and dialects spoken by the Norsemen – Danish and Norwegian Vikings. It was **cognate** with Old English, that is, they both came from the same earlier Germanic language. It seems likely that the two languages were similar enough in vocabulary for OE speakers to understand common ON words, and vice versa, so that the English and Norsemen could communicate. An Icelandic saga says of the 11th century, 'there was at that time the same tongue in England as in Norway and Denmark'. But speakers would simplify their own language when talking to the other, and OE dialects spoken in the Danelaw in time became modified in ways which were different from the Wessex, West Midland and Kentish dialects. Present-day Northern and East Anglian dialects show ON features, particularly in vocabulary.

Many OE words therefore have a similar cognate ON word, and often we cannot be sure whether a MnE reflex has come from OE, or ON, or from both. In a dictionary, the ON cognate of an OE word is given where it is known. If a word is marked *fr ON*, it means that the OE word was adopted from ON, and is proof of the close contact between the two languages. Here are some examples:

1 Examples of MnE words that are reflexes of both OE and ON

adder	OE næddre ON naðra		*lamb*	OE lamb ON lamb
bake	OE bacan ON baka		*mother*	OE mōdor ON mōðir
church	OE cir(i)ce/cyrce ON kirkja		*nut*	OE hnutu ON hnot
daughter	OE dohtor ON dōttir		*oven*	OE ofen ON ofn
earth	OE eorþe ON jorð		*plum*	OE plūma ON ploma
father	OE fæder ON faðir		*quick*	OE cwicu ON kvikr
green	OE grēne ON groenn		*road*	OE rād ON reid
hear	OE hȳran/hīeran ON heyra		*small*	OE smæl ON smalr
iron	OE īren/īsern ON īsarn		*thing*	OE þing ON ðing
knife/knives	OE cnīf /cnifas ON knifr		*wash*	OE wæscan ON vaska

From this evidence, it seems likely that an OE or ON speaker would have recognised these words spoken in the other's language.

2 OE words beginning with <sc>

The OE digraph <sc> was originally pronounced [sk], but in time the two consonants merged into the consonant [ʃ]. (The spelling ⟨sh⟩, a French convention, was not adopted until after the Norman Conquest.) This sound change did not happen in ON, however, so in the following sample of words, it is the OE pronunciation that MnE reflexes have kept.

OE	ON	MnE
sceaft	skapt	*shaft*
scell	skell	*shell*
scearp	skarpr	*sharp*
sceran	skera	*shear* (vb)
scinan	skina	*shine*
scield	skjoldr	*shield*
scufan	skufa	*shove*
sceotan	skjota	*shoot*
fisc	fiskr	*fish*
wyscan	œskja	*wish*

OE *scyrte* was cognate with ON *skyrta* and both meant *shirt*, but their MnE reflexes, *shirt* and *skirt*, have taken on different meanings.

A few MnE words beginning with ⟨sk⟩ are derived from ON words which either had no OE cognate, or have replaced the OE, for example:

OE	ON	MnE
–	skata	*skate* (fish)
–	skeppa	*skep/skip*
–	skil	*skil*
scinn	skinn	*skin*
–	skifa	*skive*
–	skufr	*skua* (sea-bird)
sceo	sky	*sky*

So one important result of Danish and Norwegian settlement in the Danelaw was its effect on the English language spoken there. English and Norse speakers lived in communities that were close enough for contact to take place, sometimes within the same settlement, or in a family after inter-marriage. A large number of proper names of Scandinavian origin can be found in late OE and early ME documents. In time, the communities merged, Norse was no longer spoken, but the English dialects spoken in different parts of the Danelaw had been modified – in pronunciation, in vocabulary, and to some extent in grammar. The earliest evidence in writing, however, does not appear until much later, during the Middle English period, because most late OE was written in the standard West Saxon dialect. The long-term effects are still with us in the present-day dialects and accents of East Anglia, the Midlands, northern England and southern Scotland.

Unlike the English, the Danes and Norwegians had not at this time developed a system of writing other than runes, and no evidence of the dialects of the Norse language spoken in the Danelaw has come down to us. Norse must have been spoken throughout, but was gradually assimilated with English.

Some evidence of this assimilation can be seen in the porch of a small church in Kirkdale, North Yorkshire, called St Gregory's Minster. A sundial dating from about 1055 has been preserved, which has this inscription carved in stone:

Text 22: Inscription, St Gregory's Minster, Kirkdale, North Yorkshire (facsimile)

+ ORM GAMAL   ÞIS IS DAGES SOL MERCA   CAN 7 TO FALAN 7 HE
SVNA BOHTESCS   HIT LET MACAN NEƷAN FROM
GREGORIVS MIN   GRVNDE XPE7SCSGREGORI
STER ÐONNE HI   VS IN EADƷARD DAGVM CNG
T ƷES ÆL TOBRO   PRS.7INTOSTI DAGVM EORL ✚
           7 HAƷARDME ƷROHTE 7 BRAND

The man who carved the stone made the letters and spaces too big to begin with, and had to cram in those in the second part of the inscription, which might have read:

> ORM ᛚAMALSUNA BOᚻTE SᛚS ᛚREᛚORIVS MINSTER ÐONNE ᚻIT
> ꝼES ÆL TOBROᛚAN ꝿ TO FALAN ꝿ ᚻE ᚻIT LET MAᛚAN NEꝼAN
> FROM ᛚRUNDE XPE ꝿ SᛚS ᛚREᛚORIVS IN EADꝼARD DAᛚUM ᛚNᛚ ꝿ
> IN TOSTI DAᛚUM EORL ꝿ ᚻAꝼARÐ ME ꝼROᚻTE ꝿ BRAND PRS

SCS = *SANCTUS* = Saint; XPE = *CHRISTE*; CNG = *CYNING* = King; PRS = *PREOSTAS* = Priests

Translation
> ORM GAMALSON BOUGHT ST GREGORY'S MINSTER WHEN IT
> WAS ALL BROKEN & FALLEN DOWN & HE CAUSED IT TO BE
> MADE ANEW FROM THE GROUND TO CHRIST AND ST GREGORY
> IN KING EDWARD'S DAYS & IN EARL TOSTI'S DAYS & HAWARTH &
> BRAND PRIEST'S MADE ME

The inscription at the top of the sundial reads: þIS IS DAGES SOL MERCA. 'This is day's sun marker'.

Tosti, or Tostig, was Earl of Northumberland and brother to Harold Godwinson, who became King of England in 1066, on King Edward's death (see also Texts 24 and 25, in section 3.5). Orm and Gamal are Norse names, but the language is English.

📖 The vocabulary of Text 22 is listed in the Word Book.

3.5.2 OE and Scandinavian surnames

The name *Orm Gamalson* looks familiar to us as the usual way of referring to people by their forename and surname. *Orm Gamalsuna* (*Orm Gamalson*) meant *Orm, son of Gamal*, and this way of creating personal surnames, by adding -*suna*/-*son* as a **patronymic** suffix (name derived from the father), was in fact a common Germanic and Scandinavian custom, which was in time adopted throughout the country.

The Anglo-Saxon patronymic suffix had been -*ing*, as in *Ælfred Æþelwulfing*, *Ælfred, son of Athelwulf*. But -*ing* was also used in an extended sense to name families or peoples as descendants from a common ancestor, and in an even more general way, meaning *place characterised by*, or denoting possession, so that *Æþelwulfing lond* means the same as *Æþelwulfes lond* – *Æþelwulf's land*. So that there is sometimes doubt as to the original meaning of names which contain the suffix -*ing*.

3.5.3 OE and Scandinavian place names

Names with the -*ing* suffix were incorporated into place names, as in *Walsingham*, *Stillington*, *Kidlington*. Other suffixes which indicate place names in OE included -*hyrst* (*copse, wood*), -*ham* (*homestead, estate*), -*wic* (*farm*), -*tun* (*settlement*) and -*stede* (*place*), as in present-day *Wadhurst, Newnham, Norwich, Berwick, Heslington* and *Maplestead*. The detailed study of place names provides much of the historical evidence for the settlement of Danes and Norwegians in England.

Activity 3.3

Use an atlas and atlas gazetteer of England to identify towns and villages with place-names ending in the Scandinavian suffixes,

(i)   -by (*town, farm*)
(ii) -thorp(e) (*village*)
(iii) -thwaite (*piece of land*)
(iv) -toft (*piece of land*)

If you find a sufficient number, and mark them on a blank map, you should find good evidence of the extent of the Danelaw. You could check the occurrence of these place names against the map of the Danelaw on p. 49.

3.5.4 The Battle of Brunanburh (1)

In the *Peterborough Chronicle* for 937 there is the briefest of entries about a battle against Norsemen from Ireland who were defeated by Æthelstan, King of Wessex (the site of the battle is not known):

Text 23: **Peterborough Chronicle** *for* AD *937 (facsimile)*

Œ 1 ꟽ.ꝺcccc xxxvii Ꝡeꞧ æðelꞧtan cýninᵹ læꝺꝺe ꝼýꞧ
ꝺe to bꞧunanbýꞧiᵹ.

Œ 2 M.dcccc xxxvii her æðelstan cyning lædde fyrde
to brunanbyrig.

WW 937. Here athelstan king led troops to brunanburh.

📖 The vocabulary of Text 23 is listed in the Word Book.

A period of twenty-five years of peace after 955 was once again broken when more attacks by Norsemen began in the 980s. Some came from Normandy across the Channel, where Norsemen (the Normans) had also settled, as well as from Denmark and Norway. In 1017, the Danish King Cnut became 'King of All England', and the line of Danish kings was not ended until 1042, when the English Edward the Confessor became king.

3.6 The Norman Conquest

In 1066 Duke William of Normandy defeated King Harold at Hastings and became King William I of England. This event had the most profound effects on the country and on the language, and when we read English texts from the 12th century onwards, we notice changes at each level of language – spelling and vocabulary, word form and grammar.

Here are two further extracts from the *Anglo-Saxon Chronicle*, one very short and the other much longer, describing the events of 1066. If you study the longer text from the *Peterborough Chronicle*, you will understand a little of how historians have to interpret original sources when writing history. The annal is written in the simple narrative style of the *Chronicle*, with each event prefaced by *and*. Reference to individuals as *he* or *him* is sometimes rather confusing. This outline of the events told in the *Chronicle* may help:

> King Edward the Confessor died on 28 December 1065, and was buried on 6 January 1066. He was succeeded by King Harold, but Duke William of Normandy also claimed the English throne, and prepared a force to attack southern England. But before this, King Harold, with Earls Edwin and Morcar, had to fend off attacks on the north of England by the Norwegian Harald Hardrada. Harold defeated the Norwegian at Stamford Bridge near York. Tostig, the Earl of Northumberland, was King Harold's brother, but he had defected to the Norwegian Harald. King Harold made a forced march southwards immediately after the battle at Stamford Bridge, but his army was defeated by William at the Battle of Hastings. Duke William was crowned William I soon after.

Text 24: **Part of the** Parker Chronicle **for 1066 (facsimile)**

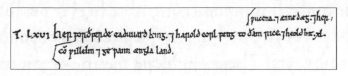

Œ 1 mlxvi. Ðer forðferde eaðuuarð king. ⁊ harolð eorl ⁊enɀ to ðam rice. ⁊ heolð hit .xl. cō rillelm ⁊ ɀe rann æn⁊la lanð.
(pucena. ⁊ ænne ðæɀ. ⁊ her)

Œ 2 mlxvi. Her forðferde eaduuard king & harold eorl feng to ðam rice. & heold hit .xl. wucena. & ænne dæg & her com willelm & gewann ænglaland.

WW 1066. Here died Edward king. & Harold earl seized the kingdom. & held it 40 of-weeks. & one day. & here came William & conquered England.

📖 The vocabulary of Text 24 is listed in the Word Book.

Text 25: part of the Peterborough Chronicle for 1066 (facsimile)

On þissū geare man halgode þet
mynster æt Westmynstre on cildamæsse dæg. ⁊ se cyng
eadward forðferde on twelfta mæsse æfen. ⁊ hine mann
bebyrgede on twelftan mæsse dæg. innan þære niwa
halgodre cyrcean on Westmynstre. ⁊ harold eorl feng
to englalandes cyne rice. swa swa se cyng hit him ge uðe.
⁊ eac men hine þær to gecuron. ⁊ wæs gebletsod to cyn
ge on twelftan mæsse dæg. ⁊ þy ilcan geare þe he cyng
wæs. he for ut mid sciphere togeanes Willelme. ⁊ þa hwi
le com Tostig eorl into   humbran mid. lx. scipū. Ead
wine eorl com land fyrde. ⁊ draf hine ut. ⁊ þa butsecarlas
hine forsocan. ⁊ he for to scotlande mid. xii. snaccū. ⁊ hi
ne gemette harold se norrena cyng mid. ccc. scipū. ⁊
Tostig him to beah. ⁊ hi bægen foran into humbran oð þer
hi coman to eoferwic. ⁊ heom wið feaht morkere eorl. ⁊
eadwine eorl. ⁊ se norrena cyng ahte siges geweald. ⁊ man
cydde harode cyng hu hit þær þær gedon ⁊ geworden.
⁊ he com mid myclū here engliscra manna. ⁊ gemette hine
æt stængfordes brycge. ⁊ hine ofsloh. ⁊ þone eorl Tostig.
⁊ eallne þone here ahtlice ofercom. ⁊ þa hwile com Willelm eorl
upp æt hestingan on sce michaeles mæsse dæg. ⁊ harold
com norðan ⁊ him wið feaht ear þan þe his here come eall. ⁊
þær he feoll. ⁊ his twægen gebroðra Gyrð ⁊ leofwine. and
Willelm þis land ge eode. ⁊ com to Westmynstre ⁊ ealdred
arceb hine to cynge ge halgode. ⁊ menn guldon him gyld.
⁊ gislas sealdon. ⁊ syððan heora land bohtan.

Œ 1

.Ꝏ.lxvi.　On þiꞅꞃū ᵹeaꞃe man halᵹoðe þet
mynꞅteꞃ æt peꞅtmynꞅtꞃe on cilða mæꞅꞅe ðæᵹ· ⁊ ꞅe cynᵹ
eaðpaꞃð foꞃðfeꞃðe on tpelꝼta mæꞅꞅe æfen· ⁊ hine mann
bebyꞃᵹeðe on tpelftan mæꞅꞅe ðæᵹ· innan þæꞃe nipa
halᵹoðꞃe ciꞃcean on peꞅtmynꞅtꞃe·⁊ haꞃolð eoꞃl ꝼenᵹ
to enᵹlalanðeꞅ cyneꞃice· ꞅpa ꞅpa ꞅe cynᵹ hit him ᵹe uðe·
⁊ eac men hine þæꞃto ᵹecuꞃon·⁊ pæꞅ ᵹebletꞃoð to cynᵹe on tpelftan mæꞅꞅe ðæᵹ· ⁊ þy ilcan ᵹeaꞃe þe he cynᵹ
pæꞅ· he ꞃoꞃ ut mið ꞅcipheꞃe toᵹeaneꞅ Willme· ⁊ þa hpi/
le cō toꞅtiᵹ eoꞃl into humbꞃan mið ·lx· ꞅcipū· Eað/
pine eoꞃl cō landꝼyꞃðe· ⁊ ðꞃaꝼ hine ut· ⁊ þa butꞅecaꞃlaꞅ
hine ꞃoꞃꞅocan· ⁊ he ꞃoꞃ to ꞅcotlanðe mið ·xii· ꞅnaccū· ⁊ hi
ne ᵹemette haꞃolð ꞅe noꞃꞃena cynᵹ mið ·ccc· ꞅcipū ⁊
toꞅtiᵹ hī to beah· ⁊ hi bæᵹen ꞃoꞃan into humbꞃan oð þet
hi coman to eoꞃeꞃpic· ⁊ heō pıð ꝼeaht moꞃkeꞃe eoꞃl· ⁊
eaðpine eoꞃl· ⁊ ꞅe noꞃꞃena cynᵹ alne ꞅiᵹeꞅ ᵹepealð· ⁊ man
cyðde haꞃo(l)ðe cynᵹ hu hit pæꞅ þæꞃ ᵹeðon ⁊ ᵹepoꞃðen·
⁊ he cō mið mycclū heꞃe enᵹliꞅcꞃa manna· ⁊ ᵹemette hine
æt ꞅtænᵹꞃoꞃðeꞅ bꞃycᵹe· ⁊ hine oꝼꞅloh· ⁊ þone eoꞃl toꞅtiᵹ·
⁊ eallne þone heꞃe ahtlice oꝼeꞃ cō· ⁊ þa hpile cō pillm eoꞃl
upp æt heꞅtinᵹan on ꞅcē michaeleꞅ mæꞅꞅe ðæᵹ· ⁊ haꞃolð
cō noꞃþan ⁊ hī pıð ꝼeahte eaꞃ þan þe hiꞅ heꞃe come eall· ⁊
þæꞃ he ꝼeoll· ⁊ hiꞅ tpæᵹen ᵹebꞃoðꞃa Gyꞃð ⁊ leoꞃpine· anð
Willelm þiꞅ lanð ᵹe eoðe· ⁊ cō to peꞅtmynꞅtꞃe· ⁊ ealðꞃeð
aꞃceb hine to cynᵹe ᵹehalᵹoðe· ⁊ menn ᵹulðon him ᵹylð·
⁊ ᵹiꞅlaꞅ ꞅealðon· ⁊ ꞅyððan heoꞃa lanð bohtan꞉

Œ 2

(abbreviations expanded)

.M.lxvi.　On þissum geare man halgode þet
mynster æt westmynstre on cilda mæsse dæg. & se cyng
eadward forðferde on twelfta mæsse æfen. & hine mann
bebyrgede on twelftan mæsse dæg. innan þære niwa
halgodre circean on westmynstre. & harold eorl feng
to englalandes cynerice. swa swa se cyng hit him geuðe.
& eac men hine þærto gecuron. & wæs gebletsod to cynge on twelftan mæsse dæg. & þy ilcan geare þe he cyng
wæs. he for ut mid sciphere togeanes Willelme. & þa hwile com tostig eorl into humbran mid .lx. scipum. Eadwine eorl com landfyrde. & draf hine ut. & þa butsecarlas
hine forsocan. & he for to scotlande mid xii snaccum. & hine gemette harold se norrena cyng mid .ccc. scipum &
tostig him to beah. & hi bægen foran into humbran oð þet
hi coman to eoferwic. & heom wið feaht morkere eorl. &
eadwine eorl. & se norrena cyng alne siges geweald. & man
cydde haro(l)de cyng hu hit wæs þær gedon & geworden.
& he com mid mycclum here engliscra manna. & gemette hine
æt stængfordes brycge. & hine ofsloh. & þone eorl tostig.
& eallne þone here ahtlice ofercom. & þa hwile com willelm eorl
upp æt hestingan on sancte michaeles mæsse dæg. & harold
com norþan & him wið feahte ear þan þe his here come eall. &

þær he feoll. & his twægen gebroðra Gyrð & leofwine. and
Willelm þis land ge eode. & com to westmynstre. & ealdred
arcebiscop hine to cynge gehalgode. & menn guldon him gyld.
& gislas sealdon. & syððan heora land bohtan.

| WW | 1066.   In this year one consecrated the
minster at westminster on children's mass day. & the king
edward died on twelfth mass eve. & him one
buried on twelfth mass day. in the new
consecrated church at westminster. & harold earl succeeded
to england's kingdom. as the king it to-him granted.
& also men him thereto chose. & was blessed as king
on twelfth mass day. & the same year that he king
was. he went out with ship-force against William. & meanwhile
came tostig earl into humber with 60 ships. Ed-
win earl came (with) land-army. & drove him out. & the shipmen
him forsook. & he went to scotland with 12 vessels. & him
met harold the norwegian king with 300 ships. and
tostig him to submitted. & they both went into humber until
they came to york. & them against fought morcar earl. &
edwin earl. & the norwegian king all victory gained. & one
told harold king how it was there done & happened.
& he came with great army of-english men, & met him
at stamford bridge. & him slew. & the earl tostig.
& all the host manfully overcame & meanwhile came william earl
up at hastings on st michael's mass day. & harold
came from-north & him against fought before his army came all. &
there he fell. & his two brothers Gurth & leofwine. and
William this land conquered. & came to westminster. & ealdred
archbishop him to king consecrated. & men paid him tribute.
& hostages gave. & then their lands bought-back.

children's mass day = Holy Innocent's Day, 28 December

twelfth mass eve = the Eve of Epiphany, 5 January

twelfth mass day = 'Twelfth Night', Epiphany, 6 January

blessed as king = consecrated as king

st michael's mass day = St Michael's Day, 29 September

📖 The vocabulary of Text 25 is listed in the Word Book.

4 Old English (II)

4.1 The language of Old English poetry

The entry recording the Battle of Brunanburh in the *Parker Chronicle* is a graphic poetical account of the battle, in complete contrast to the single terse sentence in the *Peterborough Chronicle* (section 3.5.4). Here are three short extracts from the poem.

4.1.1 The Battle of Brunanburh (2)

Text 26: From the* Parker Chronicle *for AD 937 (facsimile)

61

þær læȝ recȝ mæniȝ· ȝapū aȝeteð· ȝuma norþerna·
oꝼer rcilð rcoten· ſpilce ſcýttiſc eác· weriȝ wíȝer ræð· perreaxe ꝼóꝛð·
onðlonȝne ðæȝ· eoꝛoð cirtum· on laſt leȝðun· laþum þeoðum· heoꝛan
here ꝼleman· hinðan þearle· mecum mýlen rcearpan·

ne wearð pæl mare· ón þir
eiȝlanðe· æꝼer ȝieta· ꝼolcer ȝeꝼ̊ylleð· beꝼoran þirrū· ſpeoꝛðer
écȝum· þær þe ur recȝað bec· ealðe uðꝛitan· ſiþþan eaſtan hiðer·
enȝle 7 reaxe· up becoman· oꝼer bꝛað bꝛimu· bꝛýtene ꝛohtan·
plance piȝmiðar· peealler oꝼercoman· eoꝛlar ꝛ hꝛate· earð
beȝeatan·

OE 2 dccccc·xxxvii   Her æþelstan cyning· eorla dryhten· beorna
beahgifa· 7 his broþor eac· eadmund æþeling· ealdor langne tir·
geslogon æt sæcce· sweorda ecgum· ymbe brunanburh·

þær læg secg mænig· garum ageted· guma norþerna·
ofer scild scoten· swilce scyttisc eac· werig wiges sæd· wesseaxe forð·
ondlongne dæg· eorod cistum· on last legdun· laþum þeodum· heowan
here fleman· hindan þearle· mecum mylen scearpan·

ne wearð wæl mare· on þis
eiglande· æfer gieta· folces gefylled· beforan þissum sweordes
ecgum· þæs þe us secgað bec· ealde uðwitan· siþþan eastan hider·
engle 7 seaxe· up becoman· ofer brad brimu· brytene sohtan·
wlance wig smiðas· weealles ofercoman· eorlas ar hwate· eard
begeatan.

WW   937.   Here athelstan king. of-earls lord. of-men
ring-giver. & his brother also. edmund prince. life long honour.
won in battle. of-swords with-edges. by brunanburh. . . .

there lay man many-a. by-spears killed. man northern.
over shield shot. also scots too. weary of-battle sated. west saxons forth
throughout day. troops in-companies. on trail pursued. loathed people. hacked
from-army fugitives. from-behind harshly. with-swords millstone sharp. ...

not happened slaughter more. in this
island. ever yet. of-folk felled. before this. of-sword
with-edges. as to-us say books. ancient scholars. since from-east hither.
angles & saxons. up came. over broad seas. britain sought.
proud war smiths. welshmen overcame. earls for-honour eager. country
conquered.

📖 The vocabulary of Text 26 is listed in the Word Book.

There was no rhyme or regular syllabic metre in OE verse, which was a 'heightened' form of ordinary speech, with a strong 'falling' rhythm because of the tendency to stress the first syllable of most words. Each line is divided into two half-lines, linked by the **alliteration** of words between the half-lines of each line – that is, they begin with the same consonant or any vowel. The words carrying stress were lexical words

– nouns, adjectives, verbs or adverbs – not function words like pronouns or prepositions:

Her ⊡æ⊡ þelstan cyning. ⊡eo⊡ rla dryhten.
⊡b⊡ eorna ⊡b⊡ eahgifa. and his ⊡b⊡ roþor eac.
⊡ea⊡ dmund ⊡æ⊡ þeling. ⊡ea⊡ ldor langne tir.
ge ⊡s⊡ logon æt ⊡s⊡ æcce. ⊡s⊡ weorda ecgum.
ymbe brunanburh.

You can see from the facsimile that verse was set out like prose in OE manuscripts, not in separate lines in the way we are used to. Lines and half-lines were occasionally clearly marked with a dot like our full-stop, as in Text 26 (though this marking may be a later addition to the manuscript). Modern printing of OE verse shows the alliterative structure of the lines more clearly, with half-lines marked by a wider space, and with standard sentence punctuation added:

Her æpelstan cyning,   eorla dryhten,
beorna beahgifa   and his broþor eac,
eadmund æpeling,   ealdor langne tir.
geslogon æt sæcce   sweorda ecgum
ymbe brunanburh.

4.1.2 *Beowulf*

Here is another example of OE verse, from *Beowulf*, the most famous OE poem. It was probably written in the 8th century (though there is no external evidence and scholars of OE disagree). It is known only from a single surviving manuscript that dates from the 10th century. You will see from the facsimile that the manuscript has been damaged. It was scorched in a fire in 1731 and has deteriorated since then, so that many words on the edges are missing or only partly legible.

   The historical period of the poem's story is the 6th century, and the hero Beowulf is not Anglo-Saxon, but a Geat from southern Sweden. The tale is legendary, and the following extract from early on in the poem tells how the monster Grendel was harassing Hrothgar, the Danish king of the Scyldings, in his hall, Heorot.

Text 27: A page from the manuscript of Beowulf *(facsimile)*

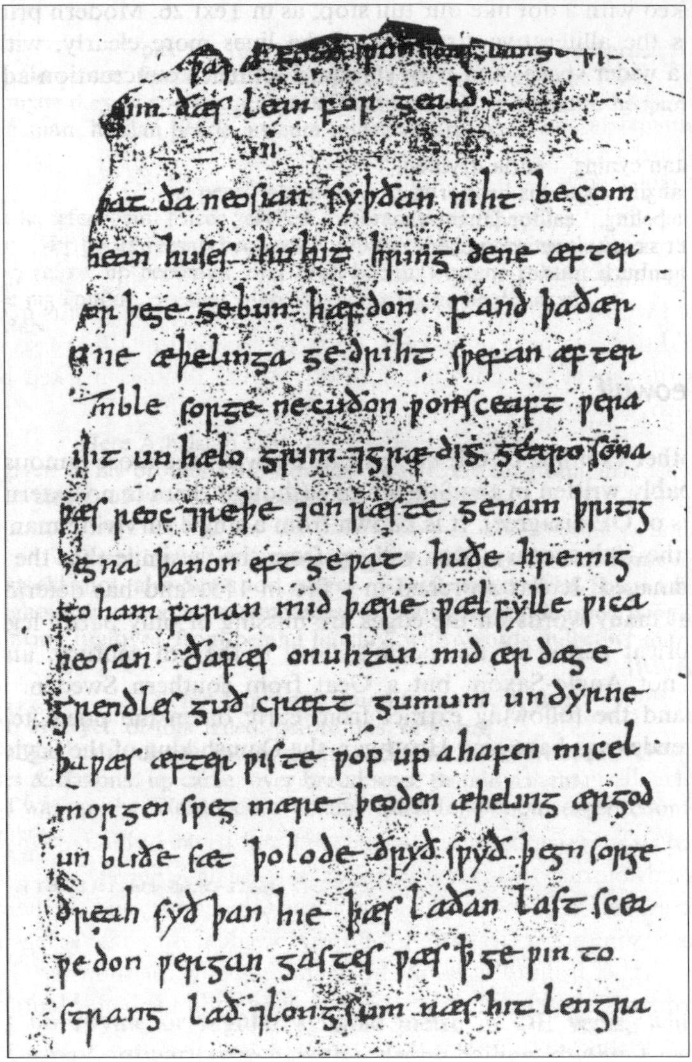

Transliterations of MS
(The lines in italics precede and follow the text of the MS page.)

Font based on the *Beowulf* MS handwriting

þanon untydras ealle onpocon
eotenas ylfe 7orcneas spylce gig-
antas þa pið gode punnon lange þrage
he him ðæs lean forgeald.

Gepat ða neosian syþðan niht becom
hean huses hu hit hring dene æfter
beore þege ge-bun hæfdon. Fand þa ðær
inne æþelinga ge-driht spefan æfter
symble sorge ne cuðon ponsceaft pera
piht un hælo grim 7grædig, gearo sona
pæs reoc 7reþe 7on ræste genam þritig
þegna þanon eft gepat huðe hremig
to ham faran mid þære pæl fylle pica
neosan. ðapæs onuhtan mid ær dæge
grendles guð cræft gumum undyrne
þa pæs æfter piste pop up ahafen micel
morgen speg mære þeoden æþeling ærgod
un blide sæt þolode ðryð spyð þegn sorge
dreah syð þan hie þæs laðan last scea
pedon pergan gastes pæs þ ge pin to
strang lað 7long sum næs hit lengra

fyrst ac ymb ane niht eft gefremede
morð beala mare 7no mearn fore
fæhðe 7fyrene

Modern printed version & word-for-word translation

þanon untydras ealle onwocon,	*Thence evil-broods all were born:*
eotenas ond ylfe ond orcneas,	*ogres and elves and goblins*
*swylce gigan*tas, *þa wið Gode wunnon*	*likewise (the) gi*ants who against God strove
lange þrage; he him ðæs lean forgeald.	(for a) long time he them their reward paid.
Gewat ða neosian, syþðan niht becom,	(He) went then (to) seek, after night came,
hean huses, hu hit Hring-Dene	(the) lofty house, how (in) it (the) Ring-Danes,
æfter beor þege gebun hæfdon.	after beer-drinking, dwelt had.
Fand þa ðær inne æþelinga gedriht	(He) found then therein of-noblemen (a) company,
swefan æfter symble; sorge ne cuðon,	asleep after (the) banquet; sorrow (they) knew not,
wonsceaft wera. Wiht unhælo,	(the) misery of-men. (The) creature damned,
grim ond grædig, gearo sona wæs,	grim and greedy, ready immediately was,
reoc ond reþe, ond on ræste genam	savage and cruel, and at rest seized
þritig þegna. þanon eft gewat	thirty thanes. Thence then (he) turned,
huðe hremig to ham faran,	(in) plunder exulting, to home go,
mid þære wælfylle wica neosan.	with that slaughter (his) dwelling to seek
Ða wæs on uhtan mid ærdæge	Then was in (the) half-light before dawn
Grendles guðcræft gumum undyrne;	Grendel's war-strength to-men revealed;
þa wæs æfter wiste wop up ahafen,	then was after (the) feast weeping, up raised
micel morgensweg. Mære þeoden,	(a) great morning-cry. (The) great prince,
æþeling ærgod, unbliðe sæt;	(a) leader good before others, joyless sat;
þolode ðryðswyð, þegnsorge dreah,	suffered (the) mighty one, thane-grief suffered
syðþan hie þæs laðan last sceawedon	when they (the) loathsome tracks looked at
wergan gastes. Wæs þæt gewin to strang,	of-(the)-accursed devil. Was the contest too fierce,
lað ond longsum. Næs hit lengra *fyrst,*	hateful and long-lasting. Nor-was it longer *time,*
ac ymb ane niht eft gefremede	*but within one night again (he) committed*
morðbeala mare ond no mearn fore,	*murder more, and no remorse felt,*
fæhðe ond fyrene	*vengeance and wickedness*

📖 The vocabulary of Text 27 is listed in the Word Book.

OE poetic diction

The 'compact' nature of OE verse is partly due to there being fewer function words when compared with MnE (see, for example, the number of bracketed determiners and pronouns marked in the translation above, which are grammatically necessary in MnE). This focuses attention on the meaning-bearing lexical words – nouns, verbs, adjectives and adverbs.

This effect is also achieved by the number of compound nouns used in OE prose and poetry. The compounds in Text 27 are contrasted with their MnE equivalents, which are usually less compact:

compound	literal translation	MnE equivalent
beorþege	beer + accepting	beer-drinking
wælfylle	the slain + plenty	large numbers of the slain
ærdæge	before + day	before dawn
guðcræft	war + skill	skill in warfare
morgensweg	morning + sound	sound made in the morning
ærgod	before + good	good before others
ðryðswyð	power + strong	very powerful
þegnsorge	thane + sorrow	sorrow for the loss of thanes

4.2 OE prose

Here are two facsimiles of texts for study, one literary (Text 28 from OE Gospels), the other 'utility' (Text 29, Wulfstan's *Canons of Edgar*).

4.2.1 OE translation of the Bible

Text 28: OE Gospels (Matthew 28: 8–19) (facsimile)

Ða feþdon hiȝ hraðlice fram þære byrȝene
mið eȝe ȝmið myclum ȝefean. ȝuþnon ȝcýð _
ðon hýt hýr leorningcnihton ȝ efne þa com ʃe
hælynð onȝean hiȝ ȝcƿæð. hale ƿe reȝé; hiȝ
ȝenealæhton ȝȝe namon hýr fet . ȝto him ȝe eað _
meððon; Ða cƿæð ʃe hælynð to heð; Ne onðræ _
ðe ȝe eop . faþað ȝcýþað minum ȝebroþþum
þ hiȝ faþon on ȝalileam þær hiȝ ȝereoð me;
þa þa hiȝ feþdon þa comon rume. þa peaþðas
on þa ceaʃtʃe ȝ cýðdon þæþa ʃaceþða ealoþum
ealle þa ðinȝ þe ðær ȝeþoþðene pæþum; ða ȝe
ʃamnuðon þa ealoþaʃ hiȝ ȝþorhtun ȝe mot. ȝ
ʃealðon þam ðeȝenum micýl feoh. ȝcƿæðon;
Secȝeað þ hýr leornincnihtaʃ comon nihteʃ ȝ
forʃtælan hýne ða ƿe ʃlepun; ȝȝýf ʃe ðema
þiʃ ȝe axað. ƿe læþað hýne ȝȝeboð eop roþh
leaʃe; Ða onfenȝon hiȝ þæʃ feor . ȝðýðon eall
ʃƿa hiȝ ȝelæþeðe pæþon; ȝþiʃ puþð þær ȝe
ƿið mæþroð mið iuðeum oð þiʃne anðpeaþðan
ðæȝ;

Ða feþdon þa enðlufun leoþnincnihtaʃ on
þone munt . þæʃ ʃe hælynð heom ðihte. ȝhýne
þær ȝeʃaþun . ȝhiȝ to him ȝe eaðmeððun; Ƿitoð _
lice ʃume hiȝ tƿeoneðon; Ða ȝenealæhte ʃe _
hælynð ȝ ʃþæc to heom þaʃ þinȝ ȝþuʃʃ cƿæð;
Mé iʃ ȝe ʃealð ælc anþealð on heoʃonan ȝ
on eoʃðan. faþað ʃitoðlice ȝlæþað ealle þeoða

Text 29: Wulfstan's Canons of Edgar *(facsimile)*

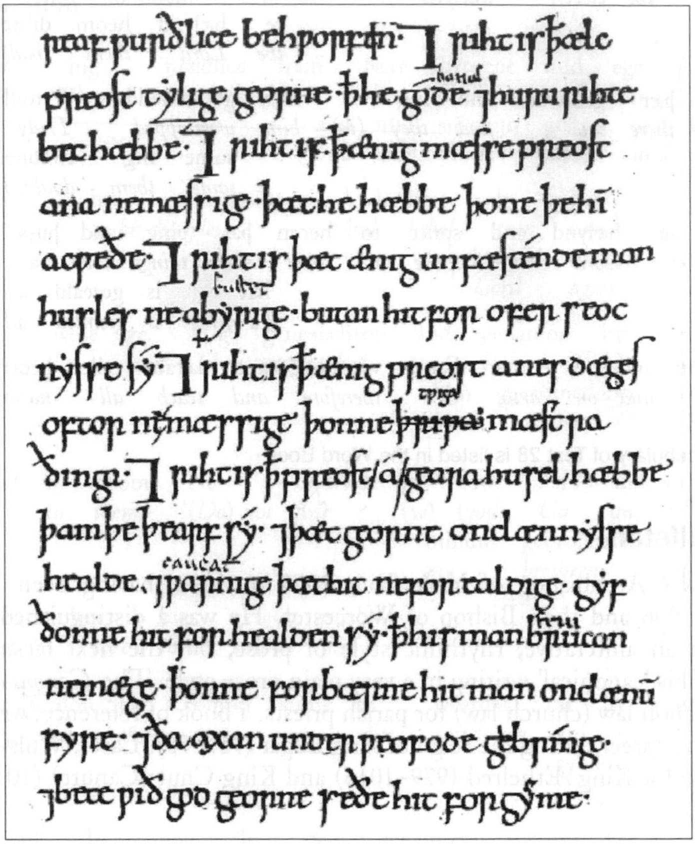

ŒE 1

ƿeaꝼ ƿuꞃðlice behƿoꞃꝼen ⁊ ꞃihꞇ iꞅ ꝥ ælc ·
pꞃeoſꞇ ꞇẏliᵹe ᵹeoꞃne· ꝥ he ᵹoꝺe ⁊huꞃu ꞃihꞇe
bec hæbbe· ⁊ ꞃihꞇ iꞅ·ꝥ æniᵹ mæſſe pꞃeoſꞇ
ana ne mæſſiᵹe·þæꞇ he hæbbe þone þe hī
acƿeꝺe· ⁊ ꞃihꞇ iꞅ þæꞇ æniᵹ unꝼæſꞇénꝺe man
huꞅleꞅ ne abẏꞃiᵹe· buꞇan hiꞇ ꝼoꞃ oꝼeꞃꞅeoc
nẏſſe ſẏ· ⁊ ꞃihꞇ iꞅ ꝥ æniᵹ pꞃeoꞅꞇ aneꞅ ꝺæᵹeꞅ
ꞇꞃiᵹa
oꝼꞇoꞃ ne mæꞅꞅiᵹe þonne ~~þꞃiƿa~~ mæſꞇꞃa
ðinᵹa· ⁊ ꞃihꞇ iꞅ ꝥ pꞃeoſꞇ a ᵹeaꞃa huꞅel hæbbe
þam þe þeaꞃꝼ ꞅẏ· ⁊ þæꞇ ᵹeoꞃne on clænnẏſſe
healꝺe· ⁊ ƿaꞃniᵹe þæꞇ hiꞇ ne ꝼoꞃealꝺiᵹe· ᵹẏꝼ
ðonne hiꞇ ꝼoꞃhealꝺan ꞅẏ· ꝥ hiꞅ man bꞃucan
ne mæᵹe· þonne ꝼoꞃbæꞃne hiꞇ man on clænū
ꝼẏꞃe· ⁊ ða axan unꝺeꞃ ƿeoꝼoꝺe ᵹebꞃínᵹe·
⁊ beꞇe ƿið ᵹoꝺ ᵹeoꞃne ꞅe ðe hiꞇ ꝼoꞃᵹẏme·

Œ 2

reaf wurðlice behworfen. & riht is þæt ælc
preost tylige georne þæt he gode & huru rihte
bec hæbbe. & riht is þæt ænig mæssepreost
ana ne mæssige. þæt he hæbbe þone þe him
acweðe. & riht is þæt ænig unfæstende man
husles ne abyrige. butan hit for oferseocnysse
sy. & riht is þæt ænig preost anes dæges
oftor ne mæssige þonne twiga mæstra
ðinga. & riht is þæt preost a geara husel hæbbe
þam þe þearf sy. & þæt georne on clænnysse
healde. & warnige þæt hit ne forealdige. gyf
ðonne hit forhealdan sy. þæt his man brucan
ne mæge. þonne forbærne hit man on clænum
fyre. & ða axan under weofode gebringe.
& bete wið god georne se ðe hit forgyme.

	And	riht	is	þæt	ælc		
	And	*right*	*is*	*that*	*each*		

preost	tylige	georne	þæt	he	gode	and	huru	rihte
priest	*strives*	*eagerly*	*that*	*he*	*good*	*and*	*at least*	*right*

bec	hæbbe.	And	riht	is	þæt	ænig	mæssepreost
books	*has.*	*And*	*right*	*is*	*that*	*any*	*mass-priest*

ana	ne	mæssige;	þæt	he	hæbbe	þone	þe	him
alone	*does not*	*say Mass;*	*that*	*he*	*has*		*him*	*who*	*for him*

acweðe.	*And	riht	is	þæt	ænig	unfæstende	man
speaks.	*And*	*right*	*is*	*that*	*any*	*not fasting*	*man*

husles	ne	abyrige,	butan	hit	for	oferseocnysse
housel	*not*	*tastes,*	*except*	*it*	*for*	*extreme sickness*

sy.	And	riht	is	þæt	ænig	preost	anes	dæges
be.	*And*	*right*	*is*	*that*	*any*	*priest*	*in one*	*day*

oftor	ne	mæssige	þonne	twiga	mæstra
more often	*does not*	*say Mass*	*than*	*two*	*most*

ðinga.	And	riht	is	þæt	preost	a	geara	husel	hæbbe
times.	*And*	*right*	*is*	*that*	*priest*	*always*	*ready*	*housel*	*has*

þam	þe	þearf	sy,	and	þæt	georne	on	clænnysse
for them	*that*	*in want*	*be,*	*and*	*that*	*desirous*	*in*	*purity*

healde,	and	warnige	þæt	hit	ne	forealdige.	Gyf
keep,	*and*	*beware*	*that*	*it*	*does not*	*decay.*	*If*

ðonne	hit	forhealdan	sy,	þæt	his	man	brucan
then	*it*	*withheld*	*be,*	*that*	*it*	*someone*	*eat*

ne	mæge,	þonne	forbærne	hit	man	on	clænum
not	*may,*	*then*	*burn up*	*it*	*someone*	*in*	*clean*

fyre,	and	ða	axan	under	weofode	gebringe,
fire,	*and*	*the*	*ashes*	*under*	*altar*	*bring*

and	bete	wið	God	georne	se	ðe	hit	forgyme.
and	*atone*	*with*	*God*	*well*	*he*	*that*	*it*	*neglects.*

*And riht is þæt ænig unfæstende man husles ne abyrige – *No one who has not fasted beforehand may receive holy communion.*

The vocabulary of Text 29 is listed in the Word Book.

4.3 OE grammar

We have to speak in sentences to convey meanings. **Words** are grouped into **phrases**, and phrases into **clauses**, and in written English one or more clauses make up a **sentence**. There are two principal ways in which words are related to form phrases and clauses and give meanings. One is using an agreed **word order**. The other is changing the form of words, either by adding **inflections** (prefixes or suffixes), or by altering part of a word.

In OE, the order of words in a clause was more variable than that of MnE, and there were many more inflections on nouns, adjectives and verbs.

4.3.1 Word order

Today, the normal unmarked order of the constituents in a declarative clause (one making a statement) is SP(C/O)(A), that is, the Subject comes first, followed by the Predicator (or Verb), then the Complements or Objects, and last the Adverbials, if any. This was the common pattern already in OE. Examples in this section and the next are from the OE versions of the stories of the Garden of Eden (Adam and Eve) or the Flood (Noah), in the book of Genesis from the Old Testament.

S	P	A
seo næddre	cwæþ	to þam wife
the serpent	*said*	*to the woman*

S	P	O
hi	gehyrdon	his stemne
they	*heard*	*his voice*

S	P	O	cj	S	P
seo næddre	bepæhte	me	and	ic	ætt
the serpent	*deceived*	*me*	*and*	*I*	*ate*

But there were also different orders of words. For example, after a linking adverb (e.g. *þa = then*) the verb came before the subject:

A	P	S	A	A
þa	cwæþ	seo næddre	eft	to þam wife
then	*said*	*the serpent*	*after*	*to the woman*

A	P	S	cj	S	P	C
þa	geseah	þæt wif	þæt	þæt treow	wæs	god to etenne
then	*saw*	*the woman*	*that*	*the tree*	*was*	*good to eat*

or the verb might sometimes come last in a subordinate clause:

S	P	A	cj	S	C	P
hi	oncneowon	þa	þæt	hi	nacode	wæron
they	*knew*	*then*	*that*	*they*	*naked*	*were*

OE word order also differed from MnE in asking questions and forming the negative:

A	P	S	O	cj	S	neg	P
Hwi	forbead	God	eow	þæt	ge	ne	æton?
Why	*forbade*	*God*	*you*	*that*	*you*	*not*	*eat?*

(= *Why did God forbid you to eat?*)

Many other examples can be found in the OE texts in Chapters 1–4 by reading the word-for-word translations.

Activity 4.1

Identify the clause elements and the order of the subjects and predicators in the following clauses (phrases are bracketed in the first set):

From Text 17a

	(Her) (nam) (breohtric cining) (offan dohter eadburge)
&	(on his dagum) (comon) (ærest) (.iii. scipu norðmanna) (of hereða lande)
&	(þa) (se gerefa) (þær to) (rad)
&	(he) (wolde drifan) (to ðes ciniges tune)
ðy	(he) (nyste)
	(hwæt) (hi) (wæron)
&	(hine) (man) (ofsloh) (þa)
	(þæt) (wæron) (þa erestan scipu deniscra manna)
	(þe)(angel cynnes land) (gesohton)

from Text 19a

	Her hiene bestæl se here on midne winter ofer twelftan niht to cippanhamme
&	Ø geridan west seaxna land
&	Ø gesetton
&	mycel þæs folces ofer sæ adræfdon
&	þæs oþres þone mæstan dæl hi geridon butan þam cynge ælfrede
&	he litle werede ȳðelice æfter wudum for & on morfestenum

4.3.2 Number, case and gender – inflections on nouns and adjectives

4.3.2.1 Number

There are only a few inflections in MnE today which mark the grammatical functions of nouns. We show the **number** of a noun, that is, whether it is **singular** (sg) or **plural** (pl), by adding [s] [z] or [ɪz] in speech, ⟨s⟩ or ⟨es⟩ in writing:

cat/cats   dog/dogs   church/churches
[kæt/kæts]   [dɒg/dɒgz]   [ʧ3ʧ/ʧ3ʧɪz]

and there are a few irregular plurals which have survived from OE, such as *men*, *geese*, and *mice*, which show plural number by a change of vowel, and *oxen*, whose *-en* plural was very common in OE as *-an*.

4.3.2.2 Case

In MnE today only the personal pronouns (except *you* and *it*) are inflected to show whether they are the subject or object in a clause.

MnE			OE		
S	*P*	*O*	*S*	*P*	*O*
I	saw	it	**ic**	seah	**hit**
you (sg)	saw	her	**þu**	sawe	**hi**
he	saw	me	**he**	seah	**me**
she	saw	him	**heo**	seah	**hine**
we	saw	you (pl)	**we**	sawon	**eow**
you (pl)	saw	us	**ge**	sawon	**us**
they	saw	them	**hi**	sawon	**hi**

Adjectives are not inflected to agree with nouns in MnE, nor is the definite article *the*, but they were in OE. The feature of the grammar which marks these functions is called **case**.

subject   ⇒   nominative case   (nom)
direct object   ⇒   accusative case   (acc)
indirect object ⇒   dative case   (dat)

In a **prepositional phrase** (PrepP) in OE, the noun was in either the accusative or the dative case, according to the preposition.

The only other MnE inflection on nouns is the ⟨'s⟩ or ⟨s'⟩ in writing to show possession – called the possessive or **genitive** case (gen). This is the only grammatical case in MnE which survives from OE in nouns. In OE the genitive noun usually preceded the noun head of the phrase:

godes cyrican (Text 18)	God's church
sweorda ecgum (Text 26)	(by the) swords' edges
sweordes ecgum (Text 26)	(by the) sword's edges

Place names often begin as genitive + noun constructions:

certices ford (Text 9a)	Cerdic's ford (*not identified*)
æþelinga ige (Text 19a)	of-princes isle = isle of the princes = Athelney
heopwines fleot (Text 7)	Ypwine's fleet (*river*) = Ebbsfleet

Phrases of measurement also contained a genitive, as in:

.iii. scipu norðmanna (Text 17a)	3 ships of-Norsemen
.xl. wucena (Text 24)	40 of-weeks
.xxxi. wintra (Text 10a)	31 of-winters = 31 years

4.3.2.3 Gender

In MnE, we have to select the correct pronoun *he*, *she* or *it*, according to the sex, or lack of sex, of the referent – *he* is **masculine** (m), *she* is **feminine** (f), *it* is **neuter** (n). This is called **natural gender**. In OE, nouns for things which today are all neuter, and nouns for a male or female person might be masculine, feminine or neuter. For example, *sunne* (*sun*) was feminine, *mona* (*moon*) was masculine, *wif* (*woman*) and *cild* (*child*) were neuter in gender. This is called **grammatical gender**.

So nouns and adjectives in OE, including the equivalent of MnE *the*, were marked by a complex system of inflections for number, case and gender. Here are a few examples; notice that sometimes the inflection is zero (Ø), like the MnE plural of *sheep*, or past tense of *cut*. The inflections are shown after a hyphen:

seo næddr-**e** cwæþ *the serpent said*	sg	nom	f
God-Ø cwæþ to **þære** næddr-**an** *God said to the serpent*	sg	dat	f
þæt wif-Ø andwyrde *the woman answered*	sg	nom	n
God-Ø cwæþ to **þam** wif-**e** *God said to the woman*	sg	dat	n
se hræfn-Ø fleah þa ut *the raven flew then out*	sg	nom	m
he asende ut **þone** hræfn-Ø *he sent out the raven*	sg	acc	m
hi gehyrdon **his** stemn-**e** *they heard his voice*	sg	acc	f
he genam hi in to **þam** arc-**e** *he took her into the ark*	sg	dat	m

> **heora** beg-**ra** eag-**an** wurdon geopenede   pl nom n
> *their both eyes became opened*
>
> ofer þære eorþ-**an** bradnysse   sg gen f
> *over the earth's broadness (= surface)*
>
> þa wæter-**u** adruwodon   pl nom n
> *the waters dried up*
>
> he abad oþre seofan dag-**as**   pl acc m
> *he waited (an) other seven days*

Proper nouns also were inflected: *ælfred cyning* (Text 19a) is subject and so nominative case; in the PrepP *butan þam cyng-e ælfred-e,* (*except king Ælfred*) (Text 19a), all three words in the NP are in the dative case, following *butan.*

4.3.3 Verbs

In MnE there are different ways of forming the **past tense** and **past participle** of verbs.

4.3.3.1 MnE regular verbs – OE weak verbs

The majority are regular, and we add [t], [d] or [ɪd] in speech and ⟨ed⟩ (usually) in writing to the verb to form both the past tense and past participle:

MnE			OE		
kiss	kissed	kissed	cyssan	cyste	cyssed
fill	filled	filled	fyllan	fylde	fylled
knit	knitted	knitted	cnyttan	cnytte	cnytted

MnE regular verbs derive from a set of OE verbs whose past tense was marked with /t/ or /d/ in a **dental suffix,** and are called **weak verbs.**

4.3.3.2 MnE irregular verbs – OE strong verbs

There is another set of common verbs in MnE, whose past tense and past participle are marked by a change of vowel, while the participle has either an ⟨en⟩ suffix (not ⟨ed⟩) or none. These are called irregular verbs. Here are a few examples, to which you could add many more:

MnE			OE		
ride	rode	ridden	ridan	rad	riden
choose	chose	chosen	ceosan	ceas	coren
drink	drank	drunk	drincan	dranc	druncen
come	came	come	cuman	com	cumen
speak	spoke	spoken	sprecan	sprac	sprecen
see saw	seen	seon	seah	sewen	
fall fell	fallen	feallan	feoll	feallen	

The irregular verbs in MnE derive from a much larger set of verbs in OE, marked by changes of vowel, which linguists have called **strong verbs.** (This is an outline only – the verb systems in both OE and MnE are more varied than shown here.)

4.3.3.3 Inflections for person and tense

OE verbs were also marked by different suffixes to agree with their subject – either 1st, 2nd or 3rd **person**, and singular or plural **number**. In MnE, the only present tense inflection is ⟨s⟩, to agree with the 3rd person singular subject:

> I/you/we/they drive he/she/it drive-**s**

In OE, this verb would have a variety of suffixes:

> ic drif-**e** þu drif-**st** he/heo/hit drif-**þ** we/ge/hi drif-**aþ**

In MnE, there are no additional suffixes to mark agreement in the past tense:

> I/he/she/it/we/you/they drove

In OE the past tense had some suffixes to mark agreement:

> ic draf þu drif-e he/heo/hit draf we/ge/hi drif-on

📖 These examples illustrate only some of the forms of inflection in OE verbs. There is a fuller discussion in the Text Commentary Book.

4.3.4 Evidence of changes in OE pronunciation and grammar

4.3.4.1 Loss of inflections in MnE

One of the important differences between OE and MnE is that MnE has lost most of the inflections of OE. We can observe the beginnings of this loss of word suffixes from evidence in the manuscripts. If you compare the spellings of the same words in the *Anglo-Saxon Chronicle* texts in Chapters 2 and 3, you will sometimes find differences in the vowel letters of unstressed syllables – suffixes that marked case in nouns, and tense in verbs (see Activity 3.2 in Chapter 3). Here are some examples, with the two text words followed by the form with the 'correct' OE suffix:

	Peterborough Chronicle	Parker Chronicle	Regular West Saxon OE form
Text 6	nefdon	næfdan	næfdon = ne hæfdon
	feordodan	fyrdedon	feordodon *or* fyrdedon
	cininge	cyningæ	cyninge
	bædon	bædan	bædon
Text 9	onfengon	onfengun	onfengon
	nemnaþ	nemneþ	nemnaþ
	rixadon	ricsadan	ricsodon
Text 16	gefuhton	gefuhtun	gefuhton
	geþingodon	geþingodan	geþingodon
Text 19	geridan	geridon	geridon
	butan	buton	butan
	sealwudu	sealwyda	sealwudu
	beheonan	behinon	beheonan
	wæron	wærun	wæron

If such spelling irregularities become frequent, we can assume that the vowel sound of these suffixes was no longer a clear [o] [ɑ] or [u], but had reduced to the vowel [ə]. This mid-central vowel is the commonest in present-day English, because we use it in most unstressed syllables, but we have never had a separate letter of the alphabet for it. The scribes of OE therefore began to use vowel letters in these unstressed syllables at random. Eventually letter ⟨e⟩ came to be generally used.

Other spelling differences are evidence of other changes in progress: *þan* (Text 9b) for *þam* (Text 9a) perhaps suggests the beginning of the loss of distinction between [m] and [n] when word-final in unstressed syllables, so that, for example, inflected forms of *tunge* (*tongue*) like *tungan* and *tungum* are both in time reduced first to *tungen* and then to *tunge*.

The spelling *cynge* (Text 19a) shows the loss of the second, unstressed syllable of *cyninge* (Text 19b) in the word's development to *king*. *Worhte* (Text 19b) for *wrohte* (Text 19a), in which the consonant [r] and vowel [o] are reversed, illustrates a process called **metathesis**, which was not uncommon in the development of OE to ME – other examples are *irnan/rinnan* (*run*), *birnan/brinnan* (*burn*), *berstan/brestan* (*burst*), *þerscan/þrescan* (*thresh*).

So although in late OE times the West Saxon dialect had become a standard for writing, and therefore did not reflect differences of pronunciation between the dialects, scribes 'mis-spelt' because other changes in pronunciation were taking place

4.4 Latin loan-words in OE

A great deal of 'Latinate' vocabulary came into English from the 16th centu onwards, during the Renaissance, or 'revival of learning', when both Latin and Gre were generally considered to be languages superior to English. These words are often long and learned, and contrast with shorter Anglo-Saxon words in their use in formal speech and writing. But Old English contained words of Latin origin also, some of which belong to the **core vocabulary** of MnE and are in no way learned or obscure.

4.4.1 Latin words borrowed before the settlement in England

Some words borrowed from Latin were in the language brought over with the Angles and Saxons in the 5th century. Old English was a Germanic language, but the Germanic people were in continuous contact with the Latin-speaking Romans. There are no written records from this period, so the evidence for the early adoption of Latin words lies in an analysis of known sound changes.

Here is a selection of words which are reflexes of OE words borrowed from Latin before the Anglo-Saxon settlement in Britain. Many such words have not survived, e.g. *cylle* from Latin *culleus* (*leather bottle*), *mese* from *mensa* (*table*), *sigel* from *sigillum* (*brooch*).

Activity 4.2

Divide the words into sets according to their meanings (e.g. domestic, household articles etc.). Consider what these sets of borrowed words might suggest about the relationship between the Germanic tribes and the Romans.

Latin	OE	MnE	Latin	OE	MnE
balteus	belt	*belt*	mulus	mul	*mule*
benna	binn	*bin*	patina	panne	*pan*
episcopus	biscop	*bishop*	pisa	pise	*pease* ⇒ *pea*
butyrum	butere	*butter*	piper	pipor	*pepper*
cattus	catt	*cat*	pulvinus	pyle	*pillow*
calx	cealc	*chalk*	pinna	pinn	*pin*
caseus	cese	*cheese*	pipa	pipe	*pipe* (musical)
cuprum	copor	*copper*	puteus	pytt	*pit*
cuppa	cuppe	*cup*	pix/picem	pic	*pitch* (tar)
discus	disc	*dish*	prunum	plume	*plum*
furca	forca	*fork*	papaver	popig	*poppy*
uncia	ynce	*inch*	pondo	pund	*pound* (weight)
catillus	cetel	*kettle*	bursa	purs	*purse*
culina	cylene	*kiln*	Saturni (dies)	Sæternes (dæg)	*Satur*(day)
cucina	cycene	*kitchen*			
linea	line	*line*	secula	sicol	*sickle*
milea	mil	*mile*	strata	stræt	*street*
molinum	mylen	*mill*	tegula	tigele	*tile*
moneta	mynet	*mint* (money)	telonium	toll	*toll* (tax)
mango	mangian/ mangere	*-monger*	vallum	wall	*wall*
			vicus	wic	*-wick* (= town)
mortarium	mortere	*mortar* (vessel)	vinum	win	*wine*

None of these words is polysyllabic or learned, and their Latin origin cannot be guessed from their form or meaning.

Although Latin would have been spoken in Britain during the Roman occupation up to the 5th century by educated Britons, hardly any Latin words were passed on from this source to the Anglo-Saxon invaders. An exception was the *-caster/-chester* suffix for place names like *Doncaster* and *Manchester*, from the Latin *castra*, meaning *camp*.

4.4.2 Latin words adopted during the Anglo-Saxon period

Other Latin words came into the language at different periods of the Anglo-Saxon settlement, many as a result of the conversion to Christianity and the establishment of the Church, because Latin was the language of the Bible and church services, and of learning and scholarship.

In the following selection of reflexes derived from Latin during this period, the date given is that of the earliest occurrence recorded in writing (taken from the *OED*). This is a 'no later than' date, and does not, of course, tell us at what earlier time the word had become common in the spoken language.

Activity 4.3

Divide the following list of words into sets according to their meanings: e.g.

(a) religion and the Church
(b) education and learning
(c) household and clothing
(d) plants, herbs and trees
(e) foods.

You will also need (f) for miscellaneous words that do not fall into sets easily.

MnE	OE	date	Latin	MnE	OE	date	Latin
anchor	ancor	880	ancora	coulter	culter	1000	culter
angel	engel	950	angelus	cowl	cugele	931	cuculla
apostle	apostol	950	apostolus	creed	creda	1000	credo
ark	arc	1000	arca	crisp	crisp	900	crispus
balsam	balsam	1000	balsamum	disciple	discipul	900	discipulus
beet	bete	1000	beta	fan	fann	800	vannus
box (tree)	box	931	buxus	fennel	finugl	700	finuclum
candle	candel	700	candela	fever	fefor	1000	febris
cap	cæppe	1000	cappa	font	fant/font	1000	fontem
cedar	ceder	1000	cedrus	ginger	gingiber	1000	gingiber
chalice	celic	825	calix	lily	lilie	971	lilium
chest	cest	700	cista	lobster	lopustre	1000	locusta
circle	circul	1000	circulus	martyr	martyr	900	martyr
cook(n)	coc	1000	cocus	mass	mæsse	900	missa

MnE	OE	date	Latin	MnE	OE	date	Latin
master	mægester	1000	magister	*radish*	rædic	1000	radicem
mat	matt	825	matta	*sabbath*	sabat	950	sabbatum
minster	mynster	900	monasterium	*sack*	sacc	1000	saccus
mussel	muscle	1000	muscula	*school*	scol	1000	schola
myrrh	myrra	824	murra	*shrine*	scrin	1000	scrinium
nun	nunne	900	nonna	*silk*	sioloc	888	sericus
organ	organe	1000	organum	*sock*	socc	725	soccus
palm	palma	825	palmum	*sponge*	sponge	1000	spongia
pear	pere	1000	pira	*talent*	talente	930	talenta
pine	pin	1000	pinus	*temple*	templ	825	templum
plant	plante	825	planta	*title*	titul	950	titulus
pope	papa	900	papa	*verse*	fers	900	versus
priest	preost	805	presbyter	*zephyr*	zefferus	1000	zephyrus
psalm	psealm	961	psalmus				

These lists of words derived from Latin during the Anglo-Saxon period of English history show how, in time, loan-words become fully assimilated into the language.

4.5 ON loan-words in OE

There is little written evidence of ON words in OE. Here is a short list of some that have MnE reflexes, with their earliest recorded occurrences in writing.

MnE	ON	date	quotation
till (in the sense of *to*)	til	800	*Inscription, Ruthwell Cross, Dumfries* Hweþræ þer fusæ fearran kwomu æþþilæ **til** anum.
awe	agi	855	*A/S Chronicle* (AD 457) þa Brettas . . . mid micle eȝe fluȝon.
call	kalla	1000	*Battle of Maldon* Ongan **ceallian** ofer cald wæter Byrhthelmes bearn.
law	lagu	1000	*Laws of Ethelred* ȝif he hine laðian wille..do ðæt be ðam deopestan aðe . . . on Engla **laȝe**, and on Dena **laȝe**, be ðam ðe heora **laȝu** si.
fellow	felage	1016	*A/S Chronicle* Beȝen ða cyningas...wurdon **feolaȝan** & wedbroðra.
outlaw	utlagi	1023	*Wulfstan Homilies* He scel beon **utlaȝa** wið me.
haven	hofn	1031	*A/S Chronicle* þa **hæfenan** on Sandwic.
knife	knifr	1100	*Gloss on Latin word – Artauus,* **cnif**.
take	taka	1100	*A/S Chronicle* (1076) Ac se kyngc . . . hine let syððan **tacan**.
their	ðeirra	1100	*A/S Chronicle* (449) On **þeora** daȝum ȝelaðode Wyrtȝeorn Angelcin hider.
wrong	wrangr	1100	*Wulfstan's Homilies* þa unrihtdeman, þe . . . wendaþ **wrang** to rihte and riht to **wrange**.

4.6 Early French loan-words

There had been close contact between the English court of Edward the Confessor (1042–66) and Normandy, and some loan-words from Norman French appear in 11th-century documents, of which a few have survived into MnE.

MnE	OF/ONF	date	quotation
sot	sot (*foolish*)	1000	Ælfric *Saints' Lives* xiii. 132 Ne bið se na wita þe unwislice leofað, ac bið open **sott**
capon	capun	1000	*Ælfric – Gloss on Latin words – Capo*, **capun**. *Gallinaccus*, **capun**.
proud	prud	1050	Pryte heaʒe utawyrpð & wiþerwyrdnyss **prute** ʒenyþerude.
castle	castel	1075	*A/S Chronicle* (1048) þa hæfdon þa welisce men ʒewroht ænne **castel** on Herefordscire.
crown	coroune	1085	*A/S Chronicle* Her se cyng bær his **corona** and heold his hired on Winceastre.
arbalest	arbaleste (*cross-bow*)	1100	*A/S Chronicle.* (1079) Mid anan **arblaste** of scoten
chaplain	capelain	1100	*A/S Chronicle* (1099) Se cyng Willim . . . Rannulfe his **capellane** þæt biscoprice on Dunholme geaf.
tower	tor/tur	1100	*A/S Chronicle* (1097), þurh þone weall þe hi worhton on butan þone **tur** on Lundenne.

5 From Old English to Middle English

5.1 The evidence for linguistic change

The ways in which we have identified and described features of the language in the Old English texts in Chapters 1–4 are those that we can systematically apply to any text of English. We look for:

- Changes in **spelling** conventions, **letter forms** and the **alphabet** used. These are our only guide in OE and ME texts to the pronunciation of the language.
- Changes in **pronunciation**, inferred from the written words.
- Changes in **word structure**, suffixes (inflections) and prefixes.
- Changes in the **grammar** and word order.
- Changes in the word-stock or **vocabulary** – new words appear, old ones are no longer used.

We call the language from about 1150 to 1450 **Middle English** (ME), because from our point of view in time it comes between the periods of Old and Modern English. The evidence for change and development in ME, before the first printing press was set up by William Caxton in 1476, lies in written manuscripts, just as for OE. Every copy of a book, letter, will or charter had to be written out by hand, but only a few of the existing manuscripts in ME are originals, in the hand of their author. Many copies of a popular book like Chaucer's *Canterbury Tales*, for example, have survived, though Chaucer's original manuscripts have been lost. On the other hand, other works are known through a single surviving copy only.

As a result of the social and political upheaval caused by the Norman Conquest (see section 5.2, following), the West Saxon standard system of spelling and punctuation was in time no longer used. Writers used spellings that tended to match the pronunciation of their spoken dialect. Scribes often changed the spelling of words they were copying to match their own dialectal pronunciation. After several copies, the writing might contain a mixture of different dialectal forms. But for students of language today, the loss of the old OE standard writing system means that there is plenty of evidence for the different dialects of ME.

5.1.1 The development of spelling and punctuation

Today we are used to reading printed books and papers in Standard English, which use a spelling and punctuation system that has been almost unchanged for over two hundred years. We are taught to use Standard English and standard spelling when we learn to write. MnE spelling is neutral to pronunciation, and written texts can be read in any regional accent. Misspelled words and nonstandard forms look 'wrong'.

The writings of most authors from the late 15th century onwards, including the plays of Shakespeare and the King James Bible of 1611, are prepared for printing in modern editions by editors who almost always convert the original spelling and punctuation into modern standard forms. For example, an early edition of Shakespeare's *Henry IV Part 1*, printed in 1598, contains these words spoken by Falstaff:

> If I be not ashamed of my soldiours, I am a souct gurnet, I haue misused the kinges presse damnablie. No eye hath seene such skarcrowes. Ile not march through Couentry with them, thats flat.

It contains several spellings that are now nonstandard – *soldiours, souct, presse, damnablie, seene, skarcrowes* – and lacks the 'apostrophe ⟨s⟩' that is now used to mark elided sounds or possessive nouns – *Ile, thats, kinges presse* for present-day *I'll, that's* and *king's press. Souct* was an alternative spelling for *soused.*

The custom of modernising the punctuation of OE and ME texts, and both spelling and punctuation of authors from the 15th century onwards, leaves us unaware of the way modern spelling and punctuation developed. We read Chaucer's original 1390s spelling, but not Shakespeare's of the 1590s. The examples of historical English texts in this book are reproduced with their original spelling. Those texts transcribed from facsimiles have their original punctuation also, because this too is part of the development of written English. Where a facsimile is not available, an edited version has to be used, which has almost certainly changed some features of the original.

But all printed versions of old texts must compromise in reproducing the originals. Facsimiles are the nearest we can get to an authentic copy, although it needs experience to be able to decipher some handwriting styles of the past.

5.2 The Norman Conquest and the English language

In Chapters 2–4 we looked at Old English in the West Saxon dialect, which had become the standard form for writing by the first half of the 11th century in all dialect areas. A standard orthography (spelling system) means that changes in pronunciation tend not to be recorded. On the other hand, any differences or inconsistencies in spelling that do occur are a clue to changes in pronunciation and word-form which were taking place (see section 4.3.4). We can see this happening in the following 12th-century copy of a text that was originally written in the 11th century (Text 30).

5.2.1 Language in transition

If you examine an ME text and compare the forms of words with their originals in OE, the evidence of changed spelling will suggest changes in pronunciation or word structure. When this is done systematically, knowledge of the probable dialectal area in which a text was written can be deduced. Building up the evidence for this in detail has been the work of ME scholars over many years. We can make use of their knowledge and examine some short texts for ourselves to see what we can find out about changes in the language after the OE period.

5.2.1.1 Old English homilies, second half of the 12th century

A homily is a sermon. The homilies in the manuscript from which the following text is taken were originally composed before the Conquest in the 11th century, but the manuscript was copied in the second half of the 12th century. So although it still has many features of the West Saxon literary standard language, there is evidence of 'a mixture of spelling traditions, West Saxon, Anglo-Norman and Latin, and also some spellings that reflect the scribe's West Midland regional dialect'. New spellings may indicate either changing pronunciation or a new spelling convention.

This short extract is the opening of a homily and consists of verses from St John's Gospel (chapter 12: 24–6), which the sermon itself expounds. It opens with a verse in Latin, which is then repeated in English.

Text 30: Old English homily, *copied second half of 12th century* (*facsimile*)

Transcription

Amen amen ðico uobiſ niſi granum frumenti caðenſ interram mortuum fuerit ipſum ſolum manet. & Rl: Soð soð ic eop ſecge ʒif þ iſapene hpætene córn feallenðe on eorðen ne bið fullice be æʒððæð. hit punæð hím ſylfenæ. ant hé cp peſt þá. ʒif hit soðlice be æʒðeð bið꞉ hit bringæð mýcele pæſtm forð. Ðe þé hiſ ſapla lufæð he for lýſt heo pitoðlice. ꝥ þe ðe hiſ ſaplæ há/ tæð ón þiſſere peorúlðe: þe héalð híre on þám ecan life. Ðe ðe me ðenæð fýliʒe hé me þenne ant þær ðær ic me ſylf béo þer bið eác min þégn. ꝥ þe ðe me ðenaþ꞉ him þon arpurðað min fǽðer almihtiʒæ þe ðe iſ on heofenū.

Modern printed version with punctuation

Amen amen dico uobis nisi granum frumenti cadens in terram mortuum fuerit ipsum solum manet. et reliqua. Soð soð ic eow secge. Gif þæt isawene hwætene corn feallende on eorðen ne bið fullice beægd(ð)æd, hit wunæð him sylfe (a)næ; ant he cwæð eft þa: Gif hit soðlice beægðed bið, hit bringæð mycele wæstm forð. Ðe þe his sawla lufæð, he forlyst heo witodlice; and þe ðe his sawlæ hatæð on þissere weorulde, þe heald hire on þam ecan life. Ðe ðe me ðenæð, fylige he me þenne; ant þær ðær ic me sylf beo, þer bið eac min þegn; and þe ðe me ðenaþ, him þonne arwurðað min fæder almihtigæ þe ðe is on heofenum.

Word for word translation

(The first sentence in Latin from St John's Gospel 12: 24 is translated in the first Old English sentence.)

Soð	soð	ic	eow	secge;	Gif	þæt	isawene	hwætene	corn
Truly	*truly*	*I*	*to you*	*say*	*if*	*the*	*sown*	*wheaten*	*corn*

		feallende	on	eorðen	ne bið	fullice
		falling	*on*	*earth*	*is not*	*fully*

beægðð̄æd	hit	wunæð	him sylfenæ;	ant	he	cwæð	eft	þa:	Gif
dead	*it*	*remains*	*to itself;*	*and*	*he*	*spoke*	*after*	*then:*	*If*

		hit	soðlice	beægðed	bið,	hit
		it	*truly*	*dead*	*is,*	*it*

bringæð	mycele	wæstm	forð.	Ðe	þe	his	sawla	lufæð,
brings	*much*	*growth*	*forth.*	*He*	*who*	*his*	*soul (= life)*	*loves*

	he	forlyst	heo	witodlice;	and	þe
	he	*loses*	*it*	*certainly:*	*and*	*he*

ðe	his	sawlæ	hatæð	on	þissere	weorulde,	þe	heald	hire
who	*his*	*life*	*hates*	*in*	*this*	*world*	*he*	*(will) hold*	*it*

	on	þam	ecan	life.
	in	*the*	*eternal*	*life.*

Ðe	ðe	me	ðenæð,	fylige	he	me	þenne;	ant	þær	ðær	ic	me sylf	beo,
He	*who*	*me*	*serves,*	*follow*	*he*	*me*	*then;*	*and*	*there*	*where*	*I*	*myself*	*am,*

þer	bið	eac	min	þegn;	and	þe	ðe	me	ðenaþ,	him	þonne
there	*is*	*also*	*my*	*servant;*	*and*	*he*	*who*	*me*	*serves,*	*him*	*then*

		arwurðað	min	fæder	almihtigæ
		honours	*my*	*father*	*almighty*

þe	ðe	is	on	heofenum.
he	*who*	*is*	*in*	*heaven.*

Earlier West Saxon standard version:
(Words in Text 30 whose spelling appears to have changed are in bold type.)

Soð roð ıc eop recȝe; Ȝıf þæt ȝerapene hpætene copn reallenðe on **eopðan** ne bıð rullıce **beaȝoð**, hıт punıað hım **rylrum**; anð he cpæð ert þa: Ȝıf hıт roðlıce **beaȝoð** bıð, hıт **bpınȝað** mýcele pærtm ropð. Ðe þe hır **raple lurað**, he roplýrt **hı** pıтoðlıce; anð þe ðe hır **raple haтıað** on **þırne** peopulðe, þe **healт** hıne on þam ecan lıre. Ðe ðe me **þeȝnað**, rylıȝe he me þenne; anð **þæn ðæn** ıc me **rylr** beo, **þep** bıð eac mın þeȝn; anð þe ðe me **þeȝnaþ**, hım þonne **appunðıað** mın ræðep ælmıhтıȝa þe ðe ır on **heoronum**.

text	OE		text	OE		text	OE
eorðen	eorðan		sawla	sawle		ðenæð	þegnaþ
beæȝðoæd	beagod		lufæð	lufað		ant	and
wunæð	wuniað		heo	hi		ðenap	egnap
sylfenæ	sylfum		sawlæ	sawle		arwurðað	arwurðıað
ant	and		hatæð	hatiað		ælmihtigæ	ælmihtiga
beæȝðed	beagod		þissere	þisre		heofenum	heofonum
bringæð	bringað		heald	healt			

The differences are slight but are evidence of the beginning of the loss of the West Saxon standard spelling system, and also of some possible changes of pronunciation.

📖 vocabulary of Text 30 is listed in the Word Book.

5.2.2 French the prestige language after 1066

After the conquest of England by William I in 1066, Norman French, not English, became the language of the ruling classes and their servants, because almost all the former English nobility were dispossessed of their lands. The chronicler Robert Mannyng, writing in 1338, refers to this:

North-East Midlands dialect
To Frankis & Normanz for þare grete laboure
To Flemmynges & Pikardes þat were with him in stoure
He gaf londes bityme of whilk þer successoure
Hold ȝit þe seyseyne with fulle grete honoure.

in stoure = in battle; *seisin* = possession of land

Here is another short account of the Conquest in an anonymous Chronicle, written in the 14th century, which still showed hostility to the Norman domination of England:

Text 31: Anonymous short metrical chronicle

South-West Midlands dialect

Chronicle	WW
Suþþe regnede a goude gome	After reigned a good man
Harold Godwynes sone	Harold Godwin's son
He was icluped Harefot	He was called Harefoot
For he was renner goud	For he was runner good
Bote he ne regnede here	But he ne-reigned here
Bot .ix. monþes of a ȝere	But 9 months of a year
Willam bastard of Normandye	William bastard of Normandy
Hym cant þat was a vilanye	Him deposed that was a villainy
Harold liþ at Waltham	Harold lies at Waltham
& Willam bastard þat þis lond wan	& William bastard that this land won
He regnede here	He reigned here
On & tuenti ȝere	One & twenty years
Suþþe he deide at þe hame	Then he died at (the) home
At Normandye at Came	In Normandy at Caen

 The vocabulary of Text 31 is listed in the Word Book.

William's policy of dispossessing the Anglo-Saxon nobility held in the Church also. French-speaking bishops and abbots were in time appointed to the principal offices, and many French-speaking monks entered the monasteries. Latin remained the principal language of both Church and State for official writing in documents, while French became the 'prestige language' of communication. We can compare the status of French in England from 1066 onwards with that of English in the British Empire in the 19th and early 20th centuries. The situation which developed is described by another verse chronicler, known as Robert of Gloucester, writing about 1300. His attitude towards Harold and William I is different from that of the anonymous chronicler of Text 31:

Text 32: Robert of Gloucester's Chronicle

(Southern dialect)

ME

þus lo þe englisse folc. vor noȝt to grounde com.
vor a fals king þat nadde no riȝt. to þe kinedom.
& come to a nywe louerd. þat more in riȝte was.
ac hor noþer as me may ise. in pur riȝte was.
& þus was in normannes hond. þat lond ibroȝt iwis . . .

þus com lo engelond. in to normandies hond.
& þe normans ne couþe speke þo. bote hor owe speche.
& speke french as hii dude at om. & hor children dude also teche.
so þat heiemen of þis lond. þat of hor blod come.
holdeþ alle þulk speche. þat hii of hom nome.
vor bote a man conne frenss. me telþ of him lute.
ac lowe men holdeþ to engliss. & to hor owe speche ȝute.

ich wene þer ne beþ in al þe world. contreyes none.
þat ne holdeþ to hor owe speche. bote engelond one.
ac wel me wot uor to conne. boþe wel it is.
vor þe more þat a mon can. þe more wurþe he is.
þis noble duc willam. him let crouny king.
at londone amidwinter day. nobliche þoru alle þing.
of þe erchebissop of euerwik. aldred was is name.
þer nas prince in al þe world. of so noble fame.

| WW |

Thus lo the English folk for nought to ground came (= *were beaten*)
For a false king that ne-had no right to the kingdom
& came to a new lord that more in right was
But their neither (= *neither of them*) as one may see in pure right was
& thus was in Norman's hand that land brought certainly . . .

Thus came lo England into Normandy's hand
& the Normans ne-could speak then but their own speech
& spoke French as they did at home & their children did also teach.
So that high-men of this land that of their blood come
hold all the-same speech that they from them took.
For but a man knows French one counts of him little.
But low men hold to English & to their own speech yet.
I believe there ne-are in all the world countries none
that ne-hold to their own speech but England alone.
But well one knows for to know both well it is
for the more that a man knows the more worthy he is.
This noble duke William him (*self*) caused to crown king
at London on mid-winter's day nobly through all things
by the Archbishop of York. Aldred was his name.
There ne-was prince in all the world of so noble fame.

The vocabulary of Text 32 is listed in the Word Book as Text 56.

5.3 The earliest 12th-century Middle English text

The manuscript of the *Anglo-Saxon Chronicle* which was written in the abbey at Peterborough is of special interest for two reasons, one historical and the other linguistic:

- It is the only copy of the *Chronicle* that describes events up to the middle of the 12th century, nearly one hundred years after the Conquest.

- It gives us the first direct evidence of the changes in the language that had taken place by the 1150s.

We know that a disastrous fire at Peterborough destroyed most of the monastery's library in 1116, including its copy of the *Chronicle*. Later, another *Chronicle* was borrowed and copied. This re-written copy has survived and is the one known as the *Peterborough Chronicle*. The entries for the years up to 1121 are all in the same hand,

and copied in the 'classical' West Saxon OE orthography. But there are two 'continuations' of the annals, probably written down by two scribes, one recording events from 1122 to 1131, and the other from 1132 to 1154, where the *Chronicle* ends.

The linguistic importance of the continuations is that the language is not the classical West Saxon OE of the older *Chronicle* to 1121, but is markedly different. It is good evidence of current English usage of that area in the first half of the 12th century. The monks of Peterborough were probably local men, and so spoke the East Midlands dialect of English. Peterborough was within the Danelaw (see section 3.4.1.1), and some influence of Old Norse might be expected too. The tradition of writing in classical OE spelling was by now lost, and as the continuations of the annals were probably written from dictation, the scribe would tend to spell English as he heard and spoke it. Scribes were also now trained in the writing of French as well as Latin, and some conventions of writing French would influence their spelling of English words, like using ⟨th⟩ for ⟨þ⟩ and ⟨qu⟩ for ⟨cw⟩.

Activity 5.1

Text 33 is part of the annal for 1140 in the second continuation of the *Peterborough Chronicle*.

(i) Read through the text to see whether you can understand the gist of it without referring to the translation.
(ii) Use the literal translation following to make a MnE version.
(iii) List any differences between the language of the text and that of the *Chronicle* annals in Texts 1–26 that you immediately notice.

📖 There is a detailed commentary in the Text Commentary Book.

Text 33: Part of the Peterborough Chronicle for 1140

.mc.xl.   On þis gær wolde þe king Stephne tæcen Rodbert eorl
of gloucestre þe kinges sune Henries. ac he ne myhte for he
wart it war. þer efter in þe lengten þestrede þe sunne 7 te
dæi. abuton nontid dæies. þa men eten. ð me lihtede candles
to æten bi ... wæron men suythe of wundred ...

þer efter wæx suythe micel uuerre betuyx þe king 7 Randolf
eorl of cæstre noht for þi ð he ne iaf him al ð he cuthe axen
him. alse he dide all othre. oc æfre þe mare he iaf heom. þe
wærse hi wæron him. þe eorl heold lincol agænes þe king 7
benam him al ð he ahte to hauen. 7 te king for þider 7
besætte him 7 his brother Willelm de Romare in þe castel. 7
te æorl stæl ut 7 ferde efter Rodbert eorl of gloucestre. 7
brohte him þider mid micel ferd. 7 fuhten suythe on
Candelmasse dæi agenes heore lauerd. 7 namen him for his men
him suyken 7 flugæn. 7 læd him to Bristowe 7 diden þar in

prisun 7 in feteres. þa was al Engleland styred mar þan ær
wæs. 7 al yuel wæs in lande . . .

þa ferde Eustace þe kinges sune to france 7 nam þe kinges
suster of france to wife. wende to bigæton normandi þærþurh.
oc he spedde litel 7 be gode rihte for he was an yuel man.
for ware se he com he dide mar yuel þanne god. he reuede þe
landes 7 læide micele geldes on. He brohte his wif to
engleland. 7 dide hire in þe castel in cantebyri. God wimman
scæ wæs. oc scæ hedde litel blisse mid him. 7 Crist ne wolde
ð he sculde lange rixan. 7 wærd ded 7 his moder beien . . .

WW 1140.   In this year wished the king Stephen take Robert earl of
Gloucester the king's son Henry's. but he ne was-able for he became
it aware. there after in the lent darkened the sun & the day.
about noontide day's. when men eat. that one lighted candles to
eat by . . . were men very amazed . . .

thereafter waxed violently much war between the king & Randolph
earl of chester (not) because he ne gave him all that he (could) demanded
from-him. as he did all others. but ever the more he gave to-them. the
worse they were to-him. the earl held lincoln against the king &
took from-him all that he ought to have. & the king fared thither &
besieged him & his brother William de Romare in the castle. &
the earl stole out & went after Robert earl of gloucester. &
brought him thither with great army. & fought violently on
Candlemass day against their lord. & captured him for his men
him betrayed & fled. & led him to Bristol & put there in
prison & in fetters. then was all England disturbed more than before
was. & all evil was in land . . .

Then went Eustace the king's son to France & took the king's
sister of France to wife. hoped to obtain normandy there-through.
but he sped little & by good right, for he was an evil man.
for where so he came he did more evil than good. he robbed the
lands & laid great taxes on. He brought his wife to
england. & put her in the castle in canterbury. Good woman
she was. but she had little bliss with him. & Christ ne wished
that he should long reign. & became dead & his mother both . . .

📖 The vocabulary of Text 33 is listed in the Word Book.

🜨 The final paragraph of Text 33 is recorded on the CD/cassette tape.

Here is a broad phonetic transcription:

θɑː feːrdə ɔstas θə kɪŋgəs sunə tɔː fraːns ənd nɑːm θə kɪŋgəs systər ɔf fraːns tɔː
wiːvə. weːndə tɔː bɪjætən nɔrmandɪ θæːrθʊrx. ɔk heː spedːə lɪtəl ənd be goːdə
rɪçtə fɔr heː was ɑːn yvəl man. fɔr warəse heː coːm heː dɪdə mɑːr yvəl θanːə
goːd. heː reːvədə θə lɑːndəs ɜnd læɪdə mɪtʃələ jeːldəs ɔn. heː brɔxtə hɪs wiːf toː
ɛŋgləland. ənd dɪdə hir ɪn θə kastəl ɪn kantəbyri. goːd wɪmːən ʃæː wæs. ɔk ʃæː
hɛdːə lɪtəl blɪsːə mɪd hɪm. ənd kriːst nɛ wɔldə θæt heː ʃʊldə lɑːŋgə riːksən. ənd
wærd dɛːd ənd hɪs moːdər beɪən

5.3.1 Loss of inflections

The most important change is the beginning of the loss of most of the inflections of OE, mainly by their reduction in sound. This leads to a greater reliance on **word order,** and the more frequent use of **prepositions** to show the meanings that formerly might have been signalled by inflections. Consequently, the *Chronicle* text reads much more like MnE to us than the OE texts. There is also the beginning of the great influx of French words into the language.

Text 34: Peterborough Chronicle *for 1137, written* c. *1154 (facsimile)*

This facsimile is a complete page by the second of the two scribes who wrote down the 'continuations' of the annals. It is part of the story of the atrocities perpetrated by the barons in the civil wars during King Stephen's reign:

✍ *A note on the handwriting*

Book hand, with the following features which distinguish it from earlier writing; it is a compressed style of book hand, with alternative shapes for several letters:

- Continental form of ⟨g⟩ e.g. *gæƀe king, hungær.*
- Insular and continental forms of ⟨r⟩, cf. *punƀeꝥ, drapen,* but the '2-form' of ⟨r⟩ after ⟨o⟩, e.g. in *foꝛbaꝥen, foꝛdon, coꝛn.*
- Insular and continental forms of ⟨d⟩, cf. *maceð, ðrapen* and *diden, ſæden,* with both forms in *ðædes.*
- Mainly 'long s' ⟨ſ⟩, but ⟨s⟩ when page final in *ſinnes.*
- ⟨þ⟩ and ⟨th⟩ both used – *þar, þꝥenȝde, þolenden, þa, þe – uuꝥythen, ꞇhꝥe, ꞇhꝥoꞇe, eꝥꞇhe.*
- ⟨ð⟩ an abbreviation for *ðat.*
- ⟨ꝥ⟩ and ⟨uu⟩ used for ⟨w⟩ – *ꝥæꝥon, ꝥunder, ſpa, noꝥiðeꝥpardeſ – uueron, uuꝥythen, uueꝥſe, uuꝥeccemen.*
- ⟨æ⟩ used for [ɛ] - *ðædes, hungær.*

Transcription

me dide cnotted ſtrengeſ abuꞇon here

hæueð . ꝸ uuꝥythen iꞇ ð iꞇ gæde ꞇo þe ᴴaerneſ . Ꝺi diden heō in quaꝥ
ꞇerne þar nadꝥeſ ꝸ ſnakeſ ꝸ padeſ pæꝥon inne . ꝸ drapen heō ſpa .
Sume hi diden in cꝥuceꞇhuꝛ ð iſ in an ceſꞇe paꞇ paſ ſcorꞇ ꝸ nareu.
ꝸ undeꝥ . ꝸ ðiðe ꝛcaeppe ſꞇaneſ þeꝥinne . ꝸ þꝥenȝde þe man þeꝥ
mne . ð hī bꝥecon alle þe limeſ . In maꝥi of þe caſꞇleſ pæron lof
ꝸ gꝥī . ð þæꝥon ꝥachenꞇegeſ ð ꞇpa oþeꝥ ꞇhꝥe men hadden onoh ꞇo
bæron onne . þaꞇ paſ ſua maceð . ð iſ fæſꞇneð ꞇo an beom . ꝸ diden an
ſcæpp iren abuꞇon þa manneſ ꞇhꝥoꞇe ꝸ hiſ halſ . ð heⁿeꝷmyhꞇe noꝥi
ðeꝥpardeſ . ne ſiꞇꞇen ne lien ne ſlepen . oc bæꝥon al ð iꝥen . Ꝟaꝥi
þuſen hi ðrapen mid hungæꝥ . I ne can ne i ne mai ꞇellen alle þe
ꝥundeꝥ ne alle þe piꝥeſ ð hi diden ꝥeccemen on þiſ land . ꝸ ð laſꞇe
ðe þa .xix. piꝥꞇꝥe þile Sꞇephne paſ kmg ꝸ auꝥe iꞇ paſ uueꝥſe ꝸ
uueꝥſe . Ꝺi læiden gæildeſ oⁿꞇhe ꞇuneſ æure ūꝥile ꝸ clepeden iꞇ
ꞇenſerie . þa þe uuꝥeccemen ne haðđen nā more ꞇo gẏuen . þa ꝥæ
ueðen hi ꝸ brenðon alle ꞇhe ꞇuneſ . ð þel þu mẏhꞇeſ faꝥen al a dæiſ
fare ſculðeſꞇ ꞇhu neure finden man in ꞇune ſiꞇꞇenðe . ne land ꞇi
leð . þa paſ corn ðaeꝥe . ꝸ flec ꝸ cæſe ꝸ buꞇere . for nan ne paeſ o þe land .
ꝥeccemen ſꞇuruen of hungæꝥ . ſume ieðen on ælmeſ þe paꝥen ſū
þile picemen . ſume flugen uꞇ of lande . Ꝟeſ næuꝥe gæꞇ mare ꝥecᶜe
heð on land . ne næure heꞇhen men peꝥſe ne ðiden þan hi ðiden .
ꝛor oueꝥ ſiꞇhon ne for baren ᴴⁱ nouꞇheꝥ ciꝥce ne cẏꝥceiærð . oc nam
al þe goð ð þaꝥinne paſ . ꝸ brenðen ſẏꞇhen þe cẏꝥce ꝸ alꞇegædere .
Ne hi ne foꝛbaren ƀ land ne aƀƀ ne preoſꞇeſ . ac reueden munekeſ
ꝸ clerekeſ . ꝸ æuric man oꞇheꝥ þe oueꝥmẏhꞇe . Gif ꞇpa men oþeꝥ .iii.
coman ꝥiðenð ꞇo an ꞇun . al þe ꞇunſcipe flugæn for heō . ꝥenðen ð
hi pæron reuereſ . þe biſcopeſ ꝸ leꝥeðmen heō cuꝥſeðe æuꝥe . oc paſ
heō nahꞇ þaꝥ of . for hi uueron al forcurſæd ꝸ forſuoren ꝸ ꝛoꝥlo
ren . par ſæ me ꞇileðe . þe eꝥꞇhe ne bar nan coꝛn. for þe land paſ al

foꞃðon . mid ſuilce ðæðeſ . & hi sæden openlice ð χꞃiſt ſlep ꞃ his ha
lechen . Suilc ꞃ maꞃe þanne þe cunnen ſæin . þe þolenðen .xix. pintꞃe
ꞃoꞃ uꞃe ſmnes .

ƀ = biscopes (*bishops'*)
aƀƀ = abbotes (*abbots'*)

<hr />

MnE

They put knotted strings round their
heads and twisted till it went to the brains. They put them in dungeons
where adders and snakes and toads were in and killed them thus.
Some they put into a 'crucet-hus', that is into a chest that was short and narrow
and shallow and put sharp stones therein and pressed the man in there
so that they broke all the limbs. In many of the castles were a 'lof
and grin' that were chains that two or three men had enough (to do) to
carry one. It was so made that (it) is fastened to a beam and (they) put a
sharp iron around the man's throat and his neck so that he might in no way
either sit or lie or sleep but bore all that iron. Many
thousands they killed with hunger. I do not know nor can I tell all the
horrors nor all the tortures that they did to wretched men in this land. And it lasted
the 19 years while Stephen was king and ever it grew worse and
worse. They laid taxes upon the villages time and again and called it
tenserie. When the wretched men had no more to give then
they robbed and burned all the villages so that you could well go a whole day's
journey and never find anyone living in a village nor land tilled.
Then corn was dear and flesh and cheese and butter because there was none in the land.
Wretched men starved with hunger; some went on alms who were once
powerful men; some fled out of the land. Was never before more wretchedness
in the land nor ever did heathen men worse than they did.
For too many times they spared neither church nor churchyard but took
all of value that was in it and afterwards burned the church and everything together.
They spared neither bishops' nor abbots' nor priests' land but robbed monks
and clerks and every man had power over another. If two or three men
came riding to a village all the villagers fled because they thought that
they were robbers. The bishops and the clergy always cursed them but that was
nothing to them because they were all accursed and forsworn and lost.
Wherever men tilled the earth bore no corn because the land was all
ruined by such deeds and they said openly that Christ slept and his
saints. Such and more than we can tell we suffered 19 years
for our sins.

Text 34a consists of three short extracts from the annal for 1137, which provide
evidence of some of the changes in the East Midlands dialect that had taken place
by the mid-12th century. It is followed by a reconstructed version in West Saxon OE
to make the changes clearer.

Text 34a: Extracts transcribed from the 1137 annal

I ne can ne I ne mai tellen alle þe
wunder ne alle þe pines ðat hi diden wreccemen on þis land. & ðat laſtede
þa .xix. wintre wile Stephne was king & æure it was uuerse & uuerſe.

þa was corn dære. & flec & cæse & butere. for nan ne wæs o þe land. wreccemen sturuen of hungær.

war sæ me tilede. þe erthe ne bar nan corn. for þe land was al fordon. mid suilce dædes. & hi sæden openlice ðat crist slep & his halechen. Suilc & mare þanne we cunnen sæin. we þolenden .xix. wintre ꝩoꝛ uꝼe ſinnes.

Version in the former OE standard written form

ic ne cann ne ic ne mæg tellan ealle þa wundor ne ealle þa pinas þe hie dydon wreccum mannum on þissum lande. ꝫ þæt læstede þa .xix. wintra þa hwile þe Stephne cyning wæs ꝫ æfre hit wæs wyrsa ꝫ wyrsa ...

þa wæs corn deore. ꝫ flesc ꝫ cese ꝫ butere. for nan ne wæs on þæm lande. wrecce menn sturfon of hungre ...

swa hwær swa man tilode. seo eorþe ne bær nan corn. for þæt land wæs eall fordon. mid swilcum dædum. ꝫ hie sædon openlice þæt crist slep ꝫ his halgan. swilc ꝫ mare þanne we cunnon secgan. we þolodon .xix. wintra for ure synna.

| WW |

I ne can ne I ne may tell all the horrors ne all the pains that they caused wretched-men in this land. & that lasted the 19 winters while Stephen was king & ever it was worse & worse ...

then was corn dear. & flesh & cheese & butter. for none ne was in the land. Wretched-men died of hunger ...

Where so one tilled. the earth ne bore no corn. for the land was all ruined. with such deeds. & they said openly that Christ slept & his saints. Such & more than we can say. we suffered 19 winters for our sins.

The vocabulary of Text 34a is listed in the Word Book.

Activity 5.2

Use the OE version to make a study of the changes that you can observe in the language. Look particularly at the following words or phrases:

OE	Chronicle	OE	Chronicle
NPs and PrepPs			
ic	I	his halgan	**his halechen**
hit	it	for ure synna	**for ure sinnes**
we	we		
hi/hie	hi	wreccum mannum	**wrecce men**
		wrecce men	**wrecce men**
man	me		
		mid swilcum dædum	**mid suilce dædes**
			⇨

OE	Chronicle	OE	Chronicle
nan	**nan**		
nan corn	**nan corn**	xix wintra	**xix wintre**
ealle þa wundor	**alle þe wunder**	cyning	**king**
ealle þa pinas	**alle þe pines**	corn (deore)	**corn (dære)**
on þæm lande	**o þe land**	flæsc/flesc	**flec**
seo eorþe	**þe erþe**	cyse/cese	**cæse**
þæt land	**þe land**	butere	**butere**
þa xix wintra	**þa xix wintre**	Crist	**crist**
on þissum lande	**on þis land**	of hungre	**of hungær**
Verbs			
ic ne mæg tellen	**I ne mai tellen**	man tilode	**me tilede**
hie dydon	**hi diden**	seo eorþe ne bær	**þe erþe ne bar**
þæt læstede	**ðat lastede**	þæt land wæs fordon	**þe land was fordon**
Stephne wæs	**Stephne was**	hie sædon	**hi sæden**
hit wæs	**it was**	Crist slep	**Crist slep**
corn wæs	**corn was**	we cunnon secgan	**we cunnen sæin**
nan ne wæs	**nan ne wæs**	we þolodon	**we þolede**
menn sturfon	**men sturuen**		

5.4 The book called *Ormulum*

Another early text dating from the late 12th century is an important source of information about the state of the language. It was written by a monk called Orm (a Danish name, as we have seen in section 3.4.1). He lived in northern Lincolnshire and wrote in an East Midlands dialect of English like the *Peterborough Chronicle* continuations.

His object was to teach the Christian faith in English, and the verses were to be read aloud. So he devised his own system of spelling, in order to help a reader to pronounce the words properly. What is especially noticeable is the number of double consonant letters. He wanted his readers and listeners to distinguish clearly between long and short vowels in closed syllables (see section 5.4.2 following), because long or short vowels could mark differences in the meaning of words. So he wrote two consonant letters (*an bocstaff write twiȝȝess*) after the short vowels. Consequently he wanted any later copier of *Ormulum* to follow his spelling system exactly.

The following transcription of Orm's description of his book sets the text in its verse lines, which were not shown in this way in the manuscript (compare the facsimile of Text 36):

Text 35: Ormulum (i)

þiss boc iss nemmned Orrmulum	this book is called Ormulum
forrþi þatt Orrm itt wrohhte.	because Orm it wrought (made).
Icc hafe wennd inntill ennglissh.	I have turned into English
goddspelles hallȝhe lare.	(*the*) gospel's holy lore,
Affterr þatt little witt þatt me.	after that little wit that me
min Drihhtin hafeþþ lenedd.	my Lord has lent (*granted*).
annd wha-se wilenn shall þiss boc.	And whoever intend shall this book
efft oþerr siþe writenn.	again another time write,
himm bidde icc þat he't write rihht.	him ask I that he it copy right,
swa-summ þiss boc himm tæcheþþ.	in the same way (*that*) this book him teaches,
all þwerrt-ut affterr þatt itt iss.	entirely after (*the way*) that it is,
uppo þiss firrste bisne.	according to this first example,
wiþþ all swillc rime alls her iss sett.	with all such rhyme as here is set (*down*),
wiþþ all þe fele wordess.	with all the many words.
annd tatt he loke wel þatt he.	And (*I ask*) that he look well that he
an bocstaff write twiȝȝess.	a letter writes twice.
eȝȝwhær þær itt uppo þiss boc	Everywhere it in this book
iss writenn o þatt wise.	is written in that way.
loke he well þatt he't wrote swa.	(*Let him*) Look well that he it wrote so,
forr he ne maȝȝ nohht elless.	for he must not else (= *otherwise*)
onn Ennglissh writenn rihht te word.	in English write correctly the word.
þatt wite he wel to soþe.	That (*should*) know he well for sure.

📖 The vocabulary of Text 35 is listed in the Word Book.

Ⓐ Here is a broad phonetic transcription of Text 35, recorded on the CD/cassette tape:

θɪs boːk ɪs nɛmnəd ɔrmʊluːm, fɔrðiːðat ɔrm ɪt wrɔxtə
ɪk haːvə wɛnd ɪntɪl ɛŋglɪʃ gɔdspɛləs halɤə laːrə
aftər ðat lɪtlə wɪt θat mɛː miːn drɪçtɪn haʋɛθ leːnəd
and hwaːse wiːlən ʃal θɪs boːk ɛft oːðər siːðȝ wriːtən
hɪm bɪd ɪk θat heːt wriːtə rɪçt, swaːsʊm θɪs boːk hɪm tæːtʃɛθ
al θwɛrtuːt aftər θat ɪt ɪs ʊpoː θɪs fɪrstə biːznə
wɪθ al swɪlk riːm als heːr ɪs sɛt, wɪθ al θe feːlə woːrdɛs
and tat heː loːkə wɛl θat heː aːn boːkstɑf wriːtə twijəs
ɛjhwær θæːr ɪt ʊpoː θɪs boːk ɪs wriːtən ɔ θat wiːzə.
loːk heː wɛl θat heːt wroːtə swaː, fɔr heː nə maj nɔçt ɛləs
ɔn ɛŋglɪʃ wriːtən rɪçt tə woːrd, θat wiːt heː wɛl toː soːðə

There are fifteen syllables to every line, without exception, and the metre is absolutely regular. Single unstressed (x) and stressed (/) syllables alternate, always with an initial and final unstressed syllable. Here is the text set out in metrical form:

```
x  / x  / x  / x  / x  / x  / x  / x
```

þiss | **boc** iss | **nemm** ned | **Orr** mu | **lum.** forr | þi þatt | **Orrm** itt | **wrohh** te.

Icc |**ha**-fe |**wennd** inn|**till** Enng|**lissh.** godd|**spell**-es |**hall**-ȝhe |**la**-re.
Aff|**terr** þatt |**litt**-le |**witt** þatt |**me.** min|**Drihh**-tin |**ha**-feþþ |**le**-nedd.

Annd |wha-se |wil-enn |shall þiss |boc. efft |o-þerr |si-þe |wri-tenn.
Himm |bidd(e) icc |þat he't |wri-te |rihht. swa-|summ þiss |boc himm |tæ-cheþþ.
All |þwerrt-ut |aff-terr |þatt itt |iss. upp|o þiss |firr-ste |bis-ne.
Wiþþ|all swillc |rim(e) alls |her iss |sett. wiþþ|all þe |fe-le |wor-dess.
Annd |tatt he |lo-ke |wel þatt |he. an |boc-staff |wri-te |twi-ȝȝess.
Eȝȝ|whær þær |itt upp|o þiss |boc. iss |wri-tenn |o þatt |wi-se.
Lok(e)he | wel þatt | he't wrote | swa. forr | he ne | maȝȝ nohht | ell-ess.
Onn |Enng-lissh |wri-tenn |rihht te |word. þatt |wit(e) he |wel to |so-þe.

The stops in the manuscript of the text mark the end of each half-line and line of verse.

Orm's spelling is consistent, and it is an attempt to reform the system and relate each sound to a symbol. For example, he used three symbols to differentiate between the three sounds that the OE letter yogh ⟨ȝ⟩ had come to represent, [g], [j] and [x]. You will notice his use of ⟨wh⟩ for OE ⟨hw⟩, e.g. *wha-se, whas* for OE *hwa swa, hwæs* (MnE *whoso, whose*); and ⟨sh⟩ for ⟨sc⟩, e.g. *shall, Ennglissh* for *sceal, Englisc*.

5.4.1 Orm's writing as evidence of language change in early ME

Orm's 20,000 or so lines of verse are important evidence for some of the changes that had taken place in the language by the late 12th century in his part of the country, just over a hundred years after the Norman Conquest. His lines are, however, monotonous to read, since they are absolutely regular in metre. Students of literature do not place Orm high on their list, but for students of language his writing is very valuable.

The following facsimile is the Dedication that begins the book. It includes part of the extract already discussed,

> Icc hafe wennd inntill Ennglissh.
> Goddspelles hallȝhe lare.

Although the book is in verse, the lines are run together and fill all the space on the parchment.

Text 36: Ormulum *(ii) (facsimile)*

✍ *A note on the handwriting*
A very compressed book hand.

- Letter ⟨a⟩ is insular (cf. the earlier facsimiles of OE).
- Insular ⟨ȝ⟩ is used for for [j], e.g. *ȝet^t* (*yet*).
- Continental ⟨g⟩, e.g. *godeſſ* (*God's*), but his own unique form.
- Insular ⟨ꝥ⟩, e.g. *bnoþeꝥꝥ*, except for small superscript form, e.g. *bnoþeꝥ^r*·
- Continental ⟨f⟩, e.g. *fulluht*.
- Long and round s – ⟨ſ⟩ and ⟨s⟩, e.g. *flæsheſſ*.
- Thorn ⟨þ⟩ and wynn ⟨ƿ⟩ used, clearly differentiated, not ⟨th⟩ or ⟨w/uu⟩.
- Few abbreviations, but ꝥ = *þæt*.

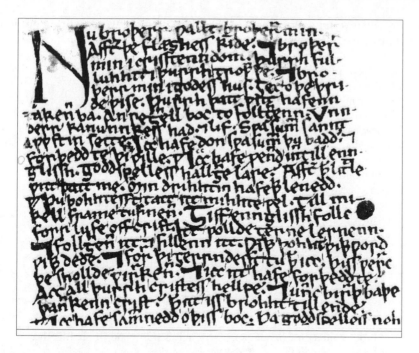

The following transcription reproduces the lineation of the text as written in the MS.

N u broþenn wallter broþer min ·
afft þe flæshess kide · 7 broþer
min i crisstenndom · þurrh ful-
luhht 7 þurrh trowwþe ·7 broþenn min i godess hus · ʒet o þe þri-
de wise · þurrh þatt witt hafenn
taken ba · an reʒell boc to follʒenn · Vnn-
derr kanunkess had ·7 lif · Swa sum sanct
appstin sette · Icc hafe don swa sum þu badd · 7
forþedd te þin wille · Icc hafe pend intill ennglissh · goddspelless hallʒe lare · Afft þ litle
witt tatt* me · min drihhtin hafeþ lenedd ·
Ʒ þu þohtesst tatt itt mihhte well · till mi-
kell frame turnenn· ʒiff ennglissh follc
forr lufe off crist · Itt wollde ʒerne lernenn ·
7 follʒen itt 7 fillenn itt · Wiþ þohht wiþ word
wiþ dede · 7 forr þi ʒerrnndesst tu þ icc · þiss werc
þe shollde wirken· 7 icc itt hafe forþedd te ·
Acc all þurrh cristess hellpe · 7unc birþ baþe
þankenn crist ⁊ þ itt iss brohht till ende ·
Ʒ Icc hafe sammnedd o þiss boc · þa goddspelless neh
(alle . þatt finndenn o þe messe boc inn all þe ʒer att messe ·)

* altered from þatt

If we write the text in its verse lines (14 syllables), with the words written out in full, the rhythmic pattern becomes clearer:

> Nu broþerr walterr broþerr min . affter þe flæshess kinde .
> 7 broþerr min i cristenndom . þurrh fulluhht 7 þurrh trowwþe .
> 7 broþerr min i godess hus . ʒett o þe þride wise .
> þurrh þatt witt hafenn takenn ba . an reʒhell boc to follʒhenn .
> Vnnderr kanunkess had 7 lif . swa summ santt Awwstin sette .
> Icc hafe don swa summ þu badd . 7 forþedd te þin wille .
> Icc hafe wennd intill ennglish . goddspelless hallʒhe lare .
> Afftr þatt little witt tatt me . min drihhtin hafeþþ lenedd .
> þu þohtesst tatt itt mihhte wel . till mikell frame turrnenn .
> ʒiff ennglissh follc forr lufe off crist . itt wollde ʒerne lernenn .
> 7 follʒhenn itt 7 fillenn itt . wiþþ þohht wiþþ word wiþþ dede .
> 7 forrþi ʒerrndesst tu þatt icc . þiss werrc þe shollde wirrkenn .
> 7 icc itt hafe forþedd te . acc all þurrh cristess hellpe .
> 7 unnc birrþ baþe þann kenn crist . þatt itt iss brohht till ende .
> Icc hafe sammnedd o þiss boc . þa goddspelless neh *alle* .
> *þatt sinndenn o þe messe boc . inn all þe ʒer att messe* .

WW

> Now brother Walter brother mine · after the flesh's nature ·
> And brother mine in Christendom · through baptism and through faith ·
> And brother mine in God's house · yet in the third way ·
> Through that we have taken both · a rule book to follow ·
> Under canon's order and life · as St Augustine set ·
> I have done as you bade · and completed you your will ·
> I have turned into English · (the) gospel's holy lore ·
> After that little wit that me · my Lord has lent ·
> You thought that it might well · to much benefit turn ·
> If English folk for love of Christ · it would eagerly learn ·
> And follow it and fulfil it · in thought in word in deed ·
> And therefore desired you that I · this work (for) you should make ·
> And I it have completed (for) you · but all through Christ's help ·
> And us two (it) befits both (to) thank Christ · that it is brought to (an) end ·
> I have gathered together in this book · almost all the gospels ·
> That are in the mass-book · in all the year at Mass ·

Orm addresses Walter, who is his brother in three ways – firstly they are natural brothers with the same parents ('affter þe flæshess kinde' – *after the nature of the flesh*); secondly, they are Christian brothers in faith, who have both been baptised into the Church; thirdly, they are both monks, brothers in the monastery where they have taken vows to follow the rule.

📖 The vocabulary of Text 36 is listed in the Word Book.

5.4.2 Open and closed syllables

If a syllable ends with a vowel (V), it is called an **open syllable**; if it ends with a consonant (C), it is a **closed syllable**. So one-syllable OE words, like *he, swa, þe, hu, to, þa, ne*, consist of open syllables, and those like *ðis, boc, is, þæt, wæs, gan*, of closed syllables.

In words of two or more syllables, if there was a sequence VCV, the consonant between the vowels was heard as part of the second syllable, as in *lare* (la-re), *ærende* (æ-rende), *siþe* (si-þe), *writen* (wri-ten), *oþer* (o-þer), *fela* (fe-la), *locaþ* (lo-caþ), *wise* (wi-se). In a sequence with two or more consonants, VCCV or VCCCV, the first consonant is heard as the end of the first syllable, which is therefore closed, as in *nemned* (nem-ned), *englisc* (en-glisc), *godspelles* (god-spel-les), *æfter* (æf-ter), *dryhten* (dryh-ten), *bocstæf* (boc-stæf).

5.4.3 Orm's spelling

Orm was anxious for his readers to read, and listeners to hear, the proper difference between long and short vowels (see section 3.1.3.1) in closed syllables, so he marked long vowels (or diphthongs) with a **single final consonant letter**, and short vowels with a **double final letter**. This is the reason why Orm wanted to be sure that his spelling was always copied correctly:

> Annd tatt he loke wel þatt he **an bocstaff write twiʒʒess**
> Eʒʒwhær þær itt uppo þiss boc iss writenn o þatt wise . . .

although there is no evidence that anyone ever did make another copy.

This is an example of using letters as **diacritics** in spelling. The doubled consonant letter did not mark the pronunciation of the consonant as double, but marked the preceding vowel as short. This convention has become a MnE spelling rule, e.g. *diner* and *dinner* are distinguished in spelling to mark the difference between the two vowels [aɪ] and [ɪ] by using ⟨-n-⟩ and ⟨-nn-⟩.

If a short vowel syllable was closed with two consonant sounds, as in the second syllable of ME *lauerd/laferd* (OE *hlaford* (hla-ford), then Orm doubled the first of the two letters – *laferrd*.

Activity 5.3

The following words are the OE originals of words from *Ormulum*, followed by Orm's spelling of the same words.

(i) Divide these OE words into syllables, and identify the syllables as open or closed.

(ii) Compare them with Orm's spellings and decide whether each word had a short or long vowel in its closed syllables. (There are also other changes in spelling and/or pronunciation that you could think about.)

OE spellings

ac	ceaster	heofones	þoht
anes	cild	hlæfdige	þus
and	eagum	milde	ure
anne	engel	modor	wencel
bliþe	findan	niht	wunden
boren	hæfdon	sum	wurdon

Orm's spellings

acc	chesstre	heffness	þohht
aness	child	laffdiʒ	þuss
annd	eʒhne	milde	ure
ænne	enngeln	moderr	wennchell
bliþe	findenn	nihht	wundenn
borenn	haffdenn	summ	wurrdenn

Orm's system of double consonant letters cannot be applied to open syllables, because they have no final consonants to be doubled. Open syllables, therefore, may be either long or short vowels in Orm's spelling, and are unmarked.

Activity 5.4

Explain why Orm spells an adverb meaning *together* (from OE *samen*) as *samenn*, but a related verb meaning *to gather* (from OE *samnian*) as *sammnenn*, when both ⟨a⟩ vowels are short.

5.4.4 Evidence of changes in pronunciation

The following list contains pairs of words, first in their OE spelling, and then in Orm's late 12th-century spelling. All these words had short vowels in closed syllables in OE.

ceaster/**chesstre**	hæfdon/**haffdenn**	niht/**nihht**	wencel/**wennchell**
cild/**child**	heorte/**herrte**	sum/**summ**	wunden/**wundenn**
engel/**enngell**	hlæfdige/**laffdiʒ**	þoht/**þohht**	wurdon/**wurrdenn**
findan/**findenn**	milde/**milde**	þus/**þuss**	

Activity 5.5

Four of Orm's words in the list above have a single consonant letter marking a closed syllable, *child*, *findenn*, *milde* and *wundenn* (not *chilld*, *finndenn*, *millde*, *wunndenn*). All the others have double letters, like *chesstre*. Orm was very consistent and accurate in his spelling. So

(i) what does the spelling tell us about the pronunciation of the vowels in these four words in Orm's Middle English? Are they long or short?

(ii) what do these words have in common that might help to explain the change?

Questions like these give you a glimpse into the problems that faced earlier students of the language. We have far too little evidence here to come to any conclusions, and must rely mostly on what generations of scholars have discovered for us, but it is a good idea to try to infer for ourselves, from historical texts, something about the changes that have taken place.

Activity 5.6

Divide the following words into two sets:

(i) those words spoken with long vowels in closed syllables in Orm's East Midland dialect (according to Orm's spelling); and

(ii) those spoken with short vowels in closed syllables.

Orm	meaning	OE source
beldenn	encourage	beldan
birde	family	ge-byrd
childenn (*fr* child)	give birth	cild
erþe	earth	eorþe
faldess	(*sheep*)-folds	fald
goddspell	gospel	godspell
himmsellf	himself	him + self
hirdess	(*shep*)herds	hirde
kinde	kinsfolk	ge-cynd
land	land	land
mannkinn	mankind	manncynn
onn	in	on
reccnedd	reckoned (= *paid*)	gerecened
sammnenn	gather	samnian
þennkenn	think	þencan
wand	wound (*wrapped*)	wand (past tense)
wurrþenn	become	worden (*fr* wurþan)

5.4.5 Commentary

According to Orm's spelling, all the following words (taken from the preceding lists) have **long vowels**, because they are in closed syllables, which he spells with a **single** consonant:

Orm	meaning	OE source
beldenn	encourage	beldan
child	child	cild
childenn	give birth	(cild)
findenn	find	findan
kinde	kinsfolk	cynd
land	land	land/lond
milde	mild	milde
wand	wound (past tense)	wand/wond

It is known that in earlier OE these words had short vowels, therefore in Orm's dialect, by the later 12th century, they were being pronounced as long vowels, which was probably caused by the fact that [ld] and [nd] are **voiced** and relatively long, and so tend to lengthen the preceding vowel. This lengthening also occurred with other combinations of voiced consonants, like [mb], but then shortened again. Sound changes in a language are seldom simple to describe and understand. They occur in some dialects and not in others, and even in some words and not in others, but here is a short list of words of this kind which have survived into MnE.

5.4.5.1 Lengthening of OE short vowels before -ld, -nd and -mb

Compare the present-day pronunciation of the following words, which all had short vowels in early OE, with their late OE and ME pronunciations.

early OE	late OE	ME	MnE
1 eald [æə]	āld [aː]	old [ɔː]	old [əʊ] RP
camb [a]	cāmb [aː]	comb [ɔː]	comb [əʊ] RP
ceald/cald [æə] / [a]	cāld [aː]	cold [ɔː]	cold [əʊ] RP
healdan [æə]	hāldan [aː]	holden [ɔː]	hold [əʊ] RP
wamb [a]	wāmb [aː]	womb [ɔː]	womb [uː]
2 feld [e]	fēld [eː]	feld [eː]	field [iː]
sceld [e]	scēld [eː]	scheld [eː]	shield [iː]
3 bindan [i]	bīndan [iː]	binden [iː]	bind [aɪ]
blind [i]	blīnd [iː]	blind [iː]	blind [aɪ]
cild [i]	cīld [iː]	child [iː]	child [aɪ]
climban [i]	clīmban [iː]	climben [iː]	climb [aɪ]
findan [i]	fīndan [iː]	finden [iː]	find [aɪ]
4 cynde [y]	cÿnde [yː]	kinde [iː]	kind [aɪ]
5 bunden [u]	būnden [uː]	bounden [uː]	bound [aʊ]
funden [u]	fūnden [uː]	founden [uː]	found [aʊ]
grund [u]	grūnd [uː]	ground [uː]	ground [aʊ]
hund [u]	hūnd [uː]	hound [uː]	hound [aʊ]
pund [u]	pūnd [uː]	pound [uː]	pound [aʊ]
wunden [u]	wūnden [uː]	wounden [uː]	wound [aʊ] (past participle of *to wind*)

There are two points to notice:

- MnE pronunciation is different from ME. This is a result of the later sound changes to long vowels which began in the 15th century, called the Great Vowel Shift (see section 15.6).
- The vowels of the first group had also changed in quality, from [aː] to [ɔː].

If a third consonant followed [ld], [nd] or [mb] after a short vowel, the vowel did not lengthen. This explains our MnE pronunciation of *child* as [ʧaɪld], and *children* as [ʧɪldren]. OE *cild* had a short vowel which became long. The ME long vowel later gradually changed from [iː] to [aɪ]. But the plural of *cild* was *cildru*, so the third [r] consonant prevented the [i] from lengthening.

Similarly, the vowel in OE *hund* (*hound*) became long, and later changed from [uː] to [aʊ], whereas the vowel of the numeral *hundred* stayed short:

5.4.5.2 *Shortening of long vowels before two consonants*

Whereas short vowels lengthened before [ld], [nd] or [mb] in late OE and early ME, long vowels which came before two consonants or a double consonant tended to become short. The clearest evidence comes from pairs of words that had the same long vowels in OE, but which are pronounced differently in MnE.

OE – all long vowels	MnE
blēde/blēdde	bleed/bled
fēde/fēdde	feed/fed
mēte/mētte	meet/met

Other pairs which show similar vowel changes are:

OE – all long vowels	MnE
cēpe/cēpte	keep/kept
clǣne (adj)/clǣnsian	clean/cleanse
hȳde/hȳdde hide/hid	wīs/wīsdōm wise/wisdom

The contrast of vowels in MnE can be explained only if the second of each pair became short, because the long vowels were all affected in the later Great Vowel Shift. The feature they all had in common was the **two** following consonants. There were many other words whose long vowel in OE shortened before two consonants, but which cannot be illustrated by using minimal pairs, e.g. OE *dūst* is MnE *dust*, not **doust* (compare OE hūs, MnE *house*).

The same shortening took place in a first long syllable in words of three syllables, so that OE *sūþ* is MnE *south*, but *sūþerne* (sū-þer-ne) now has a short vowel in MnE *southern*; an OE *hāligbut* is today a *halibut*, not a **holybut*.

Activity 5.7

What might the pronunciation of the following MnE words have been if their long vowels in OE had not shortened in early ME?

OE	MnE	OE	MnE
blēdde	bled	hāligdæg	holiday
clǣnsian	cleanse	cēpte	kept
fēdde	fed	ūttera	utter
hȳdde	hid	wīsdōm	wisdom

5.5 12th-century loan-words

5.5.1 French

We have seen in the course of these first five chapters that most of the English word-stock in the mid-11th century came from the Germanic language developed from those dialects spoken by the Angles, Saxons and Jutes in the 5th century. But there were also assimilated Latin words (see section 4.4), and a few early borrowings from French during the 10th and 11th centuries.

One of the results of the conquest of England by the Norman French-speaking William I in 1066 was the absorption, over the cenuries, of hundreds of French words into English, and the loss of many OE words. The core vocabulary of present-day English has a large number of words that were originally French but which have been completely assimilated into English in their pronunciation, structure and spelling, as we shall see in the following chapters.

Three loan-words in Text 33 from the *Peterborough Chronicle* were from Anglo-Norman, the form of Old Northern French spoken by the Normans in England – *castel* (1075), *prisun* 1123), *uuerre* (1154). Written loan-words from the Anglo-Norman dialect of French during the 12th century that have survived include:

MnE	ONF	date	MnE	ONF	date
saint	*saint*	1122	peace	*pais*	1154
abbot	*abbat*	1123	rent	*rente*	1154
prison	*prisun*	1123	standard	*estandard*	1154
prior	*prior*	1123	treasure	*tresor*	1154
cardinal	*cardinal*	1125	charity	*charité*	1175
council	*cuncile*	1125	fruit	*fruit*	1175
clerk	*clerc*	1129	grace	*grace*	1175
duke	*duc*	1129	juggler	*jouglere*	1175
chancellor	*canceler*	1131	mercy	*merci*	1175
countess	*cuntesse*	1154	oil	*olie*	1175
war	*werre*	1154	palfrey	*palefrei*	1175
court	*cort/curt*	1154	paradise	*paradis*	1175
empress	*emperice*	1154	passion	*passiun*	1175
justice	*justice*	1154	prove	*prover*	1175
legate	*legat*	1154	sacrament	*sacrement*	1175
market	*market*	1154	table	*table*	1175
miracle	*miracle*	1154			

Activity 5.8

Is there any significance in the meanings of the earliest French words in the *Chronicle* recorded in writing, and in the list, which might explain why these particular words were adopted?

5.5.2 Old Norse

There is no evidence, other than in the surviving written manuscripts, of the number and distribution of loan-words taken from the ON dialects spoken by the Danes and Norwegians of the Danelaw, and their descendants after the 9th century. We have seen that dozens of OE and ON words were similar enough to be understood by speakers of both languages. We can imagine social situations in which OE and ON speakers regularly mixed, so that one language was infiltrated by the other. In the end, ON words were assimilated into English, with many now nonstandard and confined to the regional dialects in areas of the former Danelaw. Here is a selection of ON words recorded in writing during the 12th century.

MnE	ON	date	MnE	ON	date
sister	systir	1122	both	baðar	1175
tidings	tiðendi	1125	skill	skil	1175
die	deyja	1135	thrust	ðrysta	1175
low (adj)	lagr	1150	wing	vængir	1175
swain	sveinn	1150			

6 Early Middle English – 12th century

Standard English today is not a regional variety of English but linguists classify it as a dialect in the sense that it is one variety, among many, of the English language. It is the 'prestige dialect' of the language, with a unique status (see section 1.1).

All present-day dialects of English in England, including Standard English, can be traced back to the dialects of the Middle English period (c. 1150–1450) in their pronunciation, vocabulary and grammar. Differences of spelling, vocabulary and grammar in the manuscripts are first-hand evidence of differences of usage and pronunciation, and of the changes that took place over the ME period.

We shall now look more closely at some of the evidence for change and development in the dialects of ME that a detailed analysis of a single short text provides.

6.1 Evidence of language change from late OE to early ME in Laʒamon's *Brut*

A chronicle history of Britain was written towards the end of the 12th century. The writer was called Laʒamon – 'Laʒamon wes ihoten' – and all we know about him is contained in the opening lines of the chronicle. He lived at *Ernleʒe* (now Areley Kings) in Worcestershire, 'at a noble church upon Severn's bank'. So we may assume that he was a priest and wrote in a West Midlands dialect.

He decided to write a history of the Britons and quotes three histories as his sources:

- the late 9th-century Old English translation of Bede's 8th-century Latin *Historia*;
- a Latin book by Albinus and Augustine; and
- Wace's French metrical *Roman de Brut*, finished in 1155, which was Laʒamon's principal source and expanded and edited by him.

The title *Brut* derives from the legendary story that Brutus, a great-grandson of the Trojan Aeneas (the hero of Virgil's Latin *Aeneid*), came to an uninhabited Britain with a small company of the Trojans and founded Troynovant (New Troy – later known as Londinium, London). He was thus said to have been the first king of Britain.

Laȝamon's *Brut* includes the first telling in English of the story of King Arthur – later to be more fully told in Malory's 15th-century *Le Morte Darthur* (see Texts 95 and 96 in section 14.7) – and of King Lear. It was written in alliterative verse, but in a later popular style that is different from the classical OE poetry described in Chapter 4. There is some rhyme and assonance, little poetic vocabulary, and sometimes the rhythm is counted in syllables rather than stresses. From our point of view, this is an early transitional stage of verse-writing between OE poetry and Chaucer's regular metrical rhyming couplets in the later 14th century.

The following facsimile is the first page of one of the two surviving manuscripts, copied fifty or more years after Laȝamon wrote it.

✍ A note on the handwriting

Text/textura style of book hand (also called gothic), with heavy, rounded strokes.

- Long ⟨ſ⟩ and ⟨t⟩ ligatured (tied) e.g. *preoſt, ſtaþe.*
- Round ⟨s⟩ generally word-final, otherwise long ⟨ſ⟩, but not consistently.
- 2-form of r ⟨ꝛ⟩ after ⟨o⟩, e.g. *histoꝛia, weoꝛen,*
- ⟨ő⟩ still used, e.g. *liðe, æðelen*
- ⟨ȝ⟩ used for [j], e.g. *Laȝamon, ȝond (yon),* and ⟨g⟩ for [g], e.g. *engle (English), gon (go).*
- Insular ⟨ð⟩, e.g. *leoðen, ðrihten.*
- ⟨w⟩ used, not wynn ⟨ƿ⟩, and letter thorn written like wynn.

Activity 6.1

The words of the first paragraph of Text 37 are listed on p. 113 in alphabetical order, together with their OE sources. Examine the spelling and structure of the words and identify any that you judge to be examples of:

(i)   Words that have not changed from their OE forms.

(ii) Grammatical changes.

(iii) Changes in spelling conventions that are not the result of changes in pronunciation.

(iv) Words whose spelling suggests changes in pronunciation, for example:

- the reduction to the mid-central vowel [ə] of the unstressed vowels of inflections,
- the reduction or elision of vowels,
- changes in consonants.

Text 37: The opening of Laȝamon's Brut (facsimile)

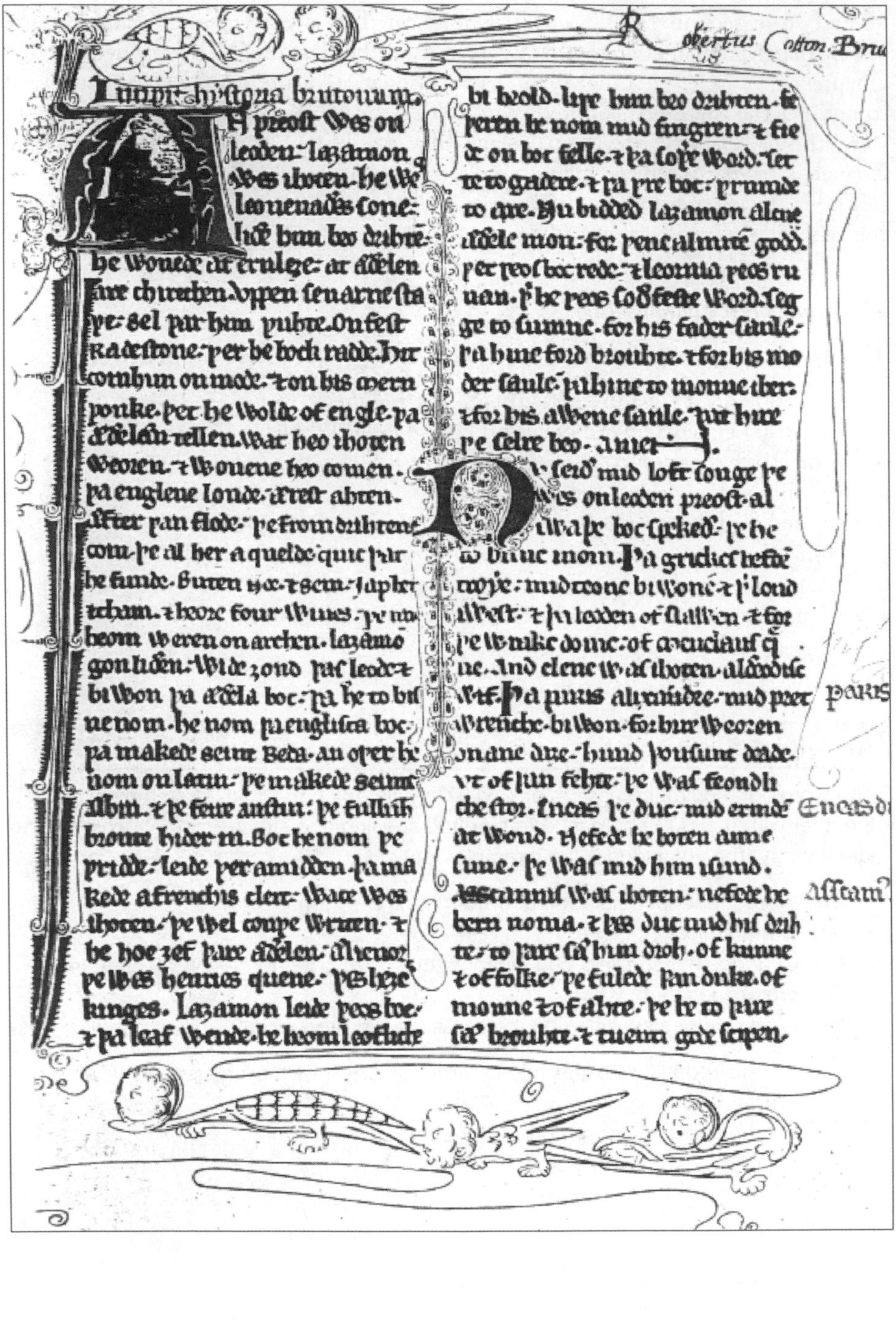

Transcription of the first paragraph to line 13, column 2

Incipit hyſtoria brutonum.

AN pꝛeoſt wes on
leoðen: laȝamon
wes ihoten. he we^s
leouenaðes ſone:
liðe him beo dꝛihtē.
he woneðe at ernleȝe: at æðelen
are chirechen. vppen ſeuarne ſta
þe: ſel þar him þuhte. on feſt
Raðeſtone: þer he bock radðe. hit
com him on moðe: ⁊ on his mern
þonke. þet he wolðe of engle þa
æðelæn tellen. wat heo ihoten
weoꝛen ⁊ wonene heo comen.
þa englene londe: æreſt ahten.
æfter þan floðe: þe from dꝛihtene
com. þe al her a quelðe: quic þat
he funðe. buten noe ⁊ sem: japhet
⁊ cham. ⁊ heoꝛe four wiues: þe mið
heom weren on archen. laȝamō
gon liðen wiðe ȝond þaſ leoðe
bi won þa æðela boc: þa he to biſ
ne nom. he nom þa engliſca boc:
þa makeðe seint Beða. an oþer he
nom on latin: þe makeðe seinte
albin. ⁊ þe ſeire auſtin: þe fulluht
bꝛoute hiðer in. Boc he nom þe
þriðde: leiðe þer amiððen. þa ma
keðe a frenchis clerc: wace wes
ihoten. þe wel couþe writen. ⁊
he hoe ȝef þare æþelen alienoꝛ
þe wes henries quene: þes heȝes
kinges. Laȝamon leiðe þeos boc:
⁊ þa leaf wenðe.he heom leofliche

be heolð: liþe him beo dꝛihten . ſe
þeren he nom mið fingren: ſie
ðe on boc-felle. ⁊ þa ſoþe woꝛð: ſet
te togaðere. ⁊ þa þre boc: þrumðe
to ane. Nu bidðeð laȝamon alcne
æðele mon. foꝛ þene almitē godð:
þet þeoſ boc reðe. ⁊ leornia þeos ru
nan: þt he þeos ſoðfeſte woꝛð: ſeg
ge to ſumne. foꝛ his ſaðer ſaule:
þa hine foꝛð bꝛouhte. ⁊ foꝛ his mo
ðer ſaule: þa hine to monne iber.
⁊ foꝛ his awene ſaule: þat hire
þe ſelre beo. ameN.

Translation

The lines in the following transcription are set out as verse, not as in the manuscript, and abbreviations are expanded.

ME

WW

Incipit hyſtoria Brutonum.
An preoſt wes on leoden: Laʒamon wes ihoten.
he wes leouenaðes ſone: liðe him beo drihten.
he wonede at Ernleʒe: at æðelen are chirechen.
vppen ſeuarne ſtaþe: ſel þar him þuhte.
on feſt Radeſtone: þer he bock radde.
hit com him on mode: 7 on his mern þonke.
þet he wolde of engle þa æðelæn tellen.
wat heo ihoten weoren wonene heo comen.
þa englene londe: æreſt ahten.
æfter þan flode: þe from drihtene com.
þe al her a quelde: quic þat he funde.
buten noe 7 sem: japhet 7 cham.
7 heore four wiues: þe mid heom weren on archen.
laʒamon gon liðen wide ʒond þaſ leode
bi won þa æðela boc: þa he to biſne nom.
he nom þa engliſca boc: þa makede seint Beda.
an oþer he nom on latin: þe makede seinte albin.
7 þe feire auſtin: þe fulluht broute hider in.
Boc he nom þe þridde: leide þer amidden.
þa makede a frenchis clerc: wace wes ihoten.
þe wel couþe writen. 7 he hoe ʒef þare æþelen alienor
þe wes henries quene: þes heʒes kinges.
Laʒamon leide þeos boc: 7 þa leaf wende.
he heom leofliche be heold: liþe him beo drihten .
feþeren he nom mid fingren: fiede on boc-felle.
7 þa ſoþe word: ſette togadere.
7 þa þre boc: þrumde to ane.
Nu biddeð laʒamon alcne æðele mon. for þene almitē godd:
þet þeoſ boc rede. 7 leornia þeos runan:
þat he þeos ſoðfeſte word: ſegge to ſumne.
for his fader ſaule: þa hine forð brouhte.
7 for his moder ſaule: þa hine to monne iber.
7 for his awene ſaule: þat hire þe ſelre beo.
ameN.

Here begins the history of Britain
(There) was a priest in (the) land, Laʒamon (who) was named;
he was Leovenath's son, gracious to him be (the) Lord.
He dwelt at Areley, at a noble church
upon Severn's bank – good there (to) him (it) seemed –
near Radestone, where he books read.
It came to him in mind, and in his chief' thought,
that he would (of the) English the noble deeds tell –
what they named were, and whence they came,
who (the) english land first possessed,
after the flood that from (the) Lord came,
that all here destroyed alive that he found,
except Noah and Shem, Japhet and Ham,
and their four wives, who with them were in (the) ark.
Laʒamon began to journey wide over this land,
he obtained the noble books which he for authority took.
He took the English book that made saint Bede;
another he took in Latin, that made saint Albin
and the fair Austin, who baptism brought hither in;
(a) book he took the third, laid there in (the) midst,
that made a French clerk, (who) wace was called,
who well could write; and he it gave to the noble eleanor,
who was Henry's queen (of) the high king.
Laʒamon laid (down) these books, and the leaves turned (over);
he them lovingly beheld – merciful (to) him be (the) Lord –
pens he took with fingers, wrote on parchment,
and the true words set together,
and the three books compressed into one.
Now prayeth Laʒamon each good man, for the Almighty God,
that this book shall read and learn this counsel,
that he these true words say together,
for his father's soul, who brought him forth,
and for his mother's soul, who him to man bore,
and for his own soul, that (for) it the better (it) be.
amen.

📖 A transcription and translation of the rest of the facsimile are in the Text Commentary Book.

In the OE column, words are given inflections corresponding to those of the ME words in the *Brut* text. Words in brackets are the base forms of nouns and adjectives or the infinitives of verbs.

Laȝamon	Old English	Laȝamon	Old English
a quelde	acwealde (acwellan)	funde	fand (findan, *pp funden*)
æfter	æfter	gon	ȝan
ærest	ærest	heo	hi/hie/heo
æþelen	æþelan	heom	him/heom
æðelen+ æðelæn	æþelum	heore	hire/hira/heora
ahte/ahten	ahte/ahton (aȝan)	her	her
alcne (alc)	æȝhwylcne (æȝhwylc)	heȝes	hean (heah)
almiten	ælmihtiȝan (ælmihtiȝ)	hine	hine
amidden	onmiddan	hoe	hi/hie/heo (*feminine acc*)
ane	anne (an)	iber	ȝebær (ȝeberan)
archen	OF arche	ihoten	ȝehaten
are	anre (an – *def. art.*)	leaf	leaf
awene	aȝene (aȝen)	leide	ȝeleȝd (lecȝan)
beo	beo (beon)	leoden	leodum
bi heold	beheold (beheoldan)	leofliche	leoflice
bi won	be + wan (winnan)	leornia	leornaþ (leornian)
biddeð	biddað (biddan)	leouenaðes	Leofnoþes
bisne	bisne (bisen)	liþe/lïðe	liþe
boc	boc (*pl* bec)	lïðen	liþan
boc-felle	boc + fell	lond/londe	land/lond
bock	boc	makede	macode (macian)
boten/buten	butan	mern	mæran
brouhte	broȝhte (brinȝan)	mid	mid
broute	broȝhte (brinȝan)	mode	mode (mod)
chirechen	cyrican (*dative*)	moder	modor
clerc	clerc	mon/monne	mann/monn
com/comen	com/comon (cuman)	nom	nam (niman)
couþe	cuþe (cunnan)	on fest	on fæst
drihten/drihtene	dryhten	oþer	oþer
engle	enȝle	preost	preost
englene	enȝlena	quene	cwene (cwen)
fader	fæder	quic	cwic
feire	fæȝer	radde	ræd (rædan)
feþeren	feþera (feþer)	rede	rætt (rædan)
fiede	feȝde (feȝan)	runan	runan (run)
fingren	finȝrum (finȝer)	saule	sawol
flode	flode (flod)	seïð	sæȝþ (secȝan)
forð	forþ	sel/selre	sel/selra
four	feower	set	sette (settan)
frenchis	frencisc		

Laȝamon	Old English	Laȝamon	Old English
sone	sunu	þonke	þanc/þonc
soþe	soþ	þridde	þridda
soðfeste	soþfæst	þuhte	þuhte (þyncan)
staþe	stæþe (stæþ)	vppen	uppon
tellen	tellan	wat	hwæt
to sumne	to sumne (sum)	wende	wende (wendan)
togadere	toȝædere	weoren/weren	wæron
þa	þa	wes	wæs
þan	þam	wide	wide
þare	þære	wif/wiues	wif/wifa
þas	þis	wolde	wolde
þat	þæt	wonede	wunode (wunian)
þe	þe	wonene	hwanon/hwonon
þene	þone	word	word
þeos	þas	writen	writan
þer	þær	ȝef	ȝeaf (ȝiefan)
þet	þæt	ȝond	ȝeond

The aim of this chapter is to assemble evidence for changes and developments in spelling, pronunciation and grammar in early ME that can be found by using as data these words from the first paragraph of Text 37.

6.1.1 Vocabulary that has not changed from OE

Most of the following words are unchanged from OE, except for the pronouns *þa, þas, þe, þene, þeos, þet*, normally unstressed and so subject to the irregular spelling of vowels that is evidence for reduction to [ə].

(The vocabulary discussed in the following sections is listed in three columns: (1) OE source; (2) Laȝamon; (3) MnE; with the Laȝamon vocabulary in bold type.)

OE source	Laȝamon	MnE	OE source	Laȝamon	MnE
æfter	**æfter**	*after*	boc (*pl* bec)	**boc**	*book/books*
ærest	**ærest**	*first*	clerc	**clerc**	*cleric, scholar*
anne (an)	**ane**	*one*	flode (flod)	**flode**	*flood*
OF arche	**archen**	*ark*	forþ	**forð**	*forth*
anre (indef art)	**are = anre**	*an*	fulluht	**fulluht**	*baptism*
beo (beon)	**beo**	*be*	hi/hie/heo	**heo**	*they*
beheold (beheoldan)	**bi heold**	*beheld*	him/heom	**heom**	*them*
			her	**her**	*here*
bisne (bisen)	**bisne**	*as an example*	hine	**hine**	*him*
boc + fell	**boc-felle**	*book-skin, parchment*	hi/hie/heo (fem)	**hoe**	*it (accusative)*

OE source	Laȝamon	MnE	OE source	Laȝamon	MnE
leaf	**leaf**	*leaves*	þis	**þas**	*this*
liþe	**liþe/liðe**	*gracious*	þe	**þe**	*that*
mid	**mid**	*with*			*(relative pn)*
mode (mod)	**mode**	*mind*	þone	**þene**	*the*
oþer	**oþer**	*other*	þas	**þeos**	*these*
preost	**preost**	*priest*	þæt	**þet**	*that*
runan (run)	**runan**	*runes =*	(?)	**þrumde**	*compressed*
		writings	þuhte (þyncan)	**þuhte**	*seemed*
sette (settan)	**set**	*set, wrote*	wende	**wende**	*turned*
		down	(wendan)		
soþ	**soþe**	*sooth = true*	wide	**wide**	*widely*
to sumne	**to sumne**	*= together*	wolde	**wolde**	*would =*
(sum)					*wished*
þa	**þa**	*then, when etc*	word	**word**	*words*

6.1.2 Changes in the grammar

6.1.2.1 Loss of prefixes and suffixes

Change in pronunciation may also produce change in the grammar. The comparative lack of grammatical inflections in present-day English is partly the result of the phonetic reduction of unstressed vowels described in section 5.3.1 which eventually led to the loss of suffixes. For example,

ȝehaten	**ihoten**	*= called*
ȝebær (ȝeberan)	**iber**	*bore*
ȝeleȝd (lecȝan)	**leide**	*laid*

The ⟨ȝe-⟩ prefix marking the past participle is reduced to ⟨i⟩ in *ihoten* and *iber*, and is elided in *leide*. But there are some grammatical changes that are caused by other processes.

Regularisation of plural suffixes

For example, in OE, nouns formed their plurals in different ways. The following nouns are paired in their singular/plural forms:

OE	MnE
cyning/cyningas	king/kings
scip/scipu	ship/ships
cild/cildru	child/children
land/land	land/lands
andswaru/andswara	answer/answers
nama/naman	name/names
gos/ges	goose/geese

OE plurals were marked with a variety of different inflections, ⟨-as, -u, -ru, -a, -an⟩, or with a zero inflection, or by a change of vowel. Today almost all plural nouns take the <s> suffix, from the OE ⟨as⟩. A few take ⟨en⟩, from the very common OE ⟨an⟩ plurals, and a small set, including *goose/geese,* are irregular, where a change of vowel signals plural number.

The OE plural of *cild* was *cildru,* which became ME *childre* or *childer.* In one dialect *childer* was given an additional ⟨-en⟩ suffix – *childeren* – which has become the Standard English *children.*

This historical process of 'making regular' – reducing a variety of forms to one – is called **regularisation**, and can be seen in several other features of the development of English. It proceeds at variable rates of change within different dialects of a language. The two changed plurals in our data are evidence of a stage in the development of regular ⟨s/-es⟩ and ⟨-en⟩ plurals in the West Midlands dialect:

⟨-en⟩ *plural suffix*

    feþera (feþer)   **feþeren**   *feathers* (= pens)

⟨-es⟩ *plural suffix*

    wifa   **wiues**   *wives*

There are two other examples of regularisation. The first also shows that adjectives were still inflected to agree with their head nouns in this late 12th-century text:

⟨-es⟩ *inflection*

    hean (heah)   **heȝes**   *high, noble*

The ⟨-es⟩ suffix marks agreement with the possessive noun *henries* in the line

    þe wes henries quene: þes **heȝes** kinges.

Vowels of strong verbs
The second example shows how the vowels of strong verbs (see section 4.4.3) came to be interchanged:

    fand (findan, *pp funden*)   **funde**   *found*

The vowel [u] of OE past participle *funden* is here used for the ME past tense, *funde,* not OE *fande.* The vowels of strong verbs interchanged in the dialects of ME, and continue to do so in present-day dialects as, for example, when *come* is used for the past tense – *I come home yesterday,* instead of Standard English *came.*

6.1.3 Changes in spelling

6.1.3.1 *French spelling conventions*

The usage of French scribes can be seen in the introduction of certain French spelling conventions into English:

⟨ch⟩ replaces OE ⟨c⟩ for [tʃ], and ⟨k⟩ or ⟨ck⟩ for [k]

The digraph ⟨ch⟩ was a very useful convention taken from Anglo-Norman. In OE, letter ⟨c⟩ clearly represented [k] in words like *camp, candel, cocc, cot* and *cuppe* – that is, before back vowels. But it had come to be pronounced [tʃ] before front vowels, as in *cese* and *cild* (*cheese, child*). So using ⟨ch⟩ and ⟨k⟩ or ⟨ck⟩ helped to clarify the ambiguous OE letter ⟨c⟩.

cyrican (dative)	**chirechen**	*church*
frencisc	**frenchis**	*French*
leoflice	**leofliche**	= *lovingly*
macode (macian)	**makede**	*made*
boc	**bock**	*book*

⟨qu⟩ replaces OE ⟨cw⟩

There were not many OE words beginning with ⟨cw⟩, and the French <qu> eventually replaced the OE. *Quake, quell, queen, quick*, from OE *cwacian, cwellan, cwen, cwic*, are surviving reflexes. Two of them are in Text 37:

cwene (cwen)	**quene**	*queen*
cwic	**quic**	*quick* (alive)

⟨ou⟩ replaces OE ⟨u⟩

The use of ⟨ou⟩ for the long vowel [uː], spelt ⟨u⟩ in OE, was French in origin. The spelling *coupe* in Text 37 is an early example of a change that was established over the next two centuries. In early ME, letter ⟨u⟩ was used for:

- back vowels [uː] (long) and [ʊ] (short) – *hus, tunge* (MnE *house, tongue*)
- the front vowel [y] in South-West dialects, *hull* (MnE *hill*)
- the consonant [v], because letters ⟨u⟩ and ⟨v⟩ were variants of the same letter until the 17th century and used both for the vowel [u] and the consonant [v] – *uertu* (*virtue*)
- the consonant [w] in the form ⟨uu⟩, and also in the new spelling ⟨qu⟩ for ⟨cw⟩.

And the ME convention of marking a long vowel by doubling the letter (e.g. *estaat, theef, goos*) would mean that ⟨uu⟩ as a long vowel would have been confused with [w] [uv] and [vu]. So the adoption of French ⟨ou⟩ (*mouse, out*) or its alternative form ⟨ow⟩ as in *cow, now*, was practical and useful.

cuþe (cunnan)　　**couþe**　　= *knew (how to)*

6.1.3.2 The influence of Latin spelling

Because so much copying by scribes was from Latin, the spelling of Latin also had some effects on the spellings of ME.

Letter ⟨o⟩ for [ʊ]

The short vowel [ʊ] in OE words like *cuman, sum, munuc, sunu, wulf* came to be spelt with letter ⟨o⟩, which has survived into MnE spelling – *come, some, monk, son, wolf*. Letter ⟨u⟩ in book hand writing could be confused with the 'minim' letters ⟨n⟩ and ⟨m⟩, as the following facsimile shows, and letter ⟨o⟩ was clearer to read.

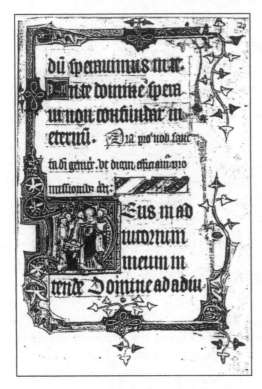

dū ſperauimus in te.
In te domine ſpera
ui non confundar in
eternū

Deus in ad
iutoʒium
meum in
tende Domine ad adiu-

There is one example of the spelling ⟨o⟩ for ⟨u⟩ in Text 37:

sunu	**sone**	*son*

6.1.3.3 *Other changes in spelling*

⟨a⟩ replaces ⟨æ⟩

The useful OE letter ⟨æ⟩, which distinguished the front vowel [æ] from the back vowel [ɑ], ceased to be used in ME writing. There were two linked reasons for the loss of the letter. First, it was not used in French spelling, and was one of the casualties of the changes brought about in the aftermath of the Norman Conquest. Secondly, the sound of the long vowel [æː] shifted towards [ɛː], and came to be spelt ⟨e⟩. (This is a simplified explanation for a complex area of sound change.)

Some examples of OE words with short [æ] which were spelt with ⟨a⟩ in ME are *æfter, æsc, cræft, græs*, which became *after, ash, craft, grass*. The following examples are from Text 37:

æȝhwylcne (æȝhwylc)	**alcne (alc)**	*each*
ælmihtiȝan (ælmihtiȝ)	**almiten**	*almighty*
fæder	**fader**	*father's* (possessive)
ræd (rædan)	**radde**	*read* (past tense)
stæþe (stæþ)	**staþe**	= *bank*
toȝædere	**togadere**	*together*
þære	**þare**	= *the*
þæt	**þat**	*that*

New letter ⟨g⟩ introduced

The 'open' form of the OE letter yogh ⟨ȝ⟩ belongs to the 'insular script' used in writing up to the 12th century. In OE, it had come to represent three sounds, according to its environment in a word – [g], [j] and [ɣ]. Text 37 shows how the 'carolingian' letter ⟨g⟩ was introduced for [g], while letter ⟨ȝ⟩, now written ⟨ȝ⟩, represented [j].

enȝle	**engle**	= *the English*
enȝlena	**englene**	= *of the English*
ȝoð	**godd**	*God*
ȝeonð	**ȝond**	= *throughout*

Variant spellings for [ʃ]

The digraph ⟨sc⟩ was pronounced [sk] in early OE, but changed to [ʃ]. It was not ambiguous like ⟨c⟩ because there were no late OE words pronounced with [sk]. But the influence of Old Norse words with ⟨sk⟩ (see section 3.4.1) led to a spelling change, with several letters or digraphs for [ʃ].

- ⟨sc⟩ became rare after the 12th century. As the sound [ʃ] did not exist in early OF, ME texts written by French-educated scribes show a wide variety of attempts to find a symbol for it.
- ⟨s⟩ was used in the 12th and 13th centuries initially and finally, as in the final letter of the single example in Text 37,

    frencisc   **frenchis**   *French*

- ⟨ss⟩ was more frequent than ⟨s⟩ in all positions.
- ⟨sch⟩ was the commonest form from the end of the 12th century to the end of the 14th century (end of the 16th century in the North).
- ⟨ssh⟩ was common from the 13th to the 16th century in medial and final positions.
- ⟨sh⟩ (perhaps a simplification of ⟨sch⟩) is regularly used in the *Ormulum* (see section 5.4). It is the usual symbol in London documents of the 14th century and in Chaucer, and from the time of Caxton onwards (*c.* 1480) it has been the established symbol for [ʃ] in all words except those like *machine, schedule, Asia*

and words ending in *-tion*, etc., which are spelt unphonetically in order not to lose the evidence of their derivation.

The *OED* lists these variant spellings for *shield*, including initial ⟨ch⟩, from OE to MnE:

> scild   scyld   sceld
> seld   sseld   sheld   cheld
> scheld   sceild   scheeld   cheeld   schuld
> scelde   schulde   schylde   shilde
> schelde sheeld
> schield   childe   scheild   shild   shylde   sheelde
> schielde   sheild
> shield

⟨gg⟩ *replaces* ⟨cȝ⟩

The single example in Text 37 shows ⟨gge⟩ replacing OE ⟨cȝ⟩ for [ʤ], as in *hegge* (*hedge*). The spelling ⟨dge⟩ was introduced in the 15th century.

> secȝe (secȝan)   **segge**   = *say*

6.1.4 Changes in pronunciation

6.1.4.1 *Reduction of unstressed vowels*

We can now apply the same methods of observation and description that began in section 4.3.4 and that were continued throughout chapter 5. The phonetic 'reduction' of vowels in unstressed syllables is so normal today that the mid-central vowel *schwa* [ə] is the commonest vowel in speech. In the late OE and early ME texts we are studying, we can see the change recorded. We assume that the vowels in OE suffixes originally spelt *-on, -an, -am, -um, -a, -u* and so on, were originally pronounced fully as [ɔ], [a] or [ʊ], and that when we find them spelt inconsistently or with ⟨e⟩, then a change has taken place. Here is evidence from the opening of the *Brut*.

⟨a⟩ ⇒ ⟨e⟩ = *pronunciation* [ə]

biddað (biddan)	**biddeð**	= *prays*
hire/hira/heora	**heore**	= *their*
sel/selra	**sel/selre**	= *good/better*
þridda	**þridde**	*third*

⟨or⟩ ⇒ ⟨er⟩ = *pronunciation* [ɔr] ⇒ [ər]

| modor | **moder** | = *mother's* |

⟨u⟩ ⇒ ⟨e⟩ = *pronunciation* [ʊ] ⇒ [ə]

| sunu | **sone** | *son* |

⟨*an*⟩ ⟹ ⟨*en*⟩ = *pronunciation* [ən]

æþelan	**æþelen**	= *noble, excellent*
onmiddan	**amidden**	= *in the midst*
butan	**boten/buten**	*but* = (except)
cyrican (dative)	**chirechen**	*church*
liþan	**liðen**	= *go, journey*
tellan	**tellen**	*tell*
writan	**writen**	*write*

⟨*an*⟩ ⟹ ⟨*n*⟩ = *elision of unstressed vowel*

mæran	**mern**	= *splendid, chief*

⟨*on*⟩ ⟹ ⟨*en*⟩ = *pronunciation* [ən]

ahte/ahton (aȝan)	**ahte/ahten**	= *owned, possessed*
com/comon (cuman)	**com/comen**	*came*
uppon	**vppen**	*upon*

⟨*um*⟩ ⟹ ⟨*en*⟩ = *pronunciation* [ʊm] ⟹ [ən]

æþelum	**æþelen**	= *noble, excellent*
	æðelæn	
finȝrum (finȝer)	**fingren**	*fingers*
leodum	**leoden**	= *country, nation*

⟨*ode*⟩ ⟹ ⟨*ede*⟩ = *pronunciation* [ədə]

macode (macian)	**makede**	*made*
wunode (wunian)	**wonede**	= *dwelt, lived*

6.1.4.2 *Other reductions and elisions*

[ɛj] ⟹ [ɛɪ] ⟹ [ɪɛ]

feȝde (feȝan)	**fiede**	= *wrote*

The transposition of the two vowels is an example of *metathesis* (see section 4.3.4.1).

OE æȝhwylcne [æjhwʏlknə] ⟹ [ælknə]

æȝhwylcne (æȝhwylc)	**alcne (alc)**	*each*

6.1.4.3 *Formation of new diphthongs*

These examples in Text 37 show the beginnings of the establishment of new diphthongs in ME, the semi-vowels [w] and [j] tending to become the vowels [ʊ] and [ɪ].

[aw] ⇒ [aʊ]

> sawol   **saule**   *soul*

[ɛj] ⇒ [ɛɪ]

> ȝeleȝd (lecȝan)   **leide**   *laid*

[æj] ⇒ [ɛɪ]

> fæȝer   **feire**   *fair*
> sæȝþ (secȝan)   **seið**   *says*

[aɣ] ⇒ [aw] (= *first stage of diphthongisation*)

> aȝene (aȝen)   **awene**   *own*

6.1.4.4 Long vowel [æː] ⇒ [ɛː]

ȝebær (ȝeberan)	**iber**	*bore*
mæran	**mern**	= *splendid, chief*
ræde (rædan)	**rede**	*reads* (present tense)
wæron	**weoren/weren**	*were*
þær	**þer**	*there*

The development of this vowel will not be discussed in detail here. Briefly, there were two sources of the long OE vowel [æː], and different pronunciations in OE dialects. One tended to develop into a half-close vowel [eː], and the other into a half-open vowel [ɛː], and both were spelt in ME with letter ⟨e⟩.

The difference between these two pronunciations of <e> is not contrastive in MnE RP, and is, very roughly, similar to the pronunciation of *get* and the Northern pronunciation of *gate* with a single vowel [geːt]. But the two contrastive vowels continued through ME into the 17th century. An attempt in the 16th century to spell the close vowel ⟨ee⟩ and the open vowel ⟨ea⟩ was made, but was not applied consistently.

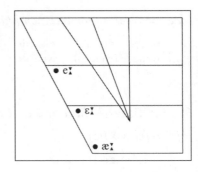

Vowel chart 4   [æː] to [eː]

6.1.4.5 Smoothing of OE diphthongs

All four OE diphthongs, long and short vowels spelt ⟨ea⟩ and ⟨eo⟩ were 'smoothed' – that is, they became single vowels – during the late OE period. Text 37 has only two examples, the long [ɛːə] of *geaf* and short [æə] of *acwealde*.

OE diphthong [ɛːə] smoothed to [ɛː]

ȝeaf (ȝiefan)	**ȝef**	*gave*
acwealde (acwellan)	**a quelde**	= *destroyed*

Here is a summary of the smoothing of the OE diphthongs (the examples are not from the *Brut*):

- **OE short ⟨ea⟩**
  The short diphthong pronounced [æə] became [æ], and so 'fell together' or merged with OE [æ]. Therefore it also became [a] in early ME, for example (not in Text 37):

OE	ME	MnE
heard	**hard**	*hard*
scearp	**scharp**	*sharp*

- **OE long ⟨ea⟩**
  The long diphthong pronounced [ɛːə] or [æːə] fell together with [æː] and so came to be spelt ⟨e⟩ and pronounced either [ɛː] or [eː]. Together with other later changes, OE [æː] words have a variety of pronunciations in their MnE reflexes, for example (not in Text 37):

OE	ME	MnE		OE	ME	MnE	
beam	**bem**	*beam*	[iː]	great	**gret**	*great*	[ɛɪ]
bread	**bred**	*bread*	[ɛ]	heafod	**heved/hed**	*head*	[ɛ]
deaf	**def**	*deaf*	[ɛ]	hleapan	**lepen**	*leap*	[iː]
deaw	**dew**	*dew*	[juː]	read	**red**	*read*	[iː]
dream	**drem**	*dream*	[iː]	sceap	**schep**	*sheep*	[iː]
eage	**eie**	*eye*	[aɪ]	sceaþ	**schethe**	*sheath*	[iː]
eare	**ere**	*ear*	[ɪə]	slean	**sle**	*slay*	[ɛɪ]
feawe	**fewe**	*few*	[juː]	stream	**strem**	*stream*	[iː]

- **OE short ⟨eo⟩**
  The short OE diphthong [eə] was smoothed and then fell together with the short vowel [e].

- **OE long ⟨eo⟩**
  The long OE diphthong [eːɔ] was smoothed and fell together with the long close [eː] vowel or sometimes with [ɔː], depending upon which of the two vowels

of the OE diphthong was more prominent, so that the MnE reflex of *ceosan* is *choose*, but the reflex of *freosan* is *freeze*.

[ɛːəw] ⇒ [uː]

> feower   **four**   *four*

The different development of long ⟨eo⟩ in OE *feower* was conditioned by the [w] following the vowel. It had the effect of smoothing the long diphthong [eːɔ] to the close back vowel [uː].

6.1.4.6 *Shifting of OE [y] and [yː]*

These OE short and long vowels were high, rounded front vowels, now heard only in a few regional accents. During the ME period they changed, but at different times and in different ways in the dialects. The result is complex:

Either	(i)	they became unrounded, and were pronounced [ɪ] and [iː] (close front vowels) *(Northern and East Midlands dialects)*;
or	(ii)	they became unrounded and shifted to [e] and [eː] (half-close front vowels) *(Southern and South-East dialects)*;
or	(iii)	at first they remained as [y] and [yː] (close rounded front vowels), but as a result of the influence of French spelling were spelt ⟨u⟩. Then they retracted and were pronounced [uː] and [uː] (close rounded back vowels). *(West Midlands and South-West dialects)*.

Here are a few examples (not in Text 37). Notice how *busy* and *bury* today have the West Midlands and South-West spelling but *busy* has the Northern and *bury* the Southern pronunciation – good examples of the irrational side of present-day English spelling.

OE short vowel /y/	Some ME spellings
byrigean	*bury/biry/bery*
bysig	*bisy/besy/busy*
cyssan	*kissen/kessen/kussen*

OE long vowel /yː/	Some ME spellings
hydan	*hiden/heden/huden/huiden*
hyran	*hire/here/hure/huire*

There is one example in Text 37, but it has ⟨i⟩ (high front vowel [i]) instead of the expected West Midlands ⟨u⟩.

⟨y⟩ ⇒ ⟨i⟩ = *pronunciation [ʏ] ⇒ [i]*

dryhten	**drihten/drihtene/**	= *God, Lord*

6.1.4.7 [a] *before a nasal consonant*

OE spelling and pronunciation of the low back vowel before [n] varied between ⟨an⟩ and ⟨on⟩. In late OE it was ⟨an⟩ except in the West Midland dialect, which is that of the *Brut*. Chaucer, in the late 14th century, has *lond*, like the *Brut*, but *land* eventually became standard.

[an] ⇒ [ɔn]

hwanon/hwonon	**wonene**	*whence*
þanc/þonc	**þonke**	= *thought, favour*

[and] ⇒ [ɔnd]

land/lond	**lond/londe**	*land*
mann/monn	**mon/monne**	*man*

6.1.4.8 *OE low back vowel* [ɑ:] *rounded* ⇒ [ɔ:]

In the four examples from Text 37, the long vowel [ɑ:] in OE has become [ɔ:] according to the evidence of the spelling.

ȝan	**gon**	= *did* (marks past tense)
ȝehaten	**ihoten**	= *called*
nam (niman)	**nom**	= *took*
be + wan (winnan)	**bi won**	*won* (= acquired)

In present-day English the word *home* (OE *ham* [hɑ:m]) is pronounced with a variety of vowels in England according to the dialectal area in which it is spoken or the social and educational background of the speaker. For example Northern [ho:m], RP [həʊm], London [haʊm], and so on. In ME, we assume that the spelling with <o> originally represented the pronunciation of a back rounded vowel in the region of [ɔ] or [o], in contrast with its neighbours like [ɑ] and [u]. We can never know what the dialectal and local variations in pronunciation were.

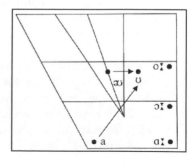

Vowel chart 5   MnE home

In Scots and some Northern dialects, however, *home* is pronounced [heːm] (spelt *hame*). Both *home* and *hame* are derived from OE *ham*, but [eː] is a *front* half-close vowel and [oː] a *back* half-close vowel.

How did this happen, and is it restricted to OE *ham*, or an example of a widespread change of the vowel [ɑː]?

Here are some short early ME texts. The words in bold type derive from OE words containing the low back vowel [ɑː]:

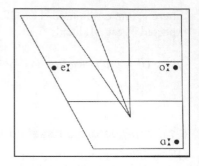

Vowel chart 6   [ɑː], [oː] and [ɛː]

OE **ahte**	þe nobeleste relike it is on þarof þat is in þe churche of Rome. So it **ouȝte** wel, hoso it understode fram ȝwanne it come. (*South-West, 13th century: St Kenelm*)
OE **agen**	(She) ledde hym to anoþer stede To hire **owen** chaumbre þat was . . . (*South-East/London, late 12th century: Kyng Alisaunder*)
OE **ban**	Alle þine **bones** he wolde tobreke (*South/South-West Midlands, 13th century: Fox and the Wolf*)
OE **cnawan**	Trewer womon ne mai no mon **cnowe** þen Ich am (*East Midlands, 13th century: Dame Sirith*)
OE **ham**	Hauelok was war þat Grim swank sore For his mete, and he lay at **hom** . . . (*East Midlands, late 13th century: Havelok*)
OE **stan**	Gold and silver and preciouse **stones** . . . (*South-East/London, late 12th century: Kyng Alisaunder*)

The evidence of these texts suggests that in these dialect areas (South-West, South-East, East Midlands), the long OE vowel [ɑː] had shifted, becoming sufficiently rounded and raised to cause writers to use the letter ⟨o⟩ to represent a sound like [ɔː].

The later development of this ME long half-open vowel [ɔː] spelt ⟨o⟩ or ⟨oa⟩ or ⟨oo⟩, to MnE [oː] or [əʊ] and its variants, is part of the later Great Vowel Shift (see section 15.6.). The following texts contain the same words as those in the preceding quotations.

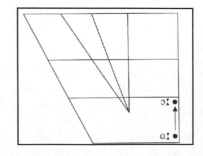

Vowel chart 7   OE [ɑː] to [ɔː]

| OE **ahte** | (He) bead to makien hire cwen of al þet he **ahte**.
(*West Midlands, late 12th century: Ancrene Wisse*) |

OE **agan**   Ich æm þin **aʒen** mon, and iseh þisne swikedom . . .
             (*West Midlands, late 12th century: Laʒamon*)

OE **ban**   Ich cwakie of grisle ant of grure, ant euch **ban** schekeð me
             (*West Midlands, late 12th century: Sawles Warde*)

OE **cnawan** For be þe thyng man drawes till
             Men schal him **knaw** for god or ill.
             (*Northern, late 13th century: Cursor Mundi*)

OE **ham**   for hwon þet he slepe oðer ohwider fare from **hame** . . .
             (*West Midlands, late 12th century: Sawles Warde*)

OE **stan**   and (hi) dide scærpe **stanes** þerinne . . .
             (*East Midlands, mid-12th century: Peterborough Chronicle*)

The use of the same spelling, ⟨a⟩, in these words could mean that:

- the vowel had not yet shifted at the time when the texts were written; or
- the shift did not occur at all in these areas, or
- the vowel shifted in pronunciation, but writers kept the same spelling in the Northern texts.

In fact, in dialects north of the Humber and in the West Midlands, the long low vowel spelt ⟨a⟩ remained until the early 14th century, when it began to shift in a different direction and eventually became a front half-close vowel [eː], as in Scots *hame*. The spelling, however, remained ⟨a⟩ or ⟨ai⟩ (letter ⟨i⟩ marking ⟨a⟩ as long), and so does not give us direct evidence. This frontward and upward shift suggests that the Northern low vowel was perhaps a more fronted [aː] rather than [ɑː].

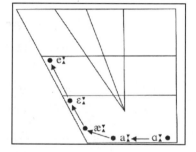

Vowel chart 8   Scots [ɑː] to [eː]

This is a warning that we cannot take the evidence of spelling only. It may not be an accurate marker of pronunciation.

We see from these examples that shifts of vowel pronunciation do not necessarily apply to a whole language, but apply to dialects of a language. Dialects differ from each other because the communities that speak them are in some way cut off from other communities and their ways of speech. The 'split' in the shift of OE long [ɑː] was probably a result of the clear geographical and political boundary marked by the rivers Humber and Lune, which prevented much direct communication between Northumbria and 'Southumbria'. The differences are still marked in present-day dialectal speech.

New words with the long low back vowel

The rounding of OE [ɑː] to [ɔː] was not the only change that we can observe between OE and ME long vowels, but it was the one in which the most marked shift took place. Most of the other vowels stayed as they were. But because the long vowel [ɑ:] shifted to [ɔ:] in Southern and Western dialects, we would expect there to be a gap in the vowel system. However, this gap did not occur, for two reasons.

First, as we have seen, French words had begun to be used in English both before and after the Norman occupation of the country (see sections 4.6 and 5.5.1). Here are some examples of adopted French words, with their first known occurrence in writing taken from the *Oxford English Dictionary*. This must be later than their use in the spoken language, but serves as a useful confirmation of a word's early assimilation into English:

age	OF eage	1325	I watȝ ful ȝong & tender of **age**.
blame (v)	OF blamer	1200	swiche men **blameð** þe prophete on þe sealm boc
cape	ONF cape	1205	A cniht mid his **capen**
cave	OF cave	1220	**Caue** ȝe [*the ant*] haueð to crepen in.
chase (n)	OF chace	1297	Mest plente of fysch . . . And mest **chase** . . . of wylde bestes.
dame	OF dame	1225	Almihti God . . . ȝiue ure **dame** his grace, so lengre so more.
face	OF face	1290	More blod þar nas in al is **face**.
grape	OF grape	1290	A luytel foul . . . brouȝte a gret bouȝ fol of **grapus** swyþe rede.
lake	OF lac	1205	Ouer þen **lac** of Siluius & ouer þen **lac** of Philisteus.
plate	OF plate	1290	He let nime **platus** of Iren sum del þunne and brode . . . And on þe berninde **plates** him casten.

These words all contained a long low (open) vowel [a:] in French, and would have been assimilated with a similar, but English, pronunciation. It began to shift to its MnE pronunciation ([e:] or [ɛɪ]) later, in the Great Vowel Shift, which suggests that it was pronounced as a front low vowel [a:] rather than the back vowel [ɑ:]. The French words must therefore have been adopted after the shift of OE [ɑ:] and began to provide new English words with a similar low vowel.

The second reason why ME continued to have words with the vowel [ɑ:] after the earlier shift to [ɔ:] needs a separate section.

6.1.4.9 Lengthening of short vowels in open syllables of two-syllable words

OE short [a] lengthens to ME long [a:]
In the following list, the ME words had the long vowel [a:] in their stem syllables:

Set 1 (not in Text 37)

OE	ME	MnE	OE	ME	MnE	OE	ME	MnE
bacan	**baken**	*bake*	lana	**lane**	*lane*	spade	**spade**	*spade*
baþian	**bathien**	*bathe*	manu	**mane**	*mane*	tacan	**taken**	*take*
crafian	**craven**	*crave*	nacod	**naked**	*naked*	talu	**tale**	*tale*
draca	**drake**	*drake*	nama	**name**	*name*	tapor	**taper**	*taper*
cnafa	**cnave**	*knave*	cwacian	**cwacien**	*quake*	wafian	**waven**	*wave*

So why had the OE vowel of these, and other words spelt with ⟨a⟩, not shifted to [ɔː] in early ME, like those just described in section 6.1.4.8?

You will find that the original OE words have in common:

- **two** syllables (i.e. they are *disyllabic*)
- **open** stem syllables (see section 5.4.2), *ba-can* etc.
- **short** stem vowels.

The OE words in the following set have:

- **one** syllable (monosyllabic)
- **closed** stem syllables
- **short** stem vowels.

Set 2

and	dranc (*drank*)	hand	ram
batt (*bat*)	hamm (*ham*)	man	sac (*sack*)

and a third set:

- **two** syllables,
- **closed** stem syllables,
- **short** stem vowels

Set 3

asse (*ass*)	catte (*cat*)	stagga (*stag*)
castel (*castle*)	mattoc (*mattock*)	thankien (*to thank*)

We now pronounce the MnE reflexes of Set 1 words with the long vowel or diphthong [eː] or [ɛɪː], but Sets 2 and 3 are still pronounced with a short vowel [æ], more or less unchanged from OE. In OE, the vowels of all three sets were short. Some feature of the Set 1 words must have caused the vowel to become long.

The evidence for this lengthening is not in the spelling of the ME words, which still used letter ⟨a⟩ and did not mark vowel length, but in their later MnE pronunciation [eː].

The significant features that all Set 1 words have in common are (a) they are **disyllabic**, and (b) the stem vowel is in an **open** syllable. The short [ɑ] vowels in open syllables of disyllabic words must have lengthened to [ɑː], otherwise they would still have been pronounced as the short vowel [æ] today.

Lengthening of [e] and [o]

This lengthening of short vowels in open syllables of disyllabic words also affected OE words with [e] and [o], as you can see from the following lists (not in Text 37):

OE	ME	MnE	OE	ME	MnE	OE	ME	MnE
bera	**bere**	*bear* (n)	peru	**pere**	*pear*	hopian	**hopien**	*hope*
beran	**beren**	*bear* (v)	specan	**speken**	*speak*	losian	**losien**	*lose*
brecan	**breken**	*break*	spere	**spere**	*spear*	nosu	**nose**	*nose*
cnedan	**cneden**	*knead*	stelan	**stelen**	*steal*	open	**open**	*open*
etan	**eten**	*eat*	swerian	**swerien**	*swear*	smoca	**smoke**	*smoke*
melu	**mele**	*meal*	wefan	**weven**	*weave*	þrote	**throte**	throat
mete	**mete**	*meat*						

The evidence for the same lengthening is clear, although the pronunciation of the MnE reflexes, spelt with ⟨ea⟩, of ME words spelt with ⟨e⟩, is variable, e.g. *bear*, *break*, *speak*. The reasons for this variation are in later sound changes (see section 15.6.1.4).

The conclusion is, therefore, that the OE vowels [ɑ], [e] and [o] in open syllables of disyllabic words lengthened in the dialects of ME in the 12th and 13th centuries. It started earlier in Northern dialects, but was complete by *c.* 1250 everywhere.

Lengthening of [ɪ] and [ʊ]

Lengthening of the two short high vowels [ɪ] and [e] only happened later in Northern and some Midlands dialects, and is complicated by the fact that the vowel tended to shift lower, so that [ɪ] became [eː] and [ʊ] became [oː]. However, only limited evidence of this remains in MnE pronunciation or spelling, e.g.

OE	Northern ME	MnE
wice	**weke**	*week*
bitol (= *mallet*)	**betel**	*beetle*
duru	**dore**	*door*

The lengthening of short open vowels in disyllabic words was probably caused by the fact that the stem vowels were stressed, and so they lengthened with the loss of the second syllable.

6.1.4.10 Consonant changes

Consonants were much less subject to change than vowels, so there are only a few features to note.

Loss of initial [h]

After the Conquest and the establishment of French-speaking government and law, English ceased to be used in most official documents. The dialect of French we call Anglo-Norman was dominant in England until the mid-14th century. There is some possible evidence in Text 37 that words with initial ⟨h⟩ were beginning to lose it.

hwæt	**wat**	*what*
hwanon	**wonene**	*whence*

though these particular words from the set of ⟨hw-⟩ words are not conclusive. The now familiar spelling ⟨wh-⟩ and the 'aspirated' pronunciation [ʍ] for some speakers suggests an assimilation of [h] and [w] rather than the loss of [h].

Word-initial ⟨h⟩ was not pronounced in French, and the borrowing of numbers of French words beginning with ⟨h⟩ has led to its irregular pronunciation in present-day English.

> All the regional dialects of Southern English lost the phoneme /h/ during the Middle English period. (D. G. Scragg, *A History of English Spelling*, 1974)

There are three possibilities in MnE:

- A few borrowed French words have lost initial ⟨h⟩ in both spelling and pronunciation, like *able*, for example:

  > OF *hable* (modern French *habile*). The initial silent *h* has been generally dropped in English from the first, though many classical scholars tried to restore it in the 16th and 17th centuries. e.g. 1678, Marvell – Apt and **habile** for any congenerous action.

- A few others are spelt with an initial ⟨h⟩ which is not pronounced, like *heir, hour, honest, honour*.
- In the majority, the ⟨h⟩ is now pronounced in RP (though not in many dialects), 'spelling-pronunciation' having been adopted – *harmony, herb, heredity* (but not *heir*), *hospital*, and so on, and in England there is divided usage over *hotel* – [ə həʊtɛl] v. [ən əʊtɛl].

[ɣ] to [h] or elision of [ɣ]

broȝhte (brinȝan)	**brouhte**	*brought*
broȝhte (brinȝan)	**broute**	*brought*

The spelling ⟨h⟩ for ⟨ȝ⟩ may or may not represent a change from the velar fricative [ɣ] to the glottal fricative [h]. The fact that the same word is spelt both *brouhte* and *broute* presents a problem that we cannot resolve without more evidence.

The change of [m] to [n] in unstressed suffixes is part of the general reduction and final loss of most inflections.

<-am> ⟹ <-an>

þam	**þan**	= *the*

6.1.4.11 Variations in ME spelling

In the preceding lists, only one ME spelling is usually quoted, which may give the impression of a fairly fixed spelling system. This was not so. The following list of words derived from OE short and long ⟨eo⟩ illustrates the variety of spellings which occur in ME manuscripts. Notice that the spelling ⟨eo⟩ persisted although the sound had changed – another illustration of the danger of accepting spelling as an accurate guide to pronunciation.

short ⟨eo⟩

OE	*ME*	*MnE*
ceorfan	keruen/keoruen/keorfen/cerue/kerue/ kerve/karve,	*carve*
deorc	dearc/derc/dorc/dorck/darc/darck/deork/durc/derk/deorke/durke/ derke/dirk(e)/dyrk/derck/dyrke/dork/darke	*dark*
geolo	ʒeolu/ʒeolo/ʒiolu/ʒeolew/ʒeoluw/ʒeolew/ʒeluw/ʒeleu/ʒelew/ ʒelugh/ʒelogh/ʒelowʒ/ʒelʒ,ʒelw/ʒealwe/ʒelwe/yelwe/ʒelou/ ʒelow/yelu/ʒelwhe/ʒelhewe	*yellow*
heofon	heofone/hefene/heofene/heouene/ houene/heauene/heofne/heoffne/ heffene/heuone/heuene/hefen/heyuen/ heiuen/hevyn/hewyn/hewin/heven/ heuin/heuon/heuun	*heaven*

long ⟨eo⟩

OE	*ME*	*MnE*
ceosan	ciose/ceose/cese/cheose/chese/chyese/chiese/chise/cheese/chees/ chess/ schese/cheyss/cheise	*choose*
freosan	freosen/frosen/freese(n)/frese(n)/frise/freys/freis/freze/frieze	*freeze*
deop	diop/deop/deop/dep/dop/deap/dup/dipe/dupe/duppe/dyep/depe/ deype/deip/deape/diep(e)	*deep*
freond	friond/frynd/friend/vriend/ frend(e)/vrend(e)/freond/vreond/ freind(e)/vrind/vryend/freend(e)/ freynd/frind(e)/frynd(e)/freyind	*friend*

6.1.4.12 Summary of changes to vowels from late OE to early ME

Chapter 5

- Reduction of vowels in unstressed syllables to [ə], leading to the eventual loss of most inflections   (section 5.3.1, *passim*).

- Lengthening of short vowels before [ld], [nd] and [mb]   (section 5.4.5.1).
- Shortening of long vowels before two consonants   (section 5.4.5.2).

Chapter 6

- OE long [æ:] shifted to [ɛ:] or [e:] and short [æ] merged with [a]   (section 6.1.4.4).
- OE diphthongs were smoothed and merged with other vowels   (section 6.1.4.5).
- OE long [y:] and short [y] shifted, but differently in dialectal areas   (section 6.1.4.6).
- OE long [ɑ:] shifted to [ɔ:] in dialect areas south of the Humber   (section 6.1.4.8).
- In early ME some short vowels lengthened if they were in open syllables of disyllabic words, mainly [a], [e] and [o]   (section 6.1.4.9).

All other vowels, long and short, remained virtually unchanged in the ME period.

6.1.5 Vocabulary

In the first paragraph of Laȝamon's *Brut*, which has been used to exemplify changes in the language in this chapter, all the words are derived directly from OE except one – *archen* (ark) from OF *arche*:

> From OF *arche*: It is possible that the OE *arc, arce* may itself have become *arch* in some dialects, but the use of this form down to the 16th C. is clearly from French. (*OED*)

We must not draw firm conclusions from the tiny amount of data that has been studied, but it seems likely that the adoption of French words was very limited in the late West Midlands dialect in which Laȝamon wrote at the end of the 12th century.

6.2 *The Owl & the Nightingale*

A poem described as 'witty and sophisticated' was written towards the end of the 12th century. It is an early example of metrical verse, in which the underlying pattern of the lines is a regular number of syllables, ending in rhyming words. *The Owl & the Nightingale* has 8-syllable lines in pairs of rhyming couplets. It contrasts with traditional alliterative Old English verse. Two lines,

> þat underyat þe king Henri   *King Henry learnt about that –*
>
> Iesus his soule do merci . . .   *(Jesus have mercy on his soul) . . .*

refer to the recent death of King Henry II in 1189, and so the poem can be fairly accurately dated to the 1190s. The original has not survived, but the facsimile Text 38, consisting of the opening lines, was probably copied after the mid-13th century.

According to a consensus of scholarly opinion, the poem was written in a South-Eastern dialect, but 'with a South-West Midland colouring'.

A note on the handwriting

Similar style to Laȝamon's *Brut* (Text 37) but with some peculiarities:

- Letter wynn is used, written with a dot over it ⟨ṗ⟩, e.g. *ṗas* (*was*).
- Letter thorn is written like wynn without a dot ⟨p⟩ (but with some confusion, e.g. line 2).
- Letter yogh is used for [ç], e.g. *niȝtingale*, and [j], e.g. *diȝele*.
- The 2-form of r <ꝛ> is written after ⟨o⟩, e.g. *ṗoꝛste* (*worst*).
- Long ⟨ſ⟩ normal, *ſtif, ſtarc, ſtrong*, with round ⟨s⟩ word-final, *ṗas* (*was*) and sometimes initial, *sval.*
- Letter ⟨a⟩ is closed.

Text 38: The Owl & the Nightingale (facsimile) – see p. 135

Here is a transcription of the first 18 lines:

	Edited version	Literal translation
Ich ṗas ın one ſum'e dale.	Ich was in one sumere dale,	I was in a summery dale
In one ſuṗe dıȝele hale.	In one suþe diȝele hale;	In a very hidden nook
Iherde ıch holde grete tale.	Iherde ich holde grete tale	Heard I hold great debate
An hule and one nıȝtıngale.	An hule and one niȝtingale.	An owl and a nightingale.
þat plaıt ṗaſ ſtıf 7 ſtarc 7 ſtrōg.	Þat plait was stif an starc an strong,	The pleading was stiff & fierce & strong
sumṗıle softe 7 lud among.	Sumwile softe and lud among;	Sometimes soft & loud now & then
An asþer* aȝen oþer sval.	And eiþer aȝen oþer sval	And each against other swelled
7 let þat wole mod ut al.	And let þat vuele mod ut al;	And let out that evil mood completely
7 eıþer ſeıde of oþeres cuſte.	And eiþer seide of oþeres custe	And each said of the other's character
þat alere ṗorſte þat hı ṗuſte.	Þat alreworste þat hi wuste;	All the worst that she knew
7 hure 7 hure of oþere ſonge	And hure and hure of oþeres songe	And especially of the other's song
hı holde plaıdıng ſuþe ſtronge.	Hi holde plaiding suþe stronge.	They held pleas very strong.
Þe nıȝtıngale bıgon þe ſpeche.	Þe niȝtingale bigon þe speche	The nightingale began the speech
In one hurne of one bꝛeche.	In one hurne of one breche,	In a corner of a clearing
7 sat upone vaıre boȝe.	And sat up one vaire boȝe	And sat upon a fair bough
þar ṗere abute bloſme ınoȝe.	Þar were abute blosme inoȝe,	Around which were blossoms enough
In ore ṗaſte þıcke hegge.	In ore waste þicke hegge	In a secure thick hedge
Imeınd mıd ſpıre 7 grene ſegge.	Imeind mid spire and grene segge.	Mingled with reeds & green sedge.

* *asþer* – probably a scribal error for *eiþer*

The vocabulary of Text 38 is listed in the Word Book.

A transcription and translation of the whole facsimile, with vocabulary, is in the Text Commentary Book.

Very few ON or OF words occur in the text. A South-East dialect would have little contact with the East Midlands and North, the area of the Danelaw, and the hundred years or so after the Norman Conquest appears to be insufficient time for more than a few French words to have been assimilated for use in the poem by a 'sophisticated' writer.

It is relatively difficult to read 12th-century ME texts. This is partly because they contain numbers of OE words that have since dropped from the language or, if a word has a MnE reflex, because the spelling does not match the MnE spelling sufficiently to make it easily recognisable. The first lines of Texts 37 and 38 illustrate the problem:

AN preoft wes on leoden: Laʒamon wes ihoten.
he wes leouenaðes sone: liðe him beo drihten.
he wonede at Ernleʒe: at æðelen are chirechen.
vppen seuarne staþe: sel þar him þuhte.

Ich was in one sumere dale,
In one suþe diʒele hale;
Iherde Ich holde grete tale
An hule and one niʒtingale

The words *leoden, ihoten, liðe, drihten, wonede, æðelen, staþe* and *sel* (Text 37) and *suþe, diʒele, hale* (Text 38) have since dropped from the language, and someone unfamiliar with OE and early ME might not recognise *are chirechen* as *a church* (Text 37) or *hule* as *owl* and *an, one* as the indefinite article *a, an* (Text 38). And the syntax of *him þuhte – it seemed to him* (Text 37) – is now archaic. It is not surprising therefore that Chaucer, writing in the late 14th century, is generally the earliest writer studied in many English literature courses. He wrote in a London dialect that resembles MnE sufficiently well in its vocabulary and structure to be relatively easily readable – if not without some need of help from a glossary. The following chapters should help in plotting the development of the language towards a greater ease of readability and familiarity.

7 Early Middle English – 13th century

7.1 *The Fox and the Wolf*

Text 39 is the opening of a poem called *The Fox and the Wolf,* dating from the early part of the 13th century.

Activity 7.1

Use the word-list following the text to compare the forms of the ME words and their OE sources, and comment on:

(i)   The use of the letters ⟨v⟩ ⟨w⟩ and ⟨u⟩ in the words *vox, wox, neuere, leuere, oueral, wous.*
(ii) The use of letter ⟨e⟩ for the main vowel in *neuere, wes, nes, erour, strete,* þen.
(iii) The spelling ⟨ou⟩ for the vowel in *out, oundred, hous, wous, hounger.*
(iv) The spellings ⟨qu⟩ and ⟨ch⟩ in *aquenche.*
(v)   The spelling ⟨o⟩ for the long vowels of *go, wo, none, so, lo*þ*, one, strok.*
(vi) The spelling and possible pronunciations of *drunche* (it rhymes with *aquenche*).
(vii) The spelling of the vowels of *half, oueral, wal/walle, leuere.*

Text 39: The Fox and the Wolf, *early 13th century*

Southern dialect (the text is edited)

ME

A vox gon out of þe wode go
Afingret so þat him wes wo
He nes neuere in none wise
Afingret erour half so swiþe.
He ne hoeld nouþer wey ne strete
For him wes loþ men to mete.
Him were leuere meten one hen
Þen half an oundred wimmen.
He strok swiþe oueral
So þat he ofsei ane wal.

WW

A fox went out of the wood (*gon . . . go = went*)
Hungered so that to-him was woe
He ne-was never in no way
Hungered before half so greatly.
He ne held neither way nor street
For to-him (*it*) was loathsome men to meet.
To-him (*it*) were more-pleasing meet one hen
Than half a hundred women.
He went quickly all-the-way
Until he saw a wall.

Wiþinne þe walle wes on hous.	Within the wall was a house.
The wox wes þider swiþe wous	The fox was thither very eager (*to go*)
For he þohute his hounger aquenche	For he intended his hunger quench
Oþer mid mete oþer mid drunche.	Either with food or with drink.

OE	text	MnE	OE	text	MnE
acwencan	**aquenche**	*quench*	an	**one**	*one*
drync	**drunche**	*drink (n)*	ofer eall/all	**oueral**	*= all the way*
æror	**erour**	*before (ere)*	hundred	**oundred**	*hundred*
gan	**go**	*go*	ut	**out**	*out*
healf	**half**	*half*	swa	**so**	*so*
hungor	**hounger**	*hunger*	stræt	**strete**	*street*
hus	**hous**	*house*	strac *fr* strican	**strok**	*= went*
leof/leofra	**leuere**	*liefer = more pleasing*	fox	**vox/wox**	*fox*
			weall/wall	**wal/walle**	*wall*
laþ	**loþ**	*loth*	wæs	**wes**	*was*
næs = ne wæs	**nes = ne wes**	*was not*	wa	**wo**	*woe*
næfre	**neuere**	*never*	fus	**wous**	*= eager, ready*
nan	**none**	*no*	þænne	**þen**	*than*

📖 The vocabulary of Text 39 is listed in the Word Book.

There is only one copy of the poem, and it is not the original. It must have been written and copied in the south of England, but it cannot be identified more closely with a particular dialectal area. But even in these few lines we find clear indications of some of the changes discussed in Chapter 6; for example, the rounding of OE [ɑː] to [ɔː], in words like *go*, *wo* and *loþ*, which had developed from OE *gan*, *wa* and *laþ*, points to a Southern dialectal form because the vowel had not changed in Northern dialects. There are no words of ON derivation in the complete poem of *c.* 300 lines, which is further evidence that it was written outside the boundaries of the former Danelaw.

📖 For a detailed description see the Text Commentary Book.

7.2 *The South English Legendary*

The South English Legendary is a manuscript containing verse legends of saints and the miracles they were said to have achieved in southern England. It includes a life of St Kenelm. There is no recorded historical evidence about him, but the legend tells of a seven-year-old boy murdered in 819, whose body was recovered and buried in a shrine at Winchcombe in Gloucestershire. (The story of St Kenelm is printed in Bennett and Smithers, *Early Middle English Prose and Verse*.)

The facsimile is from one of several surviving manuscripts, and is part of the introduction to the legend, which begins with a review of the state of England in the early 9th century with its 'five kings'.

In the transcriptions that follow, the first reproduces the facsimile with its handwriting abbreviations. The second is an edited version. The introductory lines in italics provide a suitable beginning to the facsimile. The full text is rather repetitive, so only a dozen lines are reproduced. The verse inclines to doggerel, with numbers of fillers like *iwis* and *þerto* used to make up the metre or provide a rhyme.

Text 40: Introduction to the **Life of St Kenelm** *(facsimile)*

The complete 38-line folio of the MS is reproduced with a transcription in the Text Commentary Book.

(Preceding lines)

Vif kinges þere were þulke tyme • in Engelond ido
For Engelond was god and long • & somdel brod þerto
Aboute eizte hondred mile • Engelond long is
Fram þe souþ into þe norþ • and to hondred brod iwis
Fram þe est into þe west • and also þere inne beoþ
Manie wateres god inou • as ze alday iseoþ
Ac þreo wateres principals • þer beoþ of alle iwis
Homber and Temese • Seuerne þe þridde is

Transcription

To þe noþ see humber goþ ꞅ þᵗ is on of þe befte
7 temeſe into þe eſt ſee ꞅ 7 seûne bi wefte

þıs vyf kẏnges of engelonðe ꝛ þᶜ werꞌ bı olðe ðawe
haððe herꞌpᴛ bı hē sılue ꝛ as rȝᴛ was ⁊ lawe
Þe kẏng pᵗ was of þe marche ꝛ haððe þo þe beſᴛe
Mocheðel he haððe of Engelonð ꝛ þᶜ on half al bı weſᴛe
Wnceſᴛreſchıre anð Warewẏkſchıre ꝛ ⁊ also Glouceſᴛre
þᴛ ıs neȝ al o bıſchopꞏıche ꝛ þe bıſchopes of Wırceſᴛrᵉ
he haððe alꝕo þʳᴛo cheſᴛreſchıre ꝛ ⁊ ðerbıſchıre also
⁊ Stafforðſchıre þᵗ beoþ alle ꝛ ın o bıſchopꞏıche ıðo
In þe bıſchopꞏıche of cheſᴛrᵒ ꝛ ȝut he haððe þʳᴛo
Schropſchyre sum ⁊ haluenðel ꝛ Warewẏkſchıre alꝕo ...

Edited version

To þe norþ see Humber goþ • þat is on of þe beste
And Temese into þe est see • and Seuerne bi weste
Þis vyf kynges of Engelond : þat were bi olde dawe
Hadde here part bi hem silue : as riȝt was & lawe
Þe kyng þat was of þe Marche : hadde þo þe beste
Mochedel he hadde of Engelond : þat on half al by weste
Wircestreschire and Warewykschire : and also of Gloucestre
Þat is nei al o bischopriche : þe bischopes of Wircestre
He hadde also þerto Chestreschire : and Derbischire also
And Staffordschire þat beoþ alle : in o bischopriche ido
In þe bischopriche of Chestre : ȝut he hadde þerto
Schropschire sum and haluendel : Warewykschire also

Translation

There were five kings in England at that time
For England was good and long and somewhat broad as well.
England is about eight hundred miles long
From south to north, and two hundred wide
From east to west, and therein also are
Many good rivers, as you can see any day,
But there are three principal rivers of all,
Humber and Thames, and Severn is the third.
The Humber, one of the best, flows into the north sea,
And Thames into the east sea, and Severn to the west.
These five English kings that there were in olden days
Had each their own part, as was right and lawful.
The king of the Welsh Marches then had the best.
He had a great part of England, in the west half
Worcestershire and Warwickshire and also of Gloucester
That is nearly all one bishopric, the bishop of Worcester's
He also had Chestershire and Derbyshire also
And Staffordshire, that are all in one bishopric,
The bishopric of Chester, and he had as well
Part of Shropshire and a half of Warwickshire also . . .

📖 The vocabulary of Text 40 is listed in the Word Book.

A narrative poem dealing with the Passion, Resurrection and Ascension of Christ is another of the texts in the *South English Legendary*. Like Text 40, it is written in a South-West dialect. It forms part of the story of Mary Magdalene's early morning visit to the tomb of Christ after the Crucifixion, and is based on St Matthew's Gospel, 28: 1–11, but with omissions and additions. The facsimile is not from the late 13th century original, but was probably copied in the early 14th century. The biblical text on which it is based is reproduced from the King James Bible of 1611.

IN the * end of the Sabbath, as it began to dawne towards the first day of the weeke, came Mary Magdalene and the other Mary, to see the Sepulchre.

2 And behold, there ‖ was a great earth-quake, for the Angel of the Lord descended from heauen, and came and rolled backe the stone from the doore, and sate vpon it.

3 His countenance was like lightning, and his raiment white as snow.

4 And for feare of him the keepers did shake, and became as dead men.

5 And the Angel answered, and said vnto the women, Feare not ye: for I know that yee seeke Iesus, which was crucified.

6 He is not here: for he is risen, as he sayd: Come, see the place where the Lord lay.

7 And go quickly and tell his disciples, that he is risen from the dead. And behold, he goeth before you into Galilee, there shall yee see him: loe, I haue told you.

8 And they departed quickly from the sepul-chre, with feare and great ioy, and did runne to bring his Disciples word.

9 ¶ And as they went to tell his disciples, behold, Iesus met them, saying, All haile. And they came, and held him by the feete, and wor-shipped him.

10 Then said Iesus vnto them, Bee not a-fraid: Goe tell my brethren that they goe into Galilee, and there shall they see me.

11 ¶ Now when they were going, behold, some of the watch came into the citie, and shew-ed vnto the chiefe Priests all the things that were done.

King James Bible 1611

Text 41: The Southern Passion *(facsimile)*

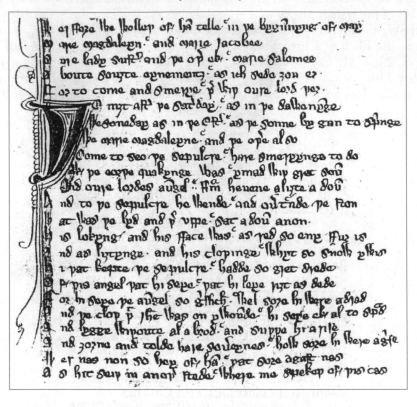

Transcription
(Initial letters of the lines of the MS are in the margin)

Þ er ffoȝe we wolleþ of hã ᴄelle ꞅ in þe bygũnyng of Ꞙꝰay

ꝳ arıe ꝳꝯagdaleyn ꞅ and ꝳꝯarıe Iacobee

O ure lady suſᴄeͬ and þe oþ⁺ ek ꞅ ꝳꝯarıe Salomee

a bouᴄe souȝᴄe oynemenᴄȝ ꞅ as ıch sede ȝou eȝ

ff oȝ ᴄo come and smerye ꞅ þꝰ wıþ oure loȝd þeȝ

P e nıȝᴄ afᴄͬ þe saᴄͬday: as ın þe dawenỹge

    þe soneday as ın þe eſᴄͬ ꞅ as þe sonne by gan ᴄo spͬınge

    þo ꝳꝯarıe ꝳꝯagdaleyne ꞅ and þe oᵱe al so

    Come ᴄo seo þe sepulcre ꞅ hare smeryynge ᴄo do

    Ak þe eoȝþe quakynge was ꞅ ymad wı greᴄ soů

    And oure loȝdes aůgel ꞅ ffm̃ heuene alıȝᴄe a doů

A nd ᴄo þe sepulcre he wende ꞅ and ouᴄͬnde þe ſᴄon

Þ aᴄ was þe lyd and þ⁺ vppe ꞅ saᴄ a doů anon

hı s lokyng and hıs ffače was ꞅ as red so eny ffuȝ ıs

a nd as lıȝᴄynge and hıs cloþınge ꞅ whyᴄ so snow ywıs

h ı þaᴄ kepᴄe þe sepulcre ꞅ hadde so greᴄ drede

O f þıs angel þaᴄ hı seye ꞅ þaᴄ hı leye rıȝᴄ as dede

ff oȝ hı seye þe aůgel so g̃ſlıch ꞅ wel soȝe hı were a drad

a nd þe cloþ þᵗ Ihe was on ywoůde ꞅ hı seye ek al ᴄo spͬd

a   nd lygge wiþoute al a bʒod ꞃ and suþþe hı arıſe
a   nd ʒoʒne and tolde hare sou^reynes ꞃ how soʒe hı were aʒ̃ſe
þ   er nas non so hey of hǎ ꞃ þat soʒe agaſt nas
a   s hıt seıþ ın anoþ^r ſtede ꞃ where me spekeþ of þıs cas

Edited text

Þer ffore we wolleþ of ham telle. In þe bygunyng of May
Marie Magdaleyn and Marie Iacobee
Oure lady suster and þe oþer ek: Marie Salomee
Aboute souʒte oynementʒ : as ich sede ʒou er
ffor to come and smerye: þerwiþ oure lord þer
Þe niʒt after þe saterday: as in þe dawenynge
Þe soneday as in þe ester: as þe sonne bygan to springe
Þo Marie Magdaleyne: and þe oþere also
Come to seo þe sepulcre: hare smeryynge to do
Ak þe eorþe quakynge was: ymad wi gret soun
And oure lordes aungel: ffram heuene aliʒte a doun
And to þe sepulcre he wende: and ouerturnede þe ston
Þat was þe lyd and þervppe: sat adoun anon
His lokyng and his fface was: as red so eny ffur is
And as liʒtynge and his cloþinge: whyt so snow ywis
Hi þat kepte þe sepulcre: hadde so gret drede
Of þis angel þat hi seye: þat hi leye riʒt as dede
ffor hi seye þe aungel so grislich: wel sore hi were adrad
And þe cloþ þat Ihesus was on ywounde: hi seye ek al to sprad
And lygge wiþoute al a brod: and suþþe hi arise
And ʒorne and tolde hare souereynes: how sore hi were agrise
Þer nas non so hey of ham: þat sore agast nas
As hit seiþ in anoþer stede: where me spekeþ of þis cas

7.2.1 Vocabulary

In the South-West dialect of this text the majority of lexical words (nouns, verbs, adjectives, adverbs) are derived from OE. The area is distant from the Danelaw, but there are two words of ON derivation, and some from French.

ON daga	**dawenynge**	*dawning*
ON systir	**suster**	*sister*
OF angele (cf. OE engel)	**angel/aungel**	*angel*
OF cas	**cas**	*case, occurrence*
OF face	**fface**	*face*
OF oignement	**oynementʒ**	*ointments*
OF sepulcre	**sepulcre**	*sepulchre*
OF soverain	**souereynes**	*sovereigns (= rulers)*
AF soun (OE son)	**soun**	*sound*

📖 The complete vocabulary of Text 41 is listed in the Word Book.

7.3 A guide for anchoresses

In the early 13th century, about 1230, a book was written for three sisters who had become anchorites (or *anchoresses*, the feminine form of the noun). The word *anchorite* derives from the Greek *anachoretes*, which means 'one who has withdrawn' – that is, withdrawn from what we would regard as a normal way of life. In medieval times monks and nuns withdrew from society into their closed communities in monasteries and nunneries, and hermits and anchorites withdrew to lead solitary lives. But the difference between a hermit and an anchorite was that an anchorite was committed to living in a single place for life, enclosed in a small cell, which was often attached to a church.

Ancrene Wisse is a book of devotional advice, written, it is believed, in a West Midlands dialect, by a canon of Wigmore Abbey in northern Herefordshire. The three anchorite sisters were enclosed nearby. Text 42 is from a section on 'fleshly and spiritual temptations' and follows a descripion of the 'unity of love'. Transcriptions and a word-for-word translation follow the facsimile, so that you can make your own study of the language.

Text 42 Ancrene Wisse (facsimile)

Al þis is iseid mine leoue sustren · þ oþer leoue
nebbes beon eauer iþent somet wið luueful semblant᷑ 7
wið spoche chere· þ ȝe beon aa wið annesse of an heorte 7
of a pil ilimet togederes · as hit iþriten is bi ure laudes
deore deciples · Multitudinis credentium erat cor unum
7 anima una· Pax uob · þis þes godes gretunge to his
deore deciples · Grið beo bimong oþ· ȝe beoð þe ancren of
englond spa feole togederes· tþenti nude oðer ma· godd
i god oþ mutli ⁚ þ meast grið is among · Meast annesse 7
anrednesse· 7 sometreadnesse of anred lif efter a riþle ᷑
Spa þ alle teoðan · alle iturnt anesþeis ⁚ 7 nan frōmard
oðer · efter þ þorð is · for þa ȝe gað þel forð 7 speded in oþ
er þei ⁚ for euch is þiðpard oþer in an manere of liflade ·
as þah ȝe þeren an cuuent of lundene 7 of oxneforc· of
schreobsburi᷑ oðer of chescer · þear as alle beoðan wið
an imeane manere · ant wið uten singularite · þ is anful
frommarðschipe · lah þing i religiun · for hit to parþed
annesse 7 manere imeane ⁚ þ ah to beon in orðre· þis
nu þenne þ ȝe beoð alle as an cuuent · is oper hehe fa
me · þis is godd icpeme· þis is nunan þide cuð · spa þet
oþer cuuent biginneð to spreaden toþard englondes
ende · ȝe beoð as þe moðerhus þ heo beoð of iscreonet ·

Edited version with modern punctuation and translation

Al	þis	is	iseid	mine		leoue	sustren,	þet		ower	leoue	nebbes
All	*this*	*is*	*said*	*my*		*beloved*	*sisters,*	*so that*		*your*	*dear*	*faces*

beon		eauer	iwent	somet	wið	luueful	semblant	ant		wið	swote
should be		*always*	*turned*	*together*	*with*	*loving*	*expressions*	*and*		*with*	*sweet*

chere,	þet	ȝe	beon	aa	wið	annesse	of	an		heorte	ant
looks;	*so that*	*you*	*should be*	*always*	*with*	*unity*	*of*	*one*		*heart*	*and*

of	a	wil	ilimet	togederes,	as	hit	iwriten	is	bi		ure	lauerdes
of	*one*	*will*	*joined*	*together*	*as*	*it*	*written*	*is*	*about*		*Our*	*Lord's*

deore	deciples:
dear	*disciples:*

Multitudinis credentium erat cor unum et anima una; pax uobis.
And the multitude of them that believed were of one heart and of one soul; peace be unto you

þis	wes	Godes	gretunge	to	his	deore	deciples:	'Grið	beo	bimong	ow.'
This	*was*	*God's*	*greeting*	*to*	*his*	*dear*	*disciples:*	*'Peace*	*be*	*among*	*you.'*

ȝe	beoð	þe	ancren	of	Englond,	swa	feole	togederes –	twenti	nuðe
You	*are*	*the*	*anchoresses*	*of*	*England,*	*so*	*many*	*together –*	*twenty*	*now*

oðer ma; Godd i god ow mutli þet meast griö is among,
or more; God in good you increase that most peace is among,

meast annesse, ant anrednesse, ant sometreadnesse of anred lif,
most unity and singleness and agreement of united life

efter a riwle, swa þet alle teoö an, alle iturnt anesweis
according to one rule, so that all pull one way, all turned in one way

ant nan frommard oðer, efter þet word is. Forþi ȝe
and no one different from the others, as the word is. Therefore you

gaö wel forö ant spedeö in ower wei, for euch is wiöward
go well forth and succeed on your way, for everyone is together with

oþer in an manere of iflade, as þah ȝe weren an cuuent
the others in one manner of living, as though you were a community

of Lundene ant of Oxnefort, of Schreobsburi, oðer of Chester, þear as
of London or of Oxford, of Shrewsbury or of Chester, where

alle beoö an wiö an imeane manere ant wiö uten singularite –
all are one with a common manner and without singularity –

þet is anful rommardschipe – lah þing i religiun, for hit
that is, individual difference – base thing in religion, for it

towarpeö annesse ant manere imeane þet ah to beon in ordre.
destroys unity and the manner shared that ought to be in an order.

þis nu þenne þet ȝe beo alle as an cuuent is ower hehe
this now, then, that you are all as one community, is your high

fame. þis is Godd icweme. þis is nunan wide cuö, swa þet
fame. This is to God pleasing. This is already widely known, so that

ower cuuent biginneö to spreaden toward Englondes ende. ȝe beoö
your community begins to spread towards England's end. You are

as þe moderhus þet heo beoö of istreonet.
like the motherhouse that they are sprung from.

📖 The vocabulary of Text 42 is listed in the Word Book.

7.4 The development of writing hands (ii) – from the 11th to the 13th centuries

In the **book hand** style of all the preceding facsimiles the letters are formed separately. When letters are joined together for greater speed in writing, **cursive** scripts are produced, and these styles developed in England from the 13th century for personal letters and business transactions. They were used in the English law-courts until the 18th century. Scripts of this kind have usually been referred to in England as either **court hands** or **charter hands**.

Although they conformed to models of style in general, scripts written by different scribes were as different in their detail as individual styles of handwriting are today, and features of scripts often changed. The short simplified surveys in sections 7.4, 12.2, 14.2, 15.1 and 17.3 are based on comprehensive studies listed in the Bibliography. The different styles which are identified do not follow each other in a straightforward chronological order, but overlap considerably, often offering alternative styles for different purposes. Some descriptions are illustrated with facsimiles of original texts, others use modern fonts which reproduce the original letter forms. The text for the latter is from the Wyclif translation of part of St Matthew's Gospel, chapter 26 (modern punctuation) –

> And Petir bithou3te on the word of Jhesu, that he hadde seid, Bifore the cok crowe, thries thou schalt denye me. And he 3ede out, and wepte bitterly.

Here is a fragment of a formal book hand in insular minuscule hand from the Domesday Book (1086). *Wermelai* is present-day Wormley in Hertfordshire:

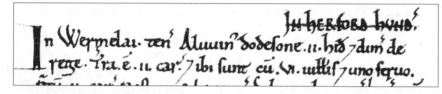

Transcription (with abbreviations expanded)

IN hERFORD hUNDREDO

In Wermelai tenet Aluuinus dodesone ii. hidas 7 dimidiam de
rege. Terra est ii. carucis 7 ibi sunt, cum vi. villanis 7 uno servo.

In Wormley Alwine son of Dodda holds 2 & a half hides of
the king. There is land for 2 ploughs & there are 2 ploughs with 6
villans & one slave . . .

After the Conquest there was at first no clear difference between the writing used for formal literary manuscripts and that used for business documents. For example, this is a charter hand of 1110, described as 'a formal book or business hand', although tending towards a cursive script:

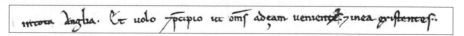

(abbreviations expanded)

> . . . in tota Anglia. Et uolo ꝛ precipio ut omnes ad eam uenientes ꝛ in ea existentes

Text hand (Textura): Later writers began to differentiate between formal book hands and charter or business hands. After *c*. 1200 a new book hand minuscule began to develop, a heavier style of Carolingian minuscule, with curves replaced by angles resembling a woven pattern (*textus* in Latin), so it was called **text hand** or **textura**. It was also called **Gothic** and lasted until the 15th century. Here is an example of early 13th-century text hand:

(abbreviations expanded)

> Omnibus ad quos presentis scripti noticia peruenerit Willelmus de Kingesford' salutem. Nouerit universitas uestra me concessisse et presenti carta mea confirmasse monachis de Bruer' unam hidam terre in Sesnecot' de feudo meo cum omnibus pertinentiis suis et . . .

Here is an example of a rather compressed form of book hand written about 1225. It comes from a copy of the devotional manual *Ancrene Riwle*, another name given to the *Ancrene Wisse*. An extract from another MS was reproduced in Text 42

Nu þe hurten
leue childʒe to þe feoʒðe ðale .
þ ı seıde schulde beō of feole fon
ðigeſ. foʒ þer beō uttre 7 ınre. 7
eıðer monı falde. Salue ıbıhet
to teachen to ʒeıneſ hā 7 bo/
te. Anð hu þaſe haueſ ham
meı Geðeren of þıs ðale con/
foʒt 7 froure to ʒaıneſ ham
alle. þat ıch þurh þe lare of
þe halı gaſt mote halde foʒep/
arðſ he hıt ʒeatı me þurh op/
re boneſ

Text hand (textura) is the most formal type of Gothic book hand (see the facsimile in section 6.1.3.2) and is the manuscript hand on which typefaces first used in the earliest printed books were based, distinguished by narrow, angular and vertical letters:

> And Petir bithouhte on the word of Jhesu, that he hadde seid, Bifore the cok crowe, thries thou schalt denye me. And he yede out, and wepte bitterli.

Handwriting font – text/textura hand

> And Petir bithouhte on the word of Jhesu, that he hadde seid, Bifore the cok crowe, thries thou schalt denye me. And he yede out, and wepte bitterli.

Printing font (16th century)

7.5 Three medieval lyrics

Here are three short extracts in facsimile, illustrating a cursive court hand, from the best known collection of ME lyric poems, in a manuscript called Harley 2253. The dialect is West Midlands. The poems were copied in the 1320s, but they were probably composed originally in the later 13th century.

Text 43: Blow northerne wynd *(facsimile)*

✍ *A note on the handwriting*

A court hand with elaborated ⟨þ⟩, long ⟨ſ⟩, ⟨w⟩ and ⟨ð⟩

- ⟨a⟩ is closed;
- closed form of ⟨s⟩ also used – ⟨σ⟩, e.g. *σyht* (*syht*);
- ⟨y⟩ is usually dotted – ⟨ẏ⟩;
- ⟨ȝ⟩ for [j], e.g. *ȝete* (*yet*). ⟨g⟩ for [g] e.g. *ſueᵹyng*
- wynn ⟨ƿ⟩ and eth ⟨ð⟩ not used.

There are ten verses altogether. The refrain *Blow northerne wynd* is repeated after each of them. The refrain and first verse are reproduced here, in transcription and in conventional verse form:

Blow norcherne wẏnð / ſenc	*Blow northerne wynd*
þou me mẏ ſuecẏng / blow	*Sent þou me my suetyng*
norþerne wẏnð blou blou blou .	*Blow norþerne wynd Blou blou blou.*
Ichoc a burðe ɪn boure brẏhc	Ichot a burde in boure bryht
þac ſullẏ· ſemlẏ ɪſ on oẏhc	þat sully semly is on syht
menrkꝼul maɪðen oꝼ mẏhc	Menskful maiden of myht
ꝼeɪr anc ꝼre co ꝼonðe	Feir ant fre to fonde.
In al þɪſ wurhlɪche won	In al þis wurhliche won
a burðe oꝼ bloð & oꝼ bon	A burde of blod and of bon
neuer ȝece ẏ nuſce non	Neuer ȝete y nuste non
luſſomore ɪn lonðe ‖ blow (*ecc*)	Lussomore in londe *Blow* (*etc.*)

The vocabulary of Text 43 is listed in the Word Book.

Text 44: Wiþ longẏng y am lad *(facsimile)*

Transcription of the first stanza

Wiþ longẏng y am lað / on molðe ẏ waxe mað / a maɪðe marreþ me/
ygreðe ẏgrone vn glað / for ſelðen y am sað / þᵗ semly forte se / leueðɪ
þou rewe me / to rouþe þou haueſc me rað / be bote of þat ẏ bað / mẏ
lẏf is long on þe /

Here is the stanza in conventional modern printing, with lineation to mark verse
patterning, metre and rhyme. The lyric has a rising duple rhythm with 3-stress lines.
There are two rhymes: a = [ad], b = [eː].

	rhyme
Wiþ longyng Y am lad	a
On molde Y waxe mad	a
A maide marreþ me.	b
Y grede Y grone vnglad	a
For selden Y am sad	a
þat semly forte se.	b
Leuedi þou rewe me!	b
To rouþe þou hauest me rad –	a
Be bote of þat Y bad!	a
My lyf is long on þe	b

The vocabulary of Text 44 is listed in the Word Book.

Text 45: Lenten ys come wiþ loue to toune *(facsimile)*

Lenten ẏs come wıþ loue to toune
wıþ bloſmen & wıþ brıꝺꝺes roune
þᵗ al þıs blıſſe brẏngeþ
ꝺaẏes eȝes ın þıs ꝺales
notes ſuete of nẏhtegales
vch foul ſong ſingeþ
þe þreſtelcoc hım þreteþ oo
awaẏ ıs huere wynter wo
when woꝺeroue sprıngeþ
þıs foules ſingeþ ferly fele
ant wlyteþ on huere wynter* wele
þat al þe woꝺe rẏngeþ

* *wynter* is said to be a scribal error for *wynn (joy)*

This poem is written in stanza form.

📖 The vocabulary of Text 45 is listed in the Word Book

7.6 *The Bestiary*

The Bestiary, or *Book of Beasts*, was a medieval collection of descriptions of the animal world, written in a variety of verse forms.

It was believed that the animal and plant world was symbolic of religious truths – 'the creatures of this sensible world signify the invisible things of God'. Later scientific knowlege shows that some of the descriptions are inaccurate, for example the description of the eagle's flight in Text 47. Some of the animals in the *Bestiary*, like the unicorn, phoenix and basilisk, are imaginary or fabulous.

There is only one surviving manuscript, written in the East Midlands dialect in the second half of the 13th century. The following facsimile of a page of the MS is a description of The Lion and its religious significance; this is followed by the first lines of The Eagle.

Text 46: The Bestiary – *The Lion (facsimile)*

✍ *A note on the handwriting*

- An unusual open form of letter wynn ⟨ꝥ⟩ is used, made in three strokes;
- eth ⟨ð⟩ is used throughout – thorn ⟨þ⟩ or ⟨ȝ⟩ are not used;
- ⟨g⟩ is used for both [g], e.g. *drageð* (*drags*), and [j], e.g. *negge* (*nigh = draw nigh*);
- 2-form of r – ⟨ꝛ⟩ – after ⟨o⟩, e.g. *foꝛ, nopoꝛ* (*nowhere*).

Text 46 set out in conventional verse form and printing

Natura leonis:

Ðe leun stant on hille . and he man hunten here
Oðer ðurg his nese smel . smake ðat he negge .
Bi wilc weie so he wile . to dele niðer wenden .
Alle hise fetsteppes . after him he filleð .
Drageð dust wið his stert . ðer he steppeð .
Oðer dust oðer deu . ðat he ne cunne is finden .
Driueð dun to his den . ðar he him bergen wille.
An oðer kinde he haueð. Wanne he is ikindled .
Stille lið ðe leun . ne stireð he nout of slepe .

Til ðe sunne haueð sinen ðries him abuten .
Ðanne reiseð his fader him mit te rem ðat he makeð .
Ðe ðridde lage haueð ðe leun . ðanne he lieð to slepen .
Sal he neure luken . ðe lides of hise egen .

Significacio:
Welle heg is tat hil . ðat is heuen riche .
Vre louerd is te leun . ðe liueð ðer abuuen .
Hu[*] ðo him likede . to ligten her on erðe .   * MS pu (wu)
Migte neure díuel witen . ðog he be derne hunte .
Hu he dun come . ne hu[*] he dennede him .   * MS wu (wu)
In ðat defte meiden . Marie bi name .
Ðe him bar[*] to manne frame.   *MS lar

Ðo ure drigten ded was . and doluen also his wille was .
In a ston stille he lai . til it kam ðe ðridde[*] dai .   *MS dridde
His fader him filstnede swo . ðat he ros fro dede ðo .
Vs to lif holden.

Wakeð so his wille is so hirde for his folde .
He is hirde . we ben sep. Silden he us wille .
If we heren to his word . ðat we ne gon nowor wille .

* MS *pu* (*wu*) – *pu* and *hu* are alternative forms, from OE *hu* or *hwu*.

Literal translation

The nature of the lion
The lion stands on a hill. If he man hunt(ing) hears
Or through (the) smell (with) his nose scents that he approaches
By whichever way he wishes to (the) dale to wend down.
All his footsteps after him he fills
Drags dust with his tail where he steps
Either dust or dew (so) that he cannot find him
Drives down to his den where he will protect himself.
Another nature he has. When he is born
Still lies the lion nor stirs he not from sleep
Till the sun has shone thrice about him
Then his father raises him with the cry that he makes.
The third law has the lion when he lies (down) to sleep
Shall he never lock (close) his eye-lids.

Significacion:
Very high is the hill that is the kingdom of heaven.
Our Lord is the lion that lives there above.
How then it pleased him to lighten here on earth
Might never (the) devil know though he in secret hunts
How he came down nor how he lodged himself
In that gentle maiden, Mary by name
Who bore him to man's advantage.

When our Lord was dead and buried as his will was
In a grave still he lay till the third day came

His father him helped so that he rose from the dead then
To hold us to life.

(He) watches so his will is as shepherd for his fold
He is (the) shepherd, we are sheep. He will shield us
If we listen to his word so that we go nowhere wrongly.

📖 The vocabulary of Text 46 is listed in the Word Book

The last three lines of the Text 46 facsimile are the beginning of the *Bestiary* account of The Eagle. John Milton used the image of the eagle 'muing her mighty youth, and kindling her undazl'd eyes at the full midday beam' in his *Areopagitica* (see Text 130, in Chapter 17).

Text 47: The Bestiary – *The Eagle*

(edited text)

ME	
Kiðen I wille ðe ernes kinde	Show I wish the eagle's nature
Also Ic o boke rede:	As I in book read
Wu he neweð his guðhede	How he renews his youth
Hu he cumeð ut of elde	How he comes out of old age
Siðen hise limes arn unwelde	When his limbs are weak
Siðen his bec is alto wrong	When his beak is completely twisted
Siðen his fligt is al unstrong	When his flight is all weak
And his egen dimme.	And his eyes dim.
Hereð wu he neweð him:	Hear how he renews himself:
A welle he sekeð ðat springeð ai	A spring he seeks that flows always
Boþe bi nigt and bi dai	Both by night and by day
Þerouer he flegeð and up he teð	Thereover he flies and up he goes
Til ðat he ðe heuene seþ	Till that he the heaven sees
Þurg skies sexe and seuene	Through clouds six and seven
Til he cumeð to heuene.	Till he comes to heaven.
So rigt so he cunne	As directly as he can
He houeð in ðe sunne.	He hovers in the sun.
Þe sunne swideð al his fligt	The sun scorches all his wings
And oc it makeð his egen brigt.	And also it makes his eyes bright.
His feðres fallen for ðe hete	His feathers fall because of the heat
And he dun mide to ðe wete.	And he down then to the water
Falleð in ðat welle grund	Falls in the well bottom
Þer he wurdeð heil and sund	Where he becomes hale and sound
And cumeð ut al newe . . .	And comes out all new . . .

📖 The vocabulary of Text 47 is listed in the Word Book.

Text 48: The Bestiary – *The Whale*

Two later 17th-century texts have the whale as their subject, Sir Thomas Browne on the subject of spermaceti, from his *Vulgar Errors* (1646), section 17.2.2.1, and an extract from John Evelyn's *Diary* in 1658, section 17.6, in which he describes the beaching of a whale at Greenwich. So it would be interesting to compare three different texts on the same topic. Here is part of the *Bestiary* account:

Edited text

ME (edited text)	WW
Cethegrande is a fis	Whale is a fish
þe moste ðat in water is . . .	The biggest that in water is
þis fis wuneð wið ðe se grund	This fish lives on the sea bottom
And liueð ðer eure heil and sund	And lives there ever healthy and sound
Til it cumeð ðe time	Till it comes the time
þat storm stireð al ðe se	That storm stirs up all the sea
þanne sumere and winter winnen	When summer and winter contend
Ne mai it wunen ðerinne	Not may it dwell therein
So droui is te sees grund	So troubled is the sea bottom
Ne mai he wunen ðer ðat stund	Not may he live there that time
Oc stireð up and houeð stille	But moves up and stays still
Wiles ðat weder is so ille	While the weather is so bad
þe sipes ðat arn on se fordriuen	The ships that are on sea driven about
Loð hem is ded and lef to liuen	Hateful to them is death and pleasing to live
Biloken hem, and sen ðis fis	They look about and see this fish
A neilond he wenen it is	An island they think it is
þerof he aren swiðe fagen	Thereof they are very pleased
And mid here migt ðarto he dragen	And with their might thereto they draw
Sipes on festen and alle up gangen	Ships on (it) fasten and all up go
Of ston mid stel in ðe tunder	Of flint with steel in the tinder
Wel to brennen one ðis wunder	Well to burn on this wonder
Warmen hem wel and heten and drinken	Warm them wel and eat and drink
þe fir he feleð and doð hem sinken	The fire he feels and makes them sink
For sone he diueð dun to grunde	For soon he dives down to bottom
He drepeð hem alle wiðuten wunde	He kills them all without wound
Significio	**Significance**
þis deuel is mikel wið wil and magt	This devil is great in deceit and strength
So witches hauen in here craft	As witches have in their sorcery
He doð men hungren and hauen ðrist	He makes men hunger and have thirst
And mani oðer sinful list	And many other sinful desire
Tolleð men to him wið his onde	Entices men to him with his breath
Woso him folegeð he findeð sonde	Whoso him follows (he) finds disgrace
þo arn ðe little in leue lage	Those are the little in faith weak
þe mikle ne maig he to him dragen	The great ne may he to him draw
þe mikle I mene ðe stedefast	The great I mean the steadfast
In rigte leue mid fles and gast	In true faith in body and spirit
Woso listneð deueles lore	Whoso listens to the devil's teaching
On lengðe it sal him rewen sore	At length it shall him grieve sorely
Woso festeð hope on him	Whoso fastens hope on him
He sal him folgen to helle dim	He shall him follow to hell dark

📖 The vocabulary of Text 48 is listed in the Word Book.

7.7 *The Lay of Havelok the Dane*

The Lay of Havelok is a poem of 3000 lines in rhyming couplets of 8-syllable lines, written in the late 13th century. The surviving, almost complete manuscript was copied in the early 14th century, and like most copies, shows evidence of modifications by the scribe. The poem was written in Lincolnshire in the East Midlands dialect. It tells the story of Havelok, a prince of Denmark dispossessed of his rightful Danish inheritance by the wicked Godard, and Goldborough, a princess of England, similarly dispossessed of her succession by the wicked Godrich. All ends well, with Havelok and Goldborough married and king and queen of both England and Denmark jointly.

The short extract in facsimile is part of the story of Havelok's rescue, as a child, from being killed. The fisherman Grim has disobeyed his orders to drown the child and has released him from being tied up and gagged. He and his wife Leve decide to raise Havelok with their family and flee to England. In the legend, the town of Grimsby is said to be named after him.

Text 49: Havelok the Dane *(facsimile)*

þ	o was haueloc a bliþe knaue
h	e ſat him up anð craueðe bred
a	nð ſeiðe ich am ney ðeð
h	wat for hunger wat for bonðes
þ	at þu leiðeſt on min honðes
a	nð for keuel at þe laſte
þ	at in mi mouth was þriſt faſte
ẏ	waſ þewith ſo harðe prangleð
þ	at i was þewith ney ſtrangleð
w	el iſ me þat þu mayth hete
G	oððoth quath leue y ſhal þe fete
B	reð an cheſe butere anð milk
p	aſtees anð flauneſ al with ſuilk
s	hole we ſone þe wel feðe
l	ouerð in þiſ mikel neðe
s	oth it is þat mē ſeyt anð ſuereth
þ	er goð wile helpē nouth ne ðereth
þ	āne ſho haueðe brouth þe mete
	haueloc anon bigā to ete
G	runðlike anð was ful bliþe
C	ouþe he nouth hiſ hunger miþe
a	lof he het y woth anð moȝe

The following edited text will demonstrate the decisions that editors of old MS texts make in producing a version for modern readers. Copyists' mistakes are corrected, abbreviations are expanded and modern punctuation is added. Words are inserted to make up the scansion of the verse line. The words that have been modified or added to the extract are in bold type:

þo was Haueloc a bliþe knaue.
He sat him up and crauede bred
And seide, 'Ich am **wel** ney ded,
Hwat for hunger, **hwat** for bondes
þat þu leidest on min hondes.
And for **þe** keuel at þe laste
þat in mi mouth was þrist **so** faste.
Y was **þerwith** so harde prangled
þat I was **þerwith** ney strangled.'
'Wel is me þat þu **maght ete**.
Goddot,' quath Leue, 'y shal þe fete
Bred **and** chese, butere and milk,
Pastees and flaunes, al with suilk
Shole we sone þe wel fede,
Louerd, in þis mikel nede.
Soth is þat **men seyth** and suereth,
þer God wile helpen, **nouht** ne dereth.'
þanne sho hauede **brouht** þe mete
Haueloc anon bigan to ete
Grundlike and was ful bliþe.
Couþe he **nouht** his hunger miþe.
A lof he **et**, y wot, and more,
For him hungrede swiþe sore.

The text has three words each of ON and OF origin,

ON band	**bondes**	*bond*	OF flaon	**flaunes**	*cakes*
ON kefli	**keuel**	*gag*	OF pastee	**pastees**	*pasties*
ON þrysta	**þrist**	*thrust*	OF strangler	**strangled**	*strangled*

which may be proportionately less than the numbers in the whole poem. Words from ON are to be expected because the poem was written in an area of high Danish settlement, and from OF because of the steady assimilation of French words into the language during the 13th century. Here are a few further examples:

Other Old Norse and Old French words in *Havelok*

þet oþer day he kepte **ok**	ON *auk*	The next day he watched out **also**
Swiþe yerne þe erles kok		Very eagerly (for) the earl's cook
Til þat he say him on þe **brigge**	ON *bryggja*	Till he saw him on the **bridge**
And bi him mani fishes **ligg** . . .	ON *lyggja*	And by him many fishes **lie** . . .
þe laddes were **kaske** and **teyte**	ON *kaskr, teitr*	The men were **active** and **eager**
Soth was þat he wolden him bynde		Truth was that he wanted to bind him
And **trusse** al þat he mihten fynde	OF *trousser*	And **pack** all that he might find
Of hise in arke or in **kiste**	ON *kista*	Of his in coffer or in **chest**
þat he mouhte in **seckes þriste**	ON *sekkr, ðrysta*	That he might in **sacks thrust**
Wiþ **poure** mete and **feble** drink	OF *povre, feble*	With **poor** food and **feeble** drink
And dide **greyþe** a **super riche**	ON *greiða*	And **prepared** a **supper rich**
	OF *soper/riche*	
Also he was no wiht **chiche**	OF *chiche*	As if he was in no way **mean**

The vocabulary of Text 49 is listed in the Word Book.

7.8 Early 13th-century loan-words, 1200–49

7.8.1 Old French

Hundreds of French loan-words were taken into English speech and writing from the 13th century onwards, and lists of common words, with their MnE reflexes, and dates of their earliest recorded occurrence, are printed in the supplementary Word Book at the end of the corresponding chapters of text word-lists. Most French loan-words from the 12th to the 14th centuries fall into one or other of the following semantic categories, which are related to the political, social and economic affairs of the time.

- Art
- Architecture and building
- Church and religion
- Entertainment
- Fashion
- Food and drink
- Government and administration
- Home life

- Law and legal affairs
- Scholarship and learning
- Literature
- Medicine
- Military
- Riding and hunting
- Social ranks

Choice of examples of loan-words

In the lists of loan-words only one spelling of each word is given, though there are often several alternatives both in Anglo-French (AF) and/or Old French (OF), and different dialectal English spellings also. Refer to the *Oxford English Dictionary* or a good etymological dictionary for details.

The lists do not give examples of loan-words that have not survived into MnE as reflexes of the originals.

The dating of loan-words

- The earliest written source that has been identified gives us a 'no later than' date, and the word would almost certainly have been in the spoken language long before it appeared in writing. The exceptions are the learned 'ink-horn terms' from Latin and Greek, created by scholars and writers from the 16th century onwards.
- Large numbers of ME manuscripts have been destroyed or lost, and with them the evidence for the appearance of many words in writing.
- Very few manuscripts can be accurately dated, and many are copies of earlier originals, so that most of the dates given with quotations in the *Oxford English Dictionary* can only be approximate.
- It is a matter of chance that a manuscript contains a particular word, which lessens even further the accuracy of dating a word's adoption.

If you compare loan-words that begin with ⟨ch⟩ in the list of 13th-century loan-words with those of later centuries, you will notice that their MnE pronunciation is [tʃ], the OF pronunciation when they were taken into English – *champion, change* etc. Later borrowings, e.g. *chevron*, are pronounced with [ʃ], because the French pronunciation had changed. Only *chivalry*, which was pronounced originally with [ʧ], but now with [ʃ] like later loan-words, is an exception.

7.8.2 Old Norse

Selected lists of Old French and Old Norse loan-words of this period can be found in the Word Book.

7.8.3 Low German

The term *Low German* is used to identify early dialects of Dutch, Flemish and northern German. Words from these languages begin to be recorded in the 13th century, and include the following:

MnE	Low German	date	quotation
bounce	bunsen	1225	*Ancrene Riwle* þer ʒe schulen iseon **bunsen** ham mit tes deofles bettles.
snatch	snacken	1225	*Ancrene Riwle* Ase ofte ase þe hund of helle keccheð ei god from þe . . . smit hine so luðerliche þet him loðie to **snecchen** eft to þe.
tackle	takel	1250	*Genesis and Exodus* And tol and **takel** and orf he [Abram] dede Wenden hom to here oʒen stede.
poll (head)	polle	1290	*South English Legendary* þe deuel . . . wolde fain henten heom bi þe **polle**.
boy	boi	1300	*Beket* ʒunge childerne and wylde **boyes** also . . . scornede hire.

7.8.4 Arabic

New words may be adopted and then passed on to other languages. Numbers of Middle English loan-words from French were in fact ultimately derived from Arabic. For example, the word *saffron* was borrowed from OF *safran* and first recorded about 1200:

Trinity College Homilies Hire winpel wit oðer maked ʒeleu mid **saffran**.

but the ultimate source is Arabic *za faran*. Similarly, the word *admiral* is first recorded about 1205,

Laʒamon þat on **admiral** of Babiloine he wes ældere.

The word's etymology is complex, and it might have been borrowed from OF, or directly from Arabic *amir al* (= *commander of*).

Loan-words taken directly into English from Arabic are not in evidence until the late 16th century. Some examples can be found in the Word Book.

8 Northern and Southern texts compared

Old English and Old Norse in the Danelaw

The Danish and Norwegian settlers in the Danelaw (see sections 3.3.1 and 3.4.1) at first spoke dialects of Old Norse, but living with or close by the Angles and Saxons of the north and east Midlands of England, their language was in time assimilated into English. No written record of the Old Norse spoken by them has survived. We believe that Old Norse and Old English were 'mutually intelligible' – much of the vocabulary was similar enough to be understood by either Danes or English. A principal difference lay in the inflections used in OE and ON to mark grammatical categories like singular/plural, past/present and so on.

Loss of inflections in ME

The loss of inflections is called **levelling**. We have already seen that the variety of the inflections of OE began to be reduced in early ME by the process we call 'regularisation' (see section 6.1.2.1). This took place more quickly in the Northern and Midland dialects spoken in or close to the Danelaw. Consequently, we find that these dialects show marked differences from the other Southern and Western dialects, with a much earlier reduction and loss of the OE inflections. The effect of the Viking settlement in the Danelaw was therefore not only an influx of Scandinavian words, but the kinds of simplification that are known to take place when people speaking similar languages communicate together, or when a pidgin language begins to be spoken.

8.1 *Cursor Mundi* – a history of the world

Cursor Mundi was written in the north of England towards the end of the 13th century. It consists of almost 24,000 lines of verse, re-telling Christian legends and the stories of the Bible from the Creation to Doomsday (*cursor* is Latin for *runner* or *messenger*; *mundi* for *of the world*). The original manuscript by the unknown author has been lost, but it was copied many times and nine manuscript copies have survived. The version transcribed below is believed to be the closest to the original poem.

Late in the 14th century another copy was written in the south of England. The writer revised the poem systematically, changing word structure, rhyme, vocabulary and spellings to match his pronunciation. It therefore provides us with some good linguistic evidence about Northern and Southern dialectal differences in the 14th century.

Here are the opening lines from Northern and Southern versions, both edited, with a literal translation of the Northern text. The author tells how people desire to read old romances and stories about princes, prelates and kings. They want to hear the things that please them best – wise men to hear wisdom, fools folly. A tree is known by its fruit, and in the present times men are esteemed only if they love 'paramours'. But bought love is false and the Virgin Mary is man's best lover – her love never fails.

Activity 8.1

(i) Examine the two texts for evidence of the changes in the language described in chapters 4–6 and summarised in section 6.1.4.12.

(ii) List some of the features by which we might identify the dialect of a text as either Northern or Southern early Middle English.

📖 The etymological origins of the words are listed in the Word Book.

Text 50: Cursor Mundi (Northern and Southern texts)

Translation	Northern version	Southern version
Man yearns to hear poems	1. Man yhernes rimes forto here	Men ȝernen iestes for to here
And (to) read romances in various styles	2. And romans red on manere sere	And romaunce rede in dyuerse manere
Of Alexander the conqueror	3. Of Alisaundur þe conquerour	Of Alisaunder þe conqueroure
Of Julius Caesar the emperor	4. Of Iuly Cesar þe emparour	Of Iulius cesar þe emperoure
Of the strong strife of Greece and Troy	5. O Grece and Troy þe strang striif	Of grece & troye þe longe strif
Where many thousand lose their life	6. þere many thosand lesis þer liif	þere mony mon lost his lif
Of Brutus that warrior bold of hand	7. O Brut þat bern bald of hand	Of bruyt þat baroun bolde of honde
The first conqueror of England	8. þe first conquerour of Ingland	Furste conqueroure of engelonde
King Arthur that was so great	9. Kyng Arthour þat was so rike	Of kyng Arthour þat was so riche
Whom none in his time was like	10. Quam non in hys tim was like	Was noon in his tyme him liche
Of marvels that befell his knights	11. O ferlys þat hys knythes fell	Of wondris þat his knyȝtes felle
That I hear tell of various adventures	12. þat aunters sere I here of tell	And auntres duden men herde telle
Like Gawain Kay and other strong men	13. Als Wawan Cai and oþer stabell	As Wawayn kay & oþre ful abul
To defend the Round Table	14. Forto were þe Ronde Tabell	For to kepe þe rounde tabul
How Charlemagne and Roland fought	15. How Charles kyng and Rauland faght	How kyng charles & rouland fauȝt
With Saracens they wished no peace	16. Wit Sarazins wald þai na saght	Wiþ Sarazines nolde þei be sauȝt
Of Tristan and his beloved Isolde	17. O Tristrem and hys leif Ysote	Of tristram & of Isoude þe swete
How he for her became a fool	18. How he for here becom a sote	How þei wiþ loue firste gan mete
Of Yonec and of Isumbras	19. O Ioneck and of Ysambrase	Of kyng Ion and of Isombras
Of Ydoine and of Amadas	20. O Ydoine and of Amadase	Of Idoyne & of amadas
Stories of diverse things	21. Storis als o serekin thinges	Storyes of dyuerse þinges
Of princes prelates and of kings	22. O princes prelates and o kynges	Of princes prelatis & of kynges
Various songs of different rhyme	23. Sanges sere of selcuth rime	Mony songes of dyuerse ryme
English French and Latin	24. Inglis Frankys and Latine	As englisshe fransshe & latyne
Everyone is eager to read and hear	25. To rede and here ilkon is prest	To rede & here mony are prest
The things that please them best	26. þe thynges þat þam likes best	Of þinges þat hem likeþ best
The wise man will hear of wisdom	27. þe wisman wil o wisdom here	þe wise man of wisdome here
The fool draws near to folly	28. þe foul hym draghus to foly nere	þe fool him draweþ to foly nere
The wicked man is loth to hear of right	29. þe wrang to here o right is lath	þe wronge to here rit is loþ

And pride is angry at obedience	30. And pride wyt buxsumnes is wrath	And pride wiþ buxomnes is wrooþ
(The) lecher has hatred of chastity	31. O chastite has lichur leth	Of chastite þe lecchoure haþ lite
Anger always wars on compassion	32. On charite werrais wreth	Charite aȝeyn wraþþe wal flite
But by the fruit may the discerning see	33. Bot be þe fruit may scilwis se	But bi þe fruyte may men ofte se
Of what virtue is each tree	34. O quat vertu is ilka tre	Of what vertu is vche a tre
Of every kind of fruit that man finds	35. Of fruit þat man schal fund	And vche fruyt þat men may fynde
It derives from the root its nature	36. He fettes fro þe rote his kynd	He haþ from þe rote his kynde
Of good pear tree come good pears	37. O gode per tre coms peres	Of good pire com gode perus
Worse tree worse fruit it bears	38. Wers tre vers fruit it beres	Werse tre wers fruyt berus
That (which) I speak of this same tree	39. þat I speke o þis ilke tre	þat i saye þus of þis tre
Symbolises man both me and thee	40. Bytakens man both me and þe	Bitokeneþ mon boþe þe & me
This fruit symbolises all our deeds	41. þis fruit alle our dedis	þis fruyt bitokeneþ alle oure dedes
Both good and ill who rightly reads	42. Both gode and ille qua rightly redis	Boþe gode & euel who so riȝte redes
Our deeds from our heart take root	43. Ovr dedis fro vr hert tas rote	Oure dedes fro oure herte take rote
Whether they deserve pain or reward	44. Quedur þai be worth or bale or bote	Wheþer þei turne to bale or bote
For by the thing that a man is drawn to	45. For be þe thyng man drawes till	For bi þat þing mon draweþ tille
Men shall know him for good or ill	46. Men schal him knaw for god or ill	Men may him for good or ille
An example about them here I say	47. A saumpul her be þaem I say	Ensaumpel herby to hem I sey
That rage in their debauchery always	48. þat rages in þare riot ay	þat rage in her riot al wey
In riot and loose living	49. In riot and in rigolage	In ryot & in rigolage
They spend the period of all their life	50. Of all þere liif spend þai þe stage	Spende mony her ȝouþe & her age
For now none is held in fashion	51. For now is halden non in curs	For now is he holden nouȝt in shouris
But (him) who can love passionately	52. Bot qua þat luue can par amurs	But he con loue paramouris
That folly love, that vanity	53. þat foly luue þat uanite	þat foles lif þat vanite
No other pleasure pleases them now	54. þam likes now nan oþer gle	Him likeþ now noon oþere gle
It is but illusion to say	55. Hit ne ys bot fantum forto say	Hit is but fantom for to say
Today it is tomorrow away	56. Today it is tomoru away	Today hit is tomorwe away
With chance of death or change of heart	57. Wyt chaunce of ded or chaunge of hert	Wiþ chaunce of deþ or chaunge of hert
What began in comfort has painful end	58. þat soft began has endyng smert	þat softe bigan endeþ ful smert
For when you most secure think to be	59. For wen þow traistest wenis at be	For whenne þu wenest hit trewest to be
From her shall you or she from thee	60. Fro hir schalt þou or scho fro	þou shalt from hit or hit from þe
He that most firmly hopes to stand	61. He þat tiithest wenis at stand	He þat weneþ stiffest to stonde
Let him take care his fall is very close	62. Warre hym his fall is nexst his hand	War him his fal is nexte at honde
Ere he so violently down is brought	63. Ar he sua brathly don be broght	Whenne he so soone doun is brouȝt
Where to go he knows not	64. Wydur to wende ne wat he noght	Whider to wende wot he nouȝt
Until his love has led him	65. Bytuixand his luf haf hym ledd	But to whom his loue haþ him led
To such reward as he him ??	66. To sli mede als he him forwit	To take suche mede shal he be sted
For then shall reward without hindrance	67. For þann sal mede witoten mer	For þere shal mede wiþouten let
Be allotted for deeds either better or worse	68. Be mette for dede or bettur or wer	Be sett to him for dew dett
Therefore I bless that loved one	69. Forþi blisce I þat þaramour	þerfore blesse we þat paramoure
(Who) when I have need helps me	70. Quen I haue nede me dos socure	þat in oure nede doþ vs socoure
That saves me from sin first in the world	71. þat saues me first in herth fra syn	þat saueþ vs in erþe fro synne
And helps me to win heaven's bliss	72. And heuen blys me helps to wyn	And heuen blisse helpeþ to wynne
For though I have been untrue at times	73. For þof I quilum haf ben untrew	For þouȝe I sumtyme be vntrewe
Her love is always constantly new	74. Hir luue is ay ilik new	Hir loue is euer I liche newe
She holds her love true always	75. Hir luue sco haldes lele ilike	Hir loue is euer trewe and lele
That is sweeter than honey from a hive	76. þat suetter es þan hony o bike	Ful swete hit is to monnes hele
Such (a one) on earth is not (to be) found	77. Suilk in herth es fundun nan	Suche oþere in erþe is founden none
For she is mother and maiden	78. For scho es modur and maiden	For she is modir & mayden alone
Mother and maiden never the less	79. Modur and maiden neuer þe lesse	Modir & mayden neuer þe les
Therefore Christ took flesh from her	80. Forþi of hir tok Crist his flesse	þerfore of hir toke ihesu flesshe
Who truly loves this mistress	81. Qua truly loues þis lemman	Who þat loueþ trewely þis lemmon
This is the love that is never	82. þis es þe loue bes neuer gan	He shal haue loue þat neuer is woon
For in this love she never fails	83. For in þis loue scho failes neuer	For in þis lif she faileþ neuer
And in that other she lasts for ever	84. And in þat toþer scho lastes euer	And in þat oþer lasteþ euer

8.1.1 Commentary

(The Northern text word is first when pairs of words or phrases are quoted. Figures refer to line numbers.)

8.1.1.1 Grammar

Verb inflections

Present tense 3rd person singular (OE -eþ, -aþ or -þ)

þam likes/hem likeþ 26	draghus/draweþ 28	bytakens/bitokeneþ (2) 40, 41
drawes till/draweþ tille 45	likes/likeþ 54	wenis/weneþ 61
saues/saueþ 71	helps/helpeþ 72	loues/ loueþ 81
scho failes/she faileþ 83	lastes/lasteþ 84	

The OE suffix is unchanged as [əθ] in the Southern text, but has become [əs], spelt ⟨-es⟩, ⟨-is⟩ or ⟨us⟩, in the Northern text. The elision of the vowel leaves the familiar ⟨s⟩ inflection of MnE 3rd person singular present tense verbs – *likes, draws, saves, fails* etc. This is evidence of the swifter 'modernisation' of the language in the north, and of the linguistic conservatism of the south, relative, that is, to Old English.

Present tense 3rd person plural (OE -aþ)

yhernes/ȝernen   1

The evidence is minimal: *yhernes* is singular following *man*, *ȝernen* is plural following *men*.

Present tense 2nd person singular (OE -est, -ast, -st)

wenis/wenest   59

Noun inflections

The variety of OE inflections marking plural nouns – ⟨-as⟩, ⟨-u⟩, ⟨-ru⟩, ⟨-a⟩, ⟨-an⟩ and zero – was discussed in section 6.2.2.1. The evidence of both texts shows a regularisation to a common [əs] or [s], the MnE inflection, with the usual variants in spelling, ⟨-es⟩, ⟨-is⟩ and ⟨-us⟩, but we would need to examine much more data to be able to confirm this as the norm.

rimes/iestes 1	ferlys/wondris 11	knythes/knyȝtes 11
Sarazins/Sarazines 16	storis/storyes 21	princes/princes 22
prelates/prelatis 22	kynges/kynges 22	sanges/songes 23
thynges/þinges 26	peres/perus 37	dedis/dedes 41, 43

Many ME noun plurals retained the [ən] suffix.

Pronouns 3rd person plural

Nominative (OE hi/hie)

> wald þai na saght/nolde þei be sauȝt   16   –/þei   18
> spend þai þe stage/–   50

Possessive (OE hira/heora)

> þer liif   6   Of all þere liif/her ȝouþe & her age   50

Dative (OE him, heom)

> þam likes/hem likeþ   26

We are unlikely to notice the use of *þai*, *þer* or *þam* (*they*, *their*, *them*) unless we remember that the OE plural 3rd person pronouns were *hi*, *hira* and *him*. This borrowing from ON of distinctive forms, all beginning with ⟨th-⟩, began early on in the Northern dialects of ME. It spread southwards, but was not completed there even at the beginning of the 15th century. In Text 50 the Southern version has the ON *þei* as subject of a clause, but retains the older forms *her* and *hem* for the possessive and object cases. Chaucer, writing in the 1390s in the London dialect, used the new form for the subject pronoun,

> And thus **they** been accorded and ysworn . . .

but the older forms for the others,

> And many a louely look on **hem** he caste . . .

> Men sholde wedden after **hir** estaat . . .

Feminine pronouns

The OE feminine subject pronoun was *heo*, beginning with ⟨h⟩ like all the personal pronouns, and therefore, potentially, easily confused with the other pronouns. The development of MnE *she* began during the early ME period, but with a variety of transitional forms (illustrated in section 9.1.1 in the next chapter), in different dialectal areas. From the limited evidence of Text 50, the Northern text form was pronounced [ʃoː] and the Southern [ʃeː].

Subject (OE heo)

> scho es/she is   78   scho failes/she faileþ   83
> sco haldes   75

Object (OE hi/hie)

> here/–   18

Possessive and dative (OE hire, hiere)

   hir luue/hir loue 74, 75   of hir/of hir 80

8.1.1.2 Pronunciation

Shifting and rounding of OE long open back vowel [ɑː] to [ɔː]

In section 6.1.4.8 it was said that this vowel change took place only south of the Humber, and the evidence of Text 50 confirms this:

wald/nolde 16	lath/looþ 29	wrath/wrooþ 30
bytakens/bitokeneþ 40, 41	knaw/knowe 46	halden/holden 51
nan/noon 54	fra/fro 71	nan/none 77
qua/who 81		

OE [y]
(See section 6.1.4.6)

   first/furste 8 (*OE fyrsta*)   –/duden 12 (*OE dydon*)

o/a before nasal consonant
(See section 6.1.4.7)

many/mony 6	hand/honde 7, 62	sanges/songes 23
wrang/wronge 29	man/mon 40	stand/stonde 61
lemman/lemmon 81		

⟨k⟩ from ON and ⟨ch⟩ from OE

The contrast here comes from the Northern use of words derived from ON, or from Northern pronunciation with [k] of OE words with [tʃ]:

rike/riche 9	ON rikr/OE rice & OF riche
like/liche 10 & ilik/I liche 74	ON likr/OE (ge)lice
suilk/ suche 77	Northern form of OE swilc, swelc
ilkon/– 25, ilka/vche 34 & alkyn/vche 35	Northern forms of ilch from OE ælc + an

8.1.1.3 Spelling

Double letters for long vowel

In order to distinguish long vowels from short, some scribes doubled the vowel letter. This accounts for most of the ⟨ee⟩ and ⟨oo⟩ spellings in MnE, but ⟨ii⟩ and ⟨aa⟩ dropped out of fashion, and ⟨uu⟩ was rarely used (see section 6.1.3.1). In Text 50 this is a feature of the Southern text only:

striif 5	fool 28	looþ 29
wrooþ 30	noon 54	woot 64

⟨*qu-*⟩ *for* ⟨*wh-*⟩

This ⟨qu-⟩ spelling is not the French convention for spelling OE ⟨cw⟩ (section 6.1.3.1) but a representation of a heavily aspirated fricative consonant, [xw]; ⟨qu-⟩ or ⟨quh-⟩ was in fact retained in Scots spelling through to the 17th century, e.g. *quhairunto, quhole* for *whereunto, whole*, from a letter by King James VI in 1586.

    quam/– 10 (= whom)   quat/what 34   quedur/wheþer 44
    qua/who 81

⟨*gh*⟩

In OE, letter yogh ⟨ȝ⟩ had come to represent three sounds – [g] [j] and [ɣ] (see sections 3.1.2 and 6.1.3.3). With the adoption of the continental letter ⟨g⟩ for [g], ⟨ȝ⟩ tended to be used for [j]. Two related sounds that occurred after a vowel, [ç] and [x], caused problems of spelling, and among different choices, ⟨gh⟩ became common; [ç] and [x] are fricative consonants, as in Scots *licht, ocht, nicht*).

    faght/fauȝt 15   saght/sauȝt 16   draghus/draweþ 28
    right/rit 29   broght/brouȝt 63   noght/nouȝt 64

The consonants [x] and [ç] came to be elided in many words eventually, e.g. *brought, sought, right, bough* (though the spelling has been retained). In others it became the fricative consonant [f], as in *cough, tough, laugh*. The single example in Text 50 helps to show how the irregularity of the MnE pronunciation of ⟨gh⟩ is the result of a fairly random choice between different dialectal pronunciations.

    þof/þouȝe 73

⟨*s*⟩, ⟨*sse*⟩ *and* ⟨*sshe*⟩ *for word-final* [ʃ]
(See section 6.1.3.3)

    Inglis/englisshe 24   Frankys/fransshe 24   flesse/flesshe 80

8.1.1.4 Vocabulary

Core vocabulary

MnE 'core vocabulary' – those words that are the most basic to the language and common in everyday use in speech – has two principal sources:

- OE words that have reflexes in the language today, which include words of ON origin. These form the basic 'Germanic' elements of the language.
- OF words that were adopted during the three to four centuries after the Norman Conquest of 1066, and which have been fully assimilated to English in their pronunciation, morphology and spelling.

If we therefore discover the proportion of OE to ON and OF words in a ME text, we have some evidence which may help in assessing its possible date and dialectal area. A text with a significantly large number of ON words is likely to be in a Northern or East Midlands dialect, the area of Danish settlement. The higher the proportion of OF words, then the later the text's composition. This, of course, needs to be done with complete texts in order to obtain any statistically significant figures, and a whole range of evidence must be studied, including spelling and pronunciation, word-forms and grammar as well as etymological derivation. The figures for OE, ON and OF derivation for the two *Cursor Mundi* texts are:

	OE	ON	OF/AN
Northern text	76%	9%	15%
Southern text	78.5%	4.5%	17%

The ON and OF vocabularies of the two texts are:

Northern text – Old Norse

ai/ay	ON ei (= *always*)	sli	ON slikr (= *such*)
both	ON baðir	tas	ON taka
brathly	ON braðliga (= *violently*)	tiithest	
ferlys	ON ferligr	?stiithest	ON tiðast/OE stiþe?
fra/fro	ON fra	till	ON til
ill/ille	ON illr	tok	ON taka, tok
rike	ON rikr	traistest	ON treystr (= *most secure*)
rote	ON rot	þai	ON þeir
saght	ON saht (= *settlement*)	þare	ON þeirra
scilwis	ON skilviss (= *discerning*)	þof	ON þo
sere	ON ser (= *various*)	wrang	ON wrang
serekin	ON ser + kyn	**23 types**	

Northern text – Old French/Anglo-Norman

amurs	OF amur (= *love*)	manere	AN manere
aunters	OF aventure	par amurs/	
charite	OF charité	paramour	OF par amurs
chastite	OF chasteté	prelates	OF prelat
chaunce	OF cheaunce	princes	OF prince
conquerour	AF conquerour	rages	OF rager (= *live wantonly*)
emparour	AN empereur	rigolage	OF rigolage
failes	OF faillir	rime/rimes	OF rime
fantum	OF fantosme	riot	OF riote
foly	OF folie	romans	OF romans
foul	OF fol (= *fool*)	ronde	AN rund
fruit	OF fruit	saues	AN sauver
lele	OF leel	saumpul	AN essaumple
lichur	AN lechur, lichur	socure	AN sucurs

sote	OF sot (= *fool*)	tabell	OF table
stabell	OF stable (= *sturdy*)	uanite	OF vanité
stage	OF stage	vertu	OF vertu
storis	AN storie	werrais	AN werreier
striif	OF strif	**37 types**	

Southern text – Old Norse

boþe	ON baðir	rote	ON rot	þei	ON þeir
ille	ON illr	sauȝt	ON saht (= *settlement*)	þouȝe	ON þo
liche	ON likr	tille	ON til	**10 types**	
nere	ON nær	wronge	ON wrangr		

Southern text – Old French/Anglo-Norman

abul	OF hable, able	lecchoure	AN lechur
age	OF eage	lele	OF leel
auntres	OF aventure	manere	AN maniere
baroun	OF barun	paramoure/-is	OF par amurs
charite	OF charité	prelatis	OF prelat
chastite	OF chasteté	princes	OF prince
chaunce	OF cheance	rage	OF rager
chaunge	AF chaunge	rigolage	OF rigolage
conqueroure	AF conquerour	riot/ryot	OF riote
dett	OF dete, dette	romaunce	OF romans
dew	OF deu	rounde	AN rund
dyuerse	OF divers	ryme	OF rime
emperoure	AN empereur	saueþ	AN sauver
ensaumpel	AN essaumple	socoure	AN sucurs
faileþ	OF faillir	storyes	AN storie
fantom	OF fantosme	strif	OF strif
foles/fool	OF fol (= *fool*)	tabul	OF table
foly	OF folie	vanite	OF vanité
fruyt/fruyte	OF fruit	vertu	OF vertu
iestes	OF geste (= *story*)	**39 types**	

8.1.1.5 Summary – identifying Northern and Southern dialects of ME

We have found the following differences between the two short extracts from the *Cursor Mundi* texts. No exact conclusions can be drawn from such limited data, but there is evidence of levelling and regularisation in both dialects.

	Northern text	Southern text	Old English
Verb inflections			
Present 2nd person singular	-is, -est	-est	-est, ast, -st
Present 3rd person singular	-es, -is, -s	-eþ	-aþ
Present 3rd person plural	-es	-en	-aþ
Nouns			
Plural inflections	-es, -s, -is	-es, -is, -us	-as, -an, -u, -ru, -a,
Pronouns			
Feminine subject	scho/sco	she	heo
Feminine object	here	*no evidence*	hi/hie
Feminine possessive	hir	hir	hire/hiere
3rd person plural subject	þai	þei	hi/hie
3rd person plural possessive	þer	her	hira/heora
3rd person plural object/dative	þam	hem	him/heom
Pronunciation/spelling			
OE long vowel [ɑ:] rounded to [ɔ:]	*no*	*yes*	
OE close front vowel [y]	⟨i⟩	⟨u⟩	
o or a before nasal consonant	⟨a⟩	⟨o⟩	
ON <k> or OE <ch>	⟨k⟩	⟨ch⟩ and ⟨k⟩	
<qu-> or <wh->?	⟨qu-⟩	⟨wh-⟩	
spelling of [ʃ]	⟨-s/ss⟩	⟨ssh⟩	

You should be able to check these findings in Chapters 9–13 on the dialects of the language in the 14th century.

Another MS of *Cursor Mundi* (facsimile)

The following facsimile of the first eleven lines of *Cursor Mundi* is from one of the other Northern manuscripts, probably copied about 1400.

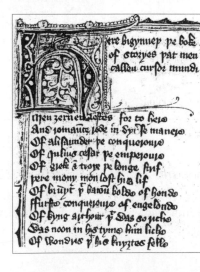

ere bigynneþ þe boke
of storyes þat men
callen curſor munði

Men ȝernen ieſtes for to here
And romaūce reðe ın ðyūſe manere   ðyuerse
Of alıſaunðer þe conqueroure
Of Iulıus ceſar þe emperoure
Of greſe ⁊ troye þe longe ſtrif
þere mony mon loſt hıs lıf
Of brüþ pt baroū bolðe of honðe
ffurſte conqueroure of engelonðe
Of kyng arthour þᵗ was so rıche
Was noon ın hıs tyme hım lıche
Of wonðrıs pᵗ hıs knyȝtes felle

Activity 8.2

Examine the next extract from *Cursor Mundi* in its Northern and Southern dialect forms and use the vocabulary lists to find evidence of change and difference in the language of the texts. (The texts are edited versions.)

Text 51: Cursor Mundi (ii)

Northern dialect	Southern dialect
1. Adam had pasid nine hundret yere	Adam past nyne hundride ȝere
2. Nai selcut þof he wex unfere	No wonder þei he wex vnfere
3. Forwroght wit his hak and spad	Al forwrouȝte wiþ his spade
4. Of himself he wex al sad.	Of his lyf he wex al made
5. He lened him þan apon his hak	Vpon his spade his breste he leyde
6. Wit Seth his sun þusgat he spak	To seeth his son þus he seyde
7. Sun he said þou most now ga	Sone he seide þow moste go
8. To Paradis þat I com fra	To paradyse þat I coom fro
9. Til Cherubin þat þe yate ward.	To cherubyn þat ȝate warde
10. Yai sir, wist I wyderward	þat kepeþ þo ȝates swyþe harde
11. þat tat vncuth contre ware	Seeth seide to his fadir þere
12. þou wat þat I was neuer þare.	How stondeþ hit fadir and where
13. þus he said I sal þe sai	I shal þe telle he seyde to sey
14. Howgate þou sal tak þe wai.	How þow shalt take þe riȝte wey
15. Toward þe est end of þis dale	Towarde þe eest ende of þe ȝonder vale
16. Find a grene gate þou sale	A grene way fynde þow shale
17. In þat way sal þou find forsoth	In þat wey shaltou fynde and se
18. þi moders and mine our bather slogh	þe steppes of þi modir and me
19. Foluand thoru þat gresse gren	Forwelewed in þat gres grene
20. þat euer has siþen ben gren	þat euer siþen haþ ben sene
21. þat we com wendand als vnwis	þere we comen goyinge as vnwyse
22. Quen we war put o paradis	Whenne we were put fro paradyse
23. Vnto þis wretched warld slade	Into þis ilke wrecchede slade
24. þar I first me self was made	þere myself firste was made
25. Thoru þe gretnes of our sin	For þe greetnes of oure synne
26. Moght na gres groue siþen þarin	Miȝte siþen no gras growe þerynne
27. þe falau slogh sal be þi gate	þat same wole þe lede þi gate
28. O paradis right to þe yate	Fro heþen to paradise ȝate

ON and OF Vocabulary

Northern text			Southern text		
ON baðir	**bather**	*both*	ON fra	**fro**	*from*
ON fra	**fra**	*from*	ON gata	**gate**	*way, path*
ON gata	**gate**	*way, path*	ON sama	**same**	*same*
ON sloð	**slogh**		ON taka	**take**	*take*
ON taka	**tak**	*take*			
ON til	**til**	*to*			
ON þo	**þof**	*though*			
ON ufoerr	**unfere**	*weak, infirm*			
OF contree	**contre**	*country*	OF mat	**mate**	*= downcast*
OF paradis	**paradis**	*paradise*	OF paradis	**paradise**	*paradise*
OF passer	**pasid**	*passed*	OF passer	**past**	*passed*
OF sire	**sir**	*sir*			

Northern dialect: ON words 8, OF   Southern dialect: ON words 4, OF 3

📖 The complete vocabulary of both versions of Text 51 is listed in the Word Book.

8.2 Later 13th-century loan-words, 1250–99

📖 Lists of Old French and Old Norse loan-words of this period, with a note on an early Arabic word, can be found in the Word Book, Chapter 8.

9 The 14th century – Southern and Kentish dialects

9.1 The dialect areas of Middle English

There were four main dialect areas of Old English – West Saxon, Kentish, Mercian and Northumbrian (see section 3.2). In Middle English, they remain roughly the same, except that the Mercian Midlands of England show enough differences between the eastern and western parts for there to be two distinct dialects, because the eastern Midlands were part of the Danelaw. So the five principal dialects of ME are usually referred to as:

- Southern
- Kentish (or South-East)
- East Midlands
- West Midlands
- Northern

When a more accurate knowledge of where a manuscript was written is known, you will often find terms, like *North-West Midlands*, which identify the area of the

Map 5   ME dialects

dialect more narrowly. Dialects have no boundaries, but merge one into the other. The dialect of Northern English spoken in what is now southern Scotland was known as *Inglis* until about 1500, when writers began to call it *Scottis* (present-day *Scots*).

French the prestige language until the mid-14th century

In the ME period no single dialect of the language was used for writing throughout the country in the way that the West Saxon dialect had become an OE written standard in the 10th and 11th centuries. After the Conquest, the language of the Norman ruling class was Old Northern French (ONF). The language of the English court in the 12th century was Parisian French, which carried more prestige than Anglo-Norman and other varieties – remember Chaucer's ironical comment in the 1390s on the Prioress's French, learned in a nunnery in east London –

> And Frenssh she spak ful faire and fetisly
> After the scole of Stratford-at-the-Bowe ...

The language of instruction in English schools was French until the second half of the 14th century. John of Trevisa wrote in 1385:

> For Iohan Cornwal, a mayster of gramere, chayngede þe lore in gramerscole and construccion of Freynsch into Englysch, so þat now, in al the gramerscoles of Engelond childern leueþ Frensch, and construeþ and lurneþ an Englysch ...

Not until 1362 was English used in the law courts and Parliament instead of French.

'Gret diversitee' in English

By the end of the 14th century the educated language of London was beginning to become a standard form of writing throughout the country, although the establishment of a recognised Standard English was not completed for several centuries. In Middle English there were only dialects, and writers or copyists used the forms of speech of their own region. Chaucer implied the lack of a standard and the diversity of forms of English at the end of his poem *Troilus and Criseyde*, written about 1385:

> Go, litel bok, go, litel myn tragedye ...
> And for ther is so gret diversite
> In Englissh and in writyng of oure tonge,
> So prey I God that non myswrite the,
> Ne the mysmetre for defaute of tonge.

as did John of Trevisa also in the same year, 'þer buþ also of so meny people longages and tonges' (see Text 57 in this chapter).

Here are some other examples of the 'diversity of tongues', taken from writings from different parts of the country in the ME period and focusing on the use of pronouns. They show some of the variations of spelling and form in the same words.

Notice how there is inconsistency within a dialectal area, and even within the same manuscript sometimes. It is difficult to know whether some of the differences are simply variations in the spelling or in the form and pronunciation of a word. As always, spelling tended to remain the same even though the pronunciation of a word had altered.

(The texts are edited versions of the originals. Word-for-word translations follow each text. References are to text and line numbers in *Early Middle English Verse & Prose*, Bennett and Smithers, 1968.)

9.1.1 Diversity of pronouns

1st person singular pronoun (MnE I)

Also Ic it o boke rede *As I it in book read*	**Ic**	(East Midlands)	XII.2
Forr Icc amm sennd off heffness ærd *For I am sent from heaven's land*	**Icc**	(Orm, East Midlands)	XIII.81
Weste Hic hit miȝtte ben forholen *Knew I it might be hidden (= If I knew . . .)*	**Hic**	(East Midlands)	VI.237
Gode þonk nou hit is þus þat Ihc am to Criste vend. *God thank now it is thus* *That I am to Christ gone*	**Ihc**	(Southern)	V.159
'Darie,' he saide, 'Ich worht ded But Ich haue of þe help and red.' 'Leue child, ful wel I se þat þou wilt to deþe te.' *'Darie,' he said, 'I were dead (= shall die)* *Unless I have of thee help and advice"* *'Dear child, full well I see* *That thou wilt to death draw.' (= you will die)*	**Ich** **I**	 (East Midlands)	 III.75
Certes for þi luf ham Hi spilt. *Certainly for thy love am I spilt. (= ruined)*	**Hi**	(Northern)	XV.22

3rd person singular feminine pronoun (MnE she)

The variant forms for *she* are evidence of a different evolution in different areas. Both the initial consonant and the vowel varied. In the Southern and West Midlands dialects the initial [h] of OE *heo* was retained, but with a variety of vowel modifications and spellings illustrated in the first group of quotations below.

The form *scho* with initial [ʃ] and vowel [o] developed in the Northern dialect, and probably evolved from the feminine personal pronoun *heo*, perhaps influenced also by the initial consonant of the feminine demonstrative pronoun *seo* in these sequences:

- from OE *seo*, [s'eo] > [s'io] > [si'o] > [sj'o] > [ʃo] and/or
- from OE *heo*, [h'eo] > [h'io] > [hjo] > [ʃo].

In the East Midlands dialect the origin of the form *sche*, with initial [ʃ] and vowel [e], which became the standard *she*, is not known. Some of these forms are illustrated in the second group:

1st group

For þan heom þuhte þat heo hadde þe houle ouercome . . . *Therefore to-them (it) seemed she had* *The owl overcome . . .*	**heo** (South-East late 12th C)	I.619
Ho was þe gladur uor þe rise *She was the gladder for the branch*	**ho** (South-East late 12th C)	I.19
And in eche manere to alle guodnesse heo drouȝ *And in every way to all goodness she drew*	**heo** (South-West 13th C)	VII.12
He song so lude an so scharpe . . . *She sang so loud and so sharp . . .*	**he** (South-East late 12th C)	I.97
He wente him to þen inne þer hoe wonede inne *He went (him) to the inn* *Where she dwelled (in)*	**hoe** (East Midland)	VI.19
God wolde hue were myn! *God grant she were mine!*	**hue** (West Midland)	VIII.K.28
ha mei don wið Godd al þet ha eauer wule *she may do with God all that she ever wishes*	**ha** (West Midland)	XVIII.74
Nu ne dorste hi namore sigge, ure Lauedi; hac hye spac to þo serganz þet seruede of þo wyne *Now ne-dared she no more say, our Lady;* *but she spoke to the servants* *that served (of) the wine . . .*	**hi** **hye** (Kentish 13th C)	 XVII.94

2nd group

þo he seghȝ hit nas nowth ȝhe . . . *When he saw it ne-was not she . . .*	**ȝhe** (East Midlands 13th C)	III.197
Leiȝande sche saide to Blaunchflour . . . *Laughing she said to Blaunchflour . . .*	**sche** (East Midlands 13th C)	III.241

She is my quene, Ich hire chalenge *She is my queen, I her claim*	**she**	(South-East early 14th C)	II.61
And te Lundenissce folc hire wolde tæcen and scæ fleh	**scæ**	(East Midlands 12th C)	XVI.262
And the London(ish) folk her wished (to) take and she fled			
Fro hir schalt þou or scho fro þe ... *From her shalt thou or she from thee ...*	**scho**	(Northern *c.* 1300)	XIV.60
Hir luue sco haldes lele ilike *Hir love she holds true constantly*	**sco**	(Northern *c.* 1300)	XIV.75
Yo hat mayden Malkyn Y wene *She is called maiden Malkin I believe*	**yo**	(Northern)	XV.47
Annd tær yho barr AllmahhtiJ Godd *And there she bore Almighty God*	**yho**	(East Midlands 12th C)	XIII.49

Some early ME dialects, as a result of certain sound changes, had come to use the word *he* for three different pronouns, MnE *he, she* and *they* (OE *he, heo* and *hi/hie*), which seems to us very confusing and ambiguous. For example:

Ambiguity of ME **he** *in different dialects*

He ne shulde nouȝth þe kyng ysee. . . *He was not allowed to see the king . . .*	**he** = *he*	(South-East)
He schal ben chosen quen wiþ honur *She will be chosen queen with honour*	**he** = *she*	(East Midlands)
þanne he com þenne he were bliþe For hom he brouhte fele siþe . . . *When he came then they were glad* *For to-them he brought many times . . .*	**he** = *he and they* 	 (East Midlands)

The assimilation of the ON plural pronouns beginning with ⟨th⟩ has already been mentioned in section 8.1.1.1. Where there was a large Scandinavian population, in the North, all three forms *they, them* and *their* replaced the older OE pronouns beginning with ⟨h⟩. In the South, the OE forms remained for much longer. In the Midlands, *they* was used, but still with the object and possessive pronouns *hem* and *hire*. The forms for *she* and *they* are therefore two of the clues which help to determine the dialect of a manuscript. Here are some examples of the variant forms for *they* and *them* in the dialects of ME:

3rd person plural pronouns (MnE they, them)

Hi holde plaiding suþe stronge . . . *They held debate very strongly . . .*	**hi**	(South-East)	I.12
An alle ho þe driueþ honne . . . *And they all thee drive hence . . .*	**ho**	(South-East)	I.66

þat þi dweole-song heo ne forlere. *That thy deceitful-song they (should) shun* (all three forms *hi, ho* and *heo* in one manuscript)	**heo**	(South-East)	I.558
And hie answerden and seyde *And they answered and said*	**hie**	(Kentish)	XVII.185
Alle he arn off onc mode *All they are of one mind*	**he**	(East Midlands)	XII.112
Nuste Ich under Criste whar heo bicumen weoren *Ne-knew I under Christ where they come were* (= *I didn't know where they had gone on earth*)	**heo**	(West Midlands)	X.33
þo þat hit com to þe time þat hoe shulden arisen ine. . . *When that it came to the time* *That they should rise in . . .*	**hoe**	(Southern)	V.263
And bispeken hou huy miȝten best don þe luþere dede *And plotted how they might best do the wicked deed*	**huy**	(South-West)	VII.38
. . . for na lickre ne beoþ **ha** *. . . for no more-like ne-are they*	**ha**	(West Midlands)	XVIII.66 .
And þilke þat beþ maidenes clene þai mai hem wassche of þe rene. *And the-same that be maidens pure* *They may them(selves) wash in the stream*	**þai/ hem**	(East Midlands)	III.53
For many god wymman haf þai don scam *For (to) many good women have they done shame*	**þai**	(Northern)	XV.29
A red þei taken hem bitwene *A plan they made them between them*	**þei/ hem**	(East Midlands)	IV.260
So hem charged þat wroþ þai were *So them burdened that angry they were*	**þai / hem**	(East Midlands)	III.178
And slæn heom alle clane . . . *And slain them all completely . . .*	**heom**	(West Midlands)	X.64
Hii sende to Sir Maci þat he þun castel ȝolde To hom and to þe baronie *They sent to Sir Maci that he the castle (should) yield* *To them and to the barons*	**hii/ hom**	(South-West)	XI.27
Godd walde o sum wise schawin ham to men *God wished in some way (to) show them to men*	**ham**	(West Midlands)	XVIII.64

þe pipins war don vnder his tung
þar ras o þam thre wandes yong   **þam**   (Northern)   XIV.281
The seeds were put under his tongue
There rose from them three young shoots

9.2 How to describe dialect differences

Dialects are varieties of a single language which are 'mutually comprehensible' (that is, speakers of different dialects can talk to and understand each other). An unfamiliar dialect may be difficult to understand at first because of the unfamiliarity of its pronunciation, or the use of unknown dialect words, but with familiarity, these difficulties disappear. This is not the case with a foreign language.

Dialects have most of their vocabulary and grammar in common, and we can therefore make a short list of features to look for when describing the differences between them.

Linguistic features marking ME dialectal differences

Spelling

- The alphabetical symbols used, and their relation to the contrasting sounds of the dialectal accent. We have to be careful not to assume that there is a one-to-one relation between sound and letter. Some differences of spelling in ME texts do not reflect differences of pronunciation, e.g. ⟨i ~ y⟩; ⟨u ~ v⟩; ⟨ȝ ~ gh⟩; ⟨ss ~ sch ~ sh⟩; ⟨þ ~ th⟩; ⟨hw ~ wh ~ qu⟩ etc. Remember that spelling tends to be conservative, and does not necessarily keep up with changed pronunciation.

Pronunciation

- Has the OE long vowel [ɑː] shifted to [ɔː] or not?
- Which vowel is used for the OE front rounded vowel [y]? For example, is *hill* (from OE *hyll*) spelt *hill*, *hell* or *hull*?
- Which vowels have developed from OE vowels spelt ⟨eo⟩, ⟨ea⟩ and ⟨æ⟩?

Word forms – pronouns

- What are the forms of personal pronouns? Have the ON 3rd person plural forms beginning with ⟨th-⟩ been adopted? What is the feminine singular pronoun?

Word forms – inflections

- On nouns, what suffixes are used to mark the plural?
- On verbs, what are:
  1 the present tense suffixes?
  2 the forms of past tense (strong or weak), past and present participles, and infinitive?
  3 the forms of the common verb *be*?

Grammar

- Examine word order within the phrase and the clause.
- How are negatives and questions formed?
- Find constructions which are no longer used in MnE.

Vocabulary

- Is the source of the words OE, ON, OF or another language, and in what proportion?

We can now use this list, or parts of it, to examine some ME texts which provide examples of the different dialects.

9.3 A South-Eastern, or Kentish dialect

The single manuscript of a book called *Ayenbite of Inwyt*, 'the remorse of conscience', is of great interest to students of the language for two reasons. First because its author and exact date are both written on the manuscript. He writes in the preface,

> þis boc is dan Michelis of Northgate/ywrite an englis of his oȝene hand. þet hatte: Ayenbite of inwyt. And is of þe boc-house of saynt Austines of Canterberi.

(*oȝene* = own; *hatte* = is called)

and towards the end of the book,

> þis boc is uolueld ine þe eue of þe holy apostles Symon an Iudas/of ane broþer of þe cloystre of sanynt Austin of Canterberi/Ine the yeare of oure lhordes beringe 1340.

(*uolueld* = fulfilled, completed; *þe eue of þe holy apostles Symon an Iudas* = October 27; *beringe* = birth)

That is, Michael of Northgate, a monk of St Augustine's, Canterbury, finished the book (a translation from a French original) on 27 October 1340. The second quotation is included in the following facsimile of part of the manuscript, towards its end.

Text 52: Kentish dialect – Michael of Northgate, Ayenbite of Inwyt, 1340 (i) (facsimile)

✍ A note on the handwriting

An informal book hand.

- ⟨ȝ⟩ used for [x] e.g. *berȝe* (= *protect*), *naȝt* (*not*) and [w] *halȝed* (*hallowed*)
- ⟨y⟩ is dotted ⟨ẏ⟩ and used for [ɪ], e.g. *ẏcome*, *ẏwyte* and for [j], e.g. *manẏere*, *ẏeue* etc.
- ⟨g⟩ for [g], e.g. *god*, *engliss*.
- thorn ⟨þ⟩ still used, e.g. *þe*, *þet*.
- ⟨w⟩ always, never wynn ⟨ƿ⟩, *wille*, *ẏwent*, etc.

- Long ⟨ſ⟩ almost always (only two examples of round ⟨s⟩ in the facsimile).
- Long ⟨þ⟩ – *ywnte* – one occurrence of the 2-form in *lhoʒd*.
- Word-initial ⟨z⟩ and ⟨u⟩ for voiced fricatives [z] and [v] – *zende* (send), *yzed* (said), *uor* (for), *uram* (from).

Transcription

        þiſ boc iſ ẏcome to þe ende:
heuene bliſſe god ouſ zende: amen. Nou ich wille þet ẏe
ẏwyte hou hit iſ ẏwent: þet þiſ boc iſ ẏwpite mid englıſſ of kent.
þiſ boc iſ ẏmad uoþ lewede men | uoþ uadeþ | and uoþ modeþ | and
uoþ oþeþ ken | ham uoþ to beþʒe uþm all manẏeþe zen | þet ıne
haþe ınwytte ne bleue no uoul wen. huo aſe god iſ hiſ name ẏzed |
þet þiſ boc made god him ẏeue þet bþead | of angleſ of heuene And
þeþto his þed | And ondeþuonge hiſ zaule huanne þet he iſ dẏad. <u>Amen.</u>
¶ẏmende. þet þiſ boc iſ uoluetd ıne þe eue of þe holẏ apoſtleſ Sẏ-
mon and Iudaſ | of ane bþoþeþ of þe cloẏſtþe of ſanẏnt Auſtın
of cantebþeþı | Ine þe ẏeaþe of ouþe lhoþdeſ beþınge. 1340
¶Vadeþ ouþe þet Aþt ıne heueneſ | ẏ halʒed bẏ þı name. comınde þı þiche.
ẏwoþþe þı wıl | Aſe ıne heuene: and ın eþþe. bþead ouþe echedaẏeſ: ẏef
ouſ to daẏ . And uoþlet ouſ ouþe ẏeldıngeſ: Aſe And we uoþleteþ ouþe
ẏeldeþeſ. and ne ouſ led naʒt: ın to uondınge: Ac vþı ouſ uþam queade: <u>zuo bẏ hıt.</u>
¶hayl maþıe | of þonke uol. lhoʒd by mid þe. ẏblıſſed þou ıne wẏmmen.
And ẏblıſſed þet ouet of þıne wombe. <u>zuo bẏ hıt</u>

WW (set out in lines to show the rhymes)

þis	boc	is	ycome	to	þe	ende,	heuene	blisse	god	ous	zende	Amen.
this	*book*	*is*	*come*	*to*	*the*	*end,*	*heaven's*	*bliss*	*God*	*us*	*send*	*Amen.*

Nou	ich	wille	þet	ye	ywyte	hou	hit	is	ywent:
Now	*I*	*wish*	*that*	*you*	*know*	*how*	*it*	*is*	*went* (= *has happened*)

þet þis boc is ywrite mid engliss of kent.
That this book is written in English of Kent

þis boc is ymad uor lewede men
this book is made for common men

uor uader and uor moder and uor oþer ken
for father and for mother and for other kin

ham uor to berʒe uram all manyere zen
them for to protect from all kind of sin

þet ine hare inwytte ne bleue no uoul wen.
so that in their conscience ne remain no foul wen.

huo ase god is his name yzed
who as God is his name said

þet þis boc made god him yeue þet bread
that this book made God to-him give the bread

of Angles of heuene and þerto his red
of angels of heaven and thereto his counsel

And onderuonge his zaule huanne þet he is dyad. <u>Amen</u>.
and receive his soul when that he is dead Amen

ymend þet þis boc is uolueld ine þe eue of þe holy apostles Symon and Iudas of ane broþer of þe cloystre of sanynt austin of canterberi ine þe yeare of oure lhordes beringe. 1340

Remember that this book was finished on the eve of the holy apostles Simon and Jude by a brother of the cloister of Saint Augustine of Canterbury in the year of Our Lord's birth 1340.

Vader oure þet Art ine heuenes	*Our father which art in heaven*
y halʒed by þi name	*Hallowed be thy name*
cominde þi riche	*Thy kingdom come*
yworþe þi wil ase ine heuene and in erþe	*Thy will be done on earth as it is in heaven*
bread oure echedayes: yef ous to day	*Give us this day our daily bread*
and uorlet ous oure yeldinges	*And forgive us our trespasses*
ase and we uorleteþ oure yelderes	*As we forgive them that trespass against us*
and ne ous led naʒt in to uondinge	*And lead us not into temptation*
ac vri ous uram queade: <u>zuo by hit</u>.	*But deliver us from evil: so be it.*
hayl marie of þonke uol	*Hail Mary full of grace*
lhord by mid þe	*The Lord be with thee*
yblissed þou ine wymmen.	*Blessed art thou among women*
and y blissed þet ouet of þine wombe	*And blessed be the fruit of thy womb*
<u>zuo by hit</u>	*So be it.*

📖 The complete vocabulary of Texts 52, 53 and 54 is listed in the Word Book.

The second reason for the manuscript's linguistic importance is that it is spelled consistently, and so provides good evidence for the South-East dialect of Kent at that time.

Ayenbite of Inwyt is therefore unique in providing an example of a Middle English dialect in an original copy whose date, author and place of writing are exactly known. It is as close to a 'pure' dialect as we can get, remembering that the written form of language can never provide a really accurate account of how a dialect was spoken.

The following edited texts from *Ayenbite of Inwyt* are short exemplary tales which illustrate the virtue of showing mercy and generosity.

Activity 9.1

Before reading the commentary which follows, examine the language under the headings provided in Section 9.2. Here are some questions to consider:

(a) How far has the Kentish dialect of 1340 lost or changed the inflections of OE?

(b) Which vowel seems to be more frequent in Kentish than in other ME dialects?

(c) What can you say about the pronunciation of Kentish from the evidence of the spellings *uram, uor, þeruore, bevil, uol, zuo, mezeyse*?

Text 53: Kentish dialect – Michael of Northgate, Ayenbite of Inwyt, 1340 (ii)

Efterward Saint Gregori telþ þet Saint Boniface uram þet he wes child he wes zuo piteuous þet he yaf ofte his kertel and his sserte to þe poure uor God, þaȝ his moder him byete ofte þeruore. þanne bevil þet þet child yseȝ manie poure þet hedden mezeyse. He aspide þet his moder nes naȝt þer. An haste he yarn to þe gerniere, and al þet his moder hedde ygadered uor to pasi þet yer he hit yaf to þe poure. And þo his moder com and wyste þe ilke dede, hy wes al out of hare wytte. þet child bed oure Lhorde, and þet gernier wes an haste al uol.

ww | Afterward Saint Gregory tells that Saint Boniface from that he was child he was so piteous that he gave often his coat and his shirt to the poor for God, though his mother him beat often therefore. Then befell that that child saw many poor that had suffering. He espied that his mother ne-was not there. In haste he ran to the granary, and all that his mother had gathered for to last the year he it gave to the poor. And when his mother came and learned the same deed, she was all out of her wit. The child prayed our Lord, and the granary was in haste all full.

Ⓑ Here is a broad phonetic transcription of Text 53, recorded on the CD/cassette tape:

ɛftərward zaınt grɛgɔrı tɛlθ ðɛt zaınt bonıfas vram ðɛt heː wɛs ʧiːld heː
wɛs zwɔː pitɛjus ðɛt heː jaf ɔftə hıs kɛrtəl and hıs ʃɛrtə tɔ ðə puːrə vor
god, ðax hıs moːdər hım bjɛːtə ɔftə ðɛːrvɔːrə. ðanɔ bɛvıl ðɛt ðɛt ʧiːld
ızeːj manıːə puːrə ðɛt hɛdən mɛzɛːjzə. heː aspiːdə ðɛt hıs moːdər nɛs
naxt ðeːr. an haːstə heː jarn tɔ ðə gɛrnıɛːrə, and al ðɛt hıs moːdər hɛdə
ıgadɛred vɔr tɔ pazı ðɛt jeːr heː hıt jaf tɔ ðə puːrə. and ðɔː hıs moːdər
coːm and wıstə ðə ılkə deːdə, heː wɛs al ut ɔf harə wıtə. ðɛt ʧiːld beːd
urə hlɔːrdə, and ðɛt gɛrnıɛːr wɛs an haːstə al vɔl.

9.3.1 Commentary

Grammar

The syntactic structures of MnE were present in Old English, and it is not surprising that the grammar of Middle English causes us few problems in conveying meaning. However, as we read older English, we are aware of phrases and combinations of words that are definitely 'old-fashioned', and which we would not use today. Sometimes the order of words is no longer acceptable; sometimes words appear to be missing or to be superfluous when compared with English today. In addition, as Michael of Northgate was translating from the French, it is possible that some constructions were not genuine ME either, so we can observe differences, but not draw any final conclusions from them without further evidence. For example:

● uram þet he wes child   from that he was child

MnE requires *from when* or *from the time that*, and the addition of a determiner in the NP, e.g. *a child*.

● he yaf ofte his kertel   he gave often his coat

The adverb *often* in MnE either precedes the verb, *he often gave*, or follows the object, *he gave his coat often*, or begins the clause 'often he gave his coat'.

● his moder him byete ofte   his mother him beat often
● he hit yaf to þe poure   he it gave to the poor

The direct object *him, it*, now follows the verb, *his mother beat him often*, *he gave it to the poor*.

● þanne bevil þet   then befell that

A MnE clause must contain a subject, and here the 'dummy subject' *it* would be used, *then it befell that*.

- þet hedden mezeyse   that had suffering

This is perhaps not ungrammatical in MnE, but it is a phrase that would sound strange.

- for to pasi þet yer   (in order) to last the year

The phrase *for to* in a structure like *I want for to go* is found in all ME texts, but is no longer Standard English, though still normal in some present-day dialects.

Double or multiple negatives

- his moder nes naȝt þer   his mother ne was not there

The OE negative *ne* preceded the verb, as in *ne wæs* (*was not*) and could be reinforced by other negatives like *næfre* (*never*):

> ond hie **næfre** his banan folgian **noldon**
> *and they **never** his murderer follow **ne-would***

In ME the emphatic *noȝt, naȝt* came to be used to reinforce the negative (it did not make it positive), as in Chaucer's

> Be wel auysed . . .
> That **noon** of us **ne** speke **noght** a word

In time, the older *ne* was dropped, leaving *not* as the Standard English negative word. However, the multiple negative remains the norm in most spoken dialects of England today – *There won't be no tradition left, will there?*

Word structure

A short text may not contain a sufficient variety of word-forms for us to come to any conclusions about the range of inflections. For example:

- There are no plural nouns in this text, so we cannot observe whether the *-es* or *-en* plurals are used. But the NP *þet gernier* shows the use of the older neuter OE pronoun *þæt* for MnE *the*, while the PrepP *to þe gerniere* has a dative case inflection *-e* on the noun, but the common form *þe* for the determiner. The NP *oure Lhorde* also has the inflection *-e* on the noun to mark dative case after *to, to our Lord.*
- There are no adjectives apart from possessive pronouns like *his* and *oure*, so there is no evidence here of the survival of inflections on adjectives.
- There is only one example of a present tense verb, *telþ*, with the 3rd person singular inflection *-(e)þ*. The past participle *ygadered* retains the prefix *y-*, from the OE *ge-*.
- The newer pronouns *she, they, them, their* are not used.

Even these limited observations, however, suggest that Kentish was a conservative dialect – that is, when compared with others it still retained more features of the OE system of inflections, even though greatly reduced. These features are very similar to those of South-Western texts, and can be compared with John of Trevisa's in the next section. This fact is not surprising when we consider the geographical position of Kent, relatively cut off and distant from the Midlands and North of England, but accessible to the rest of the South.

Pronunciation and spelling

Words spelt with the vowel letter ⟨e⟩ are much in evidence because in the Kentish dialect,

- the OE vowel [æ] had shifted to [ɛ/e], for example *þet* from *þæt, wes* (*wæs*), *hedden* (*hæfdon*), *þer* (*þær*), *dede* (*dæde*), *bed* (*bæd*) (see section 6.1.4.4),
- the OE vowel [y] unrounded and shifted to [e], as in *kertel, sserte*, from OE *cyrtel, scyrte* (see section 6.1.4.6), and
- the OE diphthong ⟨eo⟩, [eə], smoothed to [e] (see section 6.1.4.5).

The following spellings,

Kentish	uram	uor	þeruore	bevil	uol	zuo	mezeyse
MnE	*from*	*for*	*therefore*	*befell*	*full*	*so*	*misease*

suggest that the consonants pronounced [f] and [s] in other dialects were **voiced** at the beginning of a word or root syllable in Kentish, and pronounced [v] and [z]. This **initial voicing of fricative consonants** is still a feature of South-West dialects in Devon, Somerset, Dorset, Somerset, Wiltshire and Hampshire, though no longer in Kent, according to P. M. Anderson's *A Structural Atlas of the English Dialects*, 1987, pp. 141–3. It applies equally to the consonant [θ], and must have done also in ME, but has never been recorded in spelling, because the letters ⟨þ⟩ or ⟨th⟩ are used for both the voiced and voiceless forms of the consonant, as in *thin* and *then*.

Activity 9.2

Find evidence in Text 54 for changes in pronunciation, word-form and grammar from Old English, and of any special characteristics of the Kentish dialect in the 14th century.

Text 54: Kentish dialect – Michael of Northgate, Ayenbyte of Inwyt, 1340 (iii)

Efterward þer wes a poure man, ase me zayþ, þet hedde ane cou; and yherde zigge of his preste ine his prechinge þet God zede ine his spelle þet God wolde yelde an hondreduald al þet me yeaue uor him. þe guode man, mid þe rede of his wyue, yeaf his cou to his preste, þet wes riche. þe prest his nom bleþeliche, and hise зente to þe oþren þet he hedde. þo hit com to euen, þe guode mannes cou com hom to his house ase hi wes ywoned, and ledde mid hare alle þe prestes ken, al to an hondred. þo þe guode man yseз þet, he þoзte þet þet wes þet word of þe Godspelle þet he hedde yyolde; and him hi weren yloked beuore his bissoppe aye þane prest. þise uorbisne sseweþ wel þet merci is guod chapuare, uor hi deþ wexe þe timliche guodes.

| ww |

Afterward there was a poor man, as I am told, that had a cow; and heard say from his priest in his preaching that God said in his gospel that God would yield a hundredfold all that one gave for him. The good man, with the advice of his wife, gave his cow to his priest, that was rich. The priest her took blithely, and her sent to the others that he had. When it came to evening, the good man's cow came home to his house as she was accustomed, and led with her all the priest's kine, all to a hundred. When the good man saw that, he thought that that was the word of the Gospel that to-him* had restored (them); and to-him they were adjudged before his bishop against the priest. These examples show well that mercy is good trading, for it does increase the temporal goods.

* The obscure English is the result of a mistranslation of the French original, which can be found in Kenneth Sisam, *Fourteenth-Century Verse and Prose*, 1921, p. 213.

9.4 An early South-West dialect

Text 32 in Chapter 5, from a verse chronicle by Robert of Gloucester (reproduced again later in this section as Text 56), was written about 1300. The *Chronicle* was first written late in the 13th century in the Gloucester dialect by a monk of Gloucester Abbey, and ended with the death of Henry I in 1136. Robert, a monk in the same abbey, revised and continued the text to 1272, the year of the death of Henry III. Here is a short extract from the *Chronicle* in facsimile:

Text 55: Robert of Gloucester's Chronicle *(i) (facsimile)*

📖 A note on the handwriting

Book hand.

- Letter thorn written like wynn ⟨p⟩.
- Letter ⟨w⟩ used, not wynn.
- The 2-form of ⟨r⟩ after ⟨o⟩.
- Letter yogh ⟨з⟩ used for [j], *зonge* (*young*), [x], *fiзte*, and [tz], *fiз* (*Fitz*).

Transcription

A n vewe ðropeſ of reine . þer velle grete inou .

þ is tokninge vel in þis lond . þo me þis men slou .

v oʒ pretti mile panne . þis iſei roberð .

þ at verſt þis boc maðe . 7 was wel ſore aferð .

L ouᵗðingeſ þᵗ were inome . at eueſham manion .

a as ſir unfrai ðe boun . Sir Jon le fiʒ Jon .

7 simondeſ ſone . ðe moūtfoʒt ſir gwy .

s ir baudewine ðe wake . ſir Jon ðe veſcy .

s ir henri ðe haſtinges . 7 ſir Nicole iwis .

D e ſegᵃue waſ pere inome . 7 al ſo ſir periſ .

7 ſir roberð þat ſir periſ . ðe moūtfoʒt ſoneſ were .

þ uſe 7 wel mo were inome . 7 þulke moʒpre þere .

A c þe welſſe foʒ men . þat þer were manion .

a t þe biginninge of þe bataile . bigonne to fle echon .

7 come poʒu teuſkeſburi . 7 þere men of þe toune .

S lowe hom al to groūde . þat þere hii leie þᵗ ðoune .

ſ o picke biſtrete . þat reupe it was to ſe .

7 grace naððe non of hom . to fiʒte ne to fle .

þ o þe bataile waſ iðo . 7 þe goðemen aslawe were .

s ir ſimonð þe ʒonge come . to mete is faðᵗ pere .

Literal translation

A few drops of rain . there fell great enough .
this portent fell in this land . when these men were slain .
for thirty miles then . this saw Robert .
that first this book made . & was very sorely afraid .
gentlemen that were taken . at Evesham many a one .

like Sir Humphrey de Boun . Sir John Fitzjohn .
& Sir Guy, son of Simon de Montfort .
Sir Baldwin de Wake . Sir John de Vescy .
Sir Henry de Hastings . & Sir Nicolas indeed .
de Segrave was there captured . & also Sir Peris .
& Sir Robert who were Sir Peris . de Montfort's sons .
these & many more were taken . & the same murdered there .
but the Welsh footmen . that there were many a one .
at the beginning of the battle . began to flee each one .
& came through Tewkesbury . & there men of the town .
slew them all to the ground . so that there they lay down .
so thickly strewn . that pity it was to see .
& mercy had none of them . to fight or to flee .
when the battle was done . & the good men slain were .
Sir Simon the young came . to meet his father there ... ...

📖 The complete vocabulary of Text 55 is listed in the Word Book.

Activity 9.3

Use the vocabulary of Texts 55 and 56 to see whether you can find evidence for any of the following features by which southern dialects of ME are identified:

 (i)   The rounding of OE [ɑː] to [ɔː]; that is, OE words spelt with ⟨a⟩ now spelt with ⟨o⟩.
 (ii) OE ⟨y⟩ now spelt with ⟨u⟩, though remaining the same sound.
 (iii) OE ⟨eo⟩ now spelt ⟨o⟩; the diphthong has 'smoothed' and become a single vowel.
 (iv) *Verb forms:*
   ● Present tense plural and 3rd person singular suffix – ⟨-eþ⟩
   ● Present participle suffix – ⟨-inde⟩.
   ● Past participle begins with ⟨i-⟩ and has lost its final ⟨-n⟩.
   ● Infinitive has lost its final ⟨-n⟩.
 (v)   [f] at the beginning of a syllable is voiced [v], spelt ⟨v⟩ or ⟨u⟩.
 (vi) 3rd person pronoun forms still begin with ⟨h-⟩.

Text 56: Robert of Gloucester's Chronicle (ii)

þus lo þe englisse folc. vor noȝt to grounde com.
vor a fals king þat nadde no riȝt. to þe kinedom.
& come to a nywe louerd. þat more in riȝte was.
ac hor noþer as me may ise. in pur riȝte was.
& þus was in normannes hond. þat lond ibroȝt iwis . . .

þus com lo engelond. in to normandies hond.
& þe normans ne couþe speke þo. bote hor owe speche.
& speke french as hii dude at om. & hor children dude also teche.
so þat heiemen of þis lond. þat of hor blod come.
holdeþ alle þulk speche. þat hii of hom nome.

vor bote a man conne frenss. me telþ of him lute.
ac lowe men holdeþ to engliss. & to hor owe speche ȝute.
ich wene þer ne beþ in al þe world. contreyes none.
þat ne holdeþ to hor owe speche. bote engelond one.
ac wel me wot uor to conne. boþe wel it is.
vor þe more þat a mon can. þe more wurþe he is.
þis noble duc willam. him let crouny king.
at londone amidwinter day. nobliche þoru alle þing.
of þe erchebissop of euerwik. aldred was is name.
þer nas prince in al þe world. of so noble fame.

📖 The vocabulary of Text 56 is listed in the Word Book.

9.5 A later 14th-century South-West dialect

The following text, written in the 1380s by John of Trevisa, describes one man's view of the linguistic situation at that time. The complete work is a translation, with Trevisa's own additions, of a history called *Polychronicon* written in Latin earlier in the century. John of Trevisa was vicar of Berkeley near Gloucester when he translated *Polychronicon*.

It is a reminder to us of the historical origins of English and its dialects. Trevisa's attitude is not unlike that of some people today in his talk of the *apeyring* (*deterioration*) of the language, but the reasons he gives are different. He blames it on the fashion for speaking French. He is writing in the South-West dialect of ME.

Text 57: John of Trevisa on the English language in 1385 (i)

As hyt ys y-knowe houȝ meny maner people
buþ in þis ylond þer buþ also of so meny people
longages and tonges. Noþeles walschmen
and scottes þat buþ noȝt ymelled wiþ oþer
nacions holdeþ wel nyȝ here furste longage
and speche

Also englischmen þeyȝ hy hadde fram þe
bygynnyng þre maner speche souþeron
norþeron and myddel speche in þe myddel of þe
lond, as hy come of þre maner people of
Germania, noþeles by commyxstion and mellyng
furst wiþ danes and afterward wiþ normans in
menye þe contray longage ys apeyred and
some vseþ strange wlaffyng chyteryng harryng
and garryng, grisbittyng.

This apeyring of þe burþ tonge ys bycause
of twey þinges – on ys for chyldern in scole
aȝenes þe vsage and manere of al oþer
nacions buþ compelled for to leue here oune
longage and for to construe here lessons and
here þinges a freynsch, and habbeþ suþthe

As it is known how many kinds (of) people are
in this island there are also of so many people
languages and tongues. Nevertheless Welshmen
and Scots that are not mingled with other
nations hold well nigh (to) their native language
and speech.

Also Englishmen though they had from the
beginning three varieties of speech – Southern,
Northern, and Middle speech in the middle of
the land, as they came from three kinds of
people from Germany, nevertheless by mixing
and mingling first with Danes and afterwards
with Normans in many the language of the land
is impaired and some use strange stammering,
chattering, snarling and harsh gnashing.

This impairing of the native tongue is
because of two things – one is that children in
school, against the usage and custom of all
other nations, are compelled to leave their own
language and to construe their lessons and
their tasks in French, and have (done so) since

þe normans come furst into engelond.
Also gentil men children buþ ytauȝt for to
speke freynsch fram tyme þat a buþ
yrokked in here cradel and conneþ speke and
playe wiþ a child hys brouch. And oplondysch
men wol lykne hamsylf to gentil men and
fondeþ wiþ gret bysynes for to speke freynsch
for to be more ytold of . . .

þys manere was moche y-used tofore þe
furste moreyn* and ys seþthe somdel y-
chaunged Now, þe ȝer of oure Lord a þousond
þre hondred foure score and fyve, in al þe
gramerscoles of Engelond childern leueþ
Frensch, and construeþ and lurneþ an
Englysch . . .

Also gentil men habbeþ now moche
yleft for to teche here childern frensch. Hyt
semeþ a gret wondur houȝ englysch, þat ys þe
burþ-tonge of englyschmen and here oune
longage and tonge ys so dyvers of soun
in þis ylond, and þe longage of normandy ys
comlyng of anoþer lond and haþ on
maner soun among al men þat spekeþ hyt aryȝt
in engelond.

the Normans came first into England.
Also gentlemens' children are taught to
speak French from (the) time that they are
rocked in their cradle and can talk and
play with a child's brooch. And country
men want to compare themselves to gentlemen
and seek with great industry to speak French
in order to be more spoken about. . . .

This fashion was much followed before the
first plague and is since somewhat changed.
Now, the year of our Lord one thousand three
hundred four score and five, in all the
grammar schools of England, children leave
French, and construe and learn in
English.

Also gentlemen have now to a great extent
stopped teaching their children French. It
seems a great wonder how English, that is the
native tongue of Englishmen and their own
language and tongue, is so diverse in
pronunciation in this island, and the language
of Normandy is a newcomer from another land
and has one pronunciation among all men that
speak it correctly in England.

* *moreyn* – a reference to the Black Death of the 1340s

The vocabulary of Texts 57 and 58 is listed in the Word Book.

The MS was written *c.* 1400. A version from another MS is given in Text 90,
section 14.6.1, which illustrates the kinds of variation to be found in a different copy
of a text.

9.5.1 Commentary

9.5.1.1 Vocabulary

All except one of the **function words** (prepositions, determiners, pronouns and
conjunctions) are of OE origin. Such words form the 'framework' of sentences, and
are a **closed class** of words which change very slowly, if at all. The only sign of
French influence is the complex preposition *bycause of*, the origin of MnE *because –
by cause of*, being an English version of the French *par cause de*.

The adoption of words from French is much more evident in the **lexical words**,
especially the nouns (see section 9.5.1.5 following), though there are no French-
derived adverbs in this text.

9.5.1.2 Spelling

Trevisa's spelling illustrates some of the changes that had been generally adopted, although not consistently used. We have seen them all in texts of the 12th and 13th centuries and early 14th century.

- ⟨y⟩ – is interchangeable with ⟨i⟩, and represents the sound [ɪ] – *bygynnyng, chyldern/childern, bysynes.*
- ⟨u⟩ and ⟨v⟩ – the familiar present-day relationship of letter ⟨u⟩ for vowel [u] and letter ⟨v⟩ for consonant [v] is still not established; ⟨u⟩ and ⟨v⟩ were variant shapes of the same letter. In Trevisa's text, ⟨u⟩ is generally written in the middle of a word, and ⟨v⟩ at the beginning, for either sound, [u] or [v], for example, *burþ, vseþ, vsage, leue, furst.* This practice continued for a long time, for although letter ⟨v⟩ was written for the consonant sound [v] by scriveners (professional copyists) in the 15th century, it was not taken up by printers regularly until the 18th century.
- ⟨ȝ⟩ and ⟨g⟩ – yogh, ⟨ȝ⟩, is retained for [j], [x] or [ɣ], as in *ȝer* [jɛr] (*year*) or *tauȝt* [tauɣt] (*taught*). The letter ⟨g⟩ represents both [g], and also [ʒ] in borrowed French words like *vsage* [uzɑʒ]:

  > engelond, garrying, grisbittyng, gret, gramer, þinges   [g]
  > usage, gentilmen, longages   [ʒ] and [g]
  > noȝt, niȝ, þeyȝ, aȝenes, tauȝt   [j] or [ɣ] or [x]

- ⟨ch⟩ – replaced OE ⟨c⟩ for the consonant [tʃ], as in *speche* and *teche* from OE, and *brouch* and *chaunged* from OF.
- ⟨sch⟩ – is Trevisa's spelling for the OE ⟨sc⟩, [ʃ], as in *englysch* and *oplondysch.*
- ⟨th⟩ – has not replaced ⟨þ⟩ in Trevisa, although he does also use ⟨th⟩ in *suþthe* and *seþthe* where the consonant is doubled. Letter ⟨þ⟩ survived into the 15th century.

9.5.1.3 *Word-forms and inflections*

We can see how spelling was related to pronunciation by looking at the three functions of the word *a* in the text:

- as a reduced form of the preposition *an* meaning *in* or *on*, in the phrase *a freynsch* (*in French*);
- as a reduced form of the pronoun *hi* meaning *they*, in *a buþ yrokked* (*they are rocked*); and
- as the indefinite article, as in MnE, in *a þousond.*

Nouns

- The regular plural inflection is ⟨-s⟩ or ⟨-es⟩. The OE plural *men* remains, but the variant forms for the plural of *child* are interesting. The OE plural *cildru* had developed into *childre* or *childer*. In Trevisa's and other dialects, this plural was doubled by a further ⟨-en⟩ plural inflection, and Trevisa uses both *children* and *childern*.

Pronouns

- The ON 3rd person pronouns *they, them, their* have not yet reached the South-West dialect. Trevisa uses *hy/here* for *they/their*, and *hamsylf* for *themselves*.

Verbs

- The 3rd person present tense plural inflection of verbs is ⟨-eþ⟩, from OE ⟨-aþ⟩, e.g. *conneþ, spekeþ* (*they speak, know*), and the 3rd person form of *be* is *buþ* (*they are*), derived from OE *beoþ*.
- Past participles still retain the prefix ⟨y-⟩ or ⟨i-⟩, which is a reduced form of the OE prefix ⟨ge-⟩.
- The infinitive inflection is reduced to ⟨e⟩ in spelling, *leue, playe, speke, teche*, and is probably not pronounced.
- Verbs adopted from French take the structure of English weak or regular verbs. For example, the past participle suffix is ⟨-ed⟩, *apeyred, ymelled, ychaunged*, as against the irregular forms of *yknowe, yleft* and *ytauʒt* derived from OE.

9.5.1.4 Grammar

- Many of the contrasts between older and present-day English are matters of style rather than significant grammatical differences. We can read Trevisa's text without much difficulty, but it does not transcribe word for word into colloquial MnE. For example, the phrases *meny maner people* and *þre maner speche* today require the preposition *of* – *many kinds of people, three varieties of speech*. In OE the words for *people* and *speche* would have been in the genitive case, and the ME form has a similar construction.
- The phrase *a child hys broche* (*a child's toy*) is a new construction for the possessive, which survived for some time but has now been lost. It does not derive from OE.
- Infinitives which complement a main verb are marked by *for to*, e.g. *compelled for to leue . . . and for to construe, fondeþ wiþ gret bysynes for to speke frensch for to be more ytold of*.

This construction is still used in some MnE dialects, but is now nonstandard. Notice also that the last quotation is an example of a 'preposition at the end of a sentence', centuries before prescriptive grammarians ruled that the construction was 'ungrammatical'.

Activity 9.4

Make a similar study of the linguistic features of the following continuation of Trevisa's writing:

(i) *Spelling*:
  Identify and list some of the new combinations of letters and sounds.
(ii) *Inflections*:
  Do any suffixes remain from OE?
(iii) *Grammar*:
  Which constructions mark the text as ME and not MnE?
(iv) *Vocabulary*:
  What kinds of word have been taken into Trevisa's South-West dialect of ME from French and Latin?

Text 58: John of Trevisa on the English language (ii)

... also of þe forseyde saxon tonge þat is deled a þre and ys abyde scarslych wiþ feaw vplondyschmen and ys gret wondur, for men of þe est wiþ men of þe west, as hyt were vnder þe same party of heuene, acordeþ more in sounyng of speche þan men of þe norþ wiþ men of þe souþ.

þerfore hyt ys þat mercii, þat buþ men of myddel engelond, as hyt were parteners of þe endes, vndurstondeþ betre þe syde longages, norþeron and souþeron, þan norþeron and souþeron vndurstondeþ eyþer oþer.

Al þe longage of þe norþumbres and specialych at ʒork ys so scharp slyttyng and frotyng and vnschape þat we souþeron men may þat longage vnneþe vndurstonde. Y trowe þat þat ys bycause þat a buþ nyʒ to strange men and aliens þat spekeþ strangelych.

... also concerning the Saxon tongue that is divided into three and has barely survived among a few uneducated men (there) is great wonder, for men of the east with men of the west, as it were under the same part of heaven, agree more in (their) pronunciation than men of the north with men of the south.

Therefore it is that Mercians, who are men of Middle England, as it were partners of the extremes, understand better the languages on either side, Northern and Southern, than Northerners and Southerners understand each other.

All the language of the Northumbrians, and especially at York, is so shrill, cutting and grating and badly pronounced that we Southern men may that language hardly understand. I believe that this is because they are close to foreign men and aliens that speak strangely.

9.5.1.5 French vocabulary in Texts 57 and 58

There are 32 lexical word types derived from OF in the two texts, which is a higher proportion than in the 12th- and 13th-century texts we have examined. The words, with the dates of their first recorded occurrence in writing, are:

acordeþ	1123	party	1290
normandy/normans	1205	strange/strangelych	1290
brouch	1225	apeyring/apeyred	1297
frotyng	1225	scarslych	1297
lessons	1225	soun(yng)	1297
ychaunged	1230	specialych	1297
vseþ/y-vsed	1240	vsage	1297
dyvers	1250	mellyng/ymelled	1300
contray	1275	nacions	1300
gentilmen	1275	aliens	1330
maner(e)	1275	moreyn	1330
longage(s)	1290	people	1340
parteners	1290	gramer-scoles	1387

There are four words derived directly from Latin, a kind of borrowing that increases dramatically in the 16th and 17th centuries.

> commyxstion   (Trevisa's is the first recorded use in the *OED*, dated 1387)
> Germania
> compelled
> construe/construeþ

9.6 14th-century loan-words

📖 Vocabulary adopted from other languages during the 14th century is listed in the Word Book at the end of the word-lists for Chapters 9 to 13, by 20-year periods.

The words are not related to the dialect topics of each chapter.

10 The 14th century – Northern dialects

The Northern dialects of ME came from the Northumbrian dialects of OE. The dialects of Scotland and the North of England today are still markedly distinct from Standard English and other dialects in features of their grammar and vocabulary, and from RP and Southern accents in pronunciation.

10.1 A 14th-century Scots dialect

The Bruce is a verse chronicle of the life and heroic deeds of Robert Bruce (1274–1329), written by John Barbour about 1375 – *The Actes and Life of the Most Victorious Conqueror, Robert Bruce King of Scotland*. Barbour was Archdeacon of Aberdeen and had studied and taught at Oxford and Paris. The first extract comes from Book I:

Text 59: John Barbour on freedom, from The Bruce *(i) (edited text)*

A fredome is a noble thing
Fredome mays man to haiff liking
Fredome all solace to man giffis
He levys at es yat frely levys
A noble hart may haiff nane es
Na ellys nocht yat may him ples
Gyff fredome failȝhe for fre liking
Is ȝharnyt our all oyer thing.
Na he yat ay has levyt fre
May nacht knaw weill the propyrte
Ye angyr na ye wrechyt dome
Yat is cowplyt to foule thyrldome
Bot gyff he had assayit it.

Scottish Text Soc., vol. II, 1980 (eds M. P. McDiarmid and J. A. C. Stevenson)

Once you have deciphered some unusual spellings, you will find that this Northern Scots dialect is closer to MnE than Southern dialects of England at that time. Re-writing the text in present-day standard spelling makes this clearer:

Ah freedom is a noble thing
Freedom makes man to have liking
Freedom all solace to man gives
He lives at ease that freely lives
A noble heart may have no ease
Nor else nought that may him please
If freedom fails; for free liking
Is yearned over all other thing.
Nor he that aye has lived free
May not know well the property
The anger nor the wretched doom
That is coupled to foul thraldom
Unless he had assayed it.

liking = free choice

Text 59 is recorded on the CD/cassette tape.

ɑː freːdom ɪz a nɔːblə θɪŋg,

freːdom meːz man tɔ hɑːf liːkɪŋg,

freːdom al sɔːlas tɔ man gɪvz

heː lɛvz at eːz θat freːlɪ lɛvz.

ə nɔːblə hɑrt maɪ hɑːv naːn ɛːz

nɑː ɛlɪs nɔxt θat maɪ hɪm pleːz

jɪf freːdom felj, fɔr freː liːkɪŋg

ɪs jarnɪt uːr al ɔðər θɪŋg.

nɑː heː θat aɪ has lɛvɪt freː

maɪ naxt kna weːl θə prɔpərte

θɪ aŋgər na θə wrɛʃɪt doːm

θat ɪz cuplɪt tɔ fuːl θɪrldoːm

bɔt jɪf heː had asaɪjɪt ɪt

10.1.1 Commentary

The text is too short to illustrate more than a few features of this dialect, but it is at an advanced stage in its loss of the inflectional system of OE.

We might expect there to be words derived from Old Norse in a Northern dialect, but the text contains only two, *angyr* and *ay*, as against eight from Old French. Barbour was a scholar writing a literary romance, and it is therefore not surprising that he used words like *propyrte* and *solace*.

The vocabulary of Text 59 is listed in the Word Book.

10.1.1.1 Spelling and pronunciation

The metre of the verse is regular, an eight-syllable line rhyming in couplets. If you compare some of Chaucer's contemporary verses, you will see that some of Chaucer's words that end in a final ⟨e⟩ have to be pronounced to fit the metre of the verse, and some not. Perhaps this is what Chaucer was referring to when he hoped that no one would 'mysmetre' his verse (see section 9.1). For example, the final ⟨e⟩ is pronounced in these lines from *The Book of the Duchess* as indicated:

> For /nature /wold-**e** /nat suf /fys-**e**/
> /To noon /erthly /crea /ture
> Nat /long-**e** /tym-**e** /to en /dure
> Wi /thout-**e** /slep and /be in /sor-we

But it is not always pronounced, and is always elided when it precedes a word beginning with a vowel, so that none of the final ⟨e⟩ spellings is pronounced in these lines:

> /Purely /for de/faut(**e**)¿ of /slep
> That /by my /trouth(**e**) I /tak(**e**) no /kep...

> /Pass(**e**) we /over /untill /eft;
> That /wil not /be mot /ned(**e**) be /left.

The final ⟨e⟩ which was pronounced was all that was left of many of the former OE suffix inflections, and the fact that Chaucer could choose whether or not to pronounce them suggests that there was still variation between speakers.

In Barbour's verse, there is scarcely any evidence even of this remnant of the OE inflectional system. Check this in Text 60 which follows.

There are some spelling conventions to note in Barbour's writing:

- ⟨ei⟩ ⟨ai⟩ – Scots writers had adopted the convention of using ⟨i⟩ as a diacritic letter to mark a long vowel. In *haiff*, the ⟨ai⟩ represents [aː] and in *weill* the ⟨ei⟩ is [eː]. Not all uses of ⟨i⟩ following a vowel mark this feature, however. In *failȝhe* <ai> marks the diphthong derived from OF *faillir*; similarly the pronoun *thai*.
- ⟨ȝh⟩ – is written for ⟨ȝ⟩, representing the consonant [j], as in *failȝhe*, [faɪlj], and *ȝharnyt*, [jarnɪt].
- ⟨ch⟩ – is written for the ⟨ȝ⟩ or ⟨gh⟩ used in other dialect areas for the sound [x], as in *nocht*, as well as for the [tʃ] in *wrechyt*.
- ⟨ff⟩ – the doubled letters indicate unvoiced final consonants in *haiff* and *gyff*.
- ⟨y⟩ – from OE ⟨þ⟩, is used for ⟨th⟩ in some function words like *ye*, *yat* (*the*, *that*), as well as an alternative for ⟨i⟩.

10.1.1.2 Word forms and inflections

Nouns
None of the nouns is plural, but evidence of the plural inflection will be found in Text 60. The ⟨*-ing*⟩ suffix on *liking* marks a noun which derives from a verb, sometimes called a gerund.

Verbs

The infinitive has no inflection – *haiff, knaw, ples.*

Present tense: 3rd person singular inflection spelt ⟨is⟩ or ⟨ys⟩ – *giffis, levys.* Other verbs have only ⟨s⟩ – *has, mays.*

Past participle: suffix spelt ⟨yt⟩ – *ȝharnyt, levyt, cowplyt* – and the OE prefix *ge-* has been lost.

Grammar

The word order of verse is often more marked and less normal than that of prose, as in *Fredome all solace to man giffis*, in which the direct object *all solace* and adverbial *to man* precede the verb, and so cannot be reliable evidence of normal spoken usage. The relative pronoun is *that*, as in MnE, but spelt *yat*.

Activity 10.1

(i)   See if any of the following linguistic features of Scots ME Northern dialect are to be found in Texts 59 and 60.
(ii) Examine the proportion of words derived from OE, ON and OF.

- Words retaining the OE long back vowel [ɑː].
- Spelling words with <i> as a diacritic for a long vowel.
- Spelling ⟨s⟩ for [ʃ].
- Spelling ⟨quh⟩ for OE ⟨hw⟩.
- Present participle inflection of verbs ⟨-and⟩.
- Past tense 3rd person singular/plural and past participle inflections of weak verbs ⟨-it⟩ (or ⟨-yt⟩).
- Plural inflection of nouns ⟨-is⟩ or ⟨-ys⟩.
- ON form of 3rd person plural pronouns beginning with ⟨th-⟩.

Text 60: John Barbour's The Bruce (ii) (edited text)

The siege of Berwick, 1319 – the Scots are defending the town against the English

WW

Engynys alsua for to cast
Yai ordanyt & maid redy fast
And set ilk man syne till his ward.
And schyr Walter ye gud steward
With armyt men suld rid about
And se quhar yat yar war mast dout
And succour yar with his menȝe.
And quhen yai in sic degre

Machines also for to throw
They set up & made ready fast
And set each man next to his post.
And Sir Walter the good Stewart
With armed men had to ride about
And see where that there was most doubt
And bring help there with his company.
And when they in such state

Had maid yaim for defending	*Had made them for defending*
On ye Rud Ewyn in ye dawing	*On the Rood Even in the daybreak*
Ye Inglis ost blew till assail.	*The English host blew to attack.*
Yan mycht men with ser apparaill	*Then might men with various gear*
Se yat gret ost cum sturdely	*See that great host come resolutely*
Ye toun enweround yai in hy	*The town surrounded they in haste*
And assailyt with sua gret will	*And attacked with so great will*
For all yar mycht yai set yartill	*For all their might they set thereto*
Yat thaim pressyt fast on ye toun.	*Yet them advanced fast on the town.*
Bot yai yat gan yaim abandoun	*But they that had them resigned*
To dede or yan to woundis sar	*To death or else to wounds sore*
Sa weill has yaim defendit yar	*So well them defended there*
Yat leddrys to ye ground yai slang	*That ladders to the ground they slung*
And with stanys sa fast yai dan	*And with stones so fast they struck*
Yar fayis yat fele yar left liand	*Their foes that many there stayed lying*
Sum dede sum hurt and sum swonand.	*Some dead some hurt and sum swooning.*

Rud Ewyn = The eve of the Feast of the Exaltation of the Cross (Rood), that is, 13 September.

yaim/thaim = The pronoun *them* used reflexively, meaning *themselves*.

📖 The vocabulary of Text 60 is listed in the Word Book.

10.2 Another Northern dialect – York

The York Mystery Plays consist of a cycle of 50 short episodes that tell the story of the world according to medieval Christian tradition, from the Fall of the Angels and the Creation to the Last Judgement. Each trade gild of the city of York was responsible for the costs and production of a play, which was performed in procession on a pageant-wagon in the streets of York. Some of the plays were assigned to a gild whose occupation was reflected in the story. For example, the Bakers played *The Last Supper,* the Shipwrights *The Building of the Ark*, the Fishers and Mariners *The Flood*, and the Vintners *The Marriage at Cana.*

The cycle was produced each year at the feast of Corpus Christi, from the later 14th century into the early 16th century. Twelve 'stations' were set up in the streets, and each pageant-wagon moved in procession from one station to another to perform its play. They began the procession of wagons at 4.30 a.m., and the last play was probably finished after midnight. Banners were set up to mark the positions of the stations, and a proclamation was made.

Text 61: The York Proclamation for the Corpus Christi Plays, 1415 (edited text)

Oiez &c. We comand of þe kynges behalue and þe mair & þe shirefs of þis Citee þat no man go armed in þis Citee with swerdes, ne with carlill axes, ne none othir defences in distourbaunce of þe kynges pees & þe play, or hynderyng of þe processioun of Corpore Christi; and þat þai leue þare hernas in þare ines, saufand knyghtes and squwyers of wirship þat awe haue swerdes borne aftir þame, of payne of forfaiture of þaire wapen & inprisonment of þaire bodys. And þat men þat brynges furth pacentes, þat þai play at the places þat is assigned þerfore, and nowere elles, of the payne of forfaiture to be raysed þat is ordayned þerfore, þat is to say xl s . . . And þat all maner of craftmen þat bryngeth furthe ther pageantez in order & course be good players, well arayed & openly spekyng, vpon payn of lesing of c s., to be paid to the chambre withoute any pardon. And that euery player that shall play be redy in his pagiaunt at convenyant tyme, that is to say at the mydhowre betwix iiijth & vth of the cloke in the mornyng, & then all oþer pageantes fast folowyng ilkon after oþer as þer course is, without tarieing . . .

Activity 10.2

Discuss the language and style of the Proclamation, e.g.:

- the different functions of the word *þat*
- verb inflections
- noun inflections
- forms of personal pronoun
- the sources of the vocabulary – OE, ON or OF
- spelling.

10.2.1 Commentary

10.2.1.1 Grammar

As a proclamation it is written in a very formal style. The word *þat* is used frequently, and functions first as the marker of a noun clause [NCl], e.g.

> We comand þat [no man go armed . . .]

and secondly as a relative pronoun in a relative clause [RelCl], e.g.

> saufand knyghtes and squwyers of wirship [**þat** awe haue swerdes borne aftir þame]

Both uses of *þat* function to define precisely what is being commanded and to whom it applies. The formula *þat is to say* . . . is also used for this purpose, *þat* here functioning as a demonstrative pronoun. Another **formulaic** phrase is *of payne of* or *vpon payn of*, defining the penalties for not complying with the proclamation.

Verb forms

The evidence for a particular word-form in any one short text may be limited or non-existent, and this text contains few varieties of verb form. The two major classes of verb in OE, strong and weak (see section 4.3.3), continued through ME into MnE, but with many changes in individual verbs with, for example, some strong verbs becoming weak in their inflections. New verbs from French were inflected as weak, or regular verbs, with the ⟨-ed⟩ past tense and participle suffix, like *arayed*.

There were dialectal differences in verb inflections, but this text has few examples, and is also itself inconsistent, giving two different forms for the 3rd person plural present tense in the same verb, *brynges* and *bryngeth*. The common Northern inflection was ⟨-es⟩ or ⟨-is⟩, while ⟨-eth⟩ was used in the Midlands and South. York, which was a flourishing port in the 15th century, is situated on the river Ouse, or Humber, and so lies on the southern boundary of Northumbria. The people of York were therefore in direct contact with Midland dialectal speakers, and this may help to explain the use of both forms of inflection.

In John Barbour's Text 59 the inflection ⟨-ing⟩ was used in the Scots Northern dialect for a verb used as a verbal noun, or gerund, *liking*, and in Text 60 the inflection ⟨-and⟩ was used for present participles, *liand*, *swownand*. Similarly, in the York Proclamation, ⟨-and⟩ occurs on the verb *saufand* (*saving*), and ⟨-ing⟩ on the noun *hynderyng*. But ⟨-ing⟩ also occurs on other present participles – *spekyng*, *folowyng*, which was the form in other dialects. This is evidence of the mixed dialect forms of the Proclamation.

Other verb forms are similar to those familiar to us in MnE, and include the passive voice with *be* and the past participle, and the use of the subjunctive mood to indicate what must or ought to be done.

	3rd person singular
no man	go (*subjunctive*)
þat	is to say
euery player that	shall play
	be redy (*subjunctive*)
as þer course	is
	1st person plural
We	comand
	3rd person plural
þai	leue (*subjunctive*)
knyghtes & squwyers þat	awe haue
men þat	brynges (furth)
þai	play (*subjunctive*)
all maner of craftmen þat	bryngeth (furthe)
	past participle
armed swerdes	borne
(well)	arayed
	passive voice
forfaiture þat	is ordayned
the places þat	is assigned
	to be raysed
	to be paid
	present participle
(openly)	spekyng
all oþer pageantes (fast)	folowyng

Noun forms

The plural inflection is ⟨-s⟩ or ⟨-es⟩, e.g. *knyghtes, shirefs*. This was so in all Northern dialects, sometimes spelt ⟨-is⟩, as we have seen in Barbour's *Bruce*. In Southern dialects, ⟨-en⟩ as the plural inflection was widespread in ME, as well as ⟨-es⟩. It derived from the very common OE ⟨-an⟩ plural, but was eventually replaced by the regular ⟨s⟩ plural.

There is one example of the possessive inflection, also ⟨-es⟩, in *kynges*, MnE *king's*.

Pronoun forms

As we would expect, all the ON forms of 3rd person plural pronouns are used: *þai, þame* and *þaire*.

10.2.1.2 Vocabulary

There are 82 lexical word types: OE 51 = 62%; OF/AF 24 = 30%; ON 5 = 6%; Latin 2 = 2%

📖 The complete vocabulary of Text 61 is listed in the Word Book.

The sample is too small to be able to make any general inferences with certainty, but it suggests that by the end of the 14th century a large number of words of French derivation had been assimilated into English, certainly into formal written English. This is a hypothesis that can be tested by taking any historical text in English and looking up the derivation of its lexical words. Function words, as we have seen, are almost all of OE or ON derivation. Words from ON tended to be those of common speech, and many more of them survive, up to the present day, in dialectal rather than Standard English.

However, words derived from French are not necessarily specialised. Many of them are everyday words which have replaced the OE. For example, the word *city* is used, while OE *ceaster* only survives in place names like *Chester*, and *burh* in names like *Peterborough* or in the restricted meaning of *borough*. *Peace* has replaced *sibb* or *friþ*, *command* is more commonly used than *bid*, from OE *beodan*, and so on.

10.2.1.3 Spelling

Letter ⟨þ⟩ was still in use, but not consistently so in the text of the Proclamation. The digraph ⟨th⟩ appears in the second half of the text in *that, bryngeth* etc.

Typical of most ME writing is the general interchangeability of ⟨i⟩ and ⟨y⟩ for the vowel [i]; ⟨u⟩ and ⟨v⟩ were still variant forms of the same letter, and were to remain so for a long time yet. Scribes tended to write ⟨u⟩ in the middle of a word, as in *behalue, euery, course*, and ⟨v⟩ at the beginning, as in *vpon, vnwis, vertu, visage* for both the vowel [u] and the consonant [v]. Letter ⟨w⟩ was used similarly, as in *squwyers, awe, mydhowre*.

We are used to a system of 'correct spelling' in which all but a very few words have one standard spelling, to be found recorded in dictionaries. This was obviously not so for ME, as there are four different spellings for the word *pageant/pageants* in the York Proclamation: *pagiaunt/pacentes/pageantes/pageantez*. But there are no other variants apart from *furth/furthe*, which is a reminder that words were often spelt with a redundant final ⟨-e⟩, like *mydhowre*, *cloke*. Again, this was to be a feature of English spelling for a long time.

The spelling *inprisonment* uses the prefix ⟨in-⟩ as in the phrase *in prison*. The spelling was later changed to match the spoken form [ɪm], which is conditioned by the following bilabial consonant [p].

10.3 The York Plays

The only copy of the York Plays to survive was written about 1470, and was originally the property of the corporation of the city. It was probably compiled from the various prompt copies belonging to each gild that performed a play, and the language may therefore be that of the late 14th or early 15th century.

The dialect is Northern, but the scribes introduced a lot of modifications from the East Midlands dialect, the evidence for which is in the variations of spelling of the same words. The use of some East Midlands forms suggests the beginnings of a standardised system of spelling.

The plays are written in a variety of verse stanza patterns, with both rhyme and alliteration, so that they cannot be read as natural everyday speech, in spite of the liveliness of the dialogue dramatically. The following extract is from the Potters' *Pentecost Play*, which re-tells the story of the coming of the Holy Spirit at Pentecost, or Whitsuntide, after the Ascension of Christ. It fills out the story in the *Acts of the Apostles*, chapter 2.

The play does not attempt to portray the actual coming of the Spirit as it is told in the Bible.

> A ND when the day of Pentecost was fully come, they were all with one accord in one place.
> 2 And suddenly there came a sound from heauen as of a rushing mighty wind, and it filled all the house where they were sitting.
> 3 And there appeared vnto them clouen tongues, like as of fire, and it sate vpon each of them.
> 4 And they were all filled with the holy Ghost, and began to speake with other tongues, as the spirit gaue them vtterance.

King James Bible 1611, Acts 2: 1–4

The following extract from the play spans the coming of the Holy Spirit, which is represented by the singing of the ancient hymn *Veni Creator Spiritus* ('Come Creator Spirit'). Two 'Doctors' speak contemptuously of the claim of the apostles that Jesus is alive again. After the hymn, Mary and Peter celebrate the coming of the Spirit.

Text 62: *From the York Potters'* Pentecost Play, c.1470 (facsimile)

j doctor
Harke maistir for mahoundes peyne
Howe þat þes mabbardis maddis nowe
Yei maistir þat oure men haue slayne
Hase garte þame on his tri fullid trowe

ij doctor
Ye lurdayns saie he lefis agayne
þat mater may yai nevir avowe
ffor as yei herde his prechyng pleyne
He was away yai wiste noyt howe

j doctor
They wiste noyt whenne he wente
þarfore fully yai faile
And saie þam shall be sente
Grete helpe thurgh his counsaille

iij doctor
He myghtte nowdir sende clothe nor clowte
He was naked but a wreche alway
But samme oure men ond make a shoute
So shall we beste þone foolis flaye

iiij doctor
Saye nay yai will yei dye for doute
I rede we make noyt mekill dray
But wisly wayte whan þai come oute
And martre þame þenne if þat we may

ij doctor
Now certis I assente yer tille
Yitt wolde I noght yei wiste
Yone carles þan shall we kill
But yai liffe als vs liste

Angelus tunc cantare *veni creator spiritus*
Maria
Honnoure and blisse be euer nowe
With worshippe in þis worlde alwaye
To my soueraygne sone Jhesu
Oure Lorde allone þat laste shall dy
Nowe may we triste his talis ar trewe
Be dedis þat here is done þis day
Als lange as ye his pase pursue
Ye fende ne fendis your for to flay
ffor his gast halygaste
He lathis here on you lende
Myrthis and trewthe to taste
And all misse to amende

petrus
All mys to mende nowe haue we myght
þis is þe mirthe oure maistir of mente
I myghtti noyt loke so was it lyght
A loued be þat lorde þat it vs lente
Now hase he holden þat he vs hyghte
His holygaste here haue we hente
Like to þe sonne itt semed in sight
And sodenly þanne was itt sente

ij aplis
Itt was sente for oure sele
Itt giffis vs happe and hele
Me thynke slike forse I fele
I myghtt felle folke full feele

         —— Iº doctor

harke maiſtir foȝ mahoundes peyne
howe þat þes mobbaȝðis maððis nowe
þeȝ maiſtir þat oure men haue ſlayne
haſe garte þame on his trifullis trowe

         —— IIº doctor

þe lurðayne ſais he leffis agayne
þat mater may þei neueð avowe
ffoȝ as þei heȝðe his pȝechyng pleyne
he was away þai wiſte noȝt howe

         —— Iº doctor

they wiſte noght whenne he wente
þeȝfoȝe fully þei faile
and ſais þam ſchall be ſente
Gȝete helpe thurgh his counſaille

         —— IIº doctor

he myghte nowðir ſende clothe nor clowte
he was neuere but a wȝecche alway
But ſamme oure men and make a ſchowte
So ſchall we beſte yone foolis flaye

         —— Iº doctor

Nay nay þan will þei ðye foȝ ðoute
I reðe we make noȝt mekill ðȝay
But waȝly wayte when þai come oute
And maȝȝe þame þanne if þat we may

         —— IIº doctor

Now ceȝtis I aſſente þeȝ tille
Yitt wolde I noght þei wiſte
ȝone carles þan ſchall we kill
But þei liffe als vs liſte
Angelus tunc cantaȝe *veni creatr ſptus*
honnoure and bliſſe be euer nowe   *Maria*
With woȝſchippe in þis woȝlde alwaye
to my ſouerayne ſone Ihu (*Ihesu*)
Oure loȝðe allone þat laſte ſchall ay
Nowe may we triſte his talis ar trewe
Be ðeðis þat heȝe is ðone þis ðay
Als lange as ȝe his paſe purſue
þe ſende ne* fendis yow foȝ to flay *written for 'he'*
ffoȝ his high hali gaſte
he lattis heȝe on ȝou lenðe
Mirthis and trewthe to taſte
and all miſſe to amenðe

         —— Petrus

all mys to mende nowe haue we myght
þis is the mirthe oure maiſtir of mente
I myght noȝt loke, ſo was it light
A loueð be þat loȝðe þat itt vs lente
Nowe haſe he holden þat he vs highte
his holy goſte heȝe haue we hente
Like to þe ſonne itt ſemeð in ſight
and ſoðenly þanne was itt ſente

         —— IIº Apostolus

hitt was ſente foȝ oure ſele
hitt giffis vs happe and hele
Me thynke ſlike foȝſe I fele
I myght felle folke full feele

Angelus tunc cantare *veni creatr ſptus* = *Angel then to sing Come Creator Spirit*
his pase pursue = follow in his steps
þe fenðe he fenðis yow for to flay = *he prevents the devil from frightening you*

📖 The vocabulary of Text 62 is listed in the Word Book.

☉ Phonetic transcription of part of Text 62 beginning *Honnoure and blisse* . . . , recorded on the cassette tape:

> ɔnuːr ænd blɪs be ɛvər nuː
> wɪθ wɔrʃɪp ɪn θɪs wɔrld alwaɪ
> tɔ mi sɔvəraɪn sʊn ʒeːzju
> uːr lɔrd əlɔːn θæt læːst ʃæl aɪ.
> nuː maɪ weː trɪst hɪs taːls aːr treʊ
> bɛ deːds θæt heːr ɪs dʊn θɪs daɪ.
> als læŋg as jeː hɪs paːs pʊrsuː
> θə feːnd heː fɛnds juː for to flaɪ.
> fɔr hɪs hiːç haːlɪ gaːst
> heː læts heːr ɔn juː lɛnd,
> mɪrθs ænd treʊθ tɔ taːst,
> ænd al mɪs to amɛnd
>
> *Petrus*
> al mɪs to mɛnd nuː hæv weː miːçt
> θɪs ɪs θə mɪrθ uːr maɪstɪr ɔf mɛnt.
> iː miːçt nɔxt loːk, sɔ wæs ɪt liːçt,
> aː lʊvd beː θæt lɔrd θæt ɪt ʊs lɛnt.
> nuː hæs heː hɔːldən θæt heː ʊs hiːçt,
> hɪs hɔːlɪ gɔːst heːr hæv we hɛnt.
> liːk to θə sʊn ɪt seːmd ɪn siːçt,
> ænd sudənlɪ θæn wæs ɪt sɛnt.
>
> *II Apostolus*
> hɪt wæs sɛnt fɔr uːr seːl,
> hɪt gɪvz ʊs hæp ənd heːl,
> mɛ θɪŋk slɪk fɔrs iː feːl,
> iː miːçt fɛl fɔlk fʊl feːl

10.3.1 Commentary

10.3.1.1 *The verse*

Metre

This part of the play divides into patterned stanzas of twelve lines, the first eight having eight syllables and the last four having six, in a rising duple (or iambic) rhythm x / x / x / x /

First stanza

x	/	x	/	x	/	x	/	8 syllables, 4 stressed
Harke	**mais**	tir	**for**	ma	**houn**	des	**peyne**	

Howe þat þes mobbardis maddis nowe
Þer maistir þat oure men haue slayne
Hase garte þame on his trifullis trowe

Þe lurdayne sais he leffis agayne
Þat mater may þei neuere avowe
For as þei herde his prechyng pleyne
He was away þai wiste noʒt howe

  x   /   x   /   x   /   6 syllables, 3 stressed
They **wiste** noght **whenne** he **wente**
Þerfore fully þei faile
And sais þam schall be sente
Grete helpe thurgh his counsaille

Rhyme-scheme

The first eight lines of each stanza have two rhymes only, *abababab*, and the last four two rhymes *cdcd*.

Second stanza

He myghte nowdir sende clothe nor **clowte**
He was neuere but a wrecche **alway**
But samme oure men and make a **schowte**
So schall we beste yone foolis **flaye**

Nay nay þan will þei dye for **doute**
I rede we make noʒt mekill **dray**
But warly wayte when þai come **oute**
And marre þame þanne if þat we **may**

Now certis I assente þer **tille**
Yitt wolde I noght þei **wiste**
ʒone carles þan schall we **kill**
But þei liffe als vs **liste**

Alliteration

Each line has marked alliteration on some of the stressed syllables:

Third stanza

Hon [n]oure and blisse be euer [n]owe
With [w]orschippe in þis [w]orlde al [w]aye
To my [s]ouerayne [s]one Ihesu
Oure [l]orde al [l]one þat [l]aste schall ay
Nowe may we [t]riste his [t]alis ar [t]rewe
Be [d]edis þat here is [d]one þis [d]ay
Als lange as ʒe his [p]ase [p]ursue
Þe [f]ende he [f]endis yow [f]or to [f]lay

For h̲is h̲igh h̲ali gaste
He l̲attis here on ʒou l̲ende
Mirthis and t̲rewthe to t̲aste
And all m̲isse to am̲ende

This sophisticated patterning of sound and rhythm combines the Old English tradition of alliterative verse with the newer French metrical rhymed verse (compare *The Owl and the Nightingale*, Text 38, section 6.2).

10.3.1.2 Spelling and pronunciation

We have seen that one of the principal changes in the language has been the gradual erosion of OE unstressed suffixes, for example [um] > [un] > [ən] > [ə] ~ Ø. There were long periods when dialects varied in their progress towards an almost uninflected language, so that a word-final [ə] spelt ⟨e⟩ might still be pronounced as a grammatical inflection in one part of the country, but not in another. The evidence for this is very striking in verse writing, because poets would have a choice of current pronunciations with and without the final syllable to help in writing metrical verse (see section 10.1.1.1).

But none of the word-final letters ⟨e⟩ which might represent the unstressed vowel [ə] are pronounced in the last stanza of Text 62, and it is one part of the evidence that Northern dialects changed more rapidly in this process of grammatical simplification than those of the Midlands and South. The spelling of words with a redundant final letter ⟨e⟩ continued into the 17th century well after the letter was not pronounced in any dialect, as a glance at any of the later facsimiles will show.

10.3.1.3 Word-forms and inflections

Nouns

The plural suffix is spelt *-is* (*mobbardis, trifullis, dedis, mirthis, foolis*), except for the single occurrence of *-es* in *carles*. The evidence of the verse patterning suggests that the words were pronounced with a final [s] only – *mobbards, trifulls, deds, mirths, fools*.

The one example of a possessive noun is *mahoundes*.

Verbs

There are by now considerably fewer verb inflections in this Northern dialect, with *-is* common to both singular and plural 3rd person present tenses. All other inflections have been reduced to *-e*.

Present tense

1st person singular	*-e*	(*I*) *rede, assente, wolde, myght, fele*
3rd person singular	*-is*	(*he*) *sais, leffis, fendis, lattis, giffis*
		(*he*) *hase, schall, myghte, is, thynke*

1st and 3rd person plural	-is	(*þei*) *maddis, sais*
	-e	(*þei*) *haue, faile, will, ar, is*
		(*we*) *may, schall, haue*
singular subjunctive	-e	*liste, be, pursue*
plural subjunctive	-e	(*we*) *make, wayte, marre*
		(*þei*) *come, wiste, liffe*

Past tense

singular	-e	(*he*) *was, wente, mente, lente, highte, semed*
plural	-e	(*þei*) *herde, wiste*
past participle		*slayne, garte, sente, done, loued, holden, hente, sente*
imperative	-e	*harke, samme, make*
infinitive	-e	*trowe, avowe, be, sende, flaye, dye, kill, laste, triste, flay,*
		lende, taste, amende, mende, loke, felle

Personal pronouns

The Scandinavian 3rd person plural personal pronouns have been adopted in all forms: *þei/þai, þam/þame, þer.*

10.3.1.4 Sources of vocabulary

Word types: OE 140 = 77%; ON 14 = 8%; OF/AF 28 = 15%.

10.3.1.5 Grammar

We have examples of a number of developing grammatical features in Text 62:

- The relative pronoun is *þat,* e.g. *þer maistir **þat** oure men haue slayne* (cf. OE *þe*).
- The passive verb construction with *be,* e.g. *was sente, schall be sente.*
- Perfective aspect with *have,* e.g. *haue slayne, hase garte, hase holden, haue hente.*
- Perfective aspect with *be,* e.g. *is done.*
- Northern form of present tense plural of *be – ar.*
- Modal verbs:

may	*may avowe, may triste*
might	*myghte sende, myght noȝt loke, myght felle*
shall	*schall be sente, schall kill, schall laste, schall flaye*
will	*will dye*
would	*wolde*

- Negative with *not* only, without the particle *ne,* e.g. *wiste noȝt, make noȝt, wolde noght.*
- Survival of dative pronoun without *to,* e.g. *þam schall be sente* (*to them shall be sent*).
- Impersonal verb construction, e.g. *as vs liste, me thynke* (*as it pleases us, it seems to me*).

The play is in verse, so we cannot draw conclusions about the word order of the everyday spoken and written language, but there is some variation from the unmarked *Subject – Predicator (Verb) – Object – Adverbial* order of clause constituents:

Od	*P-*	*S*	*A*	*-P*		
Þat mater	may	þei	neuere	avowe		

Oi	*P*		*S*		*A*	
þam	schall be sente		Grete helpe		thurgh his counsaille	

cj	*P-*	*S*	*A*	*Od*	*-P*	
So	schall	we	beste	yone foolis	flaye	

Od	*A*	*P-*	*S*	*-P*		
ȝone carles	þan	schall	we	kill		

cj	*Od*		*S*	*P-*	*A*	*A*	*-P*
For	his high hali gaste		He	lattis	here	on ȝou	lende

Od		*P*				
Mirthis and trewthe		to taste				

cj	*Od*	*P*				
And	all misse	to amende				

Od	*P*	*A*	*P*	*S*	*Od*	
All mys	to mende	nowe	haue	we	myght	

Od	*A*	*P-*	*S*	*-P*		
His holy goste	here	haue	we	hente		

10.4 Northern and Midlands dialects compared

John de Thoresby became Archbishop of York in 1352. He found many of his parish priests ignorant and neglectful of their duties, and as one remedy for this he wrote a *Catechism* in Latin, setting out the basic doctrines of the faith. It was translated into English by a monk of St Mary's Abbey in York in 1357. This version is called *The Lay Folk's Catechism*. An extended version was written a little later by John Wyclif. He had been born in the North Riding of Yorkshire, but because he had lived and worked for a long time in Oxford and Leicestershire, his writings are in a variety of West Midlands dialect.

We can therefore clearly see some of the differences between Northern and West Midlands dialects by comparing the two versions of Archbishop Thoresby's *Catechism*.

Texts 63 and 64: The York Lay Folks' Catechism

Text 63: 1357, Northern dialect

> This er the sex thinges that I have spoken of,
> That the lawe of halikirk lies mast in

That ye er al halden to knawe and to kun,
If ye sal knawe god almighten and cum un to his blisse:
And for to gif yhou better will for to kun tham,
Our fadir the ercebisshop grauntes of his grace
Fourti daies of pardon til al that kunnes tham,
Or dos their gode diligence for to kun tham . . .
For if ye kunnandly knaw this ilk sex thinges
Thurgh thaim sal ye kun knawe god almighten,
Wham, als saint Iohn saies in his godspel,
Conandly for to knawe swilk als he is,
It is endles life and lastand bliss,
To whilk blisse he bring us that bought us. amen

Text 64: Wyclif's version, West Midlands dialect

These be þe sexe thyngys þat y haue spokyn of
þat þe law of holy chirche lys most yn.
þat þey be holde to know and to kunne;
yf þey schal knowe god almy3ty and come to þe blysse of heuyn.
And for to 3eue 3ow þe better wyl for to cunne ham.
Our Fadyr þe archiepischop grauntys of hys grace.
forty dayes of Pardoun. to alle þat cunne hem
and rehercys hem . . .
For yf 3e cunnyngly knowe þese sexe thyngys;
þorw3 hem 3e schull knowe god almy3ty.
And as seynt Ion sey þ in hys gospel.
Kunnyngly to know god almy3ty
ys endles lyf and lastynge blysse.
He bryngge vs þerto þat bow3t vs
With hys herte blod on þe cros Crist Iesu. Amen.

to kun = to learn
kunnandly/conandly = clearly
swilk = such
whilk = which

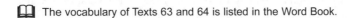 The vocabulary of Texts 63 and 64 is listed in the Word Book.

Activity 10.3

Compare the following words and phrases (line numbers in brackets) from the two versions of *The Lay Folk's Catechism* and explain the differences.

- er / be (1)
- halikirk / holy chirche (2)
- mast / most (2)
- halden to knawe / holde to know (3)
- sal / schal (4)

- cum / come (4)
- til al / to alle (7)
- kunnes tham / cunne hem (7)
- kunnandly / cunnyngly (9); conandly / kunnyngly (12); lastand / lastynge (13)
- saies / seyþ (11)

A commentary on Activity 10.3 is in the Text Commentary Book.

10.5 Chaucer and the Northern dialect

In Chaucer's 'The Reeve's Tale' there are two undergraduate characters, 'yonge poure scolers',

> Iohn highte that oon and Aleyn highte that oother
> Of oon town were they born that highte Strother
> Fer in the north, I kan noght telle where.

Chaucer makes their Northern origins clear by marking their speech with some of the features that his readers would recognise as different from the educated London dialect that he used (see Chapter 13). Here is an extract from the Tale. The Northern words are printed in **bold italic** type. Aleyn and Iohn have come to a mill and greet Symkyn, the miller. They intend to supervise the grinding of their corn, as millers were notorious for cheating their customers.

Activity 10.4

Discuss and explain the Northern features in the following text (words in **bold italic**). Some are marked for pronunciation and some for different inflections. There are also some dialectal differences of meaning, listed in the table following the text.

A commentary on Activity 10.4 is in the Text Commentary Book.

Text 65: From Chaucer's 'The Reeve's Tale'

> Aleyn spak first: Al hayl Symkyn in faith
> How *fares* thy faire doghter and thy wyf?
> Aleyn welcome, quod Symkyn, by my lyf
> And Iohn also. How now what do ye here?
> By god, quod Iohn, Symond, nede has *na* peere.
> Hym *bihoues* serue hymself that has *na* swayn
> Or ellis he is a fool, as clerkes sayn.
> Oure maunciple, I *hope* he wol be deed,
> *Swa werkes* ay the wanges in his heed.
> And therfore *is* I come and eek Alayn
> To grynde oure corn and carie it *heem* agayn . . .

It *sal* be doon, quod Symkyn, by my fay.
What wol ye doon whil that it is in hande? . . .

By god, right by the hoper wol I stande,
Quod Iohn, and se how the corn *gas* in.
Yet saw I neuere by my fader kyn
How that the hoper *wagges til* and *fra* . . .

Aleyn answerde: Iohn, wiltow *swa?*
Thanne wil I be byneth by my crown
And se how that the mele *falles* down
Into the trogh. That *sal* be my desport.
For, Iohn, in faith I may been of youre sort,
I *is* as *ille* a millere as *ar* ye.

OE feallan	**falles**	*falls*
OE faran	**fares**	*fares*
OE gan	**gas**	*goes*
OE ham	**heem**	*home*
OE hopian	**hope**	*hope* (= believe)
OE behofian	**hym bihoues**	= *he must*
OE is	**is**	*is*
OEnan	**na**	*no*
OE sceal	**sal**	*shall*
OE swa	**swa**	*so*
OE wagian	**wagges**	*wags*
OE wyrcan	**werkes**	*works* (= aches)
OE wang	**wanges**	= *back teeth*
OE *Northern*	**ar/ arun**	*are*
ON fra	**fra**	*fro*
ON illr	**ille**	*ill* (= bad)
ON sveinn	**swayn**	*swain* (= servant)
ON til	**til**	*till* (= to)

This is only part of the dialogue between the miller and the two 'clerkes'. Other words in the Tale which give away their dialect are:

OE alswa	**alswa**	*also*
OE ban	**banes**	*bones*
(*not known*)	**fonne**	= *fool*
OE gan	**ga/gane**	*go/gone*
OE lang, ON langr	**lang**	*long*
OE nan (ne + an)	**naan**	*none*
OE ra, ON ra	**ra**	*roe* (deer)
OE sang	**sang**	*song*
OE sawol	**saule**	*soul*

OE wat, fr witan	**waat**	= *knows*
OE hwa	**wha**	*who*
ON baðir	**bathe**	*both*
ON illr ON heill	**il-hail**	*bad luck*

📖 The vocabulary of Text 65 is listed in the Word Book.

10.6 Loan-words, 1320–39

📖 A selection of loan-words recorded during this period can be found in the Word Book, after the word-lists for Chapter 10.

11 The 14th century – West Midlands dialects

In the Anglo-Saxon invasion and settlement of Britain, the Angles occupied the Midlands and North of England, and what is now southern Scotland. Their dialect of OE is called Anglian as a general term, but its northern and southern varieties were different enough for two dialects to be recognised – Northumbrian (north of the river Humber) and Mercian (south of the Humber).

During the ME period, the Mercian (Midlands) dialect itself developed in different ways. The east Midlands were part of the Danelaw (see section 3.3.1.1), the west Midlands were not, so the language of the east Midlands changed, partly under the influence of the Danish Old Norse speakers who had settled there. As a result, OE Mercian became two ME dialects, East Midlands and West Midlands.

The two texts chosen to illustrate the West Midlands dialect are sufficiently similar to be called the 'same dialect', but show differences which lead scholars to place one in the north and the other in the south of the West Midlands.

11.1 A North-West Midlands dialect – *Sir Gawayn and þe Grene Knyȝt*

Sir Gawayn and þe Grene Knyȝt is a romance in alliterative verse which tells a story of the legendary court of King Arthur. The one surviving manuscript was probably written towards the end of the 14th century, and scholars are agreed that the dialect is that of Cheshire or south Lancashire. The author's name is not known.

A note on the use of letter ⟨ȝ⟩ in the poem

We think of MnE spelling as being irregular and inconsistent in the relationship of letters to sounds. This, however, began long before modern times, and the manuscript of *Sir Gawayn* provides a good example of the use of a single letter to represent several different sounds. The letter ⟨ȝ⟩ was used in writing this poem to represent several sounds, because it had developed from two sources, first from the OE letter ⟨ȝ⟩ (see section 3.1.3.3) and secondly as a form of the letter ⟨z⟩. It was therefore used for all the following sounds (the words are from Texts 66 and 67):

- [j]   3ederly, *promptly*; 3olden, *yielded*; 3eres, *years*; 3et, *yet*. (We use ⟨y⟩ in MnE.)
- [ç]   Similar to the sound in German *ich*, [ıç], and usually followed by [t] as in ⟨3t⟩, e.g. kny3t, *knight*; hy3t, *height*; ly3tly, *lightly*; ly3t, *light*. (We use ⟨ght⟩ in MnE, though the sound of the ⟨gh⟩ has now been lost in these words.)
- [x]   Similar to Scots *loch* [lox] or German *bach* [bax] after [a], [o] or [u], e.g. þur3, *through*; ra3t, *reached*; la3t, *laughed*; bo3e3, *boughs*; fla3e, *fled*; la3e, *laugh*. Again ⟨gh⟩ is used in MnE, and the sound has either changed to [f], e.g. *cough*, or has been lost.
- [w]   A developing sound change from OE [ɣ], e.g. þa3, *though*; also, elsewhere, ar3e, *arrow*; sa3e, *saw*; bro3e3, *brows*. Letter ⟨w⟩ is also used in the poem for this sound, e.g. *blowe*, *lawe*.
- [s]   ⟨3⟩ and ⟨t3⟩ were both used for letter ⟨z⟩. Letters ⟨z⟩ and ⟨tz⟩ had been used in Old French for the sound [ts], which changed to [s] and later to [z]. This French convention was used in the poem for the sound [s], e.g. hedle3, *headless*; resoun3, *reasons*; hat3, *has*.
- [z]   ⟨3⟩ represented the voiced sound [z] in ⟨-es⟩ noun and verb suffixes, e.g. discouere3, lokke3, renkke3, bo3e3, cachche3, steppe3, stryde3, halde3, etc. However, letter ⟨s⟩ is also used in the text, e.g. houes, *hooves*; bones; schonkes, *shanks* etc.; y3e-lydde3, *eye-lids* illustrates the use of letter yogh as [j] and [z].

The poem is written in 101 stanzas which have a varying number of unrhymed alliterative lines followed by five short rhymed lines. Like all OE and ME verse, it was written to be read aloud to an audience.

Text 66: *From* Sir Gawayn and þe Grene Kny3t *(i) (facsimile)*

The story so far:

During the New Year celebrations at King Arthur's court a Green Knight rides in, carrying a battle axe, and challenges any knight to strike him a blow with the axe, provided that he can give a return blow a year and a day later. Gawain takes up the challenge.

✍ A note on the handwriting

- letter thorn written like OE wynn – ⟨p⟩;
- 2-form of ⟨r⟩ after <o> – ⟨ɤ⟩;
- unusual form of ⟨w⟩.

Transcription

The grene knyȝt vpon groūde graypely hȳ ðreſſes
a littel lut wᵗ pe heðe pe lere he ðiſcoueʳȝ
his longe louelych lokkeȝ he layð ou' his croū
let pe nakeð nec ꞇo pe noꞇe ſchewe.
Gauan grippeð ꞇo his ax ⁊ geðeres hiꞇ on hyȝꞇ
pe kay foꞇ on pe folðe he be foꞃe ſeꞇꞇe
let hiꞇ ðoū lyȝꞇly lyȝꞇ on pe nakeð
paꞇ pe ſcharp of pe ſchalk ſchynðereð pe bones
⁊ ſchrāk purȝ pe ſchyire grece ⁊ ſcaðe hiꞇ ī twȳne
paꞇ pe biꞇ of pe broū ſꞇel boꞇ on pe groūðe.
pe fayre heðe fro pe halce hiꞇ ꞇo pe erpe
paꞇ fele hiꞇ foyneð wyꞇh her feꞇe pere hiꞇ forth roleð.
pe bloð brayð fro pe boðy pᵗ blykkeð on pe grene
⁊ nawper falꞇˑeð ne fel pe freke neu' pe helðer
boꞇ ſꞇyply he ſꞇarꞇ forth vpon ſꞇyf ſchonkes
⁊ ruyſchly he raȝꞇ ouꞇ pere as renkkeȝ ſꞇoðen
laȝꞇ ꞇo his lufly heð ⁊ lyfꞇ hiꞇ vp ſone
⁊ ſypen boȝeȝ ꞇo his blonk pe bryðel he cachcheȝ

ſteppeȝ īto ſtelbawe ⁊ ſtrydeȝ alofte
⁊ hıs heðe by þe here ī hıs honðe halðeȝ
⁊ as ſaðly þe ſegge hȳ ī hıs ſaðel ſette
as non vnhap ha ð hȳ ayleð paȝ heðleȝ he were
ī ſteððe
he brayðe hıs bluk aboute
þat vgly boðı þat bleððe
monı on of hȳ ha ð ðoute
bı þat hıs reſoūȝ were reððe

Edited version

The grene knyȝt vpon grounde grayþely hym dresses
A littel lut with þe hede, þe lere he discouereȝ
His longe louelych lokkeȝ he layd ouer his croun
Let the naked nec to þe note schewe.
Gauan gripped to his ax ˥ gederes hit on hyȝt
þe kay fot on þe fold he before sette
Let hit doun lyȝtly lyȝt on þe naked
þat þe scharp of þe schalk schyndered þe bones
& schrank þurȝ þe schyire grece & scade hit in twynne,
þat þe bit of þe broun stel bot on þe grounde.
þe fayre hede fro þe halce hit to þe erþe
þat fele hit foyned wyth her fete þere hit forth roled.
þe blod brayd fro þe body þat blykked on þe grene
& nawþer faltered ne fel þe freke neuer þe helder
Bot styþly he start forth vpon styf schonkes
& ru[n]yschly he raȝt out, þere as renkkeȝ stoden,
Laȝt to his lufly hed & lyft hit vp sone
& syþen boȝeȝ to his blonk, þe brydel he cachcheȝ
Steppeȝ into stelbawe & strydeȝ alofte
& his hede by þe here in his honde haldeȝ
& as sadly þe segge hym in his sadel sette
As non vnhap had hym ayled, þaȝ hedleȝ he were
in stedde.
He brayde his bluk aboute
þat vgly bodi þat bledde
Moni on of hym had doute
Bi þat his resounȝ were redde.

(with some re-ordering of words)

The green knight on (the) ground readily him(self) arranges
A little bend with the head the flesh he uncovers
His long lovely locks he laid over his crown
Let the naked neck in readiness show.
Gawain gripped (to) his axe & gathered it on high
The left foot on the ground he before set
Caused it (to) land swiftly down on the naked (flesh)
(So) that the sharp (blade) of the man sundered the bones
& cut through the fair flesh & severed it in two,
(So) that the blade of the bright steel bit on the ground

The fair head from the neck hit to the earth
That many it kicked with their feet where it forth rolled.
The blood spurted from the body that gleamed on the green
& neither faltered nor fell the man never the more
But stoutly he started forth upon sturdy shanks
& fiercely he reached out where men stood
Seized his lovely head & lifted it up at once
& then turns to his steed, the bridle he snatches,
Steps into (the) stirrup & strides aloft
& his head by the hair in his hand holds
& as steadily the man settled him(self) in his saddle
As (if) no mishap had troubled him though he headless were
in that place.
He twisted his trunk about
That ugly body that bled
Many (of them) of him had doubt
By (the time) that his reasons were declared.

📖 The vocabulary of Text 66 with Text 67 is listed in the Word Book.

☉ A broad phonetic transcription of the text recorded on the CD/cassette tape:

> ðə greːn kniːçt ʊpɒn gruːnd graɪðlɪ hɪm dresəs
> ə lɪtəl luːt wɪð ðə heːd, ðə leːr heː dɪscʊvərɛz,
> hɪs lɒŋ lʊvlɪç lɔkəs heː laɪd ɔːvər hɪs kruːn,
> lɛt ðə naːkəd nɛk tɔ ðə nɔːt ʃɛwə.
> gawan grɪpəd tɔ hɪs æks ænd gədərəs hɪt ɒn hiːçt,
> θə kaɪe fɔːt ɒn θə fɔːld heː bɛvɔːr sɛt,
> lɛt hɪt duːn liːçtlɪ liːçt ɒn θə naːkəd,
> θæt θə ʃarp ɔv θə ʃælk ʃɪndərd θə bɔːnəs
> ænd ʃrænk θʊrx θə ʃiːr greːs ænd ʃaːd hɪt ɪn twɪn,
> θæt θə bɪt ɔv θə bruːn steːl bɔːt ɒn θə gruːnd.
> θə faɪr heːd frɔ θə hæls hɪt tɔ θə ɛrθə,
> θæt feːlə hɪt fɔɪnd wɪð hər feːt ðer hɪt fɔrθ rɔld.
> θə bloːd braɪd frɔ θə bɒdɪ θæt blɪkɪd ɒn θə greːn
> ənd naːʊðər faltərd nɛ fɛl θə freːk nɛvər θə hɛldər,
> bʊt stiːθlɪ heː start fɔrθ əpɒn stɪf ʃɒŋkəs
> ænd rʊnɪʃlɪ heː raːxt uːt, θer æs reŋkes stoːdən,
> laxt tɔ hɪs lʊvlɪ heːd ænd lɪft hɪt ʊp soːn,
> ænd sɪðən boːɣɛz tɔ hɪs blɒŋk, θə briːdəl heː cætʃɛs,
> stɛpez ɪntɔ steːlbawə ænd striːdez əlɔft,
> ænd hɪs heːd bɪ θə heːr ɪn hɪs hoːnd haːldəz,
> ænd æs sædlɪ θə sɛdʒ hɪm ɪn hɪs sædəl sɛt
> æs noːn ʊnhæp hæd hɪm aɪld, θax heːdlɛs heː weːr
> ɪn stɛd.
> heː braɪd hɪs blʊk əbuːt,
> θæt ʊglɪ bɒdɪ θæt blɛdə.
> mɔnɪ oːn ɔv hɪm hæd duːt,
> bɪ θæt hɪz reːzunz wɛr rɛdə

📖 A commentary on the spelling and pronunciation of Text 66 is in the Text Commentary Book.

11.1.1 Alliteration and rhyme

The poem is evidence that the oral traditions of Old English alliterative verse were unbroken (see section 4.1.1). In *Sir Gawayn* each line divides into two, with a short break (or cesura) in the middle. There are usually four stresses in a line, two in the first half and two in the second, three of which alliterate together, but this could vary, e.g.

/Gauan /gripped to his /ax	& /gederes hit on /hy3t
þe kay /fot on þe /fold	he be/fore /sette /
Let hit doun /ly3tly	/ly3t on þe /naked
Þat þe /scharp of þe /schalk	/schyndered þe /bones
& /schrank þur3 þe /schyire grece	& /scade hit in /twynne
Þat þe /bit of þe /broun stel	/bot on þe /grounde

Each stanza ends with a group of rhyming lines. The first short line was called the 'bob', which rhymed with two alternate lines of the following four, called the 'wheel' – ababa:

> in **stedde**.
> He brayde his bluk **aboute**
> Þat vgly bodi þat **bledde**
> Moni on of hym had **doute**
> Bi þat his resoun3 were **redde**.

11.1.2 Grammar

Personal pronouns

A short extract from *Sir Gawayn* will not include all the pronouns, but Texts 66 and 67 provide the following:

		singular			*plural*
1st person	**subject**	I			
	object	me			
—	**genitive**	—			
2nd person	**subject**	þou			
	object	þe			
	genitive	—			
		masculine	*feminine*	*neuter*	
3rd person	**subject**	he		hit	þay
	object	hym		hit	
	genitive	his		his	her
Relative pronoun		þat			

Activity 11.1

Complete the chart using the following lines from *Sir Gawayn* to identify the remaining pronouns (printed in bold type).

- **Scho** made hym so gret chere
  þat watȝ so fayr of face . . .

- **Ho** commes to þe cortyn and at þe knyȝt totes.
  Sir Gawyn **her** welcumed worþy on fyrst
  And **ho** hym ȝeldeȝ aȝayn ful ȝerne of hir wordeȝ,
  Setteȝ *hir* sofly by *his* syde and swyþely *ho* laȝeȝ . . .
  (*totes* = peeps; *ȝeldeȝ* = replies; *worþy* = courteously; *ȝerne* = eager; *swyþely* = very much; *laȝeȝ* = laughs)

- He sayde, ȝe ar welcum to welde as **yow** lykeȝ;
  þat here is, al is **yowre** awen to haue at **yowre** wylle and welde . . .
  (*welde* = use; *þat here is* = that which is here; *welde* = control)

- Where is now **your** sourquydrye and **your** conquestes?
  (*sourquydrye* = pride)

- Where schuld I wale **þe**, quoþ Gauan, where is **þy** place? . . .
  (*wale* = find)

- Bot ȝe schal be in **yowre** bed, burne, at **þyn** ese . . .
  (*burne* = knight)

- **I** schal gif **hym** of my gyft þys giserne ryche . . .
  (*giserne* = battle-axe; *riche* = splendid)

- To wone any quyle in þis won, hit watȝ not **myn** ernde . . .
  (*wone* = remain; *won* = place; *ernde* = errand)

- And **we** ar in þis valay verayly **oure** one;
  Here ar no renkes **vs** to rydde, rele as **vus** likeȝ.
  (*oure one* = on our own; *renkes* = men; *rydde* = separate; *vus likeȝ* = (it) pleases us)

- A comloker knyȝt neuer Kryst made **hem** þoȝt.
  (*comloker* = comelier, nobler; *hem þoȝt* = (it) seemed to them)

- And syþen on a stif stange stoutly **hem** hanges . . .
  (*syþen* = afterwards; *stange* = pole)

- As fortune wolde fulsun **hom** . . .
  (*fulsun* = help)

- How ledes for **her** lele luf **hor** lyueȝ han auntered . . .
  (*ledes* = knights; *her lele luf* = their true love; *lyueȝ* = lives; *han auntered* = have risked)

Noun inflections

Plural nouns in the text are:

> lokke3 bones fete schonkes renkke3 resoun3

With the exception of *fete*, which still retains its OE vowel change to mark the plural, they are marked by the ⟨s/3⟩ or ⟨es/e3⟩ suffix. It derives from the former OE strong masculine ⟨-as⟩ plural, and is now the regular MnE plural suffix.

Verb inflections

We know that a principal feature of ME is the progressive change and eventual loss of most OE inflections, and also that one marker of ME dialects is the variety of verb inflections which was the result. Text 66 provides some information about verb inflections in the North West Midland dialect. Where it does not, other words from *Sir Gawayn* are listed in brackets:

Present tense			
1st person singular	I	-e / Ø	bere, craue, telle, ask
2nd person singular	þou	-es / -e3	rede3, hattes, hopes, deles
3rd person singulars etc.	he ho hit	-es / -e3	dresses, gederes, discouere3, bo3e3,
plural	we 3e þay	-en	fallen; helden; 3elden
Past tense			
1st person singular	I	*weak vb* -ed	lakked, cheued = *got*
		strong vb	se3 = *saw*
2nd person singular	þou	-ed / es(t)	fayled; kyssedes = *kissed*
			gef = *gave*
3rd person singular	he ho hit		**Strong verbs:**
			bot, fel, let, schrank, start
		-ed	**Weak verbs:**
			blykked, faltered, foyned, gripped,
			roled, schyndered, brayde/brayd
		-d / -t	hit, layd, la3t, lyft, ra3t, scade,
			sette, bledde
plural	we 3e þay	-en	stoden, maden
infinitive			schewe (tak, gif, prayse)
imperative			(gif = *give*; kysse; lepe; lach = *seize*)
present participle			sykande = *sighing*
			wre3ande = *denouncing*
past participle		-ed	lut, ayled payed hunted
		-(e)n	slayn

Several of these inflections are familiar in MnE, and the loss of many OE inflections is clear.

Inflections in ME

As a result of the Viking settlement in the Danelaw, levelling and regularisation (see section 6.1.2.1) – the loss or reduction of most of the OE inflections – took place earlier in the Northern and Midlands dialects than in the south.

The barrier to the easy reading of *Sir Gawayn* is not its grammar, but its poetic diction and the large number of West Midlands dialect words which have not survived into Standard English.

Activity 11.2

Text 67 is the next stanza of the poem (in an edited version) and tells what happened when Gawain took up the Green Knight's challenge to strike a blow with the axe. Make some analysis of its language.

Text 67: Sir Gawayn and þe Grene Kny3t (ii)

For þe hede in his honde he halde3 vp euen
Toward þe derrest on þe dece he dresse3 þe face
& hit lyfte vp þe y3e-lydde3 & loked ful brode
& meled þus much with his muthe, as 3e may now here:
Loke, Gawan, þou be grayþe to go as þou hette3
& layte as lelly til þou me, lude, fynde,
As þou hat3 hette in þis halle, herande þise kny3tes.
To þe grene chapel þou chose, I charge þe, to fotte
Such a dunt as þou hat3 dalt – disserued þou habbe3 –
To be 3ederly 3olden on Nw 3eres morn.
Þe kny3t of þe grene chapel men knowen me mony;
For þi me for to fynde if þou frayste3, fayle3 þou neuer.
Þerfore com, oþer recreaunt be calde þe behoues.
With a runisch rout þe rayne3 he torne3,
Halled out at þe hal dor, his hed in his hande,
Þat þe fyr of þe flynt fla3e fro fole houes.
To quat kyth he becom knwe non þere,
Neuer more þen þay wyste fram queþen he wat3 wonnen.
What þenne?
Þe kyng & Gawen þare
At þat grene þay la3e & grenne
3et breued wat3 hit ful bare
A meruayl among þo menne.

📖 The complete vocabulary of Text 67 with Text 66 is listed in the Word Book.

The manuscript has four rather crudely drawn colour illustrations, the clearest of which is reproduced here in black and white. Gawain has undertaken his New

Year quest to seek the Green Knight, and on his journey comes to 'a castel þe comlokest þat euer kny3t ahte' (*a castle the comeliest that ever knight owned*). He is made welcome by the lord of the castle, whose lady, 'wat3 þe fayrest in felle, of flesch and of lyre' (*was the fairest in complexion, body and face*). Following the conventions of medieval courtly love, Gawain 'kisses her comlyly' and 'aske3 to be her seruant sothly'. While the lord of the castle is deer-hunting, and 'Gawayn þe god mon in gay bed lyge3', he hears a sound, 'a little dyn' – 'hit wat3 þe ladi, loflyest to beholde . . . '. She tells him,

3e ar welcum to my cors	*You are welcome to my body*
Yowre awen won to wale,	*Your own pleasure to take,*
Me behoue3 of fine force	*It behoves of sheer necessity*
Your seruant be and schale	*That I be your servant, and shall be*

11.2 A South-West Midlands dialect – *Piers Plowman*

Piers Plowman is one of the most famous medieval poems. It must have been a very popular work, because over fifty manuscripts have survived. The poem is an allegory of the Christian life, and of the corruption of the contemporary Church and society, written in the form of a series of dreams, or 'visions':

Ac on a May mornyng on Maluerne hulles
Me biful for to slepe ...
And merueylousliche me mette, as y may telle.

hulles = hills; *mette* = dreamed

Piers Plowman, a humble poor labourer, stands for the ideal life of honest work and obedience to the Church.

The author was William Langland, but almost nothing is known about him except what can be inferred from the poem, though we must remember that the 'dreamer' of the visions is a character in the story, and may not always be identified with the author. For example, his name, *Will*:

A louely lady of lere in lynnene yclothed
Cam doun fro þe castel and calde me by name
And sayde '*Wille*, slepestou?' . . .

Ryht with þat ran Repentaunce and rehersede his teme
And made *Will* to wepe water with his eyes.

lere = face

or William *Langland*:

> I haue lyued in *londe*, quod Y, my name is *Longe Wille* . . .

If his nickname is 'Long Will', he must have been a tall man, and unfit for hard physical work:

> Y am to wayke to worche with sykel or with sythe
> And to long, lef me, lowe to stoupe
> To wurche as a werkeman eny while to duyren

to worche = too weak; *to long . . . lowe to stoupe* = too tall to stoop low; *to duyren* = to last, endure

He lived in London, in Cornhill, with Kit and Calote (perhaps his wife and daughter, though there is no other evidence), and in the country:

> Thus y awakede, woet god, whan y wonede in Cornehull
> Kytte and y in a cote . . .
>
> And so y leue yn London and opelond bothe.
>
> . . . and riht with þat y wakede
> And calde Kitte my wyf and Calote my douhter.

woet god = God knows; *cote* = cottage; *opelond* = in the country

He was sent to university *(scole)*:

> When y ȝong was, many ȝer hennes
> My fader and my frendes foende me to scole . . .

many ȝer hennes = many years ago; *foende* = provided for

There are three versions of the poem, today called the A, B and C texts, which show that Langland continually revised and extended the poem from the 1360s until the 1380s, when the C text was probably completed. It is a fine 14th-century example of the tradition of alliterative verse in English. The dialect is of the South-West Midlands, 'but rather mixed'. There are many variant spellings in the 50 different manuscripts, quite apart from the successive versions of the text itself.

In the Prologue the writer dreams of a 'fair field full of folk', the world of contemporary society:

Text 68: Piers Plowman (i)

> In a somur sesoun whan softe was þe sonne
> Y shope me into shroudes as y a shep were
> In abite as an heremite vnholy of werkes,
> Wente forth in þe world wondres to here
> And say many sellies and selkouthe thynges.
> Ac on a May mornyng on Maluerne hulles
> Me biful for to slepe, for werynesse of-walked
> And in a launde as y lay, lened y and slepte
> And merueylousliche me mette, as y may telle.
> Al þe welthe of the world and þe wo bothe

Wynkyng, as hit were, witterliche y sigh hit;
Of treuthe and tricherye, tresoun and gyle,
Al y say slepynge, as y shal telle
Estward y beheld aftir þe sonne
And say a tour – as y trowed, Treuthe was there-ynne.
Westward y waytede in a while aftir
And seigh a depe dale – Deth, as y leue,
Woned in tho wones, and wikked spiritus.
A fair feld ful of folk fond y þer bytwene
Of alle manere men, þe mene and þe pore,
Worchyng and wandryng as þis world ascuth . . .

(C text, ed. Derek Pearsall, Edward Arnold, 1978)

📖 The vocabulary of Text 68 is listed in the Word Book.

⊕ The CD/cassette tape contains a reading of the first nine lines.

> ɪn ə sʊmər sɛːzun, hwæn sɔft wæs θə sʊnːɜ
> iː ʃɔːp meː ɪnto ʃruːdəs æz iː ə ʃeːp weːr
> ɪn abiːt æz æn herəmiːt ʊnhɔːlɪ ɔv wɛrks,
> wɛnt fɔrθ ɪn ðə wɔrld wʊndrəs fɔr tɔ heːr,
> ænd saɪ manɪ sɛlɪz ænd sɛlkuːθ θɪŋɡəs.
> ak ɔn ə maɪ mɔrnɪŋg ɔn malvɛrn hyləs,
> meː bifyl fɔr to sleːp, fɔr weːrɪnɛs ɔfwalkəd,
> ænd ɪn ə land æs iː laie, lɛnəd iː ænd slɛpt,
> ænd mɛrvɛɪlʊslɪç meː mɛtːə, æz iː maɪ tɛlːə

The printed Text 68 is edited, that is, it is based upon one of the C text manuscripts, but uses other manuscript readings or makes changes where the manuscript does not make good sense. Abbreviations are also filled out, and modern punctuation has been put in. We are therefore not reading exactly what is in a manuscript.

Remember also that the manuscripts used by the editor are copies, and not the original, and so may include changes by the scribe. Consequently, any observations we make about either Langland's dialect, or the South-West Midlands dialect in general, would need to be verified from much more evidence.

Activity 11.3

Refer to section 9.2 on how to describe dialect differences, and comment on some of the linguistic features of Text 68.

📖 There is a descriptive commentary in the Text Commentary Book.

11.2.1 Wrath and Patience in *Piers Plowman*

Among the ME manuscripts which have come down to us, very many are in the form of sermons or homilies which set out the ideals of the Church and the Christian life. A typical example is contained in 'The Parson's Tale' in Chaucer's *Canterbury Tales* (see section 13.1.2), in which the first prominent theme is sin and repentance for sin, or penitence:

> Seint Ambrose seith that penitence is the plenynge of man for the gilt that he hath doon and namoore to doon any thyng for which hym oghte to pleyne.

The second theme is the Seven Deadly Sins, those sins which were thought to be the most offensive and serious:

> Now is it behouely thing to telle whiche ben dedly synnes, that is to seyn chieftaynes of synnes. . . . Now ben they clepid chieftaynes for as muche as they ben chief and sprynge of alle othere synnes.

The Seven Deadly Sins were pride, envy, wrath, sloth, covetousness, gluttony and lust. Chaucer's Parson defines wrath (*anger*, or *ire*) as:

> This synne of ire, after the discryuyng of seint Augustyn, is wikked wil to ben auenged by word or by ded.

In *Piers Plowman*, the dreamer vividly personifies each of the Seven Deadly Sins as men or women seeking repentance. In Text 69, Wrath appears:

Text 69: Piers Plowman *(ii) (facsimile of Bodleian MS Douce 104)*

Wrath, one of the Seven Deadly Sins

Transcription

> Nau a waked wrathe : wıþ two whıte eyes
> and wıþ a neuelyng noſe : nypped hıs lıppys
> I am wraþ qd þat wyᵉ : wold gladely smyte
> Boþ wıþ ſtone ⁊ wıþ ſtaf : ⁊ ſtel a pon my enemy
> To sle hym ſleylıeſt : sleȝthes y þynke
> Ɣeȝth y ſite ın þıs seuen ȝere : I schuld noȝt wel tel
> þe harme þat I haue do : wıþ hand ⁊ wıþ tong
>
> I haue auntte to none : and an abbeſſe
> hır wer leuer swoune or swolte : þan ſuffer ony payne
> I haue be koke ın hır kechene : ⁊ þe couent ſerued
> many monthes wıþ hem : and wıþ monkes boþe
> I was þe pryoures potager : and oþer poˊ ladıes
> and made hem ıoutes of ıangelyng : how dā ıohān was baſtard
> ⁊ dam clarıce a kneȝthes doȝtˊ : a kokowold was hyr syre
> ⁊ dam þnel a pᵣſtes filıe : prıores worþ sche neuer
> for scho had chıld ī a caponıs cort : scho worþe chalāget at þᵉ eleccıoū

pus paı ſetē softe : sū tyme and dıſputē
to pou lyyeſt ⁊ pou lıyeſt : be lady ouer hē all
and pan awaked I wrathe : ⁊ wold be a uenged
and pan I cry and I craſſe : wıp my kene nayles
bıte ⁊ bete ⁊ bryng forp : such pewes
pat al ladıes me lopep : pat louep ony wırchıp

Edited version

Nau awaked Wrathe, wiþ two white eyes
And wiþ a neuelyng nose, and nypped his lippys.

'I am Wraþ,' quod þat weye, 'wold gladely smyte,
Boþ wiþ stone and wiþ staf, and stel apon my enemy
To sle hym sleyliest sleʒthes Y þynke.
þeʒth Y site in þis seuen ʒere I schuld noʒt wel tel
þe harme þat I haue do wiþ hand and wiþ tong.

I haue auntte to none and an abbesse.
Hir wer leuer swoune or swolte þan suffer ony payne.
I haue be koke in hir kechene and þe couent serued
Many monthes wiþ hem and wiþ monkes boþe.
I was þe pryoures potager and oþer pour ladies
And made hem ioutes of iangelyng – how dame Iohan was bastard
And dame Clarice a kneʒthes doʒter, a kokowold was hyr syre,
And dame Purnel a prestes filie – priores worþ sche neuer
For scho had child in a caponis cort scho worþe chalanget at þe eleccioun.
þus þai seten softe sum tyme and disputen
To 'þou lyyest' and 'þou liyest' be lady ouer hem all.
And þan awaked I wrathe and wold be auenged.
And þan I cry and I crasse : wiþ my kene nayles
Bite and bete and bryng forþ such þewes
þat al ladies me loþeþ þat loueþ ony wirchip.'

MnE translation

Now awoke Wrath, with two white eyes
And with a snivelling nose, and nipped his lips.
'I am Wrath,' quoth that man, 'would gladly smite,
Both with stone and with staff, and steal upon my enemy
To slay him (with) slyest tricks I think (up).
Though I sit for seven years I should not well tell
The harm that I haue done with hand and with tongue . . .

I haue a nun, (who is) an abbess, for an aunt,
She would rather swoon or die than suffer any pain.
I have been cook in her kitchen and the convent served,
Many months with them and with monks both.
I was the prioress's and other poor ladies' cook
And made them soups of squabbling – how dame Iohan was a bastard
And dame Clarice a knight's daughter (her sire was a cuckold)
And dame Purnel a priest's daughter – prioress would she never be,
For she was challenged at the election that she had a child in a hen-yard.
Thus they sit softly some time and dispute
Till 'thou liest' and 'thou liest' be lady over them all.
And then awakened I, Wrath, and would be avenged.
And then I cry and I scratch with my keen nails,
Bite and beat and bring forth such manners
That all ladies that love any honour loath me.'

The lexical vocabulary of Text 69 is listed in the Word Book.

11.2.2 Editing and printing a medieval text

The texts of modern printed books of older writers are all edited – that is, the surviving copies of a work are compared and a 'best' version is prepared by the editor for publication. This may be a version that does not correspond exactly to any of the originals, but draws on all of them. A typical heading in a printed text will read:

Edited from MS. Laud. Misc. 656
with variants from all other extant MSS.

To give you a short example of the problems of an editor, here are facsimiles of the same corresponding lines from two of the C text manuscripts of *Piers Plowman* – Texts 70 and 71.

Activity 11.4

(i) Compare the facsimiles, Texts 70 and 71, and make your own edited version to produce a single text. Explain your choices.

(ii) Compare your version with that printed beneath as Text 72.

The editor of the version containing Text 72 used one 'base' MS, a second to correct the first where it was clearly faulty, and two more to supply better readings where both the others were unsatisfactory. None of the MSS were Langland's original.

Text 70: Piers Plowman *(iii) (facsimile)*

(MS Cotton Vespasian B XVI f. 64v)

¶What is pfut pacience . quod actiua uita.
mekeneffe and mylde fpeche . and men of on wil
þe whiche wile lóue lede . to oure lordes place
and þat is charite chaumpion . chef of alle vertues ————

¶Anð þat ıs poːe pacıence . alle pereles to ſuffre
wheþer pouerte anð pacıence . plece moːe goð al mẏȝtí
þan do rıthful rıcheſſe . anð reſonableli to ſpenðe ————
¶ȝe quıs eſt ılle quoð concıence . quık lauðabımus eū
þaw men reðen of rıcheſſe . rıth to þe worlðes enðe
anð whan he ðrou hım to þe ðeþ . þat he ne ðrat hym ſarre
þan enẏ poːe pacıent . anð þat ı pːeue bı reſoū————————

Text 71: Piers Plowman *(iv) (facsimile)*

(MS Bodleian Douce 104)

what ıs pfite pacıens : qð actíua vıta
mılðenes anð mylð ſpech : anð mē of on wıll
þe woth wıl loue leð : to hour lorðıs place
anð þat ıs charıte : champıoū chef of al uertues
anð þat poːe pacıens : al peles to ſuffer
wher pou²te anð pacıens : pleſeþ moːe goð al myȝtẏ
þan rıȝthful rıches : anð reſonable to ſpenðe
ȝe quıs eſt ılle qð pacıens : quıke lauðam⁹ eum
þoȝth men reðe of rẏȝth rıche : to þe worlðıs enð
þan whan he ðraueþ to þe ðeþe : þᵗ he ne ðreð ſorer
þan onẏ poːe pacıens : ⁊ þat pue I be reẏſoū

In the first line the question *What is parfit pacience?* is put to Patience by Activa Vita (Active Life). Patience answers, and a second question is put – *wheþer pouerte and pacience . plece more god al myȝti?* They are allegorical characters in the poem. Piers Plowman is seeking how to live a good life, and the next Passus (section) goes on to describe the life of Dowel – that is, 'how to do well'. The text is from Passus XV, beginning at line 274:

Text 72: Piers Plowman (v) – edited version of Texts 70 and 71

(There are 18 surviving manuscripts of the C text, and the following edited version is not based on either of the facsimile texts, but mainly on the manuscripts known as Huntingdon Library MS HM 143 and British Museum MS Add.35157.)

> 'What is parfit pacience?' quod Actiua Vita.
> 'Meeknesse and mylde speche and men of o will,
> The whiche wil loue lat to our lordes place,
> And þat is charite, chaumpion, chief of all vertues;
> And þat is pore pacient, alle perelles to soffre.'
> Where pouerte and pacience plese more god almyhty
> Then rihtfullyche rychesse and resonableyche to spene?'
> '3e, *quis est ille?*' quod Pacience, '*quik laudamus eum!*
> Thogh men rede of rychesse rihte to the worldes ende
> I wiste neuere renke þat riche was, þat whan he rekene sholde
> Then when he drow to þe deth, that he ne dradd hym sarrore
> Then eny pore pacient, and þat preue y be resoun.'

> (C text, ed. Derek Pearsall, 1978)

where = whether

📖 The lexical vocabulary of Text 72 is listed in the Word Book.

Typical markers of ME West Midlands dialects include:

- OE long vowel [ɑː] has shifted; now spelt ⟨o⟩.
- OE vowel [y] remains, but spelt ⟨u⟩, e.g. *hull* for MnE *hill*.
- Suffix ⟨-ed⟩ sometimes 'devoiced' and spelt ⟨-et⟩.
- Pronouns: 3rd person feminine *ha* or *heo*; 3rd person plural possessive *hare*.
- Verbs: 3rd person plural present tense suffix ⟨-eþ⟩; present participle suffix ⟨-ende⟩.

11.3 Loan-words, 1340–59

📖 A selection of loan-words recorded during this period can be found in the Word Book, after the word-lists for Chapter 11.

12 The 14th century – East Midlands and London dialects

12.1 The origins of present-day Standard English

One of the reasons for learning about the development of the English language is to understand the relationship between dialects and Standard English in present-day English. In the conglomeration of different dialects that we call 'Middle English', there was no one recognised standard form. If we were to study the political, social and economic history of England in relation to the language, we would observe that the conditions for a standard language were beginning to emerge by the later 15th century. From the 16th century onwards, there is evidence that the need for a standard in spelling, pronunciation and grammar was being actively discussed. This naturally raised the question of which dialect or variety of the language was to be used for the standard.

What is a standard language?

One definition of a standard language, in modern sociological terms, is:

> The Standard is that speech variety of a language community which is legitimised as the obligatory norm for social intercourse on the strength of the interests of dominant forces in that society.   (Norbert Dittmar, *Sociolinguistics*, 1976)

That is, the choice is made by people imitating those with prestige or power in their society, while the latter tend to prescribe their variety of the language as the 'correct' one to use. A standard language is not superior in itself as a language for communication – all dialects are regular and 'rule-governed' – but in its adoption and development it is the language of those with social and political influence, although advocates of a standard will often claim an intrinsic superiority for it.

In 1589 the poet George Puttenham published a book called *The Arte of English Poesie*. In it he gave advice to poets on their choice of language to use. It must be that of educated, not common people:

> neither shall he follow the speach of a craftes man, or other of the inferiour sort, though he be inhabitant or bred in the best towne and citie in this Realme. But he shall follow generally the better brought vp sort, . . . ciuill and graciously behauoured and bred;

The recommended dialect was therefore Southern, not Northern or Western;

> the usuall speach of the Court, and that of London and the shires lying about London within lx. myles, and not much aboue.

(Text 113, section 16.1.2, is a longer extract from Puttenham's book.)

This defines the literary language already in use in the 16th century, and clearly describes it as the prestigious language of the educated classes of London and the south-east. London was the centre of government, trade and commerce, and so the language of the 'dominant forces' in society would carry prestige, and others would seek to copy it.

This is a simplified explanation of a complex state of affairs, but it helps to explain why the educated London dialect formed the basis of the standard language as it developed. If the centre of government and commerce had been York, the Northern dialect probably would have formed the basis for Standard English today.

The London dialect in the later 14th century derived from a mixture of ME dialects, but was strongly influenced by the East Midlands dialect in particular. London naturally attracted large numbers of men and women and their families from other areas of the country to find work, bringing their own dialectal speech with them. Historians have identified a considerable migration of people from the east Midlands to London from the late 13th century to the mid-14th century, some of whom must have become the 'dominant social class' whose language carried prestige and was imitated by others. But because people migrated into London from other parts of the country as well, there are features of Southern and Kentish also in the London dialect.

So present-day Standard English derives in its origins principally from the East Midlands dialect of Middle English, and this explains why it is comparatively easy to read Chaucer's English of the late 14th century, and other East Midlands texts. It will not be necessary therefore to examine the texts in this chapter in the detail given to those already described. You can apply the same principles of analysis to them, if you wish.

12.2 The development of writing hands (iii) – the 14th century

Anglicana is the name given to a formal cursive script used as a book hand in England in the 14th century. It originated in Italy in the 13th century, spread to France, and then to England. The first text here is an early example, written in 1291.

euome scilicet fetorem per confessionem et refrigerabit te scilicet per satisfaccionem . . .

The following example of Anglicana hand was written in 1381. The text was copied in the formal script, but with a commentary in a less formal and more cursive variety. This extract shows the last four lines of Latin text and first four of commentary.

Transcription
(abbreviations are expanded)

> **Addendo semper vnum formabis in anno.**
> **Bisexti binos iungas numero preeunti.**
> **Quod superat 7 retine septemque iacendo.**
> **Per concurrentes curres annis quater apta.**
>
> || hic agit autor de concurrentibus. vnde concurrens
> est numerus non excedens septenarium qui simul
> iunctus cum regulari feriali sit quota feria men-
> sis quuilibet incipiat et ideo dicitur concurrens a con. . . .

Contrast the following extract, also written about the mid-14th century. It is a book hand, not cursive, and shows the survival of Text hand for formal writing:

Transcription with abbreviations	Abbreviations expanded
E ANIMA ſedm ſeipam ın p̄ cedentı lıbꝛo dıctū eſt. ſⱬ quıa nō tantū ſcd²m ſeipām qʼrım̄ᵘ cong noſcᶜe aiam. ſⱬ 7 opa eı⁹ 7 paſſio neſ. 7 ea que c̄c̄ opat̄ᵘ 7 a quıb⁹	(D)E ANIMA. secundum seipsam in precedenti libro dictum est. set quia non tantum secundum seipsam querimus congnoscere animam. set et opera eius et passiones. et ea que circa operatur et a quibus . . .

When scribes were used to writing two or more different scripts, a new script would sometimes emerge in developing a cursive style, with characteristics of both. In paleographic studies these are called **bastard scripts**.

Bastard Anglicana was a fusion of Gothic Text hand with Anglicana to form a cursive, formal book hand. The first of the following examples of bastard Anglicana hand was written *c*. 1400, and the second, showing developments in style, *c*. 1460.

Transcription
(abbreviations are expanded)

fuerint homines reddent de eo racionem in
die iudicii. Ociosum quippe verbum est
quod aut vtilitate rectitudinis aut racione iuste necessitatis caret.

Henricus quintus filius Henrici iiiᵗⁱ Princeps (tumulatur)*
Wallie Dux Cornubie et Comes Cestrie apud Monemouth in
Wallia natus vicesimo die Marcii videlicet in festo sancti Cuthberti Episcopi et
Confessoris accidente tamen Dominica in passione domini apud Westmonasterium
coronatur

tumulatur belongs to the preceding line.

A new style of calligraphy, a French document hand, was introduced as a book hand into England during the 14th century and adopted widely during the 15th century. Called **Secretary hand**, it became the main script for cursive writing in the 16th century (see section 14.2; the Cely letters Texts 97–9 in Chapter 14; and the Lisle letters, Texts 100–2 in Chapter 15).

12.3 A South-East Midlands dialect – *Mandeville's Travels*

The Travels of Sir John Mandeville was one of the most popular books written in the 14th century, and over 300 manuscripts of it have survived, but its title is misleading. The original book was written in French in the 1350s by a doctor of Liège called Jehan de Bourgogne. He probably never travelled outside France, and based the stories on other men's travel writings, filling them out from his own imagination. It is believed that he adopted the name Sir John Mandeville, and wrote a preface claiming to be an Englishman born in St Albans, although the facts are not known for certain. The text in English is therefore a translation from the French by an unknown English writer using a South-East Midlands dialect. It is unlikely to be a translation by the French author, because it is sometimes an inaccurate rendering.

Another version was written in verse form. The verse original was in a North-East Midlands dialect, but the only surviving manuscript is in a 'modernized version' of the 15th century. It gives us some idea of the standard literary language that had evolved and that writers were beginning to use. Unfortunately, part of the manuscript that corresponds to Text 73 is missing, but enough remains for comparison.

Text 73: The Travels of Sir John Mandeville (i)

> Now schall I seye ʒou sewyngly of contrees and yles þat ben beʒonde the contrees þat I haue spoken of. Wherfore I seye ʒou, in passynge be the lond of Cathaye toward the high Ynde, and toward Bacharye, men passen be a kyngdom þat men clepen Caldilhe, þat is a full fair contre. And þere groweth a maner of fruyt, as þough it weren gowrdes; and whan þei ben rype, men kutten hem ato, and men fynden withinne a lytyll best, in flesch, in bon, and blode as þough it were a lytill lomb, withouten wolle. And men eten bothe the frut and the best: and þat is a gret mervueylle. Of þat frute I haue eten, allþough it were wondirfull: but þat I knowe wel, þat god is merueyllous in his werkes.

sewyngly = 'followingly' = in what follows (fr OF *suir/sewir*, to follow)

Text 74: The Boke of Mawndevile

> ...That bereth applis grete plente
> And who þat cleueth an appul atwyn
> A litille beest he fyndith thereyn.
> To a litille lombe liche it ys
> Of bloode and bone and eke of flessh
> And welle shapen atte folle
> In al thinge saufe it hath noo wolle
> And men and women þere meest and leest
> Eten of þat frute so with þat beest.

atwyn = apart, in two; *atte folle* = at full, in every detail; *saufe* = save, except that; *meest and leest* = most and least = greatest and lowliest.

📖 The lexical vocabulary of Texts 73 and 74 is listed in the Word Book.

Here is part of a page in facsimile from one of the manuscripts of the *Travels*, with a transcription.

Text 75: **The Travels of Sir John Mandeville** *(ii) (facsimile)*

Egipt is a ſtrong contre
7 manye plious hauenys
ben therin fo: there lith
in eche heuene toū gret
ryches in the entre of the
hauene / Toward the eſt
is the reðe ſe that rēnyth
right to the cete of coſ
tantyn the noble / The
contre of egipt is in
lenthe v iorneis / but not
bᵗ iij in breðe for deſert⁹
that aryn there / Betwȳ
egip 4 the lonð that is
callyd / Nūðynea arn
xii ioūneis in deſertis
the folk that wonyðe
in that contre arn criſ
tene men but thy arȳ
blake of colō for the oū
gret hete that is there
and brennynge of the ſonne

The lexical vocabulary of Text 75 is listed in the Word Book.

12.4 The London dialect – Thomas Usk

From the late 14th century onwards we begin to find many more examples of everyday language surviving in letters and public documents than we do for earlier English. Literary language draws upon the ordinary language of its time, but in a special way, and we cannot be at all sure that the literature of a period tells us how people actually spoke.

London in Chaucer's day was, from time to time, the scene of violence and demonstration in the streets, and the following text describes one such series of incidents in the 1380s. Thomas Usk was involved with what turned out to be the wrong side in the political factions of his day, for he was unsuccessful in the appeal from which Texts 76 and 77 are taken, and later executed.

The Appeal is 'an example of the London English of a fairly well-educated man'. The original spelling is retained, but the punctuation is modern.

Text 76: From Thomas Usk's Appeal, 1384 (i)

I Thomas Vsk . . . knowleched thes wordes & wrote hem with myn owne honde.
. . . Also, that day that Sir Nichol Brembre was chose mair, a non after mete kom John Northampton to John Mores hows, & thider kom Richard Norbury & William Essex, & ther it was accorded that the mair, John Northampton, sholde sende after the

persones that thilk tyme wer in the comun conseil of craftes, and after the wardeyns of craftes, so that thei sholde kome to the goldsmithes halle on the morwe after, & ther the mair sholde speke with hem, to loke & ordeigne how thilk eleccion of Sir Nichol Brembre myght be letted; &, nad it be for drede of our lord the kyng, I wot wel eueri man sholde haue be in others top. And than sente he Richard Norbury, Robert Rysby, & me, Thomas Vsk, to the Neyte, to the duk of lancastre, to enforme hym in thys wyse: 'Sir, to day, ther we wolden haue go to the eleccion of the mair in goddes peas & the kynges, ther kom jn an orrible companye of criers, no man not whiche, & ther, with oute any vsage but be strength, chosen Sir Nichol Brembre mair, a yein our maner of eleccion to forn thys vsed; wher fore we preye yow yf we myght haue the kynges writ to go to a Newe eleccion.' And the duk seide: 'Nay, certes, writ shul ye non haue, auise yow amonges yowr selue.' & her of I appele John Northampton, John More, Richard Norbury, & William Essex.

Text 77: From Thomas Usk's Appeal, 1384 (ii)

Also, atte Goldsmithes halle, when al the people was assembled, the mair, John Northampton, reherced as euel as he koude of the eleccion on the day to forn, & seyde that truly: 'Sirs, thus be ye shape for to be ouer ronne, & that,' quod he, 'I nel noght soeffre; lat vs rather al be ded atones than soeffre such a vylenye.' & than the comunes, vpon these wordes, wer stered, & seiden truly they wolde go to a nother eleccion, & noght soeffre thys wrong, to be ded al ther for attones in on tyme; and than be the mair, John Northampton, was euery man boden gon hom, & kome fast a yein strong in to Chepe with al her craftes, & I wene ther wer a boute a xxx craftes, & in Chepe they sholden haue sembled to go to a newe eleccion, &, truly, had noght the aldermen kome to trete, & maked that John Northampton bad the poeple gon hoom, they wolde haue go to a Newe eleccion, & in that hete haue slayn hym that wolde haue letted it, yf they had myght; and ther of I appele John Northampton.

(R. W. Chambers and Marjorie Daunt (eds) *A Book of London English, 1384–1425,* 1931)

📖 Selected vocabulary from Texts 76 and 77 is listed in the Word Book.

Activity 12.1

Choose any of the texts in this chapter and use the following check-list to find evidence of their being written in the East Midlands or London dialect.

Features of East Midlands and London dialects

Pronunciation and spelling:

- OE long [aː] has rounded to [ɔː] , spelt ⟨o⟩ or ⟨oo⟩.
- OE short [æ] written ⟨æ⟩ is now [a] and written ⟨a⟩.
- OE ⟨eo⟩ has smoothed and is now spelt ⟨e⟩.
- OE [y] has unrounded to [i], spelt ⟨i⟩, but there are inconsistencies in the London dialect, and some words originally with OE [y] use Kentish [e] or Southern [u].

Pronouns

- 3rd person plural, East Midlands *he*, *here*, *hem*; London, *they*, *hir*, *hem*.

Verbs

- 3rd person singular present tense suffix ⟨-eþ⟩.
- 3rd person plural present tense suffix ⟨-en⟩.
- Past participle suffix ⟨-en⟩ retained, but prefix ⟨y-⟩ lost generally in East Midlands, but not consistent in the London dialect, which sometimes retains prefix ⟨y-⟩ and drops the suffix ⟨-en⟩.
- Infinitive suffix ⟨-en⟩ generally retained (East Midlands), but may be dropped in London dialect (Southern dialect influence).

12.5 Loan-words, 1360–79

📖 A selection of loan-words recorded during this period can be found in the Word Book, after the word-lists for Chapter 12.

13 The London dialect – Chaucer, late 14th century

13.1 Chaucer's prose writing

Geoffrey Chaucer was born in the 1340s and died in 1400. He was acknowledged in his own day as the greatest contemporary writer, not only in poetry but also in the arts of rhetoric and philosophy. The following tribute to Chaucer after his death is from a poem by Thomas Hoccleve:

> Alas my worthy mayster honorable
> Thys landes verray tresouur and rychesse
> Deth by thy deth hath harme irriparable
> Vnto vs don; hir vengeable duresse
> Despoyled hath this land of the swetnesse
> Of rethorik, for vnto Tullius
> Was nere man so lyk amonges vs.
> Also, who was hier in philosophy
> To Aristotle in our tonge but thou?
> The steppes of Virgile in poesie
> Thow filwedist eek, men wot wel enow . . .

Tullius = Marcus Tullius Cicero, d. 43 BC, Roman writer and orator
Aristotle = Greek philosopher, d. 322 BC
Virgile = Virgil, Roman poet, d. 19 BC, author of the epic *The Aeneid*

Chaucer wrote in the London dialect of the ME of his time, that is the literary form of the language based on the speech of the educated class. The dialect of the mass of ordinary people living in London must have been as different from Chaucer's, in both form and pronunciation, as the present-day Cockney and London area dialectal accent is from educated RP and Standard English.

13.1.1 'The Tale of Melibeus'

The Canterbury Tales is Chaucer's best known work, but some of the tales are much more widely read than others. Most of them are in verse, and it is unlikely that the two tales in prose will ever be popular, since their content and style are now out of fashion. The first prose tale is supposed to be told by Chaucer himself, after his comic satire on narrative romances, 'The Tale of Sir Thopas', has been interrupted by the Host:

Namoore of this for goddes dignytee . . .

Chaucer agrees to tell 'The Tale of Melibeus',

I wol yow telle a litel thyng in prose
That oghte like yow as I suppose
Or ellis certes ye be to daungerous.
It is a moral tale vertuous . . .

dangerous = difficult to please, fastidious

The tale is a translation from a French prose work which is itself based on a Latin original. Here are the opening paragraphs:

Text 78: Chaucer's 'The Tale of Melibeus' (facsimile)

A ẏong man called Melıbeus mẏghty and rẏche
bygat vpon hıs wyfe that called was Prudnce a doughteȝ
whıche that called was Sophıe vpon a day by fell that he
for hıs dıfpoȝte ıs went ın to the ffeeldes hym to play hıs wyfe
and eke hıs doughteȝ hath he lafte wyth ın hıs houfe of
which the doȝes weȝen fafte ẏ fhette thre of hıs olde foes
han ıt efpıed and fetten laddeȝs to the walles of hıs houfe
and by wyndowes ben entred and betten hıs wyfe and
wounded hıs doughteȝ wyth fyue moȝtall woundes ın

fyue places sondჳy that is to seyn in heჳ fete in her handis
in heჳ heჳes in heჳ nofe and in heჳ mouthe and leften heჳ foჳ
ðeðe and wenten away / Whan Melibeus ჳetoჳned was in
to his houfe and sey all this myfchefe he lyke a maðde man
rentyng hif clothef gan to wepe and crye. Prudence his
wyfe as feჳthfoჳth as she ðurfte byfought hym of his wepჳg
foჳ to stynte but nought for thy he gan* to crye and wepen
euyჳ the lengeჳ the moჳe

nought for thy meant 'nevertheless'. The verb *gan* in *he gan to crye and wepe in* was used as an auxiliary verb, to indicate past time – *he wept*.

📖 The lexical vocabulary of Text 78 is listed in the Word Book.

13.1.2 'The Parson's Tale'

The second prose tale has already been referred to in section 11.2.1 – 'The Parson's Tale'. It is a translation of two treatises in Latin, the first on penitence and the second on the Seven Deadly Sins. The following text is the commentary on gluttony in the second treatise.

Text 79: Chaucer's 'The Parson's Tale' (facsimile)

Aftere auarice comyth Glotenye Which is expres a gayne the cōmaundmēt
of god What Gloteny is Glotenye is vnmeſurable appetit to ete or
to drinke or ellys to don ynogh to the vnmeſurable apetit and deſordeynee
coueitiſe to ete or to drinke this synne corrumped all this world . as is
wel shewd in the synne of adam and of Eue

he þ^t is vſaunt to this synne of Glotenye he ne may noo
synne w^tſtonde he mote ben in servage of all vices ffor it is the deuell
hoord there he hideth hym and reſteth him this synne hath manye
spices Of diurſe speces of Glo^e þ^e firſt is drōkenneſſe The firſte is dronkynneſſe
that is the horryble sepulture of mannes ʒeſon and þ⁹for whan a man
is dronken . he hathe loſt is reſoun and this is dedly synne But sothely
whan that a man is not wont to ſtronge drinke and peruenture ne
knoweth not the strenght of the drinke or hathe ffebleſſe in his hedd
or hathe trauayled þoʒow the whiche he drinketh the moʒe al be he
sodenly caught w^t drinke, it is no dedly synne but venyall The *(end of page)*

The seconde spece of Glotenye is þ^t the spirit of a
man wexeth all trouble for dronkeneſſe bireueth hym the diſcrecyoū
of his wytte The iijᵈᵉ spece of Glo^e The therde spece of Glotenye is
wh^anne a man deuoureth his mete and hathe no ryghtfull man⁹e of
etynge. The iiij^{te} spice of Glo^e The iiij^{te} spece of Glotenye is wh^anne
thourgh the grete habundaunce of his mete the humõs of his body
ben deſtemperyd The v̄ spece of Glo^e The fyfte is foryetylneſſe by
to muchell drinkeynge ffor which som tyme a man foʒgeteth er the
moʒwe what he ded at evyn or on the nyght before . . .

Theſe ben the v fyngers of the deueles hand by
Whiche he draweth folk to synne.

📖 The vocabulary of Text 79 is listed in the Word Book.

Activity 13.1

Use the check-list in section 13.3.1 to describe some of the word-forms and
grammar of Texts 78 and 79.

13.2 Chaucer's verse

Here are facsimiles, from two manuscripts known as the Harley MS and the
Hengwrt MS, of an extract from the Prologue to Chaucer's 'Friar's Tale'. It follows
the 'Summoner's Tale' about corrupt friars, so the friar is about to cap it with a story
about a summoner.

Text 80: Chaucer's 'The Friar's Tale' (i) (facsimile)

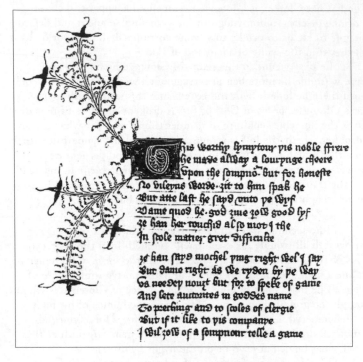

Facsimile from Harley MS 7334

Τhis woʒthy lymytour þis noble ffrere
he made alway a lourynge cheere
upon the ſompnoᵘ. but foʒ honeſte
Ño vileyns woʒðe. ʒit to hım ſpak he
But atte laſt he ſayd vnto þe wyf
Dame quoð he. god ʒiue ʒow good lyf
ʒe han her touchıð alſo mot 1 the
1n ſcole maτieρ gret dıfficulte
ʒe han ſayð mochel pıng rıght wel 1 ſay
But ðame rıght as we ryðen by þe way
Vs neeðep nouʒt but foʒ to ſpeke of game
Anð lete auctoɹıtes ın goððes name
Τo pɹechıng anð to ſcoles of clergıe
But ıf ıt lıke to pıs companye
1 wıl ʒow of a ſompnour telle a game

📖 Selected vocabulary from Text 80 is listed in the Word Book.

Text 81: Chaucer's The Friar's Tale (ii) (facsimile)

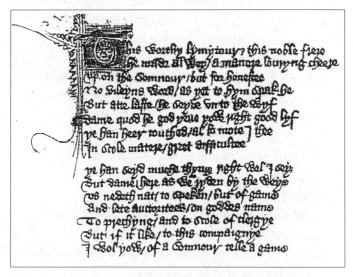

Hengwrt MS

This woɹthy lẏmẏtour / thıs noble fıeɹe
He maðe al weẏ / a manere lourẏng cheere
vp on the Somnour / but for honeſtee
Ïlo vıleẏns worð / as yet to hym spak he
But atte laſte / he seẏðe vn to the wyf
ðame quoð he / goð yeue yow rıght gooð lyf
ye han heer toucheð / al ſo mote I thee
Ïn scole matere / gɹ̣et ðifficultee

ye han seẏð muche thyng / rıght wel **1** seẏe
But ðame / here as we rẏðen bẏ the weẏe
Vs neðeth nat / to speken / but of game
And lete auctoɹ̣tees / on goððes name
Ϲo prechẏng / and to scole of clergẏe
But ıf ıt lıke / to thıs compaıgnẏe
I wol ẏow / of a Somnour telle a game

The following facsimile of the same part of the 'Friar's Tale' is from Caxton's first printed edition. It has either been taken from a poor copy, or else it has been inaccurately typeset, as several lines fail to scan fluently. Compare it line by line with the Harley and Hengwrt MSS.

> This nobyl lymytour this worthy frere
> He made alwey a maner lourynge chere
> Vp on the sompnour but for honeste
> No vileyns wordz as yet spak he
> But atte laste he sayde vnto the wyf of bathe
> Dame qd he god pou euer kepe fro scathe
> For here pe haue touchidz also moot y the
> In scole mater a ful greet difficulte
> Pe haue saidz muche thingz right coriouslp
> But dame here as pe ridep be the Wey
> Ws nedith not to speke but of game
> Andz lete auctours be a goddis name
> To prechinge andz to scole of clergye
> Andz yf it likith vnto this gentil companye
> I Wolde pou of a sompnour telle a game

🜨 A reading of the Hengwrt MS text is recorded on the CD/cassette tape.

> ðıs wɔrðı lımıtuːr, ðıs nɔːblə freːr
> heː maːd alweı ə mæneːr luːrıŋg ʧeːr
> ʊpɔn ðə sʊmnuːr, bʊt fɔr ɔnesteː,
> nɔː vıleınz wɔrd æz jet to hım spæk heː.
> bʊt ætːə læst heː seıd ʊnto ðə wiːf,
> 'daːmə' kwɔd heː 'gɔd jeːv juː rıçt goːd liːf,
> jeː hæn heːr tʊʧed, al sɔ moːt iː θeː,
> ın scoːl mæteːrə greːt dıfıkʊlteː.
> jeː hæn seıd mʊʧə θıŋg, rıçt wel iː seıjə.
> bʊt daːm, heːr æz weː riːdən bı ðə weıjə,
> ʊs neːdɛθ nat to speːkən bʊt ɔv gaːmə,
> ənd leːt aʊktɔriteːz, ɔn gɔdez naːmə,
> to preıʧŋg ænd to skoːl(ə) ɔv klerʤiːə.
> bʊt ıf ıt liːkə to ðıs kɔmpaınjiːə,
> iː wɔl juː ɔv ə sʊmnuːr tel ə gaːmə

13.2.1 Verse form

The verse form of the *Canterbury Tales* was what we now know as 'rhyming couplets' – each pair of lines rhymes – and in a metre traditionally called 'iambic pentameter'. The unit of rhythm is said to be a 'foot' containing an unstressed syllable (x) followed by a stressed syllable (/) – x /, which is called an **iamb**, and there are five of these in a line of verse (*penta* means *five* in Greek, hence **penta-meter)**. Therefore a regular iambic pentameter line contains ten syllables of alternating unstressed and stressed syllables: x / x / x / x / x / . Here is a regular couplet from the 'Friar's Tale':

> He was if I shal yeuen him his laude
> A theef and eek a somnour and a baude

> He **was** / if **I** / shal **ye** / uen **him** / his **laude**
> A **theef** / and **eek** / a **som** / nour **and** / a **baude**

yeuen = give; *laude* = due honour; *eek* = also

Lines of verse are not always absolutely regular, but with this pattern in mind, we have plenty of evidence in Chaucer's verse about the number of syllables in words, and their pronunciation and stress patterns. For example, if we assume that the following couplet from the 'Friar's Tale' is metrically regular,

> Thy body and this panne been myne by right
> Thou shalt with me to helle yet to nyght

then it is clear that the word *panne* is pronounced as one syllable [pæn], but that *helle* has probably two syllables [hɛl – lə],

> Thy **bo** / dy **and** / this **panne** / been **myne** / by **right**
> Thou **shalt** / with **me** / to **hel** / le **yet** / to **nyght**

which is important evidence about the status of suffixes like ⟨-e⟩ in Chaucer's English. The final ⟨e⟩ was not pronounced in *panne*, but it was in *helle*. The probable reason in this case is that in the phrase *to helle*, the ⟨e⟩ of *helle* is a surviving inflection from Old English, marking the grammatical category called 'case'.

What it shows is that in Chaucer's day, some final ⟨-e⟩ suffixes were pronounced, and some were not, varying from one dialect area to another as the last of the Old English suffixes finally disappeared in pronunciation, and so changed the grammar of the language. Chaucer had a choice, which helped him in making his lines of verse flow easily. However, when reading his verse, remember that a final ⟨-e⟩ before a word beginning with a vowel or ⟨h⟩ is elided, and not pronounced, as in the lines,

> Thann(e) hau(e) I get(e) of yow maistrie quod she
> Sith I may gouern and ches(e) as me list.

In Text 82 following, the form *thest* for *the est* (l. 12) in the Harley MS demonstrates this kind of elision of a final ⟨e⟩ (though it is not a suffix in this case), but the form *the Est*, in the Hengwrt MS, shows an equally acceptable variation in pronunciation in which the vowel is not elided.

Today we pronounce words like *execution*, *fornication* and *defamation* as 4-syllable words, with the final syllable pronounced as [ʃən]. The evidence from Chaucer's verse is that these words were pronounced with 5 syllables, *ex-e-cu-ci-on*, as in line 68, *That boldely did execucion*. If you say this using present-day pronunciation, there are only 8 syllables *That / bold / ly / did / ex / e / cu / tion*. We can infer therefore that Chaucer's *boldely* had 3 syllables, and *execucion* 5, to make a regular 10-syllable line:

That	**bold**	e	**ly**	did	**ex**	e	**cu**	ci	**on**
1	2	3	4	5	6	7	8	9	10

13.3 Editing a text

Now follow transcriptions of two pages from each of the two manuscripts, Harley and Hengwrt, which include Texts 80 and 81.

Punctuation in the manuscripts

Activity 13.2

Select a part of the texts, and write out your edited version, choosing what you think is the better text when there are differences between the two manuscripts. Add present-day conventions of punctuation. Discuss any problems you found.

The Harley MS

The Harley MS has virtually no punctuation. Speech is not indicated by quotation marks, there are no commas or full-stops to mark off units of grammar, and capital letters mark the beginning of each line of verse, not of sentences. There are no apostrophes to mark the possessive of nouns – *the freres tale*, (the friar's tale), *hir liues ende* (their lives' end), *in goddes name* (in God's name), *euery tounes eende* (every town's end). Apostrophes for this purpose were not introduced until the end of the 17th century.

The Hengwrt MS

Each line is divided into two by a *virgule*, the sign ⟨ / ⟩, which marks a **cesura**, or short pause in the line.

Text 82: End of 'The Summoner's Tale' and beginning of 'The Friar's Tale'

Harley MS
Thanne haue I gete of yow maistrie quod she
Sith I may gouern and chese as me list
ȝe certis wyf quod he I hold it best
Kys me quod sche we ben no lenger wroþe
ffor by my trouþe · I wol be to ȝow boþe
This is to say ȝe boþe fair and good
I pray to god þat I mot sterue wood
But I be to ȝow also good and trewe
As euer was wyf siþþen þe world was newe
And but I be to morow as fair to seen
As eny lady emp(er)esse or queen
That is bitwixe thest and eek þe west
Doth by my lyf right euen as ȝow lest

Hengwrt MS
Thanne haue I gete / of yow maistrye / quod she
Syn I may chese / and gouerne as me lest
Ye c(er)tes wyf quod he / I holde it best
Kys me quod she / we be no lenger wrothe
ffor by my trouthe / I wol be to yow bothe
This is to seyn / ye bothe fair and good
I pray to god / that I mote steruen wood
But I to yow / be al so good and trewe
As euere was wyf / syn þ(a)t the world was newe
And but I be to morn / as fair to sene
As any lady / Emperice / or Queene
That is bitwix the Est / and eek the West
Do with my lyf and deth / right as yow lest

Cast vp þe cortyns and look what þis is

And whan þe knyght saugh verrayly al þis

That sche so fair was and so ȝong þerto

ffor ioye he hent hir in his armes tuo

His herte bathid in a bath of blisse

A thousand tyme on rowe he gan hir kisse

And sche obeyed him in euery þing

That mighte doon him pleisauns or likyng

And þus þay lyue vnto her lyues ende

In parfyt ioye and ihū crist vs sende

Housbondes meke ȝonge and freissche on bedde

And grace to ouer byde hem þat we wedde

And eek I pray to Jhū schort her lyues

That wil nought be gouerned after her wyues

And old and angry nygardes of despense

God sende hem sone verray pestilence

There endith þe Wif of Bathe hire tale

There bygȳneth þe p(ro)log of þe ffreres tale.

This worthy lymytour þis noble ffrere
he made alway a lourynge cheere
Vpon the sompno¹. but for honeste

No vileyns worde . ȝit to him spak he

But atte last he sayd vnto þe wyf

Dame quod he · god ȝiue ȝow good lyf

ȝe han her touchid al so mot I the

In scole matter gret difficulte

ȝe han sayd mochel þing right wel I say

But dame right as we ryden by þe way

Vs needeþ nouȝt but for to speke of game

And lete auctorites in goddes name

To preching and to scoles of clergie

But if it like to þis companye

I wil ȝow of a sompnour telle a game

Par de ȝe may wel knowe by þe name

That of a sompnour may no good be sayd

I pray ȝow þat noon of ȝow be euel a payd

A Sompnour is a renner vp and doun

Wiþ maundemētz for fornicaciū

And is y bete at euery tounes eende

Our oste spak a sir ȝe schold been heende

And curteys as a man of ȝour estaat

In company we wol haue no debaat

Telle ȝour tale and let þe sompno¹ be

Nay quod þe sompnour let him say to me

What so him list whan it comeþ to my lot

By god I schal him quyten euery grot

I schal him telle which a gret honour

Is to ben a fals flateryng lymytour

Cast vp the Curtyn / looke how þ(a)t it is

And whan the knyght / say verraily al this

That she so fair was / and so yong ther to

ffor ioye he hente hir / in his armes two

His herte bathed / in a bath of blisse

A thousand tyme a rewe / he gan hir kisse

And she obeyed hym / in euery thyng

That myghte do hym plesance / or likyng

And thus they lyue / vn to hir lyues ende

In p(ar)fit ioye / and I(es)u crist vs sende

Housbondes meke / yonge and fressh a bedde

And grace / tou(er)byde hem that we wedde

And eek / I praye I(es)u short her lyues

that nought wol be gou(er)ned /by hir wyues

And olde / and angry nygardes of dispence

God sende hem soone / verray pestilence

Here endeth the Wyues tale of Bathe

The prologe of the ffreres tale.

This worthy lymytour / this noble frere
He made alwey / a manere louryng cheere
Vp on the Somnour / but for honestee

No vileyns word / as yet to hym spak he

But atte last / he seyde vn to the wyf

Dame quod he god yeue yow right good lyf

Ye han heer touched / al so mot I thee

In scole matere / greet difficultee

Ye han seyd muche thing / right wel I seye

But dame / here as we ryden by the weye

Vs needeth nat to speken / but of game

And lete Auctoritees / on goddes name

To prechyng / and to scole of clergye

But if it like / to this compaignye

I wol yow / of a Somnour telle a game

Pardee / ye may wel knowe by the name

That of a Somno(ur) / may no good be sayd

I praye / that noon of yow / be ypayd

A somnour / is a rennere vp and doun

With mandementz / for fornicacioun

And is ybet / at euery townes ende

Oure hoost tho spak / a sire ye sholde be hende

And curteys / as a man of your estaat

In compaignye / we wol no debaat

Telleth youre tale / and lat the Somno(ur) be

Nay quod the Somno(ur) / lat hym seye to me

What so hym list / whan it comth to my lot

By god / I shal him quyten euery grot

I shal him telle / which a gret honour

It is / to be a flaterynge lymytour

And his offis I schal him telle I wis
Oure host answerd and sayd þe sompno¹ þis
And after þis he sayd vnto þe frere
Telleþ forþ ȝour tale my maister deere

W Thilom þer was duellyng in my conutre
  An erchedeken a man of gret degre
  That boldely did execucion
In punyschyng of fornicacion
Of wicchecraft and eek of bauderye
Of diffamacioun and auoutrie
Of chirchereues and of testamentes
Of contractes and of lak of sacraments
And eek of many anoþer cryme
Which neediþ not to reherse at þis tyme
Of vsur and of symony also
But certes lecchours did he grettest woo

And of / many another maner(*e*) cryme
Which nedeth nat rehercen / for this tyme
And his office / I shal hym telle ywys
Oure hoost answerde / þees namoore of this
And after this / he seyde vn to the frere
Tel forth your tale / leeue maister deere

Here endeth the prologe of the Frere
and bigynneth his tale

W Hilom / ther was duellynge in my contree
  An Erchedekne / a man of hy degree
That boldely / dide execuciou(*n*)
In punysshyng of Fornicaciou(*n*)
Of wicchecraft / and eek of Bawderye
Of diffamaciou(*n*) / and auoutrye
Of chirche Reues / and of testamentz
Of contractes / and eek of lakke of sacramentz

Of vsure / and of Symonye also
But certes / lecchours / did he grettest wo

13.3.1 Word-forms and grammar

Activity 13.3

Use the following list to identify some of the differences in the word-forms and grammatical structures of Chaucer's English which contrast with modern Standard English.

Nouns
- What are the noun inflections for plural number and possessive case? Can you suggest a reason why some plural nouns in the texts are marked with ⟨-z⟩ rather than ⟨-s⟩?
- What forms of possessive structures can you find in the texts?

Pronouns
- What are the forms of the personal pronouns to be found in the texts – 1st, 2nd and 3rd person, singular and plural?
- Which relative pronouns are used? Quote the examples in the texts.

Verbs
- Compare the forms of the infinitive in both MS texts.
- What other verb inflections are there in the texts? Compare them with present-day English verb inflections.

- Examine forms of the past tense for evidence of strong (irregular) and weak (regular) verbs and compare their MnE forms.
- Does *have* as an auxiliary verb mark perfective aspect in a verb phrase?
- Are there any examples of the passive voice?
- Can you explain the constructions *as me list* (l. 2), *What so him list* (l. 58) and *vs needeþ nouʒt* (l. 42), when the MnE forms would be *as I please, whatever he pleases* and *we need not*?
- Identify the forms of the verb *be*.
- What is the meaning of *doon* (do) in *That mighte doon him pleisauns* (l. 21), and of *did* in *lecchours did he grettest woo* (l. 77)?

Grammar
- How is the negative formed?
- What is the meaning of *but* in,

> *But I be to ʒow also good and trewe*   (l. 8)
> *And but I be to morow*   (l. 10)
> *Vs needeþ nouʒt but for to speke of game*   (l. 42)

- Comment on word order.
- Are any constituents missing that would be expected in present-day English?

13.3.2 Vocabulary

Any text taken from Chaucer's writing will produce a fair proportion of words assimilated from French. This, of course, is not reliable evidence of the amount of French vocabulary in the common speech of uneducated men and women. The number of words of French origin in the present-day **core vocabulary** of English would be indirect evidence, and some knowledge of the loss of common Old English words would also help to indicate the extent of the infiltration.

Function words
Almost all function words derive from Old English. MnE *they, them, their* are important exceptions. They derive from the Old Norse dialects of Danish Viking settlers, adopted first in Northern England, and gradually moving south. Chaucer writes *they*, but still used OE *her* and *hem*.

Lexical words in Text 82
Word types: 229, of which OE 156 = 68%, ON 7 = 3% (71%); OF 61 = 27%. Middle Dutch 2 words; Latin/Greek 3 words.

Loan-words in Text 82
Chaucer's vocabulary in Text 82 has just over a quarter of its lexical words derived from French. A list of the words derived from OF or ON and the very small number from Latin or Middle Dutch follows. The Harley MS words are in the left-hand column.

From Old Norse

nygardes	*nygardes*
angry	*angry*
gete	*gete*
housbondes	*housbondes*
cast	*cast*
meke (= *meek*)	*meke*
nay	*nay*

From Latin or Greek

difficulte	*difficultee*
erchedeken	*erchedekne*
testamentes	*testamentz*

From Old French

auctorites	*auctoritees*
auoutrie (= *adultery*)	*auoutrye*
bauderye	*bawderye*
certis/certes	*certes*
cheere	*cheere*
clergie	*clergye*
company(e)	*compaignye*
contractes	*contractes*
cortyns	*curtyn*
countre	*contree*
cryme	*cryme*
curteys	*curteys*
dame	*dame*
debaat	*debaat*
degre	*degree*
despense	*dispence*
diffamacioun	*diffamaciou(n)*
emperesse	*emperice*
estaat	*estaat*
execucion	*execuciou(n)*
flateryng	*flaterynge*
fornicacion	*fornicacioun*
freissche	*fressh*
frere/ffrere/ffreres	*frere/ffreres*
gouern(ed)	*gou(er)n(ed)*

grace	*grace*
honeste	*honestee*
honour	*honour*
ioye	*ioye*
lecchours	*lecchours*
lymytour	*lymytour*
maister	*maister*
maistrie	*maistrye*
maundementz	*mandementz*
–	*manere*
matter	*matere*
noble	*noble*
obeyed	*obeyed*
offis	*office*
host/oste	*hoost*
par de	*pardee*
parfyt	*p(ar)fit*
payd	*ypayd*
–	*pees*
pestilence	*pestilence*
pleisauns	*plesance*
preching	*prechyng*
pray	*pray/praye*
p(ro)log	*prologe*
punyschyng	*punysshyng*
quyten	*quyten*
reherse	*rehercen/reherse*
sacraments	*sacramentz*
symony	*symonye*
sir	*sire*
sompnour	*somnour*
touchid	*touched*
vsur	*vsure*
verray	*verray*
verrayly	*verraily*
vileyns	*vileyns*

From Middle Dutch

grot (= *fragment*)	*grot*
lak	*lakke*

📖 A complete word-list, including the OE vocabulary, is in the Word Book.

📖 A detailed commentary on Text 82 is in the Text Commentary Book.

13.4 Loan-words, 1380–99

📖 A selection of loan-words recorded during this period can be found in the Word Book, after the word-lists for Chapter 13.

14 Early Modern English I – the 15th century

You will have seen that the 14th-century texts in Chapters 12 and 13 are relatively easy to read without much help from a glossary – at least it is usually possible to make out the sense of late ME writing in the East Midlands and London dialects. The following 15th century is for us, looking back, a period of transition to present-day English, and we talk of the **Early Modern English** period (**EMnE**), from about 1450, in the development of the language.

14.1 The beginnings of a standard language

Standard, official languages, with their rules of word structure and grammar and choices of vocabulary, are all written in the same way, but may be spoken in a variety of dialectal accents. An agreed writing system has many advantages, and the consensus of educated opinion towards conformity in spelling and grammatical usage is part of social history.

> From 1066 to 1400, while Latin and French were the official written languages in England, there was no official English standard. English writing was regional and individual. During the 15th century an official standard began to emerge.
>
> (J. H. Fisher et al. (eds), *An Anthology of Chancery English*, 1984)

It is important to remember that this does not entail standard speech, either in pronunciation or in vocabulary and grammar, although in contemporary England, certainly, there are social pressures towards conformity which ignore the continuing wide diversity of dialectal English.

In the 15th century, the City of Westminster, two miles distant and separate from London, had been the centre of government administration since the second half of the 12th century. The Chancery (originally *chancelery*) was the Court of the Lord Chancellor, and the written English that developed there in the 15th century was to become a standard, both in its style of handwriting ('Chancery hand') and in its vocabulary and grammar, because the use of English in administrative documents, rather than French, was re-established after about 1430.

14.2 The development of writing hands (iv) – the 15th century

Secretary hand was briefly mentioned at the end of section 12.2, having been first introduced into England at the end of the 14th century. It was widely adopted by scribes during the 15th century, but did not develop into a universally acceptable cursive style until the end of the century (for 16th-century examples, see section 15.1).

Here are two examples of 15th century Secretary book hand. The first is from a Latin commentary on Psalm 118, written *c*.1430:

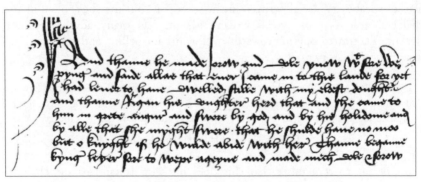

Transcription

(Ώerito ergo repellitur quia maledicto dignus est quia polluit magis et impedit opus quod

negligenter putauerit exequendum . Consieremus ergo vtrum bonitas sit repelli ab opere negli /

gentem an vero retineri et ymaginem rei huius ex aliis sumamus artibus . Curat medicus …

The second is from *The Brut in English*, *c*.1470. This facsimile is from the section which was the source of Shakespeare's play *King Lear*.

And thanne he made sorow and Dole ynow w^t sore We-
pyng⁹ and saide allas that euer I came into this lande for yet
I had leuer to haue Dwelled stille with my eldest doughter⸝
And thanne Rigan his Doughter herd that and she came to
him in grete angur⁹ and swore by god and by his holidome and
by alle that she myght swere that he shulde haue no moo
but o knyght if he wulde abide with her⁹ Thanne beganne
kyng⁹ leyer⁹ sore to wepe ageyne and made mech Dole 7 sorow …

Bastard Secretary was the name given to a group of cursive hands which began to develop in the late 14th century with the need for faster writing by clerks and scriveners. It combined features of formal Text hand with French Secretary, and was later called Bastard Secretary by teachers of writing in the early 16th century – it was in fact the precursor of English Secretary hand, and not derived from it as the name suggests. There are many varieties of this hand, for example:

And Petir bithoughte on the word of Jhesu, that he hadde seid, Bifore the cok crowe, thries thou schalt denye me. And he zede out, and wepte bitterli.

The following example of Bastard Secretary is a notary's certificate of 1396.

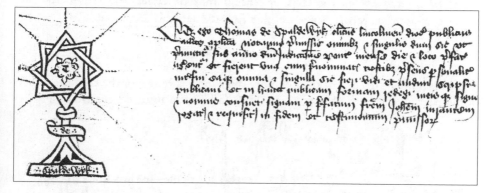

Transcription
(abbreviations expanded)

> Et ego Thomas de Spaldewyk clericus lincolniensis diocesis publicus
> auctoritate apostolica notarius premissis omnibus & singulis dum sic vt
> premittitur sub anno domini indiccione Pontificatu mense die & loco prefatis
> agerentur et fierent vna cum prenominatis testibus presens personaliter
> interfui eaque omnia et singula sic fieri vidi et audiui scripsi
> publicavi et in hanc publicam formam redegi meisque signo
> & nomine consuetis signaui per prefatum fratrem Johannem iurantem
> rogatus et requisitus in fidem et testimonium premissorum.

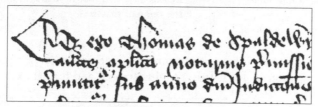

Enlarged top left-hand corner of above text

The term **Court hand** is used in a variety of ways by scholars, referring generally to (i) types of cursive script used for business and letter writing, in contrast to the Textura type of script used as a formal book hand, (ii) any document hand produced by one of the official offices of government, such as the **Court of Common Pleas hand** or the **Chancery hand**, a distinctive hand used in the royal chancery – an Anglicana hand modified by a continental business hand that had developed in Italy and France from the 13th to the 14th centuries.

Court of Common Pleas hand

Chancery hand

This portion of a document in Common-law hand is a return of the Commissioners administering the Oath of Supremacy, 1579. This is an informal cursive style.

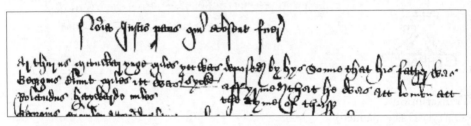

Transcription
(abbreviations expanded)

Nomina Justiciariorum Pacis Qui Absentes Fuerunt ~

(names of Justices of the Peace who were absent)

Arthurus Manwarynge miles	ytt was deposed by hys Sonne that his father was sycke
Georgius Blunt miles	itt was affyrmed that he was att london att the tyme of thassizes.
Rolandus Haywarde miles	

Here is the first line of a document from the same group of Common-law hands written a century later in 1682. It is a highly stylised and formal example.

Transcription
(abbreviations expanded)

Et predictus Willelmus in propria persona sua venit et defendit ius suum quando etc et ...

Here are some examples of **Chancery hand**, the first dated 1480:

Enlarged left-hand portion of the MS

Transcription (abbreviations expanded)

Excellentissimo principi domino Edwardo dei gracia ...
Reges regnant et principes dominantur. Quia ...
Johannem Foune filium Johannis Foune de duobus ...
pasture cum pertinenciis in holyngton' que de ...
tenore presencium significo curiam meam ...
consimili cum acciderit. In cujus rei testim ...
primo die Octobris anno regni vestri vic ...

The second is part of a Chancery decree of 1562.

Transcription

To haue and to holde the said rectorie and parsonage together with all other the premisses with the
appertenaunces vnto the said Sir Thomas Pope knight his heires and assignes to the onlie vse of the
said Sir Thomas Pope his heires and assignes for euer by force whereof the said Sir Thomas
Pope was seased of the said rectorie and parsonage and other the premisses in his demeane as of fee ...

To haue and to holde the said rectorie ...
appertenaunces vnto the said Sir Thomas ...
said Sir Thomas Pope his heires and ...
Pope was seased of the said rectorie ...

Enlarged left-hand portion of MS,
showing Chancery hand letters

The following letter was dictated to a clerk by King Henry V, who was with his army in France before Rouen, 'afore Roan', on 29th November 1418. It is the king's response to the breaking of a truce between him and the Duke of Brittany, and calls for 'reparation and restitution' for any violations of the truce. It is written in Chancery hand, but its size makes a clear reproduction of the detail of the handwriting difficult here – a transcription and a modernised version follow.

Text 83: Letter of King Henry V, 1418 (facsimile)

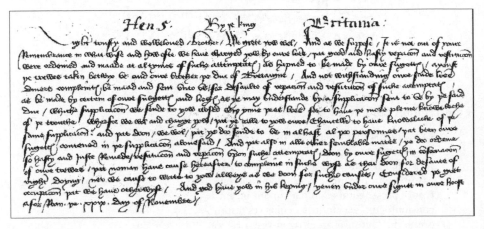

Transcription

Hen 5   By þe king   **Britania:**

Right truſty and welbeloued / brother / We grete yow wel / And as we ſuppoſe / It is not out of youre remembrance in what wiſe and how ofte we haue charged yow by oure lres / þat good and haſty repacon and restitucon were ordeined and maade at altymes of ſuche attemptat⁹ as hapned to be made by oure ſugettes / ayenſt þe trewes taken betwix vs and oure brother þe duc of Bretaigne / And not withſtanding oure ſaide ltres diuers compleint⁹ be maad and ſent vnto vs / for Defaulte of repacon and restitucon of ſuche attemptat⁹ as be made by certein of oure ſubgett⁹ and lieg⁹ as ye may vnderſtand by a ſupplicacon ſent to vs by þe ſaid duc / whiche ſupplicacon we ſende to yow cloſed wiþ ynne þees ltr⁹ for to haue þe more pleine knoweleche of þe trouthe / wherfor we wol and charge yow / þat ye calle to yow oure Chancellr to haue knowelache of þe ſame ſuppliccacon and þat doon / we wol þat ye doo ſende to vs in al haſt al þoo perſonnes / þat been oure ſugett⁹ contened in þe ſupplicacon aboueſaid / And þat alſo in alle other ſemblable mat⁹es / ye doo ordeine ſo haſty and Iuſte remede / reſtitucon / and repacon vpon ſuche attemptat⁹ doon by oure ſugettes in coſeruacon of oure trewes / þat noman haue cauſe hereafter to complaine in ſuche wyſe as þai doon for defaute of right doyng / ner we cauſe to write to yow alweys as we doon for ſuche cauſes / Conſidered þe gret occupacon þat we haue otherwyſe / And god haue yow in his keping / yeuen vnder oure ſignet in oure hooſt afor Roan. þe .xxix. day of Nouembre

attemptate – 'a violent or criminal attempt; an attack, assault, outrage, raid, incursion'.

we woll – we will, i.e. 'it is our will that . . .', 'we require . . .'

ye doo sende – *doo* is a causative verb, i.e. 'that you cause to be sent . . .'

semblable – similar

Abbreviations
The scribe writes a final 'flourish' for ⟨-es⟩ in *attemptates, sugettes, compleintes, lieges.*

ltres	**lettres**	*letters*
repacon	**reparacion**	*reparation*
restitucon	**restitucion**	*restitution*
ſupplicacon	**supplicacion**	*supplication*
matꝰes	**materes**	*matters*
coseruacon	**conservacion**	*conservation*
occupacon	**occupacion**	*occupation*

Modernised spelling and punctuation

Right trusty and well beloved brother, we greet you well, and as we suppose it is not out of your remembrance in what wise and how often we have charged you by our letters that good and hasty reparation and restitution were ordained and made at all times of such attempts as happened to be made by our subjects against the truce taken between us and our brother the Duke of Brittany. And notwithstanding our said letters, divers complaints [have] be[en] made and sent unto us for default of reparation and restitution of such attempts as be made by certain of our subjects and lieges, as you may understand by a supplication sent to us by the said Duke. Which supplication we send to you [en]closed within these letters, for [you] to have the more plain knowledge of the truth. Wherefore we will and charge you that you call to you our Chancellor to have knowledge of the same supplication; and that done, we will that you *cause to be sent* to us in all haste all those persons that *are* our subjects contained in the supplication above said. And that also in all other similar matters you do ordain so hasty and just remedy, restitution and reparation upon such *violations* done by our subjects, in conservation of our truce, that no man have cause hereafter to complain in such *a way* as they do for default of right doing, nor [that] we *are compelled* to write to you always as we do for such causes, considered the great occupation that we have otherwise. And God have you in his keeping. Given under our signet in our host afore Rouen. the 29th day of November.

📖 The lexical vocabulary of Text 83 is listed in the Word Book.

14.3 Chancery English

14.3.1 Spelling

The Chancery clerks fairly consistently preferred the spellings which have since become standard. ... At the very least, we can say that they were trying to limit choices among spellings, and that by the 1440s and 1450s they had achieved a comparative regularization.

(J. H. Fisher et al. (eds), *An Anthology of Chancery English*, 1984)

The 14th-century spellings that conform to contemporary Standard English are unremarkable for readers today, so that we tend to be unaware of the choices that the Chancery clerks made. Here are some examples of spellings that are now standard, except for the persistent redundant final ⟨e⟩, which continued to be used for another two centuries.

Preferred Chancery spelling	Other spellings less frequently used
such(e)	sich, sych, seche, swich, sweche
much(e)	moch(e), mych(e)
which(e)/whych(e)	wich, wech
not/noght	nat
many	meny
any	eny, ony
but	bot
and	ond, ant
if/yf	yif, yef

This short selection of spellings recorded in the *Oxford English Dictionary* will illustrate the extent of spelling variation in the ME period:

realm   reaume, reeaum, reawme, reome, reem(e), regm(e), rem(e), reame, reyme, reiem, reamme, reum(e), rewm(e), realme

poor   pouere, povere, pouer, pover, poeuere, poeure, pouir, poer, powere, poyr, power, powar, poure, powre, pour, pore, poore

people   peple, pepule, pepul, pepull(e), pepille, pepill, pepil, pepylle, pepyll, peeple, poeple, poepul, peopel, peopull, puple, pupile, pupill, pupyll, pupul, peuple, pople.

receive   rasawe, rassaif, rassave, recave, receave, receawe, receiuf, receive, receve, receyf, receyve, recieve, reciffe, recive, recyve, resaf, resaif, resaiff, resaive, resave, resawe, resayfe, resayff, resayve, resaywe, rescaive, rescayve, resceive, resceve, rescewe, resceyve, reschave, reschayfe, rescheyve, rescyve, reseve, reseyve, ressaif, ressaive, ressave, ressawe, ressayf, ressayve, resseve, resseyve, reycive.

We have seen how the spelling of the vowels in unstressed syllables varied in the OE period (in, for example, section 5.3.1), because the pronunciation of unstressed vowels was almost certainly [ə], the mid-central vowel *schwa*, for which there is no corresponding Roman letter. The same inconsistency of spelling is in early Chancery documents, alternating between *e, i, o* and *u*, with a 'drift towards standardisation' by using letter ⟨e⟩ more often. So *goodis* or *goodus* are in time consistently spelt *goodes*, before the final loss of the unstressed vowel in *goods*.

14.3.2 Word structure and grammar

As, in Chancery English, the beginnings of Standard English can be seen, a survey of its grammatical structures will contain much that is common to present-day English, like the plural and the possessive markers ⟨s/es⟩, the pronouns *he/him/his* and *she/her/her* and the Northern plural subject pronoun *they* (although both *them* and *hem* are used for the object pronoun). Negatives are now marked by *not* only (or *nat*, *noght*, *nought*, *nowht* etc.), and the older *ne* has gone.

When we read texts from the 15th century onwards, we have to compare an increasingly familiar language with its earlier stages of ME and OE in order to notice the changes taking place. There is still plenty that is not present-day English in spelling, vocabulary and grammar, but less and less as time progresses.

14.4 Early 15th-century East Midlands dialect – *The Boke of Margery Kempe*

Margery Kempe (*c.*1373–*c.*1439) was a woman from King's Lynn in Norfolk who gave up married life as a result of her mystical experiences, to devote herself to religion. She made many pilgrimages during her lifetime, and afterwards in the 1420s dictated a book describing her visions, temptations and journeys.

As the book was written down from Margery Kempe's own dictation, this is probably as close as we can get to ordinary speech of the early 15th century. The dialect is East Midlands, but we cannot tell how accurate was the scribe's reproduction of Margery's speech, or that of the only surviving manuscript, which was copied in the mid-15th century.

Here she describes her early marriage. Throughout the book she refers to herself as 'this creature':

Text 84: The Boke of Margery Kempe *(i)*

> Whan þis creatur was xx ȝer of age or sumdele mor sche was maryed to a worschepful burgeys of Lyn and was wyth chylde wyth in schort tyme as kynde wolde. And aftyr þat sche had conceyued sche was labowrd wyth grett accessys tyl þe chyld was born & þan what for labowr she had in chyldyng & for sekenesse goyng beforn she dyspered of hyr lyf, wenyng she mygth not leuyn.

| MnE | When this creature was 20 years of age or something more, she was married to a worshipful burgess of Lynn and was with child within a short time as nature wished. And after (that) she had conceived she was in labour with great fevers till the child was born & then what for labour she had in childbirth & for sickness going before, she despaired of her life, thinking she might not live. |

Here her first mystical vision is described:

Text 85: The Boke of Margery Kempe *(ii)*

> On a nygth as þis creatur lay in hir bedde wyth hir husbond she herd a sownd of melodye so swet & deletable hir þowt as she had ben in paradyse. And þerwyth she styrt owt of hir bedde & seyd Alas þat euyr I dede synne, it is ful mery in hevyn. Thys melodye was so swete þat it passyd alle þe melodye þat euyr mygth be herd in þis world

wyth owtyn ony comparyson, & caused þis creatur whan she herd ony myrth or melodye aftyrward for to haue ful plentyuows & habundawnt teerys of hy deuocyon wyth greet sobbyngys & syhyngys aftyr þe blysse of heuen, not dredyng þe shamys & þe spytys of þe wretchyd world.

MnE One night as this creature lay in her bed with her husband she heard a sound of melody so sweet & delectable to-her (it) seemed as she had been in Paradise. And therewith she started out of her bed & said 'Alas that ever I did sin, it is full merry in heaven. This melody was so sweet that it passed all the melody that ever might be heard in this world without any comparison, & caused this creature, when she heard any mirth or melody afterward for to have full plenteous and abundant tears of high devotion with great sobbings & sighings after the bliss of heaven, not dreading the shames and the spites of the wretched world.

Text 85 is recorded on the CD/cassette tape.

> ɔn ə nɪxt as ðɪs kreːtʊr læi ɪn hɪr bɛd wɪð hɪr hʊzbənd ʃiː heːrd ə suːnd ɒv mɛlɔdi sɔ sweːt ænd dɛlɛtabəl hɪr θɒt æz ʃiː hæd ben ɪn pærædiːs. ænd ðɛrwɪθ ʃiː stiːrt ut ɒv hɪr bɛd ænd sæɪd, 'alæs ðæt ɛvər iː dɛd sɪn, ɪt ɪz fʊl mɛri ɪn hɛvən'. ðɪs mɛlɔdi wæs sɔ sweːt ðæt ɪt pasɪd al ðɔ mɛlɔdi ðæt ɛvər mɪçt bɛ herd ɪn ðɪs wɔrld wɪðutən ɔnɪ kɒmpærɪzon, ænd kɔuzɪd ðɪs kreːtʊr hwæn ʃiː herd ɔnɪ mɪrθ ɔr mɛlɔdi æftərward fɔr to hæv fʊl plentjus ænd æbʊndənt tiːrɪs ɒv hɪx dɛvɔsɪɔn wɪð greːt sɒbɪŋgz ɜnd sɪçɪŋgz æftər ðə blɪs ɒv hɛvən, nɒt drɛdɪŋ ðə ʃæːmɪs ənd ðə spɪːtɪs ɒv ðə wrɛtʃɪd world

Here is the opening of the manuscript in facsimile:

Text 86: **The Boke of Margery Kempe** *(iii) (facsimile)*

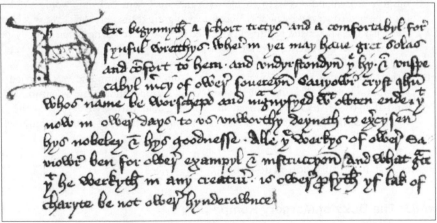

✎ A note on the handwriting

● The forms of ⟨þ⟩ and ⟨y⟩ are written identically, both as ⟨y⟩.

- The digraph ⟨th⟩ is now normally used for [θ] and [ð]; ⟨y⟩ for ⟨þ⟩ is word-initial in a restricted number of function words, which are often abbreviated – *yeı* (*they*), *yᵉ* (*the*), *yᵗ* (*that*), and in Text 87 *yā* (*than/then*), *yᵘ* (*thou*), *yʳ for* (*therefore*), *yi* (*thy*).

Here begynnyth a ſchort tretys and a comfortabyl for
ſynful wrecchys. wher ın yeı may haue gret solas
and cōfort to hem. and vndyrſtondyn yᵉ hy. & vnſpe
cabyl mʳcy of ower ſouereyn Sauyowr cryſt Ihū
whos name be worſchepd and mᵃgnyfyed wᵗowten ende. yᵗ
now ın ower days to vs vnworthy deyneth to exʳcyſen
hys nobeley & hys goodneſſe. Alle yᵉ werkys of ower Sa
viowr ben for ower exampyl & ınſtruccyon and what gᵃce
yᵗ he werkyth ın any creatur. ıs ower pſyth yf lak of
charyte be not ower hynderawnce.

Edited version (using letter thorn)

Here begynnyth a schort tretys and a comfortabyl for
synful wrecchys. wher in þei may haue gret solas
and comfort to hem. and vndyrstondyn þe hy & vnspe
cabyl mercy of ower souereyn Sauyowr cryst Ihesu
whos name be worschepd and magnyfyed wythowten ende. þat
now in ower days to vs vnworthy deyneth to exercysen
hys nobeley & hys goodnesse. Alle þe werkys of ower Sa
viowr ben for ower exampyl & instruccyon and what grace
þat he werkyth in any creatur. is ower profyth yf lak of
charyte be not ower hynderawnce.

The next extract is typical of many descriptions of Margery Kempe's religious experiences, her tears of repentance, and sense of sin and guilt.

Text 87: **The Boke of Margery Kempe** *(iv) – sin and God's forgiveness (facsimile)*

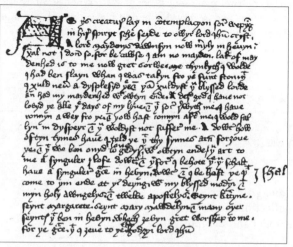

As ys creatur lay ın cōtemplacyon ſor wepȳg
ın hır ſpıryt ſche ſeyde to owyr lord Ihū cryſt .
A lord maydenys dawnſyn now mᵣyly ın heuyn :
xal not I don ρο. for be cawſe I am no mayden. lak of may
denhed ıs to me now gret ſorwe. me thynkyth I wolde
I had ben ſlayn whan I was takyn fro ye ſunt ſton yᵗ
I xuld neuʳ a dyſpleſyd ye. & yā xuldyſt yᵘ blyſſed lorde
an had my maydenhed wᵗ owtyn ende. A der God I haue not
lovyd ye alle yᵉ days of my lyue & yᵗ ſor rᵉwyth me. I haue
ronnyn a wey fro ye & yow haſt ronnyn aftʳ me. I wold ſal
lyn ın dyſpeyr & yᵘ woldyſt not ſuffer me. A dowtʳ how
oftyn tymes haue I teld ye yᵗ thy ſynnes arn forȝoue
ye & yᵗ we ben onyd ın loue to gedyr wᵗ owtyn ende / yᵘ art to
me a ſynguler loſe dowtʳ. & yʳfor I behote yᵉ yᵘ ſchalt
haue a ſynguler gᵃce ın hevyn. dowtyr & I be heſt ye yᵗ   I ſhal
come to yın ende at yī deyng wᵗ my blyſſed modyr &
myn holy awngelys. & twelve apoſtelys. Seynt Kattᵣyne.
ſeynt Margarete. Seynt Mary Mawdelyn. & many oyer
ſeyntyſ yᵗ ben ın hevyn. whech ȝevyn gret worſhep to me.
for ye gᵃce yᵗ I ȝeue to ye. thy God. yı lord Ihū

Edited text, original punctuation

As þis creatur lay in contemplacyon ſor wepyng in hir spiryt sche seyde to owyr lord
Ihesu cryst. A lord maydenys dawnsyn now meryly in heuyn : xal not I don so. for be
cawse I am no mayden, lak of maydenhed is to me now gret sorwe. me thynkyth I
wolde I had ben slayn whan I was takyn fro þe funt ston þat I xuld neuyr a dysplesyd
þe. & þan xuldyst þou blyssed Lorde an had my maydenhed wyth owtyn ende. A der
God I haue not lovyd þe alle þe days of my lyue & þat ſor rewyth me. I haue ronnyn
a wey fro þe, & þow hast ronnyn aftyr me. I wold fallyn in dyspeyr & þou woldyst not
suffer me. A dowtor how oftyn tymes haue I teld þe þat thy synnes arn forȝoue þe &
þat we ben onyd in loue to gedyr wyth owtyn ende / þou art to me a synguler loſe
dowtyr. & þerfor I behote þe þou schalt haue a synguler grace in hevyn, dowtyr & I
be hest þe þat I shal come to þin ende at þi deyng wyth my blyssed modyr & myn
holy awngelys. & twelve apostelys. Seynt Katteryne. Seynt Margarete. Seynt Mary
Mawdelyn. & many oþer seyntys þat ben in Hevyn. whech ȝevyn gret worshep to me.
for þe grace þat I ȝeue to þe. thy God. þi lord Ihesu /

📖 The lexical vocabulary of Texts 84–7 is listed in the Word Book.

Activity 14.1

Describe the linguistic features of these early 15th-century texts by Margery Kempe
which contrast with the grammar of MnE. A check-list follows.

Word structure and grammar
- Forms and inflections of nouns.
- Forms of personal and demonstrative pronouns.

- What determines the choice of the pronouns *my/myn* and *þi/þin*, both used as determiners?
- Definite and indefinite articles.
- Prepositions and phrasal verbs, conjunctions.
- Strong and weak verbs and verb inflections for tense.
- Development of the verb phrase.
- Word order in clause and phrase.

Vocabulary
- Examine and comment on the derivation of the vocabulary in these texts.

Spelling
- Describe the principal features of the spelling which are to be contrasted with present-day spelling.

📖 A commentary on Activity 14.1 is in the Text Commentary Book.

14.5 Later 15th-century East Midlands dialect – the Paston letters

The Pastons were a prosperous Norfolk family, and a large collection of their letters written between the 1420s and 1500s has survived. The letters cover three generations of the family, and are a valuable source of evidence for historians as well as students of language. Much of the period was troubled by the political upheavals of the Wars of the Roses, and this is reflected in the Pastons' letters.

The first letter, Text 88, is to the first-generation William Paston from his wife Agnes.

Text 88: Letter from Agnes to William Paston, 1440

Agnes to her husband William Paston, probably written in 1440, 20 April

> Dere housbond I recomaunde me to yow &c blyssyd be god I sende yow gode tydynggys of þe comyng and þe brynggyn hoom of þe gentylwomman þat ye wetyn of fro Redham þis same nyght ~~ae~~ acordyng to poyntmen þat ye made þer for yowre self and as for þe furste aqweyntaunce betwhen John Paston and þe seyde gentilwomman she made hym gentil chere in gyntyl wyse and seyde he was verrayly yowre son and so I hope þer shal nede no gret trete be twyxe hym | þe parson of Stocton toold me yif ye wolde byin here a goune here moder wolde yeue ther to a godely furre þe goune nedyth for to be had and of coloure it wolde be a godely blew or ellys a bryghte sanggueyn | I prey yow do byen for me ij pypys of gold | yowre stewes do weel | the Holy Trinite have yow in gouernaunce wretyn at Paston in hast þe Wednesday next after Deus qui errantibus for defaute of a good secretarye &c
>
> Yowres
> Agnes Paston

do byen – the auxiliary *do* is used as a 'causative': 'get someone to buy for me . . . '

stewes – fish-ponds.

Deus qui errantibus – a day in the Church calendar, known by the Latin opening of a text used on that day.

MnE edited and punctuated

Dear husband, I recommend me to you &c. Blessed be God I send you good tidings of the coming and the bringing home of the gentlewoman that you know of from Redham this same night, according to (the) appointment that you made there for yourself. And as for the first acquaintance between John Paston and the said gentlewoman, she made him gentle cheer in gentle wise and said he was verily your son. And so I hope there shall need no great treaty between them.

The person from Stockton told me (that) if you would buy her a gown, her mother would give thereto a goodly fur. The gown needs to be had, and of colour it would be a goodly blue or else a bright sanguine.

I pray you, have bought for me two pipes of gold.

Your stews do well.

The Holy Trinity have you in governance. Written at Paston in haste the Wednesday next after Deus qui errantibus for default of a good secretarye &c

Yours

Agnes Paston

The next text is a Valentine letter from Margery Brews to the third-generation John Paston, to whom she was engaged to be married.

Text 89: Margery Brews to John Paston, February 1477

Edited version, not punctuated

Vn to my ryght welbelouyd voluntyn John Paston squyer be þis bill delyuered &c

Ryght reuerent and wurschypfull and my ryght welebeloued voluntyne I recommaunde me vn to yowe full hertely desyring to here of yowr welefare whech I beseche almyghty god long for to preserve vn to hys plesure and ȝowr hertys desyre | and yf it please ȝowe to here of my welefare I am not in good heele of body ner of herte nor schall be tyll I here from yowe

> For þer wottys no creature what peyn þat I endure
> And for to be deede I dare it not dyscure

And my lady my moder hath labored þe mater to my fadure full delygently but sche can no more gete þen ȝe knowe of for þe whech god knowyth I am full sorry | but yf that ȝe loffe me as I tryste verely that ȝe do ȝe will not leffe me þerfor. for if þat ȝe hade not halfe þe lyvelode þat ȝe hafe, for to do þe grettyst labure þat any woman on lyve myght I wold not forsake ȝowe

> and yf ȝe commande me to kepe me true where euer I go
> iwyse I will do all my myght ȝowe to love and neuer no mo
> and yf my freendys say þat I do amys þei schal not me let so for to do
> myn herte me byddys euer more to love ȝowe truly ouer all erthely thing
> and yf þei be neuer so wroth I tryst it schall be bettur in tyme commyng

no more to yowe at this tyme but the holy trinite hafe yowe in kepyng and I besech ȝowe þat this bill be not seyn of non erthely creature safe only our selfe &c and thys lettur was yndyte at Topcroft wyth full heuy herte &c

beȝour own M B

📖 The lexical vocabulary of Texts 88 and 89 is listed in the Word Book.

They were married later that year. The letter is written on a broad sheet of paper, and cannot be reproduced in facsimile here unless it were reduced in size so much as to make the words too small to read. The first line, for example, reads:

Ryght reuerent and wurschypfull and my ryght welebeloued voluntyne I recommaunde me vn to yowe full hertely desyring to here of yowr welefare

Here is a corner of the letter to illustrate the writing hand:

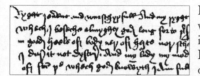

Ryght reuerent and wurschypfull and my right . . .
whech I beseche almyghty god long for to preserve . . .
in good heele of body ner of herte nor schall . . .
I dare it not dyscure. And my lady my moder . . .
of for þe whech god knowyth I am full . . .

This is Margery's signature to a letter written two years later. It seems clear from her own writing hand that her letter to John Paston (Text 89) was dictated to a clerk:

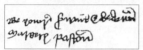

Be your^e s^er_u^au_t & bedewom^an

Margery Paston

(A *bedewoman* is a woman who prays for another (OE (*ge*)*bed*) = prayer.)

📖 The letter is recorded on the CD/cassette tape.

> ʊnto mi rixt wɛlbɛlʊvid vɔlʊntiin, ʤɔn pæstən, skwijər, bi ðis bil dɛlivərd
> rixt rɛvərənt ænd wʊrʃipfʊl ənd mi rixt wɛlbɛlʊvid vɔlʊntin, iː rɛkɔmound mi ʊnto
> ju, fʊl hertəli dɛziriŋ to hiːr ɒv jur wɛlfæːr. hwitʃ i bɛsiːtʃ almixti gɒd lɒŋ fɔr to
> prɛzɛrv ʊnto his pleːzjuːr ænd jur hertis dɛzir,
> ænd if it pleːz ju to hiːr ɒv mi wɛlfæːr i æm nɒt in guːd heːl ɒv bɒdi ner ɒv hert
> nɔr ʃæl bi til i hiːr frɒm juː
>
> fɔr ðer wɒtis no kreːtjur hwæt pæin ðæt i ɛndjur
> ænd fɔr to bi deːd i dæːr it nɒt diskjur
>
> ænd mi læidi mi mʊdər hæθ læːbɔrd ðə mæːtər to mi fæːdʊr fʊl dɛliʤəntli b t ʃi
> kæn nɔ mɔr gɛt ðen ji knɒʊ ɒv, fɔr ðə hwɛtʃ gɒd knɔʊwiθ i æm fʊl sɔri,
> bʊt if ðæt ji lʊf mi æz i trist vɛrəli ðæt ji doː, ji wil nɒt leːv mi ðerfɔr. fɔr if ðæt ji
> hæd nɒt half ðə livlɒd ðæt ji hæv, fɔr to doː ðə greːtest læːbʊr ðæt æni wʊmən ɒn
> liv mixt, i wɒld nɒt fɔrsæːk ju.
>
> ænd if ji kɒmænd mi to kiːp mi tru hwer ɛvər i gɔː
> iwis i wil duː al mi mixt ju tu lʊv ænd nɛvər no mɔː,
> ænd if mi freːndz sæi ðæt i doː əmis ðæi ʃæl nɒt mi lɛt so fɔr tɔ doː,
> min hert mi bidis ɛvər mɔr to lʊv ju triuli ɒvər al ɛrθli θiŋg,
> ænd if ðæi bi nɛvər so wrɒθ, i trist it ʃæl bi bɛtər in tiim cʊmiŋg.
> no mɔr to ju æt ðis tiim, bʊt ðə holi triniti hæf ju in kipiŋg, ænd i bɛsitʃ ju ðæt ðis
> bil bi nɒt siːn ɒv nɔːn erθli kreːtur sæːf ɔnli ur self, ænd ðis lɛtər wæs indit æt
> tɔpkrɔft wið fʊl hɛvi hert, bi jur ɔːn M B

14.6 Late 15th-century London English – William Caxton

William Caxton is known as the first English printer, and the setting-up of his printing press in London in 1476 was the beginning of a revolution in the production of books, which no longer had to be separately copied by hand. Copying did not, of course, cease, and the professional scriveners were employed for some time – the copying by hand of documents went on in government departments, legal and business offices etc. by clerks into the early 20th century, until the use of typewriters and then computers took over.

This facsimile illustrates the copying of handwriting letter shapes in early printing – it is from the *Prologue* of the first edition of one of Caxton's earliest printed books, Chaucer's *Canterbury Tales*. He brought this font, based on a Burgundian script, from the Low Countries to Westminster when he set up his own printing house in 1476. It is one of eight different fonts which he eventually used in his printed books

Caxton himself was, however, more than a printer of other people's writing. He himself translated into English and edited many of the books that he printed, and he provided a considerable number of prefaces and commentaries.

14.6.1 Caxton's revision of *Polychronicon*

In 1482 William Caxton printed a revised text of Trevisa's 1385 translation of Higden's *Polychronicon* (see Texts 57 and 58 in Chapter 9). This provides an excellent example of some of the changes that had taken place in the language within a hundred years. Caxton evidently found Trevisa's English old-fashioned and out of date, as he said in an Epilogue:

> . . . I William Caxton a symple persone haue endeuoyred me to wryte fyrst ouerall the sayd book of Proloconycon and somwhat haue chaunged the rude and old Englyssh, that is to wete certayn wordes which in these dayes be neither vsyd ne vnderstanden.

Caxton's 15th-century modernised version of John of Trevisa's description of the languages of Britain is printed below following the 14th-century text. This Trevisa text is taken from a different manuscript and slightly expanded, and shows some interesting differences from Texts 57 and 58. This illustrates the lack of standardisation in Middle English and the way in which differences in the dialects of ME were reflected in writing. Some features of Caxton's punctuation, like his use of the virgule ⟨/⟩, are reproduced, but modern punctuation is added also.

> ### Activity 14.2
>
> (i) Describe the changes that Caxton has made to 'the rude and old Englyssh' of the 14th-century text.
>
> (ii) Comment on the differences between the 14th-century text in this version and in Texts 57 and 58. Do they suggest significant differences in the pronunciation or grammar of the language, or simply in spelling conventions?

Text 90: John of Trevisa, 1385

As it is i-knowe how meny manere peple beeþ in þis ilond þere beeþ also so many dyuers longages and tonges; noþeles walsche men and scottes þat beeþ nouȝt i-medled wiþ oþer naciouns holdeþ wel nyh hir firste longage and speche ...

Also englische men þey þei hadde from þe bygynnynge þre maner speche norþerne sowþerne and middel speche in þe myddel of þe lond, as þey come of þre manere peple of Germania, noþeles by comyxtioun and mellynge firste wiþ danes and afterward wiþ normans in meny þe contray longage is apayred and som vseþ straunge wlafferynge chiterynge harrynge and garrynge grisbitynge.

This apayrynge of þe burþe tonge is bycause of tweie þinges; oon is for children in scole aȝenst þe vsage and manere of alle oþere naciouns beeþ compelled for to leue hire owne langage and for to construe hir lessouns and here þynges a frensche, and so þey haueþ seþ þe normans come first in to engelond.

Also gentil men children beeþ i-tauȝt to speke frensche from þe tyme þat þey beeþ i-rokked in here cradel and kunneþ speke and playe wiþ a childes broche; and vplondisshe men wil likne hym self to gentil men and fondeþ wiþ greet besynesse for to speke frensce for to be i-tolde of ...

þis manere was moche i-vsed to for firste deth and is siþþe sumdel i-chaunged. For Iohn Cornwaile, a maister of grammer, chaunged þe lore in gramer scole, and construccioun of frensche into englische; and Richard Pencriche lerned þe manere techynge of hym and oþere men of Pencrich; so þat now, þe ȝere of oure Lorde a þowsand þre hundred and foure score and fyue, in alle þe gramere scoles of engelond children leueþ frensche and construeþ and lerneþ an englische ...

Also gentil men haueþ now moche i-left for to teche here children frensche. Hit semeþ a greet wonder houȝ englische, þat is þe burþe tonge of englissh men and her owne langage and tonge, ys so dyuerse of sown in þis oon ilond, and þe langage of normandie is comlynge of anoþer londe and haþ oon manere soun among alle men þat spekeþ hit ariȝt in engelond.

... also of þe forsaide saxon tonge þat is i-deled a þre and is abide scarsliche wiþ fewe vplondisshe men is greet wonder; for men of þe est wiþ men of þe west, as it were vndir þe same partie of heuene, acordeþ more in sownynge of speche þan men of þe norþ wiþ men of þe souþ.

þerfore it is þat mercii, þat beeþ men of myddel engelond, as it were parteners of þe endes, vnderstondeþ bettre þe side langages, norþerne and souþerne, þan norþerne and souþerne vnderstondeþ eiþer oþer.

Al þe longage of þe norþumbres and specialliche at ȝork is so scharp slitting and frotynge and vnschape þat we souþerne men may þat longage vnneþe vnderstonde. I trowe þat þat is bycause þat þey beeþ nyh to straunge men and aliens þat spekeþ strongliche.

Text 91: Caxton's version, 1482

As it is knowen how many maner peple ben in this Ilond ther ben also many langages and tonges. Netheles walshmen and scottes that ben not medled with other nacions kepe neygh yet theyr first langage and speche /

also englysshmen though they had fro the begynnyng thre maner speches Southern northern and myddel speche in the middel of the londe as they come of thre maner of people of Germania. Netheles by commyxtion and medlyng first with danes and afterward with normans In many thynges the countreye langage is appayred / ffor somme vse straunge wlaffyng / chytering harryng garryng and grisbytyng /

this appayryng of the langage cometh of two thynges / One is by cause that children that gon to scole lerne to speke first englysshe / & than ben compellid to constrewe her lessons in Frenssh and that have ben vsed syn the normans come in to Englond /

Also gentilmens childeren ben lerned and taught from theyr yongthe to speke frenssh. And vplondyssh men will counterfete and likene hem self to gentilmen and arn besy to speke frensshe for to be more sette by.

This maner was moche vsed to fore the grete deth. But syth it is somdele chaunged For sir Johan cornuayl a mayster of gramer chaunged the techyng in gramer scole and construction of Frenssh in to englysshe. and other Scoolmaysters vse the same way now in the yere of oure lord / M.iij/C.lx.v. the /ix yere of kyng Rychard the secund and leve all frenssh in scoles and vse al construction in englissh.

And also gentilmen have moche lefte to teche theyr children to speke frenssh Hit semeth a grete wonder that Englyssmen have so grete dyversyte in theyr owne langage in sowne and in spekyng of it / whiche is all in one ylond. And the langage of Normandye is comen oute of another lond / and hath one maner soune among al men that speketh it in englond . . .

Also of the forsayd tong whiche is departed in thre is grete wonder / For men of the este with the men of the west acorde better in sownyng of theyr speche than men of the north with men of the south /

Therfor it is that men of mercij that ben of myddel englond as it were partyners with the endes vnderstande better the side langages northern & sothern than northern & southern vnderstande eyther other.

Alle the langages of the northumbres & specially at york is so sharp slytyng frotyng and vnshape that we sothern men may vnneth vnderstande that langage I suppose the cause be that they be nygh to the alyens that speke straungely.

14.6.1.1 Vocabulary change

- About 14% of the words appear in one of the texts only (partly because of the omissions and additions that Caxton made to the Trevisa text).

- There are 46 pairs of words that are identical in spelling (about 25%).
- More than half the vocabulary has minor variants that indicate changes in spelling convention only (about 53%). For example:

  - ⟨th⟩ / ⟨þ⟩
  - ⟨y⟩ / ⟨i⟩
  - redundant ⟨e⟩
  - doubled letters
  - unstressed vowel variants

  - metathesis of ⟨re⟩ / ⟨er⟩
  - ⟨ou⟩ / ⟨o⟩
  - ⟨-cion⟩ / ⟨-tion⟩
  - ⟨ssh⟩ / ⟨sch⟩ / ⟨sc⟩
  - ⟨ȝ⟩ / ⟨gh⟩ / ⟨y⟩

- The only examples of the substitution of one word for another are:

  comlynge / comen   seþ – syn (= *since*)
  holdeþ / kepe   trowe / suppose

- There are two developments in the grammar, however – the loss of the 3rd person plural present tense inflection ⟨-eþ⟩, and of the past participle prefix ⟨i-⟩ (from the OE prefix ⟨ge-⟩):

Trevisa	Caxton	Trevisa	Caxton
beeþ	ben	i-deled	departed
haueþ	have	i-knowe	knowen
lerneþ	lerne	i-left	lefte
leue, leueþ	leve	i-medled	medled
vnderstonde(þ)	vnderstande	i-vsed	vsed
vseþ	use		

📖 The lexical vocabulary of Texts 90 and 91 is in the Word Book.

14.6.2 Caxton on 'dyuersite & chaunge of langage'

A standard form of a language develops in a nation or society only at a particular time of its social and political evolution, when the need becomes evident and pressing. We define the Middle English period partly by the fact that there was no one dialect that was accepted or used throughout the country as a standard in writing. The invention of printing was one factor in the complex interaction of political and economic changes in England by the end of the 15th century, which led in time to the establishment of a written standard form of English.

One of Caxton's problems as printer and translator is clearly shown in a famous story which he tells in the Preface to his translation of a French version of Virgil's Latin poem *The Aeneid*, called *Eneydos*. A revolution in communications was brought about by the printing of books. A book might be bought and read anywhere in the country – which dialect of English should a printer use? For example, there were two words for *egg*, one derived from OE, the other from ON.

From OE: æȝ, aig, ey(e), ay(e), ȝey; *plural* æȝru, **eyren**(e), eyron, eyroun.
From ON: eg, egg, egge, ege, hegge – **egg, egges**.

The story in Text 92 is about the difficulty of asking for eggs for breakfast, but for Caxton it illustrates the problem of choice of language in translation,

> Loo what sholde a man in thyse dayes now wryte, egges or eyren?

This is just one of the problems that had to be overcome in the establishment of an agreed standard literary form of English over the next two hundred years.

If you were to examine Caxton's language in detail, you would find that he did not devise a consistent and regular spelling system, and that many of his decisions about spelling and grammatical form were already old-fashioned for the language of the 1480s.

Activity 14.3

(i) Examine Caxton's texts for evidence of his inconsistency of choice in spelling and word form.

(ii) Describe those features of Caxton's English by which we we would describe it as 'archaic' in comparison with MnE.

📖 A commentary on Caxton's spelling is in the Text Commentary Book.

Text 92: Caxton on the diversity of English, 1490

(Caxton has decided to translate *Eneydos*)

> And whan I sawe the fayr & straunge termes therin / I doubted that it sholde not please some gentylmen whiche late blamed me, sayeng that in my translacyons I had ouer curyous termes whiche coude not be vnderstande of comyn peple / and desired me to vse olde and homely termes in my translacyons. and fayn wolde I satisfye euery man / and so to doo, toke an olde boke and redde therin / and certaynly the englysshe was so rude and brood that I coude not wele vnderstande it. And also my lorde abbot of westmynster ded do shewe to me late, certayn euydences wryton on olde englysshe, for to reduce it in-to our englysshe now vsid / And certaynly it was wreton in suche wyse that it was more lyke to dutche than englysshe; I coude not reduce ne brynge it to be vnderstonden / And certaynly our langage now vsed varyeth ferre from that whiche was vsed and spoken whan I was borne / For we englysshe men / ben borne vnder the domynacyon of the mone, whiche is neuer stedfaste / but euer wauerynge / wexynge one season / and waneth & dyscreaseth another season / And that comyn englysshe that is spoken in one shyre varyeth from a nother. In so moche that in my dayes happened that certayn marchauntes were in a shippe in tamyse (*the river Thames*), for to haue sayled ouer the see into zelande (*Holland*) / and for lacke of wynde, thei taryed atte forlond (*Foreland*), and wente to lande for to refreshe them; And one of theym named sheffelde (*Sheffield*), a mercer, cam in-to an hows and exed for mete (*food*); and specyally he axyd after eggys; And the goode wyf answerde, that she coude speke no frenshe. And the marchaunt was angry, for he also coude speke no frenshe, but wolde haue hadde egges / and she vnderstode hym not / And thenne at laste a nother sayd that he wolde haue eyren / then the good wyf sayd that she

---

vnderstod hym wel / Loo, what sholde a man in thyse dayes now wryte, egges or
eyren / certaynly it is harde to playse euery man / by cause of dyuersite & chaunge of
langage . . . but in my Iudgemente / the comyn termes that be dayli vsed, ben lyghter
(*easier*) to be vnderstonde than the olde and auncyent englysshe /

📖 The lexical vocabulary of Text 92 is listed in the Word Book.

Here are two examples of Caxton's printing. The first is an advertisement, dating
from about 1478, for Caxton's edition of the *Sarum Ordinal* (an ordinal is a book of
church services; Sarum is the older name for Salisbury).

Text 93: Caxton's advertisement (facsimile)

If it pleſe onẏ man ſpirituel or temporel to bẏe onẏ
pẏes of two and thre comemoraciõs of ſaliſburi uſe
enprẏntid after the forme of this preſẽt lettre whiche
ben wel and trulẏ correct, late hẏm come to weſtmo
neſter in to the almoneſrẏe at the reed pale and he ſhal
haue them good chepe

Supplico ſtet cedula

📖 The lexical vocabulary of Text 93 is listed in the Word Book.

The second is one page from Caxton's own translation of a Dutch version of one of
Aesop's fables, *Die Hystorie van Reynaert du Vos*, printed in Gouda in 1479. He
completed the translation and printed it in 1481. This facsimile is from the second
edition in 1489.

Text 94: Caxton's The Historye of Reynart the Foxe, *1489 version (facsimile)*

¶ Hou the lyon kynge of alle beestys sent out hys maundementys that alle beestys sholde come to hys feest and court/
¶ Capitulo   Primo

IT was aboute þ tyme of penthecoste or whytsontyde that the wodes comynly be lusty and gladsom/ And trees clad with leuis & blossoms and þ ground wyth herbes & floures swete smellyng & also the foulkes and byrdes syngen melodyously in thepr armonye Thenne the lyon the noble kynge of al beestis wold in the holy dayes of this feest holde an open court at staden/ whyche he dyde to knowe ouer alle in his lande/ ¶ And commanded by strayte commyssyons and maundements that euery beest sholde come thider in suche wyse that alle the beestys grete and smale cam to the courte sauf Reynard the foy/ For he knewe hym self falsty and gylty in many thynges ageynst many beestys that thyder sholde comen that he durste not auenture to goo thyder/ whan the kynge of alle beestys had assemblyd alle hys court / Ther was none of them alle / But that he had compleyned sore on Reynard the foy.

¶ The fyrst complaynt made isegrym the woulf on reynard
Capitulo   ij°

Isegrym the woulf wyth hys lynage and frendes cam and stode to fore the kynge. And sayde hye & myghty prynce my lord the kynge I beseche yow that thurgh your grete myght. ryght and mercy that ye wyl haue pyte on the grete trespas and the vnresonable mysdedes that Reynart the fox hath don to me and my wyf that is to wyte he is comen in to myn hous ayenst the wille of my wyf ¶ And there he hath beppyssed my chyldren whereas they laye in suche wyse as they therof ben woxen blynde/ whereupon was

a   i

¶ How the lyon kynge of alle beftys fent out hys maūde
mentys that alle beeftys fholde come to hys feeft and court/
¶ Capitulo   Primo

IT was aboute þᵉ tyme of penthecofte or whytfontyde
that the wodes comynly be lufty and gladfom/And
trees clad with leuis & bloſſoms and þᵉ ground wyth
herbeſ & floures fwete fmellyng & alfo the fowles and byr:
des fyngen melodyoufly in theyr armonye Thenne the lyon
the noble kynge of al beftis wold in the holy dayes of this
feeft holde an open court at ftaden/whyche he dyde to knowe
ouer alle in his lande/¶And commanded by ftrayte com
myſſyons and maūdements that euery beeft fhold come thi
der in fuch wyfe that alle the beeftys grete and fmale cam
to the courte fauf Reynard the fox/For he knewe hym felf
fawty and gylty in many thynges ageynft many beeftys
that thyder fhold comen that he durfte not auenture to goo
thyder/whan the kynge of alle beeftys had aſſemblyd alle
hys court/Ther was none of them alle/But that he had
compleyned fore on Reynard the fox.
¶The fyrft complaynt made ifegrym the wulf on reynard
Capitulo   ij°

ISegrym the wulf wyth hys lynage and frendes cam
and ftode to fore the kynge. And fayde hye & myghty
prynce my lord the kynge I befeche yow that thurgh your
grete myght.ryght and mercy that ye wyl haue pyte on the
grete trefpas and the vnrefonable myfdedes that Reynart
the fox hath don to me and my wyf that is to wyte he is
comen in to myn hous ayenft the wille of my wyf ¶And
there he hath bepyſſed my chyldren where as they laye in
fuche wyfe as they therof ben woxen blinde/wherupon was . . .

📖 The lexical vocabulary of Text 94 is listed in the Word Book.

14.7 The medieval tales of King Arthur

In 1485 Caxton published a 'noble and joyous book entytled *Le Morte Darthur*'. He
describes it in these words:

> . . . a book of the noble hystoryes of the sayd Kynge Arthur and of certeyn of his
> knyghtes after a copye unto me delyvered. Whyche copye Syr Thomas Malorye dyd
> take oute of certeyn bookes of frensshe and reduced it into Englysshe.

We know that Sir Thomas Malory made his translations and adaptations from the
French while he was in prison. He wrote at the end of one of the books which make
up the collection,

> And I pray you all that redyth this tale to pray for hym that this wrote, that God sende
> hym good delyveraunce sone and hastely. Amen

but he died in prison in 1471.

Caxton's printed book was the only known source of Malory's version of the legends of King Arthur until 1934, when a manuscript was found in the Fellows' Library of Winchester College. It is not Malory's own hand, but more authentic than Caxton's book, which has many alterations, emendations and omissions.

Here is the opening of the fourth story, *The War with the Five Kings*, in the first of the books of the Winchester MS, *The Tale of King Arthur*.

Text 95: Sir Thomas Malory, c.1460–70 (i) (facsimile)

SO aftır thes queſtıs of Syr Gawayne Syr
tor anð kynge Pellynoꝛe Than hıt befelle that Merly/
on felle ın ðotage on the ðameſell that kynge Pellynoꝛe
brought to courte anð ſhe was / one of the ðameſels / of the Laðy of the
laake that hyght Nenyve But Merlıon wolðe nat lette her haue
no reſte but / all wayes / he wolðe by wyth. her Anð eu⁹ ſhe maðe
M[erlıon] good chere tylle ſche hað lerneð of hym all man⁹ of thyng
that ſche ðeſyreð anð he was aſſoteð vppon hır that he
myght nat be from hır // So on a tyme he tolðe to kynge
Arthure that he ſcholðe nat enðure longe but for all
hıs craftꝭ he ſcholðe be putte ınto the erthe quyk / anð ſo
he tolðe the kyng many thyngıs that ſcholðe be falle
but allwayes he warneð the kyng to kepe well hıs ſwer//
ðe anð the ſcawberðe * *for he told hym how the swerðe and the scawberðe*

ſcholðe be ſtolyn by a woman frome
hym that he moſte truſteð // Alſo he tolðe kyng Arthure
that he ſcholðe myſſe hym . Anð yett hað ye levɪr than all
youre lonðɪs haue me agayne // A ſayðe the kyng ſyn ye
knowe of youre evɪl aðuenture purvey for hɪt anð putt
hɪt a way by youre crauft⁹ that myſſeaðuenture / Nay ſeyðe
M[erlɪon] hɪt woll not be .

* The scribe omitted these words.

📖 The lexical vocabulary of Text 95 is listed in the Word Book.

📖 A short commentary is in the Text Commentary Book.

Activity 14.4

The first six lines of Text 95 were written by the principal scribe, and the rest by a second scribe. The handwriting is clearly different. Does the second scribe's spelling differ from that of the first?

The second extract from *Le Morte Darthur* comes from the final book in the Winchester MS, *The most piteous tale of the Morte Arthur saunz guerdon*. King Arthur has sustained a 'grevous wounde' in battle, and Sir Bedwere (Bedivere) has twice disobeyed the king's command to throw the jewelled sword Excalibur into the waters of the lake from which it first came.

Text 96: Sir Thomas Malory (ii) (facsimile)

Transcription
(There are some small holes in the manuscript causing the loss of a few letters.)

> ↑han ſ: Beð/
> were ðep(ar)teð anð wente to the ſwerðe anð lyghtly toke hıt vp
> anð ſo he wente vnto the watırs ſyðe anð there he bounðe
> the gyrðyll aboute the hyltıs anð threw þᵉ ſwerðe as far
> ın to the watır as he myʒt / Anð there cam an arme anð an honðe
> above the watır anð toke hıt anð *cleyʒt hıt anð ſhoke hıt thryſe
> anð braunðyſſheð anð than vanyſſheð wᵗ the ſwerðe into the
> watır // So ſ: Beðyvere cam agayne to the kynge anð tolðe
> hym what he ſaw // Alas ſeyðe the kynge helpe me hens for
> I ðreðe me I haue taryeð ouʳ[l]onge // Than ſ: Beðwere toke
> the kynge vppon hys bak anð ſo wente wᵗ hym to the watırs
> ſyðe anð whan they were there evyn faſte by the banke hoveð
> a lytyll barge wyth many fayre laðyes ın hıt anð amonge
> hem all was a quene anð all they hað blak hooðıs anð all
> they wepte anð ſhrykeð whan they ſaw kynge Arthur //
> Now put me ın to that barge ſeyðe the kynge anð ſo he ðeð
> ſofftely anð ther[e re]ſceyveð hym ıij. laðyes wᵗ grete mõnyng
> anð ſo they ſette hem [ð]owne anð ın one of þʳ lappıs kyng
> Arthure layðe hys [h]eðe anð than the quene ſeyðe a my
> ðere brothır why [ha]ue ye taryeð ſo longe frome me alas
> thys wounðe on youre heðe hath cauʒt ouʳ much coulðe
> anð anone they roweð from warð the lonðe anð ſ: Be
> ðyvere be hylðe all þo laðyes go frowarðe hym

cleyʒt = clutched

📖 The lexical vocabulary of Text 96 is listed in the Word Book.

14.8 Late 15th-century London dialect – the Cely letters

A collection of letters and memoranda of the Cely family, written in the 1470s and 1480s, gives us authentic handwritten evidence of London English a century after Thomas Usk's, and contemporary with the later Paston letters.

The Celys were wool merchants, or staplers. They bought woollen fleeces in England and sold them on the Continent in Calais and Bruges. The letters and accounts provide direct evidence for historians of the workings of a medieval English firm. They also give language students plenty of examples of late medieval commercial English, and are evidence of the speech and writing habits of middle-class Londoners of the period.

The collection contains letters by forty different people, but most are from two generations of the Cely family, father and sons. Like the Paston letters they show that there was as yet no fully standardised written English among private individuals (unlike scriveners and clerks). The spelling is not good evidence for the pronunciation of spoken English, partly because we do not know for certain the sounds given to particular letters, but also because spelling between different writers is somewhat irregular. There is comparatively little inconsistency of spelling by an individual, however. Variants are often to do with the addition of ⟨e⟩ or the choice of vowel letter in unstressed syllables:

afftyr/after	last/laste
caleys/calles/call₃ (*Calais*)	lord/lorde
com/come	mche/meche
dessesset/dessett (*deceased*)	non/none
dewke/dwke	trobellett/trobellytt
frenche/frensche/frynche	wryte/wrytt
gret/grete/grett	you/yow
hathe/hatth	

but the choice of some spellings does not seem to be based on any written standard, for example:

boshop	*bishop*	trobellett	*troubled*
dyssprowett	*disproved*	tytyng	*tiding*
grasse	*grace*	whas	*was*
hodyr	*other*	whelcom	*welcome*
ordenons	*ordnance*	whisse	*wise*
saffte	*safety*		

The following three texts consist of facsimiles and transcriptions, followed by versions in MnE spelling and punctuation.

Activity 14.5

List the principal lexical and grammatical features of the Celys' London English which mark its difference from MnE.

📖 A short commentary is in the Text Commentary Book.

Text 97: George Cely in Calais to Richard Cely in London, 12 March 1478 (facsimile)

Transcription

Ryght rewerent and whorſhypffull ffadyr afftyr all dew recomen-
daſyon pᵣtendyng I recomeavnd me vn to yow in the ~mo~ moſt lowly
eſt whiſſe that I con or may ffor dyr mor pleſythe ytt yow to
vndyr ſtond that I come vn to calles the thorſſeday afftyr my dep
tyng ffrom yow in ſaffte y thanke god and y whas whelcom vn
to my ffrendis ffor tyll my brodyr com to calles ther whas none
hodyr tydyng⁹ ther but I whas dede // etc // pleſythe ytt yow to vndᵣ
ſtond ther ys now none mᵣchant⁹ at call⁹ nor whas but ffew thys
monythe / and as ffor any hodyr tydyng⁹ I con none wrytt vn to
yow as ʒett tyll y her mor and be the next wryttyng þt I
ſent ʒe ſhall vndyr the ſalle of yowr ffellis wt mor be the
graſſe of god ~whah~ who hawe yow and all yowrs in hys kepyg
amen wrytt at calles the xij th day of mᵣche a lxxviij

> p yowr ſon
> G cely

MnE spelling and punctuation

Right reverent and worshipful father, after all due recommen-
dation pretending, I recommend me unto you in the most lowliest wise that I can or may. Furthermore, pleaseth it you to
understand that I came unto Calais the Thursday after my dep(ar)-

ting from you, in safety I thank God, and I was welcome unto my
friends, for till my brother came to Calais there was none other
tidings there but (= *except*) I was dead etc. Pleaseth it you to understand there is now none merchants at Calais nor was but few this
month, and as for any other tidings, I can none write unto
you as yet till I hear more, and by the next writing that I
send ye shall under(*stand*) the sale of your fells with more, by the
grace of God, who have you and all yowrs in his keeping,
amen. Writ at Calais the 12th day of March, a(*nno*) 78.

per your son,
G Cely

📖 The lexical vocabulary of Text 97 is listed in the Word Book.

Text 98: Richard Cely (the father) in London to Agnes, Richard and George Cely in Essex, 12 August 1479 (facsimile)

Transcription

I grete you wyll I late you wyt of ſeche tytyng as I here
Thomas blehom hatth a letter from caleys the weche
ys of a batell done on ſater^day laſte paſte be ſyde tyrwyn
be the dwke of borgan & the frynche kyng the
weche batell be gane on ſater day at iiij of the
cloke at after non and laſte tyll nyght & meche
blodc ſchede of bothe pertys and the dwke of
borgan hathe the fylde and the worſchepe the dwke
of borgan hathe gette meche ordenons of frenche
kyngys and hathe ſlayne v or vj ml frensche men
wryte on thorys day noe in haſte

p Rc cely

Modern English spelling and punctuation

> I greet you well. I let you wit of such tiding as I hear.
> Thomas Blehom hath a letter from Calais, the which
> is of a battle done on Saturday last past beside Tirwin
> by the Duke of Burgundy and the French king, the
> which battle began on Saturday at 4 of the
> clock at afternoon, and lasted till night, and much
> blood shed of both parties, and the Duke of
> Burgundy hath the field, and the worship. The Duke
> of Burgundy hath got much ordnance of (the) French
> king's and hath slain 5 or 6 thousand Frenchmen.
> Writ on Thursday now in haste.
>
> > per Richard Cely

📖 The lexical vocabulary of Text 98 is listed in the Word Book.

The following text is not a letter, but a jotted down note of political events and rumours in the troubled times preceding the deposing of Edward V and the accession of the Duke of Gloucester as Richard III. The first five items are written as facts; the rest, beginning with 'If', are rumours. The jottings were written on the back of an old memorandum, and are not always grammatically clear.

Lord Hastings, the Lord Chamberlain, had been executed in June 1483. The Chancellor was Thomas Rotherham, Archbishop of York; 'my lorde prynsse' was the Duke of York, Edward V's brother. The Earl of Northumberland and John Howard were supporters of the Duke of Gloucester.

Text 99: Note of events (June 1483) and memoranda by George Cely (facsimile)

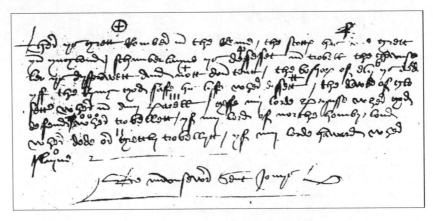

Transcription

> Ther ys grett romber ın the reme / the ſcottys has done gret
> yn ynglond / ſchamberlayne ys deſſeſſet ın trobell the chavnſe
> ler ys dyſſprowett and nott content / the boſhop of ely ys dede

yff the kyng god ʃʃaffe hɪs lyffe wher deʃʃett / the dewke of glo
ʃett⁹ wher ɪn any parell / geffe my lorde prynʃʃe wher god
defend wher trobellett / yf my lord of northehombyrlond
wher dede or grettly trobellytt / yf my lorde haward wher
ʃlayne

De movnʃewer sent jonys

'movnsewer sent jonys' (Monsieur St John) is a pseudonym – to disguise the name
– for Sir John Weston, from whom George Cely presumably got the rumours.

Modern English spelling and punctuation

There is great romber in the realm. The Scots has done great
in England. (The Lord) Chamberlain is deceased in trouble. The Chance
llor is disproved and not content. The Bishop of Ely is dead.
If the King, God save his life, were deceased. (If) the Duke of Gloucester were in any peril. If my Lord Prince were, God
defend, were troubled. If my Lord of Northumberland
were dead or greatly troubled. If my Lord Howard were
slain.

From monsieur Saint John

romber = rumour, disturbance, upheaval
disproved = proved false
troubled = molested

📖 The lexical vocabulary of Text 99 is listed in the Word Book.

The modernised versions of the letters help to clarify what are mainly difficulties of
word recognition because of the spelling. A few phrases are listed below:

Text 97   George Cely

pretending   *extended* = having been given
fells   *wool fleeces*
per (Latin)   *by*

Text 98   Richard Cely

wyt   *know*

Text 99   George Cely

romber   *disturbance* (obsolete meaning of rumour)
disproved   *proved false*
troubled   *molested*

14.9 15th-century loan-words

📖 A selection of loan-words recorded during this period can be found in the Word Book, after
the word-lists for Chapter 14.

15 Early Modern English II – the 16th century (i)

15.1 The development of writing hands (v) – the 16th century

From the late 15th century into the 16th there was a significant increase in business transactions, which led to the popular use of the hand that was both familiar to read and quick to write – **Secretary hand**.

> And Petir bithoughte on the word of Jhesu, that he hadde seid, Bifore the cok crowe, thries thou schalt denye me. And he yede out, and wepte bitterli.

At least three types of Secretary hand were taught at first, sometimes called *engrossing*, *upright* and *sloped* (*engrossing* – 'the action of writing out a document in a fair or legal character' – was a style used for formal documents rather than personal or business correspondence). A single distinctive, upright style was widely adopted *c.*1550.

The following letters of the alphabet, demonstrating a Secretary hand, are taken from a writing manual:

Here are two 16th-century orthodox examples of the hand; the first is the beginning of a letter written in the 1530s.

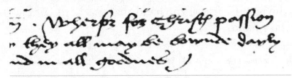

Transcription

> honorable my dutie don to yow^r maiſterſchip after moſt due man⁹ / So it is that albeit
> that yow^r m⁹cyfull goodnes is and hath ben mor to me than I am or can be able to
> recompenſe: yeth nature conſtraynith me (remembryng the greate pitie in yow)

This enlarged portion of the bottom right-hand corner of the letter will help you to examine the letter shapes more easily:

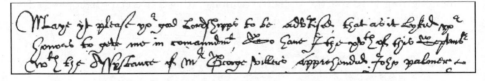

> ... Wherfor for Chriſts paſſion
> ... they all may be bownde dayly
> ... and in all goodnes /

This second example of Secretary hand is from a letter to the Council written in 1586:

> Maye yt pleaſe yor good Lordſhipps to be adv^rtiſed that as it lyked yor
> honors to geve me in comaundment, So have I the xvth of this Septembr
> with the aſſyſtance of Mr. George Villers apprehended John palmer ...

You will find a more detailed commentary on the letter shapes of Secretary, as written by Sir William Kingston to Lord Lisle in the 1530s, in section 15.2.2.

Another cursive hand was introduced from the Continent into England during the 16th century, which eventually became commonly used as an alternative to Secretary hand for all purposes, but especially for correspondence. It was known as **Italic** (also 'roman' or 'italian'), and is described as a 'humanistic' hand.

> *And Petir bithoughte on the word of Jhesu, that he hadde seid, Bifore the cok crowe, thries*
> *thou schalt denye me. And he yede out, and wepte bitterly.*

The following informal example of humanistic cursive hand is from a set of sermon notes, *c*.1530; it contrasts markedly with Secretary hand.

Transcription (abbreviations expanded)

Math. 19.	Si vis perfectus esse, vade & vende omnia quae habes, et sequere me.
Math. 10.	Nolite possidere aurum neque argentum neque pecuniam in zonis vestris.
Math. 8.	~~Volucres caeli nidos~~ Vulpes foveas habent, et volucres caeli etc.
Math. 17.	& aparto ore ejus invenies staterem (hoc est duplex didragma).
	& illum sumens da eijs pro me & te.
Actuum 4°.	Dividebant singulis prout cuique opus erat.

The fact that scriveners were expert in several contrasting styles of writing can be illustrated by the following extract from Sir Thomas More's *Treatise on the Passion*, written *c*.1550. **Italic** hand is used for the heading in Latin, **Bastard Secretary** hand for the translation which follows, and **Secretary** for the commentary.

15.2 The Lisle Letters

In Chapter 14 we saw how the private letters of the Pastons and the Celys in the 15th century give us some idea of everyday speech at the time. Another large collection, the Lisle Letters, from the early 16th century, provides us with examples of the language 50 years on.

The fact that writers at that time were not using a nationally standardised form of spelling does not mean that their spelling was haphazard, or that they simply 'wrote as they spoke'. There were some inconsistencies within an individual's spelling, especially in the use of a redundant final ⟨e⟩ on many words, but they had clearly learned a system. Variations occurred because there were no dictionaries or spelling books to refer to until later in the 16th century.

These letters were written to and by Lord Lisle, his family, friends and staff, when he was Governor of Calais for King Henry VIII, from 1533 to 1540. The French town was at that time an English possession. The letters provide examples of a wide range of correspondence, both formal and informal, and are therefore first-hand evidence of the state of the language then.

15.2.1 George Bassett to his parents

Here is an example of a letter by a 14-year-old boy. George Bassett was Lady Lisle's son by her first marriage, and as part of his education he was 'put to service' in the household of Sir Francis Bryan. The letter is 'purely formal: the boy has nothing to say and he says it in the approved Tudor manner' (Muriel St Clare Byrne, editor of *The Lisle Letters*).

Text 100: George Bassett to Lord and Lady Lisle, written 1 July 1539 (facsimile)

Transcription

> Right honoȝable and my moſt deȝe and ſingleȝ goode loȝde
> and ladye / ın my moſt humble maneȝ I ȝecōmaunde me vnto yow
> beſechynge to have yoȝ dailye bleſſynge / and to heȝe of yoȝ goode
> and pȝoſpus helth / foȝe the conſeȝvatıone of whıche / I pȝaye
> dailye vnto almyghty godde. I ceȝtıfye youe by theys my
> ȝude lȝēs* that my Maıſteȝ and my Ladye be ın goode helthe /   *letters
> to whome I am myche bounde. ffuȝtheȝmoȝe I beſeche
> yoȝ loȝdeſhepe and ladeſhepe to have me heȝtılye ȝecōmēdyde
> vnto my Bȝotheȝ and Syſteȝs. And thus I pȝaye godde to conſeȝve
> yoȝ loȝdeſhepe and ladıſhepe eveȝ ın goode / longe / and
> pȝoſpeȝus helthe wᵗ honoȝ. ffȝom Wobuȝn the
> fıȝſte daye of Julye
>   By yoȝ humble and
>   owne Son Geoȝge
>   Baſſette

George Bassett's formal 'duty letter' to his parents does not tell us much about him, except that he can write very competently in a neat Secretary hand. He uses the **strike** or **virgule** [/] as a mark of punctuation, and the occasional full-stop, then called a **prick**. There are some of the conventional abbreviations, similar to those you will have noticed in the Cely and Paston letters and in all the MS facsimiles in the book, such as the **line** over the vowel preceding one of the nasal consonants ⟨n⟩ or ⟨m⟩, especially if the consonant was double, and writing post-vocalic ⟨r⟩ and other combinations of letters as a superscript.

The lexical vocabulary of Text 100 is listed in the Word Book.

15.2.2 Sir William Kingston to Lord Lisle

The next letter is from Sir William Kingston, who was a member of the King's Privy Council and Constable of the Tower at the time. Sir William recommends a servant and, as there is no news to pass on, gossips about the King's activities and asks Lord Lisle to look out for some hawks for him. Notice the ironical reference to the usefulness of praying to St Loy (the saint whom Chaucer's Prioress swears by) – Lady Kingston's horse has been lame ever since she prayed for it. The letter is an example of an educated man's style of writing which, at first glance, would be unacceptable today in its presentation because there is no punctuation or paragraphing.

Kingston's informal cursive handwriting here is his personal style of the common current Secretary hand. Some of the letter shapes will be unfamiliar in their execution, which makes the letter difficult to decipher at first.

- abbreviations: e.g. the ⟨er⟩ in *understand* and *master*
  (l. 2) is reduced to a small curl joined to the
  previous letter – *understand* – *master*.

- letter ⟨d⟩: ⟨ð⟩, e.g. in *gud lord* (l. 4). This phrase also illustrates how some words end with a descending 'flourish' which does not represent a letter.

- letter ⟨h⟩: ⟨ℎ⟩ – word-initial in *his* and *harry* (l. 3); also a more cursive form of ⟨h⟩ for speedy handwriting in *here* (l. 7), *thay* (l. 7), *with* (l. 8).

- letter ⟨k⟩: ⟨𝑘⟩ – *kyng hawk(es)* and *goshawk(es)* (l. 11).

- 2-form of letter ⟨r⟩ mostly: ⟨𝑟⟩ – *ther, gerfawken or yerkyn* (l. 14) – except the word *your*, and the final word, *power*.

- long ⟨s⟩: ⟨ʃ⟩ word-initial and medial – *und(er)stand, mast(er)* (l. 2) small ⟨s⟩ word-final: ⟨s⟩ – *ys* (l. 12), *charges* (l. 16).

- ⟨u⟩ and ⟨v⟩ are still different forms of the same letter, ⟨v⟩ used when word-initial, and ⟨u⟩ elsewhere, cf. *gud, vnto, vnderstand* (ll. 1 and 2).

- his ampersand, a shorthand for *and*, is a curved flourish.

Activity 15.1

Examine the spelling of the words in the letter, and discuss any that seem unusual to you. Is the spelling significantly irregular or inconsistent? How many words have more than one spelling?

Text 101: Sir William Kingston to Lord Lisle, 26 September 1533 (facsimile)

Transcription

my gud loꝛð I ꝛecõmaunde me vnto your gud loꝛðſhyp yf ıt may pleſe
your loꝛðſhyp to vndᵒſtand that maſtᵒ nevell fᵣ eðwaꝛð hath
ðeſyꝛeð me to wꝛıt vnto you ın the fauᵒ of hys fᵣuant haꝛy
fomᵒ thys beyꝛer wech the kyng ys gud lorð vnto I
thynke you ſhall lyke hym well for he hath cõtenewed

ın the cort mony yeres wıth maſteꝰ nevell my loꝛd to
aduꝰtyſe you of newes heꝛe be non as ꝫıt for now thay be
abowt the peſſe ın the mꝰches of ſcotland ⁊ wıth goddꝰ
gꝛace all ſhalbe well ⁊ as ꝫıt the kyngꝰ gꝛace hathe
haꝛd now woꝛd fꝛom my loꝛd of Wyncheſtꝰ ⁊ ſo the
kyng hawkꝰ euꝰy day wıth goſhawkꝰ ⁊ otheꝛ hawkꝰ
that ys to ſay laynꝰs ſpaꝛhawkꝰ ⁊ mꝰlıons both affoꝛe
none ⁊ aftꝰ yf the wetheꝛ ſve I pꝛay you my loꝛd yf
theꝛ be hony geꝛfawken oꝛ yeꝛkyn to help͡ᵐᵉ to both yf ıt
may be ⁊ foꝛ lak of bothe to haue wun ⁊ to ſend me
woꝛde of the chaꝛges theꝛ of ⁊ then your loꝛdſhyp doſe meche
foꝛ me I ⁊ my wyfe both Ryght haꝛtely ꝛecōmaunde huſ
vnto my gud lady ⁊ we thanke my lady foꝛ my token foꝛ ıt
cam to me ın the chuꝛche of the blak fꝛeꝛes ⁊ my wyf
waſe Deſpoſed to haue offeꝛd ıt to ſaynt loy at hyr hoꝛſe
ſhuld not halt ⁊ he nevꝰ went vp ꝛyght ſyne I beche your
loꝛdſhyp to haue me ın your ꝛeymembꝛance to maſtꝰ poꝛtꝰ
⁊ my lady ⁊ to maſtꝰ mꝰſhall ⁊ my lady ⁊ to maſtꝰ mayes
⁊ my lady ⁊ thus oꝰ loꝛd ın heyvın ſend you meche honꝰ
⁊ all your company well to faꝛe fꝛom waltham abbay
the fꝛyday affoꝛe myhylmas ͡ᵈᵃʸ wıth the hand of all
yours to my power

Wıllm Kyngſton

pesse = peace; *freres* = friars; *saynt loy* = St Eligius (*St Eloi* in French); *syne* = since

The following words are names of birds used in hawking or falconry:

goshawkes	(goshawks)	*layners*	(lanners)
sparhawkes	(sparrowhawks)	*merlions*	(merlins)
gerfawken	(gerfalcon)	*yerkyn*	(jerkin = male gerfalcon)

MnE spelling and punctuation

My good lord I recommend me unto your good lordship.

If it may please your lordship to understand that Master Neville, Sir Edward, hath desired me to write unto you in the favour of his servant Harry Somer, this bearer, which the King is good lord unto. I think you shall like him well, for he hath continued in the Court many years with Master Neville.

My lord, to advertise you of news, here be none as yet, for now they be about the peace in the Marches of Scotland, & with God's grace all shall be well. And as yet the King's grace hath heard no word from my Lord of Winchester, & so the King hawks every day with goshawks & other hawks, that is to say lanners, sparrowhawks & merlins, both afore noon & after, if the weather serve.

I pray you my lord, if there be any gerfalcon or jerkin to help me to both, if it may be, & for lack of both to have one, & to send me word of the charges thereof, & then your lordship does much for me.

I & my wife both right heartily recommend us unto my good lady, & we thank my lady for my token, for it came to me in the church of the Black Friars & my wife was disposed to have offered it to Saint Loy that her horse should not halt, & he never went upright since.

I beseech your lordship to have me in your remembrance to Master Porter & my lady, & to Master Marshall & my lady, & to Master Mayes & my lady. And thus our Lord in heaven send you much honour & all your company well to fare.

From Waltham Abbey the Friday afore Michelmas Day, with the hand of all yours to my power

William Kingston

15.2.2.1 Commentary

The spelling is consistent. Most words when repeated are spelt identically, for example, *affore, gud, lordshyp, recommaunde*. The only exceptions are three pairs of words with and without an additional ⟨e⟩, a common feature in writing and printing up to the 18th century – *hath/hathe, word/worde* and *wyf/wyfe*.

The complete absence of punctuation makes an initial reading more difficult for us, but obviously was not regarded as a problem in private letters in the 1530s. The version printed above with present-day conventions of spelling, punctuation and paragraphing helps to remove much of the strangeness of the text. Idiom and style are also unfamiliar, but the letter is fully grammatical for its time.

📖 The lexical vocabulary of Text 101 is listed in the Word Book.

15.2.3 The Bishop of Carlisle to Lord Lisle

The Bishop of Carlisle, John Kite, was a contemporary of Lord Lisle's and an active statesman as well as a churchman. He was a friend of Cardinal Wolsey and had been sent on several diplomatic missions in the 1510s and 1520s. This letter contains nothing of importance but is of interest as there is a postscript written in the bishop's own hand, which contrasts in penmanship with the main part, dictated to a clerk/scrivener. He refers to Sir William Kingston, the writer of the previous letter (Text 101).

Text 102: Letter from the Bishop of Carlisle to Lord Lisle, December 1533 (facsimile)

Modernised spelling and punctuation

My lord I commend me heartily unto you right glad ye be in good health &c.
Sir, Roland your servant was with me this day and gave me commenda-
tions upon your behalf, whereof I do much heartily thank you.
And further, he showed me that your Lordship did not a little marvel,
so many letters as ye had sent unto me, that ye heard nothing
from me again. Sir, I asssure you, since our being together I received
no letter from you or otherwise, but only commendation by your

letters sent unto Mr Kingston. Further. your said servant showed
me that your lordship hath provided for me ~~three~~ two barrels of herring.
I pray you heartily to cause the same to be conveyed unto me, and I
shal consider thereof the charge and pay it gladly at the sight.
I pray you that I may be heartily commended unto my good lady
your bedfellow. Thus fare your lordship as well as I would my
self. From Carlisle Place, the 17th of December.

Sir William Kingston and his good wife recommen-
deth them unto you & to your good honour. And
I pray you that this mine own handwriting
may be taken in party of recompense for a letter
which I received from your good honour's ladyship
this day, as above written. By the hand of yours
with his at commandment,

John Carlisle

📖 The lexical vocabulary of Text 102 is listed in the Word Book.

15.3 Formal prose in the 1530s

An example of formal written language contemporary with the Lisle Letters is Sir
Thomas Elyot's *The boke named the Gouernour*, printed in London in 1531. Its
proheme, or preface, dedicates the book to King Henry VIII:

Text 103: Proheme to The Gouernour *(facsimile)*

> **The Proheme.**
> **The proheme of Thomas Elyot knyghte
> vnto the moste noble ꝛ victorious prince
> kinge Henry the eyght kyng of Eng-
> lande and Fraunce / defender of
> the true faythe / and lorde
> of Jrelande.**

Elyot's purpose was 'to describe in our vulgare tunge / the fourme of a iuste publike
wcale' – for *weale* or *weal*, now an archaic word, we would use *welfare* or *prosperity*.
He named it *The Gouernour* 'for as moch as this present boke treateth of the
education of them / that hereafter may be demed worthy to be gouernors of the
publike weale'. He wrote it in English, but in common with all educated men
regarded Latin and Greek the essential languages of education and learning, as the
following short extracts show.

The first chapter of the book deals with:

> **The firſte Boke.**
> **¶ The ſignificacion of a publike**
> **weale/and why it is called**
> **in latin Reſpublica.**

Text 104: Sir Thomas Elyot, The Gouernour, 1531 (i) (facsimile)

A publike weale is a body lyuyng/cōpacte *publyke*
oʒ made of ſondry aſtates and degrees of *weale.*
men/whiche is diſpoſed by the oʒdre of e‑
quite/and gouerned by the rule and mode‑
ration of reaſon. In the latin toinge hit is
called Reſpublica/of the whiche the woʒde *Reſpub*‑
Res/hath diuers ſignifications/ꜩ dothe nat *lica.*
only betoken that/that is called a thynge/
whiche is diſtincte from a perſone/but alſo
ſignifieth aſtate/condition/ſubſtance/and
plebe. pʒofite. In our olde vulgare/pſite is called
weale: And it is called a welthy contraye/
wherin is all thyng that is pʒofitable: And
he is a welthy man/that is riche in money
and ſubſtance. Publike(as Parro ſaith)is
diriuied of people: whiche in latin is cal‑
led Populus. wherfoʒe hit ſemeth that men
haue ben lōge abuſed in calling Rempublicā ꜩ
cōmune weale. And they which do ſuppoſe
it ſo to be called foʒ that/that euery thinge
ſhulde be to all men in cōmune without di‑
ſcrepance of any aſtate oʒ condition/be ther
to moued moʒe by ſenſualite/than by any
good reaſon oʒ inclinatiō to humanite. And
that ſhall ſone appere vnto them that wyll
be ſatiſſied either with autoʒite/oʒ with na‑
turall oʒdre and example.
Fyʒſt the ppʒe ꜩ trewe ſignification of the
woʒdes publike ꜩ cōmune/whiche be boʒo‑
wed of the latin tonge foʒ the inſufficiécie of
our owne lāgage/ſhal ſufficiétly declare the
blyndenes of them/whiche haue hitherto
holden and maynteyned the ſayde opiniōs.

Transcription into MnE spelling and punctuation, with grammar and vocabulary unchanged

A public weal is a body living, compact
or made of sundry estates and degrees of
men, which is disposed by the order of
equity, and governed by the rule and mode-
ration of reason. In the Latin tongue it is
called *respublica*, of the which the word
res hath divers significations, & doth not
only betoken that, that is called a *thing*,
which is distinct from a person, but also
signifieth *estate*, *condition*, *substance*, and
profit. In our old vulgar, *profit* is called
weal; and it is called a wealthy country,
wherein is all thing that is profitable; and
he is a wealthy man, that is rich in money
and substance. *Public* (as Varro saith) is
derived of *people*, which in Latin is called
populus, wherfore it seemeth that men
have been long abused in calling *rempublicam*
a *common weal*. And they which do suppose
it so to be called for that, that everything
should be to all men in common without
discrepancy of any estate or condition, be thereto
moved more by sensuality, than by any
good reason or inclination to humanity. And
that shall soon appear unto them that will
be satisfied either with authority, or with
natural order and example.
First, the proper & true signification of the
words *public* & *common*, which be borrowed
of the Latin tongue for the insufficiency of
our own language, shall sufficiently declare the
blindness of them, which have hitherto
holden and maintained the said opinions.

Elyot refers to 'the insufficiencie of our owne langage' when defining the words *publike* and *commune* 'whiche be borowed of the latin tonge'. Elyot's *commune* is MnE *common*, and is used in the sense of the word *commoner* as against *noble*. We know now that both words had been taken from Old French during the ME period, but their source was the Latin *publicus* and *communis*, and Elyot, like other scholarly writers of the period, himself Englished many Latin and Greek words in order to express his meaning. Sir Thomas Elyot sets out a programme of education for young noblemen in which learning Latin begins before the age of seven:

> **The ordre of lernynge that a noble man ſhulde be trayned in before he come to thaige of seuen yeres. Cap.v.**

Text 105: Sir Thomas Elyot, The Gouernour, 1531 (ii) (facsimile)

> But there can be
> nothyng moꝛe conuenient/than by litle and
> litle to trayne and exercise them in spekyng
> of latyne : infourmyng them to knowe firſt
> the names in latine of all thynges that co-
> meth in syghte / and to name all the partes
> of theyꝛ bodies :

It is clear from the next extract from *The Gouernor* that in Elyot's day, just as today, strong feelings could be aroused over accent and pronunciation. Here he is recommending the kind of nurse and serving-woman that a young nobleman under seven should have:

Text 106: Sir Thomas Elyot, The Gouernour, 1531 (iii) (facsimile)

> But to retourne to my
> purpose ; hit ſhall be expedient / that a no-
> ble mannes sonne in his infancie haue with
> hym continually/onely suche/as may accu-
> ſtome hym by litle and litle to speake pure
> and elegant latin. Semblably the nourises
> ⁊ other women aboute hym / if it be poſſi-
> ble/to do the same: oꝛ at the leſte way/that
> they speke none englisſhe but that/whiche
> is cleane/polite/perfectly/ and articulately
> pꝛonounced/omittinge no lettre oꝛ sillable/
> as foliſhe women often times do. of a wan-
> tonneſſe/wherby diuers noble men/and gē-
> tilmennes chyldꝛen (as I do at this daye
> knowe) haue attained coꝛrupte and foule
> pꝛonuntiation.

semblably = similarly; *nouriſes* = nurses

We can use these texts from *The Gouernour* not only for the interest of their subject matter and style, but to observe those features of grammar and lexis which clearly mark Elyot's language as still archaic in terms of MnE, but yet much closer to our Standard English than the earlier texts we have studied.

15.3.1 Commentary

15.3.1.1 Spelling

There are only a few alternative spellings in the Elyot texts, which show a transitional stage in the development of a standard:

1 Words may or may not have a redundant letter ⟨e⟩: *latin/latine/latyne; onely/only; ther/there; thinge/thyng/thynge; which/whiche.*
2 The OE neuter pronoun *hit* is beginning to lose its initial consonant: *hit/it.*
3 Some nouns end in either ⟨-cio(u)n⟩ or ⟨-tio(u)n⟩. The alternative ⟨c⟩ or ⟨t⟩ derives from the dual source of such words, from OF with the spelling ⟨-cion⟩, or from the original Latin suffix ⟨-tio / -tion(em)⟩: *significacions/signification, pronounced/pronuntiation, shal/shall.*
4 Abbreviations used in the writing of manuscripts are carried over into printing:

- a macron marks the omission of a following nasal consonant ⟨n⟩ or ⟨m⟩, e.g. cōpacte (*compact*), cōmune (*common*), inclinatiō (*inclination*), lāgage (*language*), opiniōs (*opinions*), lōge (*long* etc.
- the use of ⟨p⟩ for *pro*: e.g. ₰fite (*profit*), ₰pꝛe (*proper*).

5 The use of variant letter forms according to their position in a word:

- Long ⟨ſ⟩, in word-initial and medial positions; round ⟨s⟩ is word-final – e.g. *aſtates.*
- Letters ⟨u⟩ and ⟨v⟩ are still alternative forms of the same letter, used for both the vowel [u] and the consonant [v], their use depending upon their position in the word:

  word-initial ⟨v⟩ – consonant *vulgare, vertue, violently*; vowel *vnto, vniuersall.*
  word-medial ⟨u⟩ – consonant *soueraigne, moreouer, haue*; vowel *naturall, studie, tunge.*

  This can be clearly seen in the spelling of *deuulgate*, a now obsolete form of *divulgate* or *divulge.*
- Letter ⟨j⟩ is not yet used for [ʤ] – *maiestie, iuge, subiectes, iuste.*

  ⟨ꝛ⟩ (usually following letter ⟨o⟩) and ⟨r⟩ – e.g. *oꝛdre.*
  ⟨ð⟩ (word-initial) and ⟨d⟩ (word-medial and final) – e.g. *ðiſpoſed.*

15.3.1.2 Punctuation

- Full-stops mark the end of sentences, which begin with capital letters.
- The virgule ⟨/⟩ is used where we would expect a comma ⟨,⟩.
- The colon ⟨:⟩ is occasionally written.
- The ampersand for *and* resembles the older OE form like a figure seven, ⟨7⟩.

15.3.1.3 Vocabulary

There are 130 lexical words (nouns, verbs, adjectives, adverbs) in Texts 107–9.

Their proportions by derivation are: OE/ON 58 = 44.6%; OF/AF 61 = 46.9%; Latin 11 = 8.5%. If you compare these figures with those of any of the ME texts in earlier chapters, you will see that by the 16th century there is a much larger proportion of words from French and Latin in formal educated prose like Elyot's *The Gouernour* – roughly 55% to 45% from OE. In other words, there is a scholarly vocabulary of words which do not belong to the native **core vocabulary** of English, which generally consists of surviving reflexes from OE, and OF words that had been fully assimilated into English in spelling and pronunciation by the 14th century.

📖 The lexical vocabulary of Texts 103–6 is listed (i) alphabetically, and (ii) by derivation and date, in the Word Book.

15.3.1.4 Grammar

Verb inflections

The only significant difference from the present-day grammatical system in the texts is the 3rd person present tense inflection ⟨-eth⟩, *all thyngs that* **cometh**, *& **dothe** nat only betoken, but also* **signifieth**, *wherfore hit* **semeth**. But the verbs in *that they* **speke** and *do suppose* are uninflected, and so we would need more data to establish the norm.

Other differences lie in the use of the system rather than in the system itself, for example the choices made then and now in the selection of pronouns.

Relative pronouns

Today *who* is the relative pronoun used to refer to human subjects, and *which* for non-human referents only, but in Elyot's syntax *which* refers to both human and non-human:

> *a publike weale . . .* **whiche** *is disposed by . . .*
> *a thynge* **whiche** *is distincte from a persone*
> *And they* **which** *do suppose it so to be called . . .*
> *the blyndenes of them /* **whiche** *haue hitherto . . .*

Elyot also uses *that* as a relative pronoun for both human and non-human referents, as in present-day usage:

> *that /* **that** *is called . . .*
> *wherin is all thyng* **that** *is profitable*
> *he is a welthy man /* **that** *is riche in money and substance*
> *them* **that** *will be satisfied . . .*

Neuter pronouns

Elyot uses both the older form of neuter pronoun *hit*, surviving from OE, and *it*, which suggests that usage had not yet become standardised:

> *and why* **it** *is called in latin Respublica*
> *In the latin tonge* **hit** *is called Respublica*
> **hit** *shall be expedient*
> *if* **it** *be possible*

*And **it** is called a welthy contraye . . .*
*wherfore **bit** semeth . . .*
*they which do suppose **it** so to be called . . .*

15.4 A different view on new words

Sir Thomas Elyot expressed a scholar's view on the superiority of the resources of Latin and Greek, from which languages hundreds of words were 'Englished'. These words were disparagingly referred to as 'inkhorn terms' – words coming from the scholar's horn of ink and therefore pedantic – and there was a lot of controversy over this. For example, George Puttenham called the introduction of Latin and Greek words 'corruption' of language, the result of the 'peeuish affectation of clerks and scholers', because it introduced polysyllabic words into English:

Text 107: George Puttenham on inkhorn terms (1589) (facsimile)

but now I muſt recant and con-
feſſe that our Normane Engliſh which hath growen ſince *William*
the Conquerour doth admit any of the auncient feete , by reaſon of the many *polyſillables* euen to ſixe and ſeauen in one word,
which we at this day vſe in our moſt ordinarie language : and
which corruption hath bene occaſioned chiefly by the peeuiſh affectation not of the Normans them ſelues, but of clerks and ſcho-
lers or ſecretaries long ſince, who not content with the vſual Normane or Saxon word, would conuert the very Latine and Greeke
word into vulgar French, as to ſay innumerable for innombrable,
reuocable, irreuocable, irradiation, depopulatiō & ſuch like, which
are not naturall Normans nor yet French, but altered Latines, and
without any imitation at all : which therefore were long time de-
ſpiſed for inkehorne termes, and now be reputed the beſt & moſt
delicat of any other.

auncient feete means the verse rhythms of the classical Latin and Greek poets. A foot is a unit of rhythm.
peeuish is here used as an adjective of dislike, 'expressing rather the speaker's feeling than any quality of the object referred to' (*OED*).

📖 The lexical vocabulary of Text 107 is listed, alphabetically and by derivation and date, in the Word Book.

But there were those who did not not accept Sir Thomas Elyot's view on 'the insufficiencie of our own langage', and who disliked any borrowing from other languages, not just the creation of 'inkhorn terms'. Richard Verstegan's view, published in 1605, is typical of many 16th-century writers:

Text 108: Richard Verstegan, A Restitution of Decayed Intelligence, 1605 (facsimile)

> Since the tyme of *Chaucer*, more Latin & French,
> hath bin mingled with our toung then left out of it,
> but of late wee haue falne to ſuch borowing of
> woords from, Latin, French , and other toungs, that
> it had bin beyond all ſtay and limit, which albeit ſome
> of vs do lyke wel and think our toung thereby much
> bettred, yet do ſtrangers therefore carry the farre leſſe
> opinion thereof, ſome ſaying that it is of it ſelf no lan-
> guage at all, but the ſcum of many languages, others
> that it is moſt barren, and that wee are dayly faine to
> borrow woords for it (as though it yet lacked ma-
> king) out of other languages to patche it vp withall,
> *Our toung* and that yf wee were put to repay our borrowed
> *diſcredited* ſpeech back again, to the languages that may lay
> *by our lan-* claime vnto it ; wee ſhould bee left litle better then
> *guage-bor-* dumb, or ſcarſly able to ſpeak any thing that ſhould
> *rowing .* bee ſencible.

📖 The lexical vocabulary of Text 108 is listed, alphabetically and by derivation and date, in the Word Book.

However, if we compare the etymologies of the lexical words in these two texts, which are roughly equal in length, we find that a quarter of Puttenham's vocabulary derives directly from Latin, in spite of his attack on the 'peevish affectation' of inkhorn terms.

Puttenham			
Lexical word types: 56	OE	18	32.1%
	OF/AF	23	41.1%
	Latin	14	25.0%
	not known	1	1.8%
Verstegan			
Lexical word types: 49	OE/ON	35	71.5%
	OF/ONF	12	24.5%
	not known	2	4.0%

15.5 John Hart's *An Orthographie*

During the 16th century the first dictionaries, spelling-books and grammars of English were published. The writers were responding to a growing sense that the language needed an agreed form of spelling, grammar and vocabulary. People saw that the letters of the alphabet were too few to match the sounds of English, and that the spelling of many words did not match their pronunciation. Puttenham's view of the language as 'corrupted' was shared by many others.

One of the earliest books which advocated a reform of English spelling was John

Hart's *An Orthographie*, published in 1569. In the following extract he is justifying the need for his new spelling system, 'the new maner':

Text 109: John Hart's An Orthographie, 1569 – howe euerye language ought to bee written (facsimile)

Which is vppon the consideration of the seuerall voices of the speach, and the vse of their seuerall markes for them, which we cal letters. But in the moderne & present maner of writing (as well of certaine other languages as of our English) there is such confusion and disorder, as it may be accounted rather a kinde of ciphring, or such a darke kinde of writing, as the best and readiest wit that euer hath bene, could, or that is or shalbe, can or may, by the only gift of reason, attaine to the ready and perfite reading thereof, without a long and tedious labour, for that it is unfit and wrong shapen for the proportion of the voice. Whereas the new maner hereafter (thoughe it seeme at the first very straunge, hard and vnprofitable) by the reading only therof, will proue it selfe fit, easie and delectable, and that for whatsoeuer English may be written in that order.

Hart's argument begins with the 'fiue differing simple soundes or voyces' – that is, the five vowels written ⟨a e i o u⟩ and sounding, in stressed syllables, something like [æ/a ɛ ɪ ɒ/ɔ ʊ] as short vowels and [æː/aː eː iː oː uː] as long vowels. They should, he says, each represent one sound, but 'they haue bene and are abused in diuers soundes'. He illustrates their proper pronunciation with this sentence:

The pratling Hosteler hath dressed, curried, and rubbed our horses well.

and adds,

none of the fiue vowels is missounded, but kept in their proper and auncient soundes.

As you read that sentence, remember two things. First, that the present-day RP and Southern English pronunciation of *curried* and *rubbed*, with the short vowel [ʌ], did not exist then. The vowel was [ʊ]. Secondly, that the ⟨r⟩ in *horses* was pronounced, and the vowel in *Hosteler* and *horses* was the same. A possible phonetic version of the sentence reads,

[ðə pɹætlɪŋ hɒstələɹ hæθ dɹɛst kuɹɪd ænd ɹʊbd uːɹ hɒɹsɪz wəl]

Hart pointed out two spelling conventions which are still part of the modern English system, but which he did not use in his reformed spelling. The first was the use of a final ⟨e⟩ as a diacritic letter to mark a preceding long vowel, as in MnE *hate/hat*, *site/sit*. The second was the use of double consonants to mark a preceding short vowel, as in MnE *matting/mating* and *robbing/robing*. He preferred to use a dot under the letter to mark a long vowel, e.g. ⟨i̇⟩:

> I leaue also all double consonants: hauing a mark for the long vowell, there is therby sufficient knowledge giuen that euerye unmarked vowell is short . . .

The interest of Hart's book for us is not so much in the reformed alphabet that he invented, but in the authentic evidence it indirectly provides about changes in the pronunciation of English. Here is a facsimile of the opening of the first two pages of the second part of the book, which is printed in Hart's new spelling, followed by a transcription into MnE spelling.

Activity 15.2

Identify the sound changes that Hart describes in this extract from his book.

Text 110: John Hart's new alphabet and spelling system (facsimile)

An exercise of that which is said: wherein is declared, how the rest of the consonants are made
by th'instruments of the mouth: which
was omitted in the premisses, for that
we did not much abuse
them. Chapter vii

I n this title above-written, I consider of the ⟨i⟩ in exercise, & of the
⟨u⟩, in instruments: the like of the
⟨i⟩, in title, which the common man,
and many learned, do sound in the
diphthongs ⟨ei⟩, and ⟨iu⟩: yet I
would not think it meet to write them, in those
and like words, where the sound of the vowel only, may be as well allowed in our speech, as that of
the diphthong used of the rude: and so far I allow
observation for derivations. / Whereby you may
perceive, that our single sounding and use of letters, may in process of time, bring our whole nation
to one certain, perfet and general speaking. –
/ Wherein she must be ruled by the learned from
time to time. / And I can not blame any man
to think this manner of new writing strange, for
I do confess it is strange to my self, though before

I have ended the writing, and you the reading of
this book, I doubt not but you and I shall think
our labours well bestowed. / And not-with-stan-
ding that I have devised this new manner of writing for our /English, I mean not that / Latin
should be written in these letters, no more then the
/ Greek or /Hebrew, neither would I write t'any
man of any strange nation in these letters, but
whenas I would write / English. – / And as I would
gladly counterfeit his speech with my tongue, so would
I his writing with my hand. – Yet who could
let me t'use my pen the best I could, thereby t'
attain the sooner to the perfect pronunciation, of a-
ny strange speech: but writing / English, we may
(as is said) use for every strange word, the same
marks or letters of the voices which we do find in
speech, without any other regard to show by writing whence the word is borrowed, then as we do in
speaking. / For such curiosity in superfluous letters, for derivation or for difference, and so forth,
is the disordering and confounding, of any writing: contrary to the law of the perfection thereof, and against all reason: whereby, it should be o-
bedient unto the pronunciation, as to her lady
and mistress: and so, add or diminish as she shall
in success of time command.

The opening lines of text 113 are recorded on the CD/cassette tape.

an ɛksɛrsiz ɒv ðat hwiʧ ɪz sɛːd hwerɪn ɪz dɛklard, həʊ ðə rɛst ɒv
ðə kɒnsɒnants ɑr mad bəɪ ðɪnstruments ɒv ðə məʊθ, hwiʧ waz
ɔmitɛd ɪn ðə premɪsɛz, fɔr ðat wi dɪd nɒt muʃ abjuz ðɛm.

ʧaptɛr sɛvən

ɪn ðɪs tiːtəl abuv wrɪtən, əɪ kɒnsɪdər ɒv ðɪ iː ɪn ɛksɛrsiz, and ɒv
ðə u ɪn *instruments* ðə ləɪk ɒv ðə i ɪn *tiːtəl* hwiʧ ðə kɒmən man,
and manɪ lernd, duː səʊnd ɪn ðə dɪphθɒŋgz əɪ and ju. jɛt əɪ wʊld
nɒt θɪŋk ɪt miːt tʊ wrəɪt ðɛm, ɪn ðoːz and ləɪk wuːrdz, hweːr ðə
səʊnd ɒv ðə voɛl oːnlɪ, mɛː bi aswɛl ələʊɛd ɪn əʊr spiːʧ, as ðat ɒv
ðə dɪfθɒŋg juzd ɒv ðə rɪud, and so fɑr əɪ aləʊ ɒbsɛrvasɪɒn fɔr
derɪvasɪɒns. hwerbəɪ ju mɛː pɛrseːv, ðat əʊr sɪŋgəl səʊndɪŋg and
jus ɒv letərz, mɛː ɪn prɒsɛs ɒv təɪm, brɪŋg əʊr hoːl nasɪɒn tu oːn
sertɛn, perfɛt and ʤenɛral speːkɪŋg. hwerɪn ʃi mʊst bi rɪulɛd bəɪ
ðə lernɛd frɒm təɪm tə təɪm

15.5.1 Commentary

Hart apparently believed that a reformed spelling, in which there was only one letter
for each sound, would in time put an end to social and regional dialectal accents, and

bring our whole nation to one certain, perfet and general speaking.

Believing that writing 'should be obedient unto the pronunciation', he sets out some of his objections to the current spelling system:

- **Superfluous letters** – some of the letters of the Roman alphabet are redundant and could be dropped.
- **Derivation** – a 'strange word' (i.e. a loan-word from another language) should be written according to its English pronunciation, and not to match its foreign derivation.
- **Difference** – he also rejects the use of different spelling for words which are pronounced alike. If there is no confusion when we speak them, then there can be none when we write them.

15.6 The Great Vowel Shift

Between the time of Chaucer in the late 14th century, and Shakespeare in the late 16th century, all the **long vowels** in English spoken in the Midlands and south of England shifted in their pronunciation. It happened in English only, not in Continental languages, and no similar shift is known to have taken place at other times. It is called the Great Vowel Shift (GVS). Scholars are not agreed on the causes of the shift, and research is still active and controversial.

The shift was not complete in 1569, and there was much variation between regional and social dialect speakers, but in time all the long vowels were either raised or became diphthongs. In spite of Hart and other reformers up to the present day, our spelling system has never been altered to fit the changed pronunciations.

John Hart published three books on spelling reform between 1551 and 1570, and is the chief authority for the pronunciation of the time. He was clear that the 'beste and moste perfite English' was the speech of educated Londoners, maintaining that they took the best features and left the worst of contemporary dialects. He is an authentic source of evidence for the shifting of the long vowels at a transitional stage.

15.6.1 Evidence for the Great Vowel Shift in *An Orthographie*

Hart's statement,

> The sound of the vowel only, may be as well allowed in our speech, as that of the diphthong used of the rude.

means that there were two current pronunciations of the vowel spelt ⟨i⟩ in *exercise*. One was 'the vowel only', ME [iː], a simple or pure vowel. The other was a diphthong which Hart spells ⟨ei⟩. This diphthong was probably pronounced [əi]. There were also clearly two pronunciations of the ⟨u⟩ of *instruments* – [u], and the newer [ɪu] or [ju]. The changes had occurred among 'rude common men',

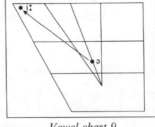

Vowel chart 9

and therefore marked a social dialect. What is interesting is that the 'vulgar' pronunciations have now taken over in prestigious speech – [əɪ] eventually shifted further to MnE RP [aɪ]. Similarly, [ju] is the RP pronunciation of many (but not all) words with ⟨u⟩, like *tune, music* and *fuel*.

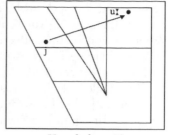

Vowel chart 10

This illustrates two of the problems of trying to make a spelling system that accurately represents pronunciation. First, which of two alternatives do you select, the conservative or the new? Secondly, because pronunciation is continuously changing over time, is spelling to be altered when a new pronunciation has clearly taken over?

John Hart spelt words in his new alphabet according to his own interpretation of their current 1560s pronunciation. All the words in the following lists are taken from the section printed in Hart's new spelling in *An Orthographie*. There is sufficient evidence here to confirm the general movement of the long vowels which was taking place in the 16th century. The spelling of the words in the following lists is transcribed from Hart's new alphabet, illustrated in Text 110.

15.6.1.1 Words spelt with letter <i>

In ME, long vowels spelt with ⟨i⟩ were pronounced [iː]. Hart's spelling shows two pronunciations, already referred to. Some are conservative,

Hart's pronunciation [iː]

advertised	devised	reciteth	sight
aspiring	exercise	right	strikes
derived	high	rightly	title

others are pronounced with the diphthong [əɪ], which Hart spelt ⟨ei⟩:

Hart's pronunciation [əɪ]

describe	find	line	tie
desire	I	lively	time
devise	idly	mind	trifle
divers	life	mine	wise
divide	like	pipe	write

15.6.1.2 Words spelt with letter <y>

The adverbial suffix ⟨-ly⟩ is today pronounced with a short [ɪ] in RP, an unstressed syllable. In Hart's book such adverbs, e.g. *diversely, especially* and *presently*, and the verb *crucify*, are spelt with ⟨ei⟩, pronounced [əɪ], which developed into [aɪ] (see section 18.3.2 on Dryden's rhymes at the end of the 17th century). Present-day pronunciation of the suffix as [ɪ] results from later sound changes in unstressed syllables. Hart spells *softly* with ⟨i⟩ however, which suggests that the change from [iː] to [əɪ] was not complete.

The single-syllable words *by*, *my*, *thy* and *why* are spelt with ⟨ei⟩ and so pronounced [əɪ]. They were therefore beginning the shift of long [iː] to its present-day [baɪ], [maɪ], [aɪ] and [ʍaɪ].

15.6.1.3 Words spelt with <ee>

More quotations from John Hart's book inform us about other changes in pronunciation.

> We call the e, in learning the A.B.C. in the sound of i, and do double the e, for that sound, as in see the Bee doth flee.

That is, the name of the letter ⟨e⟩ is pronounced [iː], and the sound is often spelt ⟨ee⟩. The words *see*, *bee* and *flee* derive from OE *seon*, *beo* and *fleon*. The ⟨eo⟩ diphthongs 'smoothed' to [eː] in the ME period, and the spelling ⟨ee⟩ marked the long vowel [eː] at that time.

But by the mid-16th century, Hart tells us that the pronunciation was [siː], [biː] and [fliː], which it is today. Therefore, ME [eː] (a half-close front vowel) had shifted and raised to the close vowel [iː].

In Hart's new spelling the vowels of *be*, *even*, *Hebrew*, *these* and *we* were spelt ⟨e⟩ and therefore pronounced [eː], the older ME sound. *She* was spelt with ⟨i⟩, however, which is evidence of the incomplete shifting of [eː] to [iː].

All the following words were written with ⟨i⟩ in Hart's new spelling and therefore pronounced [iː]:

chiz (*cheese*)	mit (*meet*)	prosideth (*proceedeth*)	spidier (*speedier*)
Grik (*Greek*)	nid (*need*)	si (*see*)	switnes (*sweetness*)
kip (*keep*)	nidful (*needful*)	spich (*speech*)	tith (*teeth*)

These words, all formerly pronounced with [eː] in ME and spelt ⟨e⟩ or ⟨ee⟩, had all raised to the close vowel [iː].

John Hart's evidence helps to explain also why the pronunciation of the ⟨i⟩ vowel in *exercise* and *title* was shifting to the diphthong [əɪ] in the mid-16th century. Both shifts were part of a general 'push–pull' movement of the long vowels. If [eː] vowels were raised far enough to be confused with [iː], which is a close vowel, and cannot be raised any higher, words

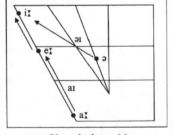

Vowel chart 11

with [iː] can only remain contrastive by using a glide to make a diphthong – at first probably [ɪiː], then [əɪ], which widened further to [aɪ], as it now is in MnE RP.

These changes only happened within some speech communities, and slowly, by degrees, so that the older and newer pronunciations would be heard at the same time.

15.6.1.4 Spellings with <ea>

In some dialects of ME there had been two contrasting long front vowels, close [eː] and open [ɛː], both spelt ⟨e⟩ or ⟨ee⟩. For example, in Chaucer's *Prologue* we find the following contrasting rhymes. *Breeth* and *heeth* derived from words with OE [æː], which had raised to open [ɛː], but *seke* and *seeke*, with close [eː], derived from OE [eː] and the smoothed diphthong [eːə]. The two front vowels [eː] and [ɛː] did not rhyme.

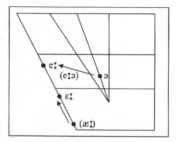

Vowel chart 12

OE source	ME rhyme	ME pronunciation	MnE reflex
bræþ	**breeth**	[brɛːθ]	breath
hæþ	**heeth**	[hɛːθ]	heath
sēcan	**seke**	[seːk]	seek
sēoc	**seeke**	[seːk]	sick

During the 15th century, scribes had begun to use the spelling ⟨ea⟩ for words of French origin with open [ɛː], so that, for example, *raison* came to be spelt *reason*. Letter ⟨a⟩ is here used as a diacritic. In the 16th century, the spelling was extended to words from OE with the same vowel; *mele* and *herte* were re-spelt *meal* and *heart*. Unfortunately for us, what might have been a very neat solution has been made complicated:

- The re-spelling was not used or applied consistently.
- Pronunciation of these two front vowels differed between regional and social dialects in ME. In some dialects the distinction was not made.
- ⟨ea⟩ words with [ɛː] shifted to [eː] in the GVS, but were raised further to [iː] in some dialects, so that they came to be pronounced like ⟨ee⟩ words.
- There were therefore marked dialectal differences in the pronunciation of ⟨ea⟩ words in the 16th and 17th centuries.
- This variation in the pronunciation of ⟨ea⟩ words, with further changes, continued into the 18th century when present-day pronunciations were settled. RP derives from the prestige varieties of pronunciation.

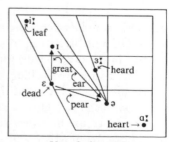

Vowel chart 13

Present-day English clearly reflects these variations and later changes, as in the words *leaf* [iː], *great* [ɛɪ], *dead* [ɛ], *heart* [ɑː], *heard* [ɜː], *ear* [ɪə], *pear* [ɛə].

The vowels of *heart, heard, ear, pear* were affected by the later loss of post-vocalic ⟨r⟩, which tends to lower the vowel, but the differences can only be accounted for as a result of the fortuitous 'selection' from different social or regional dialectal accents.

Most words which we now spell with ⟨ea⟩ have the letter ⟨e⟩ for the long vowel [eː] in Hart's spelling,

ber (*bear* – vb)	**brethd** (*breathed*)	**lev** (*leave*)	**redi** (*ready*)
brek (*break*)	**esi** (*easy*)	**meneth** (*meaneth*)	**rezon** (*reason*)
breth (*breath*)	**gret** (*great*)	**ner** (*near*)	**resonabl** (*reasonable*)
breth (*breathe*)	**lern** (*learn*)	**plez** (*please*)	**spek** (*speak*)

These words had probably shifted to [eː] from the open ME [ɛː], but Hart did not provide separate letters for the two vowels [eː] and [ɛː].

If you examine the pronunciation of these ⟨ea⟩ words today, you will see that there have been subsequent changes which have affected words selectively. Many now have the high vowel [iː], and there is evidence that this was already happening in Hart's day, because he spells a few words, including *read, reading* and *appear*, with the letter ⟨i⟩ – *rid, riding* and *apir*.

15.6.1.5 Spellings with <o>, <oo> or <oa>

Here is another quotation from Hart:

> ... and o, single or double in the sound of u, as, they two come to do some good, which is the mere sound of the u.

That is, the vowel pronounced [u] is sometimes spelt with ⟨o⟩ or ⟨oo⟩, as in *two, come, to, do, some* and *good*. The explanation for these words, all pronounced alike according to Hart, is more complicated, and involves different sound changes or spelling conventions.

- OE *twa* [twɑː] (low back vowel) had 'rounded' to *two* [twɔː] (half-open back vowel) in early ME, and later to [twoː] (half-close back vowel). The [w] was lost before the rounded back vowel, but letter ⟨w⟩ was retained in the spelling. In the GVS, the [oː] was raised to [uː], so that OE [twɑː] had now changed to [tuː].
- Both *to* and *do* were long half-close back vowels in OE and ME, [toː], [doː], and raised to close [uː] in the GVS – [tuː] [duː].

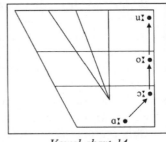

Vowel chart 14

- The alternative spelling of, for example, OE *cuman* and *sum* with ⟨o⟩ was adopted in ME to avoid the confusion of ⟨u⟩ with minim letters – ⟨n ~ m ~ w⟩ – *comen* and *som*, but the pronunciation was unchanged. The GVS did not affect them, because they were short vowels, [kʊm] and [sʊm].
- The vowel of ME *gōd* meaning *good*, was long, so it shifted to [uː] in the GVS,

together with *blōd* (*blood*) and *fōde* (*food*). Their different pronunciations today – RP [gʊd ~ blʌd ~ fuːd] are the result of later changes.

Just as in ME there were two mid-front long vowels which were contrastive, close [eː] and open [ɛː], there were also two back vowels, close [oː] and open [ɔː], both spelt with the letter ⟨o⟩ or ⟨oo⟩. In the 16th century, some writers and printers began to spell the vowel of long open [ɔː] with ⟨oa⟩, the letter ⟨a⟩ not representing a sound, but acting as a diacritic, like the ⟨a⟩ in ⟨ea⟩. But Hart does not provide different letters for these two vowels any more than he did for the two ME ⟨e⟩ vowels, and the evidence of pronunciation from his spelling is as follows:

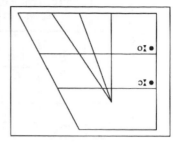

Vowel chart 15

[o] [oː]				[u] [uː]	
Hart	*MnE*	*Hart*	*MnE*	*Hart*	*MnE*
both	*both*	thoh	*though*	behuf	*behoof*
hop	*hope*	besto	*bestow*	buk	*book*
not	*note*	boro	*borrow*	fulish	*foolish*
on	*one*	kno	*know*	gud	*good*
onli	*only*	knoledg	*knowledge*	skul	*school*
voel	*vowel*	sho	*show*	suth	*sooth*
huo	*who*	aproch	*approach*	tuk	*took*
huoz	*whose*	brod	*broad*	understud	*understood*
oht	*ought*				

There is evidence of these two contrasting pairs of front and back vowels in other 16th-century **orthoepists** (writers on pronunciation). The next facsimile is a page from William Bullokar's *Boke at Large* (1580), showing another 'amendment of ortography' (revised alphabet) with separate letters proposed for the long vowels [eː], [ɛː], [oː] and [ɔː]. It is clear that in the late 16th century they were still separate phonemes.

Text 111: William Bullokar's Boke at Large, 1580 (facsimile)

The names of the letters accoding to this amendment of ogtographp, appéerc in this Table, by the which ye may name the letters in the wzitten Copies following.

a / a	b / b	cée / c	kee / c	chée / ch	D / D	e : ea / e : æ	ée / e
f / f	gée / g	ga / g tyrn a into e.	hée / h	i / i	k / k	l / l	hl / l
m / m	hm / m	n / n	hn / n	o / o	betwèn o : ɛ : b / ω	p / p	phée / ph
quée / q	r / r	er / r	ſ / ſ	ſhée / ſh	t / t	thée / th	théeſ / th
b / b	ou / þ	bée / u	wée / w	whée / wh	r / r	yée / y	zée / z

Bullokar printed several versions of his new alphabet, with his own comments in verse – here is one of them:

a.b.c.c.ch.d.e.æ.e.f.g.g.h.i.k.l.l.m.m.n.n.o.ω.
p.ph.q.r.r.ſ.ſh.t.th.th.v.y.y.w.wh.x.y.z.&.

*Howh thæz figurz vnto your siht, at first sem to be ſtrang.
Ye may soon fynd by litl hed, they do no far way rang
From the old vzd ortografy, grǣt gayn iz in the chang.*

How these figures unto your sight at first seem to be strange,
Ye may soon find by little heed, they do no far way range
From the old used orthography, great gain is in the change.

Bullokar's proposals for the letters for the two mid-front vowels [ɛ] and [e] (short and long) are shown as ⟨e æ é⟩, representing the sounds [ɛ ɛː eː]. Words containing these letters in Bullokar's text in his new spelling include, for example:

⟨e⟩	= [ɛ]	sent, qestion, terror
		sent, question, terror
⟨æ⟩	= [ɛ:]	mæning, thærfore, encræse, decræse, whær, læu
		meaning, therefore, increase, decrease, where, leave
⟨é⟩	= [e:]	bréf, agré, bé, béiing, énglish, kép, wé, yéld.
		brief, agree, be, being, English, keep, we, yield

The letters for the mid-back vowels, approximately [ɔ] and [o] (short and long), are ⟨o⟩ and ⟨oo⟩. Letter ⟨oo⟩ is glossed 'betwén o & u', which is evidence of the raising of long [o:] towards [u:]. Examples are:

⟨o⟩	= [ɔ]	qestion (*3 syllables*), prosody, diphthong, wrongd
		question, prosody, diphthong, wronged
⟨o⟩	= [ɔ:]	wo, on
		woe, one
⟨oo⟩	= [o:] ‑ [u:]	untoo, too, dooth
		unto, to / too, doth

(Of course, in spite of Hart's and Bullokar's advocacy, followed by other keen reformers in the following centuries up to George Bernard Shaw in the 20th, English spelling has never been revised or updated.)

15.6.1.6 Spellings with <ou> or <ow>

The digraph ⟨ou⟩, also spelt ⟨ow⟩, was originally taken from French spelling to represent the OE and early ME long close back [u:]. Hart's phonetic spelling with ⟨ou⟩ rather than ⟨u⟩ tells us that this vowel had become a diphthong, probably then pronounced [əʊ]. Examples from Hart's book are (in present-day spelling):

account	doubt	out	touch
bound	found	pound	without
brought	four	pronounce	allow
confound	mouth	round	down
counsel	noun	sought	how
counter	our	sound	

15.6.1.7 Spellings with <a>

The OE long vowel [ɑ:] had long before rounded and shifted to [ɔ:] in the South and Midlands, and words with this vowel were spelt with ⟨o⟩, e.g. OE *stan* and *ban* became *stone* and *bone*. The 'gap' in the system was filled in time with words of OF derivation like *grace* and *task*, and by OE disyllabic words whose short [a] vowels became long, e.g. OE *nama* and *lana* became *name* [naːmə] and *lane* [laːnə]. Words with a long vowel spelt with letter ⟨a⟩ in ME did not follow the pattern of the OE words which had earlier shifted to the back vowel [ɔː]. The ME vowel must have either been, or shifted forwards to become, a front open vowel, [aː] ~ [æː], and then [ɛː] ~ [eː]. *Name*, for example, is now pronounced [nɛːm] or [neːm].

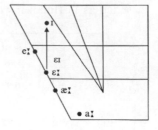

Vowel chart 16

In Hart's new orthography, all the following words were spelt with the letter ⟨a⟩, and were therefore still pronounced with [aː] or [æː]. This suggests that the shift upwards to [ɛː] or [eː] was not yet evident in Hart's time.

any	labours	nation	strange
change	lady	observation	table
blame	late	place	take
derivation	made	same	vary
grace	many	shape	
have	name	spake	

15.6.1.8 Summary of changes to long vowels and diphthongs from ME to MnE

A few examples of words with long vowels in the two pages of Hart's new spelling in Text 110 have been sorted into sets below. Hart's subscript dot or 'prick' to mark a long vowel has been used as a criterion (though he did not print it consistently).

Source (OE/OF)	ME	Hart's spelling	MnE (RP)
1		⟨ei⟩	
OE tīma [iː]	time [iː]	**teim** = [əɪ]	time [aɪ]
2		⟨i⟩	
OF exercīse [iː]	exercisen [iː]	**exersiz** = [iː]	exercise [aɪ]
3		⟨i⟩	
OE mē [eː]	me [eː]	**mi** = [iː]	me = [iː]
OE rǣdan [æː]	reden [eː]	**rid** = [iː]	read = [iː]
OE spēc [eː]	speche [eː]	**spich** = [iː]	speech = [iː]
4		⟨e⟩	
OE specan [ɛ]	speken [ɛː]	**spek** = [eː]	speak [iː]
OF perceivre [ɛ]	perceiven [ɛː]	**persev** = [eː]	perceive [iː]
		⟨e⟩	
OE mæg [æj]	mai [æɪ]	**me** = [eː]	may [eɪ]

5

OF blamer [a]	blamen [aiː]	**blam** = [aː]	blame [eɪ]
OE hlǣfdige [æː]	ladi [aː]	**ladi** = [aː]	lady [eɪ]
OE macode [a]	made [aː]	**mad** = [aː]	made [eɪ]

6 ⟨o⟩

OE ānlic [ɑː]	onli [ɔː]	**onli** = [oː]	only [oː] or [əʊ]
		⟨o⟩	
OE ān [ɑː]	on [ɔː]	**on** = [oː]	one [wʌn] or [wʊn]

7 ⟨u⟩

OE dōn [oː]	don [oː]	**du** = [uː]	do [uː]
		⟨u⟩	
OE bōc [oː]	bok [oː]	**buk** = [uː]	book [ʊ]

8 ⟨ou⟩

OE mūþ [uː]	mouth/muth [uː]	**mouth** = [əʊ]	mouth [aʊ]
OE ūre [uː]	oure/ure [uː]	**our** = [əʊ]	our [aʊ]

📖 A larger selection of words from Hart's *An Orthographie* is in the Word Book.

15.6.2 The Great Vowel Shift – a summary

There is still disagreement among scholars about the causes and precise development of the GVS. The sound changes were gradual, but sufficiently noticeable for men like John Hart and other writers on pronunciation and spelling in the 16th and 17th centuries to attempt to describe them. Their concern was often with social correctness and a concern to make the language 'perfect', but what they described is as near first-hand evidence as we can get.

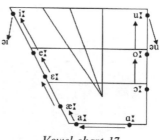

Vowel chart 17

We can summarise the GVS in terms of a 'drift upwards' of the long vowels, with the close or high vowels [iː] and [uː] becoming diphthongs, at first [əɪ] and [əʊ] and eventually (in RP) [aɪ] and [aʊ] – eg *ride, house*.

The diagram over-simplifies the process, because there are exceptions to the pattern of drift. To take one example, the ME long vowel [uː] of words like *cupe* (*coop, basket*), *drupen* (*droop*), *rum* (*room*), *wund* (*wound*, noun), *tumbe* (*tomb*) did not diphthongise. They all have a labial consonant before or after the vowel – [p ~ m ~ w] – which had the effect of retaining the vowel [uː]. You will notice, however, that the vowel of the past participle *wound* of the verb *wind* did become the diphthong [aʊ], which warns us not to over-generalise in terms of rules of sound change.

Northern dialects of ME were not affected so immediately by the shift of long vowels. Present-day Scots, for example, still retains the old pronunciation of *house* [huːs].

15.7 Punctuation in 16th-century texts

The facsimiles of written and printed texts will have shown some differences from present-day conventions in punctuation, especially in the OE and ME texts. John Hart provides a useful summary of the situation in the 1560s in *An Orthographie*:

> I will brieflye write of distinction or pointing. . . . For it sheweth us how to rest: when the sentence continueth. . . .
>
> The first marked thus , the Greekes call comma, for which the Latines and other vulgares haue used a strike thus / . . . alwayes signifying the sentence unfinished.
>
> The second marked thus : the Greekes call colon. . . . And the last of these three is a pricke thus . to signifie the ende of a full and perfite sentence.

He also describes the *Parenthesis* ( ), the *interrogatiue* ?, and the *admiratiue* !

15.8 Loan-words, 1500–49

A selection of loan-words recorded during this period can be found in the Word Book, after the word-lists for Chapter 15.

16 Early Modern English III – the 16th century (ii)

16.1 The development of the standard language

We saw in earlier chapters that there was no ME standard language, but a number of inter-related dialects. English today consists of a much greater number of inter-related dialects, spread throughout the world, but in England people now tend to regard the Standard English dialect as 'the English language', and may look on the other regional and social dialects as substandard or inferior. Hence they talk of 'good English' or 'correct English', and devalue the status of the regional dialects.

This point of view is not new, of course, and we have seen evidence of concern over the differences between the dialects at least as far back as the 14th century, in John of Trevisa's discussion of the language (Texts 57 and 58). Both Chaucer in the 1380s and Caxton in the 1480s refer to the 'diversity' of the English language.

First to develop was a written standard. Educated men and women wrote in the standard but many continued to speak in the dialect of their region. John Aubrey, writing in the mid-17th century, says of Sir Walter Ralegh (1552–1618),

> Old Sir Thomas Malett, one of the Justices of the King's bench *tempore Caroli I et II*, knew Sir Walter, and I have heard him say, that notwithstanding his so great Mastership in Style and his conversation with the learnedest and politest persons, yet he spake broad Devonshire to his dying day.

Aubrey perhaps implies that this was unusual, and that gentlemen in his time did not speak in regional dialects at court. There is also the hint that dialect does not somehow fit with learning and polite behaviour.

We have already noted in Chapter 14 how, by the end of the 15th century, there is less and less evidence in printed books and in manuscripts of the range of dialects of English. Regional and social varieties still flourished, as they do today, but the evidence for them is much more difficult to find. There are no written records of colloquial speech as authentic as sound-recording makes possible for present-day English. The language of informal letters or the dialogue of characters in prose drama are probably the nearest we can get to everyday speech of the time.

16.1.1 'The best and most perfite English'

John Hart in *An Orthographie* insisted that writing should represent speech, 'we must be ruled by our speech'. But he also recognised the problem that the diversity of dialects posed in using his new alphabet to write English as it sounded – whose dialect do you choose?

Text 112: John Hart's An Orthographie – *the speech of 'the learned sort'*

Notwithstanding, he should haue a wrong opinion of me, that should thinke by the premisses, I ment any thing shoulde be printed in London in the maner of Northerne or Westerne speaches: but if any one were minded at Newcastell uppon Tine, or Bodman in Cornewale to write or print his minde there, who should iustly blame him for his Orthographie, to serue hys neyghbours according to their mother speach, yea, though he wrate to London, to whomsoeuer it were, he could be no more offended to see his writing so, than if he were present to heare him speake: and there is no doubt, but that the English speach, which the learned sort in the ruled Latin, togither with those which are acquainted with the vulgars Italian, French, and Spanish doe vse, is that speach which euery reasonable English man, will the nearest he can, frame his tongue therevnto: but such as haue no conference by the liuely voice, nor experience of reading, nor in reading no certaintie how euery letter shoulde be sounded, can neuer come to the knowledge and vse, of that best and moste perfite English: which by Gods grace I will the neerest I can follow, leauing manye an Inckhorne terme (which I could vse) bicause I regarde for whose sake I doe it.

This is clear evidence of Hart's advocacy of educated London speech as 'the best and most perfite', spoken by 'euery reasonable English man'.

16.1.2 *'The vsuall speach of the Court'*

George Puttenham's advice to writers about choosing the best variety of English was briefly quoted in section 12.1. Here is a longer extract which illustrates his awareness of the range of available regional and social varieties before Standard English was a fully accepted and defined variety.

Activity 16.1

(i) Describe the assumptions about language which are evident in the text. Comment particularly on:

    (a) his use of the word *corruptions* to describe changes in a language,

    (b) the reference to a language which is *naturall*, *pure* and *the most vsuall*,

    (c) his contrasting of *good townes and Cities* with other places,

    (d) his references to *the inferiour sort* of men and women,

    (e) the attitude implied in *any speach vsed beyond the riuer of Trent*.

(ii) Are Puttenham's attitudes still current today?

Text 113: George Puttenham on the best language, from Book III, Chapter IIII, Of the Arte of English Poesie, **1589 (facsimile)**

But after a fpeach is fully fafhioned to the common vnderftanding,& accepted by confent of a whole countrey & natiõ,it is called a language,& receaueth none allowed alteration,but by extraordinary occafions by little & little,as it were infenfibly bringing in of many corruptiõs that creepe along with the time: ....

This part in our maker or Poet muft be heedyly looked vnto,that it be naturall, pure, and the moft vfuall of all his countrey : and for the fame purpofe rather that which is fpoken in the kings Court,or in the good townes and Cities within the land, then in the marches and frontiers, or in port townes, where ftraungers haunt for traffike fake *, or yet in Vniuerfities where Schollers vfe much peuifh affectation of words out of the primatiue languages, or finally, in any vplandifh village or corner of a Realme,where is no refort but of poore rufticall or vnciuill people: neither fhall he follow the fpeach of a craftes man or carter,or other of the inferiour fort, though he be inhabitant or bred in the belt towne and Citie in this Realme,for fuch perfons doe abufe good fpeaches by ftrange accents or ill fhapen foundes, and falfe ortographie. But he fhall follow generally the better brought vp fort, fuch as the Greekes call [*charientes*] meh ciuill and gracioufly behauoured and bred.Our maker therfore at thefe dayes fhall not follow *Piers plowman* nor *Gower* nor *Lydgate* nor yet *Chaucer*, for their language is now out of vfe with vs: neither fhall he take the termes of Northern-men,fuch as they vfe in dayly talke,whether they be noble men or gentlemen, or of their beft clarkes all is a matter : nor in effect any fpeach vfed beyond the riuer of Trent,though no man can deny but that theirs is the purer Englifh Saxon at this day, yet it is not fo Courtly nor fo currant as our Southerne Englifh is, no more is the far Wefterne mãs fpeach : ye fhall therfore take the vfuall fpeach of the Court, and that of London and the fhires lying about London within lx. myles,and not much aboue. I fay not this but that in euery fhyre of England there be gentlemen and others that fpeake but fpecially write as good Southerne as we of Middlefex or Surrey do,but not the common people of euery fhire, to whom the gentlemen, and alfo their learned clarkes do for the moft part condefeend,but herein we are already ruled by th'Englifh Dictionaries and other bookes written by learned men, and therefore it needeth none other direction in that behalfe.

Condescend to meant *adjust to* – that is, gentlemen everywhere could speak 'good Southerne', but talked to the common people in dialect.

Puttenham was expressing a point of view which is probably common in all societies. There is evidence earlier in the 16th century in the books on spelling and grammar which Puttenham mentions, that "diversity" in the language worried writers and scholars. The implications of this point of view are, however, more serious, because it is not limited simply to specifying a choice of language for writers:

● Varieties of the language are marked by social class and education. Social classes speak differently and can be recognised by their speech. Written and spoken English have prestige varieties.
● Once a written standard language also becomes the norm for speech in the educated class, the division between that class and regional dialect speakers is complete.

Such differences of language are a part of every society, but in different degrees. Standardisation of language is a necessary development in a society, but brings with it social consequences which are, therefore, the background to our continuing study of the development of Early Modern English in the 16th and 17th centuries.

16.2 Evidence for some 16th-century varieties of English

16.2.1 National dialects

The dialogue of characters in plays cannot be taken as completely authentic evidence of the spoken language, but may indicate the more obvious dialectal features of speech. In Shakespeare's *The Life of Henry the Fift* there are comic episodes involving four captains – Gower, Fluellen, Mackmorrice and Iamy. Their names give them away as an Englishman, a Welshman, an Irishman and a Scotsman.

The facsimile is reproduced from the Fourth Folio of 1685.

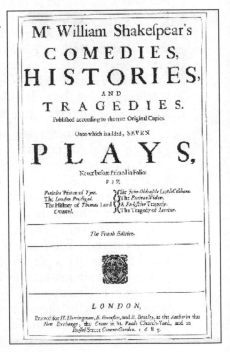

Mr William Shake{pear's

C O M E D I E S,

H I S T O R I E S,

AND

T R A G E D I E S.

Publi{hed according to their true Original Copies

Unto which is added, SEVEN

P L A Y S,

Never before Printed in Folio:

v i z.

Pericles Prince of Tyre.	Sir John Oldcastle Lord Cobham.
The London Prodigal.	The Puritan Widow.
The Hi{tory of Thomas Lord	A York{hire Tragedy.
Cromwell.	The Tragedy of Locrine.

The Fourth Edition.

L O N D O N,

Printed for H. Herringman, E. Brewster, and R. Bentley, at the Anchor in the New Exchange, the Crown in St. Paul's Church-Yard, and in Ru{sel-Street Covent-Garden. 1 6 8 5.

Activity 16.2

Describe the dialectal features of the characters' speech which is indicated by the spelling, vocabulary and syntax of the dialogue.

📖 Activity 16.2 is discussed in the Text Commentary Book.

Text 114: Shakespeare, The Life of Henry the Fift *(facsimile)*

Enter Gower.

Gower. Captain *Fluellen*, you muſt come preſently to the Mines ; the Duke of Glouceſter would ſpeak with you.

Flu. To the Mines ? Tell you the Duke, it is not ſo good to come to the Mines : for look you, the Mines are not according to the Diſciplines of War ; the Con-eavities of it is not ſufficient : for look you, th' adver-ſary, you may diſcuſs unto the Duke, look you, is digt himſelf four yards under the Countermines : by *Cheſhu*, I think a will plow up all, if there is not better dire-ctions.

Gower. The Duke of *Glouceſter*, to whom the Order of the Siege is given, is altogether directed by an Iriſh

man, a very valiant Gentleman, I'faith.

Welch. It is Captain *Makmorrice*, is it not ?

Gower. I think it be.

Welch. By *Cheſhu* he is an Aſs, as in the World, I will verifie as much in his Beard : he ha's no more directi-ons in the true diſciplines of the Wars, look you, of the *Roman* diſciplines, than is a Puppy-dog.

Enter. Makmorrice, *and Captain* Jamy.

Gower. Here a comes, and the *Scots* Captain, Captain *Jamy*, with him.

Welch. Captain *Jamy* is a marvellous valorous Gen-tleman, that is certain, and of great expedition and know-ledge in th'aunchiant Wars, upon my particular know-ledge of his directions ; by *Cheſhu* he will maintain his Argument as well as any Militarie man in the World, in the Diſciplines of the priſtine Wars of the *Romans*.

Scot. I ſay gudday, Captain *Fluellen*.

Welch. Godden to your Worſhip, good Captain *James*.

Gower. How now, Captain *Makmorrice*, have you quit the Mines ? have the Pioners given o're ?

Iriſh. By Chriſh, Law, tiſh ill done : the Work iſh give over, the Trompet ſound the Retreat. By my Hand I ſwear, and my father's Soul, The Work iſh ill done : it iſh give over : I would have blowed up the Town, ſo Chriſh ſave me, law, in an hour. O tiſh ill done, tiſh ill done : by my Hand tiſh ill done.

Welch. Captaine *Makmorrice*, I beſeech you now, will you vouchaſe me, look you, a few diſputations with you, as partly touching or concerning the diſciplines of the War, the *Roman* Wars, in the way of Argument, look you, and friendly communication : partly to ſatiſfie my Opinion, and partly for the ſatisfaction, look you, of my Mind, as touching the direction of the Mi-litary diſcipline, that is the Point.

Scot. It ſall be vary gud, gud feith, gud Captens bath, and I ſall quit you with gud leve, as I may pick occaſion : that ſal I marry.

Iriſh. It is no time to diſcourſe, ſo Chriſh ſave me : The day is hot, and the Weather, and the Wars, and the King, and the Duke : it is not time to diſcourſe, the Town is beſeech'd : and the Trumpet calls us to the Breach, and we talk, and by Chriſh do nothing, 'tis ſhame for us all : ſo God ſa'me 'tis ſhame to ſtand ſtill, it is ſhame by my hand : and there is Throats to be cut, and Works to be done, and there iſh nothing done, ſo Chriſh ſa'me law.

Scot. By the Mes, ere theiſe eyes of mine take them-ſelves to ſlomber, ayle de gud ſervice, or Ile ligge i'th' grund for it ; ay, or go to death - and Ile pay't as va-lorouſly as I may, that ſal I ſurely do, the breff and the long ; marry, I wad full fain heard ſome queſtion 'tween you tway.

16.2.2 Using thou/thee and ye/you

The grammatically singular forms *thou/thee* and plural *ye/you* were used as markers of social difference. A superior used *thou* to an inferior, who had to address his superior with *you*. A friendly relationship was also marked in this way. You began to use *thou* when you reached a more intimate relationship with a person. We have lost this distinction in most parts of England, although *tha/thee* is still used in West Yorkshire speech.

This social meaning of *thou* and *ye* had been established well before the 16th century. Here is an example from the 1390s in Chaucer's 'The Knight's Tale'. Arcite, in prison, addresses the gods Mars and Juno at first with *thow* as individuals, and then with *youre* as a pair. Immediately he goes on to address his absent love Emelye, whom he has seen but not yet met, with *ye*. He is the suppliant, and she is far above him in his estimation, so *thow* would not be appropriate, as it would mark an established intimacy:

> Allas *thow* felle Mars, allas Iuno,
> Thus hath *youre* ire oure lynage al fordo . . .
>
> *Ye* sleen me with *youre* eyen, Emelye,
> *Ye* been the cause wherfore that I dye

Elsewhere in *The Canterbury Tales* the Host addresses the Cook with *thou*,

> Now tel on, gentil Roger, by *thy* name
> But yet I praye *thee* be nat wrooth for game . . .

but uses *ye* to the Monk, his social superior,

> Now telleth *ye*, sire monk, if that *ye* konne . . .

In the following extract from Shakespeare's *Much Adoe About Nothing*, Don Pedro and Claudio are unaware that their friend Benedicke has been told to 'kill Claudio', so they indulge in witty cross-talk in which Benedicke does not join.

Activity 16.3

Discuss the evidence for the misunderstanding in the relationship between Claudio and Benedicke from their use of the pronouns *you/your* or *thee/thou/thy/thine*.

Text 115: **Much Adoe About Nothing,** *Scene 14 (Act 5, Scene 1)*

DON PEDRO	See see, heere comes the man we went to seeke.
CLAUDIO	Now signior, what newes?
BENEDICKE	(*to Don Pedro*) Good day my Lord.
DON PEDRO	Welcome signior, **you** are almost come to parte almost a fray.
CLAUDIO	Wee had likt to haue had our two noses snapt off with two old men without teeth.

DON PEDRO	Leonato and his brother what thinkst **thou**? had we fought, I doubt we should haue beene too yong for them.
BENEDICKE	In a false quarrell there is no true valour, I came to seeke **you** both.
CLAUDIO	We haue beene vp and downe to seeke **thee**, for we are high proofe melancholie, and would faine haue it beaten away, wilt **thou** vse thy wit?
BENEDICKE	It is in my scabberd, shal I drawe it?
DON PEDRO	Doest **thou** weare thy wit by thy side?
CLAUDIO	Neuer any did so, though very many haue been beside their wit, I will bid **thee** drawe, as wee doe the minstrels, draw to pleasure vs.
DON PEDRO	As I am an honest man he lookes pale, art **thou** sicke, or angry?
CLAUDIO	What, courage man: what though care kild a catte, **thou** hast mettle enough in **thee** to kill care.
BENEDICKE	Sir, I shall meete **you**r wit in the careere, and **you** charge it against me, I pray **you** chuse another subiect.
CLAUDIO	Nay then giue him another staffe, this last was broke crosse.
DON PEDRO	By this light, he chaunges more and more, I thinke he be angry indeed.
CLAUDIO	If he be, he knowes how to turne his girdle.
BENEDICKE	*(aside to Claudio)* Shall I speake a word in **you**r eare?
CLAUDIO	God blesse me from a challenge.
BENEDICKE	**You** are a villaine, I ieast not, I will make it good howe **you** dare, with what **you** dare, and when **you** dare: doe me right, or I will protest **you**r cowardise: **you** haue killd a sweete Lady, and her death shall fall heauie on **you**, let me heare from **you**.
CLAUDIO	Well I wil meet **you**, so I may haue good cheare.
DON PEDRO	What, a feast, a feast?
CLAUDIO	I faith I thanke him he hath bid me to a calues head & a capon, the which if I doe not carue most curiously, say my kniffe's naught, shall I not find a woodcoke too?
BENEDICKE	Sir **you**r wit ambles well, it goes easily.
DON PEDRO	Ile tell **thee** how Beatrice praisd thy witte the other day: I said **thou** hadst a fine witte, true said she, a fine little one: no said I, a great wit: right saies she, a great grosse one: nay said I, a good wit, iust said she, it hurts no body: nay said I, the gentleman is wise: certaine said she, a wise gentleman: nay said I, he hath the tongues: that I beleeue said shee, for he swore a thing to me on munday night, which hee forswore on tuesday morning, theres a double tongue theirs two tongues, thus did shee an houre together trans-shape thy particular vertues, yet at last she concluded with a sigh, **thou** wast the properst man in Italy.
CLAUDIO	For the which shee wept heartily and saide she cared not.
DON PEDRO	Yea that she did, but yet for all that, and if she did not hate him deadly, she would loue him dearely, the old mans daughter told vs all.

CLAUDIO	All all, and moreouer, God sawe him when he was hid in the garden.
DON PEDRO	But when shall we set the sauage bulles hornes on the sensible Benedicks head?
CLAUDIO	Yea and text vnder-neath, here dwells Benedick the married man.
BENEDICKE	Fare **you** wel, boy, **you** know my minde, I wil leaue **you** now to **you**r gossep-like humor, **you** breake iests as braggards do their blades, which God be thanked hurt not: (*to Don Pedro*) my Lord, for **your** many courtisies, I thanke **you**, I must discontinue **your** company, **your** brother the bastard is fled from Messina: **you** haue among **you**, kild a sweet and innocent lady: for my Lord Lacke-beard there, hee and I shal meet, and till then peace be with him. (*exit*)
DON PEDRO	He is in earnest.
CLAUDIO	In most profound earnest, and ile warrant **you**, for the loue of Beatrice.
DON PEDRO	And hath challengde **thee.**
CLAUDIO	Most sincerely.
DON PEDRO	What a pretty thing man is, when he goes in his dublet and hose, and leaues off his wit!

📖 A detailed commentary is in the Text Commentary Book.

📖 A lexical word-list of the vocabulary of Text 115 is in the Word Book.

(Section 17.3.4. discusses George Fox on *thee/thou* in the mid-17th century.)

16.2.3 Regional dialects

By the end of the 16th century the educated language of London was clearly established as the standard for writing in England, so that there is little evidence of the regional dialects apart from occasional references. Here is another extract from Richard Verstegan's *A Restitution of Decayed Intelligence* (see Text 108) which gives us just a little information. He is discussing 'alteration and varietie' in related languages like Danish, Norwegian and Swedish, and is saying that they do not borrow 'from any extrauagant language' (the word *extrauagant* here meant *outside the boundaries*, that is, *foreign*):

Text 116: Richard Verstegan (1605) on regional dialects (facsimile)

> This is a thing
> that eafely may happen in fo fpatious a toung as this,
> it beeing fpoken in fo many different countries and
> regions, when wee fee that in fome feueral partes of
> *England* it felf, both the names of things and pro-
> nountiations of woords are fomwhat different, and
> that among the countrey people that neuer borrow
> any woords out of the Latin or French, and of this
> different prónountiation one example in fteed of
> many fhal fuffife, as this: for pronouncing according
> as one would fay at *London*, J would eat moꝛe cheefe pf
> J had it, the northern man faith, Ay fud eat mare cheefe
> gin ay hadet, and the wefterne man faith: Chud eat moꝛe
> cheefe an chad it. Lo heer three different pronountia-
> tions in our own countrey in one thing, & heerof
> many the lyke examples might be alleaged.

Activity 16.4

Identify and describe the differences between the three dialectal sentences quoted in Text 116:

I would eat more cheese yf I had it.
Ay sud eat mare cheese gin ay had et.
Chud eat more cheese an chad it.

There is little additional evidence of contemporary regional dialect in Shakespeare's plays apart from Text 114, but an example can be found in *The Tragedie of King Lear*. Edgar, the Duke of Gloucester's son, banished by King Lear, disguises himself as a madman – a Tom a Bedlam. The speech he assumes is often inconsequential but not obviously dialectal, for example,

> Away, the fowle fiend followes me, thorough the sharpe hathorne blowes the cold wind, goe to thy cold bed and warme thee.

but at one point, defending his blinded father, his speech becomes clearly dialectal for one short episode:

Text 117: Shakespeare, The Tragedie of King Lear *(facsimile)*

(*Gloster does not recognise Edgar as his son, and cannot see him. The Steward believes Edgar to be a beggar.*)

> *Glou.* Now good Sir, what are you?
> *Edg.* A moſt poor man, made tame to fortunes blows
> Who, by the Art of known, and feeling ſorrows,
> Am pregnant to good pitty. Give me your hand,
> I'le lead you to ſome biding.
> *Glou.* Hearty thanks :
> The bounty, and the benizon of Heaven
> To boot, and boot.
>
> *Enter* Steward.
>
> *Stew.* A proclaim'd prize : moſt happy:
> That eyeleſs head of thine, was firſt fram'd fleſh
> To raiſe my fortunes. Thou old, unhappy traitor,
> Briefly thy ſelf remember : the Sword is out
> That muſt deſtroy thee.
> *Glou.* Now let thy friendly hand
> Put ſtrength enough to't.
> *Stew.* Wherefore, bold Peazant,
> Darſt thou ſupport a publiſh'd traitor? hence,
> Leſt that th'inteƈtion of his fortune take
> Like hold on thee. Let go his Arm.
> *Edg.* Chill not let go Zir,
> Without vurther caſion.
> *Stew.* Let go, Slave, or thou dy'ſt.
> *Edg.* Good Gentleman go your gate, and let poor volk
> paſs : and'chud ha'been zwagged out of my life, 'twould
> ha'been zo long as 'tis, by a vortnight. Nay, come not
> near th'old man : keep out che vor'ye, or ice try whither
> your Coſtard, or my Ballow be the harder; chill be plain
> with you.
> *Stew.* Out Dunghil.
> *Edg.* Child pick your teeth Zir : come, no matter vor
> your foyns.
> *Stew.* Slave thou haſt ſlain me · villain, take my purſe;
> If ever thou wilt thrive, bury my body,
> And give the Letters which thou find'ſt about me,
> To *Edmud* Earl of *Gloſter :* ſeek him out
> Upon the Engliſh party. Oh untimely death, death.
> *Edg.* I know thee well. A ſerviceable Villain,
> As duteous to the vices of thy Miſtris,
> As badneſs would deſire.
> *Glou.* What, is he dead?
> *Edg.* Sit you down Father : reſt you.

Activity 16.5

(i) Which of Richard Verstegan's examples of dialect in Text 116 does Edgar's speech resemble?

(ii) The scene of the play is set in Kent. The words *ice try* stand for *I sal try. Sal* for *shall* and *gate* for *way* are both Northern forms. Is Shakespeare accurately reproducing a regional dialect?

(iii) Describe the differences in Edgar's language when he is talking to Gloster and the Steward, which mark it as a dialect.

(iv) Explain the changing use of the 2nd person pronouns *thou/thee/thine* and *ye/you/your*.

16.2.3.1 Commentary

Edgar's dialect

> Chill not let goe Zir without vurther casion
> chill be plain with you
> Chill* picke your teeth Zir

*Folio has *Child*

The initial ⟨ch⟩ represents the 1st person singular pronoun (MnE *I*), and is the consonant /ʧ/ of OE *ic*, ME *ich*. The vowel has been elided, and the word is attached to its following verb in *chill / I will*.

> and **'chud** ha' bin zwagged out of my life . . .

and here means *if*, a common usage in ME and EMnE; *'chud* is *I would/should*; *zwagged* is used to mean *forced by blustering language*.

> keep out **che** vor'ye . . .

Che is the dialectal form of the pronoun *I*.

Zir, vurther, volk, zwagged, zo, vortnight, vor all show the same feature of pronunciation. The initial voiceless fricative consonants [s] and [f] of *Sir, further, folk, swagged, so, fortnight* are all voiced. This was the pronunciation in all the dialects of the South at the time, and is still to be heard in the South West of England in rural dialects. *Vor* is perhaps a reduced form of *warn?*

Casion is *occasion*; *Costard* originally meant *apple*, but was used jokingly for *head*. *Ballow* appears to be a misprint for *batton* or *baton*. The *Oxford English Dictionary* says,

> Only in the Shakespeare Folio of 1623, and subsequent editions, where the Quartos have *battero*, and *bat* (*stick, rough walking-stick*); besides which, *batton, battoun*, (*stick, cudgel*) is a probable emendation.

The scene in the play is set in Kent, and the dialectal features described so far probably fit. But in *ice try*, *ice* presumably represents the pronunciation *I sal* for *I shall*, and *gate* means *way*. Both of these are Northern forms, so it looks as if Shakespeare was using a few easily recognisable conventions for indicating a 'rustic' character, and not accurately reproducing Kentish.

These Northern forms, using [s] for Southern [ʃ] in *shall*, can be seen in Text 114 from *The Life of Henry the Fift*, in the speech of the Scots Captain Iamy:

> It **sall** be vary gud . . . I **sall** quit you . . . that **sall** I mary

whereas the Irishness of Captain Mackmorrice is marked by his use of [ʃ] for [s] or [z] in two words only, *Christ* and *is*:

> By **Chrish**, Law, **tish** ill done: the Worke **ish** give over . . .

Thou/thee and you

The *Lear* text illustrates the supposed inferiority of Edgar, playing the part of a poor beggar, in relation to the Steward. Hence Edgar uses *you/your* as well as *Zir* and *good Gentleman* to show respect and an inferior social position, while the Steward addresses Edgar with *thou/thee/thine* to match the contemptuous *bould Peazant, Slave* and *Dunghil*. On the death of the Steward, Edgar resumes his normal rank, and so addresses the body with 'I know *thee* well'. Speaking to Gloster, the Steward uses *thou*, in spite of Gloster's rank, as a form of insult in the circumstances in which he finds him and Edgar.

16.3 English at the end of the 16th century

Reading texts from the 16th century onwards, we find fewer and fewer features of vocabulary and grammar which are archaic and unfamiliar, and it becomes more difficult to specify exactly what differences there are between older and contemporary English. This is especially so if the spelling of older texts is modernised. Facsimiles or exact reproductions make the language look more unfamiliar than it really is. But it is worth trying to sum up the principal differences between English in 1600 and Standard English today. Many of them have already been described in relation to the printed texts.

16.3.1 Spelling and punctuation

OE and ME ⟨þ⟩ is no longer in use, except in the conventional abbreviations for *the* and *that*, ⟨yᵉ⟩ and ⟨yᵗ⟩. ⟨u⟩ and ⟨v⟩ are still used for both vowel [u] and consonant [v], determined by their position in the written or printed word. Similarly, long ⟨ſ⟩ and short ⟨s⟩ continue to be written and printed according to their position in the word.

Letter ⟨j⟩ is not yet in general use for the consonant, only as a variant of letter ⟨i⟩. Letters ⟨i⟩ and ⟨y⟩, are generally interchangeable for the vowel [i]. The redundant final <e> is still added to many words, long after the unstressed vowel [ə] has disappeared. The comma ⟨,⟩, colon ⟨:⟩ and full-stop (prick) ⟨.⟩ are used, with question and exclamation marks ⟨?⟩, ⟨!⟩. The virgule or strike ⟨/⟩ was no longer in general use by 1600. The apostrophe ⟨'⟩ to mark the possessive has not yet appeared.

16.3.2 Pronunciation

The raising or diphthongisation of long vowels in the Southern and Midlands dialects (the Great Vowel Shift) has taken place, but is not yet complete. For some time, until after the 16th century, there were no words with the long back vowel [ɑː]. ⟨ee⟩ words were generally pronounced [iː], ⟨ea⟩ words [eː] or [ɛː], ⟨oo⟩ words [uː] and ⟨oa⟩ words [oː], but there was considerable irregularity and variation. Many words spelt with ⟨ea⟩ and ⟨oo⟩ were pronounced with either a long or a short vowel in different dialects. This diversity led to a growing demand for **regularity** and **standardisation**.

16.3.3 Vocabulary

The assimilation of large numbers of classical Latin and Greek words into the written language had been made easy because of the previous borrowing of hundreds of French words. At the same time, numbers of new prefixes and suffixes were also taken into the language, and used with English words, for example:

prefixes		suffixes	
circum–	non–	-able	-ant/-ent
co–	pre–	-acy	-ate
dis–	re–	-age	-ess
en–/em–	semi–	-al	-ician
inter–	sub–	-ance	-ise
		-ancy/-ency	-let

Words had been borrowed from several other languages, as the lists of examples of loan-words in the Word Book show. Some were adopted through travel and exploration, others from foreign literature and culture. Many were borrowed indirectly, via another language.

16.3.4 Grammar

In general terms, the grammar of 16th-century English is that of Modern English, and only a few features mark it as an earlier form.

Personal pronouns

Both 2nd person pronouns, *thou/thee/thy/thine* and *ye/you/your*, and the neuter pronouns *hit/his* were still in use. The unstressed form *a*, written for *he* in Shakespeare's *The Life of Henry the Fift*, when Mistress Quickly describes Falstaff's death, probably reproduces a common spoken form.

> *a* made a finer end, and went away and it had beene any Chriftome Childe: *a* parted eu'n iuft betweene Twelue and One . . . and *a* babeld of greene fields . . . fo *a* cryed out, God, God, God, three or foure times . . . fo *a* bad me lay more Clothes on his feet . . .

Relative pronouns

That and *which* were most common, and *which* was used with a human subject – *Our Father **which** art in heaven* . . ., but *who/whom* began to be used in the late 16th century.

Verbs

- In the verb phrase, the **modal system** was established, with the verbs *will/would*, *shall/should*, *can/couthe-coude*, *dare/durst*, *may/might-mought* and *mote/must*.
- The **passive** was fully in use.

- **Perfect aspect** was expressed with *have*, and also with *be* when the verb was intransitive, e.g. *I am come*. Some complex verb phrases were recorded but they were still to develop in general use.

- The **3rd person singular present tense** was marked by both ⟨-eth⟩ (the Southern form) and ⟨-s⟩ (the Northern form), e.g.

> Beautie **doth** varnifh Age, as if new borne,
> And **giues** the Crutch the Cradles infancie.
> O tis the Sunne that **maketh** all thinges fhine.

(Loues Labours Lost, Act IV, sc. 3)

but ⟨-s⟩ eventually became standard. The *King James Bible* of 1611 kept the old-fashioned ⟨-eth⟩ suffix, as the translation was based upon the early 16th century translations of Tyndale and Coverdale. Poets continued to use both forms, because they provided different metrical and syllabic patterns. The evidence that both the ⟨-eth⟩ and ⟨-s⟩ suffixes were acceptable for this purpose is in William Bullokar's *Boke at Large* of 1580 (versified, and printed in his reformed spelling):

> Ano, ʒ, foꝛ,cth,may chaṅǵed be   ʒ, chaṅǵ'd
> tꝏ ȝeld fom ʋérs hiȝ ǵráé trulȳ.   for,eth,at
>   end.

And ⟨s⟩ for ⟨eth⟩ may changed be
To yield some verse his grace truly.

Interrogatives and negatives

The inversion of subject and verb in the simple present and past for the interrogative was still common – *knowest thou?*, *came he?* – but the MnE form with *do* had also come into use – *dost thou know?*, *did he come?*

Similarly, the negative *not* was still used with inversion – *I know not* – but was now also used with *do* – *I do not know*. It is at about this time that the multiple negative ceased to be standard usage, though it was and still is normal usage in the dialects.

There *and* it

The filling of the subject slot in a clause with the 'dummy' *there* or *it* had been established well before the beginning of the century, e.g. in Chaucer,

> With vs **ther was** a doctour of phisik
> In al this world ne was ther noon hym lik . . .

> **It is nat** honeste, **it may noght** auance
> For to deelen with no swich poraille . . .

and this led to the loss of the OE and ME **impersonal verb** constructions without a subject, such as,

> **Me thynketh** it acordant to resoun . . .

> A yeman he hadde and seruantz namo
> At that tyme for **hym liste** ryde so.

which were replaced with *It seems to me* . . . and *It pleased him to ride so*.

Nouns

The plural with ⟨-s⟩ or ⟨-es⟩ was the regular form, and most ⟨-en⟩ forms like *eyren* (*eggs*) and *shoon* (*shoes*) had gone, at least from literary language.

16.4 Loan-words, 1550–99

📖 A selection of loan-words recorded during this period can be found in the Word Book, after the word-lists for Chapter 16.

17 Early Modern English IV – the 17th century (i)

In Chapters 14–16 we have been following the establishment of educated London English as a standard language. Although all varieties of 17th- and 20th-century writing are clearly contrasted in style, the underlying grammatical differences between 17th-century and present-day English are relatively small, so there are fewer developments in the grammar to record. As the spelling of words becomes more and more regular, the look of the printed page becomes more familiar, though we still find less conformity to a standard spelling and punctuation in handwriting until the mid-18th century. The vocabulary is, of course, always losing and gaining words according to the needs of communication.

The remaining chapters of the book therefore consist of a series of texts which provide some typical examples of the uses of the language – ordinary uses, letters and diaries for example, and examples of literary prose both colloquial and rhetorical – together with sections on some of the evidence for changes in pronunciation during the century.

17.1 Evidence for changes in pronunciation

All living languages are in a constant state of change in their grammar and vocabulary. The grammar of a standard language, however, changes slowly, because new forms tend to be resisted, and the very fact of its being standard means that it is regarded as fixed and unchangeable.

At the same time as the establishment of a standard in vocabulary and grammar, social standards of pronunciation are also set up, and the speech of those with prestige or authority is imitated by others. In this way there is a polarisation of opinion in attitudes to language use, which is derived from differences of social class and education. In the 17th and 18th centuries rural and artisan speech was referred to as *barbarous*, meaning *uncultured* or *unpolished* as against *polite* or *civilised*. In the 19th century, the Dean of Canterbury in 1864 in *The Queen's English* referred to 'persons of low breeding and inferior education' who 'leave out the aspirate' and are therefore below the mark in intelligence (see Text 182, section 21.2).

In England today, if a man or woman were said to have 'a good accent', we would understand that they spoke in Received Pronunciation (RP). It is sometimes asserted that such speech 'has no accent', and to say of someone that 'she speaks with an accent' is to imply a nonstandard or regional way of speaking.

The evidence for pronunciation in the 17th century is much less easy to interpret than that for the vocabulary, spelling and grammar, in spite of a series of books on spelling and pronunciation, because unlike today, there was no International Phonetic Alphabet to provide an agreed reference for the relationship of sounds to letters. Other evidence comes from a study of the rhymes in poetry. Some of this evidence is discussed in section 18.3.2.

17.1.1 Occasional spellings in handwritten sources

Another indirect source of knowledge about changing pronunciation is in the spelling of written manuscripts. Printers in the 17th century tended to regularise spelling more and more, even though there were still variations and no fixed standard spelling yet. In private letters, however, even educated writers sometimes used 'phonetic' spellings, and these provide some clues to their pronunciation. The concept of a 'spelling mistake' had not yet been established.

Here is a small selection of 'occasional spellings' that are evidence of differences in pronunciation. The range of differences in dialectal pronunciation would have been much greater then than now. People moved from all parts of the country into London, and their varieties of dialectal accent were in competition with each other for acceptability. Sometimes it was the 'vulgar' speech which eventually became the social standard.

The following activity is designed to show the kind of evidence that scholars draw upon in building up their knowledge of changes in the language. The words do not come from any one particular social class. The ME source, the spelling found in a written 17th-century source, and the MnE reflex are given for each word.

Activity 17.1 – vowels

What changes in the pronunciation of the vowels do the spellings of each group show?

ME	17th-C writing	MnE reflex
[aː]		[ei]
came	ceme	came
cradel	credyll	cradle
take	teke	take
[eː]		[iː]
semed	symed	seemed
stepel	stypylle	steeple
[ɛː]		[iː]
discrete	discrate	discreet
retrete	retrate	retreat

[ʊɪ] or [ɔɪ]		[ɔɪ]
joinen	**gine**	join
puisun/poisoun	**pyson**	poison
rejoissen	**regis**	rejoice
[iː]		[ai]
defiled/defyled	**defoyled**	defiled
[ɛr]		[ɜː]
certein	**sarten**	certain
derþe	**darth**	dearth
diuert	**divart**	divert
lernen	**larne**	learn
merci	**marcy**	mercy
persoun	**parson**	person/parson

Although consonants are more stable than vowels, there have been a number of changes for which there is evidence in written letters.

Activity 17.2 – consonants

Describe any changes of pronunciation in the consonants indicated by the spelling in these words:

ME	17th-C writing	MnE reflex
doughter	**dafter**	daughter
boght	**boft**	bought
fasoun	**fessychen**	fashion
instruccion	**instrocshen**	instruction
issu/issue	**ishu**	issue
suspecious	**suspishious**	suspicious
seute/siute	**sheute**	suit
morsel	**mosselle**	morsel
persoun	**passon**	person/parson
portion	**posshene**	portion
scarsliche	**skasely**	scarcely
excepte	**excep**	except
often	**offen**	often
wastcotte	**wascote**	waistcoat
linnene	**lynand**	linen
los	**loste**	loss
syns	**synst**	since
vermine	**varment**	vermin/varmint

There is a commentary on Activities 17.1 and 17.2 in the Text Commentary Book.

17.1.2 Evidence of change from musical settings

Sir Walter Raleigh's poem *What is our life?* was set to music by Orlando Gibbons in 1612. The first two lines are:

What is our life? a play of paſſion,
Our mirth the muſic of diviſion . . .

The music sets *passion* to three syllables on separate notes, *pas/si/on*, and *division* to four, *di/vi/si/on*, so the pronunciation of the words must have been ['pæsi,on] and [dɪ'vɪzi,on], with secondary stress on the final syllable [on]. The reduction of the last two syllables led to today's pronunciation, ['pæʃən] and [dɪ'vɪʒən]. The loss of secondary stress in many words marks one of the differences between 16th- and 17th-century pronunciation and today's.

17.1.3 Evidence of change from verse

Hundreds of lines of verse were written in the late 16th and early 17th centuries by William Shakespeare, Ben Jonson and other dramatists, using the iambic pentameter line (see section 13.2.1), which in its regular form consists of ten syllables of alternating unstressed and stressed syllables, as in Ralegh's poem and in these lines from Shakespeare,

What **ſay** / you **can** / you **loue** / the **Gen** / tle **man?**
This **night** / you **ſhall** / be-**hold** / him **at** / our **feaſt**

This gives us the patterning of stressed syllables in words of two or more syllables, and shows whether the distribution of stress has since changed. For example, the word *proportion* in these lines,

I thought King Henry had reſembled thee,
In Courage, Courtſhip, and Proportion:

must have four syllables to complete the second line:

In **Cour-** / age **Court-**/ ſhip **and** / Pro-**por-**/ ti-**on**

and reinforces the musical evidence about the pronunciation of *passion* and *division*.

Activity 17.3

What is the stress pattern of the italicised words in the following lines from Shakespeare, and in present-day speech?

1   . . . I do *coniure* thee,
    Who art the Table wherein all my thoughts
    Are viſibly *Character'd*, . . .

2   Ay, and peruerſly, ſhe *perſeuers* ſo:

---

3 Goe to thy Ladies graue and call hers thence,
   Or at the leaſt, in hers, *ſepulcher* thine.

4 Madam: if your heart be ſo *obdurate*:
   Vouchſafe me yet your Picture for my loue,

5 Nephew, what meanes this paſſionate *diſcourſe*?

6 She beares a Dukes *Reuenewes* on her back,
   And in her heart ſhe ſcornes our Pouertie:

7 *Pernitious* Protector, dangerous Peere . . .

8 Away: Though parting be a fretfull *coroſiue*,
   It is *applyed* to a deathfull wound.

9 Cloſe vp his eyes, and draw the Curtaine cloſe,
   And let vs all to *Meditation*.

10 Is it for him you do *enuie* me ſo?

17.2 Sir Thomas Browne

Sir Thomas Browne (1605–82), after studying medicine on the Continent, practised as a physician in Norwich for the rest of his life, but he is remembered today as a writer. His first book, *Religio Medici* ('The Faith of a Doctor'), had been written as 'a private Exercise directed to myself', but a pirated edition had been published 'in a most depraved Copy', so he decided to publish his own version.

The book explores the tension that then existed between religious faith and new scientific ideas. This conflict had been expressed earlier by John Donne in his poem *An Anatomy of the World* in 1611,

> And new Philoſophy calls all in doubt,
> The Element of fire is quite put out;
> The Sun is loſt, and th'earth, and no mans wit
> Can well direct him where to looke for it . . .
> 'Tis all in peeces, all coherence gone;
> All juſt ſupply, and all Relation.

17.2.1 *Religio Medici*

The following short extract from *Religio Medici* expresses Sir Thomas Browne's religious faith:

Text 118: Sir Thomas Browne (i), Religio Medici, 1642

As for thoſe wingy Myſteries in Divinity, and airy ſubtleties in Religion, which have unhing'd the brains of better heads, they never ſtretched the *Pia Mater* of mine. Methinks there be not impoſſibilities enough in Religion for an active faith; the deepeſt Myſteries ours contains have not only been illuſtrated, but maintained, by Syllogiſm and the rule of Reaſon. I love to loſe my ſelf in a myſtery, to purſue my Reaſon to an *O altitudo!* 'Tis my ſolitary recreation to poſe my apprehenſion with thoſe involved Ænigma's and riddles of the Trinity, with Incarnations, and Reſurrection. I can anſwer all the Objections of Satan and my rebellious reaſon with that odd reſolution I learned of *Tertullian, Certum eſt quia impoſſibile eſt.*

Pia Mater – a membrane in the brain.
Syllogism – a logical argument consisting of two propositions and a conclusion.
Certum est quia impossibile est – Latin for *It is certain because it is impossible.*

📖 The lexical vocabulary of Text 118 is listed in the Word Book.

Students of literature today value Browne's writings for their style rather than for their content, and style is of interest to students of language too, in showing how a writer exploits and expands the resources of the language of the time.

17.2.2 *Vulgar Errors*, 1646

Sir Thomas Browne's learning is illustrated in the volumes of *Pseudodoxia Epidemica, or Enquiries into Very many received Tenents, and commonly presumed Truths,* which are more popularly known as *Vulgar Errors* – *vulgar* in the sense of *common.* He examines a variety of beliefs which were commonly held, in the light of three criteria: (i) **authority** (what had been written about the subject), (ii) **rational thought**, and (iii) **experience.** The outcome is often, to a modern reader, quaint and amusing, but the book gives us valuable insights into the 'world view' of the early 17th century, still largely a late Medieval view in spite of the beginnings of scientific experiment at that time.

17.2.2.1 *Of Sperma-Ceti*

The following extract shows the alternation of direct observation and appeal to antiquarian authorities (now long since forgotten), which he applies to the problem of 'what is spermaceti?', a substance found in whales, and used both in medicine and in the manufacture of candles. Notice also his literal acceptance of the Old Testament account of Jonah and the whale. (This is the second of three texts on the whale – see Text 48 from the medieval *Bestiary* and Text 131 from John Evelyn's *Diary.*)

Activity 17.4

(i) Divide the lexical words into two sets, formal and core vocabulary, using your own judgement. Then look up the derivation of the words and see if there is any correlation between formality and derivation.

(ii) Discuss how the grammatical structures that Browne uses tend to make the style of his writing formal and unlike ordinary speech.

Text 119: Sir Thomas Browne (ii), Vulgar Errors (i)

Of Sperma-Ceti, and the Sperma-Ceti Whale.

What Sperma-Ceti is, men might juftly doubt, fince the learned *Hofmannus* in his work of Thirty years, faith plainly, *Nefcio quid fit*. And therefore need not wonder at the variety of opinions; while fome conceived it to be *flos maris*, and many, a bituminous fubftance floating upon the fea.

That it was not the fpawn of the Whale, according to vulgar conceit, or nominal appellation Phylofophers have always doubted, not eafily conceiving the Seminal humour of Animals, fhould be inflamable; or of a floating nature.

That it proceedeth from a Whale, befide the relation of *Clufius*, and other learned obfervers, was indubitably determined, not many years fince by a Sperma-Ceti Whale, caft upon our coaft of *Norfolk*. Which, to lead on further inquiry, we cannot omit to inform. It contained no lefs then fixty foot in length, the head fomewhat peculiar, with a large prominency over the mouth; teeth only in the lower Jaw, received into flefhly fockets in the upper. The Weight of the largeft about two pound: No griftly fubftances in the mouth, commonly called Whale-bones; Only two fhort finns feated forwardly on the back; the eyes but fmall, the pizell large, and prominent. A leffer Whale of this kind above twenty years ago, was caft upon the fame fhore.

The difcription of this Whale feems omitted by *Gefner, Rondeletius*, and the firft Editions of *Aldrovandus*; but defcribeth the latin impreffion of *Pareus*, in the Exoticks of *Clufius*, and the natural hiftory of *Nirembergius*; but more amply in Icons and figures of *Johnftonus* . . .

Out of the head of this Whale, having been dead divers days, and under putrifaction, flowed ftreams of oyl and Sperma-Ceti; which was carefully taken up and preferved by the Coafters. But upon breaking up, the Magazin of Sperma- Ceti, was found in the head lying in folds and courfes, in the bignefs of goofe eggs, encompaffed with large flakie fubftances, as large as a mans head, in form of hony-combs, very white and full of oyl . . . And this many conceive to have been the fifh which fwallowed *Jonas*. Although for the largenefs of the mouth, and frequency in thofe feas, it may poffibly be the *Lamia*.

Some part of the Sperma-Ceti found on the fhore was pure, and needed little depuration; a great part mixed with fetid oyl, needing good preparation, and frequent expreffion, to bring it to a flakie confiftency. And not only the head, but other parts contained it. For the carnous parts being roafted, the oyl dropped out, an axungious and thicker parts fubfiding; the oyl it felf contained alfo much in it, and ftill after many years fome is obtained from it . . .

nescio quid sit – Latin for *I do not know what it is*

nominal appellation – a name given without reference to fact

Seminal humour – sperm; *humour* meant *a body fluid*

flos maris – Latin for *a flower of the sea*

axungious – greasy, like lard

depuration – purifying

17.2.2.2 Commentary

Formal vocabulary

Sir Thomas Browne's writing is highly 'literary' or 'formal'. Our judgement of the formality or informality of a text is subjective, and neither word can be precisely defined, but we can probably reach a consensus on most of the formal words in this text in terms of:

- their unfamiliarity, or
- their relative infrequency of use, or
- the context in which they are usually used.

The following list of formal vocabulary from Text 119 is based on a personal reaction to the text, and is therefore open to any reader to discuss and amend or criticise. The list omits words like *men, work, saith, years, weight, mouth, shore, first, head, dead, taken, large, oil,* which are short, familiar and common and so belong to the 'core vocabulary'. We want to find out whether there is any linguistic evidence to explain a selection that is based only on such intuitive judgement.

amply	Exoticks	inflamable	proceedeth
Animals	expression	inform	prominency
appellation	fetid	inquiry	prominent
axungious	figures (*n*)	learned (*adj*)	putrifaction
bituminous	fleshly	Magazin	received
carnous	forwardly	nominal	relation
conceived	frequency	observers	Seminal
consistency	frequent (*adj*)	obtained	sockets
contained	gristly	omit	spawn (*n*)
depuration	humour	peculiar	Sperma-Ceti
describeth	Icons	Phylosophers	subsiding
Editions	impression	preparation	substance
encompassed	indubitably	preserved	vulgar

Only one word, *fleshly,* comes directly from OE (*flæsclic*). Three others are later ME or EMnE derivations from OE word-stems, *learned* (adj) (1340), *gristly* (1398) and *forwardly* (1552). Only two other words were recorded before the 14th century – *divers* and *socket.*

There are 33 words from French (62%) and 16 from Latin or Greek (30%). The figures for the earliest occurrence of the words are as follows:

OE	1.8%	*15th C*	21.4%
13th C	3.6%	*16th C*	28.6%
14th C	33.9%	*17th C*	10.7%

We can therefore suggest a hypothesis, for which there is some evidence, to support our intuitive classification of the formal words in the text: *that words classified as formal tend to be those which were taken into English from French, Latin or Greek from the late 14th century onwards.*

All the formal vocabulary consists of lexical words – nouns, verbs, adjectives or adverbs. The complete text contains 442 words (tokens), some of them occurring more than once, giving a total of 231 different words (types). The structure of a text is held together by the function words – pronouns, determiners, conjunctions and prepositions – which almost all derive from Old English and form a small closed class of words. These function words make up about two-fifths of the vocabulary of the text.

📖 A complete list of the lexical vocabulary with dates and derivations is in the Word Book.

Formal syntax

Choice of vocabulary is important, but words alone do not make up language use. The way they are ordered into sentences in writing is an essential feature of the style of the writing, and is usually correlated with the lexical choices. Grammatical complexity is often a feature of formality of style. Clauses may be embedded into other clauses or phrases and made subordinate to another clause. Each level of the grammar – sentences, clauses, phrases and words – may be coordinated together. The normal, unmarked order of the elements of a declarative clause (one that makes a statement) is:

Subject (S) – Predicator (P) – Complement (C) or Object (O) – Adverbial (A).

If the normal order of a clause is changed, then this may be stylistically significant too, and the focus of information in the clause is altered. The potential for variety and complexity of style is great. We can take the first sentence as an example:

What Sperma-Ceti is, men might justly doubt, since the learned *Hofmannus* in his work of Thirty years, saith plainly, *Nescio quid sit*.

Main clause	O = NCl	S	P-	A	-P
	[What Sperma-Ceti is],	men	might	justly	doubt,
	theme				

The grammatical object of the verb in this opening main clause (MCl) is itself an embedded clause, [*What Sperma-Ceti is*], functioning like a noun and therefore a noun clause (NCl), and comes first, so the question *What Sperma-Ceti is* is made grammatically prominent and announces the theme of both the clause and the text. The 'unmarked order' of the clause constituents is:

S	P	O = NCl	A
Men	might doubt	[what Sperma-Ceti is]	justly

This main clause is followed by an adverbial clause which includes the Latin quoted clause *Nescio quid sit* – *I don't know what it is*, functioning as the object of *saith*.

	scj	S	A	P	A
AdvCl	[since	the learned *Hofmannus*	in his work of Thirty years,	saith	plainly],
(quoting)					
		O			
quoted clause		[*Nescio quid sit*].			

The grammar of the text is marked by similar kinds of complexity, with the re-ordering and embedding of clause elements.

📖 A list of the lexical vocabulary of Text 119 is in the Word Book, and a more detailed grammatical analysis is in the Text Commentary Book.

17.2.2.3 Of the Badger

It was a 'vulgar error' of the times that a badger's legs were longer on one side than the other. Sir Thomas Browne discusses this.

Activity 17.5

Discuss the distribution of words of OE, French and Latin derivation, and their effect upon the style of the writing.

Text 120: Sir Thomas Browne (iii), Vulgar Errors (ii), Of the badger

The Third Book, Ch V.

Of the Badger

That a Brock or badger hath the legs on one ſide ſhorter then of the other, though an opinion perhaps not very ancient, is yet very general; received not only by Theoriſts and unexperienced believers, but aſſented unto by moſt who have the opportunity to behold and hunt them daily. And for my own part, upon indifferent enquiry, I cannot diſcover this difference, although the regardable ſide be defined, and the brevity by moſt imputed unto the left.

Again, It ſeems no eaſie affront unto reaſon, and generally repugnant unto the courſe of Nature; for if we ſurvey the total ſet of Animals, we may in their legs, or Organs of progreſſion, obſerve an equality of length, and parity of Numeration; that is, not any to have an odd legg, or the ſupporters and movers of one ſide not exactly anſwered by the other. Perfect and viviparous quadrupeds, ſo ſtanding in their poſition of proneneſs, that the oppoſite points of Neighbour-legs conſiſt in the ſame plane; and a line deſcending from their Navel interſects at right angles the axis of the Earth . . .

📖 There is a complete list of the vocabulary of the text in the Word Book.

🜨 Text 120 is recorded on the CD/cassette tape.

ɔv ðə bædʒər

ðæt ə brɒk ɔr bædʒər hæθ ðə lɛgz ɒn oːn səid ʃɔrtər ðen ɒv ðə ʊðər, ðoː ən ɔpɪnjɒn pərhæps nɒt vɛrɪ eːnsjənt, ɪz jɛt vɛrɪ dʒɛnərəl, rɪsiːvd nɒt ɒnlɪ bəi θiərɪsts ænd ʊnɛkspɪrɪənsd bɪliːvərz, bʊt asɛntɛd ʊntu bəi moːst hu hæv ðɪ ɒportjunɪti tu bɪhoːld ænd hʊnt ðəm deːli. ənd for məi oːn pɑrt, əpɒn ɪndɪfərənt ɛnkwəiri, əi kænɒt dɪskʊvər ðɪs dɪfərəns, ɒldoː ðə rɪgɑrdəbəl səid bi dɛfəind, ænd ðə brɛvɪti bəi moːst ɪmpjutɪd ʊntu ðə lɛft. ageːn, ɪt siːmz no izi əfrɒnt ʊntu rizən, ænd dʒɛnərəli rɪpʊgnənt ʊntu ðə kɔːrs ɒv netjur, for ɪf wi sʊrveː ðə tɔtəl sɛt ɒv ænɪməlz, wi meː ɪn ðeːr lɛgz, ɔr

ɔrgənz ɒv prəgresɪən, ɒbsɛrv æn ɪkwalɪtɪ ɒv lɛŋθ, ænd pæriti ɒv
njuməresɪən, ðæt ɪz, nɒt æni tu hæv æn ɒd lɛg, or ðə səpɔrtərz ænd
muːvərz ɒv oːn sɜːid nɒt ɛgzæktli answərd bəi ðɪ uðər. pɛrfɛkt ænd
vɪvɪparʊs kwadrʊpɛdz, so stændɪŋ ɪn ðeːr pɔzɪsɪən ɒv proːnɪːes, ðæt ðɪ
ɒpəzɪt pɔɪnts ɒv neːbʊr lɛgz kɒnsɪst ɪn ðə seːm pleːn, ænd ə ləin dɛsɛndɪŋ
frɒm ðeːr neːvəl ɪntərsɛkts æt rəit æŋgəlz ðɪ æksɪs ɒv ðɪ ɛrθ.

17.3 The development of writing hands (vi) – the 17th century

Two hands, Secretary and Italic, were being taught and used simultaneously in the 17th century, so it is not surprising that a mixed bastard style developed. By the end of the century, in its many personal varieties, it became the established English national **round hand**, familiar today. This early example of a mixed hand is dated 1635, and is from the 'Minute Book of Commissioners to enquire into Fees of Courts':

Transcription

Vpon consideracion taken this day of the small
Letter written ~~somety~~ in entring the Pleadings in
the Courts at the Comon lawe, and of the
secretary hand in the English courts mixed
with the Italian hand, wch is conceived will in
short tyme ~~will~~ weare and become illegible
that it bee Certified by the Com$^{?s}$ in some fitt
place upon their next Certificates of the Officers
of those Courts to His M^{ty} as deseruinge
reformacon ./

The following extract from a letter written by John Dryden in 1683 is an example of the national round hand, which had developed from the fusion of Secretary and Italic hands:

This example is a petition to the Privy Council in 1640. It shows how different hands were in use at the same time for different purposes, and that clerks were very skilled in writing them. The petition itself is in the mixed hand, the heading 'To the right hono^{ble} . . .' in italic hand, and the Council's decision, beginning 'At the Court . . .' in another italic hand:

Transcription

To the Right Hono^{ble} the Lordes and others of
His Ma^{is} most hono^{ble} Privy Councell.

The humble peticon of Richard Beaumont
Apprentice vnto James James an Apothecary, London,
Humbly sheweth

That yor pet⁹ *(peticioner)* was sent for by warrn^t from the right hono^{ble} S^r ffrancis
Windebanke k^t principall Secretary of State and therevpon was
examyned by his hono^r for speaking some vnaduised wordes, wch hee
did not deny; And vpon report to yor LL^{pps} of yor pet⁹s humble
confession, hee was iustly comitted by yor hono^rs to the prison of
the ffleete.

Your Pet^r most humbly beseecheth yor LL^{pps} in
regard that hee is heartily sorry that ever hee spake
such wordes, and doth purpose never to offend in the
like kinde That yor hono^rs out of yor accustomed
clemency wilbee pleased to give order for his
enlargement./ And yor pet^r will pray etc.

At the Court at Whitehall the 20th of May 1640
Mr. Secretary Windebanke is prayed to consider
of this Pet^{on} and to take such order therein as
with the advise of Mr. Attorney Generall hee shall
thinck good./   Edw. Nicholas

17.3.1 Printing fonts

Whereas today hundreds of fonts are available to use in printing and word-processing, the two principal types of font from the late 15th to the 17th centuries are illustrated in some of the facsimiles. The first fonts were based upon the formal book hands (see the facsimiles of Caxton's printing, Texts 93 and 94), sometimes called black letter fonts:

> And Petir bithouhte on the word of Jhesu, that he hadde seid, Bifore the cok crowe, thries thou schalt denye me. And he yede out, and wepte bitterli.

A much less ornate font had evolved during the 16th century (contrast, for example, Texts 107 and 108 with Text 109 in Chapter 15:

> **And Petir bithouhte on the word of Jhesu, that he hadde seid, Bifore the cok crowe, thries thou schalt denye me. And he yede out, and wepte bitterly.**

The following tables illustrate letter shapes of the alphabet for some of the writing hands which have been described, and the two printing fonts:

	Lower case handwriting fonts						Printing fonts	
Old English	Textura	Bastard Secretary	Secretary	Common Pleas	Chancery	Italic	Black letter	17th C print
a	a	a	a	a	a	a	a	a
b	b	b	b	b	b	b	b	b
c	c	c	c	c	c	c	c	c
ꝺ	d	d	d	d	ꝺ	d	d	d
e	e	c	e	o	e	e	e	e
F	f	f	f	f	f	f	f	f
ꝫ	g	g	g	g	g	g	g	g
h	h	h	h	h	h	h	h	h
i	t	i	i	ı	i	i	i	i
—	t	i	i	j	j	j	j	j
k	k	k	k	k	k	k	k	k
l	l	l	l	l	l	l	l	l
m	m	m	m	m	m	m	m	m
n	n	n	n	n	n	n	n	n
o	o	o	o	o	o	o	o	o
p	p	p	p	p	p	p	p	p
q	q	q	q	q	q	q	q	q
r	r	r	r	r	r	r	r	r
r ſs	ſ	6 ſ	ꝛ ſ	ſs	ꝛ ſ	s ſ	s	s ſ
t	t	t	t	t	t	t	t	t
u	u	u	u	u	u	u	u	u
v	v	v	v	v	v	v	v	v
p	w	w	w	w	w	w	w	w
x	x	x	x	x	x	x	x	x
ẏ	y	y	y	y	y	y	y	y
z	z	z	z	z	z	z	z	z

347

	Upper case handwriting fonts						Printing fonts	
Old English	Textura	Bastard Secretary	Secretary	Common Pleas	Chancery	Italic	Black letter	17th and 18th C print
A								A
B								B
C								C
D								D
E								E
F								F
G								G
H								H
I								I
								J
K								K
L								L
M								M
N								N
O								O
P								P
Q								Q
R								R
S								S
T								T
U								U
V								V
W								W
X								X
Y								Y
Z								Z

17.4 George Fox's *Journal*

George Fox (1624–91) was the son of a Leicestershire weaver. He experienced a religious conversion, an intense spiritual conviction of 'the Inner Light of Christ', and left home in 1643 to become a preacher and the founder of the Society of Friends, or Quakers. At this time, however, failure to conform to the doctrines and practice of the Church of England meant civil penalties and often persecution. He was imprisoned many times, and it was during his long stay in Worcester jail between 1673 and 1674 that he dictated an account of his experiences to his fellow prisoner Thomas Lower, who was Fox's son-in-law. The *Journal* is a moving account of his life but in addition, for students of language, an insight into everyday spoken language of the later 17th century.

17.4.1 The written *Journal*

Here is a short example in facsimile from the manuscript of the *Journal* in Thomas Lower's handwriting, describing events in 1663. Writing ⟨ye⟩ for ⟨the⟩ and ⟨yᵗ⟩ for ⟨that⟩ was common, the ⟨y⟩ representing the old letter ⟨þ⟩ in these conventional abbreviations.

Text 121: George Fox's **Journal** *1663 (facsimile)*

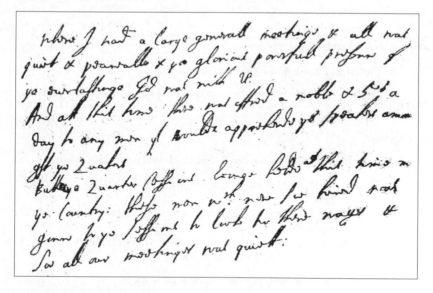

Transcription

> (*And soe from Will: Pearsons I past through ye Countryes*
> *visitinge freinds till I came to Pardsey Cragge*)
> where I had a large generall meetinge & all was
> quiet & peaceable & ye glorious powrfull prefence of
> ye euerlaftinge God was with us.

> And att this time there was offred a noble & 5s. a
> day to any men y^t coulde apprehende ye ſpeakers amon
> gſt ye Quakers
> Butt ye Quarter Seſsions beinge helde^{at} this time in
> ye Country: theſe men wch were ſoe hired was
> gonne to ye Seſsions to looke for there wages &
> ſoe all our meetinges was quiett.

17.4.2 George Fox's own handwriting

The next facsimile is in Fox's own handwriting, from his account of his appearance at the Sessions in Lancaster in 1652, on a charge of blasphemy. The argument is theological, Fox often interpreting Scripture literally, and finding texts from the Bible to support his point of view. Fox's own spelling is more individual and idiosyncratic than his son-in-law's.

The references in the left margin are to New Testament texts (*Corinthians, Ephesians, 2 Peter, Galatians*). The letter ɑ precedes Fox's answers to the charges against him – what he is alleged to have said:

Text 122: George Fox's handwriting (facsimile)

Transcription

firſt that he did aferm that he had the devenety ecenſhelly in him.—

Co^{rn} 6 16   a   for the word eſanſhally it is a expreſhon of ther one but that the ſeants ar the tempells of god

epef 4 6   & god doeth dwell in them that i witnes & the criptuer doeth witnes: & if god doeth dwell in

2 Peter 1 4   them the . . . devenety dwelleth in them & the criptuer ſeath ye ſeants ſhall be maed par takers of the divin nator this i witns

2 boeth baptiſme & the lordſ ſuper ar vnlowfull.

ɑ

glaſh 3 27   as for the word vnlowfull it was not ſpoken by mee but the ſprinkling of enfants i deny

Some extracts follow in which Fox speaks of some of his many clashes with individuals and institutions.

17.4.3 The origin of the name 'Quaker'

The name 'Quaker' was at first a term of abuse, which has since been adopted by the Friends, and its original connotations have been lost. Fox and his followers called themselves Children of the Light, Friends of Truth, or simply Friends. He described Quakers in a book called *Instructions for Right Spelling*, 1673 (see section 18.2.1):

> Quakers, they are in Deriſion ſo called by the Scorners of this Age; but their proper Name is, Children of the Light; and though they are accounted a Sect of Hereticks newly ſprung up, by ſome who have raſhly paſſed Judgment uppon them, yet upon a ſerious and diligent Search into their principles and Examples, they will appear to be led by a *Chriſtian* Spirit.

George Fox explained in the *Journal* how the name Quaker came about,

> ... this was Juſtice Bennett of Darby yᵗ firſt called Us Quakers becauſe wee bid yᵐ tremble att ye Word of God & this was in ye year 1650.

and referred to this in a letter addressed to Justice Bennett:

Text 123: George Fox's Journal, 1650

> *Collonell Bennett that called the ſervants of the Lord Quakers*
> *G.F. paper to him: Collonell bennett of darbe 1650.*
>
> ... thou waſt the firſt man in the nation that gave the people of god the name quaker And Called them quakers, when thou Examineſt George in thy houſe att Derbey (which they had never the name before) now A Juſtice to wrong name people, what may the brutiſh people doe, if ſuch A one A Juſtice of peace give names to men, but thou art Lifted upp proud and haughty and ſoe turneſt Againſt the Juſt one given upp to miſname the ſaints, and to make lyes for others to beeleve.
>   Thus ſaith the LORD, The heaven is my throne, and the earth is my footſtool: where is the houſe that ye build unto me? and where is the place of my reſt? For all thoſe things hath mine hand made, and all thoſe things have been, ſaith the LORD: but to this man will I look, even to him that is poor and of a contrite ſpirit, and trembleth at my word. (Iſaiah Ch. 66, 1–2)

The spelling and punctuation of the written *Journal* are typical of the time in their lack of conformity to the developing printed standard, but if a transcription is made using present-day spelling and punctuation, it becomes easier to examine the features of vocabulary and grammar which mark the narrative style.

Transcription into modern spelling and punctuation

> ... Thou wast the first man in the nation that gave the people of God the name 'Quaker' and called them 'Quakers', when thou examine(d)st George (*Fox*) in thy house at Derby (which they had never the name before). Now, a Justice to wrong name people! What may the brutish people do, if such a one – a Justice of Peace – give names to men? But thou art lifted up proud and haughty, and so turnest against the just. (*Thou art*) one given up to misname the saints, and to make lies for others to believe ...

There can be little doubt that this is a record of speech, with its exclamation 'now a Justice to wrong name people', and the verb *wrong name*, but its only marked difference from MnE is the use of *thou* in addressing the Justice, which Fox insisted upon.

17.4.4 Saying 'thou' to people

The use of *thee/thou/thine* (see sections 16.2.2 and 16.2.3.1) began to become old-fashioned and out of date in polite society during the 17th century. The grammarian John Wallis in 1653 considered that the use of *thou* was 'usually contemptuous, or familiarly caressing', and that 'custom' required the plural *you* when addressing one person. George Fox took a different view. He believed that the use of *thou* to address one person was a mark of equality between people, whereas it had long been used to mark social superiority or inferiority. So he published a pamphlet in 1660:

Text 124: George Fox, A Battle-Door for Teachers and Professors (facsimile)

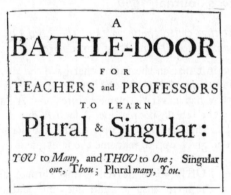

Fox's *battle-door* (more fully *battledore-book*) was a simpler and later form of *horn-book*, which was so called from its usual shape – 'a leaf of paper containing the alphabet, protected by a thin plate of translucent horn, and mounted on a tablet of wood with a projecting piece for a handle'. A *battledore* consisted of the tablet without the horn covering.

Fox practised what he preached, addressing Justices of the Peace as *thou*, and refusing to take off his hat in court – both of which were regarded as insulting behaviour.

Text 125: George Fox's Journal, 1651 – *thee and thou (i)*

... & before I was brought in before him ye garde faide It was well if ye Juftice was not drunke before wee came to him for hee ufed to bee drunke very early: & when I was brought before him becaufe I did not putt off my hatt & faide thou to him hee afkt ye man whether I was not Mafed or fonde: & hee faide noe: Itt was my principle: & foe I warned him to repent & come to ye light y^t Chrift had enlightened him withall y^t with it hee might fee all his evill words & actions y^t hee had donne & acted & his ungodly ways hee had walked in & ungodly words hee had fpoaken ...

The next extract from the *Journal* describes events at Patrington in the East Riding of Yorkshire in 1651.

Text 126: George Fox's Journal, *1651 – thee & thou (ii)*

... And afterwards I paffed away through ye Country & att night came to an Inn: & there was a rude Company of people & I afkt ye woman if fhee had any Meate to bringe mee fome: & fhee was fomethinge ftrange becaufe I faide thee & thou to her: foe I afkt her if fhee had any milke but fhee denyed it: & I afkt her if fhee had any creame & fhee denyed y^t alfo though I did not greatly like fuch meate but onely to try her.

And there ftoode a churne in her houfe: & a little boy put his hande Into ye churne & pulled it doune: & threw all ye creame In ye floore before my eyes: & foe Itt manifefted ye woman to bee a lyar: & foe I walkt out of her houfe after ye Lord God had manifefted her deceite & perverfeneffe: & came to a ftacke of hay: & lay in ye hay ftacke all night: beinge but 3 days before ye time caled Chriftmas in fnowe & raine.

17.4.5 The steeplehouse

The use of a particular word may cause offence when its connotations are not shared. For George Fox, the *Church* meant *the people of God*, and he refused to use the word for the building in which religious worship took place. This, like much of Fox's preaching, his use of *thee* and *thou*, and his principled refusal to remove his hat before a magistrate, caused offence. Here is one of many references to this in his *Journal*:

Text 127: George Fox's Journal, 1652 (i)

(1652) ... And when I was at Oram before in ye fteeplehoufe there came a profeffor & gave me a pufh in ye breft in ye fteeplehoufe & bid me gett out of ye Church: alack poore man faide I doft thou call ye fteeplehoufe ye Church: ye Church is ye people whome God has purchafed with his bloode: & not ye houfe.

professor = one who professes religion, in Fox's view, one who pretends to be religious, but is not truly so.

17.4.6 George Fox persecuted

The *Journal* is full of accounts of violent attacks on Fox and his followers for their faith and preaching. The following extract is typical. Barlby is about twelve miles south of York, and Tickhill about six miles south of Doncaster.

Activity 17.5

Examine the grammatical structure of the narrative, and describe those features which mark the text as written down from dictation, in contrast to, for example, Sir Thomas Browne's prose.

📖 An analysis can be found in the Text Commentary Book.

Text 128: George Fox's Journal, 1652 (ii)

... then we went away to Balby about a mile off: & the rude people layde waite & ftoned us doune the lane but bleffed be ye Lorde wee did not receive much hurte: & then ye next firft day* I went to Tickill & there ye freinds* of y^t fide gathered togeather & there was a meeting.*

And I went out of ye meetinge to ye fteeplehoufe & ye preift & moft of ye heads of ye parifh was gott uppe Into ye chancell & foe I went uppe to y^m & when I began to fpeake they fell upon mee & ye Clarke uppe with his bible as I was fpeakinge & hitt mee in ye face y^t my face gufht out with bloode y^t I bleade exceedingly in ye fteeplehoufe & foe ye people cryed letts have him out of ye Church as they caled it: & when they had mee out they exceedingly beate mee & threw me doune & threw mee over a hedge: & after dragged mee through a houfe Into ye ftreet ftoneinge & beatinge mee: & they gott my hatt from mee which I never gott againe.

Soe when I was gott upon my leggs I declared to y^m ye worde of life & fhowed to y^m ye fruites of there teachers & howe they difhonored Chriftianity.

And foe after a while I gott Into ye meetinge againe amongft freinds & ye preift & people comeinge by ye houfe I went foorth with freinds Into ye Yarde & there I fpoake to ye preift & people: & the preift fcoffed at us & caled us Quakers: but ye Lords power was foe over y^m all: & ye worde of life was declared in foe much power & dreade to y^m y^t ye preift fell a tremblinge himfelfe y^t one faide unto him looke howe ye preift trembles & fhakes hee is turned a Quaker alfoe.

first day – Fox's term for *Sunday*
freinds – members of the Society of Friends
meeting – the Quaker term for a religious service

📖 The lexical vocabulary of Texts 121–8 is listed in the Word Book.

17.5 John Milton

George Fox gave offence to the religious and civil authorities both during the Commonwealth under Oliver Cromwell in the 1650s, and following the Restoration of Charles II after 1660. John Milton (1608–74), on the other hand, devoted years of political activity to the Puritan cause in the 1640s and 1650s, writing books and pamphlets on behalf of, for example, religious liberty (against bishops), domestic liberty (for divorce) and civil liberty (against censorship).

One of his best known pamphlets was *Areopagitica* (the *Areopagus* was the highest civil court of Ancient Athens):

A Speech of Mr. John Milton for the Liberty of Vnlicenc'd Printing,
to the Parlamant of England,
Printed in the Teare 1644.

It is called a speech, though printed, as if it were written to be spoken, and uses the rhetorical model of Greek and Latin oratory. Its style is in complete contrast to the artless narrative of George Fox.

Text 129: John Milton, Areopagitica (i) (facsimile)

> be affur'd, Lords and Commons, there can no greater tefti-
> mony appear, then when your prudent fpirit acknowledges and o-
> beyes the voice of reafon from what quarter foever it be heard fpea-
> king; and renders ye as willing to repeal any Act of your own fet-
> ting forth, as any fet forth by your Predeceffors.
>
> If ye be thus refolv'd, as it were injury to thinke ye were not, I
> know not what fhould withhold me from prefenting ye with a fit
> inftance wherein to fhew both that love of truth which ye eminent-
> ly profeffe, and that uprightneffe of your judgement which is not
> wont to be partiall to your felves; by judging over again that Order
> which ye have ordain'd *to regulate Printing. That no-Book, pamphlet, or*
> *paper fhall be henceforth Printed, unleffe the fame be firft approv'd and li-*
> *cenc't by fuch,* or at leaft one of fuch as fhall be thereto appointed. . . .
>
> I deny not, but that it is of greateft concernment in the Church
> and Commonwealth, to have a vigilant eye how Bookes demeane
> themfelves, as well as men; and thereafter to confine, imprifon, and do
> fharpeft juftice on them as malefactors: For Books are not abfolute-
> ly dead things, but doe contain a potencie of life in them to be as a-
> ctive as that foule was whofe progeny they are; nay they do preferve
> as in a violl the pureft efficacie and extraction of that living intellect
> that bred them. I know they are as lively, and as vigoroufly produ-
> ctive, as thofe fabulous Dragons teeth; and being fown up and down,
> may chance to fpring up armed men. And yet on the other hand' un-
> leffe warineffe be us'd, as good almoft kill a Man as kill a good Book;
> who kills a Man kills a reafonable creature, Gods Image; but hee
> who deftroyes a good Booke, kills reafon it felfe, kills the Image of
> God, as it were in the eye. Many a man lives a burden to the Earth;
> but a good Booke is the pretious life-blood of a mafter fpirit, imbal-
> m'd and treafur'd up on purpofe to a life beyond life.

Activity 17.6

Comment on the stage of development in spelling and grammar which has been reached in Text 129, in comparison with the 16th-century texts of chapters 15 and 16. Use the following examples:

Spelling and punctuation

(i)   The distribution of the letters ⟨u⟩ and ⟨v⟩, ⟨i⟩ and ⟨j⟩.
(ii) The distribution of long and short ⟨ſ⟩ and ⟨s⟩.
(ii) The use of ⟨-y⟩ in the spelling of *testimony, injury* etc.
(iii) What does the spelling ⟨'d⟩ in *assur'd, treasur'd* etc. imply about pronunciation?
(iv) What was the probable pronunciation of *armed*?
(v)   Comment on these spellings:

   (a)   *Bookes* and *Books, Booke* and *Book*.
   (b)   *Dragons teeth* and *Gods Image*.
   (c)   *potencie* and *efficacie*.

Grammar

(i)   Comment on the grammar of:

   (a)   *ye*
   (b)   *I know not / I deny not*
   (c)   *doe contain / do preserve*
   (d)   *who kills a Man kills a reasonable creature*
   (e)   *that order which ye have ordain'd / whose progeny they are / hee who destroyes*

(ii) What is the inflection of the 3rd person singular present tense of verbs?

The second text from *Areopagitica* is often quoted as an example of the 'high style' of rhetorical writing, and for Milton's vision of an approaching Golden Age in England. Its content and imagery derive largely from the older Medieval world view.

The 'spirits' and the 'vital and rational faculties' refer to the belief that the human body contained both a 'vegetable soul', which conducted unconscious vital bodily processes, and a 'rational soul', which controlled understanding and reason.

The comparison of the Nation to an eagle depends upon an ancient 'vulgar error' which Sir Thomas Browne did not in fact discuss. The description of the eagle in a 13th-century bestiary can be found in section 7.6.

Text 130: John Milton, Areopagitica *(ii) (facsimile)*

Activity 17.7

Discuss the style and rhetoric of this extract.

> For as in a body, when the blood is frefh, the fpirits pure and vigorous, not only to vital, but to rationall faculties, and thofe in the acuteft, and the perteft operations of wit and futtlety, it argues in what good plight and conftitution the body is, fo when the cherfulneffe of the people is fo fprightly up, as that it has, not only wherewith to guard well its own freedom and fafety, but to fpare, and to beftow upon the folideft and fublimeft points of controverfie, and new invention, it betok'ns us not degenerated, nor drooping to a fatall decay, but cafting off the old and wrincl'd skin of corruption to outlive thefe pangs and wax young again, entring the glorious waies of Truth and profperous vertue deftin'd to become great and honourable in thefe latter ages. Methinks I fee in my mind a noble and puiffant Nation roufing herfelf like a ftrong man after fleep, and fhaking her invincible locks: Methinks I fee her as an Eagle muing her mighty youth, and kindling her undazl'd eyes at the full midday beam; purging and unfcaling her long abufed fight at the fountain it felf of heav'nly radiance; while the whole noife of timorous and flocking birds, with thofe alfo that love the twilight, flutter about, amaz'd at what fhe means, and in their envious gabble would prognofticat a year of fects and fchifms.

📖 A stylistic analysis can be found in the Text Commentary Book.

📖 The lexical vocabulary of Texts 129 and 130 is listed in the Word Book.

17.6 John Evelyn's *Diary*

John Evelyn (1620–1706) travelled widely on the Continent and had a great variety of interests – he published books on engraving, tree-growing, gardening, navigation and commerce, and architecture, but is now best known for his diary, which covers most of his life.

During the Civil Wars of the 1640s Evelyn was a royalist in sympathy. After the execution of King Charles I in 1649 a Commonwealth was set up, with Oliver Cromwell later named Lord Protector. One of the many ordinances or regulations imposed by the Puritan regime abolished the celebration of Christmas and other Church festivals. On Christmas Day 1657 John Evelyn went with his wife to the chapel of Exeter House in the Strand, London, where the Earl of Rutland lived. He recorded in his diary what happened.

Text 131: John Evelyn's diary for 25 December 1657

I went with my Wife &c: to *Lond:* to celebrate *Chriftmas day*. Mr. *Gunning* preaching in *Excefter* Chapell on *7: Micha 2.* fermon Ended, as he was giving us the holy facrament, The Chapell was furrounded with fouldiers: All the

Communicants and Affembly furpriz'd & kept Prifoners by them, fome in the houfe, others carried away: It fell to my fhare to be confined to a roome in the houfe, where yet were permitted to Dine with the mafter of it, the Counteffe of *Dorfet, Lady Hatton* & fome others of quality who invited me: In the afternoone came *Collonel Whaly, Goffe* & others from *Whitehall* to examine us one by one, & fome they committed to the *Martial*,* fome to Prifon, fome Committed: When I came before them they tooke my name & aboad, examind me, why contrary to an Ordinance made that none fhould any longer obferve the fuperftitious time of the *Nativity* (fo efteem'd by them) I durft offend, & particularly be at *Common prayers*, which they told me was but the *Maffe* in *Englifh*, & particularly pray for *Charles ftuard*, for which we had no fcripture: I told them we did not pray for *Cha: fteward* but for all *Chriftian Kings, Princes & Governors*: They replied, in fo doing we praied for the K. of *fpaine* too, who was their Enemie, & a *Papift*, with other frivolous & infnaring queftions, with much threatening, & finding no colour to detaine me longer, with much pitty of my Ignorance, they difmiff'd me: Thefe were men of high flight, and above Ordinances: & fpake fpitefull things of our B: Lords nativity: fo I got home late the next day bleffed be God: Thefe wretched mifcreants, held their mufkets againft us as we came up to receive the facred Elements, as if they would have fhot us at the Altar, but yet fuffering us to finifh the Office of Communion, as perhaps not in their Inftructions what they fhould do in cafe they found us in that Action:

Martial – Marshal, the title of a senior Army officer.

The object of the raids on churches was political as well as religious, as the authorities were afraid of royalist plots against the government. A newspaper, *The Publick Intelligencer*, printed an account on 28 December 1657.

Text 132: The Publick Intelligencer, 28 December 1657

This being the day commonly called *Chriftmas*, and divers of the old Clergymen being affembled with people of their own congregating in private to uphold a fuperftitious obfervation of the day, contrary to Ordinances of Parliament abolifhing the obfervation of that and other the like Feftivals, and againft an exprefs Order of his Highnefs and his Privy-Council, made this laft week; for this caufe, as alfo in regard of the ill Confequences that may extend to the Publick by the Affemblings of illaffected perfons at this feafon of the year wherein diforderly people are wont to affume unto themfelves too great a liberty, it was judged neceffary to fupprefs the faid meetings, and it was accordingly performed by fome of the foldiery employed to that end; who at *Weftminfter* apprehended one Mr *Thifs crofs*, he being with divers people met together in private; In *Fleet ftreet* they found another meeting of the fame nature, where one Dr *Wilde* was Preacher; And at Exeter-houfe in the ftrand they found the grand Affembly, which fome (for the magnitude of it) have been pleafed to term the Church of *England*; it being (as they fay) to be found no where elfe in fo great and fo compact a Body, of which Congregation one Mr *Gunning* was the principal Preacher, who together with Dr *Wilde*, and divers other perfons, were fecured, to give an account of their doings: fome have fince been releafed, the reft remain in cuftody at the White-Hart in the ftrand, till it fhall be known who they are:

Thiss cross was the paper's version of *Thurcross*. Timothy Thurcross was a Doctor of Divinity and priest.

Activity 17.8

Compare the language of Evelyn's account of the events with that of the newspaper.

📖 A descriptive analysis can be found in the Text Commentary Book.

The following entry in the Diary describes a whale that was stranded in the Thames Estuary, and is an interesting contrast to Sir Thomas Browne's account in Text 119, section 17.2.2.1, and that in the medieval *Bestiary* in Text 48, section 7.6.

Text 133: John Evelyn's diary for 2 and 3 June 1658

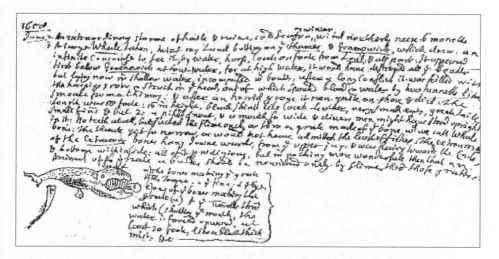

<u>1658</u>   as winter

<u>June 2.</u> An extraordinary ftorme of haile & raine, cold feafon, ∧ wind northerly neere 6 moneths.
3 A large <u>Whale</u> taken, twixt my Land butting on yᵉ <u>Thames</u> & <u>Greenwich</u>, which drew an
infinite Concourfe to fee it, by water, horfe, Coach on foote from *Lon'd*, & all parts: It appeared
firft below <u>Greenwich</u> at low-water, for at high water, it would have deftroyᵉd all yᵉ boates:
but lying now in fhallow water, incompaffd wᵗʰ boates, after a long Conflict it was killed with
the harping yrons, & ftruck in yᵉ head, out of which fpouted blood and water, by two tunnells like
fmoake from a chimny: & after an horrid grone it ran quite on fhore & died: The
length was 58 foote: 16 in height, black fkin'd like Coach-leather, very fmall eyᵉs, greate taile,
fmall finns & but 2: a piked* fnout, & a mouth fo wide & divers men might have ftood upright
in it: No teeth at all, but fucked the flime onely as thro a grate made of yt bone wᶜʰ we call Whale
bone: The throate yᵉt fo narrow, as woud not have admitted the leaft of fifhes: The extreames
of the <u>Cetaceous</u> bones hang downewards, from yᵉ upper jaw, & was hairy towards the Ends,
& bottome withinfide: all of it prodigious, but in nothing more wonderfull then that an
Animal of fo greate a bulk, fhould be nourifhed onely by flime, thru thofe grates:

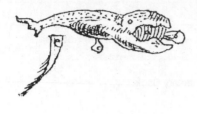

a) The bones making y^e grate.
b) The Tongue, c. y^e finn:d y^e Eye:
e) one of y^e bones making the
grate (a) f y^e Tunnells thru
which ſhutting y^e mouth, the
water is forced upward, at
leaſt 30 foote, like a black thick
miſt. &c:

piked = pointed

17.7 The Royal Society and prose style

The Royal Society of London for the Improving of Natural Knowledge, usually called just The Royal Society, was founded in 1662 under the patronage of King Charles II, who had been restored to the throne in 1660. Evelyn was a founder member of the Society, whose members met regularly to present and discuss scientific papers. The poet John Dryden was also a member, and two verses of a poem called *Annus Mirabilis – The Year of Wonders 1666* contain what he called an 'Apostrophe to the Royal Society'. (An apostrophe is a term in rhetoric which means 'a figure in which a writer suddenly stops in his discourse, and turns to address some other person or thing'.)

> This I fore-tel, from your auſpicious care,
> Who great in ſearch of God and nature grow:
> Who beſt your wiſe Creator's praiſe declare,
> Since beſt to praiſe his works is beſt to know.
>
> O truly Royal! who behold the Law,
> And rule of beings in your Makers mind,
> And thence, like Limbecks, rich Ideas draw,
> To fit the levell'd uſe of humane kind.

Evelyn's diary entry on the whale shows his interest in the detailed scientific observation of natural phenomena, expressed obliquely in Dryden's poem as 'the Law and Rule of beings in your Makers mind'.

Members of the Royal Society like John Evelyn and John Dryden were dedicated to new ways of scientific thinking and experiment, and the style of writing which they began to adopt in the 1660s also changed. The following statement, about the prose style being developed by members of the Society in their scientific papers, was written by Thomas Sprat, Secretary of the Royal Society, in 1667.

Text 134: Thomas Sprat's The History of the Royal Society, 1667 (facsimile)

Thus they have directed, judg'd, conjectur'd upon, and improved *Experiments*. But lastly, in these, and all other businesses, that have come under their care; there is one thing more, about which the *Society* has been most sollicitous; and that is, the manner of their *Discourse*: which, unless they had been very watchful to keep in due temper, the whole spirit and vigour of their *Design*, had been soon eaten out, by the luxury and redundance of *speech*. The ill effects of this superfluity of talking, have already overwhelm'd most other *Arts* and *Professions*; insomuch, that when I consider the means of *happy living*, and the causes of their corruption, I can hardly forbear recanting what I said before; and concluding, that *eloquence* ought to be banish'd out of all *civil Societies*, as a thing fatal to Peace and good Manners.

Sect. XX.
Their manner of Discourse.

For now I am warm'd with this just Anger, I cannot with-hold my self, from betraying the shallowness of all these seeming Mysteries; upon which, *we Writers*, and *Speakers*, look so bigg. And, in few words, I dare say; that of all the Studies of men, nothing may be sooner obtain'd, than this vicious abundance of *Phrase*, this trick of *Metaphors*, this volubility of *Tongue*, which makes so great a noise in the World. But I spend words in vain; for the evil is now so inveterate, that it is hard to know whom to *blame*, or where to begin to *reform*.

They have therefore been most rigorous in putting in execution, the only Remedy, that can be found for this *extravagance* : and that has been, a constant Resolution, to reject all the amplifications, digressions, and swellings of style: to return back to the primitive purity, and shortness, when men deliver'd so many *things*, almost in an equal number of *words*. They have exacted from all their members, a close, naked, natural way of speaking; positive expressions; clear senses; a native easiness: bringing all things as near the Mathematical plainness, as they can : and preferring the language of Artizans, Countrymen, and Merchants, before that, of Wits, or Scholars.

It is very clear from Thomas Sprat's attack on 'the luxury and redundance of speech' that he would have disapproved of a little book published by Joshua Pool four years before in 1663. Pool's *Practical Rhetorick* was a school text-book, and one in a long series on the subject published between the 16th and 18th centuries. Rhetoric in medieval times was the first of the three parts of a university education, with Grammar and Logic. It included *Invention* (finding new ways of expressing things) and *Disposition* (the art of ordering and interweaving themes), but the subject of Joshua Pool's book was *Elocution*, which was concerned with style, and especially with figures of speech, called *tropes* and *figures*.

The first 33 pages of *Practical Rhetorick* are taken up with variations on a single short sentence – *Love ruleth all things* – which exhaustively illustrate the tropes and figures listed in the margins, as you can see from the facsimile of the first two pages, below. Clearly, this is Sprat's 'superfluity of talking', which he sums up pejoratively as *eloquence* – 'this vicious abundance of *Phrase*, this trick of *Metaphors*, this volubility of *Tongue*, which makes so great a noise in the World'.

Text 135: Joshua Pool's Practical Rhetorick, 1663 (facsimile)

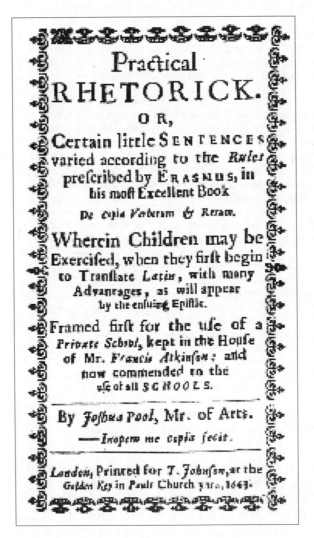

---

2   *Practical Rhetorick,*

Love *ruleth* all things:
All things *are ruled* by love.
Love *mastereth* all things:
All things *are mastered* by love.

Heterosis (seu Metataxis) Numeri.

Love *throws down* all before it:
All things *are thrown down* before love.
Love *conquers* every thing:
Every thing *is conquered* by love.
CUPID *overcomes* every thing:
Every thing *is overcome* by CU-PID.

Periphrasis.

V E N U S *Son* overcomes all things:
All things are overcome by VE-NUS *Son.*
The blind God conquers every thing:
Every thing *is conquered by that blind God.*
CYTHEREA's *Son* quells all things:
All things are quelled by CY-THEREA's *Son.*
The PAPHIAN *Prince* ruleth all things.
All things are ruled by the PA-PHIAN *Prince.*

The

Practical Rhetorick.   **3**

The CYPRIAN *Queen's blind boy,* subdues all things:
All things are subdued by *the* CYPRIAN *Queens blind Boy.*
Love overcometh *many* things:
Love overcometh *great* things:
Love overcometh *no few* things:
Love overcometh *no small* things.

Meiosis, Tapeinosis, seu Diminutio.

Litotes.

All things *yield to love:*
There is *nothing,* that doth *not yield to love.*
There is *nothing,* that is *not* overcome by love:
There can be nothing, that love doth *not overcome.*

Heterosis, seu mutatis affirmativorum negativia.

Love *triumphs over all* things:
There is *nothing,* over which Love doth *not triumph.*
Love *reigns as Lord and King* in all things:
There are no *things,* in which love doth *not reign as Lord and King.*
Love *is the Conqueror* of all things:
There is nothing, of which Love is *not the Conqueror.*
Love *exerciseth his power* in all things:

Mutatio Verborum Nomine.

B 2   *There*

17.8 Loan-words, 1600–49

A selection of loan-words recorded during this period can be found in the Word Book, after the word-lists for Chapter 17.

18 Early Modern English V – the 17th century (ii)

18.1 John Bunyan

John Bunyan (1628–88) was the son of a Bedfordshire brass-worker, and followed his father's trade after learning to read and write in the village school at Elstow. He served in the Parliamentary army during the Civil War in the 1640s, and joined a Nonconformist church in Bedford in 1653 and preached there. His first writings were against George Fox and the Quakers. But he too came into conflict with the authorities in 1660 for preaching without a licence, and spent twelve years in Bedford jail, during which time he wrote nine books. In 1672 he returned to the same church, and was again imprisoned for a short time in 1676, when he finished the first part of *The Pilgrims Progress*. The book was published in 1678, and a second part in 1684.

The Pilgrims Progress is an allegory, in which personifications of abstract qualities are the characters. The story is in the form of a dream, in which the narrator tells of Christian's progress 'from this World to that which is to come'.

The Pilgrims now, to gratify the Flesh,
Will seek its Ease; but oh how they afresh
Do thereby plunge themselves new Grief into!
Who seeks to please the Flesh, themselves undo.

The following text, reproduced in facsimile, is from the 1678 first edition of the book. Christian's religious doubts have caused him to lose hope and fall into despair. In the terms of the allegory, he and his companion Hopeful have been caught by Giant Despair and thrown into the dungeon of Doubting Castle.

Bunyan's use of the language brings us close to hearing the colloquial, everyday speech of the 1670s. It is 'the language of artizans, countrymen and merchants', not of 'wits and scholars', that Thomas Sprat commended.

The text shows us that in printed books, spelling was by now standardised in a form which has hardly changed since. There are only a few conventions that are unfamiliar, like the use of long ⟨s⟩, the capitalising of some nouns and adjectives, and the use of italics to highlight certain words; and also the absence of an apostrophe in the title – *The Pilgrims Progress*.

Text 136: Bunyan's The Pilgrims Progress, Doubting Castle (facsimile)

Neither could they, with all the skill they had, get again to the Stile that night. Wherefore, at laſt, lighting under a little ſhelter, they ſat down there till the day brake; but being weary, they fell aſleep. Now *They ſleep in the grounds of Giant Deſpair.* there was not far from the place where they lay, a *Caſtle*, called *Doubting Caſtle*, the owner whereof was

Giant Deſpair, and it was in his grounds they now were ſleeping; wherefore he getting up in the morning early, and walking up and down *He finds in his Fields*, caught *Chriſtian* and *them in his Hopeful* aſleep in his grounds. Then *ground, and carries* with a *grim* and *ſurly* voice he bid *them to* them awake, and asked them whence *Doubting* they were? and what they did in his *Caſtle.* grounds? They told him, they were Pilgrims, and that they had loſt their way. Then ſaid the *Giant*, You have this night treſpaſſed on me, by trampling in, and lying on my grounds, and therefore you muſt go along with me. So they were forced to go, becauſe he was ſtronger then they. They alſo had but little to ſay, for they knew themſelves in a fault. The *Giant* therefore drove them be-*The Grievouſneſs of their Impriſonment* fore him, and put them into his Caſtle, into a very dark Dungeon, naſty and ſtinking to the ſpirit of theſe two men: Here then they lay, from *Wed-* *Pſ. 88. 18. neſday* morning till *Saturday* night, without one bit of bread, or drop of drink, or any light, or any to ask how they did. They were therefore here in evil caſe, and were far from friends and acquaintance. Now in this place,

Chriſtian had double ſorrow, becauſe 'twas through his unadviſed haſte that they were brought into this diſtreſs.

Well, on *Saturday* about midnight they began to *pray*, and continued in Prayer till almoſt break of day.

Now a little before it was day, good *Chriſtian*, as one half amazed, brake out in this paſſionate Speech, *What a fool, quoth he, am I thus to lie in a ſtinking Dungeon, when I may as well walk at liberty?* I have a *A Key in* Key in my boſom, called *Promiſe*, that *Chriſtians, boſom called Pro-* will, I am perſuaded, open any Lock *miſe, opens* in *Doubting Caſtle*. Then ſaid *Hopeful, any Lock* That's good News; good Brother *in Doubt-* pluck it out of thy boſom and try: *ing Caſtle.* Then *Chriſtian* pulled it out of his boſom, and began to try at the Dungion door, whoſe bolt (as he turned the Key) gave back, and the door flew open with eaſe, and *Chriſtian* and *Hopeful* both came out. Then he went to the outward door that leads into the *Caſtle yard*, and with his Key opened the door alſo. After he went to the *Iron* Gate, for that muſt be opened too, but that Lock went *damnable* hard, yet the Key did open it; then they thruſt open the Gate to make their eſcape with ſpeed, but that Gate, as it opened, made ſuch a creaking, that it waked *Giant De-ſpair*, who haſtily riſing to purſue his Priſoners, felt his Limbs to fail, ſo that he could by no means go after them. Then they went on, and came to the Kings high way again, and ſo were ſafe, becauſe they were out of his Juriſdiction.

📖 A list of the lexical vocabulary of Text 136 is in the Word Book.

Bunyan was not a scholar of the Universities in Latin and Greek. His own use of the language was influenced by his reading of the King James Bible of 1611, but at the same time reflects popular everyday usage. We can therefore use *The Pilgrims Progress* with reasonable confidence as evidence of ordinary language use in the 1670s.

Although there has been little change in the basic grammatical patterns of the language since the 17th century, there are recognisable features of vocabulary and grammar, part of the idiom and usage of that period, which date it.

Activity 18.1

Discuss the vocabulary and grammar of the following sets of sentences from *The Pilgrims Progress*

Text 137: *The language of* The Pilgrims Progress

1
- his reaſon was, for that the Valley was altogether without *Honour*;
- ... but he could not be ſilent long, becauſe that his trouble increaſed.
- So the other told him, that by that he was gone ſome diſtance from the Gate, he would come at the Houſe of the *Interpreter* ...
- ... all is not worth to be compared with a little of that that I am ſeeking to enjoy.

2
- ... by reaſon of a burden that lieth hard upon me:
- The ſhame that attends Religion, lies alſo as a block in their way:
- Why came you not in at the Gate which ſtandeth at the beginning of the way?
- How ſtands it between God and your Soul now?

3
- ... but the ground is good when they are once got in at the Gate.
- I thought ſo; and it is happened unto thee as to other weak men.
- So when he was come in, and ſet down, they gave him ſomething to drink;
- There was great talk preſently after you was gone out ...

4
- Then ſaid *Pliable*, Don't revile;
- My Brother, I did not put the queſtion to thee, for that I doubted of the truth of our belief my ſelf ...
- Well then, did you not know about ten years ago, one *Temporary*?
- Nay, methinks I care not what I meet with in the way ...
- Why came you not in at the Gate which ſtandeth at the beginning of the way?

5
- But my good Companion, do you know the way. . . ?
- ... doſt thou ſee this narrow way?
- Wherefore doſt thou cry?
- But now we are by our ſelves, what do you think of ſuch men?
- ... how many, think you, muſt there be?
- Know you not that it is written . . .?
- Whence came you, and whither do you go?

6
- Oh, did he light upon you?
- Know him! Yes, he dwelt in *Graceleſs* ...
- I thought I ſhould a been killed there ...
- If this Meadow lieth along by our way ſide, lets go over into it.
- But did you tell them of your own ſorrow? Yes, over, and over, and over.
- ... the remembrance of which will ſtick by me as long as I live.

- Jofeph was hard put to it by her . . .
- . . . but it is ordinary for thofe . . . to give him the flip, and return again to me.
- He faid it was a pitiful low fneaking bufinefs for a Man to mind Religion.
- . . . let us lie down here and take one Nap.

7

- I befhrow him for his counfel;
- . . . and he wot not what to do.
- Who can tell how joyful this Man was, when he had gotten his Roll again!
- The Shepherds had them to another place, in a bottom, where was a door in the fide of an Hill.
- He went on thus, even untill he came at a bottom . . .
- . . . out of the mouth of which there came in an abundant manner Smoak, and Coals of fire, with hideous noifes.
- And did you prefently fall under the power of this conviction?
- But is there no hopes for fuch a Man as this?
- They was then afked, If they knew the Prifoner at the Bar?
- . . . but get it off my felf I cannot
- . . . abhor thy felf for hearkning unto him

8

- The hearing of this is enough to ravifh ones heart.
- A Lot that often falls from bad mens mouths upon good mens Names.

📖 A commentary on these sentences is in the Text Commentary Book.

18.2 Spelling and pronunciation at the end of the 17th century

18.2.1 George Fox and Ellis Hookes's *Instructions for Right Spelling*, 1673

Instructions for Right Spelling is one of many books on spelling, reading and writing which were regularly published throughout the 17th and 18th centuries. One section of the book lists pairs of words 'which are alike in Sound, yet unlike in their Signification' – *homophones* – and so give us data on pronunciation changes both before and after 1673.

As there is no indication of pronunciation using any kind of phonetic symbols, we only have the claim by Fox and Hookes that the words are pronounced alike. And does 'alike' mean 'exactly the same'? Of two words which are now clearly different in pronunciation, we would like to know which pronunciation made them alike in 1673.

For example, in the pairing *advice / advise*, we now distinguish noun from verb by voicing the final consonant of the verb, [ædvaɪs / ædvaɪz]. There is now a similar contrast between *copies / coppice, decease / disease, lose / loose* etc. Were these contrasts not made then?

However, we can make a reasonable guess at the pronunciation of pairings like *best / beast, reason / raisin, seas / cease* – probably the mid-front vowel [ɛ] or [e], whereas with *meet / meat / mete* we perhaps have evidence of the final raising of some ⟨ea⟩ vowels to [i] in the Great Vowel Shift.

The list offers much interesting speculation. Here is a facsimile of the frontispiece and the first two pages of homophones, which are put into simple sentences in the book in order to clarify their meaning:

Text 138: Fox and Hookes, Instructions for Right Spelling, 1673 (facsimile)

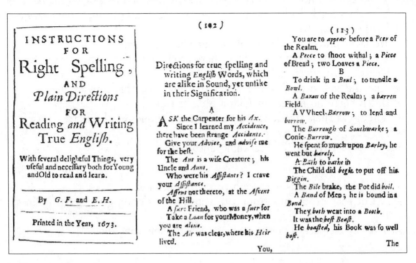

Here is the complete list (including those in Text 138) of the pairs of homophones in *Instructions for Right Spelling*, but without their illustrative sentences:

Activity 18.2

Take a selection of examples, and

- (i) identify those pairs of words that are homophones today;
- (ii) see how far you can describe and explain the changes in each set.

A	B	
aſk / ax	boul / bowl	boaſted / boſt
accidence / accidents	baron / barren	bark / barque
advice / adviſe	barrow / borrow	Barbarie / barbara
ant / aunt	burrough / burrow	bill'd / build
aſſiſtants / aſſiſtance	barley / barely	bald / baul'd
aſſent / aſcent	bath / bathe	bad / bade
ſure / ſuer	begin / biggin	by / buy
a loan / alone	bile / boil	bolt / boult
air / heir	band / bond	bow / bough
appear / a peer	both / booth	bore / boar
a peece / a piece	beſt / beaſt	brows / browz
		blew / blue

brute / bruit
bred / bread
bare / bear

C
copies / coppice
coughing / coffin
cough't / caught
chaps / chops
chare / chair / cheer
currents / corrants
coſt / coaſt
cauſes / cauſeys
quoteth / coateth
cool'd / could
call / caul
couſin / cozen
council / counſel
cruel / crewel
crue / crew

D
deer / dear
dun / done
does / doſe
device / deviſe
deceaſe / diſeaſe
deſert / deſart

E
eaſt / yeaſt
earn / yarn / yern
eat / ate
eminent / imminent

F
fraiſe / phraſe
fare / fair
fens / fence
fur / fir
form / fourm
flie / flee
feign / fain
feed / fee'd
find / fin'd
fold / foal'd
forth / fourth
furz / furs
ſoul / fowl
Francis / Frances
freez / freeſe
flower / flowr

G
guardian / garden

gueſs / gueſts
ghoſt / go'ſt
galls / gauls
gilt / guilt
gliſter / clyſter

H
hare / hair
holy / wholy
hole / whole
haſt / haſte
hoop / whoop
hire / higher / hy her
here / hear
homely / homilie
hens / hence
holly / holy

I
idle / idol
eyes / ice
eye / I
ire / eyer
incite / in ſight / inſight

J
jet / jeat
jointer / joynture
jerking / jerkin

K
kennel / channel
knots / gnats

L
lines / loins
lane / lain
low / low (*vb*)
laught / loft
lead / led
leaſes / leaſers
lothe / loth
lyes / lice
light (*vb*) / lite
Latine / latten
low'd / loud
leaſt / leſt
leſſon / leſſen
leapers / lepers
lo / low
loſe (*the knot*) / looſe
(*hiſ labour*)

M
meet / meat / mete

meſſage / meſſuage
manner / manor
mote / moat
moan / mown
mouſe / mows
mite / might
mower / more
mantle / mantil
millions / melons
Mary / marry
moles / moulds

N
neece / neeſe
needleſs / needles
neither / nether
nay / neigh
naught / nought

O
ore / oar / ower
ours / hours
of / off
own / one
ought / oft

P
pains / panes
plot / plat
principal / principle
place / plaſe
paſt / paſte
price / prize
pare / pear / pair
palait? (= *palate*) / pallet
parſon / perſon
princes / princeſs
praiſe / preys
pillars / *cater*-pillers
pride / pry'd
profit / prophet
power / pour

R
rain / reign / rein
raiſe / rayes
rancour / ranker
red / read
rear / rere
reaſon / raiſin
rite / right
write / wright
rinde / Rhine
roe / row
roſe (*vb*) / roſe (*n*)

roes / rows
rower / roar
wrot / rot
rapt (= *rapped*) / wrapt
roads / Rhodes
room / Rome
rung / wrung / rough (*sic*)
rack / wrack
reed / read
wrought / wrote / rote
raze / raiſe
raſour / raiſer
reſt / wreſt

S
ſavers / ſavors
ſeas / ſeize
ceaſing / ſeſſing
ſeller / cellar
centurie / centory
ſheer (= ſhear) / Hampſhire
cite / ſight
ſole / ſoul
ſound / ſwoon
ſtrait / ſtraight

ſlight / ſleight
ſuccour / ſucker
ſum / ſome
ſun / ſon
ſhoots / ſutes / ſuits
ſivs / ſives
ſithes / ſighs
ſower / ſowr
ſex / ſects
ſteed / ſtead
ſlow / ſlough
ſeas / ceaſe
ſhoes / ſhews
Stanes (= *Staines*) / ſtains
ſheep / ſhip

T
tax / tacks
thyme / time
tide / ty'd
toe / towe
toad / toed / towed
too / two / to
treatiſe / treaties
then / than
thrown / throne

through / thorow
there / their
tongs / tongues
tail / tale
tomb / tome

V
vein / vain
viol / vial
vale / vail
vacation / vocation
victuals / vital

W
weight / wey / way
wait / weight
were / wear / ware
waſt / waſte
wreſt / wriſt
wiſt / wiſht

Y
yew / you
ewer / ure
ye / yea
earn / yarn

There is a descriptive analysis in the Text Commentary Book.

18.2.2 Christopher Cooper's *The English Teacher*, 1687

Christopher Cooper, 'Master of the Grammar School of Bishop-Stortford in Hartfordshire', published *The English Teacher or The Discovery of the Art of Teaching and Learning the English Tongue* in 1687. He has been described as 'the best phonetician and one of the fullest recorders of pronunciation that England (and indeed modern Europe) produced before the nineteenth century, the obscure schoolmaster of a country town' (E. J. Dobson, *English Pronunciation, 1500–1700*, 1968). An examination of Christopher Cooper's book will therefore provide good evidence about the pronunciation of English in his time.

Cooper's description of the relationship of letters to sounds is, like that of all the orthoepists of the 16th and 17th centuries, not always easy to follow, because there was then no phonetic alphabet to act as a reference for the sounds. His first concern is the spelling of the vowels and consonants, to which he relates the variety of sounds which they represent. He made no proposals for spelling reform, but aimed at teaching the spelling system in general use at that time.

There was still a clear distinction of quantity between short and long vowels with the same quality, as in OE and ME, but this had become complicated as a result of the Great Vowel Shift (see section 15.6), which was not fully complete until about the end of the 17th century. As the shift of the long vowels took place in the South of England, and not in the North, the educated speech of London and the Home Counties – the emerging standard language – was affected by it.

Activity 18.3

Examine the following lists from Cooper's *The English Teacher* in turn (Texts 139–44). Discuss the evidence they show of:

(a) Cooper's pronunciation in the 1680s and any change from Middle English as a result of either the shift of the long vowels, or other causes;

(b) later changes which have taken place in the pronunciation of any of the words.

📖 A commentary on Activity 18.3 is in the Text Commentary Book.

18.2.2.1 'Of the Vowel a'

Text 139: Christopher Cooper's The English Teacher, 1687 (i) (facsimile)

> 34   *Of the Vowel* a.
>
> C H A P. II.
>
> *Of the Vowel* a.
>
> A Hath three founds, which, for diftinction fake, I have expreft in writing after this manner a *a a*. The firft of thefe, for the moft part, is pronounced long in its own found before *nch*, and *s* when another Confonant follows, and before *r* unlefs *fh* follows. But when *e* is put to the end, it is then pronounced in a more flender found, to wit, the lengthning of *e* fhort ; but it is to be obferv'd that in all thefe words, except in *cane, wane, ftrange-r, manger, mangye,* and before *ge*; as in *age, u* guttural is put after *a* ; which *u* is nothing elfe but a continuation of a naked murmur after *a* is formed : for by reafon of the flendernefs, unlefs we more accurately attend, the tongue will not eafily pafs to the next confonant without *u* coming between. The difference will plainly appear to thofe ears, that can diftinguifh founds, in the Examples placed in the following order.

a fhort	a long	*a* flender
Bar	*Barge*	*Bare*
blab	*blaft*	*blazon*
cap	*carking*	*cape*
car	*carp*	*care*
cat	*caft*	*cafe*
dafh	*dart*	*date*
flafh	*flasket*	*flake*
gafh	*gafp*	*gate*
grand	*grant*	*grange*
land	*lance*	*lane*
mafh	*mask*	*mafon*
pat	*path*	*pate*
tar	*tart*	*tares*

It is difficult for us to interpret Cooper's description because what we are trying to discover is precisely what he could assume his contemporary readers already knew. 'Short' and 'long' vowels present no problem, but 'slender' is not a term used in phonetic description today.

He describes 'the Vowel a' as having three sounds, for which he uses three forms of the letter – ⟨a⟩, ⟨*a*⟩ and ⟨α⟩ – but he does not use the third letter in the examples in Text 139. He describes two realisations of ⟨a⟩, 'a short, a long', and one of ⟨*a*⟩, '*a* slender'. Their probable pronunciations were:

a short:	[a] or [æ]
a long:	[aː] or [æː]
a slender:	[ɛː].

We cannot know the precise realisation of 'a short' and 'a long', but know that they were front vowels. Remember that ⟨ar⟩, as in *bar, car, tar, barge, carking, carp, dart* and *tar*, was not yet a digraph for the low back vowel [ɑ] in RP and other English dialects. The ⟨r⟩ was pronounced like any other consonant, [aɹ], as it still is in rhotic dialects, which have kept the pronunciation of post-vocalic [r].

He distinguishes between the ⟨a⟩ of *car* and *care*. The '*a* slender' of *care* is compared to a 'lengthning [sic] of *e* short', followed by '*a* guttural', what he calls 'a naked murmur after *a* is formed'. Cooper's '*u* guttural' was the short vowel [ə], so this must be the evolution of a diphthong in the word, pronounced [kɛəɹ], and the origin of today's RP pronunciation of *care* as [kɛə].

Cooper differentiated the vowels in certain pairs of words which today are identical homophones in RP and other dialects. These words have remained different in Scotland, parts of the north of England and in East Anglia. For example, *pane* with a pure vowel [peːn] and *pain* with a diphthong [peɪn] (see J. C. Wells, *Accents of English*, vol. 1 (Cambridge University Press, 1982), ch. 3 Section 3.1.5).

The contrast is not the same as that in Cooper's speech, however, where the spelling ⟨ai⟩ represents '*a* pure' and ⟨a-e⟩ is a diphthong. He describes the difference in this way:

Text 140: Christopher Cooper's The English Teacher, 1687 (ii) (facsimile)

let him confider the following Examples, in which *ai* pronounced gently hath the found of *a* pure, as in *cane*, but
where *a* onely is written *u* guttural is founded after it ; as

Bain	*Hail*	*Maid*
bane	*hale*	*made*
main	*lay'n*	*pain*
mane	*lane*	*pane*
plain	*fpaid*	*tail*
plane	*fpade*	*tale*

18.2.2.2 'Of the Vowel e'

The original purpose of the digraph ⟨ea⟩ was to distinguish the more open of the two long front vowels [ɛː] from the closer vowel [eː], usually spelt ⟨ee⟩ (see section 15.5.1.4). Cooper's description is:

> That found which is taken for the long e is expreſt by putting *a* after it; as *men*, *mean*.

His 'long e' was the vowel [ɛː].

18.2.2.3 'Of the Vowel o'

The following facsimile from *The English Teacher* lists some words pronounced with the vowel [u] or [uː], spelt either ⟨o⟩ or ⟨oa⟩ or ⟨oo⟩.

Activity 18.4

Consider the contemporary pronunciation of the words in Cooper's list, some of which have changed from [u] or [uː] since the 1680s. Do they have any feature in common which might explain the change?

Text 141: Christopher Cooper's **The English Teacher,** *1687 (iii)* *(facsimile)*

Rule 2.

o oa ou in theſe following is founded *oo.*

A-board	*con-courſe*	*court-ſhip*	*fourſe*	*whom*
ac-cou-tred	*could*	*force*	*ſword*	*whore*
aſ-ford	*courſe*	*forces*	*ſworn*	*who-ſo-e-ver*
be-hoves	*courſes*	*move*	*tomb*	*womb*
boar	*court*	*mourn*	*two*	*worn*
born	*cour-ti-er*	*ſcourſe*	*un-couth*	*would*
bourn	*court-li-neſs*	*ſhould*	*who*	

In all others this found is written *oo*; as *look*, *roof*. But *Board*, *forth*, *prove*, *ſloup*, are better written *boord*, *foorth*, *proove*, *ſloop*.

Blood-i-ly, good-ly-neſs, *flood*, *hood*, *brother-hood*, *ſiſterhood*, *neighbourhood*, *falſehood*, *ſoot*, *ſtood*, *wood*, *wool*; have the found of *o* la-bial ſhort. *O* in *women* is founded as *i*. in *Damoſel* not at all.

See *o* for *x* guttural, Ch. 6. Rule 6. *O* for *ou* labials, Ch. 7. Rul. 4.

Commentary

These words are still pronounced with the short [ʊ] or long [uː]:

accoutred	uncouth
behoves (or [əʊ])	who
could	whom
move	whosoever
should	womb
tomb	
two	would

All the others are now pronounced with the vowel [ɔː] in RP and most English dialects. In each word the vowel was followed by post-vocalic [r], which had the effect of lowering the vowel, which either lengthened or became a diphthong when [r] ceased to be pronounced.

18.2.2.4 'Improper diphthongs'

Cooper differentiated diphthongs in pronunciation from digraphs in writing. He did not, however, use the word *digraph* but the phrase *improper diphthong* for pairs of letters which represented only one sound. Here he is describing the different pronunciations of words with ⟨ea⟩ in the 1680s, which we have already seen as a feature of spelling today (as in *leaf, great, dead, heart, heard, ear, pear*)

Cooper's 'e short' meant [ɛ], 'e long' [ɛː], 'ee' [iː], 'a' [ɛː] and 'a' [æː].

Text 142: Christopher Cooper's The English Teacher, 1687 (iv) (facsimile)

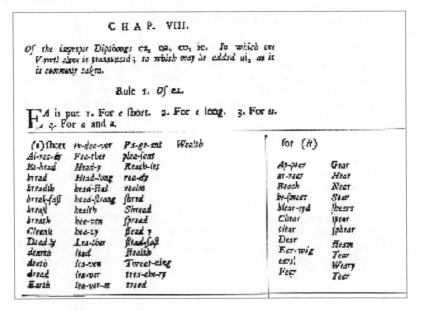

(í) long

Ap-peal	fina-vers	feat	ples-der	Trach	for (o)
ap-peal	cer-ceal	jar-fwear	pla-frog	teal	
Bea-con	congeal	freak	piech	team	Biar
Head	creak	Glean	fra-eack	team-tale	beard
brea-dir	cream	gerak	feal	trea-tife	Earl
hur-gle	crea-ture	grear	preath	Veal	rar-ly
beak-er	Crea-gue	great	Qveen	Week-ard	tare
bean	deal	grea-ry	quea-fi	ural	ear-ceff
blea	dead	Heal	Reaco	wear	Liein
bea	decea	heap	wean	wear	Re-hearfe
beat	di-ceafe	hear	reap	jeal	Serjeaw
bea-ver	de-feat	hea-cock	treu	jeal	fearce
br-fea-gant	de-trea-our	hea-then	rr-fmife	wear	fearch
br-earth	di-eale	heau	re-peal		heard
be-queath	dream	fea-preach	re-beat		fwear
be-neath	Each	ix-plead	re-treat		Tear [rend]
heath	eagle	je-creafe	repeal		Wear
black	eagle	Leach	Sea		wea-riby
breach	ear	leen	fleam	
break	ea-fe-ment	hea-ing	feal-ing	for (a)
bream	ea-fon	lean-ers	feat	
Ceafe	eafe	leap	jheaf	Dif-bear-ten
cheap	ea-fier	leafd	beat	Jheart
cheat	eat	leave	brea-th	hear-ten
clean	e-craft	Mead	hearth	hearth
clean-er	e-treat	weal	fqueak	hear-ty
	e-beat	mein	fqueat	heart-leff
	e-treat	weat	fqueat	
	re-bean	Neat	Jeal	
	Fea-l-ty	Steak	llrea-ger	
	feaft	Plea	fweat	

Some of this kind are written otherwise, and perhaps better ; as *breik, bcom, eck, tear. Appear, buck, clear, chur, etr, sheart.*

18.2.2.5 'Barbarous speaking'

The pronunciation of rural and urban dialects has always been regarded as inferior by those who consider themselves to be in a superior social class. Cooper, as a teacher, shows this in his chapter 'Of Barbarous Speaking', in which he implies that a person's pronunciation will determine his spelling:

Activity 18.5

(i) Read the two pages 77 and 78 *Of Barbarous Dialects* in Text 143.

(ii) Are any of the 'barbarous' pronunciations to be heard today, in (a) Received Pronunciation or (b) any of our regional dialects?

(iii) Does this provide any evidence that some features of Received Pronunciation, the socially prestigious accent of English today, have derived from regional accents?

Text 143: Christopher Cooper's The English Teacher, 1687 (v) (facsimile)

18.2.2.6 'Words that have the same pronunciation'

Other lists in Cooper's book are useful to us in our study of changing pronunciation. For example, there are several pages of 'Words that have the same pronunciation, but different signification and manner of writing', as in Fox and Hookes's *Instructions for Right Spelling*. Most of them are pronounced alike today, though not necessarily with the same vowels as in the 1680s. For example, *seas* and *seize* are homophones today, [siːz], but would have been pronounced [seːz] or [seːz] in Cooper's time, the final raising to [iː] not yet having taken place.

Some of the words confirm changes since ME. For example, the pairing of *rest* / *wrest*, *right* / *wright* and *ring* / *wring* shows the loss of [w] from the OE and ME initial consonant group ⟨wr⟩ to be complete. John Hart's *An Orthographie* showed that the ⟨w⟩ was still pronounced in the 16th century.

Here are a few of the pairs which have remained homophones.

altar / alter	chewes / chuse (*choose*)	in / inn
assent / ascent	dear / deer	lesson / lessen
bare / bear	hair / hare	pair / pare / pear

Others show that at least one word in each pair or group has changed since the 1680s, for example, the pronunciation of *are*, *one*, the *-ure* of *censure*, *gesture* and *tenure*, the *oi* of *oil* and *loin*, and the *ea* of *flea*, *heard*, *least*, *rear*, *reason*, *shear* and *wear*.

Activity 18.6

Compare Cooper's list with Fox and Hookes's in section 18.2.1.

Text 144: Christopher Cooper's The English Teacher, 1687 (vi)

are / air / heir / ere	hard / heard / herd	pour / power
ant / aunt	i'le / isle / oil	rare / rear
bile / boil	jerkin / jerking	raisins / reasons
censer / censor / censure	jester / gesture	share / shear
coat / quote	kill / kiln	shoo (*shoe*) / shew (*show*)
comming / cummin	least / lest	stood / stud
cool'd / could	line / loin	tenor / tenure
coughing / coffin	mile / moil (*hard labour*)	to / two / toe
car'd / card	nether / neither	war / wear / ware
doe / do / dow (= *dough*)	own / one	woo / woe
flea / flay	pastor / pasture	yea / ye
fit / fight	pick't her / picture	

18.2.2.7 Words spelt with ⟨oi⟩

The study of sound changes is complex, but here is a short explanation of one particular change, in which two sets of words with different vowels in ME and MnE fell together for a time.

From the evidence of the preceding list, *boil*, *oil*, *loin* and *moil* had the same pronunciation as *bile*, *isle*, *line* and *mile*. This can be checked in the poetry of the 17th and early 18th centuries, in which many similar pairs of words consistently rhyme together (see section 18.3.2 on John Dryden). However, this did not mean that their pronunciation at that time was either [baɪl] or [bɔɪl].

⟨boil⟩

The verb *boil*, like many other words spelt with the ⟨oi⟩ digraph, came from French and was pronounced [buɪl] in ME, though it was usually spelt with ⟨oi⟩. The diphthong was 'unrounded' during the 17th century and changed to [ʌɪ].

We saw evidence in John Hart's *An Orthographie* of the shift of the long vowel [iː] to the diphthong [əɪ], which is almost the same in sound as [ʌɪ], by the 1560s. As a result, words formerly with [iː] and [ʌɪ] fell together, and both were pronounced with the diphthong [əɪ].

After about 1700 the first element of the diphthong shifted further to its present-day pronunciation [aɪ] in words like *bile*. Why, then, do we pronounce *boil* (and similar words) today as [bɔɪl] and not [baɪl]?

The reason is that there was in ME a second set of words spelt with ⟨oi⟩, for example, *choice* and *noise*, with a diphthong pronounced [ɔɪ], not [ʊɪ]. Evidence from the orthoepists suggests that [ʊɪ] words were also pronounced [ɔɪ] by some speakers. Eventually, helped by the spelling, all words spelt with ⟨oi⟩ came to be pronounced [ɔɪ], so that *bile*, by then pronounced [baɪl], ceased to rhyme with *boil*, pronounced [bɔɪl].

18.3 John Dryden

John Dryden (1631–1700), one of the great writers in the English literary tradition, was a poet, dramatist and critic. He was largely responsible for the 'cherished superstition that prepositions must, in spite of the incurable English instinct for putting them late ... be kept true to their name & placed before the word they govern' (H. W. Fowler, 1926). Dryden 'went through all his prefaces contriving away the final prepositions that he had been guilty of in his first editions' (ibid.). This is incidental, however, to his recognised eminence as a prose writer.

18.3.1 Dryden on Chaucer

Dryden admired Chaucer's poetry, but some aspects of his assessment of Chaucer throw as clear a light on Dryden himself, and the way he and his contemporaries thought about language and writing, as they do on Chaucer. His summary of Chaucer's achievement is often quoted,

> 'Tis ſufficient to ſay according to the Proverb, that here is God's Plenty.

His remarks on Chaucer's language are relevant to our survey of the development of Standard English, and of attitudes to acceptable usage. The earliest English for us is Old English, in texts written as far back as the 9th century. Dryden was concerned with the idea of the 'purity' of English, and the notion that it had reached a state of perfection in his day:

> From Chaucer the Purity of the Engliſh Tongue began ... Chaucer (lived) in the Dawning of our Language.

For Dryden, Chaucer's diction 'stands not on an equal Foot with our present English',

> The verſe of *Chaucer*, I confeſs, is not harmonious to us. ... They who liv'd with him, and ſome time after him, thought it Muſical. ... There is the rude Sweetneſs of a *Scotch* tune in it, which is natural and pleaſing, though not perfect.

and he criticised the editor of an earlier late 16th-century printed edition of Chaucer,

> ... for he would make us believe the Fault is in our Ears, and that there were really Ten Syllables in a Verſe where we find but Nine: But this Opinion is not worth confuting; 'tis ſo groſs and obvious an Errour, that Common Senſe ... must convince the Reader, that Equality of Numbers in every Verſe which we call *Heroick*, was either not known, or not always practiſ'd in *Chaucer's* Age. It were

an eafie Matter to produce fome thoufands of his Verfes, which are lame for want of half a Foot, and fometimes a whole one, and which no Pronunciation can make otherwife . . .

Chaucer, I confefs, is a rough Diamond, and muft firft be polifh'd e're he fhines.

Dryden's 'polishing' of Chaucer was done by re-versifying some of the *Canterbury Tales*, making his choice from those Tales 'as savour nothing of Immodesty'. In his Preface to the Fables he quotes from Chaucers's *Prologue*, where the narrator 'thus excuses the Ribaldry, which is very gross . . .' Dryden then goes on to discuss Chaucer's language:

You have here a *Specimen* of *Chaucer's* Language, which is fo obfolete, that his Senfe is fcarce to be underftood; and you have likewife more than one Example of his unequal Numbers, which were mention'd before. Yet many of his verfes confift of Ten Syllables, and the Words not much behind our prefent *Englifh*.

The following texts consist of the same extract from Chaucer's *Prologue* to *The Canterbury Tales*, first as quoted by Dryden in 1700 from an early printed version, as an example of Chaucer's 'obsolete' language and rough versification, and then in a modern edition based on the manuscripts.

Text 145: Lines from Chaucer's Prologue

Dryden's version	Modern edition from the manuscripts
But firft, I pray you, of your courtefy,	But first I pray yow of youre curteisye
That ye ne arrete it nought my villany,	That ye n'arette it noght my vileynye
Though that I plainly fpeak in this mattere	Though that I pleynly speke in this mateere
To tellen you her words, and eke her chere:	To telle yow hir wordes and hir cheere
Ne though I fpeak her words properly,	Ne thogh I speke hir wordes proprely.
For this ye known as well as I,	For this ye knowen al so wel as I
Who fhall tellen a tale after a man	Whoso shal telle a tale after a man
He mote rehearfe as nye, as ever He can:	He moot reherce as ny as euere he kan
Everich word of it been in his charge,	Euerich a word if it be in his charge
All fpeke he, never fo rudely, ne large.	Al speke he neuer so rudeliche and large,
Or elfe he mote tellen his tale untrue,	Or ellis he moot telle his tale vntrewe
Or feine things, or find words new:	Or feyne thyng or fynde wordes newe.
He may not fpare, altho he were his brother,	He may nat spare althogh he were his brother
He mote as well fay o words as another.	He moot as wel seye o word as another.
Chrift fpake himfelf full broad in holy **Writ**,	Crist spak hymself ful brode in hooly writ
And well I wote no Villany is it.	And wel ye woot no vileynye is it.
Eke *Plato* faith, who fo can him rede,	Eek Plato seith, whoso that kan hym rede,
The words mote been Coufin to the dede.	The wordes moote be cosyn to the dede.

There is a commentary in the Text Commentary Book.

Activity 18.7

(i) Study the two versions and comment on the differences between them.

(ii) Read section 13.2.1, which briefly describes the pronunciation of Chaucer's verse.

(iii) Discuss the possible reasons for Dryden's criticism of Chaucer's 'unequal Numbers', that is, his belief that many of Chaucer's lines have fewer than the ten syllables which the verses should have.

(iv) What was 'obsolete' for Dryden in Chaucer's vocabulary and grammar?

18.3.2 Evidence of pronunciation from rhymes in Dryden's *Aeneis*

When you read poetry from the 16th to the 18th centuries, you will often find pairs of words that should rhyme, but do not do so in present-day pronunciation. It is therefore interesting to examine a few examples at the end of the 17th century, and relate them to what we have learned about pronunciation from the two orthoepists John Hart in the 16th century (in Chapter 15) and Christopher Cooper in the 17th century (in this chapter, section 18.2.2).

The following rhymes from John Dryden's translation of Virgil's Latin *Aeneis* occur many other times, and are not single examples which might be explained as false or eye rhymes.

Text 146: Couplets from Dryden's Aeneis, 1697 *(ea)*

appear	Amidſt our courſe Zacynthian Woods **appear;** And next by rocky Neritos we **ſteer:**	III 351
	At length, in dead of Night, the Ghoſt **appears** Of her unhappy Lord: the Spectre **ſtares,** And with erected Eyes his bloody Boſom **bares.**	I 486
Sea	He calls to raiſe the Maſts, the Sheats **diſplay;** The Chearful Crew with diligence **obey;** They ſcud before the Wind, and ſail in open **Sea.**	V 1084
	Long wandring Ways for you the Pow'rs **decree:** On Land hard Labours, and a length of **Sea.**	II 1058
	Then, from the South aroſe a gentle **Breeze,** That curl'd the ſmoothneſs of the glaſſy **Seas:**	V 997
Year	When riſing Vapours choak the wholſom **Air,** And blaſts of noiſom Winds corrupt the **Year.**	III 190
	Laocoon, Neptune's Prieſt by Lot that **Year,** With ſolemn pomp then ſacrific'd a **Steer.**	II 267

⟨i⟩
Wind   His Pow'r to hollow Caverns is **confin'd**,
There let him reign, the Jailor of the **Wind**.   I 199

⟨oi⟩

For this are various Penances **enjoyn'd**;
And fome are hung to bleach, upon the **Wind**;   VI 1002

Did I or Iris give this mad **Advice**,
Or made the Fool himſelf the fatal **Choice**?   X 110

The paſſive Gods behold the Greeks **defile**
Their Temples, and abandon to the **Spoil**
Their own Abodes . . .   II 471

But that o'reblown, when Heav'n above 'em **ſmiles**,
Return to Travel, and renew their **Toils**:   X 1144

. . . Reſolute to **die**,
And add his Fun'rals to the fate of **Troy**:   II 862

⟨a⟩

The reſt, in Meen, in habit, and in **Face**,
Appear'd a Greek; and ſuch indeed he **was**.   III 778

Yet one remain'd, the Meſſenger of **Fate**;
High on a craggy Cliff Celæno **ſate**,
And thus her diſmall Errand did **relate**.   III 321

Then, as her Strength with Years increaſ'd, **began**
To pierce aloft in Air the ſoaring **Swan**:
And from the Clouds to fetch the heron and the **Crane**.   XI 868

⟨ar⟩

O more than Madmen! you your ſelves ſhall **bear**
The guilt of Blood and Sacrilegious **War**:   VII 821

Loaded with Gold, he ſent his Darling, **far**
From Noiſe and Tumults, and deſtructive **War**:
Committed to the faithleſs Tyrant's **Care**.   III 73

⟨oo⟩

She ſeem'd a Virgin of the Spartan **Blood**:
With ſuch Array Harpalice **beſtrode**
Her Thracian Courſer, and outſtri'd the rapid **Flood**   I 440

His Father Hyrtacus of Noble **Blood**;
His Mother was a Hunt'reſs of the **Wood**:   IX 223

. . . The Brambles drink his **Blood**;
And his torn Limbs are left, the Vulture's **Food**.   VIII 855

Reſume your ancient Care; and if the **God**
Your Sire, and you, reſolve on Foreign **Blood**:   VII 516

⟨oa⟩

His knocking Knees are bent beneath the **Load**:
And ſhiv'ring Cold congeals his vital **Blood**.　　　　　XII 1308

Maids, Matrons, Widows, mix their common **Moans**:
Orphans their Sires, and Sires lament their **Sons**　　　XI 329

⟨-y⟩

Aceſtes, fir'd with juſt Diſdain, to ſee
The Palm uſurp'd without a **Victory**;
Reproch'd Entellus thus …　　　　　　　　　　　　　V 513

The Paſtor pleaſ'd with his dire **Victory**,
Beholds the ſatiate Flames in Sheets aſcend the **Sky**:　　X 573

… the Coaſt was **free**
From Foreign or Domeſtick **Enemy**:　　　　　　　　III 168

He heav'd it at a Lift: and poiz'd on **high**,
Ran ſtagg'ring on, againſt his **Enemy**.　　　　　　　XII 1304

⊕ The rhyming pairs are recorded on the CD/cassette tape.

appear	[ir]	confin'd	[aɪnd]	relate.	[rɛleːt]	God	[gɒd]
steer	[ir]	Wind	[aɪnd]			Blood	[blɒd]
				began	[bɛgæn]		
appears	[erz]	enjoyn'd	[aɪnd]	Swan	[swæn]	Load	[lɒd]
stares	[erz]	Wind	[aɪnd]	Crane	[kræn]	Blood	[blɒd]
bares	[erz]						
		Advice	[aɪs]	bear	[beːr]	Moans	[moːnz]
display	[eː]	Choice	[aɪs]	War	[weːr]	Sons	[sʊnz]
obey	[eː]						
Sea	[eː]	defile	[aɪl]	far	[fɛːr]	see	[siː]
		Spoil	[aɪl]	War	[weːr]	Victory	[vɪktəriː]
decree	[iː]			Care	[kɛːr]		
Sea	[iː]	smiles	[aɪlz]			Victory	[vɪktəraɪ]
		Toils	[aɪlz]	Blood	[blɒd]	Sky	[skaɪ]
Breeze	[iːz]			bestrode	[bɛstrɒd]		
Seas	[iːz]	die	[aɪ]	Flood	[flɒd]	free	[friː]
		Troy	[aɪ]			Enemy	[ɛnəmiː]
Air	[ɛːr]			Blood	[blʊd]		
Year	[ɛːr]	Face	[fæs]	Wood	[wʊd]	high	[haɪ]
		was	[wæs]			Enemy	[ɛnəmaɪ]
Year	[iːr]			Blood	[blʊd]		
Steer	[iːr]	Fate	[feːt]	Food	[fʊd]		
		sate	[seːt]				

It seems odd at first that *enemy* could apparently rhyme with both *free*, MnE [friː],
and *high*, MnE [haɪ]. But in Dryden's time the vowel of *high* was still in the process
of shifting from [iː] to [aɪ], and the vowel of *free* from [eː] to [iː], and at a variable
rate in different dialects. Dryden was able to make use of such variant
pronunciations. The shifting of these two vowels explains the following word-play

in Shakespeare's *The Two Gentlemen of Verona* a century earlier. The dialogue is between Protheus, 'a gentleman of Verona' and Speed, 'a clownish seruant'. The word *Ay* (*yes*) is spelt *I*; *noddy* meant *foolish*.

Text 147: Shakespeare's The Two Gentlemen of Verona

PROTHEUS But what faid fhe?
SPEED (*Nods, then faies*) I.
PROTHEUS Nod-I, why that's noddy.
SPEED You miftooke Sir: I fay fhe did nod; and you afke me if fhe did nod and I fay I.
PROTHEUS And that fet together is noddy.

18.4 North Riding Yorkshire dialect in the 1680s

It was said in an earlier chapter that from the later 15th century it becomes increasingly rare to find texts which provide evidence of regional forms other than those of the educated London dialect which became established as the standard. Once the grammar and vocabulary of written English were standardised, other dialects were recorded only in texts written for the purpose of presenting dialects as different.

During the 17th century there was a revival of interest in antiquarian studies and of language, two of the many topics discussed by members of the Royal Society. Writing on language included descriptions of the Saxon language of the past, and of contemporary dialects.

One form that this interest in dialect took can be seen in George Meriton's *A Yorkshire Dialogue*, published in York in 1683. Meriton was a lawyer, practising in the North Riding town of Northallerton. The Dialogue is a lively representation of a Yorkshire farming family, written in verse couplets, and deliberately full of proverbial sayings. It is therefore only indirect evidence of the authentic spoken North Riding English of the time, but nevertheless gives us plenty of examples of dialectal and traditional vocabulary and grammar.

The spelling of written English had remained virtually unchanged in spite of the efforts of spelling reformers like John Hart in the 16th century, and took no account of the shifts of pronunciation that had taken place since the 14th century. Consequently, the spelling of standard English did not at all accurately indicate the 'polite' accent of the late 17th and early 18th centuries. But when writing in dialect it was (and still is) usual to spell many of the words 'as they were spoken', so that features of dialectal pronunciation were shown as well as the vocabulary and grammar.

In the following short extract, the two young women in the family, Tibb the daughter and Nan the niece, talk about their sweethearts. There are no 'stage directions', so their movements have to be inferred from the dialogue.

Activity 18.8

(i) List some of the probable dialectal pronunciations which the spellings suggest.

(ii) In what ways does the grammar of the dialect differ from the standard English of the late 17th century?

Text 148: George Meriton's A Yorkshire Dialogue, 1683

A York-fhire DIALOGUE, In its pure Natural DIALECT: As it is now commonly Spoken in the North parts of *York-Shire* Being a Mifcellaneous difcourfe, or Hotchpotch of feveral Country Affaires, begun by a Daughter and her Mother, and continued by the Father, Son, Uncle, Neefe, and Land-Lord.

(The extract begins at line 155 of the original. The Yorkshire dialectal pronunciation of *the* is spelt in the Dialogue as 'th.) *F.* = Father, *M.* = Mother, *D.* = Daughter, *N.* = Niece.

⸢WW⸣

Modern English

F. What ails our Tibb, that fhe urles feay ith Newke,
Shee's nut Reet, fhe leauks an Awd farrand Leauke.

D. Father, Ive gitten cawd, I can fcarce tawke,
And my Snurles are feay fayr ftopt, I can nut fnawke,

N. How duz my Cozen Tibb Naunt I mun nut ftay,
I hard fhe gat a Cawd the other day,

M. Ey wallaneerin, wilta gang and fee,
Shee's aboun 'ith Chawmber, Thou may Clim up 'th Stee.
Shee's on a dovening now gang deftly Nan,
And mack as little din as ee'r Thou can.

N. Your mains flaid, there's an awd faying you knawe
That there's no Carrion will kill a Crawe:
If fhe be nut as dead as a deaur Naile,
Ile mack her flyer and femper like Flefh Cael,
What Tibb I fee, Thou is nut yet quite dead,
Leauke at me woman, and haud up thy head.

D. Ah Nan fteeke'th winderboard, and mack it darke,
My Neen are varra fayr, they ftoun and warke.

F. What ails our Tibb, that she crouches* so in the nook,
She's not right, she looks an old fashioned look.

D. Father, I've gotten (a) cold, I can scarce talk,
And my nostrils are so sore stopped (up), I can not inhale,

N. How does my Cousin Tibb aunt I must not stay,
I heard she got a Cold the other day,

M. Ey alas, wilt thou go and see,
She's above in the Chamber, Thou may Climb up the ladder.
She's in a doze now go gently Nan,
And make as little din as ever Thou can.

N. You're very worried, there's an old saying you know
That there's no Carrion will kill a Crow:
If she be not as dead as a door Nail,
I'll make her laugh and simper like meat broth,
What Tibb I see, Thou is not yet quite dead,
Look at me woman, and hold up thy head.

D. Ah Nan shut the window-board, and make it dark,
My eyes are very sore, they smart and ache.

They are ſeay Gummy and Furr'd up ſometime.

I can nut leauke at'th Leet, nor ſee a ſtime.

N. Come come, I can mack Thee Leetſome and blythe,

Here will be thy awd Sweet-heart here Belive.

He tell's me ſeay I ſay him but laſt night

O Tibb he is as fine as onny Kneet.

D. Nay Nan Thou dus but jeſt there's neay ſike thing,

He woes another Laſſe and gave her a Ring.

N. Away away great feaul tack thou neay Care,

He ſwears that hee'l love thee for evermare.

And ſayes as ever he whopes his Saul to ſeave,

Hee'l either wed to Thee, or tull his greave

. . .

They are so Gummy and Furr'd up sometime.

I can not look at the Light, nor see a thing.

N. Come come, I can make Thee Lightsome and blithe,

Here will be thy old Sweet-heart here soon.

He tells me so I saw him but last night

O Tibb he is as fine as any Knight.

D. Nay Nan Thou dost but jest there's no such thing,

He woos another Lass and gave her a Ring.

N. Away away great fool take thou no Care,

He swears that he'll love thee for evermore.

And says as ever he hopes his Soul to save,

He'll either wed to Thee, or till his grave (= *die*).

* *urles* cannot be accurately translated into one Standard English word. A contemporary gloss (1684) on the word was 'To Vrle, to draw ones self up on a heap'; a later one (1808) was 'to be pinched with cold'.

📖 A descriptive analysis can be found in the Text Commentary Book.

18.5 Loan-words, 1650–99

📖 A selection of loan-words recorded during this period can be found in the Word Book, after the word-lists for Chapter 18.

19 Modern English – the 18th century

A standard language is achieved when writers use prescribed and agreed forms of the vocabulary and grammar, regardless of the dialectal variety of the language which each one may speak. As a result, regional and class dialects, which are themselves no less rule-governed and systematic than an agreed standard, tend to be regarded as inferior. This chapter presents some of the evidence about attitudes towards, and beliefs about, the standard language and the dialects in the 18th century.

19.1 Correcting, improving and ascertaining the language

During the 18th century many pamphlets, articles and grammar books were published on the topic of correcting, improving and, if possible, fixing the language in a perfected form. One word which recurred time and time again in referring to the state of the English language was *corruption*. You will find it in the following text, an extract from an article written by Jonathan Swift (1667–1745) in 1710, in the journal *The Tatler*. The complete article took the form of a supposed letter written to *Isaac Bickerstaff*, a pseudonym for Jonathan Swift.

19.1.1 'The continual Corruption of our English Tongue'

Activity 19.1

(i) Discuss what the word *corruption* implies as a metaphor of language. Is it a plausible and acceptable concept?

(ii) List the features of contemporary language use that Swift objected to.

(iii) Discuss Swift's argument and his own use of language, for example his irony, and the connotations of words like *Errors, Evils, Abuses, deplorable, Depravity, Corruption, suffer, Barbarity, Disgrace, betrayed, Mutilations, Coxcomb*.

(iv) Are there any significant differences between Swift's punctuation and present-day conventions?

(The dots in the second Letter (....), quoted within the main letter addressed to 'Isaac Bickerstaff', are part of the punctuation which Swift objected to ('the Breaks at the End of almost every Sentence'). Elsewhere (. . .) they mark omissions from the original longer text. A few words are explained at the end.)

Text 149: *From* The Tatler, *no. 230, 26 September 1710*

The following Letter has laid before me many great and manifeſt Evils in the World of Letters which I had overlooked; but they open to me a very buſie Scene, and it will require no ſmall Care and Application to amend Errors which are become ſo univerſal . . .

> *To* Iſaac Bickerſtaff *Eſq;*
>
> *SIR,*
> There are ſome Abuſes among us of great Conſequence, the Reformation of which is properly your Province, tho', as far as I have been converſant in your Papers, you have not yet conſidered them. Theſe are, the deplorable Ignorance that for ſome Years hath reigned among our Engliſh Writers, the great depravity of our Taſte, and the continual Corruption of our Style . . .
> Theſe two Evils, Ignorance and Want of Taſte, have produced a Third; I mean, the continual Corruption of our Engliſh Tongue, which, without ſome timely Remedy, will ſuffer more by the falſe Refinements of twenty Years paſt, than it hath been improved in the foregoing Hundred . . .
> But inſtead of giving you a Liſt of the late Refinements crept into our Language, I here ſend you the Copy of a Letter I received ſome Time ago from a moſt accompliſhed perſon in this Way of Writing, upon which I ſhall make ſome Remarks. It is in theſe Terms.

> > SIR, I *Cou'dn't* get the Things you ſent for all *about Town*.... I *th'𝑡* to *ha'* come down my ſelf, and then *I'd ha' br'ut 'um;* but I *han't don't,* and I believe I *can't do't,* that's *Pozz*.... *Tom* begins to *gi'mſelf Airs* becauſe *he's* going with the *Plenipo's*.... 'Tis ſaid, the *French* King will *bambooz'l us agen,* which *cauſes many Speculations.* The *Jacks,* and others of that *Kidney,* are very *uppiſh,* and *alert upon't,* as you may ſee by their *Phizz's*.... *Will Hazzard* has got the *Hipps,* having loſt *to the Tune of* Five hundr'd Pound, *th'* he underſtands Play very well, *no body better.* He has promiſt me upon *Rep,* to leave off Play; but, you know 'tis a Weakneſs *he's* too apt to *give into,* *th'* he has as much Wit as any Man, *no body more.* He has lain *incog* ever ſince.... The *Mobb's* very quiet with us now.... I believe you *thot* I *banter'd* you in my Laſt like a *Country Put*.... I *ſha'n't* leave Town this Month, &c.

This Letter is in every Point an admirable Pattern of the preſent polite Way of Writing; nor is it of leſs Authority for being an Epiſtle ... The firſt Thing that ſtrikes your Eye is the Breaks at the End of almoſt every Sentence; of which I know not the Uſe, only that it is a Refinement, and very frequently practiſed. Then you will obſerve the Abbreviations and Eliſions, by which Conſonants of moſt obdurate Sound are joined together, without one ſoftening Vowel to intervene; and all this only to make one Syllable of two, directly contrary to the Example of the Greeks and Romans; altogether of the Gothick Strain, and a natural Tendency towards relapſing into barbarity, which delights in Monoſyllables, and uniting of Mute Conſonants; as it is obſervable in all the

Northern Languages. And this is ſtill more viſible in the next refinement, which conſiſts in pronouncing the firſt Syllable in a Word that has many, and diſmiſſing the reſt; ſuch as Phizz, Hipps, Mobb, Poz. Rep. and many more; when we are already overloaded with Monoſyllables, which are the diſgrace of our Language.
. . .

The Third Refinement obſervable in the Letter I ſend you, conſiſts in the Choice of certain Words invented by ſome Pretty Fellows; ſuch as Banter, Bamboozle, Country Put, and Kidney, as it is there applied; ſome of which are now ſtruggling for the Vogue, and others are in Poſſeſſion of it. I have done my utmoſt for ſome Years paſt to ſtop the Progreſs of Mobb and Banter, but have been plainly borne down by Numbers, and betrayed by thoſe who promiſed to aſſiſt me.

In the laſt Place, you are to take Notice of certain choice Phraſes ſcattered through the Letter; ſome of them tolerable enough, till they were worn to Rags by ſervile Imitators. You might eaſily find them, though they were in a different Print, and therefore I need not diſturb them.

Theſe are the falſe Refinements in our Style which you ought to correct: Firſt, by Argument and fair Means; but if thoſe fail, I think you are to make Uſe of your Authority as Cenſor, and by an Annual Index Expurgatorius expunge all Words and Phraſes that are offenſive to good Senſe, and condemn thoſe barbarous Mutilations of Vowels and Syllables. In this laſt Point, the uſual pretence is, that they ſpell as they ſpeak; A Noble Standard for a Language! to depend upon the Caprice of every Coxcomb, who, becauſe Words are the Cloathing of our Thoughts, cuts them out, and ſhapes them as he pleaſes, and changes them oftner than his Dreſs . . . And upon this Head I ſhould be glad you would beſtow ſome Advice upon ſeveral young Readers in our Churches, who coming up from the Univerſity, full fraught with Admiration of our Town Politeneſs, will needs correct the Style of their Prayer Books. In reading the Abſolution, they are very careful to ſay pardons and abſolves; and in the Prayer for the Royal Family, it muſt be endue 'um, enrich 'um, proſper 'um, and bring 'um. Then in their Sermons they uſe all the modern Terms of Art, Sham, Banter, Mob, Bubble, Bully, Cutting, Shuffling, and Palming . . .

I ſhould be glad to ſee you the Inſtrument of introducing into our Style that Simplicity which is the beſt and trueſt ornament of moſt Things in Life . . .

I am, with great Reſpect,

SIR,

Your, &c.

Some of the contracted or colloquial forms which Swift disliked were:

banter	humorous ridicule (n), to make fun of (vb), *origin unknown, regarded by Swift as slang*
Hipps/hip	hypochondria, depression
incog	incognito, concealed identity
Jacks	lads, chaps
Mobb/mob	*originally shortened from* mobile, *from Latin* mobile vulgus, the movable or excitable crowd, *hence* the rabble
Phizz	physiognomy, face
Plenipos	plenipotentiary, representative
Put	fool, lout, bumpkin (*origin not known*)

Poz	positive, certain
Rep	reputation

The Absolution in the *Book of Common Prayer*, which Swift referred to, contains the words *he pardoneth and absolveth*.

You can see that Swift disliked certain new colloquial words and phrases, and fashionable features of pronunciation – all part of spoken usage rather than written. He specifically condemned these as features of *Style*, that is, of deliberate choices of words and structures from the resources of the language. But at the same time he referred in general terms to *the Corruption of our English Tongue*, an evaluative metaphor which implied worsening and decay, as if the style he disliked to hear could affect everyone's use of English, both written and spoken.

This attitude of condemnation, focusing upon relatively trivial aspects of contemporary usage, was taken up time and time again throughout the 18th century, and has continued to the present day. It is important to study it and to assess its effects. One obvious effect is that nonstandard varieties of the language tend to become stigmatised as *substandard*, while Standard English is thought of as <u>the</u> English language, rather than as the prestige dialect of the language.

The language and speech of educated men and women of the south-east, especially in London, Oxford and Cambridge, was, as we have already observed, the source of Standard English. This was John Hart's 'best and most perfite English' (section 16.1.1), and George Puttenham's 'vsuall speach of the Court, and that of London and the shires lying about London' (section 16.1.2).

The following text, from the 1770s, illustrates the establishment of this choice.

Text 150: James Beattie, Theory of Language, 1774 (facsimile)

Are, then, all provincial accents equally good? By no means. Of accent, as well as of spelling, syntax, and idiom, there is a standard in every polite nation. And, in all these particulars, the example of approved authors, and the practice of those, who, by their rank, education, and way of life, have had the best opportunities to know men and manners, and domestick and foreign literature, ought undoubtedly to give the law. Now it is in the metropolis of a kingdom, and in the most famous schools of learning, where the greatest resort may be expected of persons adorned with all useful and elegant accomplishments. The language, therefore, of the most learned and polite persons in London, and the neighbouring Universities of Oxford and Cambridge, ought to be accounted the standard of the English tongue, especially in accent and pronunciation: syntax, spelling, and idiom, having been ascertained by the practice of good authors, and the consent of former ages.

Activity 19.2

Discuss your response to James Beattie's assertions. Does his argument hold good for the present day?

19.1.2 Fixing the language – *A Proposal*, 1712

Swift's concern about the state of the language, as he saw it, was great enough to cause him to publish a serious proposal for establishing some sort of Academy to regulate and maintain the standards of the English language, similar to the Académie Française, which had been set up in France in 1634. The arguments used were similar to those of the *Tatler* article of 1710 (Text 149), but Swift also introduced the idea of *ascertaining* the language (*fixing, making it certain*) so that it would not be subject to further change.

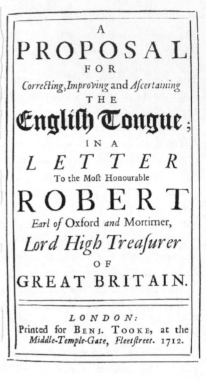

A

PROPOSAL

FOR

Correcting, Improving and *Ascertaining*

THE

English Tongue;

IN A

LETTER

To the Most Honourable

ROBERT

Earl of Oxford *and* Mortimer,

Lord High Treasurer

OF

GREAT BRITAIN.

LONDON:
Printed for BENJ. TOOKE, at the
Middle-Temple-Gate, Fleetstreet. 1712.

Text 151: From Swift's A Proposal, 1712 (facsimile)

My LORD; I do here, in the Name of all the Learned and Polite Persons of the Nation, complain to Your LORDSHIP, as *First Minister*, that our Language is extremely imperfect; that its daily Improvements are by no means in proportion to its daily Corruptions; that the Pretenders to polish and refine it, have chiefly multiplied Abuses and Absurdities; and, that in many Instances, it offends against every Part of Grammar.

I see no absolute Necessity why any Language should be perpetually changing; for we find many Examples to the contrary.

BUT what I have most at Heart is, that some Method should be thought on for *ascertaining* and *fixing* our Language for ever, after such Alterations are made in it as shall be thought requisite. For I am of Opinion, that it is better a Language should not be wholly perfect, than that it should be perpetually changing; and we must give over at one Time, or at length infallibly change for the worse:

BUT where I say, that I would have our Language, after it is duly correct, always to last; I do not mean that it should never be enlarged: Provided, that no Word which a Society shall give a Sanction to, be afterwards antiquated and exploded, they may have liberty to receive whatever new ones they shall find occasion for:

19.2   Dr Johnson's *Dictionary of the English Language*

Dr Samuel Johnson (1709–84) published *The Plan of a Dictionary of the English Language* in 1747, and completed the dictionary for publication in 1755, by which time he had written the definitions of over 40,000 words, with about 114,000 quotations to illustrate their usage. Knowledge of the etymology of words was limited in the 18th century, but Johnson's dictionary was to remain a standard reference work for over 150 years until the publication of the *Oxford English Dictionary*, completed in 1928.

THE

P L A N

OF A

DICTIONARY

OF THE

ENGLISH LANGUAGE;

Addreſſed to the Right Honourable

PHILIP DORMER,

Earl of *CHESTERFIELD*;

One of His MAJESTY's Principal Secretaries of State.

LONDON:

Printed for J. and P. KNAPTON, T. LONGMAN and T. SHEWELL, C. HITCH, A. MILLAR, and R. DODSLEY.   M DCCXLVII.

Among his objectives were

- to fix the English language – (although he recognised that this could not be attained) – 'Language is the work of man, of a being from whom permanence and stability cannot be derived.'
- 'to preserve the purity and ascertain the meaning of our English idiom' – cf. Swift's *Proposal* in section 19.1.2.

In the *Plan* he discussed the criteria he proposed to establish in preparing the dictionary:

- 'Foreign words' are to be included, whether 'naturalized and incorporated', like *zenith, meridian, cynosure, equator, satellites, category, cachexy, peripneumony*, or still 'alien', like *habeas corpus, nisi prius, hypostasis*.
- To include 'the peculiar words of every profession' (*peculiar* meaning *belonging to a group of persons, as distinct from others*).
- To include 'the names of species' even though they require no definition – *horse, dog, cat, willow, alder, dasy, rose* – because such words still require 'that their accents should be settled, their sounds ascertained, and their etymologies deduced'.
- To settle the orthography, or spelling, of words – 'The chief rule which I propose to follow, is to make no innovation, without a reason sufficient to balance the inconvenience of change; and such reason I do not expect often to find.'
- To produce a guide to pronunciation – the accentuation of polysyllables and the pronunciation of monosyllables. He saw danger in variation, when *wound* and *wind*, 'as they are now frequently pronounced', no longer rhymed with *sound* and *mind*.

- To consider the etymology or derivation of words.
- 'Interpreting the words with brevity, fulness and perspicuity'.
- Assigning words to classes – *general, poetic, obsolete, used by individual writers, used only in burlesque writing, impure and barbarous.*

Both Johnson and Swift, disliked *cant,*

> To introduce and multiply cant words is the moſt ruinous corruption in any language.   (Jonathan Swift, 1755)

> Nor are all words which are not found in the vocabulary, to be lamented as omiſſions. **Of the laborious and mercantile part of the people,** the diction is in great meaſure caſual and mutable; many of their terms are formed for ſome temporary or local convenience, and though current at certain times and places, are in others utterly unknown. This **fugitive cant,** which is always in a ſtate of increaſe or decay, cannot be regarded as any part of the durable materials of a language, and therefore muſt be ſuffered to periſh with other things unworthy of preſervation.   (Samuel Johnson, Preface to the *Dictionary,* 1755)

as did other writers on the language (see Text 171). The word *cant* was always used pejoratively, and meant variously,

- *phraseology used for fashion's sake, without being a genuine expression of sentiment,* or
- *an affected stock phrase, repeated as a matter of habit.*

It might also mean *provincial dialect, vulgar slang* – whatever the writer found distasteful.

The *Plan* was addressed to his patron, the Earl of Chesterfield, and concluded with a typical Johnsonian rhetorical peroration:

Text 152: Dr Samuel Johnson's Plan of a Dictionary, 1747 (facsimile)

THIS, my Lord, ıs my idea of an Engliſh diⅽtionary, a diⅽtionary by which the pronunciation of our language may be fixed, and ıts attainment facilitated; by which its purity may be preſerved, its uſe aſcertained, and its duration lengthened.   And though, perhaps, to correⅽt the language of nations by books of grammar, and amend their manners by diſcourſes of morality, may be taſks equally difficult; yet as it is unavoidable to wiſh, it is natural likewiſe to hope, that your Lordſhip's patronage may not be wholly loſt; that it may contribute to the preſervation of antient, and the improvement of modern writers; that it may promote the reformation of thoſe tranſlators, who for want of underſtanding the charaⅽteriſtical difference of tongues, have formed a chaoticdialeⅽt of heterogeneous phraſes; and awaken to the care of purer diⅽtion, ſome men of genius, whoſe attention to argument makes them negligent of ſtile, or whoſe rapid imagination, like the Peruvian torrents, when it brings down gold, mingles it with ſand.

19.3 The perfection of the language

Dr Johnson again refers to the idea of fixing the language in the Preface of the published *Dictionary* in 1755. He himself, as we have seen, is sceptical of the possibility of success, although he believes in the idea of the perfection and decay of a language:

> Thofe who have been perfuaded to think well of my defign, will require that it fhould fix our language, and put a ftop to thofe alterations which time and chance have hitherto been fuffered to make in it without oppofition. With this confequence I will confefs that I have indulged expectation which neither reafon nor experience can juftify.
>
> ... tongues, like governments, have a natural tendency to degeneration; we have long preferved our conftitution, let us make fome ftruggles for our language.

> (from the Preface to Dr Johnson's *Dictionary*, 1755)

Both Swift and Johnson thought that the century from the beginning of Queen Elizabeth's reign in 1558 to the Civil Wars in 1642 was a kind of Golden Age of Improvement in the language, though they did not believe that it had yet reached a 'state of Perfection'. The belief that languages could be improved and brought to a state of perfection was common (though we may not believe it today). Confusion between *language* and *language use* causes the one to be identified with the other, and a period of great writers is called a period of greatness for the language. We have already seen Swift identifying a *style* which he disliked with corruption of the *language*.

19.3.1 The Augustan Age and Classical perfection

Some writers thought that the 'state of perfection' would come in the future, but later 18th-century grammarians placed it in the early and mid-18th-century language of writers like Addison, Steele, Pope and Swift himself. This period is known as the 'Augustan Age' (from the period of the reign of the Roman Emperor Augustus, 27BC–AD14, when great writers like Virgil, Horace and Ovid flourished). The language and literature of Classical Rome and Greece were still the foundation of education in the 18th century. Writers copied the forms of Classical literature, like the epic, the ode, and dramatic tragedy, while the Latin and Greek languages were models of perfection in their unchangeable state, which writers hoped English could attain. The influence of the sound of Latin and Greek helps to explain Swift's dislike of 'Northern' consonant clusters (see Text 149):

> Confonants of moft obdurate Sound are joined together, without one foftening Vowel to intervene; and all this only to make one Syllable of two, directly contrary to the Example of the Greeks and Romans; altogether of the Gothick Strain, and a natural Tendency towards relapfing into barbarity, which delights in Monofyllables, and uniting of Mute Confonants; as it is obfervable in all the Northern Languages.

The vernacular Latin language of the 1st century had, of course, continued to change, so that after several centuries its many dialects had evolved into dialects of French, Italian, Spanish and the other Romance languages. But Classical Latin was fixed and ascertained, because its vocabulary and grammar were derived from the literature of its greatest period. This state seemed to be in complete contrast to contemporary English, and so following Swift, many other writers and grammarians sought to 'improve' the language. Somewhere, in the past or the future, lay the perfected English language.

19.4 'The Genius of the Language'

There are few references to the language of ordinary people by 18th-century writers on language – the grammarians – 'it is beneath a grammarian's attempt' (Anselm Bayly in 1772). But even writers whom they admired were not necessarily taken as models of good English either. Authors' writings were subjected to detailed scrutiny for supposed errors. Grammarians sometimes spoke of 'the Genius of the Language' or 'the Idiom of the Tongue' as a criterion for judgement, the word *genius* meaning sometimes *character* or *spirit*, or simply *grammar*. But this concept in practice meant little more than the intuition of the grammarian, what he thought or felt sounded right, expressed in the Latin phrase *ipse dixit* ('he himself has said'). Sometimes this reliance on personal opinion was clearly stated:

> ... *to commute to* I look upon not to be Englifh.

> It will be eafily difcovered that I have paid no regard to authority. I have cenfured even our beft penmen, where they have departed from what I conceive to be the idiom of the tongue, or where I have thought they violate grammar without neceffity. To judge by the rule of Ipfe dixit is the way to perpetuate error.

(on the wrong use of prepositions)

> ... even by Swift, Temple, Addifon, and other writers of the higheft reputation; fome of them, indeed, with fuch fhameful impropriety as one muft think muft fhock every Englifh ear, and almoft induce the reader to fuppofe the writers to be foreigners.
>
> (Robert Baker, *Reflections on the English Language*, 1770)

Notice that Baker condemns *ipse dixit* when applied to 'the best penmen', but not when applied to himself. Often appeals were made to *Reason*, or *Analogy* (a similar form to be found elsewhere in the language):

> In doubtful cafes regard ought to be had in our decifions to the analogy of the language ... Of 'Whether he will or *no*' and 'Whether he will or *not*', it is only the latter that is analogical ... when you fupply the ellipfis, you find it neceffary to ufe the adverb *not*, 'Whether he will or will *not*'.
>
> (George Campbell, *Philosophy of Rhetoric*, 1776)

Grammarians were not always consistent in their arguments, however. They recognised that the evidence for the vocabulary and grammar of a language must be derived from what people actually wrote and spoke, referred to sometimes as Custom:

> Reaſon permits that we give way to Cuſtom, though contrary to Reaſon. Analogie is not the Miſtreſs of Language. She preſcribes only the Laws of Cuſtom.

> *(Art of Speaking*, 1708)

This point of view is argued in greater detail in the following text.

Activity 19.4

Discuss Joseph Priestley's assessment of the relative values of *custom, analogy, the genius of the language*, and *the disapproval of grammarians* in deciding the forms of a standard language.

Text 153: *Joseph Priestley,* Rudiments of English Grammar, *1769*

> It muſt be allowed, that the cuſtom of ſpeaking is the original, and only juſt ſtandard of any language. We ſee, in all grammars, that this is ſufficient to eſtabliſh a rule, even contrary to the ſtrongeſt analogies of the language with itſelf. Muſt not this cuſtom, therefore, be allowed to have ſome weight, in favour of thoſe forms of ſpeech, to which our beſt writers and ſpeakers ſeem evidently prone; forms which are contrary to no analogy of the language with itſelf, and which have been diſapproved by grammarians, only from certain abſtract and arbitrary conſiderations, and when their deciſions were not prompted by the genius of the language; which diſcovers itſelf in nothing more than in the general propenſity of thoſe who uſe it to certain modes of conſtruction? I think, however, that I have not, in any caſe, ſeemed to favour what our grammarians will call an irregularity, but where the genius of the language, and not only ſingle examples, but the general practice of thoſe who write it, and the almoſt univerſal cuſtom of all who ſpeak it, have obliged me to do ſo. I alſo think I have ſeemed to favour thoſe irregularities, no more than the degree of the propenſity I have firſt mentioned, when unchecked by a regard to arbitrary rules, in thoſe who uſe the forms of ſpeech I refer to, will authorize me.

19.5   Bishop Lowth's *Grammar*

One in particular of the many grammar books of the 18th century had a lasting influence on later grammars which were published for use in schools in the late 18th century and throughout the 19th century – this was Robert Lowth's *A Short Introduction to English Grammar*, 1762. Lowth's attitude was **prescriptive** – that is, he prescribed or laid down what he himself considered to be correct usage:

Text 154: Robert Lowth, A Short Introduction to English Grammar, *1762*
(i) (facsimile)

A SHORT

INTRODUCTION

TO

ENGLISH GRAMMAR.

GRAMMAR.

GRAMMAR is the Art of right-
ly expreſſing our thoughts by
Words.

Grammar in general, or Univerſal Grammar, explains the Principles which are common to all languages.

The Grammar of any particular
Language, as the Engliſh Grammar, applies thoſe common principles to that particular language, according to the eſtabliſhed uſage and
cuſtom of it.

B   Gram-

Text 155: Robert Lowth, A Short Introduction to English Grammar, *1762*
(ii) (facsimile)

*The principal deſign of a Gram-
mar of any Language is to teach us
to expreſs ourſelves with propriety in
that Language, and to be able to
judge of every phraſe and form of
conſtruction, whether it be right or
not. The plain way of doing this,
is to lay down rules, and to illuſ-
trate them by examples. But be-
ſides ſhewing what is right, the
matter may be further explained by
pointing out what is wrong.*

The words *propriety* and *right* in Text 155 are important, because Lowth was not *describing* the language in its many varieties, but *prescribing what ought to be written* in a standard variety of English, and pointing out 'errors' and 'solecisms', with examples from authors like Milton, Dryden and Pope. He described other varieties of usage only in order to condemn them.

The following text is an extract from the Preface, and it typifies this particular attitude to language use. What people actually say and write, even though they may be socially of the highest rank, or eminent authors, is subject to Lowth's prescriptive judgement.

Text 156: Robert Lowth, A Short Introduction to English Grammar, 1762 (iii) (facsimile)

It is now about fifty years since Doctor Swift made a public remonstrance, addressed to the Earl of Oxford, then Lord Treasurer, of the imperfect State of our Language; alledging in particular, "that in many instances it "offended against every part of "Grammar." Swift must be allowed to have been a good judge of this matter. He was himself very attentive to this part, both in his own writings, and in his remarks upon those of his friends: he is one of our most correct, and perhaps our very best prose writer. Indeed the justness of this complaint, as far as I can find, hath never been questioned; and yet no effectual method hath hitherto been taken to redress the grievance of which he complains.

But let us consider, how, and in what extent, we are to understand this charge brought against the English Language. Does it mean, that the English Language as it is spoken by the politest part of the nation, and as it stands in the writings of our most approved authors, oftentimes offends against every part of Grammar? Thus far, I am afraid, the charge is true.

Lowth's book was intended for those already well educated. This can be inferred from part of the Preface to his *Grammar*:

> A Grammatical Study of our own Language makes no part of the ordinary method of inftruction which we paſs thro' in our childhood ... (p. vii)

The use of the first person *we* implies that his readers, like him, will have studied Latin and Greek at school – the *ancient* or *learned* languages. This, however, did not in his opinion provide them with a knowledge of English grammar, even though they lived in polite society and read English literature, activities not followed by most of the population at the time.

Text 157: Robert Lowth, A Short Introduction to English Grammar, 1762 (iv) (facsimile)

> *Much practice in the polite world, and a general acquaintance with the beſt authors, are good helps, but alone will hardly be ſufficient: we have writers, who have enjoyed theſe advantages in their full extent, and yet cannot be recommended as models of an accurate ſtyle. Much leſs then will what is commonly called Learning ſerve the purpoſe; that is, a critical knowledge of ancient languages, and much reading of ancient authors:*
>
> *In a word, it was calculated for the uſe of the Learner even of the loweſt claſs. Thoſe, who would enter more deeply into this Subject, will find it fully and accurately handled, with the greateſt acuteneſs of inveſtigation, perſpicuity of explication, and elegance of method, in a Treatiſe intitled* HERMES, *by* JAMES HARRIS *Eſq; the moſt beautiful and perfect example of Analyſis that has been exhibited ſince the days of Ariſtotle.*

class in this extract does not mean *social class*, but *grade* or *standard of achievement*.

19.6   'The depraved language of the common People'

The standard language recognised by 18th-century grammarians was that variety used by what they called 'the Learned and Polite Persons of the Nation' (Swift) – *polite* in the sense of *polished, refined, elegant, well-bred*. By definition, the language of the common people was inferior. This had far-reaching social consequences, as we shall see later in the chapter. Here is some of the evidence, which also explains why we know much less about the regional, social and spoken varieties of 18th century English, except what we can infer from novels, plays, letters and other indirect sources – they were not worth the attention of scholars:

Text 158: On the language of common people

... *themfelves and Families* (from the *Monthly Review*) ... a very bad Expreffion, though very common. It is mere **Shopkeepers cant** and will always be found contemptible in the Ears of perfons of any Tafte.

(Reflections on the English Language, Robert Baker, 1770)

(on *most an end* for *most commonly:*) ... is an expreffion that would almoft difgrace the mouth of **a hackney-coachman.**

(Remarks on the English Language, Robert Baker, 1779)

... though fometimes it may be difficult, if not impoffible to reduce **common fpeech** to rule, and indeed it is beneath a grammarian's attempt.

(Plain and Complete Grammar, Anselm Bayly, 1772)

No abfolute monarch hath it more in his power to nobilitate a perfon of obfcure birth, than it is in the power of good ufe to ennoble words of **low** or **dubious extraction;** fuch, for inftance, as have either arifen, nobody knows how, like *fib, banter, bigot, fop, flippant,* among **the rabble,** or like *flimfy,* fprung from the **cant of the manufacturers.**

(Philosophy of Rhetoric, George Campbell, 1776)

My Animadverfions will extend to fuch Phrafes only as People in decent Life inadvertently adopt ... Purity and Politenefs of Expreffion ... is the only external Diftinction which remains between **a gentleman and a valet; a lady and a Mantua-maker.**

(Aristarchus, Philip Withers, 1788)

A mantua was a loose gown, so a *Mantua-maker* was a *dress-maker.*

Such comments as these clearly show that the divisions of 18th-century society were marked by language as much as by birth, rank, wealth and education.

19.7   'Propriety and perspicuity of language'

19.7.1   Formal literary style

19.7.1.1   Dr Samuel Johnson

You will have noticed that the style of Lowth and other grammarians is very formal, its vocabulary and structure unlike that of everyday conversation. Literary prose adopts fashionable choices from the resources of the language at different periods, while ordinary language in speech and writing continues, generally unremarked.

Activity 19.5

Discuss the features of vocabulary and syntax that distinguish this literary style of writing.

Text 159: Samuel Johnson, from The Rambler, no. 38, July 1750

The advantages of mediocrity

… Health and vigour, and a happy conftitution of the corporeal frame, are of abfolute neceffity to the enjoyment of the comforts, and to the performance of the duties of life, and requifite in yet a greater meafure to the accomplifhment of any thing illuftrious or diftinguifhed; yet even thefe, if we can judge by their apparent confequences, are fometimes not very beneficial to thofe on whom they are moft liberally beftowed. They that frequent the chambers of the fick, will generally find the fharpeft pains, and moft ftubborn maladies among them whom confidence of the force of nature formerly betrayed to negligence and irregularity; and that fuperfluity of ftrength, which was at once their boaft and their fnare, has often, in the latter part of life, no other effect than that it continues them long in impotence and anguifh.

Vocabulary
Lexical words 61, of which, OE 23 = 37.7%; French 32 = 52.5%; Latin 6 = 9.8%.

The words taken from French after the 14th century are: *accomplishment, consequences, impotence, irregularity, beneficial, performance, constitution, distinguished, enjoyment, formerly*; and from Latin, *confidence, requisite, frequent, illustrious, corporeal*.

The words and phrases are often balanced in pairs, in rhetorical parallel – for example:

> *to the enjoyment of the comforts*
> *and*
> *to the performance of the duties of life*

which provide the syntactic formality of this style (compare the informal style of Text 163).

📖 There is a full analysis in the Text Commentary Book.

19.7.1.2 Edward Harwood and 'elegance of diction'

A new translation of the New Testament was published in 1768:

Text 160: Edward Harwood's Liberal Translation of the New Testament (i) (facsimile)

The author's intention was,

> to cloathe the genuine ideas and doctrines of the Apoftles with that propriety and perfpicuity, in which they themfelves, I apprehend, would have exhibited them had they *now* lived and written in our language. … I firft carefully perufed every chapter to inveftigate and difcover the ONE true meaning of the Author with all the accuracy and fagacity I could employ. … When I

A

LIBERAL TRANSLATION

OF THE

NEW TESTAMENT;

BEING

An Attempt to translate the SACRED WRITINGS

WITH THE SAME

Freedom, Spirit, and Elegance,

With which other English Translations from the Greek
Classics have lately been executed:

The DESIGN and SCOPE of each Author being strictly and
impartially explored, the TRUE SIGNIFICATION and
FORCE of the Original critically observed, and, as much
as possible, transfused into our Language, and the Whole
elucidated and explained upon a new and rational Plan:

With SELECT NOTES, Critical and Explanatory.

BY E. HARWOOD.

Ταυτην μονην ευρισκον Φιλοσοφιαν ασφαλη τε και συμφορον,
This have I found to be the only safe and useful Philosophy!
JUSTIN MARTYR, p. 225. Edit. Paris. 1636.

VOL. I.

LONDON:

Printed for T. BECKET and P. A. DE HONDT, in the Strand; and
J. JOHNSON, in Pater-noster Row; T. CADELL, at Bristol;
J. GORE and J. SIBBALD, at Liverpool; and T. BANCKS, at
Warrington.

M.DCC.LXVIII.

apprehended I had found out the *true* signification of the Original, and the *precise* ideas of the writer at the time he wrote, my *next* study was to adorn them in such language as is *now* written. . . .

Elegance of diction, therefore, hath ever been consulted, but never at the expense of truth and fidelity, which ought ever to be sacred and inviolable in an interpreter of Scripture.

It is pleasing to observe, how much our language, within these very few years, hath been refined and polished, and what infinite improvements it hath lately received.

Harwood attributes *elegance, harmony, copiousness and strength* to the language, and so to his translation, contrasting it with the Authorized Version of the Bible published in 1611, which he calls

'the bald and barbarous language of the old vulgar version.'

In present-day linguistic terms, Harwood is really talking about *language use* or *style*, the way in which the resources of *the language* are employed by writers. We would also want to question his principles and beliefs about the separation of *ideas* from the way they are *cloathed in language*. We can best assess his style by comparing one of the most famous passages from St Paul's letters in his version and that in the *bald and barbarous language* of the Authorized Version of 1611:

Text 161: St Paul's Letter to the Corinthians, chapter 13, from the King James Bible, 1611 (facsimile)

CHAP. XIII.

1 *All gifts,* 2, 3 *how excellent soeuer, are nothing worth without charitie.* 4 *The praises thereof, and* 13 *prelation before hope and faith.*

Though I speake with the tongues of men and of Angels, and haue not charity, I am become as sounding brasse, or a tinckling cymball.

2 And though I haue the gift of prophecie, and vnderstand all mysteries, and all knowledge; and though I haue all faith, so that I could remoue mountaines, and haue no charity, I am nothing.

3 And though I bestow all my goods to feed the poore, and though I giue my body to be burned, and haue not charity, it profiteth mee nothing.

4 Charity suffereth long, and is kind: charity enuieth not: charity vaunteth not it selfe, is not puffed vp,

5 Doeth not behaue it selfe vnseemely, seeketh not her owne, is not easily prouoked, thinketh no euill,

6 Reioyceth not in iniquity, but reioyceth in the trueth:

7 Beareth all things, beleeueth all things, hopeth all things, endureth all things.

8 Charity neuer faileth: but whether there be prophecies, they shall faile; whether there be tongues they shall cease; whether there bee knowledge, it shall vanish away.

9 For we know in part, and wee prophesie in part.

10 But when that which is perfect is come, then that which is in part, shall be done away.

11 When I was a childe, I spake as a child, I vnderstood as a childe, I thought as a child: but when I became a man, I put away childish things.

12 For now we see through a glasse, darkely: but then face to face: now I know in part, but then shall I know, euen as also I am knowen.

13 And now abideth faith, hope, charity, these three, but the greatest of these is charity.

Vocabulary

Lexical words 72, of which OE/ON 50 = 69.5%; OF 20 = 27.8%.

Two words (2.7%) were adopted in the 15th century – *prouoked, vaunteth*. The rest consist largely of core vocabulary from OE and assimilated OF words, which contrasts completely with Edward Harwood's choices in Text 162.

Charity meant *the Christian love of our fellow-men*. The word has developed a more restricted meaning since the 17th century – *benevolence to one's neighbours, especially to the poor, as manifested in action, specifically alms-giving*. Harwood uses *benevolence* for *charity* in his translation; modern versions use *love*.

Text 162: Edward Harwood's Liberal Translation of the New Testament *(ii)* *(facsimile)*

Chap. xiii. *to the* CORINTHIANS. 71

quire the moſt illuſtrious of theſe ſpiritual gifts—and yet I can point out to you an endowment, that far tranſcends all theſe.

CHAP. XIII.

1 COuld I ſpeak all the languages of men and of angels, and yet had an heart deſtitute of benevolence, I am no more than founding braſs or a tinkling cymbal.

2 And was I endowed with the ampleſt prophetic powers: could I unravel all the myſteries of nature: had I accumulated all the knowledge of the ſons of men: could I exert ſuch ſtupendous powers as to remove mountains from their baſis, and transfer them at pleaſure from place to place—and yet my heart a ſtranger to benevolence, I am nothing.

3 And ſhould I give away all I had in the world in charitable contributions to the poor: ſhould I even ſurrender up my body to the flames —and yet have an heart devoid of benevolence, it would be of no avail to me.

4 Benevolence is unruffled; is benign: Benevolence cheriſhes no ambitious deſires: Benevolence is not oſtenta-

tious; is not inflated with inſolence.

5 It preſerves a conſiſtent decorum; is not enſlaved to ſordid intereſt; is not tranſported with furious paſſion; indulges no malevolent deſign.

6 It conceives no delight from the perpetration of wickedneſs; but is firſt to applaud truth and virtue.

7 It throws a vail of candour over all things: is diſpoſed to believe all things: views all things in the moſt favourable light: ſupports all things with ſerene compoſure.

8 Benevolence ſhall continue to ſhine with undiminiſhed luſtre when all prophetic powers ſhall be no more, when the ability of ſpeaking various languages ſhall be withdrawn, and when all ſupernatural endowments ſhall be annihilated.

9 For in this ſtate our knowledge is defective, our prophetic powers are limited.

10 But when we arrive in thoſe happy regions where perfection dwells, the defective and the limited ſhall be no more for ever.

11 Juſt as when I was, for example, in the imperfect ſtate of childhood; I then diſcourſed, I underſtood, I reaſoned in the erroneous manner children do — but

when I arrived at the maturity and perfection of manhood, the defects of my former imperfect ſtate were all ſwallowed up and forgotten.

12 For in this ſcene of being our terreſtrial mirrour exhibits to us but a very dim and obſcure reflection: but in an happy futurity we ſhall ſee face to face—In the preſent life my knowledge is partial and limited: in the future, my knowledge will be unconfined and clear, like that divine infallible knowledge, by which I am now pervaded.

13 In fine, the virtues of ſuperior eminence are theſe three, faith, hope, benevolence—but the moſt illuſtrious of theſe is benevolence.

CHAP. XIV.

F 4

Vocabulary
Lexical words 140, of which, 14th century and before: OE, ME & ON 36 = 26%;
OF 49 = 35%; others 3 = 2%; 15th century and after: French 28 = 20%; Latin 24
= 17%.

Over a quarter of Harwood's lexical vocabulary had been adopted in the 16th and
17th centuries from French or Latin. He deliberately used a learned, formal
vocabulary, abstract and polysyllabic. The style was justified as *elegant, refined,
polished*, but present-day readers are more likely to find it pompous and so overblown
as to read like a parody.

📖 The lexical vocabulary, with derivations, is listed in the Word Book.

19.7.1.3   *William Barnes's* A Philological Grammar *(1854)*

This attitude of social and educational superiority to 'bald and barbarous' language
was criticised in the mid-19th century by the Dorset poet and grammarian William
Barnes (1801–86) in his *A Philological Grammar*, published in 1854:

> In English, purity is in many cases given up for the sake of what is considered to be
> elegance. Instead of the expression of the common people 'I will not be put upon,' we
> are apt to consider it better language to say 'I will not be imposed upon', though the
> word *imposed* is the Latin *impositum*, put upon; from *in*, upon, and *pono*, to put. So
> that in these and other such cases we use in what we consider the better expression,
> the very same words as in the worse; or we take, instead of two English words, a Latin
> compound, which, from the laws upon which languages are constructed, and the
> limited range of choice which the human mind has in constructing expressions for the
> same idea, is made of the very simples which we reject.

The technical terminology of academic language was also criticised by William
Barnes. For example, common terms we use to describe the sounds of language were
Englished by him as follows,

	Barnes
speech	breathsound language
writing	type language
vowel	pure breathsound
consonant	clipped breathsound
labials	lip letters
labiodentals	lip–teeth letters
dentals	tongue–teeth letters
alveolars	palate letters
velars	throat letters

19.7.2 Informal style

But of course not all writing in the 18th century was in the formal literary style of Harwood and Johnson. Here is a short example taken from a diary.

Text 163: Thomas Hearne, Remarks and Collections, 1715

> MAY 28 (Sat.) This being the Duke of Brunſwick, commonly called King George's Birth-Day, ſome of the Bells were jambled in Oxford, by the care of ſome of the Whiggiſh, Fanatical Crew; but as I did not obſerve the Day in the leaſt my ſelf, ſo it was little taken notice of (unleſs by way of ridicule) by other honeſt People, who are for K. James IIId. who is the undoubted King of theſe Kingdoms, & 'tis heartily wiſh'd by them that he may be reſtored.
>
> This Day I ſaw one Ward with Dr. Charlett, who, it ſeems, hath printed ſeveral Things. He is a clergy Man. I muſt inquire about him.

Vocabulary
Lexical words of which 40, OE 21 & ON 1 = 22 = 55%; French 16 = 40 %; Latin 1 (*Fanatical*)= 2.5%; not known 1 (*Whiggish*) = 2.5%.

📖 The lexical vocabulary, with derivations, is listed in the Word Book.

Most of the words are core vocabulary from OE or OF. The words entering the language after the 14th century are: *Crew, several, notice, undoubted, clergy-man, ridicule, jambled* (= jangled), *Fanatical, Whiggish*. Syntactically, the first paragraph is a compound-complex sentence, but there is no embedding of clauses; one statement follows another ('right-branching'), so there is no difficulty in understanding. The last two sentences are short and simple.

19.8 Language and social class

Here is a short example of the writing of 'the laborious and mercantile part of the people'. It is an inventory of the goods belonging to a hand-loom weaver, Elkanah Shaw, drawn up in 1773:

Text 164: *Inventory of Elkanah Shaw's property, 1773 (facsimile)*

November 20 Day 1773 this is Atrue and Perfect
Invetary of the Goods and Chattes of Elknah
Shaw Aprised by us this day And In the year
of our Lord Abuue writen ———————— £: s: D
Purse And Aperel ———————————— 2:2:0
One Close praser ———————————— 0:12:0
towo Beds and beding ————————— 2:0:0
One pare of Lomes ————————————— 1=5=0
two Chisls —————————————————— 0=12:0
One Clock ———————————————————— 1=10:0
One Couch Chear ——————————————— 0=11:0
One Coberd ————————————————————— 0=9:0
one table ——————————————————————— 0=5=0
One Chist ————————————————————————— 0=5=0
five Chears and five Stoles ————————— 0:5=0
One Little table one Boiler pot ———————— 0=4=0
One Range and Coulrake and tangs
and Endirns —————————————————— 0=10=0
for wone tenter ——————————————— 1=10=0
for wool Died and un Died ——————— 30=0=0
for Six pieces ——————————————————— 18=0=0
for pots and all huslement —————————— 0=10=0
                                        ———————
                                        60 10 0

Samll Haigh
Do Hiles
Joshua Wrigley juner
Joseph Campinot

huslement = hustlement – an obsolete word meaning 'household goods' or simply 'lumber'.
A *tenter* was 'a wooden framework on which cloth is stretched after being milled, so that it may set or dry evenly and without shrinking'. The word survives in the phrase *on tenterhooks*.

Transcription				MnE spelling			
November 20 Day 1773 this is a true and Perfect				November 20th Day 1773 This is a true and perfect			
Invetary of the Goods and Chatles of Elknah				inventory of the goods and chattels of Elkanah			
Shaw aprised by us this day and in the year				Shaw apprised by us this day and in the year			
of our Lord abuue writen	£=	S=	D	of our Lord above written	£=	s=	d
Purse and Aperel	2 =	2=	0	purse and apparel	2 =	2=	0
One close praser	0=12=		0	one clothes press	0=12=		0
towo Beds and beding	2 =	0=	0	two beds and bedding	2 =	0=	0
one pare of Lomes	1 = 5		=0	one pair of looms	1 = 5		=0
two Chists	0=12=		0	two chests	0=12=		0
one Clock	0=10		=0	one clock	0=10		=0
one Couch Chear	0=11		=0	one couch chair	0=11		=0
one Coberd	0= 9		=0	one cupboard	0= 9		=0
one table	0= 5		=0	one table	0= 5		=0
one Chist	0= 5		=0	one chest	0= 5		=0
five Chears and five Stoles	0= 5		=0	five chairs and five stools	0= 5		=0
one Litle table one Boiler pot	0= 4		=0	one little table and boiler pot	0= 4		=0
one Range and Coulrake and tangs				one range and coal-rake and tongs			
and Endirns	0=10		=0	and andirons	0=10		=0
for wone tenter	1=10		=0	for one tenter	1=10		=0
for Wool Died and un Died	30 = 0		=0	for wool dyed and undyed	30 = 0		=0
for Six pieces	18 = 0		=0	for six pieces	18 = 0		=0
for pots and all huslement	0=10		=0	for pots and all hustlement	0=10		=0
	60 =10		=0		60 =10		=0
Saml Haigh				Saml Haigh			
Joshua Wrigley				Joshua Wrigley			
Joshua Wrigley junor				Joshua Wrigley junior			
Joseph Campinot				Joseph Campinot			

The evidence of the quotations in section 19.6 suggests that if the language of the common people was regarded as inferior by the educated upper classes in the 18th century, then their ideas and thoughts would be similarly devalued.

> The beſt Expreſſions grow **low and degenrate,** when **profan'd by the populace,** and applied to **mean things.** The uſe they make of them, infecting them with a **mean and abject Idea,** cauſes that we cannot uſe them without **ſullying and defiling** thoſe things, which are ſignified by them.
>
> But it is no hard matter to diſcern between **the depraved Language of common People,** and **the noble refin'd expreſſions of the Gentry,** whoſe condition and merits have advanced them above the other.
>
> (*Art of Speaking, rendered into English from the French of Messieurs du Port Royal,* 1676, 2nd edn 1708)

Language was regarded as 'the dress of thought' or, to use another simple metaphor, its 'mirror'. It was believed that there was a direct relationship between good language and good thinking. On the one hand there was the dominant social class, the Gentry, whose language and way of life are variously described as *polite, civilized, elegant, noble, refined, tasteful,* and *pure.* On the other hand there were 'the laborious and mercantile part of the people', shopkeepers and hackney-coachmen, the rabble, whose language was *vulgar, barbarous, contemptible, low, degenerate, profane, mean, abject, depraved.*

This view was reinforced by a theory of language which was called 'Universal Grammar'. The following quotations illustrate a belief in the direct connection between language and the mind, or soul, and in the superior value of abstract thought over the senses. They are taken from *Hermes: or a Philosophical Inquiry concerning Language and Universal Grammar*, published in 1751 by James Harris, the author who was commended by Bishop Lowth (see Text 157):

> 'Tis a phrafe often apply'd to a man, when fpeaking, that *he fpeaks his MIND;* as much as to fay, that his Speech or Difcourfe is *a publifhing of fome Energie or Motion of his Soul.*
>
> The VULGAR merged *in Senfe* from their earlieft Infancy, and never once dreaming any thing to be worthy of purfuit, but what pampers their Appetite, or fills their Purfe, imagine nothing to be *real,* but what may be *tafted,* or *touched.*

For students of language today, the differences between Standard English and regional dialects are seen to be *linguistically* superficial and unimportant. You can convey the same meanings as well in one as the other, although we cannot, in everyday life, ignore the social connotations of regional and nonstandard speech, which are still very powerful in conveying and maintaining attitudes.

In the 18th century, the linguistic differences between refined and common speech were held to match fundamental differences in intellect and morality. The gulf between the two was reinforced by the fact that education was in the 'learned languages' Latin and Greek. The classical Greek language and literature in particular were judged to be the most 'perfect':

> Now the Language of thefe Greeks was truly like themfelves; 'twas conformable to their tranfcendent and univerfal Genius.
>
> 'Twere to be wifhed, that thofe amongft us, who either write or read, with a view to employ their liberal leifure . . . 'twere to be wifhed, I fay, that the liberal (if they have any relifh for letters) would infpect the finifhed Models of *Grecian Literature* . . .
>
> (James Harris, *Hermes*, 1751)

As it was believed that the contrasts between the *refined* language of the classically educated class, and the *vulgar* language of the common people, mirrored equal differences in intellectual capabilities and also in virtue or morality, such beliefs had social and political consequences.

> The most devastating aspect of 18th century assessments of language was its philosophical justification of this notion of vulgarity.
>
> (*The Politics of Language, 1791–1819*, Olivia Smith 1984)

These social and political consequences can be demonstrated. The years of the long wars with France (1793–1815) following the French Revolution of 1789 were marked by the political oppression of popular movements for reform. Ideas about language were used to protect the government from criticism. For example, the notion of *vulgarity of language* became an excuse to dismiss a series of petitions to Parliament calling for the reform of the voting system. If the language of the 'labouring classes' was by definition inferior, incapable of expressing coherent thought, and also of dubious moral value, then it was impossible for them to use language properly in order to argue their own case.

> Liberty of speech and freedom of discussion in this House form an essential part of the constitution; but it is necessary that persons coming forward as petitioners, should address the House in decent and respectful language.
>
> (*Parliamentary Debates*, xxx.779)

Here are short extracts from three petitions presented to Parliament. The first was presented by 'tradesmen and artificers, unpossessed of freehold land', in Sheffield in 1793, and was rejected; the second, by 'twelve freeholders' from Reading in 1810, was accepted; the third was presented by non-voters from Yorkshire in 1817. At that time, only men who owned freehold land had the vote.

Activity 19.6

(i) Discuss the charge that the language of the first petition was 'indecent and disrespectful', and compare it with another comment made at the time: 'I suspect that the objection to the roughness of the language was not the real cause why this petition was opposed'.

(ii) Discuss the view expressed in Parliament at the time that the language of the second petition, 'though firm as it ought to be, was respectful'.

(iii) The Tory minister George Canning said of the third petition, 'if such language were tolerated, there was an end of the House of Commons, and of the present system of government'. What is objectionable in the language?

Text 165: *From a Petition to Parliament, 1793*

> Your petitioners are lovers of peace, of liberty, and justice. They are in general tradesmen and artificers, unpossessed of freehold land, and consequently have no voice in choosing members to sit in parliament; – but though they may not be freeholders, they are men, and do not think themselves fairly used in being excluded the rights of citizens . . .
>
> (*Parliamentary Debates*, xxx.776)

Text 166: *From a Petition to Parliament, 1810*

> The petitioners cannot conceive it possible that his Majesty's present incapable and arbitrary ministers should be still permitted to carry on the government of the country, after having wasted our resources in fruitless expeditions, and having shewn no vigour but in support of antiquated prejudices, and in attacks upon the liberties of the subject.
>
> (*Parliamentary Debates*, xvi.955)

Text 167: From a Petition to Parliament, 1817

> The petitioners have a full and immovable conviction, a conviction which they believe to be universal throughout the kingdom, that the House doth not, in any consitutional or rational sense, represent the nation; that, when the people have ceased to be represented, the constitution is subverted; that taxation without representation is slavery ...
>
> (*Parliamentary Debates*, xxxv.81–2)

(Texts 165–7 are quoted in Olivia Smith, *The Politics of Language, 1791–1819*.)

The grammar and spelling of these extracts are perfectly 'correct', but here is an example of a letter of protest against the enclosure of common land, written anonymously by 'the Combin'd of the Parish of Cheshunt' to their local landowner. Nonstandard spelling, punctuation and grammar like this in a petition to Parliament would clearly have provided an excuse for its dismissal.

Text 168: From a letter to Oliver Cromwell Esquire, of Cheshunt Park, 27 February 1799

> Whe right these lines to you who are the Combin'd of the Parish of Cheshunt in the Defence of our Parrish rights which you unlawfully are about to disinherit us of. ... Resolutions is maid by the aforesaid Combind that if you intend of inclosing Our Commond Commond fields Lammas Meads Marches &c Whe Resolve before that bloudy and unlawful act is finished to have your hearts bloud if you proceede in the aforesaid bloudy act Whe like horse leaches will cry give, give until whe have split the bloud of every one that wishes to rob the Inosent unborn. It shall not be in your power to say I am safe from the hands of my Enemy for Whe like birds of pray will prively lie in wait to spil the bloud of the aforesaid Charicters whose names and places of abode are as prutrified sores in our Nostrils. Whe declair that thou shall not say I am safe when thou goest to thy bed for beware that thou liftest not thine eyes up in the most mist of flames ...
>
> (quoted in E. P. Thompson, *The Making of the English Working Class*, 1963)

19.9   William Cobbett and the politics of language

William Cobbett (1763–1835) was the son of a farmer from Farnham, Surrey, and self-educated. From 1785 to 1791 he served in a foot regiment in Canada, and left the army after trying, and failing, to bring some officers to trial for embezzlement. He spent the rest of his life in writing, journalism and farming, and became an MP in 1832 after the passing of the Reform Act.

Cobbett began a weekly newspaper, *The Political Register*, in 1802 as a Tory, but soon became converted to the Radical cause of social and Parliamentary reform, and wrote and edited the *Register* until his death in 1835, campaigning against social injustice and government corruption.

We have seen in section 19.8 how the concept of vulgarity of language was used to deny the value of the meaning and content of petitions to Parliament. Cobbett referred to this in an edition of *The Political Register* which was written in America, where he had gone after the suspension of *habeas corpus* in England.

Text 169: William Cobbett, The Political Register, 29 November 1817

The present project . . . is to communicate to all uneducated Reformers, *a knowledge of Grammar*. The people, you know, were accused of presenting petitions *not grammatically correct*. And those petitions were *rejected*, the petitioners being *'ignorant'*: though some of them were afterwards *put into prison*, for being 'better informed'. . . .

No doubt remains in my mind, that there was more talent discovered, and more political knowledge, by the leaders amongst the Reformers, than have ever been shown, at any period of time, by the Members of the two houses of parliament.

There was only one thing in which any of you were deficient, and that was in the mere art of so arranging the words in your Resolutions and Petitions as to make these compositions what is called *grammatically correct*. Hence, men of a hundredth part of the mind of some of the authors of the Petitions were enabled to cavil at them on this account, and to infer from this incorrectness, that the Petitioners were a set of *poor ignorant creatures*, who knew nothing of what they were talking; a set of the *'Lower Classes'*, who ought never to raise their reading above that of children's books, Christmas Carrols, and the like.

For my part, I have always held a mere knowledge of the rules of grammar very cheap. It is a study, which demands hardly any powers of mind. To possess a knowledge of those rules is a pitiful qualification. . . .

Grammar is to literary composition what a linch-pin is to a waggon. It is a poor pitiful thing in itself; it bears no part of the weight; adds not in the least to the celerity; but, still the waggon cannot very well and safely go on without it. . . .

Therefore, trifling, and even contemptible, as this branch of knowledge is *in itself*, it is of vast importance as to the means of giving to the great powers of the mind their proper effect. . . . The grammarian from whom a man of genius learns his rules has little more claim to a share of such a man's renown than has the goose, who yields the pens with which he writes: but, still the pens are *necessary*, and so is the grammar.

Cobbett's writings, like Tom Paine's *The Rights of Man* in 1792 and *The Age of Reason* in 1794, were themselves practical proof that the language of men of humble class origins could be effective in argument, but both Cobbett and Paine wrote in Standard English. Cobbett was well aware of the social connotations of nonstandard language, and wrote an account of how he had taught himself correct grammar. He does not use the term *standard* himself, and follows the common practice of implying that only this variety of English has *grammar*. He wrote under the name *Peter Porcupine*.

Text 170: William Cobbett, The Life and Adventures of Peter Porcupine, 1796

One branch of learning, however, I went to the bottom with, and that the most essential branch too, the grammar of my mother tongue. I had experienced the want of a knowledge of grammar during my stay with Mr Holland; but it is very probable that I never should have thought of encountering the study of it, had not accident placed me under a man whose friendship extended beyond his interest. Writing a fair hand procured me the honour of being copyist to Colonel Debeig, the commandant of the garrison. . . .

Being totally ignorant of the rules of grammar, I necessarily made many mistakes in copying, because no one can copy letter by letter, nor even word by word. The colonel saw my deficiency, and strongly recommended study. He enforced his advice with a sort of injunction, and with a promise of reward in case of success.

I procured me a Lowth's grammar, and applied myself to the study of it with unceasing assiduity, and not without some profit; for, though it was a considerable time before I fully comprehended all that I read, still I read and studied with such unremitted attention, that, at last, I could write without falling into any very gross errors. The pains I took cannot be described: I wrote the whole grammar out two or three times; I got it by heart; I repeated it every morning and every evening, and, when on guard, I imposed on myself the task of saying it all over once every time I was posted sentinel. To this exercise of my memory I ascribe the retentiveness of which I have since found it capable, and to the success with which it was attended, I ascribe the perseverance that has led to the acquirement of the little learning of which I am the master.

Cobbett was thus convinced of the need for mastering standard grammar:

Without understanding this, you can never hope to become fit for anything beyond mere trade or agriculture. . . . Without a knowledge of grammar, it is impossible for you to write correctly; and, it is by mere accident that you speak correctly; and, pray bear in mind, that all well-informed persons judge of a man's mind (until they have other means of judging) by his writing or speaking.

(William Cobbett, *Advice to Young Men*)

He followed up his conviction by himself writing a grammar book, in the form of a series of letters addressed to his son.

Text 171: William Cobbett, A Grammar of the English Language, 1817

. . . grammar teaches us *how to make use of words* . . . to the acquiring of this branch of knowledge, my dear son, there is one motive, which, though it ought, at all times, to be strongly felt, ought, at the present time, to be so felt in an extraordinary degree: I mean that desire which every man, and especially every young man, should entertain to be able to assert with effect the rights and liberties of his country.

(Introduction)

> And when we hear a Hampshire plough-boy say, 'Poll Cherrycheek have giv'd
> I thick handkercher,' we know very well that he *means* to say, 'Poll Cherrycheek
> has given me this handkerchief:' and yet, we are but too apt to *laugh at him*, and
> to call him *ignorant*; which is wrong; because he has no pretensions to a
> knowledge of grammar, and he may be very skilful as a plough-boy.
>
> (Letter xvii)

Cobbett is himself conditioned by 18th-century notions of language when he says,
'what he *means* to say . . .'. Both sentences *mean* the same, but their differences of
expression have social connotations. We would prefer to identify and describe both
versions of the sentence as dialectal, each making different choices from the available
variants of the grammar of verbs and personal pronouns (*has given/have giv'd; me/I*),
with the ploughboy using an alternative form, *thick*, for *this*, described in the *Oxford
English Dictionary* as follows:

> thilk (archaic and dialectal), from ME. þilke
> thick is in dialect use from Cornwall and Hants to Worcester and Hereford; and also
> in Pembroke, Glamorgan, and Wexford. In many parts it has also the form *thicky*,
> *thickee*, or *thicka*. It generally means *that*, but in some parts *this* . . .

'Cobbett considered grammar, in short, as an integral part of the class structure of
England, and the act of learning grammar by one of his readers as an act of class
warfare' (Olivia Smith, *The Politics of Language, 1791–1819*).

This conclusion can be inferred from Cobbett's allusions to his own learning of
standard grammar from Lowth's *Grammar* (see section 19.5), such as shown in the
extract from *The Political Register* on p. 414.

There appear to be no significant differences in the grammar of Cobbett's writing
that separate today's language from the English of the early 19th century. What we
now call Standard English (Cobbett's *knowledge of grammar*) has been established for
over 200 years as the only form of the language for writing which obtains universal
acceptance.

This seems to contradict the linguistic statement that 'all living languages are in
a constant state of change'. But the grammatical innovations since Cobbett's day are
developments of established features, rather than fundamental changes. Once a
standard form of writing becomes the norm, then the rate of change in the grammar
is slowed down considerably. At the same time, additions and losses to the
vocabulary, and modifications in pronunciation, inevitably continue.

Text 172: William Cobbett, The Political Register, 6 December 1817 (facsimile)

Vol. 32, No. 35.---Price Two Pence.

COBBETT'S WEEKLY POLITICAL PAMPHLET

[089]   LONDON, SATURDAY, DECEMBER 6. 1817.   [1090

I have gone into detail as to this anecdote in order to show what power a knowledge of grammar gives to man. During the whole of my military life, I owed even my safety to it; and, it is that, and that alone, which enabled me to pursue and acquire knowledge of a higher order; and, every young man who shall read what I am now writing may be assured, that he can never arrive at fame; that he can never obtain and retain any great degree of influence over the minds of other men, unless he be possessed of this branch of knowledge, which, as I said before, though, *in itself*, contemptible, is the key to all the means of communicating our thoughts to others. It is by the possession of this knowledge, that, sitting here in Long Island, I am able to tell you in England, what I think; and it is the possession of this knowledge by me, that has driven the Boroughmongers to those acts of desperation, which will end in their ruin. It is very true, that *all* men are not born with the same degree of capacity for acquiring knowledge. But, nature has been too fair to give all the capacity to the Aristocracy

19.10   18th-century loan-words

A selection of loan-words recorded during this period can be found in the Word Book, after the word-lists for Chapter 19.

20 From Old English to Modern English – comparing historical texts

It should be easier for you now to recognise texts from different historical periods of the language, and to describe how they differ from contemporary English. A very short example will illustrate this. It is the first verse from chapter 3 of the Book of Genesis, and illustrates some of the changes in the language from OE to MnE which have been described.

Text 173: Genesis, chapter 3, verse 1

Late 10th-century Old English

CE 1

> eac ꞅƿylce ꞅeo næððꞃe þær ᵹeapꞃe þonne ealle þa oðꞃe nyꞇenu þe ᵹoð ᵹepoꞃhꞇe oꝼeꞃ eoꞃþan. anð ꞅeo næððꞃe cꝧæþ ꞇo þam ƿiꝼe. hꝑ ꝼoꞃbeað ᵹoð eoꝛ þæꞇ ᵹe ne æꞇon oꝼ ælcon ꞇꞃeoꝑe binnan paꞃaðiꞃum.

eac swylce seo næddre wæs geapre þonne ealle þa oðre nytenu þe God geworhte ofer eorþan. and seo næddre cwæþ to þam wife. hwi forbead God eow þæt ge ne æton of ælcon treowe binnan paradisum.

Late 14th-century Middle English

CE 2

> But the serpent was feller than alle lyuynge beestis of erthe which the Lord God hadde maad. Which serpent seide to the womman Why comaundide God to ȝou that ȝe schulden not ete of ech tre of paradis.

But the serpent was feller than alle lyuynge beestis of erthe which the Lord God hadde maad. Which serpent seide to the womman Why comaundide God to ȝou that ȝe schulden not ete of ech tre of paradis.

1611 Early Modern English

> NOw the serpent was more subtill then any beast of the field, which the L O R D God had made, and he said vnto the woman, † Yea, hath God said, Ye shall not eate of euery tree of the garden?

1961 Modern English

> The serpent was more crafty than any wild creature that the LORD God had made. He said to the woman, 'Is it true that God has forbidden you to eat from any tree in the garden?'

20.1 Commentary on Text 173

The following detailed description of the extracts gives a pattern which can be applied to the comparison of any two or more texts.

Make a series of columns, one for each text, and an extra one to record any reflexes of the older words which have survived into MnE but are not used in later translations. Write down the equivalent words or phrases from each text:

1 OE	2 ME	3 EMnE 1611	4 MnE 1961	MnE reflex
eac swylce	but	now	–	such
seo næddre	the serpent	the serpent	the serpent	the adder
wæs	was	was	was	was
geapre	feller	more subtill	more crafty	–
þonne	than	then	than	than
ealle	alle	any	any	all
þa oðre	–	any	any	the other
–	lyuinge	–	–	living
nytenu	beestis	beast	wild creature	neat (*archaic*)
þe	which	which	that	–
God	the Lord God	the Lord God	the LORD God	God
geworhte	hadde maad	had made	had made	wrought
ofer eorþan	of erthe	of the field	wild	over earth
and	–	and	–	and
seo næddre	which serpent	he	he	the adder
cwæþ	seide	said	said	quoth
to þam wife	to the woman	vnto the woman	to the woman	wife
hwi	why	–	–	why
forbead	comaundide	hath . . . said	has forbidden	forbade
eow	ʒou	–	you	you
þæt	that	–	–	that
ge	ʒe	ye	you	(ye)
ne	not	not	–	–
æton	ete	eat	eat	eat
of ælcon treowe	of ech tre	of euery tree	from any tree	of each tree
binnan paradisum	of paradis	of the garden	in the garden	paradise

This table can then be used as data to describe some of the linguistic features of the texts.

1 Vocabulary

Have any words changed meaning?

- OE *næddre* meant *snake, serpent,* and is now restricted to one type of snake, the *adder.*
- OE *wif* meant *woman,* but had a more restricted meaning in ME and after.
- OE *geworhte (wrought)* is the past tense of *gewyrcan (to work, make).* Today, *wrought* is used in a specialised sense, and the past tense of *work* is *worked.*

Have any older words been lost from the language?

- OE *eac, geapre, nytenu* (plural of *nyten* = *animal*), and *binnan* are not in the vocabulary of MnE.
- OE *swylce* = MnE *such,* but is used in the phrase *eac swylce* to mean *also, moreover.*
- OE *cwæþ, quoth* is the past tense of *cweþan, to say.* We no longer use *quoth,* an archaic form, but it was used into the 19th century. The present tense *quethe* was in use up to the early 16th century, but is now obsolete.

2 Orthography

Are there any unusual letter forms?

(see section 3.2 on insular book hand letter shapes.)

- ⟨þ⟩, ⟨ȝ⟩/⟨ȝ⟩ and ⟨ð⟩ are not Roman letters.

Can you tell if different spellings of the same word are due to sound changes, or simply different spelling conventions?

- Some spelling conventions must have changed after the OE period, e.g.

    (i)   ⟨qu-⟩ replaced ⟨cp-⟩/⟨cw-⟩, as in OE *cpæþ/cwæþ.*
    (ii) ⟨y⟩ and ⟨i⟩ were often interchangeable in ME and EMnE, e.g. *lyuynge, seide, sayd, sotyller, subtill.*
    (iii) The word *ye* is an abbreviation in EMnE for *the,* the letter ⟨y⟩ standing for the OE letter ⟨þ⟩, MnE ⟨th⟩.
    (iv) ⟨v⟩ in ⟨vnto⟩ – letter ⟨v⟩ was introduced during the ME period, and written for both the consonant [v] and the vowel [u] at the beginning of a word (word-initial), e.g. *verily, vnder;* letter ⟨u⟩ was used in the middle (word-medial) or at the end of a word (word-final), e.g. *lyuynge, vndur* (= under), *dust, thou.* They were then variant forms of the same letter, just as today we use upper and lower case variants of the same letters, e.g. ⟨A⟩, ⟨a⟩, ⟨ɑ⟩.

- The spelling is evidence of some sound changes which occurred after the OE period.

    (i)   The word *næddre* in OE now has the form *adder,* as well as becoming restricted in meaning. The pronunciation of the phrase *a nadder* is identical to that of *an adder.* The indefinite article *a/an* was not part of OE grammar, so the change of *nadder* to *adder* came later, between the 14th and 16th centuries. The dialectal form *nedder* was still in use at least into the 19th century.

(ii) The diphthong vowels of *ealle, eorþan, forbead* and *treowe* have smoothed to become single vowels.

It is not possible to recognise all the sound changes from spelling alone, because MnE spelling does not reflect them; for example, the MnE pronunciation of *was* is [wɒz] but the spelling has not changed since its earlier pronunciation as [wæs].

3 Word structure

Are there changes in word-suffixes (endings)?

- The order of the consonants *re* and *or* of *næddre* and *geworhte* has changed to *er* and *ro*. Other examples are *bird, thresh,* and *run,* which come from OE *brid, þerscan* and *yrnan.* The linguistic term for this reversal of sounds is **metathesis**.
- The pronoun *oðr-e,* however, is not an example of this. It is a shortened form of *oþer-e,* from *oðer,* and *-e* is a suffix.
- The suffixes on *eall-e, nyten-u, geworht-e, eorþ-an* have been lost.
- The plural *beest-is* has been reduced to *beast-s.*

4 Grammar

Is the OE word-order different from MnE?

- *hwi forbead god eow – why forbade God you*: the **interrogative** in OE was formed by reversing the order of subject and verb, which is no longer grammatical for the simple present and past tenses in MnE except for the simple past or present of *have* or *be*.
- *þæt ge ne æton - that ye ne eat*: the **negative** in OE was formed by placing *ne* before the verb. During the ME period a reinforcing *noght* was added after the verb; *not* is now the only negative marker, *ne* having been dropped.

20.2 'Your accent gives you away!'

The following texts are historical translations of the same story of Peter's denial, from the New Testament, St Matthew's Gospel, chapter 26, verses 69–75.

Activity 20.1

Make a contrastive study of the language, using the texts as evidence of some of the principal changes that have taken place since the Old English period in vocabulary, word and sentence structure, spelling and pronunciation.

Text 174: Late West Saxon Old English, c.1050

'þyn spræc þe gesweotolað'

69 petꞃuſ ſoðlice ſæt ute on þam caꝼeꞃtune. þa com to hȳm an þeopen ⁊ cpæð. ⁊ þu pæꞃe myð þam ȝalıleıꞃcan hælenðe. 70 ⁊ he pȳðꞃoc beꝼoꞃan eallum ⁊ cpæð. nat ıc hpæt þu ꞃeȝꞃt. 71 þa he ut eoðe oꝼ þæꞃe ðuꞃa. þa ȝeꞃeh hȳne oðeꞃ þȳnen. ⁊ ꞃæðe þam ðe þaꞃ pæꞃon. ⁊ þeſ pæꞃ myð þam nazaꞃenıꞃcan hælenðe. 72 ⁊ he pȳðꞃoc eꝼt myð aðe þæt he hȳꞃ nan þȳng ne cuðe. 73 þa æꝼteꞃ lȳtlum ꝼȳꞃꞃte ȝenealæhton þa ðe þæꞃ ꞃtoðon. ⁊ cpæðon to petꞃe. ſoðlice þu eaꞃt oꝼ hȳm. ⁊ þȳn ꞃpꞃæc þe ȝeꞃpeotolað. 74 þa ætꞃoc he ⁊ ꞃpeꞃeðe. þæt he næꝼꞃe þone man ne cuðe. ⁊ hꞃæðlice þa cꞃeop ꞃe cocc. 75 ða ȝemunðe petꞃuſ þæꞃ hælenðeſ poꞃð þe he cpæð. æꞃþam þe ꞃe cocc cꞃape. þꞃȳpa ðu me pȳðꞃæcꞃt. ⁊ he eoðe ut ⁊ peop bȳteꞃlice.

69 petrus soðlice sæt ute on þam cafertune. þa com to hym an þeowen ⁊ cwæð. ⁊ þu wære myd þam galileiscan hælende. 70 ⁊ he wyðsoc beforan eallum ⁊ cwæð. nat ic hwæt þu segst. 71 þa he ut eode of þære dura. þa geseh hyne oðer þynen. ⁊ sæde þam ðe þar wæron. ⁊ þes wæs myd þam nazareniscan hælende. 72 ⁊ he wyðsoc eft myd aðe þæt he hys nan þyng ne cuðe. 73 þa æfter lytlum fyrste genealæhton þa ðe þær stodon. ⁊ cwædon to petre. Soðlice þu eart of hym. ⁊ þyn spræc þe gesweotolað. 74 þa ætsoc he ⁊ swerede. þæt he næfre þone man ne cuðe. ⁊ hrædlice þa creow se cocc. 75 ða gemunde petrus þæs hælendes word þe he cwæð. ærþam þe se cocc crawe. þrywa ðu me wyðsæcst. ⁊ he eode ut ⁊ weop byterlice.

WW

69 Peter truly sat out(side) in the courtyard. then came to him a servant & said. & thou wast with the galilean saviour. 70 & he denied before all & said. ne-know I what thou sayest. 71 when he out went of the door. then saw him other servant.& said to-them that there were. & this (man) was with the nazarean saviour. 72 & he denied again with oath that he of-him no thing ne-knew. 73 when after little time approached they that there stood. & said to peter. Truly thou art of him. & thy speech thee shows. 74 then denied he & swore. that he never the man ne knew. & immediately then crew the cock. 75 then remembered peter the saviour's words that he spoke. before that the cock crows thrice thou me deniest. & he went out & wept bitterly.

Text 175: 14th-century South Midlands dialect (the Wycliffite Bible)

'thi speche makith thee knowun'

69 And Petir sat with outen in the halle; and a damysel cam to hym, and seide, Thou were with Jhesu of Galilee. 70 And he denyede bifor alle men, and seide, Y woot not what thou seist. 71 And whanne he ȝede out at the ȝate, another damysel say hym, and seide to hem that weren there, And this was with Jhesu of Nazareth. 72 And eftsoone he denyede with an ooth, For I knewe not the man. 73 And a litil aftir, thei that stooden camen, and seiden to Petir, treuli thou art of hem; for thi speche makith thee knowun. 74 Thanne he bigan to warie and to swere, that he knewe not the man. And anoon the cok crewe. 75 And Petir bithouȝte on the word of Jhesu, that he hadde seid, Bifore the cok crowe, thries thou schalt denye me. And he ȝede out, and wepte bitterli.

Text 176: Early 16th-century Scots, c.1520

(This Scots version was made from Text 175, and is of interest because it makes clear some of the dialectal differences between Scots and Wyclif's Midland dialect.)

'thi speche makis thee knawne'

69 Ande Petir sat without in the hall: and a damycele com to him, and said, Thou was with Jesu of Galilee. 70 And he denyit before al men, and said, I wate nocht quhat thou sais. 71 And quhen he yede out at the yet, an vthir damycele saw him, and said to thame that ware thar, And this was with Jesu of Nazarethe. 72 And eftsone he denyit with ane athe, For I knew nocht the man. 73 And a litil eftir thai that stude com and said to Petir, treulie thou art of thame; for thi speche makis thee knawne. 74 Than he began to warie and to suere that he knew nocht the man. And anon the cok crew. 75 And Petir bethouchte on the word of Jesu, that he had said, Before the cok craw, thrijse thou sal denye me. And he yede out, and wepit bittirlie.

Text 177: Early Modern English (the Rheims Bible, 1582)

'for euen thy speache doth bevvray thee'

† But Peter sate vvithout in the court: and there came to 69 him one" vvenche, saying: Thou also vvast vvith I E S V S the Galilean. † But he denied before them all, saying, I vvot not 70 vvhat thou sayest. † And as he vvent out of the gate, an other 71 vvenche savv him, and she saith to them that vvere there, And this felovv also vvas vvith I E S V S the Nazarite. † And 72 againe he denied vvith an othe, That I knovv not the man. † And after a litle they came that stoode by, and said to Peter, 73 Surely thou also art of them: for euen thy speache doth be-vvray thee. † Then he began" to curse and to svveare that 74 he knevve not the man. And incontinent the cocke crevve. † And Peter remembred the vvord of I E S V S vvhich he had 75 said, Before the cocke crovv, thou shalt deny me thrise. And going forth, "he vvept bitterly.

Text 178: Early Modern English (King James Bible, 1611)

'for thy speech bewrayeth thee'

69 ❡ * Now Peter sate without in the palace: and a damosell came vnto him, saying, Thou also wast with Iesus of Galilee.

70 But he denied before them all, saying, I know not what thou sayest.

71 And when he was gone out into the porch, another maid saw him, and said vnto them that were there, This fellow was also with Iesus of Nazareth.

72 And againe he denied with an oath, I doe not know the man.

73 And after a while came vnto him, they that stood by, and said vnto Peter, Surely thou also art one of them, for thy speech bewrayeth thee.

74 Then began hee to curse and to sweare, saying, I know not the man. And immediatly the cocke crew.

75 And Peter remembred the words of Iesus, which said vnto him, Before the Cocke crow, thou shalt deny me thrice. And hee went out, and wept bitterly.

Text 179: 20th-century Scots

"your Galilee twang outs ye"

MEANTIME, PETER WIS sittin furth i the close, whan a servan-queyn cam up an said til him, "Ye war wi the man frae Galilee, Jesus, tae, I'm thinkin."

But he denied it afore them aa: "I kenna what ye mean," said he; an wi that he gaed out intil the pend.

Here anither servan-lass saw him an said tae the fowk staundin about, "This chiel wis wi yon Nazaraean Jesus."

Again Peter wadna tak wi it, but said wi an aith, "I kenna the man!"

A wee efter, the staunders-by gaed up til him an said, "Ay, but ye war sae wi him, tae: your Galilee twang outs ye."

At that he fell tae bannin an sweirin at he hed nae kennins o the man avà. An than a cock crew, an it cam back tae Peter hou Jesus hed said til him, "Afore the cock craws, ye will disavou me thrice"; an he gaed out an grat a sair, sair greit.

(*The New Testament in Scots*, translated by William Laughton Lorimer, 1985)

Standard English version

69   Meantime, Peter was sitting forth (*outside*) in the close (*courtyard*) when a servant-quean (*girl*) came up and said to him, 'You were with the man from Galilee, Jesus, too, I'm thinking.' 70   But he denied it before them all: 'I ken not (*know not*) what you mean,' said he; 71   and with that he goed (*went*) out into the entry.

Here another servant-lass saw him and said to the folk standing about, 'This child (*fellow*) was with yon Nazarean Jesus.' 72   Again Peter would not take with (*admit to*) it, but said with an oath, 'I ken not the man!' 73   A wee (*little*) after, the standers-by goed (*went*) up to him and said, 'Aye (*yes*), but you were so (*indeed*) with him, too: your Galilee twang (*accent*) outs you (*gives you away*). 74   At that he fell to banning (*cursing*) and swearing that he had no kennings (*knowledge*) of the man of all (*at all*) (cf Fr *du tout*). And then a cock crew, 75   and it came back to Peter how Jesus had said to him, 'Before the cock crows, you will disavow me thrice'; and he goed (*went*) out and greeted (*wept*) a sore, sore (*sorrowful*) greet (*weep*).

Text 180: Modern English (New English Bible, 1961)

'Your accent gives you away!'

69   Meanwhile Peter was sitting outside in the courtyard when a serving-maid accosted him and said, 'You were there too with Jesus the Galilean.' 70   Peter denied it in face of them all. 'I do not know what you mean', he said. 71   He then went out to the gateway, where another girl, seeing him, said to the people there, 'This fellow was with Jesus of Nazareth.' 72   Once again he denied it, saying with an oath, 'I do not know the man.' 73   Shortly afterwards the bystanders came up and said to Peter, 'Surely you are another of them; your accent gives you away!' 74   At this he broke into curses and declared with an oath: 'I do not know the man.' 75   At that moment a cock crew; and Peter remembered how Jesus had said, 'Before the cock crows you will disown me three times.' He went outside, and wept bitterly.

Finally, the same Biblical extract in Bislama, a pidgin language based on English, from Vanuatu (formerly the New Hebrides) in the West Pacific. Read it aloud as if it were in phonetic script, because the spelling system is based upon the spoken language, and you should be able to match the sense with the preceding texts. For example, *yad* is pronounced [yɑːd], like English *yard*, *get* is /geːt/, like *gate*, *rusta* like *rooster*, and *save* is a two-syllable word like *savvy*, meaning *know*.

Text 181: Bislama (Gud Nyus Bilong Jisas Krais, 1971)

(Bislama is written in a phonemic script.)

'tok bilong yu i tok bilong man Galili ia'

Bislama	*Standard English version*
Pita i stap sidaon aofsaid long yad bilong haos ia.	Peter sat down outside in the yard of the house
Nao wan haosgel i kam long em, i talem long em, i se	And a house-girl came to him, spoke to him & said
'Yu tu, yu stap wetem man Galili ia, Jisas.'	'You too, you were with the Galilean, Jesus.'
Be long fes bilong olgeta evrewan, Pita i haidem samting ia.	But in front of everybody, Peter denied this.
Em i ansa, i se	He answered
'Mi mi no save samting ia, we yu yu stap talem.'	'I don't know what you are talking about.'
Nao em i goaot long get bilong yad ia.	And he went out through the gate of the yard.
Nao wan narafala gel i lukem em.	Then another girl saw him.
Nao i talem long ol man we oli stap stanap long ples ia, i se	And she spoke to the people who were standing about in that place.
'Man ia i wetem man Naseret ia, Jisas.'	'This man was with the Nazarean, Jesus.'
Be Pita i haidem bakegen, i mekem strong tok, nao em i talem se 'Mi mi no save man ia.'	But Peter denied it again, vigorously, and said 'I don't know the man.'
Gogo smol taem nomo, ol man ia we oli stap stanap long ples ia,	After a little while, the people who were standing about in that place
oli kam long Pita, oli talem long em, oli se,	came to Peter and said to him,
'Be i tru ia, yu yu wan long olgeta.	'But it's true, you are one of them.
Yu luk, tok bilong yu i tok bilong man Galili ia.'	Look! your speech is the speech of a Galilean.'
Nao Pita i mekem tok we i strong moa, i se	And Peter denied it again,
'Sipos mi mi gyaman, bambae God i givem panis long mi.	'If I'm a liar, God will punish me.
Mi mi no save man ia'	I don't know that man.'
Nao wantaem rusta i singaot.	Then straight away a rooster crowed.
Nao Pita i tingabaot tok ia we Jisas i bin talem long em, i se	And Peter thought about the talk that Jesus had said to him
'Taem rusta i no singaot yet, yu, be bambae yu save haidem tri taem, se yu no save mi'	'Before the cock crows, you will deny (me) three times, say you don't know me.'
Nao em i go aofsaid, em i kraekrae tumas.	And he went outside and cried much.

Texts 174–81 are recorded on the CD/cassette tape.

IPA transcription of Text 174: Late West Saxon Old English, c.1050

petrus soːθliːtʃə sæt uːtə ɔn ðaːm kɑːvərtuːnə. ðɑː coːm toː hɪm ɑːn ðɛːəwən and kwæθ, 'and ðuː wæːrə mɪd ðaːm galɪleːɪʃən hæːləndə' and heː wɪðsoːk bevoːrən æələm and kwæθ 'nɑːt ɪʃ hwæt ðuː seɪst' ðɑː heː uːt eːədə ɔf ðæːrə durə. ðɑː jəzej hɪnə oːðər ðyːnən, and zæːdə ðaːm ðe ðaːr wæːrən, 'ɑːnd ðes wæs mɪd ðaːm nazarenɪʃən hæːlende' and heː wɪðsoːk ɛft mɪd ɑːðə θæt heː hɪs nɑːn ðɪŋg nə kuːðə. ðɑː æftər lyːtləm fɪrstə jəneːəlæːçtən ðɑː ðɛ ðæːr stoːdən, and kwæːdən toː petrə, 'soːðliːtʃə ðuː

æərt ɔf hɪm, and ðiːn spræːtʃ ðeː jəsweətəlaθ' ðaː ætsoːk heː and swɛrədə ðæt heː næːvrə ðɔnə man nɛ kuːðə, and hrædliːtʃə ðaː kreːəw sɛ kɔk. ðaː jəmundə pɛtrus ðæs hæːləndəs wɔrd ðɛ heː kwæːθ, 'æːrðam ðɛ sɛ kɔk kraːwə, ðryːwa ðuː meː wɪðzækst' and heː eːədə uːt. and weːəp bɪtərliːtʃə.

IPA transcription of Text 175: 14th-century South Midlands dialect

and peːtər sæt wɪðuːtən ɪn ðə halə and a daməzəl caːm to hɪm and sɛːɪdə, 'ðuː wɛːrə wɪð ʒeːzu ɒv gælɪleː' and heː dəniədə bɪvoːr al mɛn, and sɛɪdə, 'iː woːt nɒt hwat ðuː sɛɪst'. and hwanə heː jeːdə uːt æt ðə jaːtə, ənoːðər daməzəl saɪ hɪm, and sɛːdə to hɛm ðat weːrən ðɛːrə, and ðɪs was wɪð ʒeːzu ɒv næzæreθ'. and ɛftsoːnə heː dəniədə wɪð an ɔːθ, 'fɔr iː kneːwə nɒt ðə man'. and ə lɪtəl æftər, ðɛɪ ðæt stɔːdən caːmən, and seɪdən to peːtər, 'trɛʊli ðuː art ɒv hɛm, fɔr ðiː speːtʃə maːkəθ ðeː knɔːwən'. ðanə he bɪgan to waːriə and to sweːrə, ðat he kneːwə nɒt ðə man. and anɔːn ðə kɒk kreːwə. and peːtər bɪθɔʊxtə ɒn ðə word ɒv ʒeːzu, ðæt he hædə sɛid, 'bɪvorə ðə kɒk krɔːwə, θriːəs ðuː ʃælt dɛniə meː. and heː jeːdə uːt, and wɛptə bɪtərli.

IPA transcription of Text 176: Early 16th-century Scots, c.1520

and peːtər sæt wɪðuːt ɪ ðə hal, and ə damɪsəl cɔːm to hɪm, and said, 'ðuː was wɪθ ʒeːzu ɒv galɪleː' and heː dɛniit bɪvɔr al mɛn, and said, 'iː waːt nɒxt xwat ðuː saɪs' and xwɛn heː jeːd uːt at ðə jeːt, ənʊðer damɪsəl saʊ hɪm, and said toː ðam ðat war ðar, 'and ðɪs was wɪθ ʒeːzu ɒv nazərɛθ' and ɛftsoːn heː dɛniit wɪθ an ɛːθ, 'fɔr iː knɛʊ nɒxt ðə man' and ə lɪtəl ɛftər ðaɪ ðat stud cɔm and said to peːtər, 'trɛʊli ðuː art ɒv ðam, fɔr ði speːtʃ maks ðeː knaʊn. ðan heː bəgan to wari and to sweːr ðat heː knɛʊ nɒxt ðə man. and anɔn ðə kɒk kreːʊ. and peːtər bɛθɒʊxt ɒn ðə wɔrd ɒv ʒeːzu, ðat heː had said, 'bɛvɔr ðə kɒk kraʊ, θriːs ðuː sal dɛniː meː' and heː jeːd uːt, and weːpɪt bɪtərli:

IPA transcription of Text 177: Early Modern English, 1582

bʊt peːtər sæt wɪðəʊt ɪn ðə kɔrt ænd ðɛːr kæːm tu hɪm oːn wɛntʃ, seiɪŋg 'ðəu alsɔ wæst wɪð dʒeːzus ðə gælɪleːən'. bʊt hi dɛnəɪd bɪfɔr ðɛm al, seiɪŋg, 'əi wɒt nɒt hwæt ðəu seiɪst'. ænd æz hi wɛnt əut ɒv ðə geːt, ənʊðer wɛntʃ saʊ hɪm, ænd ʃi seɪθ tu ðɛm ðæt wɛr ðɛːr, 'ænd ðɪs fɛlɔʊ alsɔ wæs wɪð dʒeːzus ðə næzərəit'. ænd əgein hi dɛnəɪd wɪð ɒn ɔːθ, 'ðæt əi knou nɒt ðə mæn'. ænd æftər ə lɪtəl ðɛi kæːm ðæt stuːd bəi, ænd seid tu peːtər, 'sjurləi ðəu alsɔ art ɒv ðɛm, fɔr iːvən ðəi speːtʃ dʊθ bəwrei ðiː' ðɛn hi bɪgan tu kurs ænd tu sweːr ðæt hi knɪʊw nɒt ðə mæn. ænd ɪŋkɒntɪnənt ðə kɒk krɪʊw. ænd peːtər rəmɛmbərd ðə wʊrd ɒv dʒeːzus hwɪtʃ hi hæd seɪd, 'bɛfɔr ðə kɒk krɔʊ, ðəu ʃælt dɛnəɪ mi θrəis' ænd gɔɪŋg forθ, hi wɛpt bɪtərlɪ.

IPA transcription of Text 178: Early Modern English, 1611

nəʊ peːtər sɛːt wɪðəʊt ɪn ðə pæləs, ənd a dæməzəl kɛːm ʊntu hɪm, seiiŋg, 'ðəʊ also wæst wɪð ʤeːzʊs ɒv gælɪli:' bʊt hi dənəid bəvɔr ðɛm al, seiiŋg, 'əi knɔʊ nɒt hwæt ðəu seiest'. ænd hwɛn hi wæs gɒn əʊt ɪnto ðə pɔrʧ, ənʊðər meɪd sɒː hɪm, ænd seɪd ʊnto ðɛm ðæt wɛr ðɛːr, 'ðɪs fɛlɔː wæs also wɪð ʤeːzʊs əv næzərɛθ' ænd əgɛːɪn hi dənəid wɪð ən oːθ, 'əi do nɒt knɔʊ ðə mæn'. ænd æftər ə hwəil kɛːm ʊnto hɪm ðei ðæt stud bəi, ænd seɪd to peːtər, 'sjurləi ðəʊ alsɔ art oːn ɒv ðɛm, for ðəi spiːʧ bɪwrɛːɪɛθ ði'. ðɛn bɪgæn hi to kʊrs ænd to swɛːr, seiŋg, 'əi know nɒt ðə mæn'. ænd ɪmidiətli ðə kɒk krɪuː. ənd peːtər rɛmembərd ðə wʊrdz ɒv ʤezus, hwɪʧ seːɪd ʊnto hɪm, 'bəvɔːr ðə kɒk krɔː, ðəʊ ʃælt dɛnəɪ mi θrəɪs'. ænd hi wɛnt əʊt, ənd wɛpt bɪtərlɪ.

IPA transcription of Text 179: 20th-century Scots

miːntɛɪm, piːtə wəz sɪtən fʊrθ ɪ ðə klos, ʌan ə sɛˑvən kwin kam ʌp ən sɛd tɪl ɪm, ji wəˑ wɪ ðə man frɛ galɪli, ʤizəs, teː, am θɪŋkɪn.' bət hi dɪnaɪd ɪt əfor ðəm aː, 'a kɛnə ʌɒt jɪ miːn,' sɛd hiː ənd wɟ ðat hi geːd uːt ɪntɪl ðə pend. hir ənɪðə sɛˑvən-las sɔ hɪm ən sɛd tɛ ðə fok stɔndɪn əbuːt, 'ðɪs ʧiːl wəz wi jɒn næzəriən ʤizəs.' əgen piːtə wadnə tak wi ɪt, bət sɛd wi ən eːθ, 'a kɛnə ðə man'.ə wiː aftə, ðə stɔndəz baɪ geːd ʌp tɪl ɪm ən sɛd, 'aɪ, bət ji waˑ seː wi əm, teː, jəˑ galɪli twæŋ uːts ji.' æt ðæt hi fɛl tə bænɪn ən swɛːrɪn ət hi hɛd neː kɛnɪnz ə ðə man əva. ən ðan ə kɒk krʉ, ən ɪt kam bak tɛ piːtə hu ʤizəs həd sɛd tɪl ɪm, 'əfor ðə kɒk krɔːz, ji wɪl dɪsəvu mɪ θrɛɪs.' ənd hi geːd uːt ən grat ə sɛr, sɛr griːt.

IPA transcription of Text 180: Modern English

miːnwaɪl piːtə wəz sɪtɪŋ aʊtsaɪd ɪn ðə kɔːtjɑːd wɛn ə sɜːvɪŋ mɛɪd əkɒstɪd hɪm ənd sɛd, juː wɜ ðɛə tu wɪð ʤiːzəs ðə gælɪliən. piːtə dɪnaɪd ɪt ɪn fɛɪs əv ðɛm ɔːl. aɪ du nɒt nəʊ wɒt ju miːn, hi sɛd. hi ðɛn wɛnt aʊt tə ðə getwɛɪ, wɛəˑ ənʌðə gɜːl, siːɪŋ hɪm, sɛd tə ðə piːpəl ðɛə, ðɪs fɛləʊ wɒz wɪð ʤiːzəs əv næzərɛθ. wʌns əgen hi dɪnaɪd ɪt, sɛɪjɪŋ wɪð ən əʊθ, aɪ duː nɒt nəʊ ðə mæn. ʃɔːtli aftəwədz ðə baɪstændəz kɛɪm ʌp ənd sɛd tə piːtə, ʃɔːli juː ɑːˑ ənʊðəˑ əv ðɛm jɔˑ æksənt gɪvz ju əwɛɪ. æt ðɪs hi bɹəʊk ɪntə kɜːsɪz ənd dɪklɛəd wɪð ən əʊθ, aɪ du nɒt nəʊ ðə mæn. æt ðæt məʊmənt ə kɒk kruː, ənd piːtə rɪmɛmbəd haʊ ʤiːzəs hæd sɛd, bɪfɔː ðə kɒk krəʊz ju wɪl dɪsəʊn miː θriː taɪmz. hiː wɛnt aʊtsaɪd ənd wɛpt bɪtəli

IPA transcription of Text 181: Bislama, 1971

pita i stap sɪdaʊn aʊfsaɪd lɒŋ jad bɪlɒŋ haʊs ja. naʊ wan haʊsgɛl i kam lɒŋ
ɛm, i taləm lɒŋ ɛm, i se ju tu, ju stap wɛtəm man gælɪli ja, ʤizas. be lɒŋ
fes bɪlɒŋ ɒlgɛtə ɛvrɪwan, pita i haɪdəm samtɪŋ ja. ɛm i ansa, i se mi mi no
save samtɪŋ ja, wɛ ju ju stap taləm. naʊ ɛm i goaʊt lɒŋ get bɪlɒŋ jad ja.
naʊ wan narəfalə gɛl i lʊkɪm ɛm. naʊ i taləm lɒŋ ɔl man we ɔli stap stanap
lɒŋ ples ja, i se man ja i wɛtəm man nazəret ja, ʤizas be pita i haɪdəm
bakəgɛn, i mekəm strɒŋ tɒk, naʊ ɛm i taləm se mi mi no save man ja gogo
smɒl taɪm nomɔ, ɔl man ja we ɔli stap stanap lɒŋ ples ja, ɔli kam lɒŋ pita,
ɔli taləm lɒŋ ɛm, ɔli se, be i tru ja, ju ju wan lɒŋ ɔlgɛta. ju lʊk, tɒk bɪlɒŋ
ju i tɒk bɪlɒŋ man galɪli ja. naʊ pita i mekəm tɒk we i strɒŋ moa, i se sɪpoz
mi mi gjaman, baɪmbaɪ gɒd i gɪvəm panɪs lɒŋ mi. mi mi no save man ja.
naʊ wantaɪm rusta i sɪŋaʊt. naʊ pita i tɪŋəbaʊt tɒk ja we ʤizas i bɪn taləm
lɒŋ ɛm, i se taɪm rusta i no sɪŋaʊt jɛt, ju, be baɪmbaɪ ju save haɪdəm tri
taɪm, se ju no save mi naʊ ɛm i go aʊfsaɪd, ɛm i kraɪkraɪ tumas.

21 Postscript – to the present day

The object of this book has been to describe how present-day Standard English has developed from its origins in Old English a thousand years ago, and how its development effectively ends in the 18th century, since when there have been only minimal changes in the grammar of the standard language. This is not to deny that there are clear differences between the way that the language has been written and spoken in the 18th, 19th and 20th centuries. But such differences belong rather to *style* or *language use* than to the underlying *language system* . There was in the 18th century a multiplicity of spoken regional and social dialects, largely unrecorded, and this is still so.

In addition, there are today many new 'Englishes' throughout the world as a result of the spread of English as a national and international language. American, Australian, New Zealand, South African, Indian and all other varieties, pidgins and creoles, go without commentary here.

21.1 Some developments in the standard language since the 18th century

21.1.1 Vocabulary

There is a constant change in the vocabulary of the language, and it goes without saying that there have been many losses and gains of words since the 18th century. English is a language that has taken in and assimilated words from many foreign languages to add to the core vocabulary of Germanic, French and Latin words, as is illustrated in the lists of loan-words in the Word Book.

21.1.2 Spelling

The standard orthography was fixed in the 18th century by the agreed practice of printers. Dr Johnson set down accepted spellings in his *Dictionary* of 1755, and had to record some of the arbitrary choices of 'custom':

> ... thus I write, in compliance with a numberlefs majority, convey and inveigh, deceit and receipt, fancy and phantom.

A few words that you will find in the original versions of 18th-century texts have changed, e.g. *cloathing, terrour, phantasy, publick*, but there are not many. More recently, it has become acceptable to change the ⟨ae⟩ spelling to ⟨e⟩ in a few words of Latin derivation, and to write *medieval* for *mediaeval*, *archeology* for *archaeology* and *paleography* for *palaeography*.

Some American spellings have become familiar in Britain, such as *program*, as a result of its use in computer programming. Others remain controversial still, e.g. recognize/recognise, color/colour, plow/plough. With few exceptions, it is true to say that our spelling system was fixed over two hundred years ago, and every attempt to reform it has failed.

21.1.3 Grammar

While the underlying rules of the grammar have remained unchanged, their use in speech and writing has continued to develop into forms that distinguish varieties of language use since the 18th century. In present-day English we can observe a greater degree of complexity in both the noun phrase and verb phrase.

Noun phrases

Modifiers of nouns normally precede the head of the noun phrase (NP) when they are words (usually adjectives or nouns), e.g. *a red brick*, *the* **brick** *wall*, *the* **red brick** *wall*, and follow it when they are phrases or clauses, eg *the wall* **between the houses**, *the wall* **that was blown down in the gale**. The rule of pre-modification has been developed so that longer strings of words and phrases now precede the head word in some styles of use. For example, a statement which might be written as,

> There has been a report on the treatment of suspects in police stations in Northern Ireland . . .

can be turned into a NP as,

> A Northern Ireland police station suspect treatment report . . .

in which a series of post-modifying prepositional phrases (PrepPs) – *on the treatment*, *of suspects*, *in police stations*, *in Northern Ireland* – become pre-modifying NPs within the larger NP. This style is a particular feature of newspaper headlines.

The process of converting clauses with verbs into noun phrases is called **nominalisation**. It is also a prominent marker of academic and formal writing. It enables a writer to omit the agents or actors who actually do things, e.g.

> S   P   C
> There has been   no convincing explanation of the attempt . . .

is only the beginning of a longer sentence, and might have been written,

> X has not *convinced* us by *explaining* how Y *attempted* . . .

in which main verbs are used instead of nouns or a modifying participle, and the subjects X and Y would have to be named. This is a trend in style that depends upon the fact that the grammar of English permits nominalisation readily.

Verb phrases

If you compare the possible forms of the verb phrase (VP) in contemporary English with any Old English text, you will see that OE verb phrases were generally shorter, and OE grammar lacked the forms of VP that have developed since. In MnE, it is possible to construct VPs like,

> she **has been being treated** . . .
> **hasn't** she **been being treated?**
> **won't** she **have been being treated?**

which use **auxiliary verbs** to combine the grammatical features of **tense** (past or present), **aspect** (perfective or progressive), **voice** (active or passive) and **mood** (declarative or interrogative), to which we can add,

> She **seems to manage to be able to keep on being treated** . . .

in which certain verbs, called **catenatives**, can be strung together in a chain. Such VPs are not common, perhaps, but they are possible, and have developed since the 18th century.

They are examples of the way in which English has become a much more **analytic** language since the OE period, that is, its structures depend upon strings of separate words, and not on the inflections of words. An inflecting language is called **synthetic**.

Another development in the resources of the VP is in the increased use of **phrasal** and **prepositional verbs** like *run across* for *meet, put up with* for *tolerate, give in* for *surrender*. They are more commonly a feature of spoken and informal usage, and though the beginnings of the structure of *verb + particle* can be found in OE, they have increased in numbers considerably in MnE, and new combinations are continually being introduced, often as slang, e.g. *get with it*, and are later assimilated.

21.2 The continuity of prescriptive judgements on language use

We judge others by their speech as much as by other aspects of their behaviour, but some people are much more positive in their reactions. The relationship between social class and language use in the 18th century, which was described in Chapter 19, has been maintained through the 19th and 20th centuries to the present. Here, for example, is the Dean of Canterbury, Henry Alford D.D., writing in a book called *The Queen's English: Stray Notes on Speaking and Spelling*, in 1864:

Text 182: Dean Alford, The Queen's English, 1864 (facsimile)

This attitude is that of 18th-century grammarians in their references to 'the depraved language of the common People' (see section 19.6) and of John of Trevisa in the 14th century calling Northern speech 'scharp slyttyng and frotyng and unschape'.

THE QUEEN'S ENGLISH.   37

THE

QUEEN'S ENGLISH:

Stray Notes on Speaking and Spelling.

BY

HENRY ALFORD, D.D.,
DEAN OF CANTERBURY.

LONDON: STRAHAN & Co.
CAMBRIDGE: DEIGHTON, BELL, & CO.
1864.

51. I pass from spelling to pronunciation. Pronunciation—mis-use of the aspirate. And first and foremost, let me notice that worst of all faults, the leaving out of the aspirate where it ought to be, and putting it in where it ought not to be. This is a vulgarism not confined to this or that province of England, nor especially prevalent in one county or another, but common throughout England to persons of low breeding and inferior education, principally to those among the inhabitants of towns. Nothing so surely stamps a man as below the mark in intelligence, self-respect, and energy, as this unfortunate habit: in intelligence, because, if he were but moderately keen in perception, he would see how it marks him; in self-respect and energy, because if he had these he would long ago have set to work and cured it. Hundreds of stories are current about the absurd consequences of this vulgarism. We remember in *Punch* the barber who, while operating on a gentleman, expressed his opinion, that, after all, the cholera was in the *hair*. "Then," observed the customer, "you ought to be very careful what brushes you use." "Oh, sir," replied the barber, laughing, "I didn't mean the *air* of the *ed*, but the *hair* of the *hatmosphere*."

A feature of common usage which is still taught as an error is what is called the 'split infinitive'. Here is Dean Alford:

> A correspondent states as his own usage, and defends, the insertion of an adverb between the sign of the infinitive mood and the verb. He gives as an instance, 'to scientifically illustrate'. But surely this is a practice entirely unknown to English speakers and writers. It seems to me, that we ever regard the to of the infinitive as inseparable from its verb.

The Dean is wrong in his assertion that the practice is 'entirely unknown'. The idea that it is *ungrammatical* to put an adverb between *to* and the verb was an invention of prescriptive grammarians, though its avoidance can be seen as a feature of style in writers such as Gibbon, Scott and Trollope, which was possibly the model for grammarians to turn into a 'rule'. It has been handed on as a *solecism* (violation of the rules of grammar) by one generation of school teachers after another ever since and has become an easy marker of 'good English'. Avoiding it can, however, lead to ambiguity.

The following paragraph appeared in a daily newspaper in August 1989. It shows a journalist trying to avoid the 'split infinitive' at all costs, and failing to make his/her meaning clear.

> **Correction**
> Our front page report yesterday on microwave cooking mistakenly stated that in tests of 83 cook-chill and ready-cooked products, Sainsbury's found the instructions on 10 products always failed to ensure the foods were fully heated to 70C. The story should have said the instructions failed always to ensure the foods were fully heated to 70C – that is, they sometimes failed to ensure this.

- The original *always failed to ensure* has one clear meaning, which is not the intended meaning. The adverb *always* modifies the verb *failed*, that is, *the instructions never succeeded in ensuring . . .*
- The correction to *failed always to ensure* is ambiguous, because it is not clear whether *always* modifies *failed* or *ensure*. This ambiguity between *failed always* and *always to ensure* is likely to occur in a compound verb phrase with two verbs (predicators in phase) like *failed to ensure*, because the adverb may either precede or follow the verb it modifies.
- *The instructions failed to always ensure the foods were fully heated* is not ambiguous, and *always* clearly modifies *ensure*. There is no reason why the adverb *always* should not immediately precede *ensure* after the particle *to* that follows *failed*.

Letters to the Editor on the subject of language use continue to be published. Typical is a reference in the late 1990s to 'the creeping bane of the new illiteracy beloved of the nation's youth' when the writer is deploring the form *should of*. It is true that children will write *should of*, but this is because they are writing what they <u>hear</u> – that is, the normal conversational reduction of *should have* to [ʃʊdəv], which everyone says, and which should perhaps be written as *should've* to show its derivation more clearly to the eye.

21.3 The grammar of spoken English today

The invention of sound recording, and especially of the portable tape recorder, has made it possible for us to study the spoken language in a way that students of language were formerly quite unable to do. It was always known that spoken English differed from written English, but even an experienced shorthand writer would to some extent idealise what was said, and omit features that seemed irrelevant.

Here is a transcription of some recorded informal contemporary spoken English, which uses written symbols to indicate spoken features of the language. The conventions of written punctuation are deliberately not used. The symbols represent intonation and stress patterns, contained in *tone-units* (units of information into which we divide our speech), each having a *tonic syllable* marked by stress and a change of pitch.

The speaker is an educated user of Standard English, and the topic is 'linguistic acceptability', but the transcription, even if punctuated with capital letters, full-stops and commas as if it were written, would not be acceptable as written English.

Activity 21.1

(i)   Edit the transcription, omitting all non-fluency features that belong to speech only (e.g. hesitations, self-corrections and repetitions), but retaining the identical vocabulary and word order.

(ii) Examine the edited version for evidence of differences between the vocabulary and grammar of informal spoken English and of written English.

(iii) Rewrite B's part of the conversation for her, in a style that conforms to the conventions of written Standard English.

📖 For a full analysis, see the Commentary in the Text Commentary Book.

Conventions used in the transcription:

- The end of a tone-unit (or tone-group) is marked (|).
- The word containing the tonic syllable (or nucleus) is printed in bold type.
- A micro-pause in speech is marked with a stop (.); longer breaks are marked with one or more dashes (–).
- The place where two speakers overlap is marked (⌊ ⌋)

Text 183: Contemporary spoken English

The text is part of a longer conversation between two women in their twenties. *A* is a secretary, *B* is a university lecturer.

A   well what do they **put**| . in a . computing **programme?**| – –
B   **well**| you'll hear a lot about it in due **course** | . it's what they call ⌈IL tests⌉ which
⌊*A* mm⌋

B   ⌈stands for⌉ investigating language **acceptability**|
⌊*A* mm⌋

A   mm
B   and they've done those on groups of **undergraduates**| . we don't know what
A   ⌈erm battery things⌉   ⌈*A* erm⌉
⌊   *B* erm   ⌋ erm **yes**| . erm sort of . **science** graduates| .⌊ German ⌋ graduates|
B   **English** graduates|⌈ and so on| ⌉and **asked** them| – there are various **types** of test
⌊*A* mm| mm⌋

they give them| . they give them a **sentence**| and there are four a . there are **three**
answers they can give| either it's **acceptable**| it's not **acceptable**|
A   mm| – –

B   it's **marginal**| . or you **know**| it's somewhere **between**| and then . we **they**| when they
    mark up the **results**| have a **fourth category**| which is their answer was **incoherent**|

A   **yes**|

B   if it was heard and they couldn't **hear** it| . if it was written they couldn't **read** it|

A   **mm**|

B   that's **one** type| . then there's an **operation** test| they're interested say in . well
    particularly seeing various **adverbs**| and they write something like I **entirely**| dot dot
    dot| – and the student has to complete the **sentence**| –

A   **mm**| –

B   well with **entirely**| they'll nearly all write **agree** with you|

A   **yes**| .

B   and entirely and agree ⎡go **together**|⎤ mm|
               ⎣*A* mm   ⎦

B   **collate** or **something** it's called|

A   **yeah**|

B   [*laughs* – –] and then they in fact try **another** adverb| and then there'll be an absolute
    range of verbs that ⎡go with it|⎤ you know it's quite **interesting**| the way in the **thesis**|
                          ⎣*A* mm|⎦
    they had a sentence with **entirely**| . and **got** people| to er transform it into the **negative**|

B   **mm**|

A   this is **very tricky**| . I should have thought there were .

B   **yes**| well **quite**| they do that sort of **thing** you **see**| and then they see what they've
    produced| and then they ⎡sort of⎤ they score them **up**| in a certain ⎡ way ⎤ and they'll
                      ⎣*A* yes|⎦   ⎣*A* yes|⎦
    say have they . erm – have they **done**| what they were **told** to| and if not **why** not| and
    then there are various   **reasons why not**| and they were **scored**| and given a **mark**| and
    it's quite in ⎡**credible**| ⎤

A   ⎣*A* I think that's|⎦ **one of the most valuable** things| that I've thought was
    being **done**| in .⎡in . ⎤ in the **battery** test | because it should relate| quite directly|
               ⎣*B* mm|⎦
    to| the meaning of the word| –

B   **yes**|

(Adapted from Svartvik and Quirk, *Corpus of English Conversation*)

21.4 19th- and 20th-century loan-words

📖 A selection of loan-words recorded during this period can be found in the Word Book.

Bibliography

This list is a selection of books which teachers, lecturers and advanced students will find useful for further reading and reference. Separate editions of Old, Middle and Early Modern English texts are not listed.

The history and development of English

Barber, Charles, *The English Language: A Historical Introduction* (Cambridge: Cambridge Univerty Press, 1993).

Baugh, A. C. and Cable, T., *A History of the English Language*, 4th edn (London: Routledge & Kegan Paul, 1993).

Blake, N. F., *A History of the English Language* (Basingstoke: Macmillan, 1996).

Crystal, David (ed.), *Cambridge Encyclopedia of the English Language* (Cambridge: Cambridge University Press, 1995).

Hogg, Richard M. (general editor), *Cambridge History of the English Language* (Cambridge: Cambridge University Press):
- Vol. 1: Richard M. Hogg (ed.), *The Beginnings to 1066* (1992)
- Vol. 2: Norman Blake (ed.), *1066–1476* (1992)
- Vol. 5: Robert Burchfield, *English in Britain and Overseas: Origin and Development* (1994).

Leith, Dick, *A Social History of English* (London: Routledge & Kegan Paul, 1983).

Partridge, A. C., *A Companion to Old and Middle English Studies* (London: André Deutsch, 1982).

Pyles, T. and Algeo, J., *The Origins and Development of the English Language*, 3rd edn (New York: Harcourt Brace Jovanovich, 1982).

Scragg, D. G., *A History of English Spelling* (Manchester: Manchester University Press, 1974).

Strang, Barbara, *A History of English* (London: Methuen, 1970).

Old English

Bradley, S. A. J., *Anglo-Saxon Poetry* (translation) (London: Dent, 1982).

Davis, N., *Sweet's Anglo-Saxon Primer*, 9th edn (Oxford: Oxford University Press, 1953).

Mitchell, B., *An Invitation to Old English and Anglo-Saxon England* (Oxford: Blackwell, 1995).

Mitchell, B., and Robinson, F. C., *A Guide to Old English*, 5th edn (Oxford: Blackwell, 1986).

Quirk, R. and Wrenn, C. L., *An Old English Grammar* (London: Methuen, 1957).

Quirk, R., Adams, V. and Davy, D., *Old English Literature: A Practical Introduction* (London: Edward Arnold, 1975).

Swanton, Michael, *The Anglo-Saxon Chronicle* (translation) (London: Dent, 1996).

Swanton, Michael, *Anglo-Saxon Prose* (translation) (London: Dent, 1975).

Sweet, H., *The Student's Dictionary of Anglo-Saxon* (1896; Oxford: Oxford University Press reprint, 1978).

Middle English

Bennett, J. A. W. and Smithers, G. V., *Early Middle English Verse and Prose*, 2nd edn (anthology) (Oxford: Oxford University Press, 1968).

Burnley, D., *A Guide to Chaucer's Language* (Basingstoke: Macmillan, 1983).

Sisam, K., *Fourteenth-Century Verse and Prose* (Oxford: Oxford University Press, 1921).

Early Modern English

Barber, Charles, *Early Modern English* (London: André Deutsch, 1976).

Blake, N. F., *The Language of Shakespeare* (Basingstoke: Macmillan, 1985).

Modern English

Barber, Charles, *Linguistic Change in Present-Day English* (London: Oliver & Boyd, 1964).

Foster, B., *The Changing English Language* (London: Macmillan, 1968).

Potter, S., *Changing English* (London: André Deutsch, 1969).

Quirk, R. et al., *A Comprehensive Grammar of the English Language* (London: Longman, 1985).

Development of handwriting

Denholm-Young, N., *Handwriting in England and Wales* (Cardiff: University of Wales Press, 1954).

Hector, L. C., *The Handwriting of English Documents* (London: Edward Arnold, nd).

Kelliher, H. and Brown, S., *English Literary Manuscripts* (London: British Library, 1986).

Parkes, M. B., *English Cursive Book Hands* (Oxford: Oxford University Press, 1969 and Scolar Press, 1979).

Wright, C. E., *English Vernacular Hands, 12th to 15th Century* (Oxford: Oxford University Press, 1960).

Medieval Writing – History, Heritage and Data Source: website produced and maintained by Dr Dianne Tillotson, http//medievalwriting.50megs.com

Index